Best Wishes
&
Don't Despair

Fiji: Race and Politics in an Island State

In 1987 – first in May and again in September – Fiji, which has often been regarded as a model for racial co-existence, surprised the rest of the world by staging not one but two coups. Most interpreters of the Fijian political scene saw the events as a result of tension between native Fijians and members of other ethnic groups. Michael Howard argues in this book that this interpretation is simplistic. Instead, he points out, the May coup was a strike against democratic government by elements associated with Fiji's traditional oligarchy seeking to hide behind a mask of populist communalism.

Howard traces the evolution of Fijian politics from the precolonial chiefdoms, through the colonial era and into the postcolonial period, emphasizing the developments during the latter half of the 1980s. As a close and involved observer, he draws a convincing picture of the leading actors in contemporary Fijian politics and the motives guiding their actions. He describes how the ruling élite – the Fijian chiefly families and their allies – has maintained its power by manipulating communal or racially based sentiments and how the opposition has attempted to change the situation by creating political alignments based on social class.

A perceptive case study of racial politics in the modern world and a significant new approach to the understanding of the dynamics of a non-Western political system, *Fiji: Race and Politics in an Island State* provides a timely and comprehensive analysis of recent events in this important island state.

MICHAEL HOWARD holds a joint appointment with the Centre for International Studies and the Department of Sociology and Anthropology at Simon Fraser University. From 1982 to 1987 he taught at the University of the South Pacific in Suva, Fiji. He is founding editor of the journal *South Pacific Forum* and is the author of a number of books and articles on political and economic issues in the South Pacific.

MICHAEL C. HOWARD

Fiji:
Race and Politics
in an Island State

UBC Press
Vancouver

ISBN 0-7748-0368-1

Canadian Cataloguing in Publication Data

Howard, Michael C.
Fiji : race and politics in an island state

Includes bibliographical references and index.
ISBN 0-7748-0368-1

1. Fiji – Politics and government. 2. Fiji – History.
3. Fiji – Race relations. I. Title.

DU600.H69 1991   996.11   C91-091004-9

This book has been published with the help of a grant
from the Social Science Federation of Canada, using funds
provided by the Social Sciences and Humanities Research
Council of Canada.

UBC Press
University of British Columbia
6344 Memorial Rd
Vancouver, BC V6T 1Z2
(604) 822-3259

Contents

Preface

When I first thought of writing a book on Fiji shortly after the May 1987 coup, I anticipated producing something with a fairly limited focus – the coup itself and the events leading up to it. It did not take long to realize that such an approach would not do justice to the complexities of Fijian politics, and that what was needed was a study that placed the coup carefully within a broader historical and geopolitical context. Thus the book began to grow. But as it grew, events in Fiji continued to unfold, including a second coup in September 1987, that made it essential for me to examine the May coup's aftermath as well. It then became a question of where to stop. In the back of my mind was a fear that as soon as the book went to press there would be another major development. Nevertheless, with this nagging concern in mind, I decided that an appropriate place to put a stop to what otherwise could have become an endless project was the death of Timoci Bavadra in late 1989.

Writing this book has not been easy, in large part because I found myself too close to many of the events. In looking back over the period since the May coup, I am now glad that I delayed completion of the manuscript. The delay allowed my thoughts to mature and my analysis, hopefully, to become more objective. I was also able to check on reported events more carefully. Unfortunately, this did not always mean finding the answers that I sought, and I still find myself confronted with numerous unanswered questions. Although my sense of outrage remains undiminished, I have done my best not to allow such personal feelings to distort the account that follows.

Among those that are due a special note of thanks for their assistance in preparation of the manuscript are Marian Wilkinson, Wendy Bacon, Simione Durutalo, 'Atu Bain, Bill Pinwill, John Connell, Grant McCall, and, especially, Al McCoy for his lengthy comments and support of the project. At the University of British Columbia Press, I would like to thank Jean Wilson for her support and Holly Keller-Brohman for her painstaking editorial work. I would also like to thank the numerous people in Fiji who over the years helped me to better understand Fijian politics, and to express my gratitude to Timoci and Kuini Bavadra for their friendship.

Michael Howard

Fiji: Race and Politics in an Island State

CHAPTER ONE

Race, Class, and Democracy in Fiji

Tourist brochures, travel books, and even scholarly writings often have proclaimed Fiji to be special among Third World nations. It has been called a Third World success story known for the friendliness of its people, its stability and relative prosperity, its multiracial harmony despite its ethnic pluralism, and its adherence to the principles of parliamentary democracy. It seemed almost too good to be true and, of course, it was. Yet, in comparison with many other countries, Fiji's accomplishments were considerable.

The nation of Fiji is an archipelago comprised of some 320 islands with a total land area of 18,376 sq km, 16°S of the equator and just to the west of the international dateline. Most of its 714,000 people live on the two main islands of Viti Levu and Vanua Levu. Viti Levu, where the nation's capital of Suva is located, is the largest (10,390 sq km), most populated (over 550,000), and most developed island in the archipelago. The island of Vanua Levu is smaller (5,538 sq km), much more sparsely populated (around 100,000 people), and economically less developed. Over 20 per cent of the population is concentrated around the capital of Suva and in and around the western towns of Nadi, Lautoka, and Ba. In total, some 40 per cent of the population lives in or in close proximity to urban areas.

Among the remaining islands, 150 are inhabited. Taveuni and Kadavu (each a little over 400 sq km) are the largest. Ovalau (approximately 150 sq km) contains the only town among the smaller islands, the old capital of Levuka, with a population of some 1,300. Comprising fifty-seven islands scattered over 113,900 sq km of sea with a total land area of only 460 sq km and a mere 13,000 people, the Lau Group bears special mention because of its political importance far in excess of its small population and resource base.

Almost 400 kilometers to the north of the archipelago lies the island of Rotuma which was joined to the colony by the British in 1881. It is a small island, measuring only some 40 sq km, and occupied by less than 3,000 people. An additional 4,000 Rotumans live elsewhere in Fiji.

Fiji's economy is perhaps the most developed in the region. With a per capita GDP of U.S.$1,300 which places it far ahead of many Third World countries, Fiji has the most developed economy among the Pacific island nations in terms of its complexity. Although Fiji is mainly a producer and exporter of primary resources, it has the most developed industrial base of the island states, with manufacturing accounting for over 12 per cent of the GDP. Sugar is the backbone of its economy, accounting for around two-thirds of export earnings, followed in order of importance by gold, fish, coconut products, and timber. The other major income earner is tourism. The sugar, tourist, gold, and forest industries are concentrated in western Viti Levu, while the smaller eastern islands and less developed parts of Vanua Levu rely on coconut products, a few other agricultural items (such as kava), and the spoils of political patronage.

Most of Fiji's farmers depend to some extent on cash crop production and periodic wage labour, and there are over 21,000 commercial sugar-cane farmers. There are also a relatively large number of persons in regular wage employment – over 80,000 in 1981 – representing just over 20 per cent of the adult population. This group includes everything from unskilled workers to computer technicians and medical doctors. In addition, there is a sizeable commerical class ranging from thousands of proprietors of small business enterprises to the owners of the nation's largest local companies.

The indigenous or native Fijian population accounts for a little over 45 per cent of the population. Indo-Fijians comprise the largest ethnic community, a little less than 50 per cent of the population. Most of them are descendants of indentured workers brought to Fiji to work on the sugar-cane fields in the late nineteenth and early twentieth centuries. The extent to which the two ethnic groups maintain a relatively high degree of social and cultural distinctiveness is one of Fiji's colonial legacies. The other, much smaller ethnic populations include Europeans, part-Europeans, Chinese, Rotumans, Banabans (who were settled on the Fijian island of Rabi in the 1940s), Solomon Islanders (also descendants of indentured labourers), and other Pacific islanders (mostly Tongans).

Behind simple categories and numbers, however, is a much more complex ethnic situation. To begin with, the two major ethnic communities themselves are highly differentiated. The native Fijian population speaks about fifteen distinct dialects, reflecting significant cultural and social differences.[1] The primary division is between those native Fijians in the eastern part of the country with a history of close relations with Tongans and other Polynesians and those in the west and centre of Viti Levu who are more Melanesian in character. Many of the eastern native Fijian societies developed social hierarchies similar to those found in Tonga, while those in the west were less hierarchical in nature. The eastern chiefs joined the British in the mid-nineteenth century and conquered the western peoples, incorporating them into the colony of Fiji and taking steps to impose their hierarchical social structure. Even among the eastern native Fijians, however, there are important distinctions related to tribal confederacies formed in the late eighteenth and early nineteenth centuries. Rivalries between these confederacies continue to influence native Fijian politics, just as does the internal colonialism imposed on the westerners.

The Indo-Fijian population is also divided along religious lines and according to place of origin in India. Most Indo-Fijians are Hindu with a little over 10 per cent being Muslim. The Muslim community, however, is a relatively cohesive group and has played an important political role supporting colonial and later eastern chiefly rule. Then there are regional differences, essentially between those Indo-Fijians originating from southern India and those from northern India. Related to this north-south divide is a distinction between those who came under indenture and those who came later, mostly as small businessmen from Gujarat in north-western India.

Conventional academic wisdom and political rhetoric in Fiji has tended to focus on communalism – analysing economic, political, and social relations in Fiji in terms of ethnic divisions.[2] But there is another, more recent, school of thought that subordinates communalism to class and class interests.[3] This perspective focuses on the economic basis and political manipulation of communalism in relation to intra-class and inter-class collaboration or rivalry. Putting it perhaps a little too simply, from this perspective, Fiji's ruling oligarchy has sought to promote communalism in an effort to undermine threatening class cohesion from below ('divide and rule'), while at the same time trying to ensure that communalism does not get out of control to the point where it could undermine social order. This may seem like too pat an assessment, but a closer look, especially at the period of Alliance Party rule (see chapter 3), lends support to this proposition. From this perspective, Fiji's 'specialness' looks more like an example of very successful conscious manipulation of a polity by a ruling oligarchy rather than some inherent feature of the archipelago's population.

What has been the composition of this oligarchy? Under British colonial rule (1874–1970) there were three main elements: the colonial administration, a largely expatriate business élite, and the eastern native Fijian chiefly élite. In the late nineteenth century, as Fiji's economy came to be dominated by sugar, and this industry in turn was controlled by one company, Colonial Sugar Refining (CSR) of Australia, the managerial élite of CSR came to play a major role in the colony. The business elite also was comprised of the managers and owners of other leading foreign enterprises, such as Emperor Gold Mine and the trading company Burns Philp (both Australian-based) and a handful of local European businessmen. Leadership of the eastern chiefly oligarchy was consolidated during the interwar years in the hands of a single chief, Ratu Sir Lala Sukuna (*ratu* is a title indicating chiefly status), who maintained close relations with the colony's administrative and business élite. Towards the end of colonial rule, Sukuna's mantle was passed to another chief, Ratu Sir Kamasese Mara, who became prime minister after independence. Under Mara's prime ministership the nature of the oligarchy changed slightly. The colonial administration was gone and a handful of newly wealthy Indo-Fijian businessmen were incorporated into the oligarchy. It was in the interest of this group of eastern élite chiefs, foreign business interests, and the local business élite that Mara ruled independent Fiji through his Alliance Party from 1970 to 1987.

Democratic institutions and traditions have proven weak in many postcolonial societies. Appeals to nation-building, communal sentiments, and real or imagined traditions commonly have served to justify the assumption of power by small segments of these societies not able or content to rule through democratic institutions. The island nations of the South Pacific only recently have emerged from European colonial rule. Little attempt was made by the various colonial powers to foster democracy throughout the region. It was only towards the end of colonial rule that meaningful efforts were made by the administration to provide Fiji with democratic institutions, but such reforms tended merely to institutionalize the power of indigenous élites fostered under colonial rule and to maintain the regional and ethnic divisions promoted under colonialism as a means of maintaining control.

Most formal political power in colonial Fiji was vested in the governor's office. CSR and Emperor Gold Mine, however, operated almost as independent entities, as laws unto themselves, with their

managerial élite exercising almost complete control over their particular domains through their foremen and gang-bosses. Indo-Fijians
had very few political rights and only minimal representation on the
colony's Legislative Council. The same was true of native Fijian commoners who were subject to a very rigid structure of indirect rule
under the eastern chiefly oligarchy and its institutional bases, the
Great Council of Chiefs and the Fijian Administration, both colonial
constructs. The leading chiefs were opposed to any form of democratization, and the lives of native Fijian commoners were regulated
to a high degree. Significant steps to change this structure and to
introduce greater democratic rights for Indo-Fijians and native Fijian
commoners only began to take place in the late 1950s and early
1960s when reform-minded colonial administrators began 'preparing Fiji for independence.' Even this minimal democratization, however, was resisted by the chiefs, and independent Fiji came into
being with a political system that highlighted communalism and
chiefly power.

Popular perceptions and traditional academic wisdom have
viewed the Pacific as a relatively peaceful region in which colonial
rule was fairly benign, quite unlike most of the rest of the Third
World. The ruling élites of the region's newly independent states
adhered to this view of peace and stability and used it to justify their
continued rule. As prime minister of Fiji, Mara articulated an ideology known as the 'Pacific Way,' which emphasized stability and
tradition and, by implication, adherence to chiefly rule.[4] Over the
past decade, scholars have begun to question this view of the Pacific.
Recent writings have shown that popular resistance to colonialism
and those quasi-indigenous institutions associated with colonial
rule can be found in the South Pacific, and that the history of colonial Fiji was marked by both resistance and repression.[5] Since independence such opposition has continued, with the indigenous élite
and foreign capital serving as the primary targets. During the immediate postcolonial period, opposition to the Fijian oligarchy was
diverted and co-opted through appeals to nation-building and tradition under the guise of the Pacific Way. But these appeals have worn
thin in the face of growing economic inequality and the spread of
education. Gradually, popular opposition forces have assumed
increasing importance and definition.

In many ways, Fiji has been at the forefront of the political struggle in the South Pacific between obfuscation and articulation of class
interests. Fiji's transition to independence was a classic case of a
colonial power turning governing institutions over to a handpicked
élite to ensure relative stability. In this case, it was the chiefly élite

from the eastern part of the country. Chiefly rule was maintained primarily by a network of patronage and by appeals to communalism, which provided the chiefly élite with a means to stifle criticism within indigenous Fijian society and to render opposition from Indo-Fijians ineffective. In contrast to a united oligarchy, the opposition, represented primarily by the National Federation Party, was factionally divided and restrained by its basic agreement with Mara's management of the country.

Despite the opposition's weakness, Mara's Alliance Party had almost lost power to the National Federation Party in national elections. In fact, the National Federation Party had won in 1977, but had proven unable and unwilling to actually take the government away from Mara. Such electoral threats to its power did little to endear the democratic process to the oligarchy, which clearly saw it as an irritant to be endured for its utility in securing international approval and for its facility in controlling the population through a communally-oriented political system. Behind the more public face of party politics, there was considerable dissent among the country's peasantry, working class, and owners of small businesses which cut across communal boundaries. When such dissent appeared on the verge of breaking out of its communal bounds, the government co-opted or coerced as necessary. Mara's Fiji was not a police state in the usual sense, but his government oversaw a very repressive society where there was considerable restraint on democratic expression.

In the face of such repressive conditions, Fiji's workers built a large and fairly strong union movement which in 1984 represented about 45,000 workers, or 56 per cent of wage workers. Despite constant threats of co-option and coercion by the government, Fiji's unionists built a movement that was the envy of workers in many Third World countries. On occasion, unionists had engaged directly in political dissent, but by and large they limited their concerns to economic and social issues that did not translate directly into political action, thereby seeking to avoid direct confrontation with the government.

Mara and the Alliance Party had survived the 1982 national election, but dissent was becoming much more widespread throughout Fijian society, both in relation to increasing corruption in government and to a more fundamental questioning of the nature of the way politics was structured along ethnic and regional lines. The Alliance Party was also confronted with the problem of a patronage system that was proving difficult to maintain in the face of a more educated, more urbanized, and more demanding population, and in face of the greater rewards expected. Moreover, the traditional opposition party, the National Federation Party, began to collapse as a result of internal rifts. This would have been good news for the Alliance Party except for the fact that the National Federation Party had served the useful purpose of focusing Fijian politics along communal lines and away from more fundamental and more threatening issues to the status quo. What arose to replace the National Federation Party was a very different political party, one that was non-communal and that questioned the very nature of Mara's rule. Forces opposed to existing political conditions came together to form the Fiji Labour Party in mid-1985. The backbone of this new party was Fiji's powerful union movement, which the Alliance Party had forced into confrontation.

Coalition with the remnants of the National Federation Party in late 1986 gave the opposition broad-based support among Indo-Fijians. But it was the ability to tap dissent within the native Fijian community that represented the greatest challenge to the Alliance Party. The Fiji Labour Party was able to capture the imagination of many younger, better-educated indigenous Fijians in towns and villages and to secure the support of those chafing under regional inequalities. If the Alliance Party's base was in the tradition-oriented feudal classes that had been entrenched under colonial rule and survived by state patronage, then the Labour Party's was among those seeking to break out of this constricting structure.

To the surprise of many, the Labour Party-National Federation Party coalition won the April 1987 national election following a close and bitterly fought campaign. For those who lost, the experience was unsettling if not traumatic, but, to many, the relatively smooth transition of power between parties with distinct political philosophies and different interests was seen as proof, once again, of Fiji's specialness. The nation had managed to weather the storm of a tense election and come out of it perhaps even stronger.

The new Coalition government headed by Dr. Timoci Bavadra was pledged to policies that would overcome communalism, implement socio-economic reform, and eradicate the corrupt practices that had become increasingly prevalent during the latter years of Alliance Party rule. For the country's Indo-Fijian population, in particular, the promise of an end to communal politics was viewed as a victory of major significance. Among native Fijians, the regional dimension was of considerable importance. Prime Minister Bavadra was from the western part of the country, and his victory was seen by many as a victory over the eastern chiefly oligarchy. Few missed the significance of the fact that Bavadra was a commoner who was openly critical of the system. In many ways it was also a victory for democratic principles. Not only had there been a relatively smooth transition with control of the government passing from the hands of the party that had run the country for the past seventeen years, but the new party in power was pledged to ending the worst vestiges of communalism, regional imbalance, and chiefly rule.

As will be discussed in detail in chapters 6 and 7, efforts by Alliance Party supporters were under way to destabilize the new government almost as soon as the election results were known. These plans involved demonstrations, fire-bombings, and other forms of intimidation. The destabilization campaign had its roots in those sectors within Fijian society that were dependent upon state patronage – including politicians who had become accustomed to high living, military and civilian indigenous Fijians who had been given jobs, local and expatriate businessmen who depended on Alliance Party control, and a collection of urban unemployed and more traditional peasants with a strong sense of chiefly loyalty. Especially important was a small group of young indigenous Fijians who had anticipated inheriting political power by right of birth. For this group, the shock of the Alliance Party's loss was almost unbearable. One of them went so far as to attack former prime minister Mara 'for being so stupid as to lose the election,' thereby threatening this person's 'birthright.'

But, after almost a month in office, the Coalition government seemed to have the situation in hand and opposition was on the wane. An anti-government demonstration and Alliance Party boycott of the opening of Parliament had not gone particularly well, and two Alliance Party parliamentarians had been charged for activities associated with the destablization efforts. Most important, popular support among indigenous Fijians for anti-government activities had dwindled. As the new government began implementing reforms, the country awaited an important and lively period in its political history. Shortly after parliament opened on Thursday morning, 14 May, however, a small group of Fijian army troops entered the building and arrested the Coalition parliamentarians. The leader of the South Pacific's first military takeover, Colonel Sitiveni Rabuka, proclaimed that he had acted to safeguard native Fijian interests.

The events of 14 May 1987 marked a dramatic turning point in the evolution of politics in Fiji. The coup is as important a turning point in Fiji's history as the signing of the Deed of Cession in 1874 by which Fiji became a colony of Great Britain, and the granting of independence from Britain in 1970. The coup marked the end of the postcolonial honeymoon by which conflicting interests had been contained within a parliamentary structure. A darker, more repressive side of Fijian society had always been there, but usually well in the background. Now that it had come to the fore, Fiji's future seemed suddenly bleak, the optimism of the preceding weeks suddenly shattered.

The rise and ultimate success of the Fiji Labour Party in winning national office flew in the face of accepted wisdom about the nature of the Fijian polity and the strength of communal loyalties. The racist justification given by the perpetrators of the 14 May coup was accepted by many for it allowed them to retreat into simplistic stereotypes about Fijian society and politics. There is no denying that ethnic issues were important in both the April election and the May coup, but their relevance can only be understood within a broader framework of evolving patterns of privilege, inequality, and unequal development. Moreover, as subsequent events have shown, the coup was not merely an attempt to retain the communal nature of Fijian politics, but to use communalism to create a new, more repressive order of privilege and domination.

The coup surprised most observers of Fijian politics. But it surprised people for different reasons. There were those, perhaps the majority, who were surprised because they had accepted Mara's propaganda about the Pacific Way and the special nature of Fijian society. To them a military takeover in paradise was inconceivable. But there were others who were not so much surprised that a coup had happened – for they had been concerned about the role of the military in Fijian society for some time – but only that it happened at the precise time and in the precise manner that it did.[6] The permeability of military and civilian boundary lines in Fiji had for some time given a few people cause for concern. Fiji's chiefly élite had a tradition of military service, and the army had become an integral part of the Alliance Party's patronage structure – factors that produced a close association between chiefly rule and the military. In the past when chiefly authority had been challenged by electoral politics, union actions, or by intellectuals, rumours of military action often had circulated, and in some instances the government had discussed military intervention.

The electoral victory of the Coalition and the challenge it represented to the oligarchy caused concern among members of the Coalition government that Mara and his allies might resort to the use of military force. But, by the second week of May, this threat receded as the new government settled in. Perhaps, they were overly optimistic, but the important point is that they and others of like mind did not see the use of military force as something out of character with the nature of Fijian politics. Rather, they saw it as a distinct possibility, but one that hopefully had been avoided, at least for the time being.

Recent political developments have not taken place in a vacuum. Fragile democratic institutions around the South Pacific have been under increasing strain in recent years. As in Fiji, the strain comes from a struggle between those who maintain power largely for their own ends and those who demand greater democracy and equality. Many people around the South Pacific saw the Fiji Labour Party as a symbol of the challenge to existing power structures throughout the region. And throughout the region, both those in power and those in opposition watched and responded from their different perspectives to the rise of the Fiji Labour Party and to its overthrow. Since the May coup, the South Pacific has seen continuing challenges to democratic principles in country after country until many observers have come to wonder whether the entire region may soon go the way of Fiji.

Observers outside the region have watched events in Fiji over the past couple of years to an unprecedented extent. Those opposed to communal politics in other Third World countries such as Malaysia and India observed the rise of the Fiji Labour Party with interest and optimism. Likewise, those opposed to progressive developments in the Third World looked on with alarm as it appeared as if they were about to lose a staunch ally. In this and in many other ways, the situation in Fiji assumed a broader geopolitical relevance. Most important, the South Pacific looked as if it were about to make an important move towards greater independence. It is this geopolitical dimension that caused many to question whether there was outside involvement in the coup, particularly by the United States, a subject that will be discussed in chapter 7. As they watched the country slide into a totalitarian morass, the coup and its aftermath created a growing sense of despair among those previously imbued with optimism, but it also created a sense of relief among those alarmed by the prospect of an independent, progressive Fiji.

The chapters that follow trace the evolution of élite rule in Fiji from the precolonial chiefdoms, through the colonial era, and into the postcolonial period. Moreover, the challenges to this rule by the people of Fiji which culminated in the April 1987 election defeat of the Alliance government are examined. The study also focuses on the role of communalism in the political process, not as the key political factor but as product and instrument of political competition. The May 1987 coup focused unprecedented world attention on

Fiji, but most reports interpreted events in the time-tested cliches of racial or ethnic politics. Such reports missed the point. The May coup was really a strike against popular democratic government by elements associated with Fiji's traditional oligarchy. The final three chapters examine events since the May coup as the oligarchy has sought to re-impose control in the face of popular opposition and internal divisions.

CHAPTER TWO

Colonial and Precolonial Fiji

An understanding of modern Fijian politics requires a careful look at Fiji's past – both the objective past, and the idealized past promoted by Fiji's ruling oligarchy. There are in a sense two interwoven layers of these pasts. The first layer consists of a precolonial Fiji objectively comprised of differing regional traditions, warring chiefdoms and confederacies, and with a history of growing chiefly power over the lives of commoners. The legacies of past alliances and rivalries have remained an important feature in Fijian politics, as has the use of traditional lore. The ideal version of Fiji's precolonial era is that of a uniform society modelled upon some of the eastern chiefdoms. This version focuses on the acts of the eastern chiefs and paints a picture of an almost paradisiacal village life. It is a myth that suits the interests of the chiefly rulers of modern Fiji.

The second layer is that of the colonial state. The colonial state transformed much of what had existed before, creating a neotraditional order among the indigenous Fijians which it sought to rule indirectly through a chiefly élite. The colonial economy brought with it large numbers of indentured workers from India and elsewhere in the Pacific, and the colonial state created institutions to administer them along separate lines from the indigenous population, sowing the seeds for ethnically-based, pluralistic politics in postcolonial Fiji. The popular myth of colonialism in Fiji is that of a benign colonial state in which British and chiefly rulers faced little opposition except from 'greedy' Indian migrants who had little respect for Fiji's sacred traditions. Village life, according to myth, remained idyllic and continued to adhere to precolonial traditions under the paternalistic guidance of Fiji's wise chiefs. But reality was quite different. Colonial Fiji's rulers (including its chiefs) faced almost constant dissent and even revolt, and not just from 'pushy' Indians. Communal divisions, rather than being a natural response among culturally distinct peoples, were a central feature of colonial rule and they were consciously promoted as a means of retaining the hierarchical structure of colonial society.

Academic opinion about Fiji's past is divided. On the one hand there are the traditionalists such as colonial administrator G.K. Roth, anthropologist W.R. Geddes, and historian Deryck Scarr who have written on Fiji from the perspective of the colonial government and the eastern chiefs.[1] They have sought to emphasize the unchanging nature of native Fijian society, using the eastern chiefdoms as their model, and to present a highly favourable impression of the chiefly aristocracy. Thus, Geddes argues that 'despite their exposure to alien influences the Fijians have retained their traditional social structure to a remarkable extent.'[2]

For traditionalists, the colonial impact was minimal, and the chiefs remain the people's primary safeguards against the ravages of the modern world. Roth wrote of an idealized past that continued to influence modern village life despite corrupting modern influences: 'Village life nowadays is a development of an ancient society based on the precept and practice of common service in which was stressed above all else the social and ethical value of loyalty and devotion in the service of one's fellows.'[3] He saw the chiefs as central to the people's well-being and commented sadly that in the past there was 'stricter direction by chiefs of the people's way of living, and therefore closer cohesion in the social life than there is in modern times.'[4] Contemporary traditionalists such as Scarr continue to promote a view of Fiji revolving around the chiefs and their devotion to service.

There are scholars, however, who disagree with this somewhat idyllic, paternalistic portrayal of Fijian history. Peter France's pioneering work presented a Fijian precolonial past of conflict and social variation. He characterized his approach 'as one of empirical scepticism after the manner of the Fijian chief who, when asked to explain the custom of his tribe in the matter of chiefly succession, replied that the custom was to fight about it.'[5] France also documented the extent to which Fijian traditions were modified by the colonial authorities. This is a theme that also appears in the writings of anthropologist John Clammer, who argues that much of what passes for tradition 'is entirely the child of the Colonial administration.'[6]

The response of the chiefly oligarchy to ideas such as those expressed by France and Clammer was to try to suppress them, while promoting writing and research by its supporters such as Scarr. Nevertheless, contemporary Fijian scholars like Brij Lal and Simione Durutalo have built upon the work of France, Clammer, and others to present an alternative view of Fijian history in which the chiefs uneasily must share the stage with a host of others, and in which conflict in the colonial period is no longer reduced to communal rivalries but is seen more broadly as part of a struggle between ruler and ruled, a struggle that was to carry over into the postcolonial era.[7]

THE PRE-COLONIAL PAST

Generally, it has been accepted that Fiji was first settled some three to four thousand years ago. Recent work by Gibbons and Clunie, however, has raised the possibility that settlement along a now submerged coastline may have been earlier.[8] An important implication of this is that the cultural complex that existed in Fiji around four thousand years ago, rather than having been brought to the islands whole at this time, may have been the result of a longer period of evolution in Fiji. Among those who had settled on the archipelago around this time were the so-called Lapita people.

First migrating from the Philippines and Indonesia around thirty-five hundred years ago, the Lapita people spread across much of the South Pacific over the next five hundred years. They first established themselves along the coast and on small offshore islands where they engaged in trade and exploited native coastal resources such as fish and sea-birds. As the population increased, settlement gradually expanded along the coast and then moved inland. As the Lapita occupied land away from the coast they came to rely more on agriculture, and distinctions arose between coastal and inland societies.

Oral tradition states that the first migrants to Fiji landed on the west coast of the large island of Viti Levu at Vuda (near Lautoka) under the leadership of a man named Lutunasobasoba. He is said to have remained at Vuda and is considered the founding ancestor of the *yavusa* (tribes) of western Viti Levu. Then, tradition has it, other members of this group (or perhaps from another group that arrived around the same time), under the leadership of Degei, moved northward along the Ra coast and settled near the Kauvadra Mountains. Degei is viewed as the founding ancestor of the yavusa throughout much of the remainder of Fiji.

Fijian legend records the quarrels of Degei's numerous sons and traces their movements to various parts of eastern Fiji where they founded yavusa of their own. One group moved further east to

Verata. There they divided. The first group went to Burebasaga where they founded the chiefly yavusa of Rewa. A second group went to Moturiki (near the larger island of Ovalau). A third went to the island of Moala. From there, some went on to Nayau in the central Lau Group, where they became the founders of the chiefly yavusa of Lau. After extensive wanderings as far as Tonga, the descendants of another group came to Moturiki to join the group, therein founding the chiefly yavusa of Bau. Thus, these various yavusa are seen as being related and are said to have ties to Tonga.

The traditional ideal has it that the brothers of the founding families of the yavusa formed subgroups known as *mataqali*. These mataqali were given distinctive names and over time became the custodians of particular functions. The ideal yavusa would contain mataqali carrying out five distinct functions: (1) a *turaga* or chiefly mataqali, (2) a *saturaga* mataqali which was ranked just below the chiefly mataqali and served an executive function, (3) a *mata-ni-vanua* mataqali or diplomatic mataqali whose members served as official heralds and masters of ceremony, (4) a priestly or *bete* mataqali (some of whose members are said to become possessed by the *kalou-vu* or deified ancestor), and (5) a warrior or *bati* mataqali (some yavusa also were viewed as bati). The mataqali in turn were subdivided into smaller units (known in some eastern areas as *i tokatoka*) which comprised closely related families living in a defined area who acknowledged a single relative as their head. In addition, male members of Fijian society were ranked into six grades from serfs to high chiefs.

Needless to say, this ideal structure was not always found in actual situations. As a result of war, internal factionalism, migration, and depopulation, the configurations of yavusa and mataqali changed over time. There were also important regional variations. The most notable of these was the relative egalitarianism of the so-called 'Hill Tribes' located in the interior and west of Viti Levu. This contrasted with the much more hierarchical nature of eastern Fijian societies. Social stratification in western Fiji can be seen as more closely resembling the more egalitarian societies elsewhere in Melanesia, where the powers of the chief were more limited and conditional. In much of eastern Fiji, however, the pattern was more Polynesian in character, with a fairly rigid hierarchy.

The Polynesian character of eastern Fiji no doubt reflects the relatively close links that existed with the neighbouring Polynesian islands, especially those of Tonga. In addition to periodic small-scale migrations back and forth between Tonga and Fiji, there is archaeological evidence of a large-scale invasion of eastern Fiji from Tonga around one thousand years ago. Samoan craftsmen apparently accompanied the invading Tongans. The Tongans were to invade eastern Fiji again closer to the time of arrival of the first Europeans, resulting in their establishing marked influence over much of the eastern portion of the archipelago.

Warfare between groups, spurred in part by chiefly rivalries, led to the formation of confederations known as *vanua*. Vanua were formed by chiefs powerful enough to unite a number of groups, and if the vanua held together, the position of its chief gradually became hereditary. It is worth noting that such vanua only developed after a couple of thousand years of occupation of the archipelago and, by the late eighteenth century, even the largest of these, Verata and Cakaudrove, occupied only a short stretch of coast and a couple of neighbouring islands, with their hold over subject peoples being fairly unstable.

During the early nineteenth century a larger political entity evolved, the *matanitu* or chiefdom, comprised of a number of vanua, joined together on the basis of alliance or conquest. These confederacies did not develop in western or the interior of Viti Levu and those that did exist varied considerably in terms of relative size and power. R.A. Derrick records that in 1835 there were a total of thirty-two named matanitu, but also comments that 'the claims of many of them were subsequently denied or lost.'[9] In the mid-nineteenth century, immediately prior to the cession of Fiji to Great Britain, there were ten matanitu: Bau, Rewa, Naitasiri, Namosi, Nadroga, Bua, Macuata, Cakaudrove, Lau, and Tavua. There were also two other important chieftanships: Kadavu and Ba. Serua emerged as a matanitu after cession.

European exploration of the islands of the South Pacific got off to a slow start and progressed only after the settlement of south-eastern Australia by the British. The Fijian archipelago was first sighted by the Dutch explorer, Abel Janzsoon Tasman. He sailed among some reefs in the north-western portion of the islands in 1643 and named the group Prins Willem's Islands. Dutch interest, however, was focused far to the west in Indonesia, and this initial sighting was not to be followed up for over a century. Captain Cook, during his epic voyages of exploration, sighted the island of Vatoa, in the southern Lau Group, in 1774. The larger islands were sighted by Captain Bligh in 1789, on his way to Timor after the mutiny on the Bounty, when he was chased by a canoe of native Fijians near the Yasawas. He was able to examine the group more thoroughly when he returned to the Pacific in 1792. James Wilson of the missionary ship *Duff* sailed through the northern portion of the group in 1797. These visits gave only a fragmentary picture of life in the Fijian archipelago.

It was the lure of sandalwood that finally brought Europeans ashore in Fiji. To this was soon added the search for 'heathen souls.' Sandalwood stands were discovered by the survivor of a shipwreck near Lakeba, in the Lau Group, around 1800. The sandalwood trade was difficult and dangerous, but profits could be very high. The trade began in 1804, based out of Bua Bay on Vanua Levu. By 1814 all easily accessible stands of sandalwood had been logged.

The sandalwood trade brought the first European settlers, a handful of beachcombers, including Charles Savage on Bau and Paddy Connel at Rewa. During the same period, Europeans also exported small quantities of *bêche-de-mer* (sea slugs) to China. The bêche-de-mer trade remained limited, however, so long as there were sufficient quantities of sandalwood. The first intensive period of bêche-de-mer trading lasted from 1828 to 1835, followed by a second period from 1842 to 1850. An average of three ships a year would visit the area during these periods.

The town of Levuka on the island of Ovalau grew as the centre of European settlement and of the bêche-de-mer trade after beachcomber David Whippy settled there in 1822. Another centre of European influence was Lakeba. Two Tahitian missionaries arrived at Lakeba in 1830. They were joined by Wesleyans David Cross and William Cargill in 1835. Cross sought to establish a foothold on Bau in 1838, but was unsuccessful. The following year he was able to establish himself at Rewa, where he set up Fiji's first printing press. Levuka's foreign population was around fifty by the early 1850s, there being another couple of dozen Europeans scattered around the archipelago as well.

Mapping of the Fijian islands and charting its waters came slowly. Russian ships under the comand of Thaddeus von Bellingshausen visited a portion of the Lau Group in 1820. The French explorer Dumont d'Urville conducted extensive surveys in 1827 and 1838, as did the British vessel HMS *Victor* in 1836. The first reliable chart of the area was made in 1840 by the United States Exploring Expedition under the command of Charles Wilkes.

The years between 1850 and 1858 were hard ones for European traders who had to rely largely on trade in pigs and yams. Despite depressed economic conditions, the European presence continued to grow as more Christian missionaries arrived to spread the Gospel and to instill Western values in the heathens. One important step in this direction was the introduction of Western legal concepts by the Wesleyans in 1854 in areas under their influence. The economic picture changed in 1858 when coconut oil emerged as an important commodity. The German firm, Godeffroy und Sohn, one of the leading trading houses in the region at the time, sent an agent to Fiji in that year. This led the British and Americans to respond by augmenting their commercial activities in Fiji.

Fijian politics during the first half of the nineteenthth century consisted largely of rivalries between competing chiefs and of increasing chiefly dominance over commoners. Europeans influenced both of these developments. Respect for the rights of commoners gave way increasingly to harsh exploitation, including exacting more tribute and making greater demands for labour. This was related, in large part, to the desire by chiefs for more European goods for warfare and conspicuous consumption. The early nineteenthth century witnessed the rise of the Bauan chiefs in particular. Their ascendancy was accomplished not only through traditional means but also as a result of the assistance provided by Charles Savage and European weapons. Following the death of the Bauan chief, Naulivou, in 1829, Bauan power declined.

Bau's fortunes again rose in the 1840s under the leadership of Cakobau. During the 1840s, Bau was involved in almost constant warfare. In his struggles against rival eastern chiefs Cakobau sought to monopolize the bêche-de-mer trade, and in 1841 he burned Levuka in a bid to stop Europeans from trading with other chiefs. Cakobau's fortunes suffered a reverse in the early 1850s, as opposition to him among settlers and other chiefs increased, and there were several revolts against his authority. But he was able to turn the tide with the assistance of the Tongans.

The Tongan, Ma'afu, came to eastern Fiji in 1847 and soon wielded considerable influence. Ma'afu became governor of the Tongans in Fiji in 1853 and was able to secure control over much of the eastern portion of the archipelago. Ma'afu visited Bau in 1850, and over the next couple of years relations between the Tongans and Bau were strengthened. In return for becoming a Christian and allowing Christian missionaries to settle in his territory, Cakobau was promised Tongan support against his enemies.

At the Battle of Kaba in 1855, due in large part to help provided by his Tongan allies, Cakobau crushed his opponents, who included chiefs from Rewa, his half-brother Mara Kapaiwai, and a number of rebel Bauan chiefs. Once again he was a leading force in Fiji. Ma'afu also helped to secure the position of another chief, the Tui Bua, after he became a Christian in 1855. The result was that a handful of relatively powerful regional chiefs emerged in eastern Fiji with close ties to Christianity and to European traders and settlers. Relations between these chiefs were not, however, always cordial and by the late 1850s Ma'afu and Cakobau more closely resembled rivals than allies.

Following rumours in 1860 that Fiji was to be annexed by Britain, there was a substantial influx of settlers from Australia and New Zealand. The flow of migrants declined when the rumours proved unfounded, but their number and the capital that they had brought with them were sufficient to create a minor boom in Fiji's fledgling capitalist economy. The population of Levuka was only around eighty at the outset of the boom. By 1870 it had reached five hundred. The traditional areas of economic activity, bêche-de-mer and tortoiseshell, continued to be of some importance, but the focus of economic growth was coconut oil and obtaining land for plantations. A few sheep were also raised and small amounts of coffee and sugar were grown.

The American Civil War provided a major impetus to growing cotton in Fiji, as it did in other parts of the South Pacific. Since plantations in the American South still were unable to provide Europe with much cotton immediately after the Civil War, the Fijian cotton trade was able to continue through the latter part of the 1860s. One important outcome of this boom was a sharp increase in land alienation by the settlers, with a total of 250,000 acres having been alienated by 1868. Ma'afu, in particular, was able to offer cotton planters security of tenure in the eastern islands under his control.

The Australian and New Zealand economies suffered a severe downturn in the late 1860s. The resultant increase in migration to Fiji, became a 'rush' between 1870 and 1871, when the settler population neared three thousand. Such rapid population growth served to keep the local capitalist economy lively, especially for lawyers, auctioneers, and brokers. Much of the capital was provided through loans from Godeffroy und Sohn, other overseas investors, and a few local settler capitalists. Economic production was concentrated in cotton (which accounted for 80 per cent of export earnings in 1869), with a great deal of attention also focused on land speculation.

There were intense rivalries between German, English, and American interests, with the settlers seeking to manipulate local Fijian politics to promote their own ends. The Americans were represented by an exceptionally unscrupulous group, at the forefront of which was the Polynesian Company, which engaged in land and other forms of speculation. German interests generally were represented by Godeffroy, which served as a lending agent, purchased coconut products and land, and engaged in other forms of trade. British interests (which included those of Australia and New Zealand) were dominant, but this dominance was in no way secure.

At the suggestion of the British consul, a number of eastern Fijian chiefs agreed to form a government in 1865. The Europeans saw this as a way of providing a stable atmosphere for further development of plantations and other economic enterprises. Cakobau was chosen president. The formation of this government marked yet another step in the formation of what was to become an enduring alliance between foreign business and political interests and Fiji's ranking eastern chiefs, an alliance that was to coalesce into a ruling oligarchy in colonial and postcolonial Fiji.

The chiefs involved in the first Cakobau government rarely were able to agree among themselves and when Ma'afu withdrew after an unsuccessful bid for the presidency in 1867, the government collapsed. Ma'afu and a few other chiefs then established a separate confederacy known as the Tovata or North-Eastern Confederation. The following year, Tonga decided to withdraw from Fijian affairs; Ma'afu was left without Tongan backing, and the Tovata Confederation quickly became moribund. Despite these setbacks, Ma'afu continued to exert considerable influence in the eastern islands, and in 1869 he was given the newly created title of Tui Lau by his Fijian allies.

The Franco-Prussian War began in August 1870 and French factories, the main buyers of cotton from the South Pacific, stopped purchasing Fijian cotton. The London price of cotton subsequently dropped by about three-fourths, and settlers in Fiji of all nationalities found themselves in financial trouble. The collapse of the cotton market was followed by two cyclones which caused widespread damage. In the face of such a crisis, a group of settlers in Levuka set about to form a new central government with Cakobau as its figurehead.

When the new government was formed in 1871, it did not have the support of the entire settler population, but a number of important eastern chiefs did back it, among them, Ma'afu. Cakobau was proclaimed king of Fiji and Ma'afu was named viceroy as well as commander-in-chief and governor of Lau. By the end of 1871 all of the principal chiefs in the east had accepted the new government. The last to accept it was one of Ma'afu's allies, the Tui Cakau, who arrived in Levuka 'his eyes swollen with rum' to make peace with the new government after a visit to his home island by an American warship which went there 'to conduct an inquiry into outrages against American citizens.'[10]

Initial financing of the new government proved to be something of a problem, but Cakobau and his settler associates came up with a solution. Cakobau had attacked the Lovoni people in the interior of Ovalau not too long before being proclaimed king of Fiji by the

Levuka settlers. The Lovoni people had put up stiff resistance until European missionaries convinced them to give up the struggle:

> The Lovoni people surrendered ... and were made to crawl on their hands and knees before their conquerors, bearing baskets of earth. This much, indeed, was Fijian custom, and excusable; the sequel was neither. The whole tribe, including women and children, old and young ... were marched into the native town of Levuka, bullied and hustled by the young men of Bau. They were sentenced to transportation to the plantations of the European settlers. Cakobau confiscated their lands, and later mortgaged them to Europeans who advanced money to his Government; the hapless people he 'portioned out to different applicants for their services' – in plain English, he sold them into servitude to any person willing to buy them ... Cakobau never possessed so much ready money before: from the sale of these unfortunate people he collected about £1,100, which he used to launch his new Government.[11]

This was only the beginning. Cakobau's son Epeli Nailatikau was made lieutenant governor of Ba and the Yasawas, and during the latter part of 1871 he set about to sell much of the northern Yasawas to European settlers. There had been a brief military encounter with the Hill Tribes of Ba in 1871. In 1873, using the killing of a settler family as an excuse, the Cakobau government launched an invasion against these people. Once they were defeated, Cakobau sold these people's lands to European settlers and brought about one thousand of them to Levuka with the intention of repeating what he had done to the Lovoni people. This time, however, his plans were thwarted by a visiting British naval commander who was opposed to slavery.

While the Cakobau government went about passing laws favouring its merchant-planter backers and finding ways to line the pockets of its chiefly members, it found itself facing increasing difficulties. For one thing, despite the revenue from the sale of conquered people and their land, the Cakobau government was in financial trouble. The first year's budget was a little over £20,000.

By mid-1872, finding it hard to collect the numerous taxes and other fees it had introduced, the government found itself with a deficit of about £7,000. It then sought to borrow money using public lands as security. A year later the deficit had grown to over £12,000 with liabilities in excess of £40,000. Opposition to the government, even among those who had initially supported it, was growing. In Levuka itself, settler opponents formed groups, including one called the Ku Klux Klan, and relations between the government and the citizenry of Levuka became increasingly strained. Opposition to the government among the planters also was growing. There were strains among the allied Fijian chiefs as well. Ma'afu and his associates appeared ready to secede by mid-1873. They did not, but the alliance continued to weaken, especially when a number of chiefs backing Cakobau began to express anti-Tongan sentiments aimed at Ma'afu and his allies.

As a way out of the mess, Cakobau and some of his settler friends asked the British to take over. Ma'afu initially had opposed the idea, but by early 1874 he had come to support it. An agreement between Cakobau and commissioners representing the British government was reached in March 1874, and an interim government was set up. The two main concerns of the new administration were improving the financial situation and promoting law and order. The commissioners noted that while the total capital invested in the country was around £250,000, the Cakobau government had managed to spend £124,000 and run up a debt of £87,000 in a little more than two years. As for promotion of law and order, that mostly entailed further moves to defeat the Hill Tribes of western Viti Levu and any others who stood in the way of the interests of foreign capital and the eastern chiefs.

THE COLONIAL STATE

The formal takeover of Fiji by Britain in 1874 was brought about by a breakdown in the previous collaborative mechanisms under the Cakobau government. Colonial rule represented a reconstruction of collaboration between Europeans and the eastern chiefs, but this collaboration would be more extensive and deeply rooted than in the earlier precolonial period, with the balance of power shifted to the Europeans.

Following acceptance of the annexation of Fiji by the British Parliament, Hercules Robinson, the governor of New South Wales, was deputied to go to Fiji and temporarily take up the governorship there. He arrived in September 1874 and British warships were sent to collect agreements from leading eastern chiefs to cede Fiji to Britain. This done, the cession of Fiji was celebrated in Levuka on 10 October 1874.

With a few changes, Robinson allowed the existing settler government to continue functioning, but he did take steps to establish a rudimentary colonial government. Under the central government in Levuka he set up separate administrations for Europeans and part-Europeans, on the one hand, and native Fijians on the other hand.

Four stipendiary magistrates were appointed for the former. The native Fijian administration comprised an administrative structure consisting of twelve provinces which were subdivided into eighty-four districts or *tikina* with the village or *koro* as the smallest unit. A native chief or *roko tui* and a native stipendiary magistrate were appointed at the provincial level, a headman or *buli* was appointed at the district level, and a headman or *turaga-ni-koro* at the village level.

Arthur Gordon arrived in June 1875 to take over as governor of the colony, although he did not actually assume administrative control until September. One of his first responsibilities was to deal with a measles epidemic that was raging in the colony. Measles had been brought to Fiji by Cakobau and two of his sons after a visit to Sydney sponsored by the colonial government. The epidemic cost 40,000 lives before it was over – more than 25 per cent of the native Fijian population. As for Cakobau and his sons, they were cared for by European doctors in Levuka and survived. One of Britain's responses to the loss of life was to reduce funding for Fiji by about one-third.

During the latter half of 1875, Gordon consolidated control over eastern Fiji and the coastal west. In part because of limited finances, he was forced to rely on the structure of indirect rule initiated by Robinson. Gordon clearly saw that establishment of colonial rule initially entailed working through collaborator chiefs. He sought to create a façade of responsibility among these chiefs, with European officials providing supervision and ultimately being in control. The chiefs primarily involved were those with a previous history of collaboration. To strengthen the power of the chiefs over their subjects, the British expanded the sphere of communal responsibility under chiefly control among native Fijian commoners. This was especially relevant to economic aspects of native Fijian life since economic activities had traditionally been centred on the individual household. Now more of economic life fell within the domain of chiefly rule, allowing the chiefs to orient production to help fill the colonial government's coffers and to augment their own incomes.

Linked to the strengthening of indirect rule was a policy of promoting cultural, social, and linguistic hegemony among native Fijians throughout the colony. Bauan language and social structure, in no small part because of its strongly hierarchical nature, provided the model for the rest of Fiji. This represented a major change in more egalitarian societies such as those in western Fiji and assured the eastern chiefs a position at the top of the native administration.

Resistance to British colonial rule and to the hegemony of the chiefs of Bau and Lau was to be found mainly in inland and western Viti Levu. Resistance was precipitated by Cakobau's sale to European planters of coastal and riverain lands in an area to which he had no right. The highlanders of Viti Levu felt threatened by this intrusion and sought to drive off the planters by attacking them. Cakobau's initial efforts to pacify the highlanders and to assure the security of the planters met with failure and he turned to the British for help.

In early 1876 Gordon sent his aide Walter Carew and Captain Olive in command of an Armed Native Constabulary force to establish a military and trading post in the upper Sigatoka Valley, near the centre of resistance. The inland tribes viewed this as a provocative move, especially since the Armed Native Constabulary was made up of people who traditionally were hostile to them. Between January and April the two sides sized each other up. Initially Carew sought to disarm the hill tribes through persuasion. When persuasion failed, Carew decided to try to take some of the chiefs hostage with the aim of exchanging them for guns. With this in mind, in March, he sought unsuccessfully to entice a couple of the chiefs to his camp. Meanwhile the chiefs of the Sigatoka Valley met to discuss Carew's demands. Most of the chiefs strongly opposed giving in. There were a few, however, who, as a result of bribery and flattery, decided to support the British.

Fighting broke out in April 1876. The Nabutautau and Naqaqu people threatened Christian villages that were supplying the British camp. An Armed Native Constabulary force under Ratu Luke Nakulainakoro (from Nadroga) retaliated. After this encounter, Gordon raised an army of 2,000 men, consisting of Armed Native Constabulary auxiliaries under the command of Captain Knollys. The force was aided by the procurement of 150 Snider rifles from New Zealand (where they had proved effective against the Maoris). A three-pronged attack, supported by local collaborators, was launched aginst the Hill Tribes and the inland tribes were defeated quickly. Twenty-six of the defeated chiefs were executed, and a permanent military garrison was stationed at Fort Carnarvon (where it remained until 1898). In addition, whereas other native Fijian provinces had native Fijians appointed to the primary administrative posts, in the two provinces created out of the newly conquered territories (Colo West and Colo East), European commissioners were put in charge.

At the same time that he was dealing with the Hill Tribes, Gordon was busy instituting a system of native Fijian administration for the colony that would form the basis of a structure of indirect rule. The collaborator chiefs were brought together to form a Great Council of Chiefs that was intended to serve as an advisory body to Gordon. The council was used by Gordon to help legitimate his efforts to create a stable and uniform colonial state, and his power over the council was considerable. Thus, on one occasion Gordon threatened to dissolve the council and never call another when he learned that some of the members were drunk.[12]

Most power within the structure of the native Fijian administration was vested in the Native Regulations Board which Gordon created in 1876. The board was made up of two members from the Legislative Council and six nominated members. Native law was adopted to suit the needs of the colonial administration and, at the same time, English law was applied in many areas (especially for criminal offences). Cakobau himself was pensioned off at £1,500 per year (an amount second only to the governor's salary). Other leading chiefs were given salaries in order of their importance to the colonial regime – the Roko Tui Tailevu and Roko Tui Naitasiri were given £600 each per year and Cakobau's oldest son, Ratu Epeli Nailatikau, was provided with £340 per year. The lowest salaries were given to the western chiefs at £100 per year.

The land issue was a particularly important one and it had to be handled with great delicacy. At the time of annexation virtually all of the readily accessible, fertile land already had been taken over by Europeans, amounting to less than 20 per cent of the total land available. This did not, of course, stop the settlers from wanting more. Gordon had to undertake a delicate balancing act to keep the greed of the settlers from ruining his plans for creating a stable colony that would attract large-scale investment. Using the Great Council of Chiefs to give his actions a mark of 'traditional' authority, Gordon established a standard form of land tenure throughout Fiji (the traditional systems were quite diverse) for ease of administration and to ensure greater stability. Accordingly, he instructed the Council of Chiefs to come up with a standard code that suited his needs, with the threat of dissolution should they fail to do so. A land law based on this standardization was put into effect in 1880 and thereafter enshrined as traditional. It was a law that served to stabilize the situation and gave native Fijians some security of tenure, but it was also often manipulated for the benefit of the colonial administration and foreign investors (as well as in the interests of collaborator chiefs), and on a number of occasions land was alienated in clear violation of the law.

Inspired by what he had read of the Dutch system in Java, Gordon established a produce tax for native Fijians, using the rokos to oversee tax gathering. The intent was to turn native Fijian commoners into communal producers of cash crops under the supervision of their chiefs. Produce was collected on a provincial basis and sold to merchants on tender. The main cash crop was copra, followed by bananas and sugar. By the late 1870s native Fijian taxes accounted for around 3 per cent of government revenue. Most of the surplus left over after paying taxes was spent on churches and boats. In addition to economic development, this policy sought to instill in native Fijians values favouring communal cash crop production and sought to avoid the emergence of a landless class that might prove to be a destabilizing force in the colony.

Most higher ranking chiefs were strongly opposed to allowing native Fijian commoners to work for wages since they thought that this would undermine their authority. Thus, they wanted to create a communal system of production under their supervision. Many district and village headmen, however, were not opposed to the use of wage labour since it provided them with a source of income in the form of bribes and gifts for services as labour recruiters. Despite the opposition of the higher chiefs, recruitment for wage labour was allowed, albeit in a limited fashion. In an 1876 labour ordinance, the colonial government set out conditions for recruitment, treatment, and repatriation of native Fijian workers (an additional ordinance was passed in 1877). By 1880 there were 580 native Fijians working as plantation labourers and 420 as crew on inter-island shipping.

Cash crop production by native Fijian commoners and the settler-owned plantations certainly helped the colonial economy, but they were not judged by the administration to be sufficient to create a sound economic basis for the colony. The pressure to do something to improve the situation was particularly keen after the virtual collapse of the cotton industry. When the British took over Fiji there were about six hundred European-owned plantations. Most of these were extremely small and under-financed. Even the largest of them were not, in fact, very big – and they were much too small for what Gordon had in mind.

In 1874 negotiations began with the large Australian concern, the Colonial Sugar Refining Company (CSR). It was not until 1880, however, that CSR was persuaded to invest in Fiji. An important consideration behind this decision was the assurance by the colonial government of a stable supply of cheap labour in the form of indentured workers from India. An agreement had been worked out to begin bringing indentured workers to Fiji from India on five-year contracts. A recruitment depot was opened in Calcutta in 1879 (a second one was opened in Madras in 1903).

The stage was now set for the development of the Fijian colonial state, based primarily on a sugar industry under the control of a single large foreign company which used imported indentured labour. To a lesser extent the colonial economy was also based on coconut products and other agricultural commodities grown by European planters and by native Fijian commoners who were locked up in their villages and forced to work communally under the control of a class of collaborator chiefs. The overall importance of sugar for the colonial economy increased sharply during the 1870s and 1880s. In 1875 it had accounted for only 4 per cent of the value of exports, with cotton and coconut products being of considerably more importance. By 1885 sugar products accounted for 66 per cent of the value of the colony's exports, cotton had disappeared as an export, and coconut products had declined to a 20 per cent share.

Gordon was appointed governor of New Zealand in 1880. He was replaced by William Des Voeux who had previous experience in the Caribbean and, like Gordon, he was not favourably disposed towards small-scale settler capitalists. The Des Voeux administration (1880–87) witnessed the gradual transformation of the sugar industry as CSR's presence in the colony grew. Sugar-cane production increased substantially from 1,731 tons in 1882 to 12,831 tons in 1887. Moreover, the nature of the industry began to change. European planters had agreed to sell cane to CSR at a fixed price in 1880. But planters quickly found themselves in a difficult position, caught between the price agreed to with CSR and increasing labour costs as a result of a shortage of supply and higher costs of food. Tension between CSR and the planters ensued.

During the Des Voeux administration, control of native Fijian commoners was increased (for example, internal migration was restricted) and the power of native Fijian chiefly administrators over them was enhanced. This did not occur without incident and in 1882 a rebellion had to be put down in Macuata Province. Two other events of note occurred during his administration: the colonial capital was moved from Levuka to Suva in 1882, and Cakobau died in 1883.

Charles Mitchell served briefly as governor after Des Voeux and then was replaced by John B. Thurston in 1888 (he remained as governor until he died in 1897). Thurston had first visited Fiji in 1863 and subsequently had become a cotton planter. He served as a member of the Legislative Assembly in the Cakobau government and played an active role in the move towards annexation. He had become auditor general, colonial secretary and finally lieutenant governor, and had been responsible for negotiations with CSR. His governorship witnessed the final entrenchment of the administrative and commercial processes begun by Gordon.

Even though the price of sugar began to fall in the 1880s and continued to do so into the first decades of the twentieth century, this was more than compensated for by large increases in production. Sugar exports during the final year of Thurston's governorship amounted to 26,991 tons, valued at some £323,830 (the export value of sugar in 1882 had been £58,857). By 1897, CSR was well on its way towards a complete monopoly of the industry. The company controlled 20,000 acres of freehold and leasehold land, and its mills at Nausori, Rarawai, and Labasa accounted for 87.5 per cent of unrefined sugar and cane products.

At first most of the labour in the sugar industry was provided by native Fijians and other Pacific islanders brought to Fiji as indentured labourers. Between 1877 and 1911, about 23,000 Melanesian labourers were imported to work on sugar and copra plantations. A large number of these people returned to their home islands, many died of diseases while in Fiji, but some remained.[13] By the mid-1880s, Indian indentured labourers had come to comprise the majority of workers in the rapidly expanding sugar industry. Their indenture period was for five years, working five and one-half days a week, at one shilling per day. The cost of their passage was £23, of which CSR paid two-thirds and the colonial government one-third.

In total, some 60,000 Indian workers were brought to Fiji and of these about 40,000 remained. Conditions for the workers were especially bad during the initial period up to the early 1890s, and then improved somewhat as the industry became more established. But even at the best of times, work conditions were far from ideal – even if they might have been better than those prevailing back in India. Between 1885 and 1919 there were 229 suicides among the Indian indentured workers. A protest march in 1886 by 130 Indian labourers led the colonial government to pass legislation to strengthen control over the workers. In general, however, the government left the affairs of the workers in the hands of CSR.

As the number of Indians in Fiji increased, the Indian community in the colony became more diverse. In addition to indentured workers, there were smallholder agricultural producers, hawkers, shopkeepers, artisans, and others. As they became more established, they sought to reconstitute a form of the society they had known back in India, building on remembered cultural traditions and the urgings of visiting religious and political leaders from India. Between 1897 and 1914, the government financed the establishment of eighteen Indian settlements near sugar plantations to provide a stable residential setting for about 2,000 smallholders who were able to lease 32,000 acres from the government or from native Fijians. By 1888 there were eleven Indian-owned shops in the colony.

Indian migrants were mixing freely with native Fijian commoners, and this was of growing concern to the leading chiefs who felt that this might undermine their position of domination. In addition, the chiefs were upset by evidence of Indian commercial success (European control of most commerce somehow did not seem to bother them). European landowners and businessmen, for their part, were making money from the Indians and saw little to worry about. In fact, there was a general feeling in the European community that the Indian presence was good for the economic development of the colony.

During the 1880s and early 1890s, many of the smaller European plantations and businesses in the colony went bankrupt. This coincided with CSR's growing domination of the sugar industry. Production of copra and bananas (which was initiated in 1875 and reached 10 per cent of the value of exports by the early twentieth century) fell largely into the hands of native Fijians. Native Fijian commoners carried out the work under the control of the chiefs with the government purchasing what was produced as tax and then selling it to European merchants.

In 1895 the Australian firm Burns Philp, in partnership with two other firms, purchased the year's supply of 'tax' copra from the government, giving it possession of virtually the entire output of the colony.[14] With the exception of a couple of years, this Burns Philp partnership continued to be successful in its bids until the early part of the twentieth century. Their profits were substantial. In 1904, for example, the bid was £10/10/9 per ton and the 4,000 tons of copra purchased were then sold in the Baltic for £16/10/0.

The myth was that the administration was acting in the interests of the Fijian people, which included helping to preserve their communalism. The reality was that such communalism and protection was intended to ensure the smooth operation of an exploitative trade that brought revenue to the administration and profits to large firms like Burns Philp, while also helping the chiefs at the expense of commoners.

Following the initial guidelines established by Robinson and Gordon, during the remainder of the nineteenth century, the system of administering to native Fijians was developed to serve the needs of an evolving colonial political and economic order. At the upper level, hereditary chiefs slowly were turned into colonial bureaucrats. During the initial period of colonial rule, chiefly power had been consolidated and reformed and the rights of commoners diluted. The latter part of the nineteenth century witnessed the rise of 'second-order' or 'new-type' chiefs over 'old-type' chiefs like Cakobau. These new-type chiefs usually were descended from lines opposed to Cakobau in the traditional political order or from second-order lines associated with Bau (i.e., 'lesser' lineages) or in a vassal relationship to Bau.[15]

One of these new-type chiefs was Ratu Marika Totoca, who became an important trouble-shooter for the colonial administration. He became chief native magistrate in 1875 and native lands commissioner in 1891. His appeal to colonial officials lay in his literacy and his loyalty. Another was Ratu Jone Madraiwiwi, who Timothy Macnaught refers to as 'Thurston's enthusiastic tax collector.'[16] Madraiwiwi began his career as a clerk in the audit office in 1883 and became Native Lands Commissioner in 1889. In 1896 he was made Roko Tui Ra. In 1904 he was also placed in charge of Bua Province. And, in 1912, he was made Roko Tui Tailevu. In these positions he played an important role in obtaining land for Europeans from native Fijians. This was often done under duress, with neither European nor chiefly members of the colonial administration listening to the protests of native Fijian landowners. Under Governor im Thurn (1904–11), Madraiwiwi was able to obtain large amounts of land under very favourable conditions for Europeans: 20,000 acres in Bua in 1906, another 12,000 acres in Bua in 1908, and 50,000 acres in Macuata. He was able to accumulate personal wealth in this manner as well. Thus, in 1907 he persuaded the Somosomo chiefs on Taveuni to grant him 2,000 acres of prime land which in 1912 he had converted into a Crown grant.

One other important member of this group of new chiefs was Devi Toganivalu, from a second-ranking Bauan mataqali. He began his career as a clerk in Levuka in 1880. He then moved to the Native Department and in 1908 he was elevated to the position of Roko Tui Bua, at which time he began referring to himself as Ratu.

During the latter part of the nineteenth century it became increasingly clear that hereditary right to the Roko Tui title (head chief of a province) was not automatic. Service to the colonial administration became the main criteria; office holders could be dismissed and others given the positions as rewards at the will of the governor. The effect was to remove many of the old-type chiefs from these positions and to replace them with more literate and more loyal new-type chiefs.

With the exception of Colo East, Colo West, and Colo North (the latter created after suppression of the Tuku Movement in 1892) which remained under direct European control, administration of native Fijian affairs at the provincial and district (tikina) levels was handed over to loyal native Fijians. A large number of these posts were given to those who had risen through the ranks of the colonial administration or through the military and police bodies. An important avenue of mobility for young chiefs within the colonial hierarchy was through the various bodies created for the maintenance of law and order. These included the Armed Native Constabulary, the Town and Civil Police, and the Village Constabulary. Leading eastern collaborator chiefs commonly used the Armed Native Constabulary as a stepping stone into civilian administrative posts, using it as a means to readily prove their loyalty to the colonial order. Younger lesser chiefs also joined enthusiastically, seeing this as a means of advancement.

It was the members of these lesser lineages who first recognized the importance of learning English and of Western education for advancement in the new order. And it was this that gave them a decided advantage over the old-style chiefs. But during most of the first few decades of colonial rule, opportunities for such education remained extremely limited. At the time of annexation, education was largely in the hands of the churches. The education they provided was almost exclusively in the Fijian language, and the curriculum was of little relevance for work in a Western-style bureaucracy.

While most Europeans in the colony opposed the idea of Western education for native Fijians – whether chiefs or commoners – as a waste of time, those at the higher levels of the administration came to favour it. Governors such as Thurston saw it as a means of providing less expensive personnel for the colonial administration. The two leading schools in the colony, Levuka Grammar School (established in 1879) and Suva Grammar School (established in 1883) catered mainly to Europeans. An ordinance was passed in 1882 for the establishment of two technical schools to provide education for the children of collaborator chiefs. Only one of the schools (Yanawai School on Vanua Levu), however, was ever built. The Native Medical School was founded at the Colonial Hospital in Suva in 1884, primarily to provide for the training of practitioners to assist European government doctors.

The Council of Chiefs requested a school like Suva Grammar for the children of chiefs in 1890. Initially there was little support for this idea within the colonial administration or church bodies. By the mid-1890s, however, the notion of providing such education for the children of the chiefs had gained more widespread acceptance. The Catholics took the lead, offering instruction in English in 1899. The

Methodists did the same in 1902. Queen Victoria School for boys was opened in 1906. It became an important institution for training Fiji's native élite, and by 1930 around five hundred youths had attended the school.

The situation for native Fijian commoners was somewhat different from that of the chiefs. Virtually every aspect of their lives came to be regulated by the Fijian Administration. In particular, males between the ages of fourteen and sixty could be called on to provide an increasingly wide range of services. So-called 'traditional' obligations to the chiefs and the church were expanded greatly (leading to numerous protests by commoners). Native Fijian commoners were feeling growing pressures as a result of colonial taxes, exactions of the church, administrative and traditional (lala) obligations, as well as their own consumer desires. They were especially resentful about having to grow sugar-cane for tax purposes, preferring the easier work of copra production. Most of the produce for tax purposes came from the eastern provinces where chiefly rule was strongest. In 1901 there was widespread protest about paying tax in cane in the western provinces of Serua and Namosi. The compulsion to pay taxes in kind was removed in 1908 and by 1910 no native Fijian commoners were producing cane.

Despite continued resistance by the leading chiefs, a number of native Fijian commoners continued to work for wages. In 1882 there were 2,300 working under one-year contracts, and by 1884 about 25 per cent of native Fijian adult males had worked for wages in some capacity. Demand for native Fijian labour declined as the number of indentured labourers from India grew. During the 1890s the main avenue for employment for native Fijians was on European-owned coconut plantations, which employed about 2,000 native Fijian labourers.

By the 1880s, for the most part, serious opposition to colonial rule had come to an end, but it had not disappeared entirely. In 1894 the people of Seaqaqa on Vanua Levu objected to being forced to carry a large number of heavy logs across rough terrain to be used as house posts for CSR's new installation at Labasa – a form of service imposed on them by colonial authorities. They also complained of paying taxes for which they received nothing in return. Two constables sent by the Roko Tui Macuatua were killed, and the people of Seaqaqa, led by Ramasieli and Yacadra, built a fort in defiance of colonial rule. A detachment of the Armed Native Constabulary, led by a chief from Rewa and comprised mainly of traditional enemies of the Seaqaqa people, attacked the fort and crushed the rebellion. Seven of the rebels were killed and two committed suicide. Afterwards, two more rebels were hung. This was the last armed revolt against colonial rule.

Resistance took other forms as well. One form that it took was millenarianism. Unrest stimulated by a religious cult in Ra Province came to the attention of colonial authorities in 1877. The people of Ra were among the most travelled in Fiji, having been recruited as workers on European-owned plantations since the time of the Cakobau government. The leader of the cult was a commoner turned prophet-priest named Dugumoi. He was arrested in 1878 and exiled to Lau. He was allowed to return in 1882. Upon his return he founded the *Wai ni Tuka* (the water of immortal youth) or Tuka Cult. Dugumoi claimed that the twin gods Naucirikaumoli and Nakausabaria had revealed to him that they held the key to immortality. It was a syncretic cult containing Christian and pagan elements. It was also strongly anticolonial. A date was set in 1885 when the Europeans and their Bauan allies, along with Christianity, were to be overthrown. The administration became disturbed when 'they heard that parties of men with blackened faces, and clothed in robes were carrying out military drills in the upper reaches of the Rewa River.'[17] Dugumoi was arrested again and sent into exile to Rotuma. By 1888 most of the cult followers, at least nominally, had become Catholics. Quietly, however, the cult spread into the highlands of western Viti Levu. In the eastern highlands, it was led by Senileba and known as the *Bai Tabua* (fence of whale's teeth). In the western highlands one of the most prominent cult leaders was Osea Saunivalu. These leaders too were arrested and jailed or exiled.

There was a major revival of the Tuka Cult in Ra and Ba provinces in 1892. In the face of this perceived threat to the colonial administration, Governor Thurston himself, with the assistance of Ratu Jone Madraiwiwi, led the Armed Native Constabulary against the cult followers. Several villages were destroyed and 300 adherents were exiled to Kadavu for ten years. Colo North Province was created to help contain the movement and an Armed Native Constabulary post was established at Nadarivatu.

Despite suppression by the colonial authorities, sporadic outbreaks of millenarian activity continued until the First World War. In fact, during the early years of the twentieth century cult activities became more open. In 1907 millenarian activity was noted in the middle Sigatoka Valley, involving elements of the Tuka and *Leve ni wai* (children of the water) cults. What upset the authorities the most in this instance was the participation of a number of local native Fijian officials. Moreover, during their trial they indicated that such activities were quite widespread. Cult followers built a *bure* (house) for the twin gods in 1914. Once detected by the authorities, the cult members joined the Catholic church to avoid being sent to jail.

Also worthy of mention, was a strike organized in 1890 by the Roko Tui Suva, Avarosa Tuivuya, on the Suva wharf among native Fijian workers. They sought to have the wages they received from United Steamship Navigation Company doubled to two shillings a day.

Thurston died in 1897, and by 1900 most of the European and native Fijian 'old colonial hands' were dead or in retirement. In addition, older settler commercial enterprises for the most part had been replaced by larger foreign firms. These developments set the scene for a new stage in the evolution of Fiji's colonial political economy. This new stage was to be ushered in during the governorship of Everard im Thurn. It is important to recognize, however, that the policies implemented by im Thurn were not a complete break with previous policies. They represented an intensification of a trajectory long since established.

The European population had remained roughly the same size since the 1870s and stood at 2,726 in 1906. Just under one-half of the Europeans (1,112) lived in Suva, which had become a town of roughly 5,000. Suva had grown and achieved a degree of prosperity, but it was hardly a booming metropolis. The *Cyclopedia of Fiji* of 1907 notes: 'The town can boast of nothing very substantial in the way of buildings ... The stranger on landing in Suva is likely to be not too favourably impressed with the place – apart from its great natural attractions ... For the streets of the town little can be said; they are narrow, crooked alleys.'[18] Elsewhere, towns were growing up around CSR's sugar operations at Ba, Lautoka, and Labasa. Levuka carried on, but the centre of activity clearly had shifted elsewhere. In many ways, CSR, its activities focused away from Suva, was a law unto itself with its strict ethnic hierarchy of work and residence: Europeans on top, part-Europeans in the middle, and Indians on the bottom. The Indian communities were catered to by European, Chinese, and a growing number of Indian merchants. Gujaratis began arriving from India around 1904 as goldsmiths and tailors and soon had established themselves as leaders of the Indo-Fijian business community.

The governor retained most power in the colony, with the Legislative Council serving largely in an advisory capacity. The Legislative Council consisted of six elected Europeans, two nominated native Fijians, and an official majority (with no Indian representation). In 1905 the members included local businessmen Henry Marks (one of the leading settler merchants), David Robbie (a copra trader who was shortly to be associated with an affiliate of Burns Philp), and Simeon Lazarus (of A.M. Brodziak & Company and a leader of the small local Jewish community), as well as James Turner (a planter and founding member of the Fiji Planters' Association) and William McRae (manager of the Fiji branch of the Bank of New South Wales). The native Fijian members were Ratu Jone Madraiwiwi and Ratu Kadayu Levu.

In 1903 the secretary of state for colonies issued a policy pronouncement advocating a slow departure from the communal system in favour of self-reliance and individualism for native Fijians. The process was initiated by im Thurn when he was appointed governor the following year. Both the Colonial Office and im Thurn felt that it was time to rid the colony of the paternalism of indirect rule, which was seen as standing in the way of agricultural development for native Fijians. The initiative came at a time when the colonial economy was doing relatively well (because of healthy international prices for its exports) and when the colonial administration felt secure enough to move further away from the policies that it had needed at first to control the native Fijian population.

With most of the old Fiji hands out of the way it was relatively simple to establish a new orthodoxy concerning the nature of native Fijian society that was more in keeping with the current political and economic mood. The new orthodoxy was based in large part on the ideas of the missionary and amateur anthropologist Lorimer Fison, especially his work on land tenure and his argument that chiefly power was comparatively recent and to some extent still illegitimate at the time of colonization. It was a position that had been anathema to Gordon and his chiefly allies at the time of cession. Im Thurn also felt that since the native Fijian population was declining, more of the land they occupied should be made available to others who would be able to put it to better use.

Im Thurn was critical of the excessive demands of chiefs and the church on native Fijian commoners which he felt distracted them from more productive work and better use of their capital. Much to the relief of many commoners, the compulsion to pay taxes in kind was removed in 1908 and with this the communal marketing system under the control of the chiefs collapsed. But the commoners soon found themselves at the mercy of European and Chinese merchants who bought their produce in small quantities and then sold it at considerable profit to larger firms.

There were also significant changes made in landholding during the early years of the twentieth century. Native Fijian land was made alienable in 1905. European settlers and commercial interests, commonly working through and in concert with collaborator chiefs, by 1908 had managed to buy outright 104,412 acres of accessible, fertile land and to acquire another 170,000 acres on long leases. Largely as a result of lobbying efforts by Arthur Gordon (by then Lord Stanmore) in England, the 1905 ordinance was overturned in 1908, except for a provision allowing the government to assume land that was deemed necessary for public purposes. Interestingly, this took place at a time when Gordon and his associates in the Pacific Islands Company were in the process of alienating large amounts of land on the phosphate-rich islands of Nauru, Banaba, and Makatea for as little money as possible.

While a number of the collaborator chiefs had benefitted personally from the brief period of land alienation, the chiefs as a group were in an ambiguous position since their statuses and, in part, their incomes depended on the retention of the paternalistic structure. Even someone like Madraiwiwi, who had accumulated considerable wealth under the new capitalist order, did not want to see liberal capitalist reforms go too far as to threaten the security of his status under the paternalistic order. In particular, these chiefs did not feel that they could run capitalist enterprises on their own or even in partnership with Europeans, and they certainly did not want commoners to be given the opportunity to do so. In the main, what they feared most was that the wholesale introduction of liberal capitalism at this time might make them redundant.

Madraiwiwi's son, Ratu J.V.L. Sukuna (1888–1958), became the leader of the battle to defend the position and perquisites of the eastern chiefly establishment during the first half of the twentieth century. Sukuna had been particularly well educated for a chief's son and had been sent to college in New Zealand. He was made a secretariat clerk in 1907 and then in 1912 he was sent by Bau and Lau provinces to Oxford University, making him the most educated and anglicized native Fijian of the period. He had become an important intermediary for the eastern chiefs before leaving for England, and after his return he became a leading spokesman for their interests, eventually emerging as the dominant figure in native Fijian affairs. He dominated the Great Council of Chiefs, was the leading native Fijian chief in colonial government circles, and was a trusted ally of the leading expatriate capitalists.

The native Fijian commoners were presented with an alternative vision by a man from a very different background, Apolosi Nawai, and the two men were to be rivals for the hearts and minds of the native Fijian people for a number of years – a rivalry that has lasted beyond the grave, as they remain symbols of opposing views of native Fijian society. As Macnaught comments: 'If Ratu Sukuna was to become the statesman of Fiji, Apolosi R. Nawai was its under-world hero – the only man from the ranks of ordinary villagers who rivalled the statesman for eloquence, personal *mana,* and a compel-ling vision of the future of Fijians in their own country ... When Apolosi said 'We Fijians' to people with whom he had no connection or status, he was speaking a new language cutting across the intense parochial bonds that kept the constituent groups at every level of Fijian society and administration dependent on chiefs for leadership and initiative.'[19] Nawai's vision was one that even some Europeans could appreciate, such as Robert Compton, member of the Legisla-tive Council and an active proponent of the universal application of English law and the ending of paternalism towards native Fijians (and Apolosi Nawai's legal adviser). But to the eastern collaborator chiefs, Nawai represented a threat. He had to be stopped.

Nawai was born in Nadi around 1876 of very poor, commoner parents. He became a follower of the Tuka Cult (one of the more important cults in western Viti Levu that had anti-European over-tones). Reacting to the exploitative system that he perceived around him and encouraged by the opening provided by the liberal eco-nomic principles enunciated by the colonial government, he launched the Viti Kabani (Viti Company) in 1912. As noted by Wil-liam Sutherland, 'of all the early instances of ... indigenous struggle, this was the most important in the sense that it was the first clear expression of organised struggle by the Fijian peasantry against not only colonial rule but also the underlying system of exploitation.'[20]

The initial idea of the Viti Kabani basically was to cut out the European and Chinese middlemen with whom native Fijian banana and copra producers had to contend and to take matters into their own hands. Nawai was particularly critical of the high profits being made by middlemen in the banana trade. Rather than seeing a remedy in retreating back into the paternalistic arms of the old communal system, Nawai sought to organize native Fijians on a co-operative basis to allow them to compete from a position of greater strength within the market. Thus, he was not only a threat to the collaborator chiefs but also to the settler business community, which was no more keen to see truly free competition prevail than were Sukuna and his associates.

The Viti Kabani soon became much more than a means of promot-ing economic advancement. It became a vehicle for the expression of a wide range of grievances and political discontent. Support for it spread rapidly throughout Fiji. Among those attracted to it were old-style chiefs who had not fared well under administrative reforms, and banana and copra producers. It became so effective in attracting produce, funds, and labour that European planters began to complain that they could not obtain sufficient labour since people were busy producing for the Viti Kabani. Church officials were upset by falling revenue as money that otherwise would have gone to them went to the company. In January 1915 a three-week meeting held by Nawai in Rewa to gain support for his economic plans attracted two to three thousand people.

Sukuna and other collaborator chiefs accused Nawai of treachery and urged that he be charged with sedition. Amidst unsubstantiated rumours that Nawai and some of his men were preparing to launch a rebellion, Nawai was arrested on a charge of embezzlement in May 1915. He was tried, convicted, and sentenced to eighteen months in prison. Despite this setback, his followers carried on with a new company, the Fiji Produce Agency, and were successful in petitioning to use a bloc of native Fijian land that had been sought by Europeans.

Nawai was released in September 1916 and quickly resumed his activities. His enemies launched a slander campaign accusing him of robbing the people and seducing their women. Sukuna was at the forefront of those demanding that drastic steps be taken against Nawai. On the basis of a European witness claiming that at a meeting Nawai had said 'I am the enemy of the government, I am a strong man,'[21] he was arrested on a charge of sedition in November 1917 and without a trial he was exiled to Rotuma. In part, as a result of intervention on his behalf by the Catholic bishop, Nawai was allowed to return in 1924. He was active in the Nadi area until 1930, when he predicted England's demise as a result of the depression, and he was exiled again to Rotuma (this time for ten years). He was placed on probation after his return in 1940, and it was not long before the government found an excuse to exile him. This time he was sent to New Zealand for fear that he might fall into Japanese hands if sent to Rotuma. He was brought back to Fiji in 1946 to die.

Upon his return from Rotuma in 1924, Nawai found his strongest support among *galala* farmers in western Viti Levu and it was this group, assisted by Wesleyan missionary Arthur D. Lelan, that kept the movement alive after Nawai was exiled again in 1930. Galala farmers were individual native Fijian farmers who had distanced themselves from village communalism. Provision was made in 1912 to exempt them from communal service upon evidence of their enterprise and payment of a fee. It was a move that helped to lay the basis for a native Fijian peasantry that was more independent of chiefly authority.

There were a number of other significant reforms during the period immediately before the First World War. In a move that was strongly supported by the collaborator chiefs, in 1911 the government drew up a list of mataqali (clan) members. This action served to end much of the flexibility of the land tenure system (which had tended to benefit poorer commoners) and firmly established the mataqali as the primary landholding unit of native Fijian society (rather than some smaller unit as had been recognized traditionally such as the *tokatoka*). The implication of this move was to institutionalize a landholding unit that was too large for effective commercial management by villagers, thus serving to ensure that land management remained largely in the hands of Europeans and their chiefly allies.

In 1913, the government sought to bring about even further uniformity within native Fijian society and to allow for greater centralization of administration by strengthening of the native Fijian kinship system. In the same year, European provincial magistrates were elevated to district officers and for the first time assigned direct oversight in native Fijian affairs (except in the case of the hill provinces, where they were already involved). The rokos (provincial heads) became native assistants on one-half their former salaries, and they no longer received a share of the land-rent monies. This move served to integrate the chiefs even more thoroughly into the colonial bureaucracy. A similar process was at work with the buli or district heads.

Two contingents of Europeans went from Fiji to fight for England in the First World War. Native Fijians were not allowed to join the British army, but Sukuna, ever loyal, joined the Foreign Legion to be able to fight for the Empire, and a few other collaborator chiefs joined Maori forces in New Zealand. Later one hundred native Fijians were accepted by the military to work on the docks in France.

Meanwhile, in India there was a nationalist awakening and with it growing opposition to the indenture system. In the face of growing protests by Gandhi and his associates, the indenture system was suspended in 1917. The last ship of indentured workers had left for Fiji in 1916. On 1 January 1920 the remaining indentures in Fiji were cancelled. This left Fiji's sugar-based economy in a state of crisis, a crisis that was heightened when the price of sugar dropped sharply in 1921.

The sugar industry was also facing a crisis of another sort – worker militancy. In 1916 there had been an unsuccessful attempt to organize workers on the wharf at Lautoka which served CSR's milling operations in western Viti Levu.[22] In 1919 a delegation from the

Indian community went to the colonial government to ask that measures be taken to alleviate hardships caused by the decline in wages during the war. There was no response and from January to February 1920 the Suva-Nausori area was the scene of a widespread strike by Indo-Fijian workers, and violent clashes occurred between the workers and the police. The governor at the time, Cecil Rodwell (1918–25), had previous experience in South Africa and had little sympathy for political or labour agitators. The strike was broken but matters did not end there.

Indo-Fijian cane growers and mill workers joined forces against CSR in October 1920 to form the Fiji Indian Labour Federation. In February 1921, led by Gandhi-inspired Basisth Muni, a strike was declared after the federation's log of claims was ignored. The strike lasted six months until it collapsed when growers and workers no longer were able to hold out. During the strike, Christian missionaries actively sought to dissuade native Fijians from supporting it and even recruited some native Fijians to work for those hit by the strike. The government, for its part, although supporting CSR privately, did not want to aggravate the situation further and therefore took no official action. While this strike and the earlier one were primarily over basic economic issues, there were political dimensions as well. This was pointed out negatively by the European community on numerous occasions during the strikes, and the strikes can be seen as important points in the evolution of Indo-Fijian political consciousness.

The strikes did not dissuade members of the settler élite and colonial administration from favouring further Indian migration. Further migration continued to be seen as a means of encouraging the economic development of Fiji. Part of the reason for this view was that most Europeans by now had given up any hope of economic development among native Fijians, who were seen more than ever as members of a 'dying race,' especially after the infleunza epidemic of 1918. CSR's response was to encourage Indo-Fijians to settle on 10- to 12-acre leased blocs of land and to produce sugar under contract. This initiative served to reduce CSR's direct role in the growing of cane, while still allowing it to maintain overall control of the industry. It also eliminated the bulk of the Indo-Fijian proletariat by turning wage-earners in the cane fields into peasant producers.

During the decade after the First World War, CSR was able to sustain healthy profits despite the continued decline in the price of sugar.The amount of land under cane cultivation increased by about 20 per cent, with tenant and smallholder producers accounting for an increasing amount of production: to 41 per cent in 1925, 76 per cent in 1930, and 90 per cent by 1933. This helped to reduce the cost of cane for CSR. The company was provided further assistance by the colonial administration, which exempted it from export taxes (this being made up for in part by new taxes on Indo-Fijians), and by a British imperial preferential duty.

Copra and bananas continued to be exported during the interwar years. There were attempts to promote further agricultural diversification but none of them succeeded. One new industry was tourism. The Grand Pacific Hotel was built by the Union Steamship Company in 1914 and the Suva Tourist Bureau was created in 1923. In 1926 there were 3,722 visitors, mostly businessmen, who spent an estimated £60,000 in the colony.

Also during the 1920s, there were changes in the configuration of the colony's business houses. Burns Philp and the other leading merchant house in the colony, Morris Hedstrom, bought out a number of the older European firms. At the same time, Indo-Fijian businesses appeared in greater number, but few were of sufficient size to be of concern to the European oligarchy. This was less true of the numerous small to medium Chinese firms that proliferated during the 1920s. These were particularly influential in the copra trade (the three largest accounting for 24 per cent of the trade in 1924). The fall in the price of copra during the depression hurt these firms and forced them to begin selling almost entirely to larger European merchants. Nevertheless, they remained a significant part of the colony's commercial sector.

Gold-mining emerged as a major new industry in the colony in the 1930s. Gold-mining had a sporadic history in Fiji dating back to 1886. 'It was not, however, until the world market prices for agricultural commodities plummeted and the value of gold rose in the late 1920s that large scale mining ventures could be perceived as viable.'[23] Gold production rose significantly from 1935, following the founding of Emperor Gold Mine (controlled largely by Australian interests).

After the defeat of the 1920 and 1921 strikes, it took time for labour and political leaders in the Indo-Fijian community to regain their initiative. But slowly, frequently inspired by events in India, community leaders began to organize. These activities culminated in the founding of the Kisan Sangh (Famers' Union) in 1937, representing peasant cane farmers, and the Chini Mazdur Sangh (Workers' Union) in 1938, representing mill workers (which will be discussed at the end of this chapter).

Apart from the governor and perhaps one or two other high-ranking colonial officials, the top of European society in Fiji (and hence the top of its colonial society in general) was comprised of the highest ranking CSR managers, on the one hand, and a small, tightly-knit group of Suva businessmen and lawyers, on the other hand. Significantly, by the latter part of the 1930s, the colonial administration had come to have little sympathy for either of these two groups. This colonial oligarchy had run the colony pretty much its own way since the First World War. But by the late 1930s, in the wake of serious rioting in the Caribbean and growing problems in Britain's colonies elsewhere, the British began to tighten colonial rule in an effort to keep the situation from getting out of hand.

The colonial administration decided that it was necessary to take steps to put a stop to the worst excesses of European settler élites whose actions at times were seen to be working against the long-term interests of colonial rule. Arthur Richards, who became governor in 1936, had little good to say of Fiji's oligarchy. He referred to those in the Legislative Council as 'an archaic trinity of reactionaries.' In a letter to the Colonial Office written shortly after his arrival in Fiji he commented:

> As I begin to settle down here things take on a more solid shape. It is a peculiar Colony. The presence of a resident European population, their long isolation from the world and the limitation even of recent contacts to Australia and New Zealand has bread a particular insularity of its own. A few big men have obtained a strangle-hold on the place – they have won their way to the top and mean to stay there. The underdog is under-paid and powerless. A few big men control everything behind the scenes and even Government has been run with a strong bias.[24]

While the European commercial élite was relatively secure in its ascendancy during the interwar years, its allies, the eastern chiefs, were not. They continued to dominate the positions in the colonial system left to native Fijians and remained the favoured ones of the European oligarchy and administration over other native Fijians and certainly over the Indo-Fijians. Their feeling of unease came from the threat that they perceived growing from below, where support for Apolosi Nawai had demonstrated the extent of dissatisfaction and the potential for even greater unrest.

The treatment of Nawai had convinced many native Fijian villagers, especially in western Viti Levu, that the colonial government and its chiefly collaborators were only interested in using the law for their own purposes. The 1930s (and even more so the 1940s) was a period in which there was considerable uncertainty and dissatisfaction among native Fijian commoners. In large part, these feelings were the result of the lack of channels for commoners to effectively articulate their aspirations. The collaborator chiefs were more attuned and responsive to the needs and wishes of élite Europeans than they were to those of native Fijian commoners. The reasons for this are not hard to understand: the offices held by the chiefs carried with them numerous material rewards in the form of salaries and the right to demand goods and services, including rent monies, from those under them, and 'These privileges were worth keeping and the way to keep them was to carry out orders from above.'[25]

Sukuna, the spokesman for the interests of the collaborator chiefs, was an antidemocratic traditionalist who favoured a return to the paternalistic indirect rule of the nineteenth century in the form of a revival of the Fijian Administration and the enforcement of communal market production. Sukuna was particularly aware of the threat that commoner discontent posed to the privileged position that he and his associates held.[26] While reminding chiefs of their obligations to commoners, he devoted much of his energy to countering the threat posed by the commoners through lobbying to strengthen the position of the collaborator chiefs within the colonial administration as well as seeking to divide and thwart opposition through appeals to communal loyalty, threats, patronage, and other means. He had a strongly racist view of society and felt that each ethnic community should live in isolation from the other. He saw inter-ethnic solidarity as representing perhaps the greatest threat, and the promotion of inter-ethnic suspicion and separation became the cornerstone of his design to maintain a social order that served the interests of he and his fellow chiefs.

But controlling the native Fijian masses was becoming more and more difficult, especially as an increasing number of Fijians were finding ways of supporting themselves outside of villages that were under the tight control of the chiefs and church. The 1921 census reported that the total native Fijian population was 84,475: 1,981 of these were listed as living permanently in Suva, and around 4,500 (or 5.25 per cent) were recorded as living away from villages. By 1936 the percentage living away from villages had increased to 17.5 per cent. With the end of indenture, the demand for native Fijian labour once again had increased. In the 1920s rubber planters near Suva had a need for native Fijian workers. Native Fijians accounted for about 60 to 75 per cent of the work-force at the gold-mines of Vatukoula during the latter part of the 1930s. In one peak year of employment during this period, a total of 1,713 people were employed at the mines: 1,344 native Fijians, 172 part-Europeans, 126 Europeans, and 56 Indo-Fijians. The number of galala farmers was also on the increase. Under Governor Fletcher (1929–36), who was a strong advocate of individual enterprise, there was an upsurge in the number of applications by native Fijians to be assigned the galala status. Fletcher also asked CSR to help promote individualism among native Fijians.

The other threat to chiefly power came from the growing Indo-Fijian population that had reached 60,634 in 1921. In December 1916, provision was made for one nominated Indo-Fijian member of the Legislative Council. The man appointed was Badri Dutt, who had arrived in Fiji in 1890 and subsequently become a 'man of property' who worked closely with the colonial regime. While Dutt was generally supportive of the status quo, another Indo-Fijian leader, Vishnu Deo, was a proponent of Indo-Fijian equality and advocated political reforms leading to a common electoral roll rather than a communal one. Deo was a member of the Arya Samaj Hindu sect that came to play an important role in Indo-Fijian politics.

In 1928, under growing pressure, the colonial government gave Indo-Fijians three elected seats in the Legislative Council (Europeans had six elected seats at the time). In the 1929 Legislative Council election, with 7,000 registered Indo-Fijian voters, Vishnu Deo was elected. Following the predictable defeat of a motion for a common roll put forward by Dutt shortly after assuming office, the three Indo-Fijian members walked out.

The eastern chiefly élite was becoming increasingly concerned over the prospect of losing power should more democratic conditions prevail and the Indo-Fijian population be given a greater voice in the Legislative Council. Thus, their Great Council of Chiefs moved in 1933 that: 'Fiji, having been ceded to her Majesty the Queen of Great Britain and Ireland, Her Heirs and Successors, the immigrant Indian population should neither directly nor indirectly have any part in the control or direction of matters affecting the control of the Fijian race.'[27] The following year, at its annual conference, the Viti Cauavou (Young Fijian Society), which was comprised of younger members of the eastern chiefly élite, moved that: 'India is under Britain – Britain is not under India, therefore it is not right that one belonging to India should rule over Europeans but that Indians in Fiji should be subject to the Europeans.'[28]

The response of Governor Fletcher to the chiefs was to suggest in 1935 to a wholly nominated Legislative Council. Sukuna, never the friend of democratic principles, saw this as an acceptable compromise that was preferable to a common roll, or to a communal roll in which native Fijian commoners could vote, and urged his fellow chiefs to support it in the name of 'the paramountcy of native inter-ests.' The motion was moved by K.B. Singh, a Muslim. The Muslims (about 16 per cent of the Indo-Fijian population) were, in general, a very conservative force in Indo-Fijian society, and Muslim leaders tended to side with colonial authorities against what they perceived to be Hindu interests – a notion given strength by Deo's activities on behalf of the Arya Samaj. The alliance between eastern collaborator chiefs and conservative Muslims proved to be an important one that was to continue throughout the colonial era and into the period of independence as the eastern chiefly élite assumed state power. A short time later, Deo was banned from the Legislative Council until 1937 for publishing an attack on orthodox Hinduism.

The Colonial Office worked out a compromise in 1937 that allowed for there to still be some elected members of the Legislative Council. European membership was reduced from six elected members to three elected and two nominated members. There were to be three elected Indo-Fijian members and two nominated Indo-Fijian mem-bers. And there were to be five nominated native Fijian members. Thus, there was still no provision for election of native Fijian mem-bers, which satisfied Sukuna. Deo was re-elected to the council and remained an elected member until 1959. K.B. Singh remained a nom-inated member.

War broke out in Europe in September 1939 and in the Pacific in December 1941. Japanese plans to head south to Fiji after occupying the Gilbert Islands were put on hold and then abandoned after the Battle of Midway in June 1942. The eastern chiefs, with a long mil-itary tradition, were enthusiastic about supporting the British war effort. In contrast, the Indo-Fijian community, influenced by atti-tudes in India, wanted little part of it. Thirty native Fijians were sent to the Solomon Islands as members of the Fiji Commando unit in December 1942. A larger number were sent to the Solomon Islands in April 1943. Altogether, 11,000 men passed through the Fijian Mil-itary Forces during the war, and fifty-six native Fijians died while serving with the Allied forces. The eastern chiefs were not alone in their enthusiasm for the war effort; their relatives in Tonga also provided a small contingent for the campaign in the Solomon Islands, while the queen of Tonga mounted fund drives.

The Americans assumed responsibility for Fiji's defence, but this had little impact on the colony's administration. By and large, the British authorities and their local assistants remained in charge. Allied troops stationed or on leave in Fiji did not have as dramatic an impact on the local economy and populace as they did in many other parts of the South Pacific; but the impact was not completely insignificant, and the presence of American GIs certainly added a bit of excitement to life in Suva, Nadi, and a few other towns.

The value of Fijian exports, which had been recovering after the depression when the war broke out, peaked in 1942 and thereafter declined for the duration of the war. This was despite sharp increases in the prices paid for these commodities (especially copra). Gold came to account for about one-fifth of the value of exports. Fijian sociologist 'Atu Bain comments: 'During the war years, the continued production of gold was perceived as crucial by both the colonial and home governments: to the empire as a means of earning dollars and to the colony as a means of financing defence works.'[29] Sugar, however, remained the most important export, and price increases for sugar were offset by a lower volume of production (from a peak of 131,294 tons in 1942, the volume declined steadily to 30,504 tons in 1945).

For the majority of Fijians, higher prices for export commodities were more than offset by a rise in the cost of living. Taking 1939 as a base (100), the cost-of-living index reached 156 in mid-1943, and remained at 200 or above throughout most of 1943 and 1944.[30] Wartime inflation was felt especially by those employed as wage labourers. Whereas those who were able to find employment in service areas closely related to the war effort were often paid higher wages that at least in part compensated for the increased cost of living, those employed in other areas of the economy were not so fortunate.

Mineworkers were among those who saw the value of their wages fall sharply in the face of wartime inflation. The result was that many of those employed in the mining industry sought to find work in defence and related services or to devote their energies to producing copra. This led to a crisis in the mining industry. The colonial administration responded by mobilizing additional labour, primarily among native Fijians in western and central Viti Levu, and by issuing a ruling whereby native Fijians in the mining industry had to have the governor's permission before enlisting in the military.[31]

Political developments within the Indo-Fijian community made controlling labour more difficult for CSR. By the late 1930s a new generation of Indo-Fijian cane growers, the sons of those who had come as indentured labourers, was assuming responsibility for the farms. Several factors influenced their becoming more militant than their fathers. They were less willing to cut cane for themselves, and the hiring of cane cutters became more widespread. This reduced farm profits since wages had to be paid. Generally, they also had more dependents to support, which again cut into profits. In addition, many of them simply had higher expectations than their fathers. Such a situation led to the formation of growers' associations as a means of challenging the existing system and, especially, CSR's control of the industry.

The first of these associations was the Kisan Sangh, founded in 1937. The leader of the Kisan Sangh was a north Indian, G.S. Ayodhya Prasad. Most of the members of the association were north Indians who were among the more prosperous cane farmers. The colonial administration, motivated largely by a desire to see CSR's labour management policies modernized in order to defuse what was seen as a potentially volatile situation, exerted pressure on CSR to recognize the Kisan Sangh. As the Kisan Sangh's membership grew, CSR was forced into granting concessions. Finally, in May 1941, after a dispute over the threatened eviction of seven farmers, CSR recognized the Kisan Sangh. The following year the colonial government enacted the Industrial Associations Ordinance, not only marking an important step in the evolution of industrial relations in Fiji but also the ascendancy of a policy of co-optation over one of coercion.

The Kisan Sangh's position among cane farmers soon was to be challenged. Opposition within the Indo-Fijian community was motivated in part by the conciliatory approach of the Kisan Sangh towards CSR in its hope to bring the company and growers closer together. The trigger was a campaign by the Kisan Sangh to reduce dependence of growers on Indo-Fijian shopkeepers (mostly Gujarati) through the promotion of co-operatives. This angered the shopkeepers, whose cause was taken up by a Gujarati lawyer, A.D. Patel. Gujarati business interests were able to align themselves with south Indians (many of whom were among the poorer cane farmers) under Swami Rudrananda to form the Akhil Krishak Maha Sangh (All Fiji Farmers' Union).

The Maha Sangh was founded in mid-June 1941, only two weeks after CSR had recognized the Kisan Sangh. CSR's Sydney office was pleased to learn of this development and in one document expressed the hope that the 'unions would compete for support among growers, so preventing them from launching a united attack on the company.'[32] The Maha Sangh was able to increase its support among growers by arguing that the Kisan Sangh had failed to gain any significant concessions from CSR as a result of its collaborationist approach.

In March 1943 the Kisan Sangh, worried about its loss of support among growers, asked CSR to raise the price it paid for cane. The company refused. Rather than resort to industrial action, the Kisan

Sangh appealed to the government. One of the union's officers, B.D. Lakshman, requested that the government appoint a commission of inquiry to look into the price of cane. The commission was established in July 1943 and its recommendations were to be non-binding. Members of the Kisan Sangh were divided in their response to the commission. A number of them joined the Maha Sangh in boycotting the commission. Lakshman and other more conservative members of the Kisan Sangh urged that the commission go ahead, and in September it issued a report recommending against a price increase. Those in the Kisan Sangh who had boycotted the commission, along with the Maha Sangh and the newly formed Rewa Cane Growers' Union, then demanded that the issue be taken before an arbitration tribunal whose findings would be binding. Furthermore, they announced that until this was agreed upon their members would refuse to harvest their cane. They argued that cane farmers should have a greater share of the profits that CSR was making, at a time when the cost of living for growers had increased significantly.

The strike began in July 1943, shortly after mill workers at the Lautoka and Rarawai mills had received substantial pay increases after resorting to industrial action. In an effort to end the strike, the government asked CSR to agree to pay more for the cane (which it could easily afford). CSR refused, mainly for two reasons: it did not wish to encourage further union militancy and it feared that sugar prices would fall after the war. The strike began to crumble towards the end of 1943 and ended in January 1944.

The strike failed for a number of reasons: the strikers were unable to gain the support of the government; there were divisions among growers (for example, the strikers were unable to gain the support of the more conservative Muslim farmers); and there were differences in the abilities of growers to withstand a prolonged strike. In addition, in January, Sukuna warned Indo-Fijian farmers that if they did not harvest their cane they might have trouble when it came time to renew their leases. The strike further added to communal problems since many native Fijians felt that it undermined the war effort.

Sukuna was also engaged in other activities aimed at thwarting possible threats to the status quo, while at the same time enhancing the power of the eastern chiefly élite. In part, through his urging, the Fijian Affairs Ordinance came into force on 1 January 1945.[33] This created a separate administrative body for native Fijians which was to be known as the Fijian Administration.

The Fijian Administration was under the authority of the Fijian Affairs Board, which served as something of an executive for the Council of Chiefs. The Fijian Affairs Board was comprised of a secretary (who served as chairman and sat on the Executive Council of the colonial administration), the five nominated native Fijian members of the Legislative Council, a legal adviser, and a financial adviser (the latter two posts being held by Europeans). Sukuna was named secretary of the Fijian Affairs Board. The Fijian Administration was given considerable powers over native Fijian commoners to the point that it regulated most of their daily activities in addition to having its own system of taxation and justice for native Fijians. Among the reasons for the initiative according to Governor Mitchell (1942–45) was the necessity 'to broaden the base of Native support and collaboration upon which every Colonial Government must stand.'[34] John Coulter comments that its 'first and most important purpose is to ensure continuance of the native communal system, and the customs and observances traditionally associated with it.'[35] It was to promote economic development among native Fijians in such a way as not to challenge existing political relations.

Sukuna and his wife, Lady Maraia Sukuna, were also responsible for creating another institution that became a cornerstone of eastern chiefly rule – the Soqosoqo Vakamarama. It originated as a Fijian women's association known as Ruve which was founded by Mr. and Mrs. R.A. Derrick in 1924. It did not emerge as an important mass organization, however, until its leadership was assumed by the Sukunas in 1942 (when its name was changed). Lady Sukuna, who served as president from 1942 to 1956, brought together women chiefs and the wives of male chiefs and rokos initially to knit woollen garments for soldiers.

The role of the Soqosoqo Vakamarama broadened after the war to include a wide variety of activities and more generally to serve as a women's auxiliary to the male-dominated chiefly institutions. After the founding of the Alliance Party, it served as an unofficial women's auxiliary to the Fijian Association. And after Maraia Sukuna's death, the wives of two of the most prominent eastern chiefs served as president of the organization. Adi Laisa Ganilau, the wife of Ratu Penaia Ganilau (who was to become governor general), was president from 1968 until her death in 1981. She was succeeded by Prime Minister Mara's wife, Adi Lala Mara.

The creation of the Fijian Administration strengthened the position of the eastern chiefs and served to further institutionalize the concept of separate development for native Fijians and Indo-Fijians, and thus of communal separateness as part of an overall strategy of 'divide and rule.' While binding native Fijians even more to the communal and chiefly system through the new regulations, Sukuna and his associates were all too aware of the extent to which such a move, if handled wrongly, could produce a severe backlash that might threaten the success of the entire undertaking. With this in mind, they sought to widen the scope of participation in the newly created institutions of control.

In the revised Fijian Affairs Regulations of 1949, an elective system of choosing some members of the Divisional Councils, Provincial Councils, and the Great Council of Chiefs was adopted. These reforms allowed native Fijians to feel that they were participating in the system designed to administer them without seriously threatening the ultimate power of the eastern chiefly establishment, that is, it was a means of letting off pressure. With Sukuna at the helm and with the assistance of a paternalistic colonial administration that was all too willing to allow the chiefs to control native Fijian commoners, the chiefs were prepared to meet the challenges of the postwar world through the Fijian Administration.

CHAPTER THREE

Alliance Party Rule

One political party, the Alliance Party, dominated by one man, Ratu Sir Kamasese Mara, has been in power in Fiji since independence. Ratu Sukuna, who had led the eastern chiefly oligarchy since before the Second World War, died in 1958. It was Mara who took over the mantle of chiefly leadership from Sukuna and who thus became the primary spokesman and defender of the interests of the country's chiefly and European oligarchy.

Alliance Party/chiefly rule, however, has not gone unchallenged. Mara and his party have had to contend with threats to their power from members of the Indo-Fijian community, from organized labour, from native Fijian commoners, and from western native Fijians. In seeking to meet these threats Mara and the Alliance Party increasingly resorted to the classic strategies of 'bread or the club' and 'divide and rule.' To remain in power, Mara and the Alliance Party employed patronage and intimidation; they sought to divide native Fijians from Indo-Fijians, while trying to cover over differences among native Fijians themselves, and they sought to divide the Indo-Fijian community internally.

The three main ideological themes articulated by the oligarchy have been the maintenance of stability, the paramountcy of native Fijian interests, and the denial of the relevance of class interests, or class struggle. Hegemony over the native Fijian community, in particular, which is the cornerstone of Alliance Party rule, is based on what Simione Durutalo calls the 'four R's: Ratusim, Royalism, Religion and Rugby.'[1]

Durutalo defines ratuism as 'the ideology which claims that chiefs are divinely ordained as natural rulers and hence to be obeyed unquestioningly by indigenous Fijians.'[2] In essence, the intent has been the try to ensure that native Fijians identify the maintenance of chiefy rule with the paramountcy of native Fijian interests in general. Royalism refers to the glorification of the British royal family by the chiefs in order to strengthen the belief in aristocratic rule among native Fijian commoners.The Christian religion, and especially Methodism, has been used by the oligarchy to promote the notion of loyalty to the chiefs and to foster a broader docility among native Fijian commoners. It also served to highlight differences between native Fijians and Indo-Fijians (very few of whom are Christians). Finally, it is no accident that Mara and other prominent Alliance Party leaders have held high offices in the Fijian Rugby Association and that Mara's photo is a constant feature in sports pages of the newspapers. The sport of rugby has become an integral part of the fabric of chiefly rule and the maintenance of values associated with its interests. During the postwar period rugby emerged alongside military service as a symbol of native Fijian manhood that linked manliness with Fiji's warrior past. Rugby was seen as promoting the associated values of loyalty and bravery – as well as ethnic solidarity (since it was viewed by most as a native Fijian sport). Moreover, interpersonal ties created through specific rugby clubs led to the formation of important networks of male bonding in civilian and military life that, on one level, helped to hold the oligarchy and its allies together and, on another level, often reflected factional differences within the oligarchy.

Chiefly rule and the denial of the relevance of social class is tied to the concept of the 'Pacific Way.' The term was first used by Mara in 1970 in an address to the General Assembly of the United Nations. As this author has noted elsewhere, the ideology contains 'certain central notions within an overall framework of the maintenance of tradition: communalism, consensus, conformity and uniqueness.'[3] In reference to chiefly rule in Fiji: 'One aspect of Pacific Way consensus is avoidance of substantive debate ... Moreover, it implies agreement with those in authority – the right to agree with the chiefs.'[4] On the question of social class, the Pacific Way preaches anti-materialism and anti-urbanism (with a concomitant idealization of village life) to the commoners. In arguing for the uniqueness of the South Pacific, advocates of the Pacific Way state that the concept of social class is an inapproprate import. Thus, Mara was quoted in 1977 as saying: 'We have enough difficulties in Fiji without importing the 'class war'. For to be sure it would be an imported thing; and not something imported by honest people seeking our welfare or at least with no will to harm us; it would be imported by men who thrive on unrest, and disruption of peace and an orderly form of government.'[5]

Closely associated with promotion of the Pacific Way is use of the communist bogy and, especially, its supposed threat to Christianity. This was championed by local Europeans such as close Mara associate Len Usher and by the colonial authorities in the 1950s and has become a standard feature of Alliance Party rhetoric against trade unionists and others opposed to the ruling oligarchy.[6] These are all themes that will appear over and over again in Fijian politics throughout the 1970s and early 1980s, and in the events surrounding the coups of 1987.

THE TRANSITION TO INDEPENDENCE

After the Second World War, although there were threats to the colonial order established by the alliance of colonial authorities, European businessmen, and eastern Fijian chiefs, these were soon brought under control. At the invitation of the colonial government, unions came together in 1951 to form the Fiji Industrial Workers' Council, with B.D. Lakshman as president. Militant seamen and dockworkers did not join, but, by and large, the colonial authorities had managed to create a structure of industrial relations that prevented labour from challenging the status quo. Politically-oriented agitation among Indo-Fijians that had taken place during the 1930s and 1940s had largely disappeared as well. But given the nature of the postwar world and of Fijian society in particular – whose population was more educated and urbanized, and had higher aspirations – it was unlikely that change was far off.

The situation started to heat up in 1955, when the mineworkers at Vatukoula went on strike. Then, in 1957, Lakshman was forced out of the presidency of the Fiji Industrial Workers' Council by a vote of no confidence.[7] From his base in the Nadi airport workers' union he set about to wrest control of the mill workers' union (the Chini Mazdur Sangh) in an effort to re-establish his position within the trade union movement. After promoting a series of strikes among mill workers, he succeeded in assuming leadership of the union in 1957 and promptly denounced the existing agreement with CSR. The workers went on strike in early 1959. The strike led to the establishment of a board of inquiry by the colonial government.

A much more dramatic strike took place in Suva in December 1959, involving the Wholesale and Retail Workers' General Union which was led by two young unionists associated with Lakshman –

Mohammed Apisai Tora and James Anthony – both of whom were branded communists by the other side. A riot broke out during the strike in which native Fijians and Indo-Fijians joined forces to destroy European property. The government threatened to use force against the strikers and rioters. At the same time, civic leaders, moderate unionists, and prominent native Fijian chiefs were called in to try to calm things down. The strike was broken as the chiefs succeeded in driving a communal wedge between the strikers, while Lakshman and others exerted a moderating influence over the Indo-Fijians.[8]

Labour unrest continued in 1960, with a total of fourteen disputes being recorded during the year. The most important of these was in the sugar industry. Alongside the Chini Mazdur Sangh (which represented the mill workers), and also dating back to the 1940s, were the Kisan Sangh and Maha Sangh (representing Indo-Fijian cane growers). There had been relatively little unrest in the cane fields since the 1943 strike. But in 1959 the situation began to change. The international price of sugar had dropped and, in an effort to cut costs, CSR proposed paying growers less and reducing the quantities of sugar that it bought. In the resultant dispute, the government was successful in reaching an agreement with the relatively moderate Kisan Sangh and native Fijian growers, but the members of the more militant, newly formed Federation of Cane Growers (the descendant of the older Maha Sangh) did not agree.[9]

The Federation of Cane Growers under the leadership of A.D Patel presented CSR with a far-reaching list of demands in early 1960. If implemented, the demands would have substantially altered the nature of the cane industry, and in the process would have given greater power to cane growers, while putting an end to the monopoly held by CSR. Not surprisingly, the demands were not acceptable to CSR. Tensions increased in the cane fields as CSR and the colonial authorities sought to put an end to the threat posed by the federation. A group led by Vijay Singh broke with the federation in July and joined native Fijian growers in agreeing to an interim contract and a commission of inquiry. The strike led by the federation finally collapsed in the face of dwindling support among growers. It was a bitter and costly dispute that highlighted divisions within the Indo-Fijian community, but also served to strengthen the resolve among those supporting the strike to struggle for greater political power.

Although these major strikes were suppressed, they sent a clear message to the authorities that all was not well in the colony. Specific steps were taken to contain the threat of growing militancy. The Sugar Industry Ordinance was enacted in 1961, which singled out the sugar industry for special treatment in the handling of industrial disputes. Militants were expelled from the Fiji Sugar Employees' Union and the Wholesale and Retail Workers' General Union during 1961 and 1962, leading temporarily to an end to industrial unrest. Later, in 1963, the latter union was deregistered, and then in 1964 the Trade Unions Act was passed which required registration of all unions and effectively put an end to the formation of broad-based unions. Efforts were also made for greater centralization of union activities under the unbrella of the Fiji Industrial Workers' Council, which was now under the leadership the Mohammed Ramzan. Ramzan urged workers to reject militancy and to comply with procedures laid down by the government.

There were other sources of trouble as well. Actions by the native Fijian chiefly élite were increasing communal tensions. Through the Native Land Trust Board the chiefs had begun to place land leased by Indo-Fijian farmers into native Fijian reserves when the leases expired, causing fear within the Indo-Fijian community that eventually they would be driven from the land. And more generally, it was clear that the colony faced a growing number of economic and social problems which, if not dealt with, could only serve to lead to further unrest.

During the mid-1950s, the colonial government had commissioned two reports to provide the basis for instituting economic and administrative reforms. The first of these reports was prepared by Professor Oskar Spate. The Spate report was submitted in April 1959. Its recommendations were enough to send chills down the spine of any member of the chiefly élite. In addition to its summary of the numerous economic problems facing native Fijians and to the numerous specific recommendations for economic reforms, the report called into question the fundamental orthodoxy regarding the nature of native Fijian society.

The Spate report challenged the existence of the 'communal system,' by showing that 'there are collectivist elements, but as regards the economic basis of society – the production of food and most craft-goods – that seems to have been essentially individualistic.'[10] The report then drew attention to the importance of the individual or galala farmer: 'After all, wherever he may stand in relation to the traditional system, the fact remains that the successful *gulula* is doing more for the economic strength of the Fijian people than the man who simply mends the house and plants so many *dalo* when he is told. A whole-hearted acceptance of this fact, and consequently of individualism as the general objective (which does not mean 'scrapping the communal system' forthwith or a rigid plan for all Fiji at the same tempo), would be, in my opinion, the biggest single step towards economic development which Fijian Administration could take.'[11] And in his conclusion, Spate made recommendations for increased professionalism within the Fijian Administration, greater use of cash rather than unpaid labour in villages, support for galala farmers, 'making Fijian Members of the Legislative Council representatives of territorial constituencies instead of representatives-at-large,'[12] and a number of other steps in keeping with his general theme 'that the future of the Fijians is a turn from communalism towards individualism.'[13] The significance of territorial representation, of course, is that it would become more difficult for the eastern chiefs to dominate native Fijians in other parts of the country.

The second report, by Sir Alan Burns, whose vast experience as a colonial administrator dated back to 1905, was submitted in early 1960. As with the previous report, the Fijian Administration came in for severe criticism, as did the colonial administration 'for so long adopting a paternalistic attitude and for still giving a very high priority to fostering, at this period of the 20th century, "the continuance of the Fijian communal system and the customs and observances traditionally associated with that system." '[14] The report provided more extensive recommendations for political reform. After stating that there was evidence to suggest that the Great Council of Chiefs did 'not fully represent Fijian public opinion' and arguing that ordinary native Fijians should be given the right 'to choose at least some of their representatives,' the report recommended that all native Fijians should be allowed to elect three representatives to the Legislative Council, with the Great Council of Chiefs retaining two nominated seats. It also recommended that native Fijians living in Suva be allowed to elect a representative to the Suva City Council.[15]

Needless to say, the native Fijian establishment was horrified and it was quick to let the authorities know its feelings. Thus, Legislative Council member Ravuama Vunivalu referred to the Burns report as a 'brutal attack' on 'the Fijian way of life' and stated that it made native Fijians realize that 'their position in the Colony was not as invulnerable as they had hoped it to be.'[16] As usual, the native Fijian élite sought to identify its interests with those of the native Fijian people as a whole, but it was clear that there were those in positions of influence within the colonial administration who were prepared to question the validity of this communalist view.

The two reports appeared within the context of increasing moves by Britain to rid itself of its scattered colonies around the world. The Suez Crisis of 1956 had helped to push Britain in this direction as Prime Minister Harold Macmillan, despite continued imperial posturing, sought to reduce Britain's colonial commitments and concentrate its economic priorities during the late 1950s and early 1960s. Such moves also were motivated in part by international pressure for decolonization that had been building since the founding of the United Nations, with a charter that called for self-determination of peoples and states. The U.N. subsequently issued declarations calling for decolonization and established a Committee on Decolonization. These sentiments were expressed further at the 1955 meeting in Bandung, Indonesia, that led, in 1961, to the founding of the Non-Aligned Movement at the Belgrade Conference.

Responding to these external pressures, and despite opposition from the native Fijian élite (and members of the local European élite as well), the colonial administration, starting in 1961, initiated political changes aimed at devolving power and advancing towards a ministerial system of government. The administration proposed altering the Legislative Council to consist of thirty-seven members. This was to include nineteen official members and six members to represent each of the three primary ethnic groups, four of which were to be elected and two nominated. Norman Meller and James Anthony comment that this structure 'served to legally imprint an ethnic character on political action and thereby potentially to exacerbate ethnic tensions, but it was also clear that it represented progress in terms of democratization of the colony.'[17]

Under pressure from the colonial administration, the Great Council of Chiefs agreed to having elected representatives for native Fijians. In December 1962, however, the native Fijian chiefs in the Legislative Council were able to put through a motion 'taking cognizance of the wish of the Fijian people that there should be no change in the present Constitution of the Colony until the Fijian people express their desire for further constitutional changes.'

Despite continued resistance, the colonial authorities increased the pace of political change in 1963. The administration let it be known that it favoured the development of political parties along multiracial lines. Added to this was the proposal to hold a constitutional conference in 1965 to be attended by 'leaders of representative opinion.' The implication was that political parties had to be created which could be said to be representative. For the Indo-Fijian community this was not so difficult since they had been moving in this direction, but for the native Fijian community it was a different matter.

Until his death in 1958, Ratu Sukuna had dominated native Fijian politics, promoting its strongly undemocratic character through the Fijian Affairs Board. He was supported in his efforts by a few local

Europeans who had come to play an important role in shaping Fijian chiefly politics. As Robert Norton comments:

> Conservative European lawyers with business connections played important roles in Fijian politics. Morris Scott formed ties with Fijian chiefs in the army and as legal adviser to the Fijian Affairs Board. In 1956 he encouraged them to organize the Fijian Association to counteract challenges by the European president of an Indian cane farmers' union. His interests in Fijian ex-servicemen's and rugby football associations enhanced his popularity as did friendships that his missionary forbears established with leading chiefs. John Falvey succeeded Scott as legal adviser to the Fijian Affairs Board. He helped organize Fijian cane farmers into their own unions during the 1960 farmers' strike and gave advice during the expansion of the Fijian Association and the formation of the Alliance Party in the mid-1960s.[18]

The Fijian Association was closely associated with the Fijian Affairs Board, and its leadership was drawn from the chiefly class. Political scientist Roderic Alley describes its primary aims: 'to maintain the existing hierarchy of chiefly authority, Fiji's links with the British Crown, the system of Fijian land ownership, and the primacy of Fijian consultation in any discussion with the British government preceding constitutional change. It acted as something of a watchdog over local Indian political aspirations.'[19] In practice, the Fijian Association did very little and Alley cites evidence of its being criticized not only by some Europeans linked to the colonial administration, but also by native Fijian commoners (especially those living in Suva) for being moribund and unrepresentative.

With the death of Sukuna, Mara emerged as the leading advocate of the chiefly position. Mara was born in the Lau Group in 1920 and attended Otago Medical College. While attending medical school he was selected by Sukuna as his successor and sent to Wadham College at Oxford to study administration and politics. Subsequently, he received an M.A. in economics from the London School of Economics. Mara was then promoted through the Fijian Administration with the aim of preparing him to take over from Sukuna.

Mara and others in the Fijian Affairs Board, with the assistance of close Mara associate John Falvey, responded to the 'threat' posed to chiefly hegemony by the reforms being advocated by the British, in the form of a letter, the so-called 'Wakaya letter'. In the letter, the signatories sought guarantees for the paramountcy of native Fijian interests, including a demand that future constitutional changes should be intitiated by the chiefs. They further sought to establish ties between Fiji and Britain similar to those between Britain and the Channel Islands and the Isle of Man. Those signing the letter included the leading figures in the native Fijian establishment at the time, as well as John Falvey and Morris Scott. The aim of the letter was not only to secure the paramountcy of native Fijian interests over those of other ethnic groups, but also the interests of the chiefs over native Fijian commoners. It raised another issue that was of concern to this group as well: increased participation by native Fijians within the colonial civil service (in part to ensure that jobs did not go to Indo-Fijians, while at the same time serving to provide the chiefs with a patronage network to help maintain their paramountcy within native Fijian society).[20]

The chiefs' desire to assert their right to speak on behalf of the entire native Fijian population did not go unchallenged. And, as might be expected, the challenge came primarily from the west. One group opposed to the chiefly establishment was the Bula Tale Communist Party. Its origins can be traced to a peasant movement among native Fijians in Nadroga, known as the Dra-ni-Lami (Blood of the Lamb), that was opposed to the Fijian Administration and the chiefly élite. It declined after a period of activity and then was revived in 1961 under the name of the Bula Tale (New Era) Association.

The members of the Bula Tale Communist Party disassociated themselves from native Fijian traditions by banning customs such as those related to birth, marriage, and death; by refusing to recognise the authority of chiefs; by not drinking *kava* or using the *tabua* (a traditional drink and a ceremonial whale's tooth); and broke with orthodox Christianity. Its leader, Apimeleki Ramatau, who had been a clerk in the Medical Department, stated that they sought to establish a 'communist state' within the territory they occupied. Simione Durutalo points out that, while denouncing many aspects of native Fijian custom, they sought to retain 'what they considered to be the most important aspect of Fijian tradition which was the nature and level of co-operation integral to the traditional Fijian socio-economic system.' He further argues that they were motivated primarily by 'the desire to dilute the demands of customs and ceremonies on their lives' since 'they felt the need to conserve their time and resources in order to survive economically and to meet the demands of the modern economic system.'[21]

Much to the alarm of the native Fijian establishment and colonial authorities, there was growing evidence of support for the Bula Tale Communist Party from other parts of Fiji, even from the establishment stronghold of Lau. Prominent members of the Fijian Association, such as its national president, Ratu Edward Cakobau, and Suva branch president Ravuama Vunivalu issued strong denounciations of the Bula Tale as 'a move along lines which we know well is not in keeping with the general opinion of the Fijian people.'[22]

It was left to Mara to deal with Ramatau and the Bula Tale through a policy of containment. Mara met with Ramatau in mid-August to receive assurances that the movement would not cause problems and 'advised provincial officials to try to guide it along lawful paths rather than try to suppress it.'[23] The Bula Tale Communist Party changed its name to the Dra-ni-Lami Club and continued its activities despite harassment by representatives of Fijian Affairs and colonial officials. At its highpoint in 1961 it had a membership of around one thousand and in 1962 it was able to establish a branch in Navua.

It was a radical trade unionist named Apisai Tora who was to emerge at this time as the most important critic of the chiefly establishment in the west. Tora, who had played a prominent role in the 1959 strike in Suva, was from the village of Sabeto, near Nadi. He had received support for his union activities from native Fijians as well as Indo-Fijians. He and several native Fijian cane farmers from around Ba formed the Western Democratic Party in late 1962. As can be seen from this April 1963 election broadcast by Tora, the party's platform was both anti-colonial and anti-chiefly establishment, and it sought to articulate the grievances of western native Fijians:

> You have been ruled by leaders from other areas who have treated you with calculated contempt ... Your division is the most important one because from it comes the economic lifeblood of the colony ... You deserve to be treated as first-class citizens ... You must confess that deep inside you there is a longing to see the day when your kinsmen in western Fiji, sons of the soil, speaking your own language, valuing the same values as you, would rise to become leaders in their own domain, and perhaps of the whole group ... The party offers your own kinsmen who like you come from the humble surroundings of a village, who know what it is to be ignored by officials, to be discouraged by *Rokos* and chiefs and straight-jacketed by the system under which you and I live.[24]

The British quickly made it clear that they did not agree with the sentiments expressed in the Wakaya letter and that they planned to press ahead with plans for democratization. Lack of support from the British, and the threat posed by Tora and others like him, made the chiefs realize that they needed to come up with a viable political organization to ensure maintenance of their interests. This need for a political body became even more apparent as the administration moved the colony towards an election of the Legislative Council under the new rules.

The 1963 Legislative Council elections marked the first time that the bulk of people in the country were to participate in the selection of government representatives. The powers of the Legislative Council remained limited, with most control being in the hands of the governor and his advisory council (consisting largely of colonial civil servants). Nevertheless, the intention of Britain was clear. The Legislative Council would be given full lawmaking and executive powers after a period of apprenticeship. During this period of apprenticeship – a process known as 'gradualism' – the British would guide the country towards independence in a way that it saw fitting.

The new structure of the Legislative Council, as laid out by the British, meant that all native Fijians were to elect four representatives. Under the previous system, the Great Council of Chiefs had selected representatives. Now this was to be replaced by a structure giving both men and women the right to vote regardless of their chiefly status. Thus, while maintaining the communal structure of colonial politics, the new framework also served to promote democratic politics within the native Fijian community. The British did not want to push things too far, however, and there were certain property and income qualifications required to run for office. A candidate had to post a deposit of £50 (which would be lost if the candidate received less than 10 per cent of the vote).

In view of the novelty of the situation, the government made a concerted effort to register native Fijian voters. A total of 93,598 voters were registered, representing 56.6 per cent of possible native Fijian voters, 38.6 per cent of Indo-Fijians, and 48 per cent of Europeans. While the lack of democratic traditions made the low level of native Fijian registration understandable, the even lower level of Indo-Fijian registration was harder to explain. Meller and Anthony feel that it was the result of two factors: Indo-Fijians had less of a personal concern with politics, and organized attempts to register Indo-Fijian voters were inadequate.[25]

The native Fijian candidates were drawn mainly from the chiefly establishment. One notable exception was the western native Fijian unionist and populist agitator Apisai Tora. Tora ran on behalf of the Fijian National Party against Ratu Penaia Ganilau, an eastern chief from Cakaudrove who was a sitting member of the Legislative Council. Although the establishment candidate won, Tora did receive 33 per cent of the vote – a credible showing that reflected the significant opposition to the chiefly establishment. A short time later, in July, Tora denounced the election before the U.N. as a 'farce and fraud' and called into question the right of the chiefly establishment to represent the native Fijian population.[26]

Among Indo-Fijians, the Federation of Cane Growers, in effect, had been turned into a political body known as the Citizens' Federation. Although the federation had little in the way of a formal organization and did not present a party platform, it did run a slate of candidates. Each of the candidates put forward his own platform. The platforms, however, did overlap to some extent and their concerns were mainly focused on improving conditions for cane growers. There was also general support for the idea of a common roll. Three of its candidates won seats on the Indian roll: A.D. Patel, Siddiq M. Koya, and James Madhavan.

The pace of political change hastened following the 1963 election, largely because of pressure from the British. Indo-Fijian political leaders from the Citizens' Federation met in Ba in 1964 to draft a constitution for a formal political party to be named the Federation Party. In part to avoid problems of factionalism, the structure of the party was to be highly centralized under a powerful president and a working committee. The party was launched officially in Lautoka in April 1965. Once the influential Indo-Fijian political leader A.D. Patel was elected president, the party immediately set about establishing branches in western and northern Viti Levu. Its founders and supporters saw it largely as a mechanism to advocate issues of concern to Indo-Fijians.

The Federation Party's policies focused on the land tenure system, inequities within the sugar industry, replacement of the communal roll with a common roll, removal of other vestiges of communalism within the political structure, and the elimination of colonial rule. It is significant that these last two items, in particular, had come to be seen as Indo-Fijian initiatives. They were opposed by native Fijian chiefs and members of the local European élite who sought to ensure that they were viewed in narrow communal terms. In keeping with this goal, these same elements branded the Federation Party as an instrument for achieving Indo-Fijian domination.

Once it was clear that the British meant to press ahead with their plans for political reform, and in the face of organizing activities among Indo-Fijians and western native Fijians, members of the native Fijian establishment saw the need to create a political organization of their own. Roderic Alley cites a memo on the subject prepared in January 1964 by a group of young native Fijians from the chiefly class who were studying in London. This group included David Toganivalu from Tailevu Province, who was to figure prominently in post-independence Alliance Party politics (and who was seen by many as a possible replacement or perhaps rival for Mara). Noting the apparent lack of leadership within the native Fijian community since the death of Sukuna and the growing 'threat' of Indo-Fijian dominance, the authors of the memo argued for the need to form a political party to represent native Fijian views and to provide the chiefs with 'a coherent mandate.' One of the primary aims of the party would 'be to campaign for superior Fijian representation in the legislature.'[27]

Prominent native Fijian chiefs such as Mara and Ganilau argued in favour of using the Fijian Association as the basis for a new political party that would ensure continued political control of the native Fijian community by the chiefs. One of the few dissenting voices within the native Fijian establishment was that of Dr. Rusiate Nayacakalau, who spoke in favour of creating a more democratic institution that would better represent the aspirations of ordinary native Fijians.[28] It was an idea that fell on deaf ears among Mara and his associates, who had little interest in promoting democracy within the native Fijian community.

The local European élite had formed a body called the European Electors to represent their interests. This was now transformed into the General Electors' Association to provide them with a broader political base. John Falvey and Len Usher emerged as leading spokesmen for the local European élite. They and other members of the European community sought to secure the privileges that had been given to them under the British by aligning themselves with the chiefly oligarchy.

In early 1965, Mara, Falvey, and Usher set to work laying the foundation for a broad-based coalition to champion the interests they represented. To begin with this meant revitalizing the Fijian Association and European Electors organizations and transforming them into a unified political party. They also sought to gain a foothold within the Indo-Fijian community. To secure support from Indo-Fijians, Mara and Falvey followed in the footsteps of the British by seeking to take advantage of the factionalism within the Indo-Fijian community. To promote and take advantage of such factionalism, they sought to cultivate a long-time rival of A.D. Patel, Ajodhya Prasad, who, after helping to break the back of the 1960 cane growers' strike, formed his own organization known as the National Congress. Unlike Patel and others in the Federation Party, Prasad had not placed priority on achieving a common roll. Also following British tradition, Mara and his allies sought to gain the support of the Muslim community.

While many of the more conservative chiefs in the Fijian Association were not keen on the idea of working with Indo-Fijians, the notion of forming a party comprised of representatives of the three communities was strongly supported by the colonial administration (which itself cared little for the Federation politicians). The governor himself made a speech to the Legislative Council in support of such an initiative – a speech which, as noted by Alley, 'surely strained the bounds of constitutional propriety.'[29]

A constitutional conference was convened in London in 1965 to discuss proposed constitutional changes, including the possibility of independence. It was arranged for the delegation from Fiji to represent the three main ethnic communities. The delegates were Mara, John Falvey, and A.D. Patel. The conference provoked expressions of anti-Indian sentiment among extreme native Fijian communalists. Thus, shortly before the delegates left Fiji, a meeting chaired by Ratu Etuate Cakobau (son of Adi Litia Cakobau) at Nausori demanded the exclusion of all Indo-Fijians if the colony were to become independent.[30]

During the conference, Apisai Tora sent Mara the following telegram on behalf of his party: 'very concerned about latest reports on conference. Party emphatically requests that you stand firm oppose common roll one man one vote and support common roll cross voting. To drive home into thick skulls of those Colonial Office wallahs determination of Fijian people on important issues, party suggests your and European delegation walk out of conference if one man one vote proposition not completely dropped. Drastic counter-measures especially when future of Fijian people is at stake.'

The Fijian Association prepared a submission for the conference in which it demanded that native Fijians be given an absolute majority in the legislature, that the position of prime minister could only be held by a native Fijian, that the Great Council of Chiefs and Fijian Affairs Board retain their present powers, that there be no change in the system of land tenure, and that there be a balance between native Fijians and Indo-Fijians in the public service.

The most important controversy emerged over Patel's call for a common electoral roll. This was completely unacceptable to Mara and Falvey and for a while it looked as if the conference would end in a deadlock. Finally, the British put forward a compromise proposal for a system of 'cross-voting' that was accepted by the conference. The principle of communal voting was maintained in part, but Mara and Falvey did agree to allow some voting on a partial multi-ethnic basis. As agreed, the new Legislative Council was to consist of thirty-two elected members and four nominated members (two of which were to come from the Council of Chiefs). Whereas twenty-three of the seats were to be allocated on a communal basis to the three communities (Fijian, Indian, and 'General Elector,' the latter referring to other non-islander immigrant communities, such as the Chinese, as well as Europeans), nine seats were to be selected on the basis of cross-voting. This meant that members of each community would be able to stand for three seats reserved for them, respectively, but that voters from all three communities would be able to vote for these candidates. The idea was to pressure parties to run multi-ethnic slates of candidates and to promote policies to appeal to all ethnic communities. Mara and Falvey were able to prevail at the conference with an agreement that the pace of political reform would be one agreed to by the native Fijian chiefs.

Both Mara and Falvey appeared to be relatively happy with the outcome of the conference. A number of principles of concern to them had been resolved in their favour, and their constituencies had received quite a generous allocation of seats. Mara's message to his supporters at home towards the end of the conference was 'be calm, the victory is ours.' Patel and the Federation Party were not so pleased and were quick to denounce the agreement. The Federation Party was particularly upset with the electoral formula. Nevertheless, it was clear that the British planned to press ahead with the agreement, and it was announced that a Legislative Council election would be held in 1966 under the new guidelines.

Mara and Falvey now set about to create a formal political party. The National Alliance Party was founded in March 1966. Its hastily drafted constitution created a party that was to be composed of an amalgamation of organizations, a structure influenced by the model of the Malaysian Alliance Party. The nature of these organizations was left relatively ambiguous, but primary components of the party were the Fijian Association and the General Electors' Association. Indo-Fijians were represented largely by the political wing of the Kisan Sangh, but there were also several individuals involved with no formal attachment to a communal organization. Among the Indo-Fijians involved were Vijay Singh and Ahmed Ali, who would play an important political role in years to come. Singh would become attorney general under Mara, and Ali an important ideologue for the Alliance Party. One of the problems facing the party was that of co-ordination between its constituent parts. This came to depend upon individuals such as Mara and Falvey, with each organization retaining a degree of autonomy.

The 1966 Election

In terms of sheer numbers, native Fijians and Indo-Fijians represented roughly equal portions of the electorate (approximately 48 per cent each), with the General Electors comprising about 4 per cent of the electoral community. Under the new structure, there were thirty-four elected members and two nominated members. The elected seats were divided thus: 9 Fijian, 9 Indian, and 7 General Elector communal seats; 3 Indian, 3 Fijian, and 3 General Elector cross-voting (or national) seats. This configuration meant that all the Alliance Party had to do to win was to retain control of the native Fijian and European vote and perhaps pick up a few Indo-Fijian votes to ensure that it won a couple of national seats. For the Federation Party, the task of winning the election was almost impossible, but it did need to try to make as strong a showing as possible to remain a political force in the lead-up to independence.

The Alliance Party left selection of native Fijian and European candidates up to their respective bodies, while the central administration, the Alliance Council, picked the Indo-Fijian candidates. Among native Fijians, candidates were nominated at the village level, with the Fijian Association and Alliance Council endorsing the candidate who received the largest number of nominations. This was not as democratic as it sounds since the village-level proceedings tended to be controlled by members of the chiefly class and there was strong pressure to eliminate candidates who did not support the views of the chiefly establishment. In the end, twenty-six candidates were nominated. The Alliance Party had not bothered to nominate candidates for the six Indian communal seats since it was felt that there was little chance of winning these seats.

The working committee of the Federation Party authorized Patel to gather nominations after visiting local branches and holding discussions around the country. A slate of names was then put before the party council and most of the names he had selected were nominated without dissent. The Federation Party ran only thirteen candidates: twelve candidates for the Indian communal and national seats and only one other candidate. This meant that it had no chance of winning a majority on the Legislative Council (seventeen seats).

There were thirty-nine independent candidates: 13 native Fijians, 15 Indo-Fijians, and 11 General Electors. A number of the Indo-Fijian candidates did not so much oppose the Federation Party as they sought to promote themselves as possible political intermediaries. Among the native Fijians, the Fijian Association permitted several of its members to stand against those who had been officially endorsed by the Alliance Party (believing that whoever won would make little difference to the paramountcy of native Fijian interests). Among those standing was Militoni Leweniqila who stood as an independent for the Macuata-Bua Fijian communal seat, and former Suva mayor Charles Stinson (the Stinson family being a prominent European settler family with extensive business holdings in the colony) who ran as an independent for the Suva General Elector seat (having to resign from the General Electors' Association to do so).

The Federation Party mainly campaigned among Indo-Fijian voters by appealing to communal insecurities. It stated that the London Conference had relegated Indo-Fijians to the status of second-class citizens thus paving the way to complete domination by native Fijians and Europeans once Fiji was independent. It not only complained of Indo-Fijians being given a mere one-third of the seats, but also pointed to how Indo-Fijians were disciminated against in other ways by the colonial government. The party maintained its call for a common electoral roll, invoking UN resolutions in support, and also sought to have Indo-Fijians admitted into the army in numbers equal to native Fijians. The Federation Party also had to contend with attempts by the Alliance Party to promote differences between Hindus and Muslims.

But the Federation Party also sought the support of members of other ethnic communities by appealing along class lines to sentiments against the colonial élite. Before the election the Federation Party had virtually no base within the native Fijian community. It backed two native Fijian candidates (with only one receiving formal endorsement): former trade unionist Nemani Waka (who ran against Mara) and Penaia Rokovuni. Rokovuni was a cane farmer from Ra who had been an official in Tora's Western Democratic Party and had taken an active part in the 1960 strike. He ran for a national seat in the west and was supported by Tora, who urged native Fijians in his area to vote for the Federation Party. With even less of a base of support in the European community, the Federation Party urged Indo-Fijians not to vote for the General Elector seats.

The Alliance Party campaign focused on the 'threat' posed by the Federation Party to stability in general and to the position of the native Fijian and European communities. Its native Fiijan candidates also sought support for continued chiefly rule among native Fijians and portrayed the Federation Party as seeking to undermine the position of native Fijians through its criticism of the chiefly élite. Australian anthropologist Robert Norton quotes one Alliance Party candidate, a high ranking chief, at a rally: 'Some of us who have returned from education overseas advocate the abolition of our traditions. But the tradition of chiefly rule is our natural strength. It will secure us if racial conflict should intensify. The British people kept their reverence for their chiefs even after gaining control of government; the Queen remains the highest chief in Britain today ... What do you think will hold us united in time of trouble? Our tradition, our unity under chiefly leadership.'[31] Norton cites another means by which the Fijian Association sought to ensure the support of native Fijians:

> At meetings I attended in Suva and in a nearby village the national secretary of the Fijian Association warned members against fraternizing with the enemy. For each member, he said, there was to be a 'personal card' filed at headquarters. If anyone was found to be giving information to a political party opposed to the Association, an entry would be made on his card. 'We will have agents throughout the colony to watch the movements and activities of members. If any member moves from here to the western districts and is found or suspected to be associated with Apisai Tora or the Federation Party he will be reported to headquarters.'[32]

The Alliance Party backed six Indo-Fijian candidates (three for communal seats and three for national seats). They argued for Indo-Fijian support on the basis of stability and security. In the west, the Alliance Party ran Ajodhya Prasad against A.D. Patel.

The results were much as expected, with the Alliance Party winning twenty-two seats, the Federation Party winning nine seats. The Alliance Party had won all of the Fijian and General Elector seats and the three Indian national seats; the Federation Party won only the Indian communal seats. In addition, there were three independents elected who sided with the Alliance Party. When the two nominees from the Great Council of Chiefs were added, the Alliance Party had a majority of eighteen. Ajodhya Prasad had proven to be its strongest Indian communal candidate, winning 29 per cent of the votes on the basis of longstanding rivalries and divisions within the community. Among the independents winning was Charles Stinson, who was quickly taken back into the Alliance Party (and given a ministry). The Federation Party had gained solid support from the Indo-Fijian community, while the Alliance Party had demonstrated its firm control over the Fijian and General Elector constituencies.

At one level, the election seemed to further entrench communalism within the political structure, but the election also had served to point out the limitations of electioneering based solely on ethnicity. The election left the Federation Party with little prospect of exercising much influence, let alone power. It was obvious that it would be necessary to move beyond the Indo-Fijian community to alter this situation. What was not clear, however, was how to accomplish this.

Independence

Having won the 1966 election with a large majority of seats, Mara and his allies were prepared to start taking steps toward eventual independence, but at a very slow pace. The Alliance Party looked to 1970 as a possible date for the granting of internal self-government. But once this took place, the Alliance Party was satisfied to allow an undetermined period before full independence was to be granted.

Patel and the Federation Party were not pleased with the prospect of such a long transition period. Relations between members of the Federation and Alliance parties in the Legislative Council were far from cordial. Patel referred to the Alliance Party as the 'white colonialist Alliance' and accused them of being the stooges of foreign business interests.[33] While the Alliance Party supported initiatives by the colonial government and made proposals in the Legislative Council which coincided with the interests of the administration, the Federation Party, by contrast, was vocal in its criticism of many of their positions. Indicative of its populist views, the Federation Party put forward a whole range of social justice policies which included: establishing a national standard of living, opposition to continuing salary differentials for expatriate civil servants, compensation to native Fijians for lands alienated by Europeans before the Deed of Cession, taking steps to improve the position of native Fijians in rural areas, and opposition to proposed changes in the Agricultural Landlords and Tenants Ordinance.

In September 1967, Patel put forward a proposal to hold a new constitutional conference to prepare a constitution along democratic lines rather than one that supported the interests of the colonial oligarchy. The Alliance Party responded with a motion endorsing the existing constitution and the Federation Party members staged a walk-out. The Federation Party continued to boycott the Legislative Council until the government was forced to hold by-elections the following year in all of the Indian communal seats.

By now the Federation was demanding that independence be granted promptly and according to democratic principles, and had begun actively canvassing for native Fijian support (especially in the west). Two high ranking native Fijian chiefs, Ratu Julian Toganivalu and Ratu Mosese Varasekete (from Bua and Rewa, respectively), joined the Federation Party. Both men not only campaigned on the Federation Party's behalf among Indo-Fijians, but also articulated criticisms of the colonial administration and chiefly oligarchy that were of relevance to the native Fijian community. One body that was singled out for criticism was the Native Land Trust Board, which the Federation Party accused of charging fees that were too high, of unfairly giving the chiefs too much of the rent, and of failing to assist native Fijians raise capital for development purposes. The Native Land Trust Board, it was argued, primarily served the interests of the European business community and the chiefs, while doing little for the majority of native Fijians, who were owners of the land in name only.

Further momentum was added with the affiliation of the National Democratic Party to the Federation Party in 1968. The National Democratic Party was a populist party which sought to appeal to native Fijians in the west. It was led by the two most outspoken native Fijian critics of the Alliance Party in western Fiji, Apisai Tora and Isikeli Nadalo. The parties came together to form the National Federation Party (NFP). Nadalo was made vice-president of the party and Tora was made regional organizer in the west. The Federation Party leadership felt that it had begun at last to build a political base among native Fijians.

Opposition to the Alliance Party was also mounted through the Fijian Chamber of Commerce. Supporters of the Fijian Chamber of Commerce were critical of the Fijian Association and of the chiefly establishment for ignoring the needs of common native Fijians. Three young native Fijians founded the organization in Suva in 1967. They focused on the commercial dominance of members of other ethnic communities, and especially the Europeans, and sought to establish agricultural marketing boards and company shops and to gain commercial training for native Fijians. It held its first conference in Lautoka in 1968, which was attended by an estimated 4,000 native Fiijans. Its president, Viliame Savu, was expelled from the Fijian Association (allegedly for making statements against Mara) and the organization soon collapsed. The Fijian Chamber of Commerce was not affiliated with the Federation Party, but the level of support it received served to heighten concern on the part of the Alliance Party that its hold over the native Fijian population was being undermined on the basis of appeals to regionalism and class.

Patel, Tora, Varasekete, and the others sought to unify Fijian workers and peasants across ethnic lines (they referred to native Fijian commoners as *Taukei*) in opposition to the native Fijian and European élite. The attempt to gain the support of native Fijians by the National Federation Party turned the by-elections into an important test for the Alliance Party. Mara and others in the Alliance Party spoke out in favour of the need to maintain racial differences and sought to appeal to communalism among Indo-Fijians and native Fijians.

The NFP candidates won all of the seats in the 1968 by-election by significantly larger margins than they had in the 1966 general election. In the four south-eastern seats, where Mosose Varasekete and Julian Toganivalu had been particularly active, they increased their majorities from an average of 44 to 77 per cent. In the two eastern seats the increase was from 31 to 66 per cent. And in the case of the four western seats the majority increased from 27 to 42 per cent. At a mid-September rally held after the elections, the NFP leaders proclaimed that the outcome of the election reflected the will of the entire nation which was in favour of 'freedom and equal rights' and called on the Alliance Party to hold a general election.[34]

The Alliance Party had no intention of giving in to the demands of the NFP. What it did do, through the Fijian Association, was seek to reaffirm its control of the native Fijian community by stirring up racist sentiments. The Fijian Association warned native Fijian commoners to beware of scheming Indo-Fijians who sought to reduce them to the status of second-class citizens, and it branded native Fijians who supported the NFP as traitors. A few marches and rallies were organized to demonstrate native Fijian support for the Alliance Party and to intimidate Indo-Fijians. Several native Fijians issued threats to take the land away from Indo-Fijian tenants when their leases expired, to deport Patel and others, and to disenfranchise Indo-Fijians and bar them from holding office.There were a few physical attacks on Indo-Fijians. Mara himself argued that the NFP had gone too far and that it threatened the stability of the colony. He and other leaders of the Fijian Association sought to present themselves as standing for moderation and multiracialism, holding at bay communal forces that threatened the well-being of the country – a theme that was to recur repeatedly in the years to come.

The success of the Alliance Party initiative was tested in the 1969 Ba and Nadroga-Navosa provincial council elections. The NFP fielded ten candidates out of a total of forty-five. Only one candidate, Apisai Tora, previously had held a seat. The NFP campaigned on a platform of abolishing the provincial councils in favour of multiracial ones so as to ease the financial burdens imposed on native Fijians by the councils and in an effort to promote economic development. It also brought up issues of regional significance such as improving educational facilities and providing support for economic development in the west. The Alliance Party used its standard appeal to tradition and racism as well as resorting to intimidation.

The election was a crushing victory for the Alliance Party and demonstrated just how much remained to be done if the NFP were to break the hold of the chiefs.[35] The Alliance Party viewed the elections as proof that its strategy had worked in neutralizing the threat of non-racial politics. That the NFP threat had not disappeared entirely, however, became evident in a by-election in early 1970 for the Suva-Rewa Fijian communal seat. Mosese Varasakete, relying largely upon his chiefly rank, lost in his bid for the seat, but did receive 39 per cent of the vote.

The political front was not the only one on which the governing élite faced problems. The administration was keen to encourage industrial relations that would allow a stable transition to independence. The Alliance Party supported the colonial administration in this goal and used its influence to convince workers to co-operate with employers and not demand wages that were 'too high.' The NFP took a very different stand and actively supported the demands of organized labour.

Opposition to the oligarchy also came from Tora who had succeeded in registering the Airport, Hotel and Catering Workers Union in 1965 in an effort to revitalize militant trade unionism. The business community saw Tora's actions as a direct threat to the colony's emerging tourist industry. In the 1967 Gould report, which concerned a dispute between Tora's union and Qantas, the employers' submissions portrayed Tora's union as threatening the fabric of the colonial economy through its drive for higher wages.[36] Tora refused to make a submission. The report's findings went largely against the union and in 1968 it was deregistered. In April 1969 the Fijian Association was able to muster the support of native Fijian dockworkers to also oust Tora as Suva branch president of the Dockworkers' and Seamen's Union.

The Municipal Workers' Union, led by an Indo-Fijian closely associated with the National Federation Party, staged another strike in 1967. The strike involved several hundred workers, and the governor invoked public safety regulations to restrict gatherings supporting the strike. In this instance, as with Tora's strike, the workers supporting the action included both Indo-Fijians and native Fijians. The administration and the Alliance Party had continued to support (the government more tacitly than the Alliance Party) separate unions for members of different ethnic communities. As in the 1959 strike, workers had formed a united front that transcended communalism and this was seen as a grave threat by the colonial government, the European business élite, and the chiefs.

Another potential area of trouble was the sugar industry. Both the Kisan Sangh and the National Federation of Cane Growers were pushing for a better deal from csr for growers and in the process hoping to gain support for their respective political parties. The Alliance Party was also anxious to control the Nadroga Fijian Cane Growers' Association, which represented native Fijian growers. Isikeli Nadalo was secretary of the union and, in late July 1969, the pro-Alliance president of the union was able to have him removed from office. The colonial government, in an apparent effort to placate cane growers during this sensitive time and perhaps lend support to Alliance Party efforts in the cane fields, appointed an arbitrator who was likely to, and in fact did, produce a report favourable to the growers.[37]

A.D. Patel, the pre-eminent political leader of the Indo-Fijian community, died in October 1969. He was replaced as president of the NFP by Siddiq Koya. Koya, a Muslim also from the west, was seen by many native Fijians as less threatening than Patel and seemed more likely to be able to extend the party's base within the native Fijian community. Moreover, while Patel and Mara had been bitter political enemies, Koya got along relatively well with Mara. The two parties had begun holding informal talks on constitutional change just before Patel died after attending only one meeting in August 1969. With Koya leading the NFP, it and the Alliance Party met twenty-five more times.[38] The NFP delegation consisted of five Indo-Fijians, whereas the Alliance delegation of ten consisted of five native Fijian chiefs, two Indo-Fijians, two Europeans, and one Chinese. The voice of the native Fijian commoner, the Taukei, was thus absent.

The NFP was willing to drop its demand that Fiji become a republic when the chiefs voiced their desire to maintain ties with the British Crown. Both sides also agreed not to hold an election before independence to avoid the prospect of inciting communal hostilities. Agreement on the composition of the new parliament, however, proved more difficult. The NFP's desire for a common roll and the Alliance Party's desire to ensure that the chiefs were given a significant position were two crucial issues.

When Mara proposed creation of an upper house, the NFP suggested that it be composed of the descendants of the high-ranking chiefs who had signed the Deed of Cession and that they be given veto power over legislation pertaining to native Fijian land and traditions. The NFP hoped that this would lead the Alliance Party to accept a common roll election for the Lower House. When Mara put the proposition to the Great Council of Chiefs, its members agreed only to having an upper house that had the power to safeguard the interests of the chiefs. They did not, however, want its membership to be so restricted. As for the idea of a lower house elected on the basis of a common roll, this was deemed out of the question by the members of the Council of Chiefs. A compromise was reached on the matter of the number of seats reserved for General Electors when the Alliance Party agreed to fewer than it had proposed initially, but it remained unwilling to bend on the question of a common roll.

Mara came under criticism from hard-line chiefs who saw little reason to compromise with the Indo-Fijians and who opposed independence altogether, but overall opposition to him within the Alliance Party was minimal. Koya, on the other hand, received a great deal of criticism from his party cohorts. Many were not pleased with his willingness to compromise on the issue of the common roll, and there was concern over what seemed to be too close a relationship between Koya and Mara. He was accused of turning his back on the legacy of A.D. Patel and abandoning the principles for which the party had fought since its inception. Some expressed their fear that Koya might lead them into a coalition with the Alliance Party. Such dissension was not sufficient, however, to challenge Koya's leadership of the party.

The talks continued in Fiji until March 1970. Sufficient progress was made for the parties involved to decide to move to London in April. Negotiations went quickly in London and a final agreement was reached in May. Under the terms of the agreement, Fiji would have a parliament comprised of two houses, its membership selected along communal lines. There was to be an upper house, the Senate, which was made up of nominated members; eight chosen by the Great Council of Chiefs, seven by the prime minister, six by the leader of the opposition and one by the Council of Rotuma. Parliament could pass no law affecting native Fijian land or traditions without the support of six of the eight nominees from the Great Council of Chiefs. The lower house, the House of Representatives, was to have fifty-two members: twenty-seven communal seats and twenty-five national seats divided among the three communal electorates. There was to be parity between the seats assigned to native Fijians and Indo-Fijians, each having twelve communal and ten national seats. General Electors were given a total of eight seats: three communal and five national. In addition to the safeguards provided by the Senate, the constitution contained other clauses specifically spelling out and entrenching the rights of native Fijians.

Those involved in the negotiations decided to defer a final decision on a common roll until after independence, when a royal commission would be set up to recommend the most appropriate method of selecting members for the House of Representatives. It was the intent of the compromise that the agreement to maintain a communal system of voting at this time was to be a temporary measure. It was also agreed that new parliamentary elections under the new constitution would be held within six months of independence.

Independence was proclaimed on 10 October 1970, with Ratu George Cakobau serving as governor general. In light of his subsequent political career, it is perhaps worth quoting Alliance Party ideologue Ahmed Ali, writing as an academic, on the meaning of the agreement between Mara and Koya and the manner in which independence was granted to Fiji:

> Colonial rule on its departure left Fiji in Fijian hands and might thereby be deemed to have fulfilled, at least in a political sense, its promise of the paramountcy of indigenous interests. By permitting European over-representation and facilitating an alliance of European and Fijian communities, it substantially secured the European position. As for Indians, who had been brought initially as indentured labourers but with the promise of 'enjoyment of equal rights' ... the care of their future was transferred without any special legal provisions, from the British to the new rulers of Fiji. It would be no exaggeration to conclude that the colonial regime failed to reconcile paramountcy for Fijians, over-representation of Europeans and promise of equality to Indians. Indeed the three were and are incompatible.[39]

It is, of course, unfair to hold the British responsible for all of this, although they certainly deserve a good deal of the blame. The European and Fijian chiefly oligarchy were not simply unwitting tools of the colonial administration. And it was, after all, they who fought so strongly against reforms attempted by the British to create a somewhat more democratic Fiji. Moreover, as we have seen, the British themselves were not always of one mind as to how to proceed. There were those within the colonial administration who were committed to democratic reform, but there were many others who were not. In the end, it was the latter whose views prevailed and who joined with the chiefs and European business intererests in Fiji to thwart attempts to create a more democratic nation and to move Fiji away from communal politics.

INDEPENDENT FIJI

The first half of the 1970s has been characterized by many as the 'honeymoon' years for the Alliance Party and NFP as a result of the continuing close relationship between Mara and Koya. Koya's relationship with Mara led to continued sniping at Koya within the NFP, but for the time being, no serious challenge was launched against his leadership. Moreover, the NFP rejected an offer by Mara in 1971 to join the Alliance Party in a coalition government. It did so largely because it felt that it could win the election now planned for 1972. An important factor contributing to this optimism was the belief that the NFP would be able to win the support of a significant number of native Fijian voters. With this aim in mind, it launched 'Operation Taukei' by 1969, seeking to build upon its pre-independence initiative among native Fiijans, especially in western Viti Levu and the Rewa area.

Mara became increasingly worried when a number of western native Fijians used the occasion of the drawing of electoral boundaries in 1971 to complain that the Alliance Party had a history of neglecting people in their region and of bringing in outside candidates to stand for seats in the west. To meet this challenge, towards the end of 1971, he invited about a dozen prominent western chiefs, including the Tui Nadi, Ratu Napolioni Dawai, and the Tui Vuda, Ratu Josaia Tavaiqia, to visit him at his home on Lakeba in the Lau Group. During the meeting, the chiefs formed the Confederation of Western Tui Association.

In a statement carried in the *Fiji Times*, Dawai said that the chiefs had formed the association to look after 'the political and economic welfare of their people' as a result of the number of complaints that were being aired and to counter the drive to recruit native Fijians to the NFP, and to 'strengthen our position as *tui ni vanua* (chiefs of the land).' He complained that non-westerners occupied the two western Fijian communal seats and argued that the changes going on in Fiji and the world around them meant that the chiefs had to organize to 'make us stronger and bring us closer to the people.'[40] Durutalo comments that 'this move by Ratu Mara was aimed at safeguarding his support in western Viti Levu by his apparent acknowledgement of western Fijian grievances as articulated by its chiefs.'[41] Thus, Mara sought to ensure that the western chiefs continued to support him and he sought to use them to counter the discontent among native Fijian commoners in the west. Mara's initiative was not entirely successful, and after the chiefs returned from Lakeba their unity quickly broke down as they divided between those willing to support the Alliance Party since it was the party that best represented the interests of native Fijian chiefs and those who placed greater emphasis on support for the demands and aspirations of western native Fijians.

The 1972 Election

In a survey conducted three months before the 1972 election, anthropologist Alexander Mamak found 'that sectional affiliation is a very important factor in the choice of a party for both Europeans and Fijians. It is not so clear with respect of the Indian section. Although ... the NFP would receive its major support from the Indian section, only 29 per cent of Indians were firmly committed to this party.'[42] Mamak argued that the reasons for this lack of attachment to the NFP was a reflection of several factors: (1) a general disenchantment with politics among Indo-Fijians; (2) disenchantment specifically with the NFP; (3) a lack of cohesion within the Indo-Fijian community; and (4) (related to the first two points) a low level of participation in politically-aligned voluntary associations, especially when compared with other communities.

Mamak also sought to analyse the significance of social class in relation to party support. Traditionally, the NFP had been identified with farmers and workers within the Indo-Fijian community, and his survey indicated that wealthier Indo-Fijians (especially Gujaratis) tended to identify with the Alliance Party rather than the NFP. His survey found that 59 per cent of those indicating support for the NFP cited ideology as the major difference between the parties, and he quotes several Indo-Fijian respondents who highlighted this ideological dimension: 'The Alliance works for the wealthy; the Federation works for the poor (Accounts clerk, Indian) ... Alliance is on the side of the capitalist; the NFP fights for the poor people (Primary school teacher, Indian) ... The Government (Alliance) favour themselves; the Federation is in favour of the working people (Carpenter, Indian).'[43]

In contrast, native Fijian and European support for the Alliance Party transcended class lines. Those supporting the Alliance Party tended to point to sectional factors, either seeing the Alliance Party as a defender of their particular sectional interests (native Fijians mostly) or pointed to its multiracialism versus perceived communal exclusiveness on the part of the NFP. While class consciousness among Europeans and native Fijians was limited, Mamak did turn up evidence that it was not entirely absent, as indicated in the following quotation: 'If our chiefs send us a message asking us to vote for them we vote for them. That is why I have always voted Alliance. But I recently heard Ratu Mosese [a Fijian vice-president in the NFP] speak in the senate; I read his articles; and heard him on the radio. I like what he says. I am beginning to doubt whether the Fijian people are going to stick with the Alliance for long, at least not the working-class people (Dockworker, Fijian, undecided).'[44]

The campaign for the 1972 election began in March, with voting taking place the end of April. There were fifty-two communal and national seats to be contested. The Alliance Party announced candidates for fifty seats, while the NFP ran candidates for only forty seats (22 Indian, 15 Fijian, and 3 General Elector). Under the leadership of Viliame Savu, a group of native Fijians who were disenchanted with the Fijian Association prior to independence had formed the Fijian Advancement Society. It changed its name to the Fijian Independent Party and ran six candidates in the election (5 Fijian and 1 Indian). Finally, there were twenty-six independent candidates (13 Fijian, 7 Indian, and 6 General Elector).

Selection of candidates within the NFP was ultimately in the hands of its working committee, headed by Siddiq Koya, and it received the names of potential candidates from the various branches. Communal differences were acknowledged by allowing the party's Taukei Committee to select the native Fijian candidates, although these too had to be approved by the working committee. Candidate selection for communal seats within the Alliance Party was handled through its three constituent communal bodies – the Fijian Association, the Indian Alliance, and the General Electors' Association – while selection for national seats was made by the party's national council on the basis of nominations from district councils. Many of the independents who ran were individuals who had failed to be named by the Alliance Party.

Both the Alliance Party and the NFP sought to cut across communal lines and present themselves as multiracial, national parties. Such a strategy meant avoiding or playing down issues that had the potential of promoting communal antagonism. Thus, the NFP, rather than talk of questions of land ownership, focused on seeking means to improve land utilization. In the past, the NFP had advocated a common electoral roll. This time, efforts were made to avoid the issue and to direct attention to issues relating to social and economic development. For its part, the Alliance Party took an ambiguous position on the common roll, pointing to its reservations about a common roll, but expressing a willingness to consider it at some time in the future. In the case of land, however, Alliance candidates did seek to implant the fear among native Fijians that an NFP victory would threaten their control of the land.

Clearer differences emerged between the two parties over economic issues. Koya pursued a populist approach calling for the nationalization of vital industries, the end of foreign economic domination, compulsory and free education, establishment of a minimum living wage, setting up an agricultural bank to provide low-interest loans to cane farmers, and increases in social welfare services. The NFP also made an issue of the government's 'failure' to control inflation. The Alliance Party agreed with some of these goals and claimed to be working towards them (for example, free education), but was opposed to those of a more socialistic nature. Both the Fijian Independent Party and the NFP, in a move to appeal to native Fijian voters, stated that Fiji should become a republic and that a native Fijian should replace the Queen as the head of state.

The Fijian Independent Party took a very different approach from that of the two leading parties. It denounced the other parties for 'hiding behind the skirt of multi-racialism' and campaigned to have native Fijians alone 'decide the destiny of their land.' On the land issue, it called for 'an immediate return of all Crown and Freehold lands in Fiji to the rightful Native owners with the present holders being given priority by the Native owners to lease.'

By and large, the actual campaign was a muted affair, generating little excitement or hostility, in part, because of the relatively harmonious relations that prevailed between Mara and Koya. Anthropologist Robert Norton comments: 'I gathered from what my informants said that the prime minister Ratu Mara and leader of the Opposition Siddiq Koya had a mutual understanding to discipline their campaigns to minimize tensions.'[45] One of the few things to arouse a little electoral passion was the so-called 'Labasa letter.' This letter, allegedly written in 1967 by the president of the Indian Alliance to a supporter in Labasa, appeared to be an offer of land for votes. The NFP distributed copies of the letter, but its impact was minimal.

Despite official insistence that the two parties stood for multiracialism, communal appeals were not absent. Indian Alliance candidates hinted that their defeat might lead to retribution by native Fijians. Within the NFP, there were communal appeals to both Indo-Fijians and native Fijians. This was especially true of the party's Taukei Committee, which sought to promote the view that the Alliance Party was dominated by Europeans and served European interests (the Fijian Independent Party pursued a similar line of argument).

Both parties expected to win the election. The NFP predicted that it would win twenty-eight of the fifty-two seats. The Alliance Party claimed that it expected to win between twenty-eight and thirty seats. When the actual results were known the Alliance Party had won thirty-three seats and the NFP nineteen seats (Table 1). As for the Fijian Independent Party and the independents, they received a total of only 15 per cent of the vote and many lost their deposits.

TABLE 1
Results of the 1972 election

Seats	Alliance Party	NFP
Fijian communal	12	0
Indian communal	0	12
General communal	3	0
Fijian national	7	3
Indian national	7	3
General national	4	1
Total seats	33	19

In assessing the outcome of the election, Mamak feels that the NFP could have tied or won the election had it placed a few of its more prominent candidates in some of the marginal national seats.[46] Thus, the large majority of seats won by the Alliance Party should not lead to the conclusion that it was an easy win.

The results indicated a high correlation between ethnic community and support for a party. However, in the case of the national seats, a large number of Indo-Fijians had voted for the Alliance Party. And, while the NFP had failed to gain much support from native Fijian voters (overall, it only received 2 per cent of the votes in the Fijian communal seats), its support did vary according to region. Thus, whereas the two NFP candidates for Fijian communal seats in the east received only 1 to 2 per cent of the vote, in the west its three candidates averaged 6 per cent. Nevertheless, it was clear that Operation Taukei had not succeeded in generating the support that had been anticipated.

Analysts are not in agreement concerning the extent to which the election results indicated a growing sense of communalism within Fijian politics. Robert Norton concludes: 'Despite the racial appeals, voting in the communal constituencies indicated stronger racial polarization than in 1966 when party competition dominated elections for the first time. Fijians were now more strongly united behind the Alliance, and Indians behind the Federation.'[47] Norton goes on to comment that 'many Fijians regard the Federation as a worthy option. The prevalent opinion was that the Federation was the Indians' party and that its Fijian adherents had "gone over to the Indians".'[48]

Mamak, on the other hand, argues against placing too much importance on communalism, and that while the structure of the electoral system did promote communal politics, there was evidence of various other forces at work promoting multi-ethnic politics. He notes that during the election there was an unprecedented level of co-operation across communal boundaries. In the case of the NFP, he points out:

> Not only were Fijians and other non-Indians actual candidates for the NFP, but for the first time, in such proportions, the party actively sought the 'non-Indian' vote. (The NFP sponsored a record number of Fijian candidates in the election, fifteen as compared to one in 1966.) Despite the election set-back the NFP has pledged to continue its attempts to attract greater Fijian support. In that case, with three Fijians already elected to office by the party, less conservative Fijian views will be accommodated and the possible emergence of totally sectional parties such as the FIP [Fijian Independent Party] is lessened.'[49]

Mamak's proposition concerning the likelihood of the rise of another chauvanistic party such as the Fijian Independent Party proved to be off the mark, but his comments do serve to capture a feeling of the time that, despite evidence of communalism, the situation was still a fluid one in which multi-ethnic politics were a possibility.

Restless Workers and Natives

The Fijian oligarchy and the Alliance Party came out of the 1972 election with their positions intact, if not strengthened, but the Alliance Party soon found itself beset by an array of problems. There had been some fear that independence would have an adverse effect on the nation's economy, and initially there was some slow-down in investment in certain sectors. The country's rate of economic growth as reflected in GDP in constant dollar terms, however, was relatively healthy during the first few years after independence, ranging from 6 per cent in 1970 to 12.7 per cent in 1974. But, as the impact of the

rise in oil prices was felt, the situation worsened. The rate of inflation
went from 3.9 per cent in 1969 to 14.4 per cent in 1974, the highest
level since the Second World War. The rise in inflation was followed
by the full brunt of the international recession hitting Fiji's open
economy, and through 1978, Fiji's GDP barely grew at all (ranging
between 0 and 2.3 per cent per year). Such economic conditions
created problems for labour, the peasantry, and the business sector,
and this was translated into political problems for the government.

As the level of inflation increased, organized labour sought wage
increases. As expected, the Alliance Party was hostile to these
demands and supported employers.[50] Thus, in one instance, the government went so far as to threaten to call in the army to take over
services if striking workers did not return to their jobs. The government sought to regularize things by establishing a Labour Advisory
Board with representatives from unions and the private sector, but it
proved to be ineffective.

The 1972 election had an important, if unintended, effect on industrial relations. Two of the older conservative trade unionists who had
played a role in moderating the demands of workers in the past –
Mohammed Ramzan (who from 1961 to 1972 served as general secretary of the Fiji Trades Union Congress, which had superceded the
Fiji Industrial Workers' Council) and Sakeasi Waqanivavalaqi
(general secretary of the mineworkers' union at Vatukoula from 1962
to 1972 and president of the Fiji Trades Union Congress until 1972) –
were elected to Parliament by the Alliance Party (both were given
ministerial portfolios). The removal of these two men from the union
movement occurred at the same time that a new generation of more
militant trade unionists was arriving on the scene. And soon such
unionists had taken over the mineworkers', the Nadi airport workers', timber workers', and oil workers' unions. To add to the government's worries, Apisai Tora, who had been elected to Parliament in
1972 by the NFP, continued to be associated with the airport workers
and mill workers.

Waqanivavalaqi resigned as president of the Fiji Trades Union
Congress in 1972 and the militants sought to have Tora elected in his
place. A struggle erupted and the moderates succeeded in putting
Ramzan in instead. When he in turn resigned the following year he
was replaced by one of his protégés, Joveci Gavoka. Another pro-
Alliance, moderate unionist, James Raman (national secretary of the
Union of Factory and Commercial Workers) was made general secre-
tary of the Fiji Trades Union Congress.

The response of Tora and his supporters to the triumph of the
moderates within the Fiji Trades Union Congress was to break away

and form the Fiji Confederation of Trade Unions, with Tora as president. When the Fiji Confederation of Trade Unions affiliated internationally with the Moscow-aligned World Federation of Trade Unions (the Fiji Trades Union Congress was affiliated with the anti-communist International Confederation of Free Trade Unions), this generated a 'red scare' and conservative politicians and others warned the population of a growing 'communist menace.' It is perhaps an indication of the extent to which the NFP had changed under Koya's leadership that, whereas the Fiji Trades Union Congress had close ties with the Alliance Party, the Fiji Confederation of Trade Unions could count on little support from the NFP. Tora was virtually a lone voice in Parliament speaking on behalf of labour.

Faced with a slowing of economic growth and higher inflation, the government announced in March 1973 that it was about to introduce a new Trade Disputes Bill. Not having been consulted prior to the announcement, the Fiji Trades Union Congress asked for time to examine the proposed bill. The government pressed for quick passage and, urged on by its membership, the Fiji Trades Union Congress announced plans for a one-day general strike in protest. The day before the strike was to be held, the reasons for the government's sense of urgency became clear when it announced a three-month wage freeze. This was followed by a Prices and Incomes Policy which set maximum levels for wage awards. The NFP, with the exception of Tora, was muted in its criticism of the government's actions. The Fiji Trades Union Congress and Fiji Confederation of Trade Unions continued to protest until in March 1974, when after the Fiji Trades Union Congress threatened to call a national general strike, the Alliance Party agreed to amend the policy.

The more militant unionists found the Fiji Trades Union Congress leadership too willing to compromise. This leadership found itself in a difficult position. It was not anxious to alienate the Alliance Party, with which it identified (and from which the leaders might receive future rewards as had Ramzan and Waqanivavalaqi), but it was under strong pressure from the members of affiliated unions to act. Added to this was the recognition that failure to act could drive these unions into the rival Fiji Confederation of Trade Unions. A compromise was reached in which the Fiji Trades Union Congress leadership put forward minimal demands and the government agreed to a few concessions.

The compromise did not put an end to labour unrest. Between 1974 and 1978 there were an average of sixty strikes a year. The situation became particularly tense in 1976, when strikes were threatened in the oil distribution, sugar milling, gold-mining, and other industries. There were also heated arguments between the Fiji Trades Union Congress and the Fiji Confederation of Trade Unions. The government decided to act to calm things down before the situation deteriorated further. David Toganivalu, who had a reputation for a willingness to talk, was appointed labour minister and was able to establish better relations with the unions.

In an effort to strengthen the hand of the moderate unionists, the government brought in the Trade Union (Recognition) Act in 1976, establishing guidelines for union registration and collective bargaining. But as wages fell further behind the rate of inflation, labour unrest continued. The following year, the management of Emperor Gold Mine at Vatukoula, which had a long history of close relations with the chiefly oligarchy, threatened to close the mine and lay off its 1,300 workers. A strike was called, in which the Fiji Trades Union Congress was drawn in, and the government decided to intervene. The mine was not closed (it is doubtful that this was ever really a consideration), but 700 workers lost their jobs and the union was broken (mostly non-union workers were rehired, and the union was deregistered in 1979).

By the mid-1970s, the Alliance Party was facing growing problems among rural-dwelling native Fijians as well. Opposition came from two sources: from the Rewa and from the west. Sakeasi Butadroka had been elected to parliament from Rewa in 1972 on an Alliance Party ticket. He was a small businessman who, along with others in his position, felt frustrated by the lack of support forthcoming from the government and by competition from businesses run by members of other ethnic communities.

In October 1975, claiming that the Alliance Party had failed to adequately promote native Fijian interests, Butadroka put forward a motion that: 'Indians or people of Indian origin be repatriated back to India and that their travelling expenses and compensation for their properties be met by the British government.'[51] Characterizing Indo-Fijians as a 'demanding race,' he argued that through the Agricultural Land and Tenants Ordinance they sought to strip the Native Land Trust Board of its power, which he felt was too limited as it was. He demanded that the Great Council of Chiefs be given more power and that 75 per cent of the seats in the House of Representatives should be reserved for native Fijians. He also asked that more support be provided to native Fijians to develop small businesses.

Mara dealt with the motion by adding an amendment that drew attention to the contributions made by Fiji's non-indigenous communities and expressing the belief that they were committed to helping to improve the lot of native Fijians. Mara's amendment did not, however, question some of the basic assumptions of the original motion concerning the paramountcy of native Fijian interests. After Koya sought unsuccessfully to put forward his own amendment, the motion, as amended by Mara, was passed.

In addition to making such political demands, Butadroka organized native Fijians in the countryside and threatened Indo-Fijian tenant farmers who were behind in their rents or whose leases had expired, claiming that the Native Land Trust Board was failing in its duty to the native Fijian people. His activities culminated in the founding of the Fijian Nationalist Party, which fielded four candidates in the 1975 Suva City Council election. They were defeated by the Alliance Party candidates, but out-polled the native Fijian candidates fielded by the NFP by a hefty margin.

Mara and other members of the Alliance Party condemned Butadroka and had him thrown out of the party. Butadroka's expulsion was hailed by Mara's supporters as an example of his stature as a leader for all Fijians and of the Alliance Party's support for multiracialism. But the matter was not quite that simple. Sociologist Simione Durutalo argues that: 'the Alliance Party strategy was to use Butadroka as a "straw man" to present to the Indo-Fijian population a favourable image of Prime Minister Mara, while at the same time demonstrating his concern for maintenance of the paramountcy of native Fijian interests. Thus, for the non-indigenous Fijian electorate, Butadroka was portrayed as a stupid and racist indigenous Fijian politician as opposed to the reasonableness of Mara.'[52] Durutalo refers to this as a 'strategy of "facing both ways", uttering multi-racial mumbo-jumbo to the electorate at large, particularly to the Indo-Fijian audience, while reiterating the paramountcy of Fijian interests to an indigenous Fijian audience.'[53] As was about to be demonstrated, however, the Alliance Party's strategy of using Butadroka was a dangerous one that could go very wrong.

In the west, dissent centred on the newly introduced pine industry.[54] Fiji's Sixth Development Plan (1971–75) called for increased development of pine forests in western Viti Levu (and especially for reforestation). Western native landowners felt that, although the proposed development could be of considerable benefit to them, there were numerous potential problems. They were worried that increased forest development might harm other activities such as farming and hunting, and they felt that the terms of land acquisition and lease were inadequate. They sought to ensure that they received maximum economic benefits and that they were provided a significant role in determining the manner in which the industry was developed.

The first clash between the government and western landowners took place in 1972. The government had established the 'Fiji Pine Scheme' to administer pine development in the west. Those in charge viewed it primarily as a commercial enterprise concerned with generating revenue for the government. The Divisional Forest Officer Western, Ratu Osea Gavidi, a high chief from the west who had been instrumental in gaining the acceptance of initial lease terms by landowners in the Nabou area, felt that the well-being of the landowners was not sufficiently being looked after by the government. He argued with his superiors who sought to have him transferred to Labasa in early 1973 (transfers being a common means by which the Alliance Party has handled dissent).

The Nabou area had a history of involvement in the Viti Kabani movement and with the Bula Tale Communist Party, and the villagers were not strongly supportive of the Fijian Association or the Alliance Party. They formed a delegation to visit the deputy prime minister, a chief from Bua/Cakaudrove (Mara was out of the country), to protest Gavidi's transfer. At the meeting, they were told 'not to try to dispute or question the government decision.' The response of the leader of the deputation (a western chief) was 'you are only a chief in your place, but as far as we are concerned we do not recognise you as such.'[53] The landowners were upset further by what they felt to be the insensitive and racist treatment meted out to them by the European staff of the Fiji Pine Scheme.

Gavidi resigned from his post and went to Australia. But Mara, recognizing the political importance of the dispute, asked Gavidi to return and appointed him a special forestry officer directly under the prime minister. This move resulted in a temporary reconciliation between the two men. To diffuse the situation further, Mara initiated a review of lease arrangements and staff conditions of service in the pine industry.

As a means of improving the situation, Gavidi suggested the formation of a 'Fiji Pine Incorporation' to manage the industry and to develop subsidiary industries for the landowners. He modelled the idea on the Maori Land Incorporation of New Zealand and suggested that it be comprised of representatives from the government, the Native Land Trust Board, and the western landowners. The government did not adopt the idea, and the following year western landowners in the primary regions where the pine industry was being developed formed three companies on their own: the Nabou Development Corporation, the Vakabuli Development Corporation, and the Nadroga/Navosa Development Corporation.

Trouble erupted in the west again in 1975, this time in the Drasa/

Lololo area. The landowners went on strike over unpaid money due to them for the lease of pine land and forced the closing of two pine stations. Mara intervened personally to settle the strike. Following the strike, Mara agreed to establish a committee of management comprising representatives from the government, the pine scheme, landowners, and foreign organizations such as the Commonwealth Development Corporation to assist in transformation of the Fiji Pine Scheme into a statutory body. Influenced largely by expertise provided by the Commonwealth Development Corporation, the committee prepared draft legislation, which was placed before Parliament in early 1976 in the form of the Fiji Pine Commission Bill.

In presenting the bill to Parliament, the government indicated that it saw the proposed Fiji Pine Commission as a partnership involving the government and the landowners, with the assistance of such bodies as the Commonwealth Development Corporation, in order to ensure that the landowners received 'a more equitable share of the profits from the operations on their land as well as being more closely involved in the development process itself.'[56] Moreover, it was stated that the government planned to gradually lessen its direct involvement in the commission, while the landowners 'would acquire a far greater say in what is done.'[57] In support of the bill, NFP parliamentarian Isikeli Nadolo (representing south-western Viti Levu), stated that the most important feature of the bill was that it allowed for 'full participation of the landowners in the Commission.'[58] But he also raised a question concerning the number of representatives on the commission from each party.

The bill set the number of landowner representatives at three but did not specify the number for the government. And Nadolo asked for clarification concerning the leasehold rights of the landowners. NFP parliamentarians Koya and Ramrakha raised questions about the debts to be incurred in order to finance development of the project; Koya hoped that when the scheme was turned over to the landowners, they would not be given something overburdened with debts. In the end, the bill passed with the support of both parties on a note of relative optimism.

The Street Commission

In accordance with the agreement reached during the Fiji Constitutional Conference in London on 30 April 1970, a royal commission was established on 27 March 1975 to prepare a report on the means of electing members to the House of Representatives.[59] The chairman of the commission was Professor Harry Street. Its two other members were Professor Bryan Keith-Lucas and Sir William Hart. Street was in Fiji in March and April to hold discussions with concerned parties about the commission and to make arrangements for its visit in August. At this time it became apparent that the views of the Alliance Party and the NFP differed concerning the purpose and status of the commission.[60]

The Alliance Party argued that 'the idea expressed in some quarters that the present Constitution is interim is an erroneous one,' and that Parliament was under no compulsion to make changes in the electoral system in keeping with the recommendations of the commission. The view expressed by the NFP was markedly different: 'The understanding of 1970 clearly visualised that the Royal Commission would be instrumental to establish fully the fundamental principles of democracy and representative government in this country. The 1970 constitutional arrangement was only an "interim" one and was the penultimate step in the direction of a fully representative and popular democracy. This is how the arrangement was offered to us and we accepted it in good faith.'[61] In addition, Koya noted that the compromise was part of a 'package deal' in which it had been understood that the recommendations of the commission were to be much more binding than was now indicated by the Alliance Party. Koya argued that in his view, both sides were under a 'moral obligation' to accept the recommendations of the commission, and he quoted Mara from the constitutional negotiations as stating that the recommendations 'would be taken into consideration, and then become part of the Constitution otherwise its recommendations could be subject to the whim and fancies of any Parliament.' Clearly, after the 1972 election, the Alliance Party was in no mood to tamper with the electoral system in any way that might make it possible for the NFP to do better at the polls, no matter what Mara and Falvey had agreed to in 1970.

In its submission to the commission, the Alliance Party essentially argued in favour of maintaining the status quo. Arguing that 'it was an inescapable conclusion that race was a very important fact of life in Fiji' and that therefore any attempts to bridge gaps across ethnic boundaries had to be taken very gradually, it raised the need to continue the level of representation for General Electors and the need to ensure that native Fijians were not made to feel 'insecure' by implementing changes that undermined their current status. Basically, the Alliance Party wanted to ensure that the chiefs retained their power over native Fijian commoners and that their European allies continued to hold an electorally significant number of seats.

The NFP's submission was very different. It argued that, in an ethnically plural society such as Fiji, 'a common electoral roll could bring the different peoples together in the common task of creating a genuinely united nation,' whereas the existing system 'perpetuated communal interests and led to communal confrontation and conflict.' In addition, it was felt that 'fears that Fijian interests and particularly Fijian land ownership might be jeopardised by changes in the electoral system for the House of Representatives were unreal' since 'more than adequate protection' was provided 'through the veto powers of the Upper House' and the 'entrenched clauses of the Constitution.' Finally, the NFP felt that 'the eight seats reserved for the General Electors were excessive.'[62]

Evidence was presented by a large number of other individuals and organizations. A progressive group of university-educated Fijians in Suva prepared a submission along lines similar to that presented by the NFP.[63] Tora made a submission as well, as did Ratu Napolioni Dawai and a number of other westerners. So too did the Fijian Nationalist Party. The presentations of the individuals representing the Fijian Nationalist Party were not in total agreement, but basically they argued that the present structure did not sufficiently protect native Fijian interests and asked that either all or 75 per cent of the seats in the House of Representatives be reserved for native Fijians. Voting for these seats could be on a common-roll basis if 100 per cent of the seats were reserved for native Fijians or on a communal basis if only 75 per cent of the seats were reserved.[64]

The recommendations of the royal commission, which became available in January 1976, included the following: (1) Rotuma should form a single-member constituency (at the time it was joined with the Lau Group, an Alliance stronghold, and was therefore neutralized by the Alliance Party as a potential source of trouble); (2) the existing structure of communal seats should be retained 'for the present'; and (3) 'the further step towards a fully democratic system should be taken by removing the present racial reservations from the remaining 25 seats' (the national seats), which 'would amount to the same thing as converting the national or cross-voting roll to a common electoral roll.'[65] What it suggested for the twenty-five seats was that they be divided among five constituencies, each with five members, who were to be elected on the basis of a common electoral roll with single transferable voting. It cited Malta as a country where single transferable voting had been used successfully. It was felt that such a system would promote the development of multi-ethnic parties and that it would not allow Indo-Fijians to dominate parliament. In effect, this was an attempt at a compromise that might be acceptable to all parties, while at the same time moving the country closer to a more democratic system.

The recommendations represented a threat to the Alliance Party since it stood to lose control of the five General Elector national seats and probably a couple of the Fijian national seats. Of course, it might be able to compensate for this loss in other ways under the proposed new system, but the Alliance Party appeared to be unwilling to take the chance. Mara denounced the commission's recommendations, stating that if implemented they would lead to bloodshed, and he reaffirmed his commitment to maintaining communal voting. He was supported by the Alliance Party and by the Fijian Association. Koya responded by stating that the Alliance Party was under an obligation to accept the recommendations. It was evident, however, that Mara and his party had no intention of accepting the recommendations and the matter was not even brought up for debate in parliament. For Koya and Mara the 'honeymoon' period was over – as it was for many Indo-Fijians who now held little hope that the Alliance Party would agree to democratic reforms unless forced to do so. Moreover, Mara's renunciation of the Street Commission proposals rebounded to Koya over claims that he had given Mara too much leeway in the initial independence agreement.

Trouble within the NFP

The Alliance Party was not alone in having problems. Koya's leadership of the NFP had been challenged within the party from the outset. Members of his party had questioned his leadership in the constitutional negotiations as well as after the party's defeat in the 1972 election. His close ties with Mara and other members of the Alliance Party were of particular concern. One of his more vocal critics, K.C. Ramrakha, resigned as general secretary of the party in 1973, alleging that he could no longer tolerate Koya's dictatorial style. He was convinced to retract his resignation, but the bitterness between the two men remained. Koya's falling out with Mara in 1975 only served to make matters worse.

In October 1975 the government placed a bill before parliament to alter the 1969 Agricultural Landlord and Tenant Ordinance. To be enacted the bill required the support of thirty-nine members of the House of Representatives as well as six of the eight representatives of the Council of Chiefs in the Senate. One of the main provisions of the bill concerned the duration of leases: a minimum of thirty years with a further extension of twenty years. Indo-Fijian politicians were divided. There were those who accepted the provisions, which were an improvement, as the best that could be hoped for under the present circumstances, but others considered them inadequate and argued for ninety-nine-year leases. Another provision in the bill dealt with assessment, which was to be every five years on the unimproved capital value based on the current market price. This provoked an outcry even from the Alliance-aligned Kisan Sangh. In addition, an amendment was presented that would allow for a share-cropping arrangement. The Indo-Fijian farming community strongly condemned this amendment, fearful that it would turn them into little more than labourers working for native Fijian landlords.

The bill was passed the following month, but barely. It passed the Senate with no difficulty, but in the House of Representatives it required the Speaker's vote to gain the thirty-nine votes needed as well as those of several NFP parliamentarians. In the course of the very bitter debate over the bill, the split between pro-Koya and anti-Koya NFP parliamentarians became even wider as the anti-Koya faction led by Ramrakha and Irene Narayan came out in favour of the bill while Koya and his supporters opposed it.

The political situation within the NFP deteriorated further in 1976. Early in the year, the anti-Koya faction ran its own candidate against the pro-Koya candidate in a by-election for the Ba Indian communal seat. The Koya candidate, Surendra Prasad, won, but the campaign had served to worsen relations within the party. In August, anti-Koya members of the NFP succeeded in having the offices of party president and parliamentary leader separated. A member of the anti-Koya faction, Irene Narayan, was elected president, while Koya retained the parliamentary leadership. In this state of disarray, the NFP prepared to fight the 1977 election.

But the Alliance Party was itself not in a very good position to take advantage of the NFP's factional problems. Debate over the Agricultural Landlord and Tenant Act had also served to widen divisions within the Indian Alliance. Alliance minister M.T. Khan had been removed from his portfolio over allegations of corruption. When the court failed to find him guilty he was not reinstated. When the Agricultural Landlord and Tenant Act came before parliament he refused to support it. Further problems arose when Vijay Singh was not nominated for his constituency by the party's district council (partially on the basis of native Fijian support going to his rival).

Singh then withdrew from consideration by the party's national council and in the wake of this provoked a serious split within the Indian Alliance.

THE 1977 ELECTIONS

The 1977 election presented both the Alliance Party and the NFP with problems. The NFP not only faced the same difficulties that it had in 1972, but it also had to contend with serious internal rifts. For the Alliance Party there were two main trouble spots. One was disaffection within the Indian Alliance. The other was the unknown extent to which Sakeasi Butadroka's new party, the Fijian Nationalist Party, would divide the native Fijian community. Each party sought to put on a united face in public, but it was clear to most observers that this was little more than a cosmetic gesture.

Mara launched the Alliance Party's campaign in a speech on 28 February in which he emphasized his party's record and painted a bright future if the party was returned to office and allowed to implement various economic plans. He also stressed that the party believed in racial harmony and ruled out the possibility of forming a coalition with the NFP.

When Koya made his speech to inaugurate the NFP's campaign on 2 March he took a very different approach. Koya's remarks were addressed specifically to the Indo-Fijian electorate. He listed a number of areas where the Alliance Party had failed to assist Indo-Fijians adequately: land tenure, the tax structure, industrial relations, education, various aspects of social welfare, and so forth. What he did not do was offer a detailed alternative. In the campaign, Koya did propose a series of populist reforms including lower taxes, a wide variety of free social services, and greater security of land tenure. The NFP's Taukei Committee, headed by Tora (seen as a Koya ally in the factional divide), was left with the job of pursuing a campaign to woo native Fijian voters away from the Alliance Party. Tora sought to consolidate NFP support where it was perceived to exist among native Fijians, largely in communal terms, and he concentrated on criticizing the eastern chiefly oligarchy. Thus, even more than in the past, the NFP was running two parallel campaigns.

Butadroka, on behalf of the Fijian Nationalist Party, campaigned for greater native Fijian representation in parliament, more opportunities for native Fijians in business and education, more jobs for native Fijians in government, and returning the land leased to Indo-Fijians to native Fijians. Butadroka also played upon local grievances over rule by the eastern chiefly élite and singled out Mara, personally, and the Lauans, more generally, for severe criticism. In the west, the Nationalists pointed to the discrimination faced by westerners as wealth produced in the west was diverted by Mara to support Lauans. Ratu Mosese Varasekete, a Rewan who had left the NFP and become president of the Nationalist Party also ran as a candidate. In addition, Ratu Osea Gavidi had decided to stand as an independent in an effort to gain greater recognition for the rights of native Fijians from the west.

In the campaign itself, the Alliance Party had the advantage of having considerably more money at its disposal as well as having access to government resources (which it used freely). The Alliance Party also had its traditional sources of strength within native Fijian communities (the chiefs and village-level organizations) and the unquestioning backing of the European community. The relative strength of the Alliance Party, however, led to a degree of complacency in its campaign. Dealing with the Nationalists proved a problem since both parties based their appeals for support among native Fijians on communalism. What the Alliance Party had to do was to ensure that it retained its position as the legitimate, communal native Fijian party, but if it asserted this too strongly, the view of the party as one devoted to multiracialism was endangered.

The NFP relied primarily on its traditional means of soliciting support within the Indo-Fijian community (especially the *sirdars* or cane gang leaders, school teachers, and religious leaders). In this regard, it had an edge over the Alliance Party in campaigning for Indo-Fijian votes. The NFP focused on four issues in its effort to solidify Indo-Fijian support: (1) insecurity generated by the racial politics of the Nationalists (accusing the Alliance Party of being soft on the Nationalists); (2) alleged discrimination by the government in favour of issuing university scholarships to native Fijians (which was said to be just the beginning of what would soon filter through the entire educational system); (3) a tax structure which the NFP argued discriminated against the middle class and which introduced income taxes for cane farmers; and (4) insecurity over land tenure among cane farmers in relation to the Agricultural Landlord and Tenant Act, and the fear that increased pine planting might push some cane farmers off their land.

The Alliance Party was especially worried by the extent of collaboration between Tora (and the NFP's Operation Taukei) and the Fijian Nationalist Party. Over the years, Tora had expressed many of the same views as Butadroka and boasted of having brought the Nationalists around to seeing that the economic problems of native Fijian commoners was not the fault of Indo-Fijians, but rather that blame lay with the chiefly oligarchy. Tora's claim was something of an overstatement, but the Nationalists had dropped their demand for the expulsion of Indo-Fijians (a move that Tora himself had once supported). Tora was the only native Fijian candidate on Viti Levu who was not opposed by the Nationalists, and relations between Tora and the Nationalists during the election were close. Both parties combined their efforts on many fronts to convince native Fijians to vote against the Alliance Party. In practical terms, the NFP provided financial support, and during the polling, assisted the Nationalists in getting its supporters to the polls.

The NFP leadership seems to have perceived the Nationalists as useful for two reasons: they threatened to cost the Alliance Party support among native Fijians, and the fear that they generated among Indo-Fijians was perceived to be helpful in rallying the Indo-Fijian community behind the NFP as its protector. A key to the success of this strategy was the relative independence of the native Fijian wing of the party – in this way, the NFP proved that it too could employ a version of the strategy of 'facing both ways.'

Factional tensions within the NFP remained intense throughout the campaign and served to heighten religious and linguistic differences among Indo-Fijians (primarily among Gujaratis, Muslims, and South Indians). In some instances, differences were sufficient to motivate rival factions to field candidates against one another. Koya himself was opposed by R.D. Patel for the Lautoka communal seat. R.D. Patel was the brother of the late A.D. Patel and formerly had served as Speaker of the House. Patel relied on support from the Gujarati community, while Koya received the backing of the Muslim community. In addition, Koya urged non-Muslims to back him to ensure that an NFP split did not result in a victory for Alliance Party candidates. The official candidates for the Labasa and Suva Rural seats were identified with the anti-Koya faction and were opposed by non-official candidates identified with the Koya faction (Vijaya Parmanandan, in the case of the Suva Rural seat). Ahmed Ali has argued that rather than hurting the NFP, 'the determination and dedication of each faction to maintain its strength prevented any slackening of effort' in campaigning by the NFP and in ensuring that the Alliance Party candidates were defeated no matter which factional candidate won.[66]

When the results of the election were known, the Alliance Party had lost. The NFP had won twenty-six seats, the Alliance Party twenty-four, the Fijian Nationalist Party one seat, and Ratu Osea Gavidi had won a seat as an independent. Thus, the Alliance Party had lost nine seats. It had retained all of the General Elector seats, but elsewhere it had run into serious trouble. Its support among native Fijians had declined from 83 per cent in 1972 to 67 per cent in 1977, with 25 per cent of the vote going to the Nationalists. This decline in support can be attributed, in part, to the resentment of some native Fijian voters who felt they were taken for granted by the Alliance Party. This loss of support had cost the Alliance Party one communal seat directly and contributed to its loss of a number of national seats. Its Indo-Fijian support had dwindled as well, from 24 per cent in 1972 to 16 per cent. Dissatisfaction with the NFP among Indo-Fijian voters had not translated into support for the Alliance Party, but instead went to unofficial candidates still identified with the NFP.

The one place where the Alliance Party had done better than expected was in Suva. Irene Narayan, identified with the anti-Koya faction, was the NFP candidate for the Suva communal seat, whereas the two NFP candidates for the national seats were from the pro-Koya faction. The national Suva seats were considered marginal seats and it was felt by some that Narayan, the strongest of the three NFP candidates, had made little effort to assist the two weaker NFP candidates from the rival faction. Both seats were won by the Alliance Party (Mohammed Ramzan and Mosese Qionibaravi), in part, because of ticket splitting by Indo-Fijians who voted for the NFP for the communal seat and the Alliance Party for the national seats. The NFP's failure to win these seats was of considerable importance because if it had won them, its electoral majority would have been unquestionable. As it stood, the balance of power was left in the hands of the two seats held by Butadroka and Gavidi.

Mara conceded defeat on Monday, 4 April and called upon the NFP to form the new government. Koya refrained from making a public statement, stating only that the NFP parliamentarians would meet the following afternoon. The reasons for his timidity are not entirely clear. One important factor appears to have been the factional nature of the election and the need for him to tread carefully with his colleagues before making any public pronouncements. Informally, Mara was approached about the possibility of forming a coalition government, but Mara rejected the proposal.

It would appear that Koya and others in the NFP feared that forming a weak government might lead to increased ethnic strife. Koya's critics within the NFP later argued that this was a crucial failure of will on Koya's part that was to give Mara the opportunity to out-manoeuvre him. Koya met with the governor general, Ratu George Cakobau, on the sixth and asked that he convene a joint NFP-Alliance meeting the following day. That evening, the Alliance Party announced that there was no need for the meeting since Koya had told the governor general that he would go ahead and form a government on his own. Aware of Koya's difficulties, Mara talked to the governor general and proposed that he be allowed to form a caretaker government to be composed solely of Alliance Party ministers. The government would rule until fresh elections could be held in three months. Mara emphasized that he was not prepared to form a coalition with the NFP.

The governor general met with four leading members of the anti-Koya faction within the NFP on the morning of the seventh and informed them of Mara's proposal. He told them that unless the NFP formed a government he would go along with Mara's plan. The NFP parliamentarians then met to select a parliamentary leader (since they had so far failed to do so). It was not until midday that Koya was elected parliamentary leader. The first ballot had ended in a thirteen-thirteen tie and on the second ballot he won by a narrow fourteen to twelve margin.

The leadership question having been settled, Koya telephoned the governor general at 3:15 P.M. to inform him that he was ready to have his government sworn in. The governor general asked him to come to Government House alone at 4:30 P.M. What happened next has been the subject of considerable controversy. It would appear that the governor general contacted Mara, and a short time later the two high chiefs met at Government House. Mara was then sworn in as prime minister at 4:15. When Koya arrived at 4:30, he was told that Mara had already been appointed.

The governor general argued that he had acted in accordance with powers given to him by the constitution, which stipulated that he could 'appoint as Prime Minister the member of the House of Representatives who appears to him best able to command the support of the majority of the members of the House' (clause 73.2). He further justified his actions on the basis of neither party having a clear majority and his belief that Mara 'was the person best able to command the support of the majority of members of parliament.'[67] He also claimed to have acted out of concern for national 'security,' implying that there was a threat of racial violence. What was apparent is that, faced with the prospect of losing control of the government, the chiefly oligarchy had closed ranks.

Needless to say, Koya was outraged. He argued that the governor general had acted unconstitutionally, but it was at Mara that he directed most of his anger. He claimed that Mara had acted to block an Indo-Fijian from becoming prime minister and charged Mara with wrongly accusing him of 'racialism,' for which he demanded that Mara apologize. Tora and others who had hoped for cabinet posts in a Koya government were also highly critical of the move. Members of the anti-Koya faction, however, took the matter more calmly. One of the leaders of the anti-Koya faction, K.C. Ramrakha, stated that the governor general's action was politically questionable but he felt that the governor general had acted constitutionally, and he urged people to accept what had happened while also criticizing Koya for his remarks about Mara.

The ground was now prepared for an outbreak of factional fighting within the NFP of unprecedented vehemence. Anti-Koya and pro-Koya factions set about to hold separate political meetings and sought to establish separate branches of the NFP. Narayan filed a law suit for slander against Koya, and Ramrakha called upon Koya to resign. Despite its internal problems, on 31 May the NFP was able to amend a confidence motion put forward by the Alliance Party and force a dissolution. A new election was scheduled for 17–24 September.[68]

Preparing for the second election, the NFP factions were unable to patch up their differences. The two factions went to court to see who could use the NFP name and symbol. It was ruled that each faction had to choose a new symbol. The anti-Koya faction led by Narayan and Ramrakha selected the hibiscus flower and came to be called the 'Flower' or 'Hibiscus' faction. Koya and his supporters picked the dove and were labelled the 'Dove' or 'Bird' faction. However, the Flower faction had gained the right to use the official NFP label. The Dove faction responded by claiming that it was the rightful heir to A.D. Patel's mantle.

Attempts at working together in selecting candidates failed and the two factions nominated separate candidates for all twelve of the Indian communal seats and five of the ten Indian national seats. In the intense factional fighting that followed, the two groups seemed almost oblivious to the problem of defeating the Alliance Party. Basically, the Hibiscus faction led by Narayan and Ramrakha attacked Koya along the established lines (the constitutional convention, the Agricultural Landlord and Tenant Act debate, his style of leadership, and so on), while the Dove faction devoted its energies to defending Koya.

The Alliance Party, for its part, concentrated its efforts on eliminating the threat posed by the Fijian Nationalist Party and other forms of dissent within the native Fijian community. The Fijian Association had established a task force following the first election to investigate what had gone wrong and to suggest means to regain lost native Fijian support. Butadroka went into the election claiming that the Nationalists had doubled their support among native Fijians. But the Alliance Party felt that this time around it was better prepared to take on the Nationalists. Its chances were improved when two Nationalist leaders were jailed (conveniently). Butadroka himself was sentenced under the Public Order Act, and another Nationalist candidate, the head of the dockworkers' union, Taniela Veitata, was sentenced for violation of the Trade Disputes Act. To add to the Nationalists' worries, the party's president, Ratu Mosese Tuisawau, was forced to declare bankruptcy a couple of months before the election. The Alliance Party focused on three issues to undermine support for the Nationalist Party: that it had collaborated with the NFP in the previous election, that it sought to undermine the chiefs who were central to the maintenance of native Fijian paramountcy, and that the individuals in the Fijian Nationalist Party were only out for personal gain.

In its campaign against the NFP, the Alliance Party concentrated on attacking Koya as party leader and suggested that it would be better if he were replaced. The Alliance Party said little about the members of the Flower faction, which it did not see as so inimicable to the interests of the oligarchy. What Mara appears to have wanted was for Koya to be replaced with an Indo-Fijian more willing to go along with Mara, as Koya had been in his earlier days. Mara had made it clear that he would not tolerate Indo-Fijian politicians who disagreed with him on substantive issues. He was willing to abide them only so long as they behaved much as he expected native Fijian commoners to behave towards him. Koya's Dove faction accused the Alliance Party and the Flower faction of working together, and it was only towards the end of the election that an effort was made to dispel this impression when Narayan launched a brief personal attack on Mara.

Political scientist Ralph Premdas comments that the election was essentially 'about each of the traditional parties re-arranging and sorting out its domestic ethnic affairs, and for the NFP this was an agonizing almost self-destructive process.'[69] But there was more to the election than this. In a sense, the first electoral victory for the NFP, despite widespread feelings of greater communal rivalry, had represented the success of Operation Taukei and laid the groundwork for moving Fijian politics further away from communalism towards a right-left divide. Tora, along with his native Fijian associates in the NFP, had been able to forge a relatively successful alliance among populists within the native Fijian community on the basis of region and class, in opposition to the eastern chiefly oligarchy. This alliance, as much as the prospect of an Indo-Fijian prime minister, was seen as a threat by Mara and the other members of the oligarchy. By putting Mara back in office, the governor general managed to divert the political process once more back towards communalism.

The election results the second time around were, predictably, very different. The Alliance Party won thirty-six seats (regaining 8 and winning 4 new ones) to fifteen for the NFP (12 Flower, 3 Dove), with Gavidi retaining his seat in the west as an independent. Three factors were crucial to the outcome: a low voter turnout among Indo-Fijians, the effect of the factional split, and the poor showing of the Nationalists. All of these factors were evident, for example, in the cases of the South Eastern and North Eastern Fijian and Indian national seats, which were all won by the Alliance Party after having lost them in the first election.

Two particularly important seats were the Lautoka Indian communal and Rewa/Serua/Namosi Fijian communal seats. The Lautoka seat was a contest between Koya and Jai Ram Reddy of the Flower faction. Reddy had trained as a lawyer in New Zealand and had been appointed to the Senate in 1974 by Koya. As factionalism intensified, Reddy sided with the Flower forces. The Alliance Party had sought to help Reddy by withdrawing its candidate and Reddy was able to win the seat. Butadroka had won the Rewa/Serua/Namosi seat the first time by only 596 votes. This time, he was in jail and the Alliance Party launched a concerted effort to defeat him, which they did by 1,719 votes.The election also witnessed the defeat of Tora, another thorn in the side of the Alliance Party. Only Gavidi, who based his campaign almost solely on the concerns of native landowners in his area, was able to hold on to his seat.

One particularly important factor behind the improved showing by the Alliance Party was the higher voter turnout among native Fijians, in part because of pressure put on chiefs at the village level by the Alliance Party. In the March/April election, the turnout had been 80,369, of whom 20,189 supported the Nationalists (25 per cent). In September, the turnout was 92,400, of whom about 16,000 supported the Nationalists (17 per cent). The loss of 4,000 voters might not have been so significant had it not been for the fact that there were an additional 12,000 voters for the Alliance Party as well.

The Aftermath of the 1977 Elections

After the election, the members of the Dove and Flower factions insisted on sitting separately in Parliament. The weakness of the Dove faction, however, and the electoral defeat of its leader left it in a very weakened position. Koya was replaced as parliamentary leader by Reddy from the Flower faction, the man who had defeated him in the election. Ramrakha migrated and moved to Sydney, leaving only Narayan as the senior party member.

It was Reddy's job to try to rebuild the NFP. Reddy was able to bring the two factions together again in July 1979, but relations between members of the two groups remained strained, and Reddy saw to it that members of the Dove faction were marginalized. At the same time that he sought to reunite the NFP, Reddy was able to maintain relatively good relations with Mara, similar to those enjoyed between Mara and Koya during the 'honeymoon' period. For Reddy and Mara the honeymoon lasted from 1977 until 1979, coinciding with the NFP 'reconstruction' period. By 1980, relations between the two party leaders had soured and they remained bitter into the 1982 election.

Under Reddy's leadership, the NFP turned away from its earlier populist policies towards more of a middle-of-the-road position. This new position reflected the values of the party's middle-class members (professionals, civil servants, wealthier farmers, and businessmen), who now made up a significant part of its membership, rather than those of blue-collar workers and poorer farmers. Gone were the policies of nationalizing industries, creating a comprehensive welfare structure, and providing free education. Gone too was support for a common roll. In an interview in August 1981, Reddy stated that he did not believe in any 'isms' and was opposed to anything smacking of 'class warfare.' He saw his approach as one that was 'pragmatic' and 'middle of the road.'[70] Reddy was equally anxious to avoid having the party branded as simply the party of the Indo-Fijian community. The new image was to be one of a middle-of-the-road, liberal party that catered to Fiji's middle class regardless of ethnic community, in contrast to the right-wing, traditionalist Alliance Party which pandered to the desires of the country's political and economic élite.

The Indian Alliance had come out of the second 1977 election with a reasonable number of seats, but it remained the troubled wing of the Alliance Party. Vijay Singh had been made attorney general by Mara, but in 1979 he was dismissed from the cabinet over his suspected involvement in the Flour Mills of Fiji court case and later left the Alliance Party (joining the NFP in 1982). The fortunes of the Indian Alliance continued to decline during the period between the 1977 and 1982 elections, with Mara seemingly unwilling to do much to rectify the situation.

Butadroka and the Nationalists almost disappeared from public view after the second 1977 election while he and others in the party directed their energies mainly to their own businesses and affairs. But the Fijian Nationalist Party did not disappear entirely and continued to be a force to be reckoned with in many native Fijian villages, especially along the Rewa River.

In the west, things began to heat up again towards the end of the decade. Establishment of the Fiji Pine Commission in 1976 had been seen by the Alliance government as a satisfactory arrangement for overcoming dissatisfaction among western landowners. Consultants' reports were commissioned in 1977 to assess the state of progress of the pine scheme and to make recommendations concerning future directions. The following year the Pine Commission sent out a brochure inviting foreign companies to undertake a joint venture to develop the industry once it was ready to begin its commercial phase around 1984.[71]

The Pine Commission reviewed the submissions in 1979, and the M.K. Hunt Foundation of New Zealand was asked to prepare a pre-feasibility study. The commission was not satisfied with the study and asked three other companies, who also had submitted initial proposals, to prepare pre-feasibility studies. These were: Shell Fiji Limited (in association with New Zealand Forest Products Limited), British Petroleum South West Pacific Limited, and United Marketing Corporation (registered in Arizona). The British Petroleum proposal was selected in April 1981 and British Petroleum was asked to prepare a more comprehensive report. It proposed to invest F$27.2 million and suggested that annual export earnings would reach F$21 million by around 1987 and climb to over F$26 million by 1994. Two things that helped to sell the proposal were British Petroleum's willingness to negotiate up to a 51 per cent share for the pine commission and the offer of a 20 per cent 'gift share.' The latter had been the idea of British Petroleum's general manager in Fiji, Colonel Paul Manueli. Manueli was the former commander of the Royal Fiji Military Forces and had very close ties to the Alliance Party.

The British Petroleum proposal was not the one favoured by Gavidi and the western landowners, who had been largely left out of the selection process. They supported the proposal prepared by Paul Sandblom of the United Marketing Corporation, which promised the landowners a larger share of the profits (50 per cent), higher harvesting royalties, and greater employment and training benefits for local people than the other proposals.

Those involved in the selection process had ruled out the United Marketing Corporation proposal as offering to invest too little (F$2-F$4 million) and for being 'too idealistic' and lacking 'comprehension.' There were also reports in the press linking United Marketing Corporation with the Phoenix Foundation and Sandblom himself was denied an entry visa at one point for having been convicted for fraud in 1965.[72] But the western landowners were not convinced and Gavidi pointed out that the two large transnational corporations, Shell and British Petroleum, had engaged in questionable practices as well.

The landowners hired an independent firm of consultants to evaluate the proposals. Two crucial issues were the potential of each proposal for generating revenue for the landowners and participation by the landowners in the venture. The report pointed to strengths and weaknesses in all the proposals, but two of its points were of particular interest to the landowners. First, the United Marketing Corporation proposal, although unacceptable in its present form, 'has merits and with adaptation and development, it could become an attractive one.' Second, in terms of landowner participation, none of the proposals was sufficiently clear.

Durutalo argues that the Alliance government and its associates found the United Marketing Corporation proposal unacceptable in large part because it raised the expectations of the landowners and favoured a decentralized, less capital-intensive form of development that would generate money largely for those living in the pine area. In contrast, the British Petroleum and Shell proposals (both of which were viewed as acceptable by the Alliance government) favoured big, capital-intensive development that was more centralized and more likely to generate profits for the Alliance government and its friends.[73]

The disagreement over the joint venture proposals served as a catalyst for the formation of the Western United Front on 9 July 1981.[74] To press the point that they were not happy with the way things were going, the landowners had forced five pine stations to close. Gavidi became increasingly outspoken in his criticisms of the government in March and April 1981. When Mara announced over radio in mid-April that the ban on Sandblom would remain in force, Gavidi accused Mara of having a 'dictatorial attittude' and a few days later stated that, since Mara would no longer listen to the western landowners, dialogue with the government was no longer possible. After the announcement of the decision favouring British Petroleum, Gavidi accused the government of selling out the landowners. The only one to express support for Gavidi and the western landowners at this time was Butadroka.

In May 1981, Gavidi and others began talks about establishing a new political party to represent the interests of western native landowners and to work towards toppling the Alliance government in the 1982 election. Gavidi hoped to enlist the support of other western chiefs to form a united front. Ratu Naopolioni Dawai and several others chose to remain in the Alliance camp, but there were those who were willing to go along with Gavidi.

The party was launched officially by Gavidi and Isikeli Nadalo, and an interim committee was formed, chaired by Ratu Meli Naevo (the Tui Nawaka). Its first meeting, on 16 July was attended by an estimated eight hundred native Fijians from the west (including about two hundred chiefs). Gavidi was elected president and Nadalo, secretary. In its constitution, the stated aim of the party was to protest on behalf of western native Fijians and to unify them in an effort to protect their interests. The party was attacked in the press on behalf of the Alliance Party by Ratu David Toganivalu and Apisai Tora (who had joined the Alliance camp).

There were important changes in the nation's industrial relations after the 1977 elections. During the 1970s, relations between the Fiji Trades Union Congress and international bodies such as the International Labour Organisation and International Confederation of Free Trade Unions (ICFTU) had been increasing. Following an ICFTU-sponsored workshop in December 1977, the Fiji Trades Union Congress decided to establish a permanent Workers' Education Unit with funds provided by the ICFTU. An education officer was brought in from Sri Lanka who played an important role in expanding the activities of the Fiji Trades Union Congress, while at the same time spreading the ICFTU's ideology of apolitical unionism. This manifest itself in the cane fields in 1978. The existing cane growers' organizations were closely affiliated with the two political parties. In 1978 the Fiji Trades Union Congress launched the National Farmers Union which was to 'be strictly free from party politics.'[75]

The growing involvement of these international labour organizations also was influential in promoting the idea of establishing a tripartite body with representatives from the government, labour, and employers in the private sector to deal with wages and related matters in an effort to reduce the level of conflict in the labour field. The idea took hold after a 1977 workshop. Subsequent talks between unions and the government, in the context of continuing wage demands by labour, led to the establishment of the Tripartite Forum. The main aim of the Tripartite Forum was to establish annual wage guidelines. Its most important committees were those concerned with remuneration guidelines, redundancy, industrial relations, and ability to pay. Initially at least, through the Tripartite Forum, wages kept up with inflation and there was greater industrial peace. One of the reasons for the success of this body was Mara's willingness to support the idea. It also reflected the success of moderate trade unionists in rebuilding bridges with the Alliance Party.

As the Tripartite Forum became the focal point of annual wage negotiations, total ascendancy of the Fiji Trades Union Congress over the Fiji Confederation of Trade Unions was assured. Membership in the Fiji Confederation of Trade Unions had reached a peak in 1976 when a split took place between Tora and several other trade union leaders in the Fiji Confederation of Trade Unions (including Dinsukh Lal Morarji, head of Tora's old union at Nadi airport). The split was caused, in part, by certain actions by Tora that threatened to increase ethnic tensions within the unions concerned. The result was that all the unions, except the Sugar and General Workers' Union and Building Workers' Union, left the Fiji Confederation of Trade Unions and rejoined the Fiji Trades Union Congress. Tora lost control of the sugar workers' union in 1979 and it too rejoined the Fiji Trades Union Congress. This effectively put an end to Tora's active involvement in the union movement.

Tora, finding himself out of favour in the NFP (being identified as a Dove) and having lost his trade union base, now began to cultivate relations with the Alliance Party. He sought to justify this as seeking to 'work within the system in order to change it,' but others saw it in a more cynical light. Tora's acceptance by the Alliance Party was facilitated by Mara. With militancy among western native Fijians once again on the rise, Mara felt the need to strengthen the Alliance Party in the west. Tora seemed to be the perfect answer, although many of Mara's colleagues were less than happy about having to rub shoulders with someone of Tora's background. He was made a vice-president of the Fijian Association and later was selected to run for parliament in the 1982 election.

The Fijian economy underwent a brief boom in 1979 and 1980, largely because of a substantial increase in the international price of sugar (this being tied to the global upswing in commodity prices at this time). The boom was accompanied by a spurt of inflation from 6.1 per cent in 1978 to 14.5 per cent in 1980. When the international commodity market went into a downswing after 1980, the Fijian economy went into a severe recession. The situation was made worse by continued high inflation (11 per cent in 1981). In 1982 the economy grew by less than 0.5 per cent (with inflation running at 7 per cent). With the onset of the recession, the government placed a virtual freeze on new hiring as did many private-sector firms. It was in the midst of this recession that Fiji held its next general election.

THE 1982 ELECTION

The 1982 national election was fought between the Alliance Party and a coalition formed between the NFP and the Western United Front. Both the Alliance Party and the coalition claimed to have widespread multiracial support, 'something', as noted by historian Brij Lal, 'which has remained an elusive dream ever since the emergence of party politics in Fiji.'[76] Initially, both parties did seek to promote non-racial issues, but as the campaign wore on and it appeared as if the two parties were close in their levels of support, it degenerated into the worst appeals to communalism since independence.

The coalition between the National Federation Party and Western United Front was formed in January 1982. The two parties viewed the coalition as 'a partnership of equals' with 'each party to maintain its identity and objectives.' A committee was formed to arrive at common policies for the election campaign and to draw up a joint list of candidates. For the NFP, the coalition was seen as a means of forging a multiracial front. For the Western United Front, it presented the possibility of becoming a national rather than regional party. But there were obvious problems. For one thing, the Western United Front had no base outside of the west and had only a brief period to try to build one. Coalition with the NFP also risked becoming identified as pro-Indian and thereby alienating some native Fijian support.

The ascendancy of Reddy and the weakness of Koya's Dove faction within the NFP meant that the worst vestiges of communalism within the party probably could be eliminated or kept under control, but the party itself remained firmly identified as a communal party in the minds of the electorate and most party officials. Thus, the coalition was not so much an attempt to forge a non-racial alliance as an alliance of convenience of communally-based parties. This meant that although the rhetoric of non-racialism was put forward at the outset of the campaign by the Coalition and the Alliance Party, it was clear that communalism remained an important means of seeking support, and that should the campaign prove close, the parties were likely to revert to the well-trod path of an appeal to communalism in an effort to secure victory. And if this were the case, the Western United Front would find itself in the difficult position of having to rely on regionalism while being attacked by the Alliance Party for having become the tool of crafty Indians. Moreover, in the west, the Western United Front had to contend with Tora in addition to the traditional Alliance Party support.

When nominations closed on 21 May, the Alliance Party and the coalition each had fielded candidates for all fifty-two seats. In addition, the Fiji Nationalist Party had put forward twenty-seven candidates and there were seven independents. The process of candidate selection within the two main parties had been an extremely difficult one. Mara had decided that it was time to find new blood to replace some of the older sitting members. In the past the selection committee had served as a rubber stamp for decisions made through primaries. This time Mara established a ten-member committee, with himself as head, which had the power to screen candidates and to make the final decision about their acceptability. While many party members were not happy with this new structure, only the president of the Indian Alliance, James Shankar Singh, and a few others were willing to voice their feelings in public. In the end the changes were not as great as had been anticipated, and of the thirty-six sitting members only seven were dropped.

The selection committee had not given seats to members of the Young Alliance (including its president Jone Banuve) as well as several other aspirants such as Jo Nacola, a young, educated native Fijian from Ra Province, and former Suva mayor, Joape Rokosoi. In the early years after independence, the Young Alliance had been an important political force. By 1982, however, Mara had come to see it merely in a supportive role, a fact that generated a great deal of frustration among its members. Rokosoi became a coalition candidate. In addition, the Western United Front's appeal for solidarity among Western native Fijians had cost the Alliance Party the support of an important political figure, the Tui Nadi, Ratu Napolioni Dawai.

In the meantime, the Indian Alliance was in a state of near collapse. A severe blow came in May 1982, when James Shankar Singh, the president of the Indian Alliance, left the Alliance Party claiming irreconcilable differences with Mara. He had a reputation as a man of principle who had been willing to stand up to Mara in the past. In January he had accused Mara of treating the Indian Alliance 'like a bunch of coolies.'[77]

Mara dismissed the loss of most of the Indian Alliance as insignificant. He felt that he could rely on the Alliance Party's traditional support from the Muslim and Gujarati communities and on the handiwork of his protégé, Ahmed Ali. Ali, a Fijian academic of considerable ambition, had worked behind the scenes as an adviser and speech-writer for Mara for several years. His time at the university had been a troubled one and his decision to leave was made once Mara offered him the safest Indo-Fijian seat that the Alliance Party had to offer, the Lau-Cakaudrove-Rotuma Indian national seat. As the campaign heated up, Ali came to play an important role in promoting appeals to communalism and in seeking to brand the coalition as pro-communist.

The problem facing NFP party leader Jai Ram Reddy was how to hold together the Flower and Dove factions. Tension remained and Reddy sought to strengthen his position with new candidates who were either loyal to him or neutral and, in particular, to get rid of the hard-core members of the Dove faction. A nine-member selection committee was formed with Reddy as chair. Koya was included for the sake of party unity. The names of three Koya supporters were put forward, but only one, Shardha Nand, was selected. During the negotiations Koya threatened to pull out, and the Navua branch (controlled by Nand) and a few others under Dove control threatened to revolt. Despite these problems, Reddy was able to have his way, for the most part, and in mid-April he arranged for the party to give him a unanimous vote of confidence as party leader.

Attempts to cover over factional divisions were not entirely successful and some members of the Dove faction did leave the party to join the Alliance Party. Surendra Prasad ran against Reddy in Lautoka, and Raojibhai Patel ran against former Flower leader Irene Narayan in Suva. Neither won, but they did serve as irritants. Prasad, in particular, forced Reddy to spend more time than he would have liked working in his Lautoka district.

Both parties were well funded for the campaign. The Alliance Party was able to draw upon funds from a cross-section of the business community as well as from government funds and facilities, while the NFP received funding from members of the Indo-Fijian business community. Mara also sought to revitalize the Alliance Party's campaign machinery well before the election. The party secretary, Adi Losalini Dovi, was fired for ineptitude and replaced by Isimeli Bose. Bose was young and well educated. He was a University of the South Pacific graduate and former University of the South Pacific lecturer who at the time of his appointment was a shipping manager at Burns Philp. In 1981 he was sent to Australia and Papua New Guinea to study campaign strategies. A publicity committee was formed, comprised of Bose, Ahmed Ali, and Len Usher (Mara confidant and former editor of the *Fiji Times*). In addition to preparing news releases, they briefed candidates on a regular basis and produced a newsletter that was widely circulated throughout the country. By February 1982 the party also had established six hundred village-level committees in an effort to ensure a high voter turnout among native Fijians and to thwart the activity of the Western United Front and Fijian Nationalist Party. Alliance leaders felt that it was unnecessary to produce a detailed election manifesto and published one that was only eight pages in length.

In contrast to the Alliance, the coalition's campaign was not nearly as well organized or as centralized. Poor organization was not seen as too much of a handicap within the Indo-Fijian community, but it limited its ability to campaign within the native Fijian community. The coalition did produce an impressive eighty-two page manifesto, but it was not well distributed.

At the outset, the Alliance Party campaigned on the basis of its record in office in promoting stability and economic growth as well as on the basis of its being a multiracial party. Its campaign slogan was 'Keep Fiji in Good Hands.' In addressing economic problems faced by the country, the Alliance Party argued that they were mainly the result of international factors beyond the control of anyone in Fiji (such as the rising price of oil). It also claimed that under its guidance Fiji had done much better during times of international economic difficulty than other Third World countries. And it pointed to achievements such as trade deals like the regional SPAR-TECA trade agreement that gave Fiji greater access to the New Zealand and Australian markets, and the more recent Lomé Convention that secured Fijian sugar exports to the European Economic Community. The Alliance Party campaign also placed a great deal of emphasis on Mara's personal stature as an international statesman as well as his high traditional status.

The coalition, under the banner of 'Time for a Change,' focused on economic issues and sought to overcome the NFP's image as the Indian party. It dropped previous issues promoted by the NFP that were identified as pro-Indian, such as calls for changes in the constitution and reassessments of the manner in which government scholarships were awarded. In the coalition manifesto the appeal to native Fijians was based on a call for greater decentralization and participation of native Fijians in economic activities. These were promises that it was hoped not only would appeal to westerners in relation to the pine industry, but to native Fijians in other parts of the country as well.

In substantive terms, the coalition's economic policies did not differ from those of the Alliance Party. The NFP drew attention to a report by the Financial Review Committee that Fiji faced a bleak future unless current economic trends were reversed.[78] Using this report, the NFP called for expansion and diversification of the agricultural sector, greater food self-sufficiency, more employment in rural areas, tax concessions for employers who created jobs, and measures to curb inflation. Many of the coalition's points were to be found in existing development plans, but there was some question as to the Alliance government's committment to implementing them. On the political front, the coalition argued that the country was ruled by cabinet and that parliamentary democracy had been undermined. The coalition advocated creating the means by which to increase Parliament's role in decisionmaking. Reddy also broached the idea of forming a multiracial cabinet based on the Singapore model.

The Nationalists had little money with which to campaign and only a minimal organization. The Fijian National Party's campaign positions were similar to those in 1977. It retained its call for 'Fiji for the Fijians,' but did not return to its demand for the expulsion of Indo-Fijians. Instead, it sought to emphasize improving the economic and political position of native Fijians, especially those who were not chiefs.

Up until mid-June the campaign remained relatively low-keyed. Then, suddenly, things turned nasty. The Australian television news program *Four Corners* had come to Fiji to investigate the role that a group of Australian-based consultants had played in the Fiji election. The group consisted of Alan Carroll, Jeffrey Race, Rosemary Gillespie, and Geoffrey Allen. Carroll and Race were associated with Business International and Allen was a business lobbyist. The arrangements for their work were made by Mara associate, businessman Mahendra Motibhai Patel, who at the time was also head of the Fiji Visitors Bureau. Patel had used an air ticket given to the Fiji Visitors Bureau by Qantas to fund Gillespie's trip to Fiji, with other funds apparently being channelled through his business. Gillespie came to Fiji in June to conduct a political survey. The same month, Carroll and Race visited Fiji to carry out interviews with politicians, bureaucrats, academics, jounalists, and businessmen.

The team met with Mara and his advisers between 16–20 September 1981. At this meeting, the consultants had recommended upgrading the Alliance Party organization and improving media relations. Following the meeting, Bose was sent to Australia and Papua New Guinea, and Australian Clive Speed was appointed as a media consultant attached to the Ministry of Information with a salary paid from Australian aid funds.The following month, the group produced a report entitled 'Report of Consultants to the Prime Minister of Fiji on the Economic and Political Outlook and Options for Strategy and Political Organization' or more popularly known as the 'Carroll report.'[79] The report contained the findings of the June research, a series of 'scenarios,' and recommendations. The recommendations included establishing a 'think tank,' campaigning on such themes as 'renewal' and 'multi-racial justice,' and building a 'stronger commitment to mobilizing the energies of the private sector.' The recommendations that were to receive the most notoriety included: (1) a recommendation to seek Muslim and Gujarati support through appointments and promises of appointments and other favours; (2) noting that 'the highest immediate priority is to consolidate the base of Fijian support now threatened by the growth of splinter Fijian parties,' recommendations for 'a combination of symbolic and material appeals,' and, for Butadroka, to 'either buy [him] off or take him out of running,' and, for Gavidi, 'since he is going to jail anyway ... to pile all efforts on and accelerate prosecutions so he cannot run'; and (3) a recommendation to 'combine divide and rule with stroking,' which was to include finding ways to capitalize on existing splits within the NFP, putting chiefs on the ticket to ensure native Fijian support, and seeking to make sure that those dropped from cabinet are given some reward to keep them happy while at the same time making 'sure they understand they will be sorry if they challenge the Alliance (get something on them).'[80]

The existence of the report, which in many ways simply put into writing what had been Alliance Party practice in the past, was made public by Reddy at a political rally on 22 June. At another meeting on the twenty-sixth he provided more details of the report and expressed concern over the involvement of Business International and Clive Speed in Fijian affairs. At a political rally of its own on the twenty-sixth, the Alliance Party responded by denying Reddy's allegations and accusing him of trying 'to bamboozle and mislead the electorate.' In response to Reddy's charges that the Alliance Party was relying on outside help, the Alliance Party referred to a speech made by David Coombe of the Australian Labor Party at the previous NFP national convention. The next day the Alliance Party admitted that the report existed, but claimed that it was nothing out of the ordinary ('perfectly normal practice').

Over the next few days the NFP-Western United Front coalition came to focus its campaign on the recommendations of the Carroll report and especially those of a racial nature. The Alliance Party responded by denying that it had followed the recommendations to use religious and ethnic divisions in its campaign and that Clive Speed was working with the Alliance Party. In typical Alliance fashion, Reddy was accused of inciting ethnic tension by referring to the consultants as 'expatriates.' As the debate heated up, Mahendra Motibhai Patel sought to defuse the situation by claiming that hiring the consultants was all his doing.

At this point the *Four Corners* program aired. The NFP ordered a large number of copies of the program and circulated them widely around the country. It was a strategy that was to backfire badly. Mara attacked the program 'as an act of political sabotage against a sovereign nation,' claimed that it employed language that was derogatory to native Fijian traditions, and accused those producing it of collaborating with the NFP. He also claimed that he had only just seen a complete copy of the Carroll report and stated that he found some of its recommendations 'repugnant.'[81] Mara's denial of prior knowledge was greeted with disbelief by the NFP. But the Alliance, in a characteristic manner, was able to deflect attention away from this and similar issues by focusing on the opening lines of the program which referred to Mara and other prominent native Fijian political leaders as the descendants of chiefs who 'clubbed and ate their way to power.'

The Alliance Party sought to portray the opening lines of the program as a grave insult to Fijian chiefs and to native Fijian traditions (despite the fact that it was largely true and that cannibal jokes were relatively common in Fiji) and to attack Reddy for being a party to this insult. The Alliance Party organized a group of a few hundred individuals to march on Reddy's home to demand that Reddy apologize for insulting a high Fijian chief (Mara). In addition, the Alliance Party set in motion a campaign of letter writing to the newspapers that accused Reddy of being a racist and anti-chief. The Alliance Party also highlighted a remark made by Reddy at an 18 July rally when he said that Mara would open a toilet in order to shake the hands of a few more Indo-Fijians in the hope of getting their votes.

In addition to communalism and appeals to tradition, the Alliance Party sought to secure electoral support by raising the spectre of the communist bogy. This had long been a favorite of Len Usher and now Ahmed Ali, in particular, began making accusations at political rallies that the NFP had ties with the Russians.

Polling began on 10 July as the campaign continued to heat up. In his final address in the press, Mara again was critical of the NFP–Western United Front coalition and Australian television for attacking Fijian traditions and himself personally. In addition, in a move aimed at getting more native Fijians to the polls, he stated that he would resign unless the Alliance Party won at least thirty seats.[82]

The results of the election were finalized by midday Sunday 19 July. The Alliance Party had won twenty-eight seats (no more was heard from Mara about his promise to resign if the Alliance Party won fewer than thirty seats) and the NFP–Western United Front coalition twenty-four seats, with the Fijian Nationalist Party failing to win a single seat (Butadroka losing to Tomasi Vakatora by over 4,000 votes). Within the coalition, the Western United Front suffered a setback when Gavidi lost the Nadroga-Navoso Fijian communal seat to Dr. Apenisa Kurisaqila by a slim margin (4,926 to 4,682). Analysts after the election felt that Gavidi had spent too much time campaigning nationally and not enough time in his own area, taking his support there too much for granted. Two other Western United Front candidates, however, were elected to Fijian national seats.

In light of what was to happen in the 1987 election, four seats deserve particular mention: the Suva and South Eastern national seats. The Suva constituency contained 12,969 native Fijians, 16,257 Indo-Fijians, and 2,823 General Electors. The Alliance Party realized that it needed a native Fijian candidate with strong Indo-Fijian support. The choice was Ratu David Toganivalu, who had close links with the local Gujarati community and an image of multiracialism. Pitted against him for the Fijian seat was Suva mayor, Joape Rokosoi, who had been passed over by the Alliance Party in his bid for a seat. For the Indian seat, the Alliance Party remained with former trade unionist Mohammed Ramzan. Even though he was considered a weak candidate, it was hoped that old trade union loyalties and other sources of Alliance Party support (including the Muslim community) would be enough to allow him to win. The coalition ran Mumtatz Ali, a well-known accountant and also a Muslim, who was new to politics. As expected, the outcome was close, with the Alliance Party candidates winning. The results were: Toganivalu, 13,400 or 51.2 per cent of the vote; Rokosoi, 12,234 or 46.7 per cent of the vote; Ramzan, 13,221 or 50.9 per cent of the vote; and Ali, 12,590 or 48.3 per cent of the vote.

The South Eastern constituency contained 18,786 native Fijians, 16,257 Indo-Fijians and 2,823 General Electors. The seats had been won by the NFP in the first 1977 election because of the support among native Fijians for the Nationalists, but the Alliance had regained the seats in the second election when support for the Nationalists collapsed. The Alliance Party fielded two well-known local candidates, Semesa Sikivou (former minister of education) and Beniram Bissessar (a local businessman who was active in civic affairs). The NFP fielded two candidates who were not from the area and who were new to politics. Support for the Nationalists failed to be sufficient to give the coalition an edge, in part because of the high voter turnout (Table 2). In both cases, however, it was clear that the Alliance Party could have lost these seats in the face of stronger candidates and better organized campaigns by the opposition.

TABLE 2

Voter registration and turnout in the 1972 through 1982 elections

	Per cent registered 1982	Per cent turnout 1982	Per cent turnout 1977(2)	Per cent turnout 1977(1)	Per cent turnout 1972
Fijian	96.1	85.6	77.4	71.0	77.9
Indian	94.4	85.2	75.0	76.9	84.7
General Elector	79.7	83.3	---	81.5	81.3

The Alliance Party had failed to make inroads into the Indo-Fijian community, while the NFP-Western United Front coalition had been unable to attract significant support among native Fijians. Voter turnout in all communities was its highest ever. The high turnout was in large part a reflection of the improved Alliance Party machine, the sense that it would be a close election, and, undoubtedly, the communal appeals made towards the end of the campaign. The Alliance Party garnered the highest percentage of native Fijian communal votes in any election to date: 83.7 per cent (although only marginally so, for in the second 1977 election and the 1972 election it had received 80.5 per cent and 83.1 per cent, respectively). This level of support was achieved not only because of the party's new organizational strength, but also as a result of its strategy of appealing to chiefly honour and tradition in response to the *Four Corners* program and because of the poor performances of the Western United Front and Fijian Nationalist Party at an organizational level.

The Alliance Party was able to secure 15.3 per cent of the Indo-Fijian communal vote. This was a lower percentage than in the 1972 and first 1977 elections (24.1 per cent and 15.6 per cent) and only slightly above the level of the second 1977 election (14.4 per cent), but it was a significant achievement considering the number of desertions that it had suffered before the election and the state of the Indian Alliance. It had been able to hold on to its traditional base of support among Muslims and Gujaratis and, undoubtledly, had been able to add the support of a number of disgruntled Doves. It was a close election in which, but for a few miscalculations on the part of the NFP-Western United Front coalition, the outcome could easily have been twenty-seven seats for the coalition and twenty-five seats for the Alliance Party, and once again the NFP could have found itself in a position to form a government.

The Commission of Inquiry into the 1982 Election

The Alliance Party had won the election by a slim margin and after the election the two parties continued to exchange accusations. In particular, during the election campaign the Alliance Party had made numerous accusations alleging deals between the NFP and Soviet Union. After the election, Mara decided to keep the issue alive. In an interview with Stuart Inder (an Australian journalist closely associated with Mara) during a visit to Sydney in July 1982, Mara accused the NFP of receiving F$1 million in covert aid from the Soviet Union and stated that this had been done with the knowledge of the Indian high commissioner in Suva.[83] As with the previous claims, there was no evidence to support it but Mara and his associates seemed to view it as a means of deflecting attention away from NFP charges of wrongdoing on the part of the Alliance Party in its relationship with Business International and Clive Speed.

After his return to Fiji, Mara announced that his government would ban future visits by Soviet ships and claimed that the Soviets had been trying to remove him from power since he stood in the way of their expanding their influence in the region. Irene Narayan responded: 'He is trying to portray us as pro-Russian so that all the countries like the United States, Australia and New Zealand will get together and help him.'[84]

When Parliament met on 16 August, the situation was very tense. Siddiq Koya was notable for his absence. His close associate Vijaya Parmanandan called upon Reddy to resign for losing the election and walked out of Parliament after being sworn in. There was little support for Parmandandan within the NFP, however, and the fighting continued to be focused on differences between the two parties. Mara pointedly ignored Reddy in parliament and did not follow normal procedure and consult with the opposition in selecting a speaker of the House. Tomasi Vakatora was named speaker with the opposition refusing to participate in the election. The government then announced that selection of the deputy speaker, usually drawn from the opposition, would be deferred. Two days later, Parmandandan was named deputy speaker against the wishes of the opposition and in his acceptance speeech he supported the Alliance Party's allegations that the NFP had sought to defeat the Alliance Party by attacking native Fiijan traditions and the honour of their chiefs, and that this had been done in collusion with the *Four Corners* television team.

In the midst of the internal political bickering, Mara sought to boost his image with two events. The first was the Commonwealth

Heads of Government Regional Meeting, hosted by Fiji in Suva
14–18 October. During the meeting, Mara was constantly seen in the
presence of foreign political leaders. But there was another side to
the meeting as well. The meeting played an important role in the
growing problem of corruption in Fiji. It had an impact on Alliance
Party politicians who could not help but be envious of the luxurious
life-styles of many of the relatively wealthy politicians from other
Third World countries at the meeting, who sported expensive clothing and jewellery. Then there was the matter of some two dozen new
Mercedes Benz automobiles that Mara arranged to have purchased
by the government for the event (at a time of budget restraint and
calls for 'belt tightening'). These vehicles later found their way into
government ministries and served to establish new norms of luxury
for the Alliance élite.

The second event was the visit of Queen Elizabeth II to Fiji at the
end of the month, and especially her visit to the chiefly island of Bau
on 30 October. The visit was used by the chiefly oligarchy to raise
the spectre of royalism in native Fijian villages to a frenzied level. In
the Queen's address on Bau, she praised Fiji for its political stability
and added that she was certain that the chiefs 'would continue to
extend great influence for the good and for the happiness and
prosperity of all people of this land.'[85] It was music to the ears of
Mara and the chiefly oligarchy.

The Queen's visit was followed a few days later by a meeting of
the Great Council of Chiefs on Bau. Chiefs from Ra Province,
angered at what they saw as attacks on the chiefly system during
the election, presented a motion that two-thirds of the seats in the
House should be reserved for native Fijians and that the offices of
prime minister and governor general should also be reserved for
native Fijians. The governor general's brother, Ratu Tevita Naulivou,
called for the expulsion from Fiji of those who sought to attack the
chiefs. Trade unionist Joveci Gavoka, a commoner who Mara had
made a member of the Council of Chiefs, referred to Indo-Fijians as
dogs and stated that when the chiefs were attacked this was also an
attack on the chiefs' subjects. Another Bauan chief, Ratu Semi
Komaisavai, stated that the abuse of the chiefs had to be stopped
and that his people were 'willing to be jailed or hanged to achieve
this.' The membership of the Council of Chiefs was seventy-two;
twelve were absent at the time and twenty abstained from voting on
the motion. Of the forty who did vote, twenty-five supported the
motion and fifteen were opposed.

As with Butadroka's motion in the House in 1975, Mara was able
to use the Council of Chiefs motion to advantage in trying to appear

as the man who alone could hold back the forces of racism and instability, although a few cynics noted that a number of those involved in trying to stir up the hysteria were well-known Mara mouthpieces. The NFP convened a special meeting to consider and respond to the motion. After the meeting, Reddy stated that 'this appears to be part of an emerging campaign of hatred and ill-will towards the Indian community.' The question in many people's minds was just who was behind this campaign and where was it supposed to be heading.

A short time later, towards the end of his speech on the 1984 budget, Mara proposed a government of national unity.[86] He had asked Ahmed Ali to prepare a paper on the subject in 1979 and had sent it to Reddy. Reddy had returned it without comment. In light of the Council of Chiefs resolution and problems stemming from the 1982 election, Mara argued that the time was now ripe to consider the proposal once again. Reddy stated that he would study the proposal, while others in the NFP suggested that Mara was trying to take attention away from problems facing the government.

As the barbs continued to fly, the Alliance government agreed to appoint a Royal Commission to look into the allegations and counter-allegations. In September 1982 the New Zealand government was approached and asked to assist in finding an appropriate commissioner. A retired New Zealand judge, John White, was appointed on 12 October, and a preliminary hearing was held on 14 December, with John Rabone, another New Zealander, assisting. The Alliance Party arranged to have one of its own, Jone Veisamasama, appointed secretary. John Falvey represented the Alliance Party (later he was joined by R.I. Kapadia); Bhupendra Patel, the NFP; Siddiq Koya, the Western United Front; and Sakeasi Butadroka appeared in person on behalf of the Fijian Nationalist Party.[87] The initial meeting outlined the topics to be covered and the various parties tabled outlines of their allegations. Attention was given to providing assurances that the inquiry would cover questions relating to receipt of funds from foreign powers. These matters settled, the commission adjourned until 26 January 1983.

The main allegations to be investigated were: (1) the opposition's claim that the Alliance Party had hired a team of foreign consultants to plan a 'dirty tricks' campaign and the extent to which this plan was used; (2) the opposition's claim that the journalist Clive Speed had been supplied to the Alliance Party as an election adviser by the Australian government; (3) Mara's allegation that the NFP had received financial assistance from the Soviet Union; (4) Mara's allegation that the Indian high commissioner had assisted the NFP while stationed in Fiji; (5) Mara's allegation that the husband of the Indian high commissioner served as an intermediary between the NFP and the Soviet Union; (6) the Alliance Party's claim that the NFP had paid native Fijians to stand against the Alliance Party in the election; and (7) the Alliance Party's claim that the NFP had worked in collusion with the *Four Corners* television team to undermine the chances of the Alliance Party winning the election. It was a long list, and negotiations went on at various times during the hearings to see about shortening it, but no agreement was reached and the commission continued to hold hearings from 27 January through the end of August (with a long break in February and March in addition to several shorter ones).

As the hearing dragged on, Mara, with the assistance of Len Usher, decided to go on the offensive in May by producing a photostat of a letter linking Koya to the Soviets and releasing a statement by Mara drawing attention to the importance of the letter.[88] Usher delivered the documents to the media on 17 May. The letter, bearing what was supposed to be Koya's signature, committed the NFP to allowing the Soviets, among other things, to open an embassy in Fiji should the NFP win the election. The agreement was supposed to have been made at a meeting in Sydney in March 1981. The press release claimed that the allegation of the NFP receiving F$1 million from the Soviets was 'of relatively minor importance alongside the arrangement which is indicated in the document' (the photostat). The letter that had been produced was poorly typed (rumour stated that it had been typed on Len Usher's typewriter), contained grammatical and spelling errors (including the spelling of 'rouble'), and the signature was of questionable authenticity. Koya asked Mara and Usher to produce the original of the letter, and the NFP asked John White to set other matters aside and initiate an immediate probe into the new allegations. John Falvey, for the Alliance Party, objected to this and White chose to keep the inquiry to its normal schedule.

Lawyers for the Alliance Party and the NFP fought an intense battle over the Carroll report and the *Four Corners* program in June and July. During this time Mara had told the commission that the recommendations of the report had been ignored since they went against the high values that the Alliance Party stood for and had his secretary, Dr. Israeli Lasaqa, deny that he had given Rosemary Gillespie a confidential file (the so-called 'red file') pertaining to someone the prime minister wished to discredit. Lasaqa's evidence had been dismissed by the commission and doubts persisted about the veracity of Mara's testimony.

In late July, the Alliance Party announced that for reasons of national security it would not present evidence to support Mara's allegations concerning Soviet involvement. Alliance Party lawyers then virtually withdrew from the hearings, leaving the floor to the NFP. As the hearing resumed in early August, it became public that the Alliance Party had told the commission that it was 'unable to obtain or provide evidence' to prove that Koya had signed the letter linking the NFP to the Soviets. With this, a lawyer for the Alliance Party stated that it was ready to close its case. White then announced that he would begin hearing final addresses.

Koya responded to the Alliance Party's admission that it could provide no evidence of the authenticity of the letter he was supposed to have signed by calling on the commissioner to issue a statement exonerating him. He and others were therefore surprised when on the final day of the hearings, Falvey stated that 'the Alliance maintains that the Koya letter is authentic, that the original was in fact signed by Mr. Koya and that money was paid to or for the benefit of the National Federation Party in exchange for the promises made to the USSR in that letter.'[89] Koya responded by demanding that Mara be called to testify, but the request was denied. Fijian journalist Robert Keith-Reid commented at the end of the seventy-six days of hearings: 'As the inquiry wound up, the groundswell of public opinion appeared to reflect a fairly common view among Alliance as well as NFP followers – that the NFP seemed to have won and that the credibility of the Alliance and of Mara personally had been damaged, perhaps severely.'[90]

The report of the commission was made public in November 1983. White found that the Alliance Party had commissioned the Carroll report, but he felt that there was no evidence that the strategies recommended by it had been put to use, although he admitted that the report's recommendations had not been ignored entirely. He went on to state: 'I find that the employment of the Carroll team as consultants and the implementing by the Alliance of recommendations did not amount to foreign interference as alleged.' However, White did agree that Clive Speed had been employed in a partisan manner. White rejected Alliance claims of Soviet involvement and of collusion between the NFP and the *Four Corners* team. He stated that there was no evidence that Koya had signed the Russian letter. Both sides claimed victory, but there was also widespread belief that it represented a whitewash of the darker side of the Alliance Party campaign.

The 'Russian letter affair' did not end in 1983. In April 1986, Koya decided to sue John Falvey and Len Usher for defamation in relation to the letter, claiming that the letter was a fraud.[91] On 5 June 1986,

Falvey and Usher agreed in an out-of-court settlement to have their lawyers read a letter of apology to Koya in court. In a letter to the editor of the *Fiji Times*, Koya noted that it was now apparent that the Alliance Party had purposely misled the inquiry and demanded a public apology from Usher and Falvey. In addition, he called 'upon the Prime Minister on whose instructions and authority the Koya letter was released to the media to publicly apologise to the nation and hand in the Alliance government's resignation and call for a general election now.'[92] Mara did not apologize nor did he call an election. Instead, on 11 June he had the Alliance Party issue a statement referring to Koya's letter as 'cheap political theatrics' and the call to apologize as 'malicious' and 'unnecessary.' This was not to be the end of the matter and the letter was to resurface again in 1987 in the hands of Colonel Rabuka.

CHAPTER FOUR

Fiji and the World

Fiji is not just 'another' South Pacific island nation. In many ways Fiji is the most important state in the region. It is important not only because of its relative size and wealth, but because it plays a central role as a bridge between the nation states of the Melanesian, Polynesian, and Micronesian islands – Fiji is the centre of the South Pacific. As such, the Mara government's moderate, pro-Western stance on many issues served to set the tone in foreign affairs for the region as a whole. During the late 1970s and early 1980s, as a few of the states in the region began to espouse policies that were of concern to conservative Western governments, Fiji's moderating role became even more important and it began to be courted more assiduously by the United States, France, Israel, and even South Africa.

During the colonial era, local political figures in Fiji, while focusing on internal affairs, generally shared many of the same international perspectives as the colonial administration and the expatriate business community. This was especially true of Fiji's chiefly élite, led by Sukuna and later Mara, who adopted the pro-imperial and anti-communist stances of their European advisers and colleagues. These views were reinforced by a conservative clergy and educational system. Only within the Indo-Fijian community, largely because of the ties it retained with India, was there evidence of something of a Third World perspective. From the early part of the century through the early postwar period, many prominent Indo-Fijians supported Gandhi's critical approach to the British and his lack of enthusiasm for the Allied war effort in the Second World War. After the war there was a degree of pride in the role that an independent India had assumed as a leading political force in the Third World, and there was even some support for the notion of non-alignment. Indo-Fijian leaders, however, expressed relatively little interest in foreign policy when compared to pressing local concerns, notably conditions in the cane fields. Even the trade unions, for the most part, lacked an interest in issues related to international solidarity, beyond establishing a few weak ties with unionists in neighbouring Australia as well as the United Kingdom.

GEOPOLITICS

The Second World War and the Japanese invasion brought important changes in the geopolitics of the South Pacific. With an eye to controlling regional trade after the war, Australia had offered to assume responsibility for supplying all of the islands. Although the United States had said no to the proposal, the offer indicated a growing assertiveness by Australia within the South Pacific. For its part, New Zealand came to see the islands as more important than ever for strategic reasons. Australia's and New Zealand's need for American support during the war sealed an alliance that was given expression in the ANZAC pact in 1944 and then the ANZUS treaty in 1952. The latter was intended to unite Australia, New Zealand, and the United States in 'their efforts for collective defence for the preservation of peace and security' in the Pacific region against 'armed attack' (presumably from the Soviet Union). The ANZUS treaty, in effect, served to incorporate Australia and New Zealand in America's 'war against communism,' primarily in the role of regional policeman.

The Cold War was also largely responsible for the founding of the South Pacific Commission (SPC) in 1947, following the signing of the Canberra Agreement by the region's colonial powers: Australia, New Zealand, France, the United States, and the Netherlands (which left the SPC in 1962). Ostensibly to provide technical and training assistance in social, economic, and cultural fields to the island states, strategically, the SPC was part of the Western alliance's global strategy of containment along similar lines as the SEATO and CENTO treaties which covered Southeast Asia and South Asia, respectively.

As worry over the 'Yellow Peril' faded and the Cold War heated up, the principal target of concern among the pro-Western states of the southwestern Pacific became the Soviet Union. During the 1950s and 1960s 'red scares and attempts to alert people to the supposed menace of the Soviet bogey' became commonplace on the part of colonial administrators, businessmen, journalists, and clergy throughout the colonial possessions in the South Pacific.[1] Most of this propaganda was intended for internal consumption to stigmatize trade unionists and others attempting to upset the colonial status quo, but the mindless anti-communist and pro-Western geopolitical culture that was created served to link such a perspective closely with the national political establishment that was to inherit state power after independence.

In actual fact, there was relatively little in the South Pacific to concern conservative Western powers until the latter part of the 1970s. The United States, more concerned with the northern Pacific, felt that the region could safely be ignored and left to its regional and European allies. The foundation of American policy towards the South Pacific has been 'strategic denial,' and to keep 'the Soviets out in every way possible so as to ensure that there is no threat to the control exercised by the United States and its allies over the region's people and resources.'[2] The policy was closely tied to 'the desire to ensure free passage of American ships and aircraft through the region.'[3]

Developments within the South Pacific in the late 1970s and early 1980s, however, served to draw America's attention to the region. Perceived reasons for concern by conservative Americans at this time were numerous. Tuna fishing proved a serious problem as poaching by American tuna boats in regional waters upset even islanders normally known for their strong pro-American sentiments. This trouble was highlighted with the seizure of the tuna boat *Danica* by the Papua New Guinea government in 1982 and the *Janette Diana* by the Solomon Islands in 1984.[4] Concern increased even more when Kiribati signed a fishing agreement with the Soviet Union in October 1985, in which the Soviets agreed to pay the Kiribati government an amount far in excess of what the United States and other countries had been willing to pay for the right to fish in its waters.[5] Then, Vanuatu achieved independence in 1980 under a government pledged to support non-alignment and a nuclear-free Pacific, and which also set about to establish diplomatic relations with Cuba and Vietnam and to hold discussions with Libya.

The independence struggle of the indigenous Kanaks in New Caledonia under the leadership of the socialist Kanak independence front or FLNKS was another matter of geopolitical concern for the United States. There was also evidence of growing union militancy throughout the region (as exemplified in a series of public sector strikes in the early 1980s in Western Samoa, Kiribati, and elsewhere), and the unions were becoming active in their support for a nuclear-free Pacific. An additional concern was the emergence of progressive elements within the traditionally conservative Christian churches of the region. There was nothing to indicate that the situation was comparable to that in Latin America or the Philippines, where large numbers of Christians had fallen under the influence of 'liberation theology,' but the potential for trouble was evident. For example, the Pacific Council of Churches, based in Suva, had published critical studies concerned with nuclear testing and transnational corporations.[6] The anti-nuclear movement itself, which had faded into obscurity at one point, now seemed to be coming back to life, especially in Fiji. Finally, not only were conservative Americans finding themselves confronted with these disturbing developments among the small states in the region, but there was the even more serious problem of the David Lange government in New Zealand. Such conservatives saw its anti-nuclear stance as wrecking the ANZUS alliance and leaving the entire region more vulnerable to Soviet penetration.

America's most important ally in the region remained Australia. A 1984 report prepared for Australia's Senate Standing Committee on Foreign Affairs and Defence echoed American policy concerns when it stated: 'Australia's principal strategic interest in the South Pacific is to ensure that our sea communications with Japan and the Americas remain open. It is argued that instability in the South Pacific could endanger these sea approaches. Australia is also concerned that the Soviet presence in the region be kept to a minimum militarily and diplomatically.'[7] Australia's strong support for the American position was reaffirmed by Prime Minister Bob Hawke on 19 April 1984, when he stated that Australia was not going to 'indulge in the stupidity of unilateral neutrality.' During his visit to Fiji in mid-August 1984, Hawke emphasized the importance of defence co-operation in the region in order to maintain 'security and stability.' Australia sought to back up its concern by providing military assistance through its Defence Co-operation Programme (since 1972 in the case of Fiji). Its desire to maintain stability also led Australia to support the use of Papua New Guinea troops in 1980 to assist the government of Walter Lini in Vanuatu in putting an end to the secessionist threat on Santo. The Australians had their own Operational Defence Force based in northern Queensland capable of quick intervention in any Pacific island state should the need arise,[8] but, as in the case of Vanuatu, the preference was for using 'brown-faced troops' in 'brown' countries.

The other Western power with an important presence in the South Pacific is, of course, France, with its string of colonies stretching from New Caledonia in the southwestern Pacific, to Wallis and Futuna and French Polynesia, and finally to Clipperton Island off the coast of Mexico. While other Western nations, even the United States, have been content to move gradually from control to neo-colonial influence with the South Pacific, France alone has sought to maintain a more traditional colonial presence in the region. While the United States and its allies do not object to a Western power maintaining a large military presence in the region, they are concerned that the French presence has served as a destabilizing factor and contributed to increased anti-Western sentiments. Thus, nuclear testing in French Polynesia has served to draw attention to other nuclear issues such as the passage of nuclear armed ships through regional waters and has also provided a rallying point for progressive elements. The Kanak struggle for independence has become one of the most difficult problems facing the region, with Australia, New Zealand, and the United States worrying that intransigent French policies might result in a further radicalization of the Kanaks and of neighbouring Melanesian governments.

As Western paranoia about the South Pacific increased, Fiji came to assume an ever more important role in the minds of Western strategists. It was referred to by some American officials as 'the Jamaica of the South Pacific,' in relation to its significance as a bulwark against communist domination. Not all Western diplomats or officials shared these views, and many simply saw the heterogeneous policies in the region as a reflection of the growing maturity of the region in the postcolonial era, but there were a sufficient number who could only see these small Third World countries in Cold War terms. The views of the latter prevailed in promoting additional Western support for regional military forces – forces that, in the absence of an external enemy to defend against, could be used to intervene in national civilian political affairs that had nothing to do with keeping the South Pacific free of communists.

ADMINISTRATION OF FOREIGN AFFAIRS

After independence Mara decided to keep the Foreign Affairs portfolio for himself. By and large, this decision was motivated by his desire to create an image as a 'statesman' in the international arena – partly to bolster his position at home and also because he enjoyed the role. In so doing, he was merely following in Sukuna's footsteps once again. The actual establishment and running of the Ministry of Foreign Affairs was left to a European, Robert Sanders, who served in the post as secretary until 1974, ensuring continuity with previous policies. After July 1982, Mara turned the foreign affairs ministry over to loyal followers in the Alliance Party, and earlier Sanders had been replaced by other Mara loyalists.[9] Effectively, however, Mara continued to determine the overall direction of Fiji's foreign policy after 1982 and to be the centre of attention when publicity opportunities arose.

As for the opposition National Federation Party, only rarely did its parliamentarians voice any opinion on foreign policy matters. The only dissent came from within the trade union movement and from a small group of academics. While the trade unions in the Fiji Trades Union Congress shared the conservative orientation of the International Confederation of Free Trade Unions with which the Fiji Trades Union Congress was affiliated, Tora's militant breakaway group in the mid-1970s established ties with East Bloc unions. Although this was more rhetorical than substantial, it was greeted with considerable alarm by a government unaccustomed to such an affront, especially because of the close personal identification of foreign affairs with Mara and his chiefly authority.

Soon after independence, Fiji established overseas missions at the U.N. and with Australia and the United Kingdom.[10] In these, as in earlier appointments, a pattern emerged of Mara filling the posts with useful, educated commoners as a means of patronage. In later years this pattern was to be maintained but added to it was a greater use of patronage for those of chiefly rank as well. With the growing importance of the European Economic Community as a destination for Fiji's sugar exports and as a source of foreign aid, in 1976, it was decided to appoint an ambassador to the European Economic Community in Brussels.[11] The pattern of appointing useful, educated commoners can be seen once again when Filipe Bole was named permanent representative to the United Nations in 1980, to replace Berenado Vunibobo. Bole was from Lau and was one of the most prominent young Fijians being groomed by Mara for eventual leadership within the Alliance Party. The use of ambassadorships simply as a means of rewards for service was evident in the appointment of Ratu Josua Toganivalu to succeed J.D. Gibson in London.

The budget of the Ministry of Foreign Affairs had grown to around F$1 million per year by the mid-1970s. Following the 1977 elections it began to climb sharply, until by 1982 it had reached F$3.2 million – only a little over 1 per cent of total government spending, but nevertheless a relatively large amount for such a small country under pressure for budgetary restraint. By 1982 the Ministry had thirty-nine staff: 13 in Suva, 6 in New York, 4 in Brussels, 4 in London, 4 in Tokyo (a mission opened in 1981), 4 in Wellington, 3 in Canberra, and

1 in Sydney. In addition, it owned twelve overseas properties and leased another nineteen properties. Significantly, Fiji did not have a mission in India, although one was planned to open after the 1987 election should the Alliance Party win. Initially, training of professional staff had been handled through participation in Oxford University's Foreign Service Programme, and later assistance was also provided by Australia. Such assistance did little, however, to alter the fact that the Ministry of Foreign Affairs was becoming an expensive appendage of Alliance Party patronage. (An example of this are the expenses incurred to support Fiji's participation in the Pacific Islands Development Program at the East-West Center in Honolulu, to which Filipe Bole was appointed director after the u.N. post.) In fact, after the 1982 election, there was some attempt to scale back the ministry's overseas operations in the face of overall budget constraints and it became increasingly difficult to carry out the duties expected of the overseas missions. Expansion again seemed to be in the cards in 1987, when Mara began making various promises of overseas diplomatic postings to buy off those not selected to run for office and as a means of rewarding loyalty to the Alliance Party. For this reason, one of the Labour Party-NFP coalition's campaign promises in 1987 was to reduce the size of Fiji's overseas missions.

By the end of 1973, Fiji had established diplomatic relations with twenty-three countries. Seventeen of these countries had accredited diplomatic missions in Fiji, but few had diplomatic staff in residence. Australia, New Zealand, the United Kingdom, and India had high commissions. The United States and France had embassies run by interim chargé d'affaires with their ambassadors in Wellington being responsible for Fiji. Otherwise, a handful of Western European nations had honorary consuls, and eleven other countries assigned their ambassadors in Wellington or Canberra responsibility for Fiji (including Canada, Japan, South Korea, Singapore, and Israel). In the early 1970s Fiji established diplomatic relations with the German Democratic Republic, the Federal Republic of Germany, and Chile.[12] The GDR was the first East Bloc country with which Fiji established relations, although there was no exchange of diplomatic representation. A trade mission from Taiwan to Fiji in 1971 served to strengthen ties between the Mara government and Kuomintang regime, but diplomatic ties were not established.

Between 1973 and 1982 embassies were opened in Suva by a number of Asian countries, and the United States and France upgraded their embassies. Following the lead of the United States, diplomatic relations were established with the People's Republic of China in 1975, and the following year the Chinese opened a diplomatic mission in Suva. Subsequently, embassies were opened by Japan (1978), South Korea (1980), and Malaysia (1982).

Mara's Policies

From the outset, the cornerstone of Fiji's foreign policy, as enunciated by Mara, was the Pacific Way. In his address to the General Assembly of the United Nations in 1970, he stated: 'Many speakers have commented on our peaceful transition to independence; and we ourselves are deeply grateful for our good fortune in this way. But this is nothing new in the Pacific ... We like to think that this is the Pacific Way, and that it underlines the case for a Pacific voice in this Assembly, both geographically and ideologically.'[13]

As was noted in the previous chapter, the Pacific Way has served as an ideological support for the maintenance of chiefly rule in Fiji based on a distorted view of Fiji's peaceful past and an emphasis on consensus in such a way as to mean consenting to the wishes of those in authority. Mara touched on the consensual aspect in his 1970 U.N. speech:

> I wonder whether we have not now, in our deep concern for personal liberty and freedom of expression, over-weighted the balance in favour of the individual as against the mass of people composing a society. I wonder if the over-indulgence of the angry young men, the 'way out' people and the small militant groups with their own ends has not reacted against the steady progress of society as a whole, and in particular against the large body of quiet, honest, hard-working folk throughout the world. It might be that if we devoted more of our time and energies to the progress and betterment of the whole, our overall achievement would be the greater.[14]

Here again the chief is claiming to speak on behalf of the whole and labelling dissenters as trouble-makers working against the betterment of society. Reference to the Pacific Way has become a feature of most international speeches by overseas representatives of Fiji and its central role in Fiji's foreign affairs was spelled out in the 1974 *Report on Foreign Affairs*: 'On ... global issues such as the settlement of international disputes, the elimination of all forms of racial injustice and colonial domination, and the widening gap between the rich and poor countries, the Pacific Way of continuous dialogue, peaceful change and close co-operation on the basis of partnership has been the guiding philosophy in Fiji's approach.'[15]

In practical terms, the Pacific Way has meant support for conservative Western positions under the guise of seeking a moderate path rather than siding with extremists. Thus, on the question of 'terrorism' Fiji accepted the American definition that excluded 'state terrorism', and focused instead on 'acts of politically inspired terrorism against innocent individuals and commercial aircraft.' The meaning of this view can be seen in Fiji's support for the Pinochet regime in Chile.

Whereas Mara took relations with Western countries for granted, feeling that Fiji and the West shared common values and goals, relations with other Third World nations outside of the South Pacific, and with East Bloc countries, were more ambivalent. Mara sought to establish a high profile in the Commonwealth and among the ACP (Asia, Caribbean, and Pacific) nations in their relations with the European Economic Community, in part, to establish his identity as a 'statesman' of world stature and, in part, as a result of specific economic concerns. Under Mara, however, Fiji did not identify with many of the political issues of concern to other Third World nations. Overall, its relations with the rest of the Third World were minimal. Where significant ties did develop, they tended to be with conservative governments which shared Fiji's general view of the world.

In 1974 the government's *Report on Foreign Affairs* noted that Fiji had little direct contact with East Bloc countries, but that it had 'established friendly working relations with them ... through its membership in the United Nations.' But the report also noted that there was little actual substance to these relations.[16] Concerning the issue of China, when a motion was brought before the U.N. on the seating of China and expulsion of Taiwan, 'Fiji abstained on the resolution because though it fully supported the seating of the People's Republic of China, it could not accept the expulsion of Taiwan.'[17] It was only after the United States gave the go-ahead that Fiji recognized the Chinese government.

During most of the 1970s, Mara's policies were merely taken for granted by the United States and other Western powers – Fiji was one Third World country, at least, that they didn't have to 'worry about.' However, by the latter part of the decade, as the region became more unstable, Mara's Pacific Way conservatism would take on greater importance.

REGIONAL CO-OPERATION

Founded in 1947, the South Pacific Commission (SPC) is the oldest regional body in the South Pacific. Originally comprised of the colonial powers present in the region, the SPC's membership was expanded as the colonies in the region achieved independence, beginning with Western Samoa in 1962. The SPC's offices were established in New Caledonia. Starting in 1950, the commissioners met every three years at the South Pacific Conference to adopt a work program and to discuss other matters falling within areas of concern to the SPC (the meetings became annual in 1967). With an emphasis on economic development, the SPC has sought to avoid discussion of issues of a directly political nature. Indirectly, it has served as a means of helping to promote a continued role in the South Pacific for external powers such as Britain and especially France. As the number of colonies in the region declined, the newly independent nations in the South Pacific began to see the need for another form of regional organization and, more recently, have begun to call into question the need for the SPC at all.

The South Pacific Forum (SPF) was established in 1971 'in response to a growing desire from within the region to extend the process of regional consultation and co-operation, already established by the South Pacific Commission and other regional bodies in economic and social development, into all matters of common concern through the heads of independent governments.'[18] In particular, and unlike the SPC, the SPF excluded from membership external powers such as Britain and France. The earliest members included Fiji, Western Samoa, Tonga, Nauru, the Cook Islands, Australia, and New Zealand. Thus comprised, the 'Forum' had a decidedly conservative, Polynesian orientation with Fiji's Ratu Mara playing a prominent role in its affairs.

Economic issues were of primary concern to the Pacific Island Forum members. These included regional trade, deep-sea fishing, and offshore mining. In November 1972, the Forum members decided to establish the South Pacific Bureau for Economic Co-operation (SPEC) to serve as the Forum's secretariat. It was opened in April 1973 with headquarters in Suva, and Mahe Tupouniua, from Tonga, became its first director. One of SPEC's first activities involved preparation of a report on increasing links with the European Economic Community. It also carried out a survey of regional trade by commodity and industry.

The Pacific Islands Producers' Association had been organized in 1965 to co-ordinate the production and export of copra and bananas among the Polynesian countries in the region. In 1974, the association was dissolved and absorbed into SPEC. The Committee for a Co-ordination of Off-shore Prospecting also had been established in November 1972 in response to regional concern over the growing interest in offshore mining by foreign interests in the South Pacific.

This and the deep-sea fishing industry led the Forum members to take a particular interest in the 1974 United Nations Law of the Sea Conference.

At its 1977 meeting, the Forum delegates decided to establish the South Pacific Regional Fisheries Agency and urged member states to pursue claims for two-hundred-mile economic and fishing zones (known as exclusive economic zones). The Forum Fisheries Agency was established in 1979 with its headquarters located in Honiara. The Forum Fisheries Agency has come to be probably the most important body within the SPF, playing an extremely important role in the region in fisheries negotiations.[19] Discussions had been held at meetings of the SPC and the Pacific Islands Producers' Association concerning the establishment of a regional shipping body to better serve the needs of the Pacific island nations. In 1972, SPEC undertook to prepare a study with the aim of establishing such a body. This resulted in the setting up of the Regional Shipping Council in 1974, and the members adopted a proposal to create the Pacific Forum Line in 1976.

In 1980, the SPF member states negotiated the regional SPARTECA trade agreement, which provides for the preferential entry of a range of agricultural and industrial goods from Pacific island states to Australia and New Zealand. In the case of Fiji, this encouraged development of export manufacturing within its small industrial sector (clothing in particular) and also led to tentative moves by outside interests (primarily from South Korea) to establish industries in Fiji which allowed them to get in under the Australian and New Zealand tariff barriers.

On the political front, during the early 1970s the Forum members voiced their opposition to French nuclear testing on Mururoa (which commenced in 1966), culminating in a 1975 declaration of support for the creation of a nuclear-free zone in the South Pacific. However, beyond such expressions, no concrete steps were taken to pressure the French to cease the tests. The conservative heads of state from the Pacific island nations also shared a concern over evidence of the growing strength of the trade union movement in the region. They were especially worried about the influence of overseas trade unions in promoting the development of unions in the South Pacific. One result of this was the convening of a meeting of Pacific Labour Ministers in October 1973. Subsequently, this became an annual affair.

Having been granted independence first, the Polynesian states dominated regional foreign affairs and co-operation throughout most of the 1970s. In this regard, Fiji, under Mara, was viewed as a

Polynesian nation. The situation began to change, however, by the end of the decade as non-Polynesian states gained independence, including Papua New Guinea (1975), Solomon Islands (1978), Kiribati (1979), and Vanuatu (1980). It was Vanuatu, under Prime Minister Walter Lini, in particular, that raised the spectre of a region that could no longer be taken for granted by the Western powers. Walter Lini's party set as its goal the promotion of Melanesian socialism.[20] In foreign policy terms, this translated into a non-aligned foreign policy marked by an attempt to avoid diplomatic relations with superpowers while seeking to balance relations with lesser powers, vocal support for a host of Third World issues, and condemnation of racism, colonialism, and exploitation.[21] Although, in practice, Vanuatu has tended not to live up to its radical image, its policies were still a radical departure from the prevailing policies in other countries in the region and this began to worry the United States and its Western allies. The alarm grew as other non-Polynesian states also began to assume more independent foreign policy positions. The larger geopolitical question will be discussed later in the chapter, but for now, what is worth pointing out is that this more radical stance and the political differences between Polynesian and non-Polynesian states began to influence regional co-operation.

The first real challenge to the moderate Polynesian position (of which Mara was a leading advocate) came over the question of fisheries negotiations. Seven Pacific island countries signed the Nauru Agreement in February 1982.[22] In addition to pledging themselves to close co-operation in developing their fishing industries, the signatories stated that they would collectively seek to drive hard bargains in negotiations with outside fishing nations (essentially Japan, Taiwan, South Korea, the Soviet Union, and the United States). The nations signing the agreement were those most directly involved with foreign fishing fleets since their islands sat astride the main fishing grounds in the central Pacific. The more moderate Polynesian states (most of them having relatively limited interest in deep-sea fishing) tended to shy away from such militant posturing and advocated bilateral rather than regional negotiations. The position advocated by the Nauru Agreement prevailed, by and large, but the existence of a division within the region was apparent.

Regional differences became even more obvious during the early 1980s in discussions over support for independence struggles in West Papua and New Caledonia and over the need to take further steps in creating a nuclear-free Pacific. West Papua and New Caledonia increasingly came to be seen as Melanesian concerns within the Polynesian bloc. Mara was involved in the SPF's discussions with

France over New Caledonia, in which his views tended to be much more moderate than the Melanesian representatives. Likewise, he demonstrated little resolve to pursue the anti-nuclear issue with much vigour. The stance on the part of Mara and the Polynesian bloc in general was based on the following: a desire not to offend the Western powers, upon which most Polynesian countries were heavily dependent economically; a lack of identification with other Third World countries; and a strong antipathy for anything that smacked of communism or socialism.

Even the University of the South Pacific, which served the island nations of the region and was supported jointly by the various island states, became embroiled in wranglings between the two emerging blocs. From its inception, the university had been strongly influenced not only by the policies of the Mara government (in both subtle and not so subtle ways, such as through the Fiji government's control of work permits for university employees) but also by Polynesian elements at the university at the expense of the Melanesian states. Thus, the Institute of Pacific Studies was often jokingly referred to as the 'Institute of Polynesian Studies,' and a conservative group of administrators and academics from Polynesian countries came to assume greater power as the process of localization progressed. Frustration on the part of Vanuatu, and especially the Solomon Islands, led them on occasion to threaten to pull out of the university.

By the early 1980s a growing number of educated and prominent Melanesians had come to view the Polynesians (including Mara) not only as being soft on important international issues but also as deriving an undue share of the benefits from regional and international bodies (or, generally, having too much influence in the region). Moreover, there was another view which was expressed by a Solomon Islands speaker at the University of the South Pacific during the 1983 Wantok Week (a week set aside since 1980 essentially to promote Melanesian consciousness and solidarity): 'The Polynesian nations are on their way down and we are on our way up.' Those holding such a view tend to see most of the Polynesian states as declining welfare appendages of neocolonial powers. They further point to the greater land and resource base of the Melanesian states and argue that it is these states that are escaping from dependency.[23] These sentiments began to take shape in 1982 when the concept of a Melanesian Alliance was being considered. It was a concept that Mara took the lead in opposing, arguing for the need to maintain regional co-operation. Critics of Mara's position contended that this call for co-operation was merely an attempt to thwart the development of a more independent South Pacific and to maintain the conservative hegemony of the Polynesian states.

FOREIGN AID

Fiji's first budget after independence of F$60.1 million produced a deficit of F$7.1 million. The deficit was met with relatively small amounts of domestic and foreign borrowing and foreign grants.[24] Fiji's debt service ratio was 0.8 per cent. For a newly independent nation, it was not a bad start. Over the years the budget, deficit, and debt service ratio increased, although not dramatically by Third World standards. The country's reliance on foreign grants and other forms of assistance also grew. The total public debt had reached F$421.7 million by 1983, having risen by an average of 17.5 per cent per year over the previous five years.[25] The debt service ratio was 4.2 per cent. Total foreign aid in 1983 amounted to F$35.5 million, equal to around 10 per cent of the budget and representing F$53 per capita. Thus, while foreign aid was nowhere near as important to Fiji as it was in many other Pacific island nations, it was nonetheless a significant source of revenue, especially for a government facing growing economic constraints.

Australia had long been Fiji's main source of foreign aid, followed by New Zealand and Britain. In 1983 they contributed F$10.9 million, F$3.5 million, and F$2.1 million, respectively. Various U.N. agencies also contributed significant amounts.[26] Starting in 1975, the European Economic Community began providing Fiji with small amounts of aid. In 1983 the amount forthcoming from the European Economic Community was increased substantially, to F$5.0 million, making it Fiji's second most important source of aid. Another source of assistance to Fiji was the International Labour Organisation, which had its regional office in Suva. One of the International Labour Organisation's activities included a large regional program for promoting worker education. Funded largely by Danish unions and lasting through the early 1980s, the project played a profound role in the development of unions in many South Pacific countries, as well as providing important assistance to Fiji's unions. As a result, as relations between the unions and the Mara government deteriorated, and especially after the founding of the Fiji Labour Party in 1985, the Fiji government's attitude toward the International Labour Organisation soured to the point that the Mara government threatened to pull out of the International Labour Organisation altogether.

Japan was a relative newcomer as a provider of assistance to the South Pacific. Since the late 1970s the Japanese International Co-operation Agency has become an increasingly important source of aid in the region. In Fiji, as elsewhere in the South Pacific, the Japanese have focused on assistance to the fisheries sector. Starting in 1977 with a small expert assignment program, Japanese aid to Fiji increased substantially in the early 1980s. Whereas in 1981 Japan had provided only F$300,000 in aid, the amount was increased to F$3.4 million in 1982 and to F$4.4 million in 1983, when it ranked third in importance. The biggest project began in 1986: a F$10 million fishing port in Lautoka (which was completed in May 1988).

Bilateral aid from Western European countries besides Britain had never amounted to much. The French presence in Fiji had been negligible and even after 1982 did not amount to much. The West German presence increased first following negotiations with the Hans Seidel Foundation (representing conservative political elements in West Germany) in 1982. The Hans Seidel Foundation came to play an important role in assisting the Alliance Party to train a cadre of young leaders and helped with media production and had its main office in quarters leased from Alliance Party fixer David Toganivalu in Suva. In part because of the presence of the Hans Seidel Foundation, the Friedrich Ebert Stiftung which was affiliated with the Social Democratic Party of West Germany also decided to open an office in Suva. The Friedrich Ebert Stiftung had been active in the South Pacific for several years previously, primarily funding trade union seminars and related educational activities. Its entry into Fiji was viewed with considerable suspicion by the Alliance government and the Friedrich Ebert Stiftung was forced to concentrate its efforts outside of Fiji, helping to develop regional media.

The Americans

Until the latter part of the 1970s the United States had been content to leave the South Pacific to its European and regional allies. In 1977, after the king of Tonga made reference to the possibility of creating ties with the Soviet Union, and the South Pacific Forum endorsed the concept of a nuclear-free zone in the South Pacific, the United States reacted to this grave security threat by initiating aid projects in the South Pacific, beginning in 1977 with an Agency for International Development (AID) grant of U.S.$1.3 million to Papua New Guinea. The following year, the United States established the South Pacific Regional Development Office to oversee its aid programs in the region. Operations were begun in that year in Fiji, Tonga, and Western Samoa, with other countries being included later. Total U.S. expenditure in the region by 1980 amounted to U.S.$9.4 million.

American aid was channelled through four modes: (1) regional bodies (the South Pacific Commission and the University of the South Pacific); (2) support for American-based non-governmental organizations (for example, the South Pacific Peoples Foundation, the Asia Foundation, the Summer Institute of Linguistics, and Helen Keller International); (3) the Peace Corps (Fiji being one of the larger recipients of Peace Corps volunteers); and (4) the Accelerated Impact Program which funds small, mainly rural development projects, primarily in conjunction with the Peace Corps. The use of so-called private American foundations became a particularly important part of the new initiative. As noted by Richard Herr, this was in part because the American administration doubted that it could get congressional approval for a higher level of involvement, and it also created an image of the United States not being directly involved in many activities.[27] The use of private foundations to carry out the questionable policies of various u.s. administrations was, of course, becoming an increasingly important part of American foreign policy world-wide at this time.

The first American aid projects in Fiji were quickly integrated into the Alliance Party patronage network (as was the use of Peace Corps volunteers), largely through the targeting of rural native Fijian villages for assistance. The United States provided u.s.$33,000 to the YMCA as a contribution of 13 per cent to the total budget for rural development work in twenty selected villages (the leadership of the YMCA in Fiji coming from active members of the Alliance Party). In 1979 and 1980, the Accelerated Impact Program disbursed u.s.$218,400 mainly for small rural development projects (bridges, public buildings, etc.) and u.s.$650,000 was provided in the form of Disaster Assistance. The latter became associated with the prime minister's Hurricane Relief Committee, which quickly gained a reputation within Fiji for corruption and patronage. An additional u.s.$167,600 was provided to Helen Keller International in 1980 to assist in its work with the Fiji Blind Society.

In addition to formal assistance, in the late 1970s, American officials also began to cultivate personal ties with South Pacific leaders, and with Mara in particular, who was viewed as a key figure in the region, and who was easily susceptible to flattery. This perhaps reached a peak during the tenure of American ambassador to Fiji, Fred Eckert. Appointed in 1982 to replace William Brode, Jr., Eckert's ambassadorship was a reward for his work in upstate New York on behalf of Ronald Reagan in his campaign for the presidency. Eckert had no previous experience in the Pacific or in foreign affairs, but he and Mara hit it off. Eckert is widely credited with Mara's decision in

1983 to lift the ban on visits by nuclear ships to Fiji. Eckert himself boasted that he had 'done more than any previous ambassador to bring the country [Fiji] closer to the u.s.'[28]

Six months after his arrival in Fiji, an interview with Eckert, which highlighted the strategic rationale behind America's involvement in the region, appeared in the Fiji government's publication, *Fiji Focus*.[29] In this interview, he defended America's refusal to sign the Law of the Sea Treaty, commenting: 'I don't think it's reasonable to expect the u.s. to hand over a quarter of a billion dollars in interest free loans and loan guarantees to an international body to establish a seabed mining authority that would be in a position to dictate to American companies ... that's contrary to the American way of doing things.' On the topic of anti-nuclear sentiments in the region, he stated that he saw no evidence of growing support for the anti-nuclear movement and stressed the importance of nuclear-powered vessels and their safety: 'we feel that in order to have peace in the world there must be a strong u.s. Navy, in order to have a strong u.s. Navy we must have the latest, the most efficient technology and that means nuclear-powered vessels so that they can go great distances at a minimal cost.'

When further asked in the interview about the effects of the Soviets opening an embassy in Suva, Eckert stated that 'the Government of Fiji has long made it crystal clear that it does not want a Soviet Embassy in this country' and 'we don't think that any country in the South Pacific region is anxious to have the Soviet presence.' Mentioning Afghanistan and Poland, he noted that 'many countries in the world are fed up with the Soviet presence.' On Soviet embassies, he commented: 'I presume the reason for the reservations about the Soviet Embassy in this country as in many countries of the world is that it is common knowledge that the Soviet Union uses its Embassies for espionage purposes and for, when possible, subversion.' And, finally, on America's growing awareness of the region's strategic importance, he stated that the fact that Reagan chose him as ambassador ('someone with whom he is personally acquainted') was a sign of the region's importance. Then, pointing to the region's significance for sea and air connections between the United States and its ANZUS allies he stated: 'It is critically important for the u.s. to keep a constant surveillance of the movement of adversaries. It is therefore important to be present at a reasonable level in every region of the world. So we have in recent years shown a greater interest and awareness of the South Pacific region.'

Growing American influence was marked by a string of visits by high-ranking American military personnel to Fiji and to a strengthening of ties between the Fijian and American military. For example, the commander of the United States Army Western Command, Lt. Gen. James Lee, made a visit to Fiji (and Tonga) in May 1984. During his visit, Lee made frequent public remarks about the 'Soviet threat' to the region and held talks with the commander of the Royal Fiji Military Forces (RFMF) on defence and security matters. He referred to the Fijian army as 'one of the best in the world' and mentioned that the United States was prepared to help Fiji develop a bigger and more varied weapons system.[30] When Mara visited Washington in late November 1984, he failed to get American approval for increased sugar imports from Fiji or to secure west coast landing rights for Air Pacific, but he did come home with a promise of U.S.$400,000 worth of arms for Fiji's military.[31]

The Eckert years (1982–84) witnessed marked increases in direct American assistance to Fiji as well as a tremendous expansion of activities by American non-governmental organizations. Associated with conservative religious bodies, many of these non-governmental organizations came to play an important role in rural villages. Their work was not confined to the countryside, however, as can be seen in the case of World Vision, a conservative, anti-communist religious body founded in South Korea in 1950 that came to be closely associated with right-wing Americans and specifically with the Reagan administration. Through activities such as its 'prayer breakfasts,' World Vision has sought to bring together Third World leaders and instill them with the virtues of the American brand of Christian fundamentalism, conservative American values in general, and a hatred of anything that smacks of godless communism. Among those attending the prayer breakfasts from the South Pacific were Mara and a number of other prominent members of the Alliance Party.

Until 1980, World Vision's activities in the South Pacific were modest. Since 1980, its presence in the region has grown and in 1982–83 it stepped up its activities in Fiji in particular. In late 1985, a decision was made to increase its staff in Fiji from seven to thirty. Among those hired were a number of former government employees associated with the Alliance Party who were lured by offers of high salaries. At the same time, World Vision increased its activities in targeted villages. Village leaders were approached and told that World Vision had large amounts of money and they were invited to come to Suva to discuss projects. Records of expenditures were not made public, but it soon became obvious that World Vision was indeed spending substantial sums in Fiji. When World Vision was criticized during the course of a public address at the University of the South Pacific in October 1985, several church leaders associated with World Vision signed a letter prepared by the local director which was sent to one of the local newspapers. The letter included the usual litany of 'Soviet atrocities,' warned of 'revolution and chaos,' attacked the speaker for criticizing the United States, and supported American assistance to the Fijian military.

Responding to union involvement in the anti-nuclear movement and union militancy in general, Mara agreed to allow the Asian-American Free Labor Institute (AAFLI) to open an office in Fiji in late 1984, the culmination of over two years of increased activity in the region by conservative American labour organizations. AAFLI's executive director, Morris Paladino, visited Suva in October 1982 to hold talks with Mara. Early the following year in July 1983, two representatives from the Labour Committee for Pacific Affairs, with close links to American intelligence, also visited Suva. Both the AAFLI and the LCPA subsequently launched a propaganda campaign to win the hearts and minds of regional trade unionists.

In late 1983, the LCPA sponsored an educational tour of the United States for four Fiji trade unionists which included briefings by personnel from the National Security Council and the National Information Center which drew attention to the supposed growing Soviet menace in the region. A short time later another meeting was held between Fijian unionists and LCPA representatives during which the Committee recommended that they establish closer ties with the Israeli labour body Histadrut. Then, in March 1984, the AAFLI and the International Confederation of Free Trade Unions sponsored a seminar in Honolulu for Pacific trade unionists, chaired by Paladino, on priorities for Pacific labour in the 1980s. In September 1984, the AAFLI, with the assistance of the Histadrut and the Israeli-based Afro-Asian Institute, organized a seminar on co-operatives in Suva. Attended by trade unionists from around the region, the AAFLI and the Israelis used the seminar as a venue for very strong lobbying efforts. After the meeting, a few of the trade unionists were sent on a tour to Israel and the head of the Vanuatu Trade Union Congress was sent to the United States.

A short time after this meeting, the AAFLI opened its Suva office. Valentine Suazo, the director of the AAFLI office (which, coincidently, was located next to the World Vision office) had previous experience in Chile, India, and the Philippines.[32] While the initial budget was small, before long it was increased by a few hundred thousand dollars to allow Suazo to carry out an active program throughout the region. In Fiji, in an apparent effort to increase splits within the trade union movement, Suazo sought to court union dissidents from the Fiji Trades Union Congress. He also maintained close links with trade unionists opposed to the founding of the Fiji Labour Party.

One other non-governmental organization that bears mention because of its role in promoting Cold War views in the region is the Asian Pacific Anti-Communist League. Founded in South Korea in 1954 as the Asian Peoples Anti-Communist League, chapters were established in the late 1970s in Fiji and Tonga. Its name was changed to the Asian Pacific Anti-Communist League after its general conference was held in Nadi, Fiji in 1984. While the membership of the Fiji branch was small, it included a number of influential individuals within the Alliance Party and it clearly had the support of Mara. Its 1985 general conference was held in Tonga, with 102 delegates attending from thirty-eight countries, including several from the South Pacific. It was opened with a message from the king of Tonga wishing the delegates well and with keynote addresses by two well-known regional anti-communist crusaders: Fusitu'a of Tonga and Len Usher from Fiji. In his address, Usher sought to raise alarm over supposed Soviet ties to political opponents of the Alliance Party and warned of the danger posed by the new Fiji Labour Party's policy of non-alignment.

Fred Eckert was replaced as American ambassador to Fiji by a foreign affairs professional, Edward Dillery. By this time, the staff of the American embassy in Suva had increased substantially, and soon there were discussions concerning the need to find new, larger premises. U.S. military assistance to Fiji for 1985–86 increased to U.S.$800,000, and in 1986 non-military aid grew to U.S.$1.5 million. If the amount being spent in the country by American-based non-governmental organizations is added, the United States had become one of Fiji's largest aid donors. And even more than the aid from other sources, this was aid that was targeted primarily to assist the Alliance Party and its patronage network.

THE FIJI MILITARY OVERSEAS

As a result of its participation in the Allied campaigns in the Pacific during the Second World War, native Fijians had gained a reputation as loyal soldiers, willing to serve the British empire like the Gurkhas and other so-called 'martial races' of South Asia. When Britain was confronted with the communist insurgency in British Malaya after the war, again it prevailed upon the ever loyal native Fijians, through their chiefs, to fight 'communist terrorists' and support the world-wide crusade against 'godless communism.' When the call for volunteers went out in late 1951, native Fijian villagers responded enthusi-astically.

The First Battalion of the Fiji Infantry Regiment left for Malaya in January 1952, under the command of Lt. Col. Ratu Penaia Ganilau. The Fijian battalion remained in Malaya until June 1956. During that time it suffered twenty-five deaths, while being credited with the highest number of communists killed of any battalion in the cam-paign. In selecting a career in the military, Ganilau was following in the footsteps of Colonel Ratu Sukuna and other young men of chiefly rank. He had received his initial military training in the Fiji Defence Force in 1936 and then served in the army as a regular soldier during the Second World War. Of his early training, Ganilau has this to say: 'The training was tough and strict discipline was enforced ... Anyone who has been through the army will agree that this strict discipline was essential to inculcate into every soldier a sense of loyalty, respect and unquestioning obedience.'[33] These, of course, were the same values that the chiefs desired to promote and maintain among native Fijian commoners, and it is little wonder that the army came to be seen as a key element in the eastern chiefs' campaign to maintain their status within Fiji.

Ganilau became a member of the Legislative Council and then Parliament upon his resumption of civilian life. Representing the chiefly oligarchy form Cakaudrove, he rose to the rank of deputy prime minister and then in February 1983 replaced Ratu George Cakobau as governor general. As a civilian politician he maintained a keen interest in the military and did his best to assist young officers from his home area, among them Sitiveni Rabuka. The second in command of Fiji's Malaya contingent was Lt. Paul Manueli, who was later to become commander of the Fiji Military Forces and an impor-tant figure in the Alliance Party.

During the next fifteen years leading up to independence, the Fijian army was not involved in any further overseas campaigns, but at home it continued to serve as a training ground for young native Fijians in support of chiefly power. More specifically, it was used by the chiefs and colonial authorities in strike-breaking. Thus, during the 1960 cane strike the Executive Council sent native Fijian troops to protect cane farmers who wished to harvest their cane, and native Fijian veterans were organized in Suva to stage a march opposing the strike. The response of many Indo-Fijians was to complain that such a use of troops was serving to increase communal tensions.

During the 1966 Legislative Council election campaign, the spec-tre of armed native Fijians being used against Indo-Fijians was used in an effort to undermine support for militant demands by Indo-

Fijians such as the demand for a common electoral roll. Indo-Fijian political leaders had sought to have a far greater number of Indo-Fijians enlist in the army, which was almost exclusively made up of native Fijians and Europeans, but this was strongly opposed by the chiefs. This issue of Indo-Fijians joining the army was raised in the constitutional negotiations in the late 1960s and re-emerged in elections following independence. As Fiji moved towards independence in the late 1960s, the British suggested getting rid of the army and transforming it into a police force.[34] Mara apparently agreed with this idea, but Ganilau and others in the cabinet felt that it should be retained, arguing that the army was needed to protect native Fijian interests against Indo-Fijians.

After independence, the situation remained more or less the same, with Mara and his cabinet discussing the use of troops on numerous occasions during strikes in the 1970s. At the time of independence, the Fijian army numbered 358 (including thirty officers). The army had doubled in size by 1976 when its strength reached 714 (with forty-four officers). By and large, this growth mirrored the post-independence development of other institutions within Fiji. The status of the army changed dramatically in 1978, when Mara agreed to employ Fijian troops in U.N. peacekeeping activities in the Middle East. The Fijian military contingent in Lebanon or FIJIBATT, as it came to be known, arrived in Lebanon in June 1978, its 500 men under the command of Lt. Col. Ratu Epeli Nailatikau. Its size was increased to 650 in January 1979. The decision to participate in the U.N. peacekeeping forces, as noted in Fiji's Eighth Development Plan, 'involved a significant reorientation and expansion of RFMF resources.'[35] By 1980 the total strength of Fiji's military was 2,000: 1,271 in the Regular Force; 602 in the Territorial Force (for mobilization within forty-eight hours); and 127 in the Naval Squadron (formed in 1975, and comprised of three former U.S. minesweepers and a hydrographic unit). In addition, there was a reserve which could be mobilized if required. Concerning training, the Eighth Development Plan states: 'Army training changed emphasis following the UNIFIL [the U.N. Infantry Force in Lebanon] commitment. Previously emphasis was on conventional operations of war involving tactical study weekends, command post exercises and battalion-level exercise during Annual Camp. This changed in mid-1979 to training for peacekeeping duties and internal security operations.'[36]

Between December 1979 and March 1980 an additional twenty-four Fijian soldiers served in Zimbabwe to assist Britain in monitoring the ceasefire in that country's civil war. Then, in March 1982, Mara agreed to send another 500 soldiers to the Sinai Peninsula to join other U.N. peacekeeping forces. This time, the move was openly criticized by NFP parliamentarians and University of the South Pacific students, concerned over Fiji's growing identification with Israel.

Military personnel are trained in Fiji as well as in Australia, New Zealand, Britain, India, and Malaysia through various bilateral training schemes. Fijian troops gained training experience by joining troops from New Zealand, Britain, and elsewhere who came to Fiji to carry out counter-insurgency exercises. Australia has provided training assistance to Fiji through its defense co-operation program (DCP) since 1972. To this list was added the United States in the early 1980s. American military assistance to Fiji began in 1983 with U.S.$55,000 for training purposes. As was noted above, in 1984 Mara returned from a visit with Reagan in Washington with a promise of an additional U.S.$400,000 in military assistance, and by 1984–85 this amount had doubled. An increasing number of Fijian military personnel also received training in the United States. Thus, in March 1985, military officers from Fiji joined officers from Papua New Guinea, the Solomon Islands, French Polynesia, Tonga, Vanuatu, and fifteen other countries in a Pacific Armies Management Seminar co-hosted by the United States and New Zealand.

Even with foreign assistance and the expenses met by the U.N. (averaging around F$5 million a year during the early 1980s), the cost of maintaining such a large military for Fiji has been considerable, averaging about F$4 million a year. For the Alliance Party and the chiefs, however, this was a small price to pay for the returns in the form of patronage and training of loyal cadre.

From its earliest days, the military has played an important political role in Fiji, first as an instrument of conquest by the eastern chiefs and later as a training and unifying force for the eastern oligarchy. Many of those who became prominent in the Alliance Party had prior military experience, and the military became one of the most important institutions to be brought within the party's patronage network. Moreover, the military remained in the background as a threat to those who would challenge the power of the eastern chiefs. While there was talk of there being only professional soldiers in the military and that the military should remain aloof from politics, the inter-penetrability of the civilian and military establishments meant that many officers identified strongly with the civilian oligarchy.

Among the young native Fijians attracted to a military career was Sitiveni Rabuka. Son of a teacher and a commoner, he was born in southern Vanua Levu in 1948. After attending the élite Queen Victoria School, where he became a top rugby player, he joined many Queen Victoria School graduates and in 1968 enlisted in the army. During the 1970s, he rose quickly through the ranks, undergoing periods of training in New Zealand and serving briefly in 1974 with the Gurkhas in Hong Kong. In 1979 he went to India to attend the Indian Defence Staff College in Tamil Naidu. At the college, he met other officers from around the world and, focusing on Central America and Africa, he wrote a thesis 'on the role of the military in Third World nations, as an interventionist force – in the post-coup period, re-organising a nation and running it.'[37] On his return from India, Rabuka was promoted to lieutenant colonel and sent to Lebanon as UNIFIL Chief of Operations Plans and later made Commander of the First Battalion of the Fiji Infantry Regiment in southern Lebanon. He was posted back to Fiji in 1981 and then, after attending a training course in Australia, joined the Fiji Battalion in the Sinai, where he remained, eventually as battalion commander, until mid-1985. Back in Fiji once again, and despite occasional run-ins with his commanding officers, Rabuka rose to third in order of command of the RFMF. He remained in Fiji and held the post of staff officer in charge of operations and training until May 1987 when this young careerist decided to promote himself to an even higher rank.

CHAPTER FIVE

The Fiji Labour Party

The rise of the Fiji Labour Party came as a surprise to many who had become accustomed to viewing Fiji essentially as a two-party state. True, there were minor parties besides the Alliance and National Federation parties, but these other parties had remained narrow, special interest parties without a national base. Although the NFP had, at times, seemed on the verge of total collapse, it had always bounced back if for no other reason than to claim the vacuum that its departure would have created. For observers of the Fijian political scene, the country's party politics had assumed the regularity of party politics in Australia or the United States. Or so it seemed. Thus, the surprise when a little over three years after the Alliance Party had been returned to power in the 1982 election, a new party had emerged that promised to radically alter the nature of politics in Fiji: the Fiji Labour Party.

How was it possible for such a rapid transformation to occur in what, on the surface, appeared to be such a stable political system? The answer is threefold. First, Fiji's political stability was largely illusory. The Alliance Party had not had an easy time remaining in power and its rule or, more specifically, the rule of the oligarchy constantly required a large degree of coercion and intimidation. Second, the two parties increasingly had become out of touch with the realities of Fijian society in the 1980s. The patronage system of the Alliance Party was under growing strain and it seemed out of touch with a younger generation of native Fijians. Its leader, Ratu Sir Kamasese Mara, had become even more autocratic and more distant from the world of most Fijians as he surrounded himself with a coterie of sychophants. Both parties seemed to be incapable of putting forward new ideas that appealed to a Fijian electorate that was more urbanized, more educated, and increasingly fed up with what it saw as stagnation rather than stability in the political system. Third, there was the presence of an exceptionally strong, dynamic, and well-organized labour movement that was more in tune with the goals and views of many Fijians. Fiji's labour movement, for the most part, had been ignored by political commentators who chose to focus on political parties and communalism. Yet it loomed ever larger in the background of a country with a relatively large percentage of its population employed in wage labour.

The fact that most of Fiji's labour movement was not integrated into the nation's political parties meant that it possessed a degree of political independence. Bids by the Alliance Party to co-opt the leadership of the movement had succeeded in a few instances, but most union leaders resisted what they saw as an attempt to undermine the autonomy and thwart the goals of their unions. The catalyst which was to transform this independence into political action came from two directions. Internally, it was a matter of the union movement becoming more involved in social and economic issues beyond the narrow bounds of concern for conditions at the workplace. Externally, the union leaders were forced to respond to the threat posed by Alliance Party initiatives aimed at breaking the back of what the oligarchy perceived as a movement that had grown too strong. It was a conflict that put economic issues centre stage. This time a weakened NFP was pushed aside by a new political force that was not content to focus on protection of communal interests and which chose instead to offer the voters the prospect of a new Fiji – a more egalitarian, democratic Fiji, where communal politics were to be replaced by class politics. Reaching out to garner the support of other elements within Fiji which were also opposed to the oligarchy, the Fiji Labour Party presented the Alliance Party with an unprecedented challenge.

The immediate origins of the Fiji Labour Party lay in conflicts between the Alliance Party government and organized labour.[1] Since 1977, industrial relations in Fiji had centred around the Tripartite Forum, which included representatives from the government, organized labour (the Fiji Trades Union Congress), and employers (the Fiji Employers' Consultative Association). Its primary aim was to establish wage guidelines each year, although it dealt with a range of other issues as well. Almost all unions came to accept the role of the Tripartite Forum, as did the government and a growing number of employers. An additional important element in the structure of industrial relations was the system of arbitration. A full-time permanent arbitrator was appointed in December 1982 and a relatively large number of cases were taken before the arbitrator for settlement.

Virtually all government employees are unionized and these unions are the largest and most powerful in the country. Most notable is the Fiji Public Service Association (FPSA), which is the largest union in Fiji (with over 7,000 members) and which came to assume a leading national role in raising issues related to employment conditions and to broader social concerns. It and other unions, however, had disavowed any desire to become directly involved in politics.

The Fijian economy underwent a brief boom around 1979 and 1980, in large part because of a substantial increase in revenue from sugar sales. The boom was shortlived and was accompanied by a higher rate of inflation (from 6.1 per cent in 1978 to 14.5 per cent in 1980). The economy then entered a recession. The growth rate was less than 0.5 per cent in 1982. The situation was made even worse in 1983 by two cyclones and a drought. The result was a decline in Fiji's GDP of around 5 per cent. The international price of sugar hit a postwar low in mid-1983 (Fiji is only partially covered by long-term contracts). Fiji's balance-of-payments situation worsened and this and other financial difficulties led the government in late 1983 to introduce a fairly stringent budget that contained tariff increases and an income tax surcharge.

Between 1981 and 1982, the government had placed a virtual freeze on new positions and failed to fill many existing posts. Government hiring in the civil service subsequently remained at a very low level and there was a substantial reduction in the unestablished work-force. At the same time, there was very little hiring in the private sector and redundancies, sometimes on a relatively large scale, became increasingly commonplace. In particular, many foreign firms initiated rationalization moves that entailed laying off large numbers of (mainly unionized) workers. Thus, the permanent arbitrator's first case involved establishing compensation for 188 redundant employees of the Australian-owned firm, Burns Philp. For the first time, unemployment became a significant issue in Fiji.

In early 1980, the FPSA and the Public Service Commission found themselves at loggerheads over a dispute concerning the carrying out of a job evaluation. A dispute was registered with the Ministry of Labour and in May agreement was reached to carry out an evaluation 'covering the classification, grading and structures' of all posts in the civil service. The review committee, known as the Public Service Review Team, submitted its report in mid-1982.[2] It promptly met with protests from all sides. Fiscal conservatives cared little for the financial implications. The report was attacked by the FPSA and others for seeking to widen the gap between those at the top and those at the bottom of the salary scale.

Negotiations between the FPSA and Public Service Commission over implementation of the report went on throughout the latter half of 1982. The main point of contention was the date to implement the pay increases. The FPSA and the cabinet had agreed in May 1980 to abide by the recommendations made by the Review Team in July 1981. When the report actually was submitted in July 1982, the Public Service Commission asked unions to accept an implementation date of January 1983. At this point, the FPSA was becoming increasingly critical of the attitude of employers and the government towards pay increases. At the FPSA's annual general meeting in March, its general secretary, Mahendra Chaudhry, stated that workers were being asked at every opportunity to make sacrifices in the interest of the nation while employers and the government were doing little to tackle the economic problems facing Fiji. Noting that employers in the private sector were not prepared to reduce their profit margins, he complained that the Tripartite Forum was becoming nothing more than 'a vehicle for restraining the income of workers.'

During the latter part of 1982, opposition to unions by employers and politicians became more strident. In December, the prime minister proposed a wage freeze. Employers' groups such as Fiji Employers' Consultative Association as well as various chambers of commerce and many members of the opposition party were quick to voice their support, citing the need to think of the rural poor and of companies facing financial difficulties. Politicians and employers began to tell unions to accept the freeze or face massive redundancies. Thus, economic difficulties became an excuse for anti-union rhetoric and calls for limitations on union power. The truce that had been more or less in place since 1977 was threatening to fall apart.

The union response to Mara's call for a wage freeze was a mixed one, although all the unions indicated their faith that existing structures were capable of handling the emerging crisis. A few unions, seeing no alternative, accepted wage freezes independently. Among those most vocal in their opposition to the proposed freeze were white-collar unions such as the FPSA and the Fiji Bank Employees' Union. Chaudhry had argued for some time that Fiji's relatively high wages had contributed to economic growth and favoured expansionary economic policies on the part of the government. In contrast, the Public Employees Union, whose general secretary, Joveci Gavoka, was staunchly loyal to Mara, initially supported the idea of a freeze.

Negotiations between the FPSA and the Public Service Commission continued in 1983, with the FPSA twice threatening to go on strike. No progress was made until August, when both parties agreed to go to arbitration. Later in the same month the government asked its employees to forgo the 1983 Cost of Living Adjustment that had been agreed to by the Tripartite Forum in June, claiming its inability to pay the F$4.5 million involved. Chaudhry's response was that the Tripartite Forum guidelines had shown considerable restraint and had been agreed to by all parties after careful consideration, and he added that about one-third of the money would go back to the government in taxes.

The Fiji Trades Union Congress (FTUC) and other unions rallied behind the FPSA. Even FTUC General Secretary James Raman spoke out against those seeking to make 'the workers the whipping boy for factors for which they are not responsible.'[3] On the other side, there was also considerable solidarity, within the context of a call by Mara for a 'government of national unity.' The leader of the opposition, Jai Ram Reddy, voicing the position of the Indo-Fijian business community, stated that 'it was a pity that while 1,500 sugar workers and many other workers faced redundancy, civil servants were going to arbitration for implementation of a pay report.'[4] In the same speech, he suggested temporarily abolishing minimum-wage guidelines. The pressure clearly was on to divide workers over issues of pay and redundancies.

Shortly after presentation of the controversial 1984 budget in November 1983, the FPSA membership again voted to go on strike. Under pressure from the FPSA and other unions, the Senate agreed in December to pay out a portion of what was due. Then, in late December, the permanent arbitrator issued a decision that was generally favourable to the FPSA. The FPSA responded by warning the government not to delay any longer. Meanwhile, a dispute was heating up between white-collar public sector unions and the government over announced plans to reduce staff and curtail hiring of new staff. In late February 1984, graduating education students went on a hunger strike to protest a decision by Minister of Education Ahmed Ali not to hire 134 newly qualified teachers. As it looked as if the strike could escalate, a compromise was reached. In March, however, the minister of finance announced that the government job freeze would last for another two years. He also noted that the government was considering farming out more tasks to the private sector.

The back pay for January and February 1984, alone, was paid out in March. Continued delays in paying the remainder and increasing attacks on unionists in Parliament and elsewhere led to a further deterioration of relations between the government and the FPSA with Chaudhry at one point accusing the government of 'bureaucratic bungling,' 'misguided management,' and 'unethical negotiating tactics.'[5] When the government announced in June that it wanted to pay out the remaining amount over a four-year period starting in June 1985, the FPSA responded that it wanted the entire amount paid in 1984 and filed a strike notice. The strike notice was turned down by the minister of employment and industrial relations, who was the former trade unionist Mohammed Ramzan, and the dispute was referred back to the Tripartite Forum's Consultative Committee.

The FPSA stated that it would look for alternative ways to force the government to act. Then, some 1,200 members of the Lautoka branch of the FPSA voted to impose a work-to-rule overtime ban in protest of the government's action. On 4 July, the FPSA announced that it would go on strike in defiance of the rejection of its strike notice if necessary, setting 1 August as the date. This forced the Public Service Commission to resume negotiations and, by August, a compromise was reached involving payment in installments in cash and government bonds. This matter out of the way, the FPSA turned its attention to the 1983 Cost of Living Adjustment and the government's claimed inability to pay. Submissions from the government and unions were placed before the Tripartite Forum's Inability to Pay Committee in late August. To the obvious embarrassment of the government the unions won this case as well, in part, because of the poor quality of the government's submission. And yet to come was implementation of the 1984 Cost of Living Adjustment that had been agreed to by the Tripartite Forum earlier in the year.

The struggle surrounding implementation of the Public Service Review Team's recommendations and the 1983 Cost of Living Adjustment placed a great deal of strain on the existing system of industrial relations. The unions clearly had out-manoeuvred the government. As unionists proved increasingly adept at using the system, the government seemed to be changing its mind about its utility. Towards the end of the Review Team negotiations, and coming hard on a serious strike at Nadi airport, a *Fiji Times* editorial referred to the 'drift mentality' that appeared to be present in Fiji's industrial relations.[6] The government seemed increasingly uncertain of itself, and trade unionists were becoming more sceptical of the government's willingness to abide by promises made in the course of negotiations. The sense of drift was soon, and very abruptly, to come to an end.

On 9 November 1984, the minister of finance presented the government's budget for 1985. Included in the speech was the announcement of an immediate wage freeze. A closely guarded secret, the announcement of the freeze came with no prior warning. The minister estimated that the freeze would save the government F$14 million, reduce the level of imports, and contribute to the country's economic recovery. His justification included reference to an International Monetary Fund report that stated that Fiji's salaries were 15 per cent too high. The freeze was supported enthusiastically by the various groups representing employers and by members of the opposition (although the NFP used the opportunity to blame the government for getting itself into a situation where it felt a freeze was necessary). The union response was one of outrage. Chaudhry referred to the freeze as a 'stab in the back' that allowed manufacturers to continue to 'line their pockets' and made a 'complete mockery' of the 1984 Tripartite Forum agreement. Similar responses were voiced by other trade union leaders.[7]

The FTUC executive met shortly after the announcement to discuss options for a united action in response to the freeze. They were especially upset over two issues: the failure of the government to discuss the freeze through the Tripartite Forum and the fact that the freeze contravened the 1984 Cost of Living Adjustment agreement that had been signed by Mara. Most of those present at the meeting, representing thirty-four of Fiji's unions and some 50,000 workers, supported the idea of a general strike, if necessary. But, first, it was decided to hold talks with the prime minister himself.

FTUC General Secretary Raman and Mara held informal talks, but to no avail. A short time later the prime minister addressed Parliament to reiterate the government's firmness on the freeze, while asserting that he still saw the Tripartite Forum as a viable and effective body. At a meeting the same day, the FTUC decided to pull out of the Tripartite Forum. Raman stated that the FTUC would refuse to participate in the Forum as long as the freeze remained. The FTUC leadership also decided to hold a series of public meetings in December in Lautoka, Labasa, and Suva to canvass opinions concerning the proposed general strike. The government's response was to propose an economic summit in January to which trade unions would be invited to participate. This proposal met with little sympathy from the unions. At a meeting of the FTUC the following day, a motion proposed by Chaudhry to call a general strike was passed unanimously.

The freeze triggered more than the threat of a general strike or a breakdown in the structure of industrial relations. The FTUC leadership also announced plans to form a political party: the Fiji Labour

Party. The idea of forming a labour party was not a new one. It had been broached by Dinsukh Lal Morarji, representing the airport workers at Nadi, and discussed by other unionists in the late 1970s. But the idea did not get very far. As late as early September 1984, Raman, long an outspoken advocate of unions staying out of politics, had addressed a regional seminar on co-operation sponsored by the Asian-American Free Labor Institute where he emphasized the need for trade unions to remain politically neutral. In this speech, he also urged unions to avoid becoming overly militant and to stay clear of activities that might threaten the government. Raman himself was closely identified with the Alliance Party and there was considerable speculation about his own political aspirations. Other trade unionists, however, were talking behind the scenes of the need for labour to have a political base of its own (obviously they could not use the NFP).

Since the late 1970s, there were several important developments within the trade union movement which contributed to the possibility of such a rapid change of policy on the part of the movement's leadership. For one thing, while many of the union militants in the 1970s had ceased to discuss political options in the open, except to express a willingness to work with existing parties, sympathy for ideas such as forming a labour party had not disappeared. In addition, there were younger trade union militants coming on the scene who felt less constrained by the spirit of compromise adopted by the older leaders and who tended to have less sympathy for the apolitical ideology that had come to be accepted by those in leadership positions. Also significant was the growing interest of white-collar union leaders like Chaudhry, Timoci Bavadra (also from the FPSA), and Bob Kumar (from the Fiji Bank Employees' Union) in broader social, economic, and political issues such as the role of transnational corporations and the anti-nuclear movement.

Involvement in the anti-nuclear movement proved to be important in helping to improve relations between unionists and other liberal forces in Fiji and to rebuild ties with left-leaning trade union elements elsewhere. One avenue for this was the Pacific Trade Union Forum – essentially the creation of a few Australian trade unionists like Bill Richardson, Cliff Dolan, and, especially, John Halfpenny – which held its first meeting in Nadi in November 1980. The Pacific Trade Union Forum was founded primarily to oppose testing of nuclear weapons and dumping of nuclear wastes in the Pacific. It also became involved in supporting the independence movements in New Caledonia and French Polynesia. Through the Pacific Trade Union Forum, relations with the New Zealand Federation of Labour, which had been strained under the previous FTUC leadership, had improved. Observers from the USSR were at the 1984 meeting (the United States declined to participate). Creation of the Pacific Trade Union Forum and increased union involvement in the anti-nuclear movement were important factors for increased American interest in South Pacific trade unions, with an aim to manipulating or undermining them. It was the key factor behind the decision to establish an Asian-American Free Labor Institute office in Suva in late 1984.

After lobbying efforts by the American ambassador, in mid-1983 Prime Minister Mara had decided to reverse government policy and allow nuclear-powered and/or armed American warships to visit Fiji. Academics, church leaders, and trade unionists responded by organizing the Fiji Anti-Nuclear Group (FANG) in August 1983. FANG quickly became a venue for public criticism of the Alliance Party's foreign policy. Significantly, trade unionist Bob Kumar was elected president in 1983 and re-elected in 1984.[8]

FANG held a public meeting on the eve of the FTUC's first anti-freeze rally that served to spark speculation about the emergence of a labour party. FANG had called the meeting in response to Prime Minister Mara's forthcoming visit to the United States. The meeting was addressed by Chaudhry, and the FTUC provided funds to bring two speakers from overseas (one of them being former Fiji trade unionist James Anthony).

On 5 December, speakers at the FTUC's first public meeting to discuss the freeze in Lautoka raised the idea of forming a labour party. Chaudhry urged consideration of such a step to counter 'the ganging up of the government and opposition against workers.' By this time, even Raman's position had shifted (in part, because of pressure from within his own union), and he stated that the FTUC would form a labour party if it appeared that there was no alternative. Other speakers accused the government of moving towards a 'dictatorship.' By the next day, at the meeting held in Labasa, the idea of forming a labour party seemed to have gained widespread acceptance among the trade union leaders involved, including Raman, who stated that 'we have to become political to defend the honour of workers.' By the time of the Suva meeting on the twelfth, formation of a labour party was virtually taken for granted. Raman talked at the meeting of how difficult it had been for him to support leaving the Tripartite Forum and to urge the union movement to move directly into politics, but few others expressed such difficulty.[9]

At an executive meeting of the FTUC on 15 December, Mahendra Sukhdeo (general secretary of the National Union of Municipal Workers) presented a motion to form the Fiji Labour Party. The motion was passed unanimously and the Board of Management of the FTUC was directed to draw up a party manifesto for the FTUC's biennial conference in May of the following year. In a newspaper interview, Sukhdeo outlined some of the items likely to be included in the platform: a strong anti-corruption bill, tougher immigration laws, improvements for rural people, increased social welfare projects, an overhaul of all labour legislation, job creation programs, greater encouragement of local production and import substitution, a non-aligned foreign policy, and support for a nuclear-free Pacific as well as for independence movements in New Caledonia and French Polynesia.[10]

The initial response from outside of the labour movement was predictable. Both political parties indicated that they did not see the proposed labour party as a threat. One senator from Lau, sometimes seen as a mouthpiece for Mara, argued that those advocating the new party were trying to undermine Fiji's ties with the United States, and the spectre of Soviet support for the labour party was raised. The Special Branch, which was responsible for state security, announced that it was looking 'for signs of foreign infiltration by activists, like communists' and that it would carefully watch the activities of those involved in forming the party. Former trade unionists in parliament like Apisai Tora and Jim Smith were relatively silent. In private, of course, there was much more discussion, and politicians affiliated with the NFP, in particular, seemed concerned that the proposed labour party might erode their support.

In early January 1985, Mara's attacks on the unions became even more strident. On 8 January he stated that the threatened national strike was aimed at toppling his government and that he would call on the army and police if necessary to keep the country running. This was followed by a government propaganda campaign to support the wage freeze and attack the FTUC with slogans such as: 'Think Fiji First' and 'Why a Wage Freeze Will Help Our Country.' The FTUC set 12 February as the date to begin the general strike. Mara responded by stating that he would not talk with the unions until the strike threat was lifted. The FTUC agreed to lift the threat temporarily and on 16 January a meeting was held between Mara and the FTUC executive. The FTUC suggested compromises, but it was clear that Mara was not interested. Then, Fiji was hit by two successive cyclones on the seventeenth and nineteenth that did considerable damage. Effectively, this put an end to any serious push for a general strike. It provided the FTUC with an excuse to back down without losing face, while Mara was able to use it as an opportunity to call for 'national unity' and talk of the need for 'restraint.'

When the two cyclones struck in mid-January, the government announced that it intended to pursue the idea of a national economic summit, to be held in February, and invited over two hundred delegates to attend. The government asked the FTUC to send representatives, but the union body's executive announced that it would boycott the summit, stating that it would hold a rival economic summit. The NFP followed the FTUC and declared that it would not be attending either. In his address to the government summit, Mara alluded to recent riots in Jamaica over implementation of International Monetary Fund policies and warned of 'economic disintegration and chaos' if his government's policies were not implemented.

The FTUC's alternative economic summit was held on 3–4 May. It provided a venue for criticizing government economic policies and repeating justifications for the union movement's decision to become directly involved in the political process. A nine-page communiqué dealt with issues related to job creation and offered alternatives to the wage and salary freeze. Noting that workers paid the largest share of taxes, it also made suggestions for tax reform.

In his address to the FTUC's biennial conference in May 1985, Raman stated that the union movement was in danger of breaking up: 'We see signs of cracks – by fighting external forces, we are cracking up from within.'[11] Plans to launch a labour party and debate over how to respond to the wage freeze and related issues had put the labour movement under a strain the likes of which it had not experienced in a number of years. This was especially true for unions with large native Fijian memberships, which were being lobbied strongly by the Alliance Party. There was significant disagreement within the FTUC executive, although an effort was made to put on a united front in public.

Despite disagreements, most of the more important unions in the FTUC remained united. Moreover, there were signs of growing unity among the white-collar unions. Relations between the teachers' unions and the minister of education remained strained and on 26 February the unions decided to go on strike over a Ministry plan to hire volunteer teachers at low salaries. The strike began on 28 February and lasted until 13 March, when it was agreed to take the dispute to arbitration. Not only had the two teachers' unions acted closely in the dispute, but they had been actively supported by the FPSA, which had placed a 'blackban' on the offices of the Ministry of Education.

In February, Fijian trade unionists began discussions concerning establishment of a confederation of public sector unions similar to

New Zealand's Combined State Union in order to provide a united front over pay claims. Plans to form such a confederation reflected frustration by the majority of the trade union leaders with the more conservative members of the FTUC executive (such as James Raman and Jale Toki), but these leaders did not see the confederation as an alternative to the FTUC. The Confederation of Public Sector Unions was formed in mid-April. Timoci Bavadra, president of the FPSA, was elected president and Mahendra Chaudhry was elected general secretary.

In late March, the Senate passed a motion urging a tightening of labour legislation, especially the Trade Dispute Act. During the debate, Mara's 'mouthpiece' from Lau, Senator Inoke Tabua, accused the unions of receiving support from Cuba, the Soviet Union, and Libya. Around the same time, government pressure forced the International Labour Organisation to withdraw its financial support for an FTUC seminar on 'Social and Political Options for Trade Unions.' The Alliance Party stepped up its efforts to woo native Fijian unionists. On 17 March, Deputy Prime Minister David Toganivalu attacked the proposal to form a labour party in an address to native Fijian dockworkers and employees of the Ports Authority. He appealed to them along ethnic lines saying, 'nothing can destroy Fijian solidarity.'[12] More direct means of intimidation were employed as well. In early April, the Public Service Commission warned that civil servants who took an active role in politics would face disciplinary action.

The most important attack on union militants was to come from Joveci Gavoka and his Public Employees Union. At the Public Employees Union's annual general meeting on 31 March, Gavoka criticized the FTUC for not helping to fight redundancies and also criticized white-collar unions for lining their own pockets while ignoring the needs of blue-collar workers. He announced plans to form a national organization, which by implication was to compete with the FTUC and act as a counter to the Confederation of Public Sector Unions, and which would undermine support for the proposed labour party. Over the next couple of months, Gavoka and a few other union leaders sought to gain support for the idea of a new national body by playing up real and supposed differences between blue- and white-collar workers and by appealing to communal sentiments.

The Confederation of Blue Collar Workers Unions was launched in early June. The meeting was chaired by Jim Smith, an NFP member of Parliament and general secretary of the timber workers' union. In addition to Gavoka, also prominent at the meeting were Isimeli Volavola of the hotel workers' union and Taniela Veitata of the dockworkers' union. The new confederation was to be 'non-political' and the FTUC was criticized for seeking to launch a labour party without first 'cleaning up its own backyard.' Those involved in the initiative, Jim Smith in particular, were closely associated with the local Asian-American Free Labor Institute representative, Valentine Suazo, and evidence points to his having played a major role in its formation. Speculation was that Mara planned to promote the confederation as a replacement to the FTUC should the FTUC remain obstinate, but this never eventuated as the confederation failed to get off the ground.

The position of the NFP to the proposed labour party was mixed and reflected growing factional splits within the NFP. In December 1983, party leader Reddy walked out of Parliament after a heated exchange with the speaker, vowing not to return until the speaker was replaced. Reddy resigned as leader of the opposition in April 1984. A heated contest for leadership of the NFP followed between one-time leader Siddiq Koya and his longtime rival Irene Jai Narayan. Koya was able to outmanoeuvre Narayan for leadership of the party, but the battle left the NFP badly divided once again. After Narayan was unanimously elected deputy leader, Koya refused to allow her access to the office of the leader of the opposition even though she had been allowed to use the office by Reddy.

At the annual NFP conference in September 1984, Koya refused to accept Mumtatz Ali, who was associated with non-Koya forces, as party secretary. A short time later, Koya refused to allow the NFP Youth Wing, also associated with non-Koya members, entry to a working committee meeting of the party. This action inflamed already difficult relations within the NFP as Koya was accused of attempting to assert dictatorial rule over the party. The factional fighting worsened when it came time to find a replacement to stand for the Lautoka Indian communal seat in the May 1985 by-election, a seat left vacant by Reddy's resignation. Koya chose one of his supporters, Dr. Balwant Singh Rakkha, to stand for the seat. The Youth Wing decided to challenge him by putting up their own candidate, Davendra Singh. Koya turned the election into a referendum on his leadership and offered to resign should his candidate lose. In a light turnout (4,421 of 12,260 registered voters), Davendra Singh was elected by a vote of 2,209 to 2,196. Koya refused to resign and factional fighting within the NFP worsened, to the point of occasional outbreaks of violence. Fresh from its victory, the Youth Wing announced that it would have its own candidate stand for Koya's seat in the next election.

Koya's faction went to court over the outcome of the by-election (eventually losing the case) and Koya barred the Youth Wing parliamentarian from attending a meeting of other NFP members of Parliament. In June, a Youth Wing member stated that they would consider joining forces with the Alliance Party or the proposed labour party. He noted that their policies seemed compatible with those of the labour party. In an effort to patch things up, the seven native Fijian and General Elector NFP members of Parliament threatened to break away from the party unless differences between the Youth Wing and Koya factions were overcome. But there was little chance of this. Reddy resigned as party president in August, withdrawing from any active participation in the NFP, and Koya had managed to have Narayan replaced as deputy leader by Koresi Matatolu. The NFP was more deeply divided than ever and, quietly, some senior Indo-Fijian NFP parliamentarians began exploring possibilities for themselves in the proposed labour party. Among these was Vijay Singh, who was also president of the large cane growers' association, the Kisan Sangh.

By April 1985, factional in-fighting in the cane fields had come to involve a three-way struggle focusing on the newly formed Sugar Cane Growers Council that had been established to represent cane growers. Koya and his supporters within the NFP had sought to have the council set up primarily to strengthen their own position among cane growers. But once the council was established they ran into difficulty controlling it. Koya's bid for leadership of the council was opposed in late April by a candidate backed by the Youth Wing of the NFP. This threat was easily overcome, but in late May more serious problems emerged. There was widespread opposition to a proposed F$535,000 budget prepared by Koya ally, Shardha Nand. Protest erupted again when Koya urged growers in 1985 to accept a lower price for cane from the Fiji Sugar Corporation. This time anti-Koya forces within the NFP, led by Vijay Singh, were joined by the pro-labour National Farmers Union, which was closely identified with Chaudhry. This gave rise to speculation over a Chaudhry-Singh political alliance. Such speculation was fueled in early June, when Vijay Singh made a call in Parliament for support of the reforms proposed at the FTUC economic summit. The spectre of an alliance between these two men had some of those involved in formation of the labour party worried. They feared an attempt by Singh to move into the leadership of the party. As one person put it: 'We don't need the NFP's liabilities.'

THE LAUNCHING OF THE FIJI LABOUR PARTY

The Fiji Labour Party was launched after the National Federation

Party had ceased to function as an effective opposition. The Alliance Party viewed the crumbling of the NFP under Koya's leadership almost with glee. But the lack of formal opposition had done little to lessen growing popular opposition to the Alliance Party throughout the country. There were numerous minor issues of concern to people such as Mara's reversal of the country's anti-nuclear policies and Minister of Education Ahmed Ali's high-handed manner in dealing with teacher employment. But the most important concerns were about the Alliance Party's economic policies and growing evidence of government corruption. There were numerous complaints that senior members of the Alliance Party were using their positions to enhance personal fortunes. This was given credence by the rapidly improving life-styles of many of those in government. Rumours abounded about shady loans from national financial institutions to Alliance Party officials and the line between politics and business had become excessively blurred. After the recent cyclones, the name of the prime minister's Hurricane Relief Committee had taken on a new meaning to many.

As the date for the launching of the Fiji Labour Party drew near, there were behind-the-scenes debates, schemes, and political manoeuvrings focusing on the constitution policies of the party, and the crucial question of party leadership. Many of those involved were anxious to ensure that the party did not become 'just another NFP.' At the heart of this was the ethnic question – could the Fiji Labour Party avoid becoming nothing more than a replacement for the NFP? Could it avoid becoming essentially an Indo-Fijian party? The NFP had continually tried to break out of its communal mould but failed. Many were optimistic about the proposed labour party because it appeared that the union movement itself had been able to move somewhat away from communalism, despite concerted efforts by those in power outside of the movement to divide it along communal lines.

Despite initial worries, the question of party leadership was decided smoothly. Unionists, academics, and others involved in the party came to an agreement with surprisingly little difficulty. Dr. Timoci Bavadra was elected party president without opposition at the launching of the Fiji Labour Party in Suva on 6 July 1985. Bavadra, 52 years old, was an indigenous Fijian commoner from western Viti Levu who had been born at Namoli village near Lautoka. He had studied medicine in New Zealand and at the Fiji School of Medicine and began his career in medicine in 1960 at Lautoka Hospital. Subsequently, he served as a doctor in several parts of the country as well as in the Solomon Islands. He was an active member of the Fiji Public Service Association and had served as its president since 1977. Bavadra was a member of the Ba Provincial Council and had been a member of the Alliance Party. He had resigned his position as assistant director of primary and preventive health services on 24 June and turned down a job offer from the World Health Organisation to become president of the Fiji Labour Party.

Bob Kumar, general secretary of the Fiji Bank Employees' Union and an Indo-Fijian from Suva, was selected as treasurer. Krishna Datt, general secretary of the Fiji Teachers Union, a longtime school teacher in the Suva area and an Indo-Fijian from the northern island of Vanua Levu, was chosen as party secretary. And Mahendra Chaudhry was made assistant general secretary. Twelve vice-presidents were selected. They were drawn largely from the trade union movement, but not exclusively, and it was widely recognized that an effort had to be made to move the party beyond its trade union base if it was to become a viable political force. Attention was also paid to achieving a sufficient ethnic mix to ensure that the party would not be seen as being 'Indian-dominated' and that it would be seen to embody the principle of non-racialism. These office holders formed the National Council of the Fiji Labour Party.

In his address at the launching of the party, newly elected president Timoci Bavadra outlined some of the proposed policies of the party: (1) a commitment to democratic socialism, (2) multiracialism, (3) 'putting an end to the many undemocratic features that dominate the political life of Fiji,' (4) 'ensuring that the shortcomings and benefits of the national economy are more equitably shared,' (5) nationalization of select industries (including Emperor Gold Mine), (6) taking steps to end corruption, (7) ensuring 'that free education for the poor becomes a reality,' (8) creation of a more independent judiciary, (9) creation of more employment and improvement of conditions for poorer workers, and (10) an active foreign policy of nonalignment and strong support for a nuclear-free Pacific.

By international standards this may not appear to be too radical a platform, but in the context of Fiji and the South Pacific as a whole it represented a major step in the development of progressive politics. The Fiji Labour Party became the first political party in the region to advocate the goals of democratic socialism when both of Fiji's major political parties were becoming more conservative. Its call for a nonaligned foreign policy came at a time when Prime Minister Mara was turning Fiji into little more than an agent of American interests in the South Pacific. The Labour Party's policies were also significant for their break with the 'culturalist' ideology, commonly labelled the 'Pacific Way' that continued to dominate the ideologies of most political parties in the region.[13] The Labour Party recognized the importance of 'tradition' in Fiji, but sought to place this within a progressive framework.

At its first meeting, the National Council elected a management board which was to handle most of the day-to-day affairs of the party. It met formally about once a month, and most of its members stayed in fairly regular contact with one another on an informal basis. The management board was almost exclusively drawn from the union movement. It consisted of Bavadra, Kumar, Chaudhry, and vice-presidents James Raman, Joeli Kalou, Emma Druavesi, David Eyre, and Tupeni Baba (the only non-unionist).

THE 1985 ELECTIONS

The Fiji Labour Party was very quickly faced with the need to test its electoral support. In November and December 1985, there were to be council elections in the main towns of Fiji, starting with the capital of Suva on 16 November, and two national by-elections for the North-Central Indian national seat and the Lau-Rotuma Fijian communal seat. The Lau-Rotuma seat was in an Alliance Party stronghold (including the home island of the prime minister) and the North-Central seat had a history of being closely contested by the NFP and the Alliance Party.[14] After some debate, the Labour Party decided to contest all of the elections. This was at a time when the party was only a few weeks old, but it was felt that it was important to maintain the momentum that had begun in late 1984.

The tendency in public was for Alliance and NFP politicians to dismiss the Labour Party. Its chances of appealing to voters in the two by-elections were said to be minimal since, so it was argued, the Labour Party was an urban-based party. The Alliance Party also tried to brand the Labour Party as an Indo-Fijian party that was opposed to native Fijian interests. In private, however, many politicians were worried, including the prime minister. Labour Party supporters were harassed constantly and the Alliance Party attempted to keep the party from receiving press coverage. While the intimidation did succeed in making some people afraid of openly supporting the Labour Party (for example, Labour Party T-shirts were widely sold, but many people expressed fear of wearing them in public), and there was some suppression of press coverage (especially by the government-owned radio station), by and large, the tactics were unsuccessful. In fact, Labour Party coverage in the newspapers was surprisingly good, and there was evidence of resentment of government tactics employed against the Labour Party.

Meanwhile, factional quarrelling within the NFP remained intense. Members of the anti-Koya faction began to seriously explore options outside of the NFP. These included joining the Alliance Party, joining the Labour Party, or forming a party of their own. While some seemed to favour joining the Alliance Party, the majority did not. A meeting was held with representatives of the Labour Party to discuss a possible merger. For the Labour Party, this presented something of a crisis. After considerable debate, the Labour Party decided against allowing the NFP dissidents to join the Labour Party. An important factor in this decision was the fear of giving credence to Alliance Party claims that the Labour Party was 'just another Indian party.' There was also a problem of ideological differences. As one native Fijian supporter of the Labour Party put it: 'We represent the workers, peasants and poor of Fiji while these people represent the capitalists.' Such a class perspective represented a novelty in the Fijian political consciousness and was indicative of some of the changes going on within the electorate.

The first test of electoral support for the Labour Party came with the Suva City Council election on 16 November. The Suva City Council had a long history of corruption, mismanagement, and domination by a small segment of the business community. To ensure their control of the council, local business interests had pushed through a voting procedure whereby companies were eligible to nominate three voters. Moreover, city council elections in the past had often been subject to widespread registration and voting fraud. The Labour Party faced other hurdles as well. Some of its prospective candidates were forced to withdraw by their employers or as a result of other forms of pressure. One withdrew when it was claimed that she was not registered – a claim that was later proved false. As a result, several of the final Labour Party candidates to stand for election were selected only at the last minute, and in many areas, the Labour Party was not able to play an active role in voter registration. Added to this was the fact that the Labour Party had very little money to fund a campaign, in contrast to the other parties, and the Labour Party's prospects did not seem too promising.

Despite the handicaps faced by the Labour Party, and public disclaimers to the contrary, both the NFP and the Alliance Party were worried about the election. Both parties launched campaigns of unprecedented intensity with major national political figures, including Prime Minister Mara, taking an active part. The press contained photos of Alliance Party politicians sitting on dirt floors in squatter shacks (which not too long before they had been trying to remove) and escorting Prince Charles and Lady Diana (who paid a timely visit to Fiji in light of the extent to which the oligarchy had sought to use British royalty to bolster its own position among native Fijians). The two parties were able to raise considerable amounts of money for their campaigns, while the Labour Party continued to face a shortage of funds. The Alliance Party was also able to swell the electoral roll with a large number of voters from out of town during the celebration of the 150th anniversary of the Methodist church in Fiji, which attracted visitors from all over the country. Both the NFP and Alliance Party also made liberal use of corporate nominations of voters.

The NFP, however, was plagued by internal divisions. The most serious of these arose when all NFP candidates associated with Koya rival Narayan and representing Gujarati business interests decided to stand as independents in one of the city's four wards (each ward elects five members of the city council). In their campaign, they were assisted by other anti-Koya members of the NFP.

The Labour Party campaign focused on issues with appeal to a large segment of the population. Its manifesto promised to promote dialogue between the people and the administration, to provide an honest administration, to create employment for unemployed youth, to assist in crime prevention, to improve the level of hygiene and sanitation for squatter settlements, to keep the city clean, to provide more recreational facilities, and to rationalize the use of city funds and properties. These were not earth-shattering promises, but they offered, what seemed to many voters, a credible alternative.

On election day, the NFP and the Alliance Party were able to provide far more transport than the Labour Party to bring voters to the polls. Thus, in one ward, where the NFP was particularly confident of winning, it provided around sixty passenger vehicles. The Alliance Party provided a similar number of vehicles, as well as some buses. The Labour Party was only able to garner about two-dozen passenger vehicles. Both of the major parties gave out free hats, T-shirts, cigarettes, and drinks. The Labour Party was not able to match this generosity. The prime minister and other prominent parliamentarians (with the notable exception of Koya) spent the day touring the polling booths. Each of the parties expressed confidence that they were doing well. The day before, one of the newspapers had predicted that the Labour Party would gain a large percentage of the votes, but this was dismissed by the other two parties.

The outcome gave eight seats to the Fiji Labour Party, seven seats to the Alliance Party, five seats to the independents, and none to the NFP. The distribution of votes was: 24,260 for the Alliance Party, 23,224 for the Labour Party, 6,313 for the NFP, and 6,082 for the independents. Significantly, over 60 per cent of the voters had passed through the Alliance Party voting sheds – and then a large number voted for the Labour Party. This was seen as a significant blow since, traditionally, those who passed through a party's voting shed to receive its voting cards and other handouts were then expected to vote for that party. What had happened was that some voters (native Fijian voters, especially) had been unwilling to make a public show of their opposition to the Alliance Party, while others had simply used the transportation provided by the Alliance Party to get to the polls and vote against it.

Newspaper headlines the following day in the two English-language dailies read: 'Fed Wiped Out in Poll' and 'Feds Crash: Labour Rocks Major Parties,' the latter followed by a photo of some leading NFP politicians with the caption, 'the face of defeat.' Prime Minister Mara expressed surprise and complained of people accepting the hospitality of the Alliance Party and then voting for the Labour Party before he went into seclusion to recover from the shock. Some Alliance Party politicians also sought to portray what had happened as a swing by Indo-Fijian voters away from the NFP, ignoring the fact that a large number of indigenous Fijians had also voted for the Labour Party. Said another Alliance Party politician: 'I am shocked and I still can't make out what went wrong.' Their dismay reflected the strong possibility of a Labour Party member becoming the next mayor of Suva, and then members of the two major political parties would find it more difficult to use city council patronage and funds.

As subsequent events were to confirm, the Suva City Council election signalled the emergence of the Fiji Labour Party as a major political force in Fiji, as well as signalling the end for the NFP. After the results in Suva, the Labour Party felt that it stood a good chance of winning seats in other municipal elections. On 14 December it won five of twelve seats on the Labasa Town Council, but only one of seventeen seats on the Nadi Town Council. In both instances, it was clear that enthusiasm alone would not be sufficient to win elections and that the party organization still had a long way to go before becoming a possible contender for national political power. Nevertheless, it was equally clear that the Labour Party was not simply going to disappear from the political landscape.

Alliance and NFP politicians were quick to dismiss the idea that the Labour Party victory in Suva would have a bearing on, or was an indication of, what was likely to happen with the North-Central Indian seat. Prime Minister Mara expressed the feeling that the impact would be minimal 'since rural voters were more conservative.' The NFP put forward a strong candidate, James Shankar Singh.

He had been a prominent member of Parliament for the Alliance Party, until he had a falling out with Mara in 1982 and decided not to run. His subsequent decision to join the NFP was seen as a major coup for that party. The Alliance Party candidate was James Shankar Singh's brother, Uday Singh. Uday Singh also had been active in the Alliance Party and was a large landowner in the Ba area. Added to his relative strength among Indo-Fijian voters was the expectation that the bulk of the native Fijians, who comprised about 30 per cent of the voters in the constituency would back the Alliance Party. Mahendra Chaudhry stood for the Labour Party. His support would depend heavily on union members in the area and the extent to which he could pick up dissenters from the other two parties.

All three parties affirmed their confidence in winning the by-election, although most agreed that the Alliance Party had an edge. Off the record, NFP supporters expressed the view that things were going very badly for the NFP and that many people now would throw their support behind one of the other parties. The results gave the Alliance Party a narrow victory and the vote count was: Alliance Party, 7,885 votes; Labour Party, 7,644 votes; and NFP, 5,003 votes. The Alliance Party had won by only 204 votes.

Even though it had no chance of winning, the Labour Party also fielded a candidate for the Lau-Rotuma Fijian communal seat. The seat had fallen vacant by the death of longstanding Alliance Party parliamentarian, Jonati Mavoa. It had been rumoured that Mara had planned on giving the seat to his son, Finau Mara, since it was considered one of the safest Alliance Party seats in Fiji. The Labour Party nominated Jokapeci Koroi, who was from Ono-i-Lau and general secretary of the Fiji Nurses Association, to stand for the seat, hoping that she would be able to pick up votes primarily from her own island and from Rotuma. After the Labour Party had named its candidate, Mara announced that he was bringing Filipe Bole back from Hawaii, where he had had him installed as head of the Pacific Islands Development Program at the East-West Center, to stand for the seat. When it was discovered that one of the Labour Party's nominators was ineligible, however, its candidate was not allowed to stand and Bole was able to stand without opposition.

BUILDING A PARTY

The 1985 elections demonstrated the potential of the Fiji Labour Party, but it was also made clear that a great deal of work remained to be done if this potential was to be realized. In addition, the elections raised important questions concerning the political future of the country. First, there were the structural questions. Would the political structure of Fiji remain the same with the Labour Party becoming yet another fringe party like the Fijian Nationalists or Western United Front? Would a three-party system emerge? If the dominance of the two parties did break down, then what would happen? It seemed unlikely then that a single party would be able to form a government on its own. Would this instability lead to a government of national unity or to coalitions? Was the Labour Party going to replace the NFP as the NFP continued its downward slide?

There were also questions relating to ethnicity. Under the two party structure, each party had sought to build a base within the various communities separately, without seriously challenging the fundamentals of ethnic politics. This attempt at forming a multi-ethnic coalition on the part of the NFP had succeeded in the first 1977 election. Subsequently, the parties had concentrated on securing their bases in their respective primary communal bases, but neither had given up pursuing cross-ethnic alliances. The Labour Party recognized that at least for the time being, it would have to work within this structure, but, at the same time, it saw as its goal the eradication of communal politics and its replacement with a politics based more clearly on ideology and class. The relative success at overcoming communalism within the union movement was seen as evidence that this was not an impossibility, even though, clearly it would be extremely difficult. And an important difference between the NFP and the Labour Party lay in the fact that the leadership of the latter was prepared to think in terms of non-communal politics, whereas it was clear that the leadership of the NFP found it impossible even to conceive of this. The question, then, was whether this goal was attainable or whether, even if the Labour Party succeeded in replacing the NFP, it would simply be manoeuvred into the same role as that of the NFP. The first three months of 1986 were ones of intense political activity on the part of all three parties as each sought to assess what was happening and to adapt in an appropriate manner.

Establishing the Fiji Labour Party

The Fiji Labour Party focused its efforts against the NFP on the NFP's ineffectiveness as an opposition party and on the state of factionalism within the party. This was contrasted with the record of the labour movement in fighting for the rights of its members and with the greater degree of unity within the movement. Under Koya's leadership the NFP had pursued communalistic politics with renewed vigour as the primary means of holding on to its Indo-

Fijian support base. The Labour Party sought to challenge this with a more moderate position, arguing that the Indo-Fijian community would best be served by avoidance of rhetoric that led to communal antagonism. The National Farmers Union continued to be used by Chaudhry and others to build a base for the Labour Party among Indo-Fijian cane farmers. Personal ties between Indo-Fijian trade unionists and Indo-Fijian members of the NFP also played an important role in taking support away from the NFP. A great deal of the support, however, simply came from people who were fed up with the squabbling within the NFP since Reddy had resigned and who saw the Labour Party as a needed 'breath of fresh air.'

It was the Alliance Party, of course, that was seen as the ultimate enemy, and winning elections required convincing traditional NFP supporters that the Labour Party offered a better alternative for challenging the Alliance Party. The Labour Party campaigned against the Alliance Party on a number of related fronts. At the heart of the campaign was the need to reduce the control that the Alliance Party exercised on a large segment of the native Fijian community. Many native Fijians continued to see the Alliance Party and 'the government' as one and the same and identified the Alliance Party as the only party that could safeguard native Fijian communal interests. The NFP had been trying to do this for years with, at best, limited success. The Labour Party felt that it was in a better position to accomplish this, however, since it did not view itself as a communally-based party, and since its party leader was a native Fijian.

At a general level, the Labour Party's campaign to gain support among native Fijians targeted Alliance Party corruption, regional inequalities, and the need for popular participation in native Fijian institutions such as the Native Land Trust Board. In addition, there was the need to: (1) establish Bavadra's credibility as party leader and as a possible prime minister, which, in part, meant overcoming Alliance Party propaganda that sought to picture him as merely the tool of 'wily' Indo-Fijians; (2) convince native Fijians that the Labour Party was not the same as the NFP (i.e., the Indo-Fijian party) or the Fiji Trades Union Congress (i.e., representing solely the interests of urban workers); (3) emphasize that the Labour Party was not against native Fijian traditions or even chiefs per se, but that a distinction needed to be made among traditions, government, and the Alliance Party, and that the Labour Party was opposed to the abuse or manipulation of tradition for the sake of the personal gain of a few; and (4) recruit more recognized and senior native Fijians to give the Labour Party greater legitimacy (in other words, picking off a few Alliance Party stalwarts).

One other issue raised by Labour Party leader Bavadra was the lack of a national name for the citizens of Fiji and the need for one in the name of national unity. The issue had been raised by the NFP, and even Mara himself, around the time of independence, but had then been dropped as each party opted to continue using communal tags alone. In early February 1986, Bavadra proposed using the term 'Fijian' for all people of Fiji, and an indigenous term such as i taukei for native Fijians. It was pointed out that the term 'Fijian' had originated as a corruption of Viti by Tongans and early Christian missionaries who used the word Fisi which later became 'Fiji' and thus had no traditional legitimacy. The Alliance Party responded by saying that the use of 'Fijian' for all people of Fiji would encourage further disintegration of indigenous culture. Fijian Nationalist Party leader Sakeasi Butadroka commented that 'the name "Fijian" is for the "Taukei" only and nobody else.' Harish Sharma of the NFP supported Bavadra's call for a common name and branded the Alliance Party's response as 'politically expedient' and 'consistent with its policy of racial compartmentalisation.'[15]

In one of his speeches, David Toganivalu had argued that the interests of native Fijians were being looked after through various commercial initiatives launched by the government. Bavadra responded in a speech in early March in which he said that the Native Land Trust Board's record in promoting economic development for native Fijians was 'abysmal' and that 'funds that should be given directly to the landowners were used to prop up the NLTB [Native Land Trust Board] bureaucracy.' He went on to say that the growing number of court cases against the Native Land Trust Board by native Fijians was a good indication that a review of its operations was called for. He also cited the failure of such enterprises as the Native Land Development Corporation and the Business Opportunity and Management Service (which was designed to promote business enterprises among native Fijians) and was critical of the extent to which native landowners were excluded from decision-making and profits within the forest industry.

Controlled by Mara's close associate Jeffrey Reid, Emperor Gold Mine came to feature prominently in the struggle between the Alliance Party and Labour Party for native Fijian support. On 7 July 1985, the Fiji Times, reporting on the launching of the Fiji Labour Party the previous day, had carried the headline: 'Labour Party Makes Call: Nationalise the Gold Mine.' While this was only a minor point in the hour-long speech delivered by newly elected party president Bavadra, it was considered sufficiently sensational by the press to warrant such attention.

In early 1986, the Labour Party drew public attention to a dispute between a group of native landowners near the gold-mine and the mine's management. In March 1983, a bloc of over one thousand acres belonging to Nasomo landowners was leased by the government to Western Mining (which assumed managerial responsibility for the Emperor mine in April 1983 after acquiring a partial stake in the company) for a twenty-one year period. The villagers were unhappy that there had been no prior consultation and were opposed to the lease. They approached the Labour Party for help in February 1986 after other avenues of redress had failed. The following month, with Labour Party backing, the villagers filed a F$10 million writ against Emperor Gold Mine and Western Mining.

The situation at Nasomo heated up even further in early April, when Bavadra attended a meeting at the village to form a party branch. At the meeting, Bavadra once again called for nationalization of the gold-mine at Vatukoula, stating that the Labour Party was not interested in wholesale nationalization of industries, but that this was a special case that would serve to bring about social justice. A *Fiji Sun* article reported:

> According to villagers working in the mines, a number of workers have lost their jobs since the news of the writ and meetings got to their bosses. 'A lot of people I have talked to are scared to show up today because they fear losing their jobs,' a man who said he was a miner told the meeting ... Several families from the village are staying in company quarters. They fear attending the meetings, which are now being held weekly, other villagers said. The villagers also claimed that some villagers are being 'bought' by the companies to spy on workers.[16]

With the assistance of the mine's management, the Alliance Party had a group of villagers petition the district officer expressing their lack of support for those who had filed the writ against the mining companies and for those who established the Labour Party branch. Those who had signed this petition, it was claimed by one of the village leaders, did so 'because they were told that if they did not sign then they would be sacked from their jobs.' The Alliance Party and Emperor Gold Mine also took steps to reward loyal workers. Thus, Reid, using funds borrowed from the workers' own pension fund, initiated a housing scheme for company workers, the Nasivi Housing Estate, which was opened officially by Mara in August 1986.

The case against the mine came to court in Lautoka on 23 May. Two buses brought around one hundred villagers from Nasomo. The hearing lasted only a short time and ended when the judge ordered an adjournment until 13 June to allow the mining companies' lawyers to prepare their defence. After the adjournment, the villagers held a public meeting which was addressed by Bavadra and the lawyers handling the case. At the meeting, five villagers claimed that they had been fired from their jobs at the gold-mine because of the writ and lawyer Tevita Fa announced that he would apply for an injunction to prevent the companies from touching the land in question.

Jeffrey Reid decided to respond to the Nasomo landowners and the Labour Party through a paid statement in the newspapers on 8 June under the title 'The Truth About Nasomo,' stating that the companies had paid compensation for exploration work on the land in question, including F$260 to the Nasomo chairman. The Nasomo villagers replied that they had received a small amount of money, but that it did not equal what they had been promised nor was anything paid to the village committee. The companies also sought to undermine support for the writ through traditional means. A two-member delegation consisting of an accountant employed by the companies, Ratu Meli Malani, and the Tui Nadrau was sent to visit the governor general, Ratu Penaia Ganilau, on 2 June to ask him to intervene in the dispute. But Ganilau declined to become involved 'to preserve the dignity, respect and neutrality of the Governor-General's office.'

Bavadra also involved the Labour Party in a dispute between native Fijian cocoa growers and the Alliance Party government. The dispute dated back to 1979, when Alliance Party politicians had sought to siphon off money from the Cocoa Stabilisation Fund held by the National Marketing Authority to help finance Cakadrove, Bua and Macuata Holdings Limited (a 'pork-barrel' operation run by Alliance Party members in northern Fiji). This attempt was successfully challenged in court by the growers in 1980. The growers had gone to court again in 1984 to demand payment of National Marketing Authority funds owed to them. The money from this dispute had never been paid, and in early 1986 the secretary of the Cocoa Growers' Association, Sivinia Vakarewa, approached Bavadra for assistance.

On 4 May 1986, with the assistance of the Labour Party, the cocoa growers filed a writ against the National Marketing Authority claiming that stabilization funds had been improperly distributed, and that despite a 1980 cabinet decision to allow the Cocoa Growers' Association to handle the fund, the National Marketing Authority had not relinquished it. Another writ was filed on the growers' behalf on 25 June by Tevita Fa demanding payment of F$330,393 owed to them by the National Marketing Authority under the stabilization fund and claiming F$100,000 in damages. Added pressure was placed on the government when the Fiji Public Service Association raised questions about the loss of F$130,000 by the National Marketing Authority, alleging misappropriation of funds and other irregularities. The Fiji Public Service Association also questioned the failure of the National Marketing Authority to publish annual accounts since 1981 and to answer queries on financial irregularities raised by auditors. In an effort to defuse the situation, the government promised an investigation of the National Marketing Authority.

One of the most important cases to involve the Labour Party concerned Mara's wife, Adi Lala, and her position as the sole governing director of the Nakuruvakarua Company, a holding company for the Nakuruvakarua mataqali (clan), located at Cuvu, near Sigatoka. Such companies had become an important source of funds for the eastern chiefly oligarchy, which had been able to secure trusteeships over them, and for the Alliance Party as well. This case was seen by both sides as a direct challenge to the oligarchy that struck at the very heart of its political power and financial base.

The Nakuruvakarua Company had been set up by the mataqali in 1970 to manage royalties it received from the lease of Yanuca Island to the Fijian Hotel (one of Fiji's largest resort hotels).The island was a freehold property owned by the mataqali and royalties amounted to F$20,000 per year plus 2 per cent of the resort's income above F$1.8 million. In 1973 the company's articles of association were changed to make Adi Lala Mara sole governing director of the company for life. In October 1985 mataqali members led by Ratu Epi Volavola had written to the Registrar of Companies protesting against Adi Lala's continued appointment and stating that they no longer had confidence in her. A petition was also sent the following month to Adi Lala asking her to step down. When no reply was received, the mataqali members had retained the lawyer, Tevita Fa (at the time a prominent member of the Alliance Party), on their behalf. Cognizant of the implications of these developments, representatives of Adi Lala arranged a meeting of the various parties in December and it was agreed to pay out F$60,000 to members of the mataqali immediately. This did not satisfy the mataqali members. By this time Tevita Fa had become associated with Bavadra and the Labour Party, distancing himself from the Alliance Party (of which he had held several important posts) and charging both the government and party with corruption.

On 3 April 1986, Volavola, with Tevita Fa as his lawyer, filed a writ in the Supreme Court seeking Adi Lala's dismissal on grounds that they had not been given a proper accounting of funds received by the company. Mara and his associates reacted quickly to this serious threat and called on Bulou Eta Vosailagi, the paramount chief (*Ka Levu*) of Nadroga and also the head of the Nakuruvakarua mataqali, to put pressure on the mataqali to withdraw the writ. After a hastily called meeting with mataqali members at which appeals to traditional loyalty were used to convince the members to withdraw the suit, the Ka Levu issued a statement that the majority of members of the mataqali did not support Volavola's action and that they had faith in Adi Lala. As evidence of the wisdom of Adi Lala in handling the company's funds, the Ka Levu told how she and Adi Lala had recently transferred F$50,000 from the company to pay for the entire contribution of Nadroga/Navosa to the Fijian investment scheme being promoted by the Great Council of Chiefs. To many within the mataqali, however, this was a good example of precisely what was wrong – that the chiefly oligarchy was using the mataqali's money as it pleased without discussing matters first with the mataqali. Volavola replied by pointing out that Bulou Eta herself had signed last year's petition asking Adi Lala to resign. He further asserted that he had the backing of most of the mataqali members and questioned the right of Bulou Eta to use the Ka Levu title. Her husband, Ratu Tevita Makutu, who had held the Ka Levu title, had died in 1973 and no new Ka Levu had been installed.

Appeals to tradition having failed, Adi Lala's lawyer, Kelemedi Bulewa, appealed the writ, arguing that an individual member of a mataqali could not sue on the mataqali's behalf. After a great deal of behind-the-scenes manoeuvring by Mara and others, Supreme Court Justice Rooney decided on 16 May that Volavola was entitled to file the writ. Upset, Bulewa threatened to appeal the ruling, while Tevita Fa commented that he had 'won round one.' Toward the end of July, Tevita Fa, on behalf of Volavola, sought an injunction against Adi Lala withdrawing or using funds belonging to the Nakuruvaka-rua Company (its total assets at the time amounting to around F$1 million) until the case was finished. At this time Fa was approached by two prominent members of the Alliance Party who asked him to withdraw the writ or make a settlement 'on their terms,' but Fa refused.

The question of the Ka Levu title was an important one. It had become common practice for titles to be linked to Alliance Party patronage, and disputes over chiefly titles were common. Disputes involving the installations of the Tui Ba, Tui Nadrau, and Tui Vuna

(Taveuni) had taken place recently, and there were others brewing as well (the title Tui referring to the position of high chief of a region). Commenting in late May on the number of disputes, the Tui Nadi, Ratu Napolioni Dawai, argued that they were linked to lease money since chiefs received a great deal more money than other members of the mataqali. Dawai himself received over F$25,000 a year from the Native Land Trust Board. To money, Ratu Osea Gavidi added democracy and education as contributing factors: 'People feel it is their democratic right to question something they are not happy about.' Feelings of injustice over such decisions were to become an important part of the Labour Party strategy for winning support among native Fijians.

In light of later events, one other economic issue also bears mention. Bavadra had also raised the issue of improved salaries and conditions for soldiers (comparable to other government employees) and of an inquiry into pensions for former soldiers. This elicited considerable interest in a number of village meetings and prompted one former soldier to write a letter to the editor of the *Fiji Sun*: 'If you have that type of policy in mind for the soldiers, I'm sure all the soldiers will give you the green light in your next election ... it's high time we receive reality, not promises and peanuts. The army doesn't ask for much, they ask for fairness, equality and reality, which would mean bringing all the civil servant pay to normal living standard level if need be.'[17]

Tevita Fa had been an important Labour Party convert. At the time of his break with the Alliance Party he held the position of treasurer of the Fijian Association and his office was in the Alliance Party building (which he was told to vacate in late May as a result of his involvement in the case against Adi Lala and his association with Bavadra). Quietly, other Alliance Party dissidents began visiting Bavadra to hold discussions. Among them were Solomone Momoivalu and Epeli Kacimaiwai. Momoivalu, from Kadavu, was a senior Alliance Party parliamentarian. He had held cabinet posts from 1977 to 1982, but had not been reappointed to the cabinet after the 1982 election. Kacimaiwai had held important diplomatic posts under the Alliance government and there had been a good deal of discussion about his standing for a seat with the Alliance Party, but he was also a personal friend of Bavadra's. The Alliance Party sought to keep an eye on the activities of its members who were suspected of weakening allegiance, and when they were discovered to be meeting with Bavadra they were warned not to continue.

There were a number of examples of alleged Alliance Party corruption brought up by the Labour Party. One that received considerable attention in early 1986 was the cabinet decision to award the company, Australian Publishing and Broadcasting Limited, an exclusive twelve-year contract to run a national television station. The negotiations had been carried out in relative secrecy, and there was a great deal of gossip concerning pay-offs. In a speech in late March, Bavadra asked why the issue had not been discussed in Parliament, noting that in 1981 a government committee had recommended that a television station not be approved for another seven years and that when it was introduced, the Fiji Broadcasting Commission infrastructure should be used. There had been no subsequent recommendations and Mara himself, until recently, had been opposed to introducing television in the near future. The question was, what had changed his mind? And why had he decided to give such a contract to the Australian company? Bavadra was joined in his criticism of the government decision by members of the NFP, as well as by church leaders.

One other questionable development was exposed by the Labour Party toward the end of March. The party noted that the Fiji Visitors Bureau (with a long history of involvement in questionable Alliance Party practices) had paid an advance of F$23,000, with the promise of another F$23,000 upon completion, to former U.S. Ambassador Fred Eckert to produce a picture book on Fiji. A *Fiji Times* editorial expressed concern over this, pointing out that a lot of money was involved and questioning whether Eckert was the most appropriate person to produce such a book.[18] The editorial also asked why local writers, photographers, and printers had not been given an opportunity to work on the book and commented, 'we have not been told how much Mr. Eckert himself is to make from the book.'

In terms of organization, by the end of March, the Labour Party had branches established in Suva, Ba, Nadi, Lautoka, Sigatoka, and Nausori, which provided it with a basic infrastructure in and around the capital and in the larger communities in the west. In early April, additional branches were set up in Rakiraki and Tavua to complete coverage of the west. After the April council elections, there were plans to start work in the north, on Ovalau, Vanua Levu, and elsewhere, and to seek to broaden the party's base in the west. This was not much of an organization when compared to the other two parties, but Labour Party leaders were confident that they would be able to close the infrastructural gap in time for the national election.

The Alliance Party Response

The Alliance Party had sought to entrench its position after the 1982 election by reforming the Fijian Administration in order to increase the party's coercive powers over native Fijian commoners and to strengthen its position in western Viti Levu. After the 1982 election, Mara had sought to use the Pacific Islands Development Program at the East-West Center in Honolulu to plot a course for strengthening the Alliance Party's hold on native Fijian commoners. With this in mind, an American anthropologist was hired in early 1983 as project director of the Pacific Islands Development Program's government and administrative systems project. Ostensibly, the project was to examine 'Development the Pacific Way' in the context of the conflict between Western-style development and so-called traditional cultures. Mara was angered by the anthropologist's approach to the subject and had little sympathy for views that appeared in the project reports – such as, the view that 'debate about political and social philosophy is healthy and useful in the Pacific region.' Shortly after an outburst by Mara at a Pacific Islands Development Program meeting, the anthropologist lost his job.

The Prime Minister's Office prepared a short paper that dealt more specifically with the need to strengthen the Fijian Administration and enhance chiefly power, and presented it to the Great Council of Chiefs in November 1983. To avoid a repeat of the Pacific Islands Development Program situation, a more acquiescent expatriate was found who would be more likely to come up with the sort of report desired by Mara. The man chosen, Rodney Cole, was to be assisted by an up-and-coming young member of the Alliance Party named Anare Matahau, who was perfectly aware of the political aims of the project. Funded by the United States, the project described in the report was supposed to take four to five years to complete. Among the changes recommended were a return to tikina (district) units established in the late nineteenth and early twentieth centuries instead of the ones that were presently in force, and establishment of a decentralized judicial system in which separate native Fijian courts would be set up under the direction of local chiefs to try all except major offences. Obviously, one of the aims of the reforms was to increase control of the chiefs over native Fijian youths. In 1985 the reforms began to be implemented in Bua and Macuata provinces with the intention being to extend them gradually throughout the rest of Fiji over the next few years. The Alliance Party stepped up the pace of implementation of these reforms following the founding of the Labour Party.

The Alliance Party leadership was well aware that its control of native Fijians was most vulnerable in the west. Accordingly, in 1985, under the guidance of Apisai Tora, the government stepped up public spending in this previously neglected area. For the year, it spent a record F$1 million on rural development (including over F$100,000 in aid funds). This trend continued in 1986 and in April of that year plans were announced for a F$10 million agricultural project (road building, irrigation and drainage works, etc.) in the Sigatoka Valley, 'to transform the valley into a major centre for agricultural development.' The expenditure was to be spread over a ten-year period and included a F$5 million loan from the Asian Development Bank. Then, in July, the government announced that it would be spending F$3 million each to build new bridges for the towns of Sigatoka and Ba.

On the directly political front, the *Fiji Times* noted that 'the Alliance Party is moving to consolidate Fijian support in the Western Division as part of its campaign to boost its chances in the 1987 general election. The strategy is linked to the Fijian Administration restructuring, and it is emphasised that service to traditional leaders and protection of Native rights is of paramount importance.'[19] The drive got under way with an initiative to revive the Western Chiefs' Association. On 5 February, close Mara associate Jeffrey Reid (co-chairman of Emperor Gold Mine and one of the more influential expatriates in local political and economic circles) hosted a dinner at his home near Vatukoula at which Mara was present. Those invited were the primary Alliance Party local bosses in the west, including the Tui Ba from Nailaga, the Tui Ba from Sorokoba, the Tui Navitilevu from Rakiraki, the Tui Tavua, the Tui Magodro from the highlands, and the Tui Yakete from near Lololo. The meeting focused on consolidation of Alliance Party control in the west through the restructuring of the Fijian Administration. After knowledge of the meeting became public, the Alliance Party co-ordinator in the West, Jona Qio, commented that the dynamism of the Fijian Administration 'is very much dependent on a concerted effort towards enlivening of the culture and ensuring that Fijians are delivering their own traditional obligations.'[20]

Following the meeting at Reid's house, the Alliance Party opened offices in Nadi and Ba as part of its 'groundwork for the next general election.' At the opening of the Nadi office on 16 February, Apisai Tora (at the time minister of state for rural development) warned those attending that the Alliance Party could lose the 1987 election unless it started organizing immediately. Remembering his own activities with Koya before joining the Alliance Party, he argued that the party could lose to the NFP under the leadership of Koya ('Mr.

Koya is a smart man ... The NFP is still a strong party with Mr. Koya there.'). As for the Labour Party, he said that its leaders lacked experience and that it was not much of a threat.

In the mid-February issue of the *Alliance Messenger* (the revived party newsletter) it was stated: 'There is no escaping the fact that to many people the Labour Party is just a substitute for the Flower Faction of the NFP and the NFP has never had any attraction for Fijians.' This was to become a familiar theme in Alliance Party propaganda over the next year as it sought to minimize native Fijian support for the Labour Party. The newsletter also was critical of the Labour Party's call to democratize the Native Land Trust Board and asked if this indicated that the Labour Party was against chiefly leadership. To boost its image among native Fijians, the Alliance Party also laid plans for its ministers to visit development projects around the country. The first of these visits, involving Mara and the two deputy prime ministers (David Toganivalu and Mosese Qionibaravi), was announced on 17 February. The party soon became even more ambitious, as it watched the Labour Party campaign pick up more steam, and in March announced plans to hold entire cabinet meetings in differenet locations around the country. The first of these was held on Kadavu, and it was announced that one was even to be held on Rotuma, represented by Filipe Bole, and where there were growing signs of Labour Party support. Bavadra labelled these a misuse of public funds since they constituted nothing more than campaigning for the Alliance Party.

Threat or not, the Alliance Party was taking no chances with the Labour Party, and it continued its campaign to undermine support for its opponents within the labour movement. In mid-February, a small group of native Fijian members of the Fiji Public Service Association who were linked with the Alliance Party sought to challenge Mahendra Chaudhry's re-election bid as secretary. They were led by Joe Leweniqila (a labour officer), Tevita Fa (former secretary to the Ombudsman, not the lawyer working with the Labour Party), and Jone Veisamasama (a former civil servant who had become one of the initial vice-presidents of the Labour Party). One of the means of doing so was to seek to spread dissent among native Fijian members of the union, claiming that the executive was Indo-Fijian-dominated. Their attempt failed and they were able to gain very little support from the members. Leweniqila and Fa were suspended from the Fiij Public Service Association (later they were reinstated) and Veisamasama resigned from the Labour Party.

The Alliance Party also sought to sow dissent within the Fiji Nurses Association, which had emerged as a strong supporter of the

Labour Party. Its secretary, Jokapeci Koroi, had sought to run in one of the recent by-elections for the Labour Party. In November 1985 one of its officers who was a strong supporter of the Alliance Party, Molly Tamani, had resigned because of Koroi's involvement in the Labour Party. A pro-Alliance group within the union now sought to have her reinstated at the Fiji Nurses Association's annual general meeting in February. At the opening of the annual general meeting on 20 February, the president of the Fiji Nurses Association had urged nurses to become more political:

> Health is a political activity – from identifying priorities so as to bring epidemiological needs and social preferences into line with each other, to allocating resources, to deciding on the most appropriate technology, to providing preventative action, to providing care. It is for the above reasons that I voice my belief in saying that all nurses must become politically aware if we are to fulfil our potential and take full advantage of the opportunities offered. I am quite aware of the fact that there is always a feeling of uneasiness when nurses talk about politics. However, I still strongly feel that the professional organisation is the only appropriate catalyst to release the power that is in nursing.[21]

Such expressions of growing political consciousness among trade unionists were making Mara and the Alliance Party very uneasy about the union movement, especially in light of its size and voting potential. At the same meeting, the director of energy, Suliana Siwatibau, urged nurses not to become complacent in the pursuit of social justice. Shortly after the opening speeches, a row erupted when Tamani's pro-Alliance backers sought to have her reinstated. They were blocked by the union's executive and they then staged a walkout. At this point, the executive decided to suspend the meeting. A second attempt to hold the meeting on 6 April lasted long enough to elect officers but, then, it too failed to finish when nurses supporting Tamani staged another walkout.

The Alliance Party began to put pressure on the unions in other ways as well. Labour Party councillor Nitya Reddy was fired by the Fiji Sugar Corporation, the first week of June. The government planned to bar senior civil servants from joining unions, but this idea had to be dropped under pressure from the Fiji Public Service Association. The government did, however, issue warnings to civil servants to 'stay out of politics.' The Labour Party's response to this was to point to the very active involvement of many government employees in Alliance Party affairs.

The National Council of the Alliance Party met at the Merchants

Club in Suva on 22 March. It was announced that the party was to launch a membership and fund-raising drive. The party treasurer, Malcolm Brain, noted that the budget for the 1982 election had been F$199,000 and that they were anticipating spending F$320,000 for the next election, adding that 'this is a large sum of money which has to be collected, starting now.'[22] Just before the meeting the Alliance Party had a bank balance of F$7,000.

Speaking at Nadi airport the following day, before leaving for a visit to Honolulu, Mara told the press that the Alliance Party was headed for a big victory in the national election, but did concede that the Labour Party might win eight and perhaps as many as ten seats, implying that the opposition would be divided between the Labour Party and NFP with the Labour Party possibly holding more seats than the NFP. It was a statement designed to elicit even greater fear among the NFP leadership and to heighten the struggle for support between the two parties. Bavadra responded: 'The way the [Fiji Labour Party] is progressing and receiving support, we are very positive that we are going to get at least 28 to 30 seats. We will form the next government in this country.'[23]

The National Federation Party Response

For the National Federation Party, there was a sense of desperation. Something had to be done, and quickly, if the party was to survive. Irene Narayan's group of independents (which included six members of Parliament) remained outside the party, and parliamentarian Vijaya Parmanandan had been expelled from the party's board. Added to this was the obvious fact that an increasing number of Indo-Fijians were going over to the Labour Party and that the NFP's tie to the Western United Front was under threat as well, with many of its members expressing a desire to join the Labour Party. After the North Central Indian national by-election, a group of party leaders including Harish Sharma (secretary), Shardha Nand, Navin Patel, and Koresi Matatolu decided that the only hope of reviving the party was to have Koya replaced as leader. Negotiations with Koya were handled with great care and largely away from public view so as not to cause a further division within the party.

NFP leaders met in Suva the third week of February to discuss an 'appraisal report' prepared by Sharma, Nand and Patel, on revitalizing the party. The report argued that unless the NFP took drastic action the Alliance Party would win the next national election by a large majority. It noted that the needs and demands of voters had changed considerably since independence and questioned whether the NFP had adapted to those changes. The report was highly critical of Siddiq Koya's leadership of the party, although it stopped short of recommending that he be replaced as party leader. It also questioned Ratu Osea Gavidi's usefulness to the party and asked the NFP to consider whether it should retain its association with the Western United Front. In speaking to the meeting, Nand warned that with the Labour Party splitting the Indo-Fijian vote the Alliance Party could win two-thirds of the seats in the next election and thereby be in a position to change the constitution. To avoid this, he urged making stronger appeals to communal sentiments. After the meeting, Sharma announced formation of a six-member committee to draw up plans to prepare the party for the 1987 election. An angered Koya threatened to quit after the contents of the report became known, although with no serious intention of doing so, and the sentiment among other members of the NFP executive seemed to be that, while Koya should be replaced, they did not want to be put in a position where they had to force him out: 'It has to be done with Mr. Koya's consent ... for the sake of the party' was one comment.

The committee made its report on 16 March. Its most important recommendation was that a change of leadership was essential, and it was clear that Koya would be asked to step down as leader of the opposition. The report also called for the establishment of a management committee to fill vacancies for the election created by those who had left the party and recommended that those who had defied the party not be considered for nomination. The committee was to raise funds and appoint a board to issue a newsletter to prepare for the election. Sharma and Koya were to work together to prepare a report on revising the party's constitution at the annual general meeting. Finally, it was recommended that the date of the annual general meeting be brought forward from June to 26 April to step up the pace of reform.

On the day before the report had been issued, Koya had addressed a public meeting in Nasinu. He warned that the NFP would be crushed in the upcoming election and that the 'Indian people' would be 'finished' if they failed to unite behind the NFP. Referring to the prospect of the Alliance Party winning enough seats to change the constitution, he stated that the 'the Alliance people will do legally then what Mr. Butadroka is trying to do now' and referred to racist statements made recently in Parliament by members of the Alliance Party such as Apisai Tora. He then launched into a series of personal attacks in which he accused members of the press and supporters of the Labour Party of dividing the Indo-Fijian community ('you are responsible for destroying the Indians') and stated, 'I am after your blood and I will fight you. You will be without jobs soon.' After the meeting, visibly embarrassed senior members of the NFP, who had sat through the speech with their heads lowered, apologized to the *Fiji Times* reporter present. One told the reporter: 'We did not know what he was going to talk about. If we had known we would have stopped him before he began. But we could not stop him once he had started making a public speech as it would have led to open conflict between us ... But the rest of the NFP does not feel the same way and do not have the false fears he carries.'[24]

If there had been any doubts about the need to replace Koya on the part of Sharma and his allies, this outburst had laid them to rest, and the Alliance Party wasted no time in trying to capitalize on Koya's speech, accusing him of seeking to instill 'fear in the Indian community.' The following day, the *Fiji Sun* editorial commented: 'The drum beat of racial politics is on the march again as Siddiq Koya tries to rally the fragmented National Federation Party ... Mr Koya's reversion to the politics of race is a sign of just how desperate he has become.'[25] Pointedly, the editorial asked whether the NFP continued to function as a viable opposition party. One local journalist referred to Koya as 'one of the Labour Party's most effective recruiting agents.' Nevertheless, Koya still had supporters in the party and replacing him as leader, especially if it was to be done peacefully, still remained a difficult task. And as negotiations went on, party members continued to drift to the Labour Party. In addition, some of those remaining in the party began to discuss the possibility of the two parties uniting against the Alliance Party. In early April, the secretary of the Navua branch of the NFP, Vijay Kumar, announced that he would submit a proposal along these lines at the party's annual general meeting: 'We do not regard Labour as our opponents but as a brother party.' It was a sentiment that was shared by many rank-and-file members of the NFP, but not by party leaders, who continued to see the Labour Party as a threat.

Local Council Elections

In the midst of these developments, the first chance for the three parties to test the political waters came in the Ba Town Council elections on 19 April 1986. There were five wards to be contested, each electing three councillors. Initially, the NFP and Fiji Labour Party had reached an agreement whereby each party would not contest two of the wards thus allowing the other to win them. This was a strategy designed to push out the Alliance Party, which had dominated the council previously. But the deal collapsed when the NFP announced that it would be contesting all of the wards. Some saw this as the work of pro-Koya forces within the party. The voter turnout was high (82 per cent). The NFP received 3,779 votes (more than in 1983); the Alliance Party, 3,721; and the Labour Party, 2,600. The NFP and Alliance Party had each won two wards, giving them six councillors apiece.

The Labour Party won one ward, the Yalalevu Ward, giving it three councillors.The Alliance Party had held the Yalalevu Ward and had been expected to hold on to it, on the basis of votes by native Fijians. The Alliance Party claimed that it lost because native Fijians had not voted for it, pointing out that although 325 people had passed through their voting shed, the party received only 219 votes. It was a situation similar to the one in Suva, where native Fijians had not been willing to support the Labour Party openly but had voted for it nonetheless. In particular, the Alliance Party singled out the Dra-ni-Lami society to blame for its loss. Three years earlier, the Alliance Party had arranged to guarantee a F$20,000 bank loan for the society (a typical method of securing political support) and now it was upset that the society did not appear to have supported it in the election. One Alliance Party official warned that similar loan supports might not be forthcoming in the future while another referred to the Lami group as 'traitors.' A spokesman for the society responded that it had never promised the Alliance Party political support in return for the loan guarantee, but that, generally, the group had supported the party and that in this election its members had built the Alliance Party's voting shed. 'But,' he said, 'we cannot exactly say who voted for which party' and he claimed that the Alliance Party was over-reacting since the society had only ninety-three voting members in the ward.

The results of the election left none of the parties with a majority. Immediately after the election, the NFP had suggested a three-party coalition to ensure peace and stability. Neither the Labour Party nor the Alliance Party ruled this out, the Labour Party stating that it would wait for a concrete proposal. Basically, however, the Labour Party let it be known that it was not keen on sharing power with the other parties and, Navin Patel, who had run the campaign for the NFP, said that the NFP was prepared to sit in opposition if a workable coalition could not be achieved. In the meantime, the Alliance Party sent out feelers to the NFP to indicate that it was willing to work out a deal. The Alliance Party parliamentarian for Ba, Uday Singh, was quoted as saying that he felt that 'some sort of understanding was likely between the NFP and Alliance Party' but that 'I doubt if there can be an understanding between Alliance and Labour.' When the Council met on the twenty-fifth, no deal had been agreed upon, and the Labour Party had made it clear that it was not prepared to join a coalition. Finally, a last minute deal was worked out between the NFP and the Alliance Party, and NFP councillor Ahmed Bhamji was elected mayor over Labour Party councillor Arun Singh by a vote of six to three. The deal was that, in 1986, the NFP would be given the position of mayor and deputy mayor while the Alliance Party would be given the chairmanship of the Finance Committee. The next year the positions would be reversed.

The Labour Party was relatively satisfied with the outcome and hoped to gain support based on its 'moral' stance on the matter of a coalition. It was also pleased with its ability, once again, to pick up native Fijian voters. It was this last fact that had the Alliance Party most worried, even though, overall, it had not done too badly. Generally, the election was seen as something of a victory for the NFP and for Siddiq Koya, in particular, but many observers felt that it would not be enough to 'halt the rot' and start the party on the road to recovery.

The second contest was a by-election in the Simla Ward of the Lautoka City Council resulting from the resignation of Alliance councillor Abdul Hakim who had emigrated to Australia. Initially, it looked as if the Alliance Party would be able to hold on to the seat unopposed. One local NFP leader commented that his party had decided not to field a candidate: 'There is apathy all around. Nobody seems to be interested.' Alliance Party candidate selection, however, did not go without a hitch. Three people put forward their names, but one (from the Young Alliance) dropped out, leaving former Alliance Party councillor Davendra Singh and car salesman Deo Lingham Reddy. When Deo Lingham Reddy was selected in the first week of April, Singh let it be known that he was upset at being passed over after his years of service to the party in favour of a relative newcomer. In one interview he stated: 'The godmakers of the selection committee have cheated me. The Alliance gave me a raw deal so it's pointless for me to hang on to the dead tail of a horse.' The Labour Party had not indicated whether it would field a candidate, many feeling that it would have been foolish to do so, but party leaders were active in seeking local support. A break for the party came shortly after the Alliance Party had named Reddy as its candidate. Davendra Singh and another former Alliance Party coun-cillor Mili Ah Tong announced that they were joining the Labour Party. In what was to become a familiar refrain, Mili Ah Tong stated: 'I joined the Alliance Party because of the prime minister, Ratu Sir

Kamasese Mara. But all these years I found that only prominent people are being given a place in the party not ordinary people. Despite the party rejecting me as a candidate in the Lautoka City Council's elections two years ago, I continued to be an active worker. Human beings should not be treated like this and I felt the Labour Party needed me and I joined.' On 8 April, the Labour Party announced that its candidate would be trade unionist Nitya Reddy.

A heavy turnout of between 50 and 70 per cent was predicted, and both parties put all their heavyweights to work as this was seen as an important test in which the two parties directly confronted one another without the NFP to intervene. But the high turnout did not materialize, the final tally being 44 per cent. Nitya Reddy won by a margin of 780 to 531 votes. The Alliance Party blamed its loss on the low voter turnout. Prominent Alliance Party organizer Ratu Josaia Tavaiqia complained: 'The campaign was done but the voters just did not come out and vote. We even sent transport to collect them and it came back empty.' Ratu David Toganivalu, speaking for the Alliance Party, sought to play down the loss, stating that such a local election had no bearing on national politics. But the Labour Party was jubilant. Timoci Bavadra told the press that Labour's victory was a reflection of 'the mood of the people' and that it was an indication of what was in store in next year's national election. In private, members of the Labour Party expressed pleasure at their ability to maintain momentum, but they were all too aware of how much remained to be done before the national election. As for the Alliance Party, despite David Toganivalu's dismissal of the election, there was growing anxiety.

THE COALITION

With the council elections fresh in politician's minds, on Friday, 2 May, Irene Narayan almost succeeded in defeating the government in Parliament. With many Alliance Party parliamentarians out of town or in their offices, she put forward a motion calling for a judicial inquiry into compensation claims paid to three individuals including Alliance minister Akariva Nabati and another Alliance Party associate, Eliki Bomani. The case had created a scandal which had come to cause the government some embarrassment. The Speaker, Tomasi Vakatora, called for a voice vote and declared the motion defeated, but it was clear to those present that the motion had in fact been passed since the opposition outnumbered the government eighteen to sixteen. The NFP then asked for individual votes to be taken. Vakatora stalled while Alliance Party minister Jone Naisara rushed out and gathered as many Alliance parliamentarians as he could find. The number was sufficient to defeat the motion twenty-three to twenty, but it served to emphasize just how delicate the Alliance Party's hold on the government was when confronted with an active opposition.

Meanwhile, the Labour Party had begun its campaign in the Northern Division, with Bavadra setting out to visit a number of villages on Vanua Levu. In Bua, he commented on the government's sudden decision to grade roads in the area ('Why can't it improve the roads and maintain them every year and not do it just before elections?') and sought to emphasize that the Labour Party was not anti-chief or anti-tradition, but that people 'should not follow their chiefs blindly.' He also commented on the large number of native Fijians in prison, saying that 'we should expect better of a government that is led by a group of chiefs.' Speaking at the village of Nawailevu, he criticized the Native Land Trust Board for leasing six hundred acres of land owned by the local mataqali without first getting the approval of the landowners, who erected a road blockade after learning of the decision.

The NFP's annual general meeting had been scheduled for 26 April, but it was postponed as negotiations continued with Koya over his resignation. Koya and his opponents in the NFP finally reached an agreement, and on 1 May it was announced that Koya would step down on the fifteenth. Koresi Matatolu and Shardha Nand were among those considered to replace Koya, but Matatolu was ruled out when the party executive decided that the leader had to be an Indo-Fijian; and Nand was eliminated as being too closely identified with Koya. Harish Sharma was chosen primarily because of his reputation for moderation. It was hoped that he would be able to put the party back together again, but there were few signs to justify such optimism.

When Sharma assumed the leadership on 15 May, he stated that rebuilding party unity was his first priority. As Sharma called for unity, however, the infighting continued. Noor Dean openly called for Nand's resignation because of his association with Koya, and relations between the two factions remained tense. Narayan and the other independents said they would think about it, but earlier Satendra Nandan had stated that 'I don't think that I can rejoin with a clear conscience' and indicated that he felt that the change had come too late. Krishna Datt, speaking for the Labour Party, commented, 'It is too late to do anything now. The NFP is sliding out of public life. I do not think that Mr. Sharma will be able to bring together a party that is fast fragmenting. The rot has set in.'

By the early part of May, Mara had made it clear that he was upset that those responsible in the Alliance Party for preparing its plan for the national election were taking so long. Mara and others expressed concern about finances at a meeting of the party's management board on 8 May, because many constituency councils had not paid their contributions and many Alliance Party parliamentarians had not been paying visits to their constituencies. In addition, a Suva-based group led by David Toganivalu asked the party's general secretary, Isoa Makutu, to step down. Makutu had taken over the post the year before at Mara's request when Senator Jone Banuve had indicated that he wanted to resign. The move against Makutu was prompted by his failure to organize a planned public meeting to combat the Labour Party's growing popularity in the Suva area, and by the group's worry about the Suva national seats.

Meanwhile, the Alliance Party had been busy at work trying to build support in those areas where it was perceived the party was weakest. The week after the Suva meeting, a meeting of the western high chiefs and western Fijian Association chiefs was convened in Lautoka. Tora warned the chiefs not to under-estimate the Labour Party. Plans were announced for a large meeting of Fijian Association members to take place in the west in August. Recently, the Alliance Party had brought pressure to bear on the Taukei Sawaieke of Vuda, Tevita Momoidonu, to leave the Labour Party (he was a vice-president) and rejoin the Alliance Party. Bavadra branded the Lautoka meeting as a 'blatant use of Fijian chiefly tradition for political ends.'

To the north, on 7 May, David Toganivalu left for a tour of Rotuma with a large contingent of government officials, and plans were announced to improve wharf facilities on the island using Australian aid funds. The following week, the government mooted the possiblity of setting up a separate lands commission for Rotuma (land inheritance on Rotuma is from the father or mother, whereas throughout most of Fiji it is through the male line only).

At a meeting of the Sigatoka branch of the NFP on 24 May, the branch president and NFP member for the North Central Fijian national seat, Temo Sukanaivalu, warned those present that 'there are some elements in the Alliance today who would like to see Indians leave Fiji.' As a member of the Great Council of Chiefs, Sukanaivalu reminded those at the Sigatoka meeting of the 1982 Great Council of Chiefs meeting where Indo-Fijians had been referred to as 'dogs,' where sentiments had been expressed that Indo-Fijians should leave Fiji, and where it had been resolved that two-thirds of the seats in parliament be reserved for native Fijians. He urged Indo-

Fijians to unite behind the NFP and not allow the Labour Party to split the vote. He felt that such a split would allow the Alliance Party to be re-elected with possible catastrophic results for Indo-Fijians, for there were 'people in the Alliance who would not hesitate to carry out what was resolved by the Great Council of Chiefs.'[26]

The speech led to a flurry of accusations and counter-accusations among the parties. While Sukanaivalu issued a statement saying that he stood by everything he had said in the speech, other members of his party sought to distance themselves from it. Harish Sharma made it clear that he had left the meeting before Sukanaivalu spoke and defended his record in promoting harmonious race relations. The deputy leader of the NFP, Koresi Matatolu, issued an official statement on behalf of the party denouncing Sukanaivalu's 'racial remarks' as having 'no justification' and being contrary to party policy. The Alliance Party issued a series of statements with its usual position: 'Under the Alliance government, our nation is a model for the world on how people of different backgrounds, religious creeds and racial origins can live together in peace.' The party also denounced Sukanaivalu's attempt 'to create fear of the Alliance in the minds of Indian voters.' Bavadra issued a statement on behalf of the Labour Party denouncing the speech as an insult to Indo-Fijians and calling on the NFP leadership to issue a public apology. The statement also commented that 'Mr. Sukanaivalu assumes that he can attempt with the Indians, what the Alliance attempts to do with the Fijians, and whip the Indians back into the National Federation Party camp' and argued that differences within the Indo-Fijian community were based on ideological reasons and reflected independent thinking, which was healthy and 'can only lead to greater political maturity of our people.'

Koya also had addressed the Sigatoka meeting. One of his more ironical statements criticized the Labour Party as standing for 'people with ties going around in nice cars.'[27] Only a couple of days earlier, on 21 May, the Sugar Cane Growers Council, of which Koya was chairman and which was already in trouble for the amount of money it was spending (including money on 'nice cars'), voted to double the daily travelling and subsistence allowance of councillors from F$50 to F$100, for an estimated total cost of F$102,000 per year on top of what already had been budgeted. He also passed a motion seeking revision of the Sugar Industry Act to provide for payment of loss of remunerative time for the councillors. Only nine of the 103 councillors voted against the motions. The impact of the motions was to put the council into even greater disrepute and to drive more farmers into the Labour Party camp.

Earlier in the year, Irene Narayan had secretly approached the Labour Party to explore the possibility of joining the party with some of her confederates. Sensitive to Alliance Party taunts that the Labour Party was nothing but an NFP faction and wary of Narayan's record of factional politics, the Labour Party had turned her down. The first week in June, Satendra Nandan approached the Labour Party on his own to apply for membership. This time the feeling was different and there was considerable sympathy for Nandan's application. The executive council of the Labour Party met on 10 June and decided to accept him. Commenting on the decision, Bavadra stated: 'I feel that this man has stood the test of time and he has already made some very strong pro-Labour statements. Also, we will now have a say in Parliament, which is very important.' He justified the apparent change in policy on the basis of the need to anaylse policies from time to time and on the need for change depending on the situation. Nandan told the press that he was 'delighted' with the decision, while Harish Sharma expressed disappointment: 'I expected Dr. Nandan to come back to the NFP fold and I am sorry he didn't.'[28] Members of the NFP's Suva branch called on Nandan to give up his seat. On the positive side, NFP Youth Wing parliamentarian Davendra Singh had rejoined the party on 2 June.

Another problem facing Sharma was the NFP's coalition with the Western United Front. The Labour Party had held a meeting in Cuvu on 31 May and, subsequently, the Nakuruvakarua branch was established. This was only one more sign of growing support within Western United Front territory for the Labour Party, and Western United Front leader Osea Gavidi and Labour Party leader Bavadra were known to have been holding meetings. Then on 4 June over one hundred western chiefs met in Cuvu primarily to discuss the future of the Western United Front. A large number of the chiefs favoured breaking with the NFP and joining in a coalition with the Labour Party, but it was known that Gavidi was loath to break with the NFP, partly out of a sense of loyalty to Koya. Few were prepared to create a breach in the party and embarrass Gavidi until a compromise was reached. It was decided to remain with the NFP for the time being, and a committee was formed to be led by Gavidi and include the Western United Front parliamentarians (Dawai, Nadolo, and Nalatu). The committee would explore two options: an NFP-Labour Party-Western United Front coalition or an Alliance Party-Western United Front coalition. Only five of the chiefs had indicated support for a coalition with the Alliance Party, but it was felt that the option should be explored nonetheless.

Bavadra announced the next day that he would meet with the

Western United Front committee. Party members were generally supportive of the idea of uniting with the Western United Front but few supported joining in a coalition with the NFP. Meeting at Cuvu on 15 June, the two parties agreed on the need for a coalition to defeat the Alliance Party the next year and they explored other common objectives. The Labour Party expressed its willingness to consider a coalition with the NFP. After the meeting, Bavadra commented to the press that all three of the parties shared the goal of defeating the Alliance Party and that he anticipated a series of future meetings to 'decide what sort of agreement could be reached.' He also noted, however, that 'if no agreement is reached between NFP and its partners, then WUF [Western United Front] may sever its links and join the Labour Party.'[29]

When interviewed by the press, Harish Sharma said that he was waiting for a report from the Western United Front committee on the meeting with the Labour Party, and, while not wanting to commit himself to anything, he did say that 'if the party accepts the offer then we will get the ball rolling.'[30] He emphasised, however, that the matter was up to the party as a whole. Not all NFP members were as open to the prospect of a coalition. Addressing the annual meeting of the NFP's Nausori branch on the fifteenth, Shardha Nand spoke out strongly against a coalition with the Labour Party and emphasized once again the need for Indo-Fijians to unite behind the NFP to protect their rights. The following day, Mumtatz Ali commented: 'Who the devil are they to suggest that NFP might coalesce with Labour? Who are they to preach to us? WUF [Western United Front] have gone into Parliament riding on our backs ... financially as well as vote-wise. I think their departure may well be a blessing in disguise.'[31] The next day, Sharma sought to disassociate the NFP from Ali's remarks and referred to them as 'rather unfortunate,' stressing that he viewed the Western United Front as 'an equal partner with the NFP.' On 21 June Sharma led a delegation from the NFP to meet with Gavidi and others from the Western United Front in Cuvu. The meeting ended with a statement that the NFP-Western United Front coalition remained intact and that there would be future discussions concerning a coalition with the Labour Party. Basically, opposition to the idea within the NFP remained too strong to make a deal, although there were a few who saw it as a way out of the NFP's débâcle.

When Harish Sharma had taken over as opposition leader from Koya the position of NFP president had fallen vacant. Disagreement over selection of a new president now threatened to destroy what unity remained in the party. The annual convention of the NFP had been delayed on several occasions in the hope that the internal struggles would settle down. Finally, it was decided to hold the meeting at Navua on 22 June. The Suva branch of the NFP decided to nominate Mumtatz Ali for the presidency while a group of Koya loyalists in Ba considered nominating Siddiq Koya for the post, or another member of the Dove faction. Ali was identified with Jai Ram Reddy and the Flower faction and relations between Ali and Koya had been particularly strained since Ali had arranged for a supporter of his, Dr. Balwant Singh Rakkha, to stand for the Lautoka Indian communal seat. In an effort to avoid a new outbreak of Flower-Dove factional fighting, Ali let it be known that he would not stand if opposed, and Sharma expressed hope that efforts to unify the party would not be 'spoilt by wrong actions.'

The meeting was a disaster. The morning portion of the meeting had gone smoothly, and after lunch the first item of business was to have been the election of officers. This looked as if it would go well too since Koya's followers had not fielded a candidate to oppose Mumtatz Ali, nor was Shardha Nand opposed for the position of general secretary. Then Noor Dean, the assistant secretary, announced that he had received one other nomination for the presidency – Subramani Basawaiya who was identifed with the Koya faction in Ba – as well as nominations for the general secretary position. After informal discussions, the majority opinion seemed to be that Ali should be elected president; Basawaiya, vice president; and Nand, general secretary. But Koya, who had opposed Ali's and Nand's nominations from the beginning and who favoured Basawaiya and Dean instead, blocked the compromise. Earlier in the meeting, according to Mumtatz Ali, two of Koya's supporters had approached him to offer him their group's support if he were willing to support them in blocking Nand. When he refused to go along, they made it clear that they planned to oppose him as well.

Koresi Matatolu (acting president and chair of the meeting), after consultation with Sharma and Koya, announced that there would be no election since there was no proper record of financial members. He said that the present office bearers would remain in office until the treasurer had drawn up a list of financial members, at which time a special general meeting would be convened. Immediately, several of Mumtatz Ali's supporters walked out of the meeting. Mumtatz Ali and Davendra Singh resigned and then walked out with Ahmed Bhamji and others. Before leaving the meeting, Ali told those present: 'If this is how the NFP is going to work, then I can assure you there is not much chance for this party ... I am sorry to say that today you have lost me. Good luck to your party. Go back to

Mr. Koya and make him the Leader of the Opposition.' Harish Sharma was described in the *Fiji Times* as 'shell-shocked' and he too walked out of the meeting, to regain his composure.[32] He told the press: 'All the work I have done this past month in reuniting the party has been destroyed this afternoon.' The *Fiji Times* editorial the next morning referred to the meeting as 'farcical' and commented: 'When a party becomes the preserve of a few and refuses to accept the will of the majority, it ceases to be a democratic party.' It referred to Sharma as cutting a 'sorry figure yesterday, as all his dreams for a united party lay shattered on the banks of Navua River. As party leader, he failed to stamp his authority on the meeting. He was overpowered by Mr. Koya's domineering presence.' Essentially, Koya had outmanoeuvred those who had brought about his removal, but in the process of achieving his revenge he had ruined what remained of the party's unity.

On 26 June, Sharma, Gavidi, and Bavadra met to discuss forming a united front against the Alliance Party. There was no formal agreement concerning a coalition, but a statement after the meeting referred to plans for regular meetings in the future that would include discussions of sharing seats. Two particular issues that came up for discussion which exemplify some of the common concerns and perspectives were the fake 'Russian letter' and the manner in which the government had awarded the television contract.

While negotiating and debating the merits of forming a coalition with the other opposition parties, Bavadra and other native Fijian members of the Labour Party concentrated on building support among rural native Fijians. The Labour Party felt that if the Alliance Party was going to be defeated its hold over rural-dwelling native Fijians would have to be reduced. Land disputes had become the most important means by which the Labour Party had sought to gain native Fijian support, but there was concern that this would only attract the vocal minority that had specific grudges against the Alliance government. The question of regional inequality, particularly in relation to the west, was seen as one means of broadening the Labour Party's support in the villages. With this in mind, on 19 June the Labour Party convened a meeting in the western village of Viseisei, in the Vuda tikina, to establish its sixteenth branch. Viseisei was Bavadra's home village, but it was also the home of the Tui Vuda and the minister of state for forests, Ratu Josaia Tavaiqia, and it was traditionally an Alliance Party stronghold. It was seen by both sides as something of a test of strength between the two parties.

The Alliance Party had sought to stop the Labour Party from holding meetings in villages such as Viseisei by using the power of the chiefs aligned with it. In the case of Viseisei, the Taukei Nakelo, Ratu Vuki Tavai, had forbidden that the meeting be held. The traditional means of arranging a meeting under the Alliance Party was to first ask the Taukei Nakelo, who would then consult with the Tui Vuda. The Labour Party was fully aware that it would not be given permission by either of these Alliance Party stalwarts, but it was also aware that Bavadra had been given permission earlier by the Vunivalu, Ratu George Cakobau, to hold meetings in native Fijian villages, in general. The meeting was arranged by a retired teacher, Jona Tavai Tavutunawai, who was a member of the chiefly mataqali, and who used his membership in this mataqali to convene the meeting. At the meeting, Bavadra spoke of the 'need to realize the difference between the traditional role and our democratic rights as citizens of this country' and said that he felt that a growing number of native Fijians had begun to assert their political rights in relation to their traditional obligations to their chiefs, and that this indicated 'political maturity on the part of the people.'

The day after the Labour Party's meeting, the Alliance Party announced that it would hold a meeting of the Fijian Association in Viseisei the following week. The Alliance Party sought to emphasize that the Labour Party meeting constituted a breach of traditional etiquette and that this was yet one more indication of the Labour Party's disregard for the honour of the chiefs. The Taukei Nakelo arranged to open the meeting with a ceremony 'to ask forgiveness' of the Tui Vuda on the part of the people of Viseisei for insulting him by holding the Labour Party meeting. Needless to say, the Tui Vuda 'accepted their plea.' This ceremony was followed with a speech by Dr. Apenisa Kurisaqila, who told the audience that the chiefly system was the 'mainstay of Fijian politics and leadership' and that 'no one who disregards tradition and the chiefly system will ever win in Fiji.'[33] Then Apisai Tora spoke, highlighting the Alliance Party's record in promoting the interests of native Fijians and dismissed the prospects of the proposed Labour Party-NFP-Western United Front coalition.

The Viseisei meeting was followed the next day, 28 June, with a larger meeting of the Alliance Party National Council, at the village of Narewa, near Nadi. Narewa was the home of the Tui Nadi, Ratu Napolioni Dawai, who had left the Alliance Party to join the Western United Front, and who now was under considerable pressure to rejoin the Alliance Party. He had invited Mara to hold the National Council meeting at Narewa after he and Mara had met to discuss Dawai's returning to the Alliance Party, which was expected to be announced at the meeting. Some three hundred delegates were present and the meeting began with a welcoming ceremony for Mara. In his speech, Mara commented on the great strides made by the Alliance Party, and while admitting that some mistakes had been made, told the audience that 'governing is not a matter for novices, nor the self-appointed' and laid some of the responsibility for present criticisms on the relative success of Alliance Party rule and the rising expectations that this had created. He pointed to the stability brought to Fiji by the Alliance Party, implying that this was now threatened by the Labour Party. Mara also hinted that 'someone might just call an early election.'[34] One thing that did not take place at the meeting was Dawai's announcement that he was rejoining the Alliance Party. Instead, he remained with Western United Front.

Earlier, moves had begun to revitalize the Vatukoula branch of the Fijian Association in response to the Labour Party's involvement in the Nasomo land case. Jeffrey Reid of Emperor Gold Mine had banned political meetings in the Vatukoula area, but this ban was lifted to allow Apisai Tora to organize a meeting of the local Fijian Association on 25 June. The meeting was attended by an array of prominent Alliance Party members who promised that efforts would be made to sort out problems with the mining companies.

The issue of the right to call meetings came up again in early July in Nadroga, when a meeting was called by the Tui Nalolo, Ratu Isei Vosailagi, the paramount chief of six villages and one of the founders of the Western United Front. At the Cuvu meeting, he had been one of the handful of chiefs who had backed a move for the Western United Front to join in a coalition with the Alliance Party. He stated that the people in his area now supported the Alliance Party because of assistance provided to the villages for rural development, citing F$20,000 given to two of the villages to help extend their land into mangrove areas: 'We were against the Alliance at that time, but they kept on helping us.' His support for the Alliance Party was challenged by Ratu Sitiveni Varani of Tau village (a village which had also received development assistance) who sought to call a meeting to gauge community sentiment. Vosailagi responded that he alone had the right to call meetings in the area. Nevertheless, Varani organized meetings for the six villages at which overwhelming support for the Western United Front was expressed. Furthermore, people sought to disassociate themselves from Vosailagi, who they said had consulted with almost no one before going to the Cuvu meeting; and the need to separate chiefly traditions and politics was also emphasized.

In addition to the Alliance Party pattern of seeking to use the paramount chiefs to hold onto support in villages, the dispute between Vosailagi and Varani highlights the greater sense of a democratic tradition among western native Fijians – a tradition that the eastern chiefly oligarchy had sought to stamp out since the last century. As in eastern Fiji, the Alliance Party had sought to establish control over the western villages largely through the chiefs. But in the west, this had not guaranteed support of the commoners or even lower ranking chiefs. Tora in his early years, the Western United Front, and now the Labour Party had shown the extent to which support among native Fijians in the west could not be taken for granted. This was to prove increasingly frustrating to the Alliance Party as villagers continued to form Labour Party branches in western villages in contravention of orders from the Alliance Party's chiefly henchmen.

The *Fiji Sun* of 29 June contained a piece entitled: 'The Great Debate: Politics and Fijian Tradition' and published position statements by Inoke Tabua for the Alliance Party, Sakeasi Butadroka for the Fijian Nationalist Party, Temo Sukanaivalu for the NFP, and Timoci Bavadra for the Fiji Labour Party. Senator Tabua sought to emphasize the interconnection of tradition and politics, citing the importance of tradition for native Fijians and the centrality of chiefly rule to this tradition and hence to native Fijian politics. Bavadra countered that while the Labour Party upholds the importance of tradition for native Fijians, there was a need to separate tradition and politics – and, in particular, it was wrong to use traditional authority as a means of seeking political support. As an indication of the Labour Party's respect for tradition, he pointed to how the Labour Party had sought the permission of the Vunivalu before campaigning in Tailevu Province. The Labour Party's position was reinforced the following week in a speech by another of its native Fijian members, Joeli Kalou. Kalou, a trade unionist, was also a member of the Great Council of Chiefs. Speaking in Labasa, he told a rally: 'Traditionally I was born a mata-ni-vanua and I will die as one. But my political stance is entirely my choice.'

As the Labour Party prepared for its first annual convention in Lautoka on 19 July, talks concerning a coalition with the NFP and Western United Front continued. Little progress had been made since the initial meeting, however, with the NFP remaining reticent to risk taking a back seat to the Labour Party, and the Labour Party still divided on the issue. Rank-and-file Labour Party supporters clearly did not favour a coalition with the NFP on ideological and practical grounds. The NFP was seen as too firmly committed to communal politics, as having moved too far away from its peasant roots, and as being far too fragmented to represent a credible political force.

Reports from party branches prepared for the convention indicated strong opposition to a coalition. On 6 July, speaking at the opening of a new party branch near Labasa, Labour Party secretary Krishna Datt had stated that he saw no prospect of a coalition being formed. Other party leaders such as Kalou were also strongly opposed. Bavadra himself, however, felt that it was important to continue a dialogue with the NFP and the Western United Front. Only a few days before the Lautoka convention he had expressed confidence that 'something concrete will come out of the discussions' and, in private, many NFP members felt that a coalition was the only hope for their party.

The situation for the NFP worsened on 15 July, when NFP Youth Wing parliamentarian Davendra Singh joined the Labour Party. The next day, another NFP parliamentarian, Jai Raj Singh (who had held the North West Indian national seat since 1977), also joined the Labour Party. Singh justified his move citing his feeling that the NFP had lost its grass-roots support and that a three-way electoral fight would be a disaster. (Two weeks later, the Labour Party was to gain its fourth parliamentarian, when Filimone Nalatu, who held the North Eastern Fijian national seat, crossed the floor.)

The weeks before the Labour Party convention also witnessed growing tension in the trade union movement. The government decided to withdraw recognition of the Fiji Trades Union Congress, 'to give workers a wider say in safeguarding their interests.' The primary reason behind this move was to divide the union movement and, if possible, to force those in the Labour Party to quit their union posts. The Fiji Trades Union Congress responded by organizing three public rallies, including one in Suva on 2 July. Three courses of action were proposed: taking the government to court for violation of the workers' constitutional rights, taking selective industrial actions, and going on a national strike. Shortly after the rallies, the president of the FTUC, Jale Toki, who was closely associated with the Alliance Party, questioned the propriety of having FTUC officers also serving as officers of the Labour Party. He further expressed the hope that by removing them the government might take a more conciliatory line with the union body. He had little support for this position within the FTUC, some pointing to the fact that it seemed perfectly all right for the government to allow those on the other side of the bargaining table to hold offices in the Alliance Party. James Raman, general secretary of the FTUC, remained fairly silent on the issue and there were those in the Labour Party and the FTUC who expected Raman to make his long-expected break with the Labour

Party. Raman did not leave the Labour Party and the tension between labour and the government continued to simmer.

Meanwhile, trade unionist Joveci Gavoka, who was an Alliance Party stalwart and a longtime opponent of Mahendra Chaudhry, announced plans for his Public Employees Union to initiate a move to unite blue-collar workers and eventually form a national body to rival the FTUC. The plan was for this body, comprised of pro-Alliance unions, to be recognized by the government instead of the FTUC. As with earlier attempts to form a united front of blue-collar workers to challenge Chaudhry and the others in the Labour Party, this move too failed to get off the ground. The government did, however, manage to begin a personal attack on Chaudhry, removing him from various posts he had held on statutory bodies. Thus, in mid-August he was dropped from the board of the Fiji National Provident Fund and replaced by Gavoka.

On 19 July 1986, the Fiji Labour Party held its first annual convention at the Girmit Centenary Centre in Lautoka – a western site had been chosen to emphasize the party's regional base. It was attended by over one thousand people and gave the party a chance to take stock of its progress and to present its plans for the future leading up to the national election. Party secretary Krishna Datt announced that the Labour Party was ready to fight an election and that the party would field candidates for all fifty-two seats. This decision had come after considerable debate, but it had been decided that the Labour Party was strong enough to challenge the Alliance Party throughout the country and in all communal groups, including General Electors. Success in establishing thirty branches and a women's wing were also highlighted.

Bavadra's address to the meeting was similar to the one he had given at the launching of the party a year before, and he once again outlined party policies under the general heading of the Labour Party's commitment to the principles of democratic socialism and its desire to 'unleash' the productive potential of Fiji and to further the cause of democracy, which would thus create more jobs; improve incomes; provide for basic needs; equalize regional development; improve industrial relations; create a better place for women; end corruption, nepotism, and catering to vested interests; democratize government instrumentalities; implement a non-aligned and nuclear-free foreign policy; and so forth. On the question of tradition and politics, Bavadra stated:

The Fiji Labour Party will continue to educate and inform the indigenous Fijian people so that they can grasp the difference between what can properly be deemed to be indigenous Fijian obligations demanded by tradition and his fundamental rights and freedom guaranteed in the Fiji Constitution. We in the Fiji Labour Party suspect that one of the reasons why the ruling Alliance government has failed to deliver its promise repeated at numerous meetings of the Great Council of Chiefs and Fijian Association to translate the Constitution of Fiji into the Bauan vernacular is precisely because they want to keep the indigenous Fijian people ignorant of the proper relationship between tradition and politics.

The Fiji Labour Party firmly believes that tradition and politics must be kept separate and one must not be confused for the other and we abhor the way in which the ruling Alliance Party has manipulated the vanua and chiefly system for political purposes.[35]

Bavadra also reiterated the Labour Party's plans to nationalize the gold-mine at Vatukoula, in addition to the bus industry and brewery. He cited the Fiji Sugar Corporation as an example of a well-run state enterprise and also pointed to the example of the worker and state-run international airport at Nadi. He felt that nationalization was called for when the private sector had failed to work with the government in promoting its goal of providing for basic needs and social justice. In the case of the gold-mine and the bus industry, they were often at the centre of controversy, and their ownership was closely identified with and was a major sources of funds for the Alliance Party.

Nationalization of these industries was shown to be part of an encompassing plan for the creation of a structure of producers' and workers' councils:

Essentially, what we propose is to establish a comprehensive structure of elected councils for each major productive area in our economy with a National Producers and Workers Council to provide overall co-ordination. The idea is to give a real voice to those who produce the wealth of our country. Included in this plan is a restructuring of the organisation of the sugar and pine industries to give greater say to all of those involved. In the case of the pine industries, we propose formation of a Forestry Council in which the landowners have the major say, but in which other interests will be represented. Similarly, we propose creation of a Sugar Council, with the main voice being given to cane growers, but with significant representation from workers in the cane industry as well. In these and in other instances, the relevant statutory bodies are to fall under the direction of these councils.

The proposed structure also includes a Mining Council and a Marine Products Council. These councils are to be part of a plan to provide for the democratic functioning of Emperor Goldmine and PAFCO [a local tuna canning operation], both of which we propose to nationalise. These two companies would be operated along the lines of FASA/ATS [the worker-managed body that runs Nadi International Airport].[36]

Further details of this plan were not made available at the convention, but were circulated the following month for discussion and revision among party members and at meetings in native Fijian villages. It was a bold step that threatened to destroy the very basis of Alliance Party rule and to radically transform Fijian society. And it was one that received considerable support.

The Alliance Party focused its criticism of Bavadra's speech on his plans for nationalization and the way in which the call for producers' and workers' councils would touch upon the land issue. Peter Stinson, in his opening address at the Nadi Bula Festival, accused the Labour Party of advocating 'left-wing policies' which would destroy parts of the economy and lead to higher taxes. He further added that its policies for nationalization went against the world-wide trend favouring privatization, saying, 'At last the Fiji Labour Party is showing its true colours.' An Australian consultant was brought in to criticize the call for nationalization of the bus industry, followed by critical statements from the Bus Operators Association.

The land issue had begun to heat up days before the Labour Party convention when the government announced that it was converting 4,800 hectares of Crown land into native reserve and considering conversion of another 12,000 hectares. The land involved had become Crown land as a result of the extinction of mataqali and now the proposal was to redistribute it to other mataqali. The move was primarily intended to help secure support for the Alliance Party among native Fijian villagers, and it was not by accident that most of the land involved was in Ba, Nadroga, and Navosa. It also served to raise Indo-Fijian insecurity over land leases and the fear that such conversions would be accompanied by cancellation of leases. Both the NFP and Labour Party condemned the move, although with different emphases. The NFP argued that 'these lands are Crown property and are assets of the nation. It cannot and should not be alienated without Parliamentary approval.' The NFP also focused on Indo-Fijian insecurity of tenure. The Labour Party objected to 'the political motivation of this move' and expressed concern that the land would not benefit native Fijian landowners but rather would be 'lost within the native land administration.' The Alliance Party also used this occasion to announce that it would have a 'serious and close' look into the request of native Fijians in the western interior to have a province of their own – Colo North – something that the Alliance Party had never supported in the past.

The month of August saw four important gatherings for the Alliance Party. At the South Pacific Forum at Suva in early August, Mara sought to maximize the propaganda benefits from the meeting with highly publicized photos of himself with other leaders such as Jean Marie Tjibaou from New Caledonia and Cook Islands prime minister Tom Davis. The Fiji papers ran headlines such as 'Bowen has praise for Ratu Sir Kamasese,' 'Kanak: Ratu Mara for Independence,' and 'Lange Backs Ratu Mara.' To make sure that all went well, the government kept a close watch on the media, banning some reporters, such as those working with the Australian Broadcasting Commission's *Four Corners* program, and limiting the activities of those who were present. Before the gathering, Mara also had warned the local media that he was not pleased with growing evidence of their 'irresponsible' behaviour.

Next came a 'mini-convention' of the western branch of the Fijian Association in Lautoka on 16 August. Mara's opening address was critical of the tendency for native Fijians to take land disputes to the courts and of recent court decisions concerning ownership of native Fijian land. To deal with the matter, he announced plans to set up a three-member appeals tribunal. He was also extremely critical of the Labour Party for bringing the land issue into the election ('they have made it a political issue ... the Government is only carrying out what has been laid down by law') and of the Labour Party's plans for reform in the native lands administration.[37] Once again he referred to the Labour Party as the Flower faction of the NFP. Apisai Tora told those at the convention that there was nothing wrong with mixing tradition and politics: 'Fijian traditional leadership has always been political ... The art of ruling their people is political.'[38] Two former members of the Western United Front, the Taukei Nalolo and Tui Vitogo, announced that they were rejoining the Alliance Party and were given a prominent place in the front row of the hall with other western chiefs. Tora commented, 'the stray ones have decided to return without the machinery getting out to get them.'

The third event was the third national economic summit, held in Suva from 18–20 August. At the last minute, the Fiji Trades Union Congress decided to attend the summit and sought to use it as a forum to criticize government economic policies. But the main purpose of the summit was to allow the government to claim that the economic situation had improved to the point where it was considering relaxing the wage freeze.

Finally, the meeting of the Great Council of Chiefs at Somosomo in late August did not go as well as planned. Among the topics for discussion were the draft regulation on the reorganization of the Fijian Administration, the Crown to native reserve land conversion, native Fijian education, and economic problems faced by bodies associated with the Council of Chiefs. The Alliance Party had expected to have the meeting to itself as usual, but the week before it convened, Bavadra announced that he would be attending as a Ba Provincial Council delegate, primarily to explain his party's land policy, but also to discuss its position on other matters. Bavadra's presence forced the Alliance Party chiefs to curtail discussion of some potentially embarrassing issues. Not only had the Alliance Party been unable to stop Bavadra from attending the meeting, but it was clear that there were chiefs in attendance who were sympathetic to what he had to say. Mara and other members of the chiefly oligarchy were not pleased with this small show of democracy at the Council of Chiefs. Moreover, Mara and his associates were concerned that worse problems might be in store if those native Fijians who did not share their views of the oligarchy were able to gain access to the Council of Chiefs in greater number through the Parliament and provincial councils.

Bavadra's position on reorganizing the administration of land was spelled out in greater detail in an unpublished paper. Circulated around the time of the Council of Chiefs meeting, this paper discussed the party's plan for a landowners council and a national lands and resources commission.[39] Bavadra explained that the purpose of the landowners council was 'to give the native landowners of Fiji for the first time a direct say in decision-making concerning their land rather than leaving control in the hands of a small circle of individuals.' The council was to be comprised of 'representatives from different landowning groups throughout Fiji determined on a proportional basis so as to ensure that all landowners have a voice.' He saw that 'this body will serve as the overall democratic body to debate issues related to the management of native land and to oversee the functioning of the NLTB [Native Land Trust Board].' To counter Alliance Party propaganda, he noted: 'It is important to point out that this body will not replace the Great Council of Chiefs ... Rather, it is intended to strengthen direct control by the landowners over what happens to their land, while the Great Council of Chiefs remains the ultimate guarantor of the rights of native landowners.'

Bavadra continued that the 'members of the Landowners Council will in turn select from among themselves representatives who will form the NLTB Governing Council. Members of the Governing Council will be chosen on a regional basis so as to avoid the distortion that exists at present ... These Councillors will function as an executive for the Landowners Council and it is they who will be directly responsible for overseeing the running of the NLTB in accordance with the wishes of the landowners throughout the country.' Responding to Alliance Party criticisms of the cost of these reforms, Bavadra explained:

> They will be paid for through a small percentage of the money that will be saved by the reduction of wasted and misappropriated expenditure that at present characterises the administration of native land in this country. Rather than using such funds to further entrench the political power of the Alliance Party and the vested interests of a few, we would use a portion of this money to promote real control of the land by those who own it. We have no doubt that the end result would not only be money better spent, but an actual reduction in expenditure. This, when combined with our proposal to reduce the amount of royalties that the NLTB appropriates to itself, will mean that more money will go directly to the native owners.[40]

Again, Bavadra's critique was very threatening stuff to the Alliance Party, which responded with further attempts at distortion aimed at instilling fear among native Fijians and with greater use of patronage funds – in short, to greater appeals for communal solidarity against the 'Labour threat.' Addressing another Fijian Association 'mini-convention' in late September, Mara called on native Fijians to remain united in order to hold on to the nation's leadership. The veil of multiracialism was slipping away as the pressure increased. This outburst resulted in Bavadra writing to the Office of Director of Public Prosecutions to ask for an investigation into whether Mara's remarks constituted a breach of the Public Order Act under which it was illegal to make remarks that incited racial dislike or hatred. It was, after all, this act that had provided Mara with justification for jailing Sakeasi Butadroka for six months in 1977. Mara's racial remarks were more extreme than those prevailing in previous elections, and many political observers in Fiji saw this as a sign that he was worried.

Charges of corruption and wasteful government spending had continued to mount during the latter part of the year. Debate over the government's granting of a television license to Australian Kerry

Packer's PBL Pacific Television continued with widespread rumours of government corruption. One thing that received frequent mention was a decision by the Ministry of Education to move out of government-owned offices into Marela House, a building owned by Mara. Questions arose over the propriety of such a move and over the fact that, under the lease agreement, the building's owner was paid rent above the market rate. The 1985 Auditor General's report was made public in September, documenting millions of dollars of fraud, misuse, and waste of funds by various departments, including the prime minister's. Mara was forced to call for an immediate investigation of 'irregularities.'

Mara had other problems as well. Ahmed Ali, as minister of education, had managed to alienate a large number of teachers as well as parents of school children. In October, he decided to pull Ali out of the Ministry of Education and make him head of the newly created Ministry of Information. There, Ali could devote all of his energies to the upcoming election. Mara then shifted Filipe Bole to the Ministry of Education which would give him a specific responsibility, and, because of Bole's ability to get along with people, it was hoped he could mend some fences and undo some of Ali's damage.

The Alliance Party was also confronted with the problem of the Indian Alliance, which was in complete disarray. Young Alliance member Anil Bidesi had criticized Ahmed Ali in public, and it was widely known that many members of the Indian Alliance were unhappy with Ali. Denials by Indian Alliance president Ishwari Bajpai, whose own position was threatened, convinced no one. In addition to internal factional problems, the government's decision to convert the Crown land to reserve land was known to have cost the Indian Alliance even more support. Mara's hopes for the Indian Alliance, however, were buoyed in November when Irene Narayan announced that she was crossing to join the Alliance Party. Praising Mara, she referred to the Alliance Party as 'the party that has stood the test of time.'

The end of November witnessed Mara seeking to gain political advantage from the Pope's visit, and his minister of finance announcing an election budget for the following year that included tax relief for a large number of poor farmers and a relaxing of wage restraints. Meanwhile, the opposition parties went ahead with discussions about a possible coalition. The election had to be called by September 1987, but many speculated that it would be held in May, if not earlier, partly to take advantage of the continued divisions in the opposition camp. In an interview published in *Pacific Islands Monthly*, Bavadra was 'candid enough to admit that Labour alone can hope only to become the main opposition next year. To attain power, it needs the NFP and its coalition partner, the Western United Front.'[41] Bavadra and Chaudhry had continued to pursue a dialogue with the NFP and the Western United Front even after the Lautoka convention, and by September more party members were coming to support their view that perhaps a coalition should not be ruled out – if it was the only way to overthrow the Alliance Party. Unionists were especially worried that if Mara was returned to power he would step up moves to destroy the union movement; he and other members of the Alliance Party had already given ample warnings that they planned to further curtail civil liberties.

By October, the opposition parties had secretly formed a joint committee to work out a proposed common platform. Meanwhile, the Labour Party's forty branches were again polled on the idea of a coalition and this time they all supported the move. The NFP, by now, was under no illusion as to the state of its organization and its lack of support. Sharma and others seemed to feel that a deal needed to be made as soon as possible, while they still had a party to lead. There was still opposition to forming too close an alliance with the Labour Party on the part of the pro-Koya forces, for they felt that such a coalition would weaken their position in the party even further. The committee arrived at a tentative agreement to form a coalition under the name of the National People's Unity. The coalition was to be for the election period, after which it would remain to be seen what kind of arrangement would be worked out. A draft manifesto was produced under the slogan: 'Together for Our People and Country.' The Labour Party expressed a willingness to compromise on some issues, but it was clear that it felt that it was bargaining from a position of strength. The most important item missing from the document was the Labour Party's call for nationalization.

It appeared to those involved in the negotiations between the two parties that the primary difficulty remaining was the allocation of seats among the members of the coalition. The NFP sought to retain its strong seats, leaving the more marginal seats to the Labour Party. But events elsewhere overtook the negotiations. Meeting in Ba, NFP delegates gave Sharma and his allies a mandate to form a more thorough coalition with the Labour Party. This reflected the recognition of the weakness of the NFP and the almost complete loss of power of the pro-Koya forces within the party. Sharma and his supporters now joined with representatives from the Labour Party to form a united political front. There was a feeling of urgency since both the Labour Party and the NFP knew that Mara hoped to call an election as soon as possible, in the hope of catching the two parties in disarray.

Representatives of the Labour Party and NFP met in Suva throughout the final week of November. After a meeting on Friday, the twenty-eighth, that lasted into the early hours of Saturday morning, a final agreement was reached. The debate had not been acrimonious and, by this time, the outcome was never in doubt, but the veteran trade unionists and politicians involved were cautious and sought to ensure that all elements were covered. As expected, Bavadra was to be the leader of the Coalition, as it was to be called, and Harish Sharma was to be deputy leader. Jai Ram Reddy was named as chairman of a committee to select candidates from among the eighty-eight applicants received by the NFP and from 120 by the Labour Party. Before a deal was made, the Labour Party let it be known that it did not want to inherit any of the pro-Koya forces, who, it was felt, would only cause trouble. With Reddy chairing the selection committee this was assured. Future meetings were to be held to work out the final details of the Coalition platform.

The agreement to form a coalition did not go unchallenged by pro-Koya forces. On Monday, 1 December, Shardha Nand, who had assumed leadership of the pro-Koya faction, sought to force Harish Sharma to call a meeting of NFP parliamentarians with the aim of toppling Sharma as leader. But Sharma did not agree, arguing that there was insufficient time to inform everyone. During the day, another member of the pro-Koya faction, Noor Dean, had taken a petition around to NFP parliamentarians which called for Sharma to be replaced by Nand as leader of the NFP. It was claimed that twelve parliamentarians had signed the petition. Given the composition of the coalition selection committee and the fact that the Labour Party had made it plain that it considered no seat reserved for anyone, it was clear to a number of the sitting members that they would not be asked to run again. The move to unseat Sharma failed, but it served to give the Alliance Party hope that the coalition would be a fragile one.

Parliament was dissolved on 18 December, and it was announced that a writ of election would be issued before the end of the month. Mara had sought a late February or early March election date, but the electoral commission announced that it would not be possible for it to prepare for a poll earlier than 4 April. This loss of a month did not please Mara, but he accepted it as the best that could be done and announced an election for 4–11 April.

Mara had good reason to be optimistic about the election: the

Alliance Party appeared in good shape financially and organization-
ally; his party already had begun stirring up communal sentiments
among native Fijians; state patronage funds were flowing; and, with
Irene Narayan in the Alliance Party, he had someone who should be
able to revitalize the Indo-Fijian wing of the party. Nevertheless, he
was aware that it would be a difficult race. The Labour Party had
defied initial predictions that it would never be more than another
fringe party, and the fact that a coalition had been formed at all was
amazing. As for the members of the newly formed coalition, they too
shared a sense of optimism. The Labour Party felt that it had gained
a great deal of political experience over the past eighteen months
and that along with the remnants of the NFP, purged of a Koya
faction which appeared to have little remaining electoral support, it
had a good chance of defeating the Alliance Party. Bavadra and the
others in the coalition realized, however, as did Mara, that the outcome would depend largely on the native Fijian voters. Would they
vote communally as a bloc and remain loyal to their Alliance-con-
trolled chiefs? Or would they divide along regional, class, and other
lines and against the appeals to chiefly obedience?

CHAPTER SIX

The 1987 Election and the Coalition Government

The politically charged atmosphere of 1986 was a prelude to what was to be Fiji's most bitterly fought national election in April 1987. To the surprise of most political observers, the Alliance Party lost the election, in large part because of its failure to win the four crucial seats in and around Suva and because of the ability of the Fiji Labour Party and National Federation Party to forge a united coalition. In contrast to Siddiq Koya in 1977, Dr. Timoci Bavadra had no trouble forming a new government in 1987, and he and his colleagues immediately set about instituting reforms.

Although Mara made a public show of begrudgingly accepting his party's loss, several other prominent members of the Alliance Party joined with racist extremists to launch a destabilization campaign based on appeals to native Fijian communalism and acts of violence, under the banner of a newly formed Taukei Movement. The Bavadra government proved adept at meeting the challenge as support for the Taukei seemed to wane, and a month after assuming office, the new government appeared to be in control. But the Coalition still had to contend with an array of disparate and powerful opponents.

THE 1987 ELECTION

The Alliance Party, privately fearing defeat, and the Fiji Labour Party-National Federation Party coalition, sensing the possibility of electoral victory, each sought to put forward as strong a field of candidates as possible for the 1987 election. The Alliance Party announced its fifty-two candidates on Monday, 22 December. In what was easily the most difficult candidate selection process since independence, the party had dumped eleven sitting members of

Parliament. Although, in public, the Alliance Party continued to dismiss its opponents, the consensus was that great care had to be taken to ensure that the party would win the election, even in the case of those seats with predominant native Fijian electorates.

General agreement within the party was that the ultimate choice of candidates was up to Mara, who let it be known that he wanted to improve the image of the party to give it a more dynamic and capable look. This meant easing out older ministers who were seen to belong to an earlier political era. To ensure that these individuals did not join the opposition, Mara planned to reward them with diplomatic and other posts after the election (promising a further strain on Fiji's already over-extended foreign affairs budget).

One potentially important problem within the Alliance Party came from its youth wing, the Young Alliance. Its president, Nirmal Singh, and other members of the Young Alliance were sufficiently angered when the party selected only one of their candidates, Surya Deep Singh, that they threatened to field a parallel slate of candidates. Nirmal Singh complained that their loyalty had not been rewarded while 'there are people who just walked into the party and are given seats.' He went on to comment: 'There is a feeling among the youths that they have been neglected by the party.' Under pressure from senior members of the party and out of fear of being excluded from future party patronage, the Young Alliance did not follow through with its threat. Young Alliance members soon issued statements denying any intention to do so and reaffirming their support for the Alliance Party, but evidence of a rift did not completely disappear.

The emphasis within the Coalition, as the united opposition parties came to be known, was also on projecting a new, dynamic look in an effort to distance itself from the image of the National Federation Party of Siddiq Koya and Irene Narayan, and to capture the support of younger, more educated native Fijians. In doing so, party leaders were aware of the need to gain support through traditional means as well. The Coalition's eight-member committee (five Labour and three NFP), under the chairmanship of Jai Ram Reddy, presented a preliminary list of thirty-nine candidates in mid-December, with plans to announce its final list of candidates a day or two after the Alliance Party (to allow for a last minute assessment of the strengths and weaknesses of the Alliance Party choices). On 23 December, however, the party leadership decided to wait in the hope of convincing a few more possible candidates to stand (including Jai Ram Reddy himself). The final list of candidates appeared in the middle of January.

As expected, several members of the Koya faction failed to win endorsement by the Coalition. In fact, a total of seventeen sitting members of the opposition had been dumped. Those who had not been chosen sought to mount a challenge. Shardha Nand, who held the Nausori-Levuka Indian communal seat, decided to hold a meeting of the Rewa branch of the NFP (in his district) to challenge the recent changes. Announcement of a meeting was made on 17 January. The plan was to present a list of fourteen conditions to the Coalition that appealed to Indo-Fijian communalism. These conditions included a demand that a large number of Indian seats remain in NFP hands 'as the reserved voice of the Indians of Fiji.' Members of the Koya faction also called for the creation of a Ministry of Indian Affairs (there was a department of Indian Affairs in colonial days) and to make appointments to government boards and committees and to the army and police on a communal basis. In addition, the branch criticized the Labour Party's advocacy of nationalization.The Rewa branch announced that Koya would be attending the meeting, but supporters of the Coalition said that he would not, and Koya himself remained unavailable for comment. It appeared as if he was waiting to see how things developed before committing himself, and in the meantime he had met for an hour in private with Mara, fuelling speculation that Koya had made a deal with Mara to try to sabotage the Coalition in return for some reward.

Next, members of the Koya faction who failed to win Coalition endorsement met on 23 January and decided to try to go their own way under the NFP banner. After the meeting, Koya issued a statement to the press denouncing the selection of candidates and stating that he no longer supported the Coalition – signs of a serious division within the NFP that threatened the newly formed Coalition. The Alliance Party clearly was delighted, but neither Labour nor the non-Koya faction of the NFP appeared to be particularly upset. NFP leader Harish Sharma responded merely that 'Mr Koya is entitled to his views' and noted that Koya had been present during negotiations over the formation of the Coalition and while selection procedures were outlined. The attempt to re-awaken the Dove/Flower division did not meet with much success. A number of prominent individuals, identified in the past with Koya, remained loyal to the Coalition, while the anti-Coalition group included only a handful of individuals such as Shardha Nand.[1]

The Rewa branch meeting was held the weekend of 24–25 January. It was attended by fewer than one hundred people and even Koya decided not to appear. It did not go well for Nand and the other Coalition opponents, and the meeting ended meekly with the passing of a resolution which asked the Coalition to reconsider its list of candidates. The Coalition responded with little enthusiasm for the proposal. Krishna Datt told reporters: 'It seems very unlikely that we will make any changes' and referred to the Rewa branch meeting as a 'non-event.' Bavadra indicated that he saw no reason to bow to the demands: 'We are in control of the situation.' NFP members of the Coaliton responded in a like manner.

The National Federation Party/Western United Front splinter group, the anti-Coalition dissidents, announced that it would name its own candidates at a public meeting in Labasa on 14 February. The meeting was attended by only about two hundred people and was addressed by Vijaya Parmanandan, Siddiq Koya, and Osea Gavidi. The speakers were heckled and tension grew until Koya asked a police officer present to take action to control the crowd and threatened to call for additional police if order was not restored. Only a partial list of candidates was presented which did not include Koya or Parmanandan. Koya apparently had come to realize that he stood little chance of being elected this time around and wished to avoid the embarrassment of electoral defeat. This did not, however, stop Koya from speaking out during the campaign. The final list of NFP splinter candidates included only five – among them Shardha Nand for the Nausori/Levuka Indian communal seat and Subramani Basawaiya for the Vanua Levu North and West Indian national seat.

Despite pressure from his own party to join the Coalition, Western United Front leader Gavidi continued to support Koya, and he attended the Rewa meeting with Western United Front (WUF) secretary Isikeli Nadolo, as well as subsequent meetings of the splinter group. The situation with the Western United Front was a complicated one. It was clear that the majority of its rank-and-file supporters backed the Labour Party, but most of them did not want to split publicly with party leader Gavidi. Bavadra and other Labour Party members continued to hold discussions with Gavidi in hopes of convincing him to join the Coalition, and he was promised a prominent place in the Coalition. At the same time, Gavidi was being courted by members of the Koya faction in the NFP and by the Alliance Party (he had business interests in common with Mara's son, Finau).

Gavidi vacillated on the idea of joining the Coalition, and the Labour Party became increasingly frustrated, but party members were anxious not to push too hard in the hopes of creating a united front among western native Fijians. There was also a feeling that should Gavidi be elected, he would work with the Coalition in Parliament after the election. At one point, on 21 December, it was announced that Gavidi would stand as the Coalition candidate for the Nadroga/Navosa Fijian communal seat, but after he attended the NFP-splinter meeting in Nausori he was dropped and relations between the Coalition and Gavidi cooled. The issue was never settled satisfactorily and the WUF went ahead and fielded five of its own candidates under the NFP/WUF splinter group banner – among them Gavidi, who stood once again for the Nadroga/Navosa Fijian communal seat; and Isikeli Nadolo, who stood for the South Western Fijian national seat.

The Coalition also faced dissatisfaction from within the Labour Party, although it was easily contained. The most important dissident was Suva mayor Bob Kumar, who was upset at not being nominated. Bavadra, Chaudhry, and others in the Labour Party had not been overly pleased with Kumar's handling of the city council or with his work as treasurer of the party, and they felt it was best to leave him where he was and field other, stronger, candidates in the Suva area. Kumar threatened to run on his own in Suva in an effort to pressure the Labour Party to give him a seat, but when it was obvious that this was not going to happen, he backed down quietly.

There was also the question of the relationship between the Fijian Nationalist Party and the Coalition. A number of Nationalist Party supporters had begun working for the Labour Party, and leaders of the two parties held discussions centring on their common desire to put an end to Alliance Party rule. While welcoming support from the Nationalists, the Labour Party was wary of becoming too closely identified with their racist positions. The Labour Party would have liked to have been able to depend on the support of the Nationalists, or at least not to have been opposed by them, but it was not overly worried by a failure to reach a formal agreement. Most of the seats involved were not ones that the Labour Party was likely to win on its own, but it was thought that, in a replay of 1977, the Coalition or the Nationalists might be able to beat the Alliance Party with a divided vote. Also, the Labour Party felt that it could live with the Nationalists after the election as coalition partners in parliament, if necessary. The Nationalists fielded six candidates, centring in their eastern Viti Levu strongholds. Party leader Sakeasi Butadroka himself ran for the Rewa Fijian communal seat.

Finally, there were a handful of independents. Some of these were unaffiliated individuals who felt that they had a special message for the people of Fiji, and others were persons who had failed to be given the nod by one of the main parties. The only serious candidates out of this group were Epeli Kacimaiwai (Rewa Fijian communal), Paula Sotutu (Bua/Macuata Fijian communal), and Hugh Thaggard (Western General communal). All had been aligned with the Alliance Party in the past and were running now largely because the party had passed them over. Although it was doubtful that any of them would win, they threatened to cost the Alliance Party support.

Candidates for the election filed their nominations on 9 March. The following day a few 'dummy' candidates withdrew, leaving fifty-two candidates from the Coalition, fifty-two from the Alliance Party, ten from the NFP/WUF splinter group, six from the Fijian Nationalist Party, and eleven independents.

The Campaign

Actual campaigning for the 1987 election had begun in early 1986, but the 'formal' campaign did not begin until January 1987. The Coalition unveiled its election manifesto at a public meeting attended by approximately two thousand people at Lautoka's Girmit Centenary Centre on 21 February. Published as an eight-page supplement in the newspapers on 28 January, the manifesto began: 'The Coalition reiterates its conviction that any Government in Fiji cannot be identified with race or religion or a section of our people and that any sectarian approach is contrary to our philosophy.'[2] It promised a caring government that would unite the people and that would uphold 'the values, rights and freedoms enshrined in the Constitution of Fiji.'

The bulk of the manifesto dealt with 'Policies on Economic Development.' Goals included providing work for everyone, just wages, a better standard of living for all, relief for the poor, and a more responsive public sector. It called for better use of public monies and a review of the taxation system and pledged itself to 'adopt policies that will create the environment for individual, corporate, and co-operative efforts in commerce and industry.' Along these lines it stated: 'We will encourage investment through a policy of a fair return to the investor and by providing incentive allowances/payments to export-oriented industries.' It also promised to 'introduce measures to re-orient commercial bank lending from traditional commercial activities into longer term lending for investments, particularly in agriculture and industry.' The manifesto further promised that a Coalition government would introduce legislation 'to check unfair monopoly in business' and that it would take steps to help small businesses and to bring about 'prosperity for all regions.'

On nationalization, the moderates within the party had won: 'We will not nationalise any business or industry in Fiji.' But it also warned: 'We will set up an inquiry into the Emperor Gold Mines with a view to advising the Government on the best way of operating the mines, whether through private sector, joint venture with Government or worker participation like Air Terminal Services (Fiji) Limited.' On the thorny issue of native Fijian land ownership and its administration by the Native Land Trust Board, the manifesto affirmed that the Coalition 'has never challenged the ownership rights of the Fijian people to their land' and that no changes would ever be made 'without the full consultation and approval of the Great Council of Chiefs.' What the Coalition did want to do was to 'streamline' the Native Land Trust Board to make it 'more efficient' while also setting up a 'National Lands and Resources Commission which will work in full co-operation with the NLTB ... to maximise the use of Fiji's major natural resources.'

The remainder of the document dealt with social services, a 'Programme for Fair and Open Government,' that included a promise to review the Official Secrets Act, adoption of a Code of Conduct for parliamentarians, extension of the powers of the Ombudsman, and, finally, a discussion of foreign policy. As with economic policy, the manifesto's position on foreign policy was an extremely moderate one. It reasserted the Coalition's desire to pursue a non-aligned policy, while pledging not to open a Soviet embassy in Fiji. It did, however, retain its support for a nuclear-free Pacific and its opposition to 'the carriage, testing, storage, and manufacture of nuclear weapons or the dumping of nuclear waste within the South Pacific region,' but did not raise the issue of American ship visits.

On balance, it was a document aimed at assuring voters and overseas powers and interests that a Coalition government would be a moderate one and that the Labour Party had no intention of turning Fiji into another Cuba or turning the country over to the Indo-Fijians. In the campaign, the Coalition focused on 'bread and butter' issues such as unemployment, crime, corruption, and the Alliance Party's failure to deliver on its promises. The *Sunday Sun* headline the day after the launching of the manifesto read: 'Poll Promises – Corruption, Crime Top Coalition Manifesto.'[3]

One important part of the campaign that got under way early in the year was an effort to bolster Bavadra's image. In past campaigns, the Alliance Party had made a great deal out of Mara's image as a national and international leader. The Alliance Party had already begun this time to use the same strategy to promote Mara as a leader in comparison with Bavadra. In mid-February the Coalition published a glossy pamphlet on the life and achievements of Bavadra. The Alliance Party countered the Coalition initiative by seeking to belittle Bavadra as a party leader. Thus, under the heading 'Timoci WHO?' an Alliance Party advertisement in mid-March read: 'Eighteen months ago the FLP [Fiji Labour Party] made Timoci Bavadra its head and armed him with speeches written by others. Then a faction in the NFP in its GREED for power decided to absorb the FLP but kept Bavadra as the front-man. Jai Ram Reddy, the real boss of that NFP faction now pulls the strings and Bavadra dances.' Such advertisements appeared alongside almost daily photos in the press of Mara meeting ambassadors, dedicating schools, bridges and the like, and attending traditional ceremonies. A related theme in Alliance Party speeches was that ruling Fiji should be left in the hands of the chiefs and, by implication, commoners like Bavadra were unfit to be prime minister.

The Coalition's position on the role of chiefs reflected Bavadra and the other's awareness of the delicacy of the issue and the extent to which it lent itself to Alliance Party propaganda. Many of the native Fijian supporters of the Labour Party backed it largely because of their anti-chiefly sentiments, but the Labour Party leadership was all too aware that it was too dangerous to be seen in public attacking the chiefs. Therefore, they continued to seek the support of chiefs where possible and to emphasize the need to distinguish between traditional chiefly authority and modern politics. As the campaign progressed, it was apparent from the growing stridency of the Alliance Party in defending the role of the chiefs that the Labour Party's strategy was working. Thus, speaking at a fund-raising dinner for the Alliance Party in Lautoka attended by Indo-Fijian businessmen on 13 March, David Toganivalu stated that Timoci Bavadra, Tupeni Baba, and Joeli Kalou sought to 'remove chiefs from politics' and warned that 'this will destroy the inseparable link between the *Turaga* (chief) and the *Vanua* (land).' Toganivalu argued that 'the Fijian chiefs must remain a force for moderation, balance, and fair play' and that the chiefs were the 'bulwark' of security for native Fijians as well as 'the protectors of the rights of Indians and General Electors.' He concluded that removal of the chiefs from politics would 'pave the way for instability.'[4] A short time later, the Alliance Party began spreading a rumour that the Coalition planned to remove Ratu Penaia Ganilau as governor general, if it won the election. At a large rally at Suva in late March, Bavadra responded that the rumour was a 'blatant lie' and that 'the Coalition has no intention of interfering with the neutrality of this high office.'

The Labour Party's strategy of using the courts to challenge the chiefly oligarchy was used against Mara himself in late January when pro-Labour lawyer Tevita Fa took up a case by a Vunabalavu farmer. The farmer, Alipate Fatafehi, claimed that Mara had seized some three hundred acres belonging to his family at Drano, Loma-

loma. Part of the land had been used by the government to build an airstrip, and about eight acres had been fenced off by the prime minister for a copra plantation. Fatafehi asserted that the land had been given to his family by the first Tui Lau, Enele Ma'afu, and wanted Tevita Fa to initiate proceedings for a judicial review to establish rightful ownership. As with the other cases, this one had broader implications in that it might lead to additional claims against lands taken by Mara over the years and that once again a commoner had sought to challenge a high chief. (Although it did not surface during the election, relatives of Mara were also upset over land that they felt he had taken from them.)

Other aspects of Mara's personal rule came under scutiny, including a look at some of his friends. While attending a Commonwealth Heads of Government Meeting in Nassau in October 1985, Mara met with one of the local hotel developers, Edward St. George, who provided encouragement for Mara's interest in developing casinos in Fiji: 'I learnt a lot from him on the casinos. It is not such a vulnerable animal as we learnt at home.' He also praised Bahamas prime minister Lynden Pindling, against whom the United States was seeking an indictment on drug-related charges. Mara proposed to establish casinos in Fiji after his return, but was forced to drop the idea in the face of opposition, especially from the churches. This parallelled efforts by Australian interests, supported by Alliance Party cabinet minister Peter Stinson, to allow greyhound racing in Fiji. Such developments also upset the churches, and they objected so vehemently that Mara was forced to back off. Mara also befriended numerous controversial religious figures such as Indian guru Chandra Swamiji Maharaj, who turned up in Fiji for a visit at one point in the private jet of another Mara associate, well-known international arms merchant Adnan Khashoggi. The circumstances under which the Mara cabinet had awarded the exclusive twelve-year television contract to a company owned by Australian financier Kerry Packer (which subsequently had been taken over by a company controlled by Alan Bond) also surfaced frequently in the campaign. There was widespread suspicion that government ministers had been bribed.

The Labour Party became concerned about rumours of ties between members of the Mara government, such as Peter Stinson and Apisai Tora, and Australian criminal elements who had invested in Fijian hotels and other properties. The Labour Party circulated a document it had obtained relating to Australian investigations into the activities of Abe Saffron, Errol Leon Fifer, and other suspected underworld figures, in which the names of Apisai Tora and Ratu Josaia Tavaiqia turned up in connection with negotiations surrounding the Mana Island Resort in the 1970s. In one passage the report noted: 'FIFER could not reach agreement with TORA because the latter demanded $15,000 goodwill money before considering other financial transactions ... After FIFER'S unsuccessful bid he commented that "TORA is a bloodsucker who only wants money." '

During the latter part of 1986, Australian reporter Wendy Bacon published an article in the *Times of Sunday* on Peter Stinson's involvement in the Soqulu Plantation affair in the 1970s that drew public attention in Fiji once again to Stinson's questionable financial activities. Bacon's report prompted the *Fiji Sun* to publish a story on Soqulu in November 1986.[5] While Stinson was working in Hong Kong in 1977, his family's company, the Stinson Pearce Group, gave Trois Investments, owned by Australian financier Barry Loiterton, exclusive rights to market its Soqulu Plantation development to overseas investors. Loiterton was involved in the project with another Australian, Colin Coghill, and the two men traded lots in the project back and forth to boost their own profits. In late 1986 Coghill was facing a charge in Melbourne concerning an alleged A$78 million sales tax fraud. The other investors were not so lucky. Although they made payments for the land, they did not receive title for it, in part, because Trois Investments had not forwarded the duties owed to the Fiji Lands Office. In addition to smaller investors, among those putting money into Soqulu Plantation were four individuals linked to the 'Mr. Asia' drug syndicate.

In 1981 the Stinson Pearce Group accepted the partially paid-off contracts back from Trois Investments in lieu of being paid for the land that already had been sold. A short time later the National Bank of Fiji, which had provided substantial financing for the development and held charge over the assets of the company, placed a caveat over the titles. This placed it in a position to claim the land if necessary. Stinson had extricated himself from the affairs by 1983, but it had ruined the family company, which had put some F$7 million into the project and questions remained concerning Stinson's knowledge of the transactions and of the shady characters involved.

In various speeches during the campaign in March 1987, Baba, Chaudhry, and other Labour Party candidates made reference to a F$4 million loan from the National Bank of Fiji to the Stinson Pearce Group in relation to its financial troubles resulting from the Soqulu Plantation fiasco. They asserted that the loan had been 'written off,' a charge which Stinson denied. Claims of financial irregularities also were made with respect to the election campaign itself. Speaking at a rally in Lautoka on 26 March, Coalition candidate Bhupendra Patel

Above left
Press conference by Colonel Rabuka,
15 May 1987, to announce his overthrow of the Bavadra government

Above
Filipe Bole and Taniela Veitata
outside Parliament, 12 May 1987

Left
Ratu Mara playing golf at Pacific
Harbour, Deuba, August 1988

All photos courtesy Fiji Times

Members of the deposed Coalition cabinet, June 1987

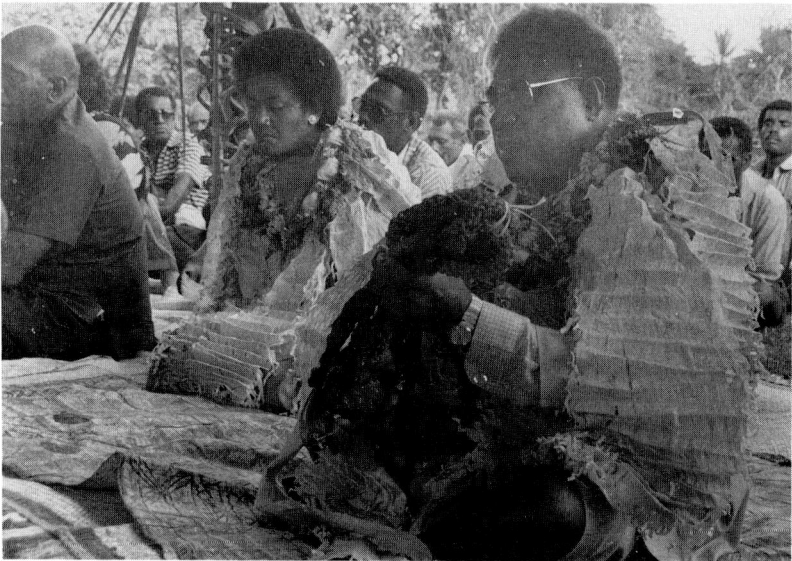

Timoci and Kuini Bavadra, installation ceremony for the newly elected prime minister, 2 May 1987

Veitata, Kubuabola, and other Taukei leaders at march in Suva, 25 April 1987

Former Brigadier General Epeli
Nailatikau, June 1987

Taukei protest march, Suva,
25 April 1987

Veitata addressing protesters outside Parliament prior to the May coup, 1987

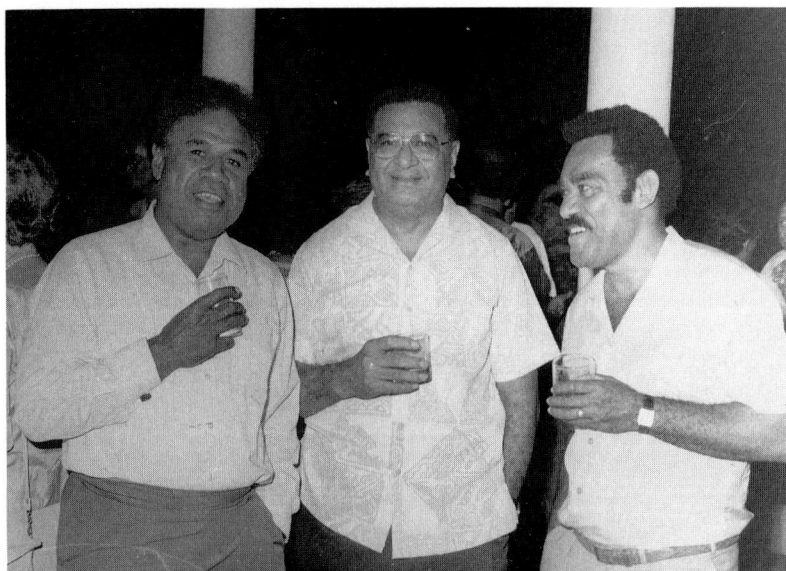

Prime Minister Bavadra (left) at reception, 2 May 1987

linked the Alliance government's failure to implement the recommendations of a garment industry tribunal for establishing minimum wages in the industry to a F$52,000 campaign donation given to the Alliance Party by owners of garment companies. At the same rally, Chaudhry claimed that two other large businesses had each given the Alliance Party F$100,000 towards its campaign.

The Nasomo land claim and Emperor Gold Mine featured prominently in the campaign. After the mine's manager Jeffrey Reid and Bavadra exchanged letters in the newspapers in November 1986, tensions had simmered. The situation heated up considerably towards the end of the campaign. On 2 April, Bavadra, as leader of the Coalition, published a large newspaper advertisement entitled, 'An Open Letter to the People of Fiji – The Truth About Nasomo,' charging the Alliance Government of being 'willing to abandon the Nasomo people to the dubious dealings of the Vatukoula mining companies.' In response to criticism of the companies' policies, Reid placed a half-page advertisement in the 4 April issues of the newspapers and he accused Bavadra of having 'grossly and unfairly maligned the companies, and in doing so manipulated people's minds for cheap political mileage.' He warned that 'your tactics of winning votes by falsely maligning companies like ours does not augur well for the future of our country and its people.' Bavadra's response was another advertisement in which he stated: 'You have at last been smoked out. Only you are so overwhelmed by the smokey FACTS of Nasomo that you can only sputter a feeble response.' The advertisement concluded: 'You are doing a sterling job as henchmen for the Alliance government. But despite your combined energies and resources, you cannot continue to deceive our people.' [6]

Alliance Party propaganda sought to promote the idea that the Coalition's campaign was being run from behind the scenes by former NFP leader Jai Ram Reddy and that Bavadra and other native Fijians were merely the dupes of this wily Indian. This theme was picked up by the pro-Alliance *Pacific Islands Monthly* magazine in its June 1987 issue in an article stating that Reddy 'masterminded the whole strategy of the Coalition during the election campaign.'[7] Reality was quite different. Reddy played an important role, but he was only one of many who influenced campaign decisions. Many of the most important decisions were made by Bavadra himself after consultation with a wide range of people associated with the party. Negotiation and consensus among members of the Coalition was a common feature of decisionmaking. In general, ideas were circulated and discussed as widely as was practical before being formulated into policy or strategy.

The Alliance Party launched its election manifesto on 18 March. Promising a stable government and greater economic prosperity, the sixteen-page document claimed responsibility for all the good since the last election. In addition, it tried to highlight the central role that Mara had played in creating a stable and prosperous nation. Among the manifesto's promises was one to create 35,000 jobs within five years. This was despite Bureau of Statistics figures indicating no growth in employment over the past few years and Fiji National Provident Fund figures recording only 425 new jobs between 1981 and 1985 – but it was typical of previous Alliance Party promises. The manifesto also opposed nationalization and, in fact, called for selective privatization of enterprises. In addition, it called for the creation of 'economic producing zones' for export industries; something that it had promised before but that had yet to materialize.

For its native Fijian and General Elector audience the manifesto stated: 'The Alliance will strenuously oppose any suggestion of Constitutional change that would weaken or destroy the principle of guaranteed representation of Fiji's major racial groups in the House of Representatives.' This was yet another attempt to create an image that the Coalition wanted to change the consititution to turn the country over to the Indo-Fijians. It added that it would 'resist any attempt to weaken the authority or independence of the Native Land Trust Board.' This was aimed at ensuring that any attempt to wrest control of the board from Mara and his cronies was seen as a challenge to native Fijian land rights. It also promised to establish an Institute of Fijian Language and Culture and to continue providing large numbers of scholarships to native Fijians.

One of the more curious passages in the document concerned foreign affairs: 'The Alliance Government will maintain its non-aligned status.' In general, however, the manifesto contained little that was new and simply promised business as usual. The night before its launching, at a fund-raising dinner in Lautoka, David Toganivalu stated that he felt that the Coalition had not been raising issues and accused it of 'turning racial' in its campaign.

The reasons for the Alliance Party's strident appeals to communal sentiments are not hard to find. Not only was it concerned with evidence of growing support for the Labour Party among native Fijians, but it also had to contend with a resurgent Fijian Nationalist Party. Throughout February and March, the Alliance Party indicated publicly that it expected to win a 'landslide victory.' A survey conducted for the party in late December and early January by Inoke Sikivou had indicated that the Alliance Party was likely to win thirty-nine seats. But, privately, Mara and other political veterans were not so certain and urged the party to keep up the pressure. Their concerns were well founded as subsequent polls would show.

A report compiled for the Alliance Party in late January warned of 'Butadroka fever' throughout the Rewa delta that threatened to cost the Alliance Party the Rewa Fijian communal seat currently held by House Speaker Tomasi Vakatora. Of the native Fijian voters polled for the report, 67 per cent had said that they would vote for Butadroka, 21 per cent for the Alliance Party, and 12 per cent were undecided. Accurate or not, the report was extremely upsetting for the party, not only because it indicated that this important seat was threatened but also because it raised the spectre of losing other seats where Nationalists had influence. Mara and others in the Alliance Party began to worry about a repeat of the April 1977 election when Butadroka won this seat and the Alliance Party lost the election – and this time they did not have the Flower-Dove factionalism and Koya's weaknesses as a party leader to fall back on. To counter the Nationalists in the Rewa region, the report suggested calling in Apisai Tora, who was popular in the delta for many of the same reasons that Butadroka was popular, to assist Vakatora.

A poll conducted by Sikivou among General Electors in late February and early March indicated a significant shift with a greater number of part-Europeans, in particular, supporting the Coalition. Following this survey, Sikivou predicted that the Alliance Party might win only thirty seats. This was still enough to defeat the Coalition, but a worrisome trend was indicated with just over a month left before the election dates. *Fiji Sun* journalist Nemani Delaibatiki pointed to another concern for the Alliance Party, the increase in the number of registered Indo-Fijian voters, which spelled trouble for the Alliance Party in several crucial national seats.[8]

The Alliance Party was also concerned about the Bua/Macuata Fijian communal seat. Mara had backed down from dumping Militoni Leweniqila from this seat because of Leweniqila's continued influence in the area. Leweniqila, however, faced a strong challenge from Coalition candidate Koresi Matatolu and from a former Alliance member, who was now an independent, Paula Sotutu. One of the most serious outstanding issues concerned irregularities and related financial problems facing the Macuata Development Corporation, which Leweniqila had headed. A number of chiefs who had been important Alliance Party supporters had threatened not to back the Alliance if it selected Leweniqila. Faced with this problem, Mara himself was forced to intervene to keep the chiefs loyal.

Under the guidance of Len Usher and Ahmed Ali, the printed propaganda of the Alliance Party became increasingly hysterical as the election date neared. Advertising in March focused on the land question and sought to instill fear in the minds of native Fijians that the Coalition was up to something. 'All Landowners Beware' read a typical heading in large bold print. In early April, another typical Alliance Party advertisement bore the heading: 'The Communist Coalition?' This particular advertisement began: 'It is common knowledge that the FLP [Fiji Labour Party] is socialist,' and continued 'but everyone knows that the path to socialism is through communism.' Focusing on Tupeni Baba, a Coalition candidate for Suva, the Alliance Party advertisement cited an article in the *Weekend Australian*, written after the author spoke with Tupeni Baba, purporting that the Coalition intended to 'make Fiji an ally of Cuba which is a close friend of Russia.' Next the advertisement asserted that Baba had 'stated that the FLP-NFP will take over Big Estates and Cut Them Up to Give away' and that Krishna Datt after a visit to the Soviet Union had said that the Labour Party would give away land, noting that 'this is what was done in All Communist States.' The theme of the advertisement then shifted to Coalition 'secrecy': 'Can Anyone trust his or her future in the hands of FLP-NFP which has Hidden Plans' was placed below 'Bavadra and Baba Want to Remove Chiefs from Politics – What is the Next Step?'

Ali and Usher had written similar advertisements which raised the spectre of communism in previous elections, but, in this election, the tone was more strident, and the anti-communist smears were repeated with greater frequency. The Alliance Party also made use of Labour Party defector Mahendra Sukhdeo, who claimed that Labour Party secretary Krishna Datt had sought financial help from the Soviets during a visit to Moscow and East Berlin. No proof was offered. Out in the villages, such claims about the Labour Party were made orally in speeches and discussions with villagers.

The Alliance Party continued its efforts to attack the Labour Party along communal lines. Among native Fijians, it sought to portray the Labour Party as an extension of Reddy's wing of the National Federation Party and, more simply, as the 'Indian party.' Irene Narayan and Ahmed Ali took a different approach among Indo-Fijians. They claimed that 'Labour only pretends to be multiracial' and accused the Labour Party of working secretly with the racist Fijian Nationalist Party. Mara himself took part in the Alliance Party's usual wooing of Muslim voters. For example, at an address in Lautoka on 8 February, he praised them for running an orphanage and spoke of the religious freedom in Fiji that had allowed Islam to flourish: 'In Fiji today, mosques are as much a part of our scenic grandeur as temples and churches.'[9]

The Alliance Party also made use of its control of the government to bolster support. The cabinet announced on 13 March that it was granting a 5.5 per cent pay increase to members of the pro-Alliance Public Employees Union (which included a large number of native Fijian voters in Suva). As it became apparent that the Alliance Party was not getting much electoral support in public housing and squatter settlements, the government initiated crash programs to provide facilities to these communities. Linked to political troubles in Tailevu Province was a government announcement on 26 March that a F$500,000 tar sealing project for the Kings Road in the province was soon to get under way. The Alliance government also poured a great deal of money into the western side. The largest project promised was one for F$10 million over ten years for the Sigatoka Valley. Mara spoke of this when the Alliance Party held its largest rally of the campaign to date at Sigatoka on 21 March. The rally was attended by about seven hundred people, a somewhat disappointing turnout, but the rally itself was indicative of the importance that the Alliance Party placed on the region. In addition, the Alliance government held frequent meetings in native Fijian villages during the campaign to promote acceptance of the reforms it wished to implement within the Fijian Administration.

In his speech at the Sigatoka rally, Mara described the Coalition as a 'political cyclone which has suddenly developed from a depression' and warned that it 'is bent on bringing destruction to all that we have achieved together as a nation.'[10] The Alliance Party had used the theme of stability versus instability in past elections and did so again in this campaign, usually in conjunction with references to the importance of maintaining chiefly authority.

There were numerous threats and acts of violence carried out against Coalition candidates and supporters. Thus, in early March, a gang of youths smashed Tupeni Baba's car window while he was addressing a gathering in Raiwaqa. Then, a bus carrying Coalition supporters near Labasa was stoned on 24 March. Elsewhere in the country, there were rock-throwing incidents, and threatening telephone calls were common. There were other forms of harassment as well. David Eyre, the Coalition candidate for the Eastern General national seat had initially been granted permission to take his annual leave to allow him to campaign, but on 10 March he received notice that his employer, Air Pacific, had altered its decision to grant him paid holiday leave.

The Alliance government/party brought pressure on the press, and accused the nation's two newspapers of a pro-Labour bias. Thus, after reporting that 150 people had walked out of an Alliance meeting on 9 March, *Fiji Times* reporters were banned from a meeting in Labasa on the eighteenth: 'You people support Labour. You cannot be allowed here. You can come in if you apologise for the Valebasoga meeting.'[11] The Alliance Party was especially upset with the balanced coverage of Coalition rallies. In late March the Alliance Party brought pressure to bear on the two newspapers to stop such coverage. Meanwhile, as in the past, the government sought to use Radio Fiji to assist the Alliance Party campaign. Radio news was strongly biased in favour of the Alliance Party, ignoring Coalition rallies while reporting even the smallest utterance of an Alliance Party candidate.

The Alliance Party was also concerned with the number of voters registered. The number of native Fijian voters registered was satisfactory, although experience with recent by-elections and the Suva City Council election meant that their loyalty could not be assumed. More worrisome was the rise in the number of registered Indo-Fijian voters since some of the national seats were likely to be close races. Registration of voters, of course, was not the same as actually getting them to the polls, and it was here that the Alliance Party felt that it had the edge (Table 3).

TABLE 3
Voter registration in the 1982 and 1987 elections

	1982	1987
Total Fijian voters registered	141,845	169,398
Total Indian voters registered	142,529	174,611
Total General voters registered	7,966	9,682
Total voters registered	292,341	353,691

The Koya/Nand splinter group from the NFP and Ratu Osea Gavidi from the Western United Front tried to work together during the campaign. Their efforts did not go smoothly. For one thing, few besides Gavidi in the Western United Front shared his sense of allegiance to Koya, the majority of Western United Front supporters favouring the Labour Party. It was also apparent that support for the NFP splinter group within the Indo-Fijian community was small. General attendance at their meetings was low, and many of those present seemed to come to cause trouble rather than to show their support for the splinter group. Despite the evidence of poor support, Shardha Nand indicated that he hoped that his splinter group would hold the balance of power after the election. Similarly, the

Alliance Party counted on the splinter group to divide the opposition and anticipated that this would help it win a number of important seats.

The Nationalists hoped to win a few seats and were fully aware of the extent to which their support worried the Alliance Party. Speaking at a Nationalist Party rally in Suva on 20 March, Butadroka challenged Mara to a debate 'on matters regarding Fijians' with Bavadra serving as chairman. He said that such a debate would also serve to give Bavadra a chance to put forward his party's position. The Nationalists' message had changed little since previous campaigns, and they blamed the Alliance Party for growing disparity in wealth between native Fijians and Indo-Fijians. As in the past, the Alliance Party responded by raising the spectre of an Indian-dominated government should it be defeated. This did bring about a few defections, but not enough to dampen the Nationalist campaign.

Tensions ran extremely high in early April as the election dates drew near. The level of campaign rhetoric became more and more strident. Both sides predicted victory. In private, leading figures in the Labour Party were not so sure and most in the Coalition felt that it would be close. The Alliance Party's public optimism, however, had come to be matched by a private confidence that they had maintained enough support to defeat the Coalition and that they would be able to win most of the seats about which they had been concerned.

As usual, the Lau seats were counted a day ahead of the others, and at a separate locale, so that Mara's victory in his own seat could be proclaimed ahead of other results. The evening of Friday, 10 April, Alliance Party supporters began celebrating their election victory around Suva and elsewhere in the country. The nation awoke the next morning to headlines announcing that Mara had been re-elected to Parliament. With this out of the way, Fiji waited to hear the results for the remaining seats which would come in some time on Sunday the twelfth. As it became apparent that it was going to be a very close election, the pace of counting slowed.

The Outcome

When the counting was over mid-Sunday, the Coalition had won twenty-eight seats to twenty-four for the Alliance Party (results for each seat are to be found in Appendix A). By ethnic breakdown, the Coalition had 7 Fijian seats, 19 Indian seats, and 2 General Elector seats. The Alliance Party had 15 Fijian seats, 4 Indian seats, and 5 General Elector seats. The turnout had been lower than in 1982; 71

per cent instead of 85 per cent. The Alliance Party had been able to retain the same level of Indo-Fijian support as in 1982 (15 per cent), but it had lost support among native Fijians and General Electors; a drop of 5 per cent among native Fijians, down to 77 per cent, and a drop of 9 per cent among General Electors, down to 80 per cent. The extent to which the Alliance Party lost support among these two electorates is reflected both in the voting percentages and in the low voter turnout. Despite its appeals to racist sentiment and loyalty to the chiefs, and despite widespread intimidation, a reorganized and well-funded party, and the advantages of incumbency, almost one-quarter of the native Fijians voting had voted against the Alliance Party, and another significant percentage had expressed their uncertainty over continued Alliance Party rule by not voting at all.

The May issue of *Pacific Islands Monthly*, a magazine well known for its sympathy towards the Mara government, stated that 'the main reason for the coalition's victory is its multi-racial approach.'[12] In fact, this was only one of many factors that contributed to the Coalition's victory. As in the past, candidate selection had a great deal to do with the outcome. In several instances, Alliance Party mistakes cost it dearly and many of these reflected the extent to which Mara had surrounded himself with sycophants. The Coalition's appeal to 'bread and butter' issues like unemployment, crime, and, especially corruption had also played an important role. So, too, had the regional factor among native Fijians, especially in the west and Rewa area.

The Coalition more than proved itself a match for the Alliance Party in terms of organizational skill. The experience of veteran NFP politicians and trade unionists within the Labour Party allowed the Coalition to counter an Alliance Party machine which was handicapped by Mara's growing inability to grasp the forces at work in a changing Fiji. He could only see the Coalition as another version of the NFP and fought the election with the tactics that had won past elections. In effect, the election was a victory of the politics of multi-racialism over the politics of communalism. It appeared as if a party had finally been able to break the grip of communalism. Significantly, among native Fijians, it was also a victory over Lauan chiefly domination.

Four swing seats played a key role in the Coalition victory – the same four seats that had been so important in past elections. These were the Suva Fijian national seat, the Suva Indian national seat, the South Eastern Fijian national seat, and the South Eastern Indian national seat. Coalition candidates won all four of these seats with small majorities after hotly contested campaigns.

The Suva Fijian seat pitted two strong candidates against one another and cost the Alliance Party one of its senior parliamentarians. In 1982, Alliance Party candidate David Toganivalu had won by a margin of 13,400 to 12,234 votes. This time, however, Coalition candidate Tupeni Baba received 12,452 votes to Toganivalu's 11,902 votes. The Alliance Party had sought to ensure Toganivalu's victory by making a deal with Suva city councillor and former Labour Party member Iliesa Duvuloco to stand as an independent, in the hope of splitting the Labour vote. Duvuloco had little personal support and this move angered voters. He received only 204 votes. Both Toganivalu and Baba waged relentless campaigns, moving from house to house and taking every opportunity to speak and meet people. Toganivalu's source of support in Suva traditionally was based on his being able to count on overwhelming support among native Fijians while also being popular among segments of the Indo-Fijian community, especially the important Gujarati business community. His loss of support among members of this latter group, in part because of anger directed at Irene Narayan for switching parties, was a crucial factor in his defeat. But he also lost votes among native Fijians to Baba.

Mara's faith in the ability of NFP defector Narayan to bring Indo-Fijian voters into the Alliance Party camp proved badly mistaken. If anything, she cost the party support, and Coalition candidate Navin Maharaj, who had strong support among the Indo-Fijian community in Suva, easily capitalized on displeasure with Narayan. In the past, she had been able to win her communal seat handily and it was expected that she would have little trouble with the national seat. In 1982, the Alliance Party candidate Ramzan had won the seat by a margin of 13,221 to 12,590 votes, despite his weak appeal. In 1987, the Alliance Party miscalculated badly and many of those who had supported Narayan in the past now chose either to remain loyal to the Coalition or failed to vote. Narayan lost the Suva Indian national seat by 659 votes, 11,772 votes to Maharaj's 12,431. She did not take her defeat gracefully and considered demanding a recount. However, she was talked out of this by Toganivalu, who had accepted his defeat with a degree of dignity, telling the press that he would probably concentrate on his business activities for a while.

The Alliance Party had expected to win the two South Eastern national seats. Coalition candidate and trade unionist, Joeli Kalou, won the South Eastern Fijian national seat by a majority of 939 votes. Kalou received 13,445 votes to Alliance Party candidate Ratu George Tu'uakitau Cokanauto's 12,506. Some Alliance Party strategists had considered Cokanauto's selection for this seat to have been a mistake since he was identified by Rewans with the rival Kabuna Confederacy. Kalou himself was from Ovalau and was able to make a great deal out of the regional issue. Despite these misgivings, Coka-nauto was selected as one of the new faces that Mara was keen to bring into Parliament and on Mara's faith that the influence of his wife, Adi Lala, who was from Rewa, would be able to overcome opposition among native Fijians. While Adi Lala did continue to exert some influence, there was a growing number of native Fijians in the area who no longer saw her in very favourable terms. The Labour-backed court case against her for mismanagement of native lands had made Adi Lala Mara a symbol of chiefly exploitation. Sentiment against the chiefly oligarchy helped to give Fijian Nationalist Party candidate Emoni Rakadrudru 2,474 votes – votes that otherwise would have probably gone to Kalou.

The Coalition victory in the South Eastern Indian national seat came as even more of a surprise. Its candidate, Fida Hussein, was a relative newcomer to politics. He was, however, from Rewa and had worked very hard to try to sway Muslim voters to the Labour Party during the Suva City Council election. The Alliance Party, in retro-spect, made a serious error in selecting Major Veer Vijay Singh as the candidate for this crucial seat. He was selected not only over the sitting member, Ben Rambisheswar, who was relatively popular, but also over a candidate put forward by the Young Alliance. Singh himself was a relative unknown in the area and had trouble picking up Indo-Fijian support. He also had trouble with native Fijian voters, who outnumbered Indo-Fijian voters in this national seat by 22,228 to 19,974. While this would have worked in the Alliance Par-ty's favour with most national seats, this was not the case with the South Eastern seat which had been a base of support for the Nationalists (who did not field a candidate of their own) and could be counted on to contain many Labour Party sympathizers. The combination of these factors and Singh's overall poor performance as a candidate – in contrast to Hussein, who received the support of the vast majority of Indo-Fijians as well as pro-Labour and some pro-Nationalist native Fijians – meant that Hussein was able to defeat Singh by 14,138 to 13,341 votes.

Two of the Fijian communal seats that were won by the Alliance Party, but which the party had been at considerable risk of loosing, bear special mention. The first of these is the Nadroga/Navosa Fijian communal seat, which includes the town of Sigatoka and the interior settlements along the Sigatoka River. A portion of the area encom-passed by this seat had a tradition of support for the Western United Front. Western United Front leader Gavidi and Dr. Apenisa Kurisaqila had run against one another in 1982, and Gavidi had lost by only 244 votes, 4,682 to 4,926. This time around, Gavidi polled 3,791 votes to 4,829 votes for Kurisaqila of the Alliance Party, while the Coalition's candidate Rev. Mosese Naisoroi, received only 406 votes. The poor showing by the Coalition candidate (who was from the Labour Party) reflected the overlap between support among voters for the Labour Party and the Western United Front. Many rank-and-file Western United Front supporters had wanted Gavidi to join the Coalition, but when he did not they remained loyal to him. Also the Coalition did not pursue this seat as vigorously as it might have out of deference to Gavidi. Had the opposition to the Alliance Party been unified, it is possible that Kurisaqila might have been defeated.

The other significant seat is the Rewa/Serua/Namosi Fijian communal seat which included voters from the western Suva suburb of Lami west of the town of Navua, as well as the island of Beqa, famous for its firewalkers. This was a five-way contest involving the Alliance Party, Coalition, Western United Front, Fijian Nationalist Party, and an independent candidate. The Alliance Party candidate, Tomasi Vakatora, received 6,002 votes to 4,102 votes for Fijian Nationalist Party leader Sakeasi Butadroka. The Coalition's candidate received only 351 votes and the Western United Front, a mere 84. Independent, Epeli Kacimaiwai, formerly a prominent member of the Alliance Party suspected of shifting his sympathy to the Labour Party, received 287 votes. Had Kacimaiwai run a stronger campaign either as an independent or with the Labour Party, it is possible that Butadroka could have beaten Vakatora.

THE COALITION GOVERNMENT

As the final votes were tabulated and it was clear that the Coalition had won, supporters gathered at Labour Party headquarters in Suva and elsewhere around the country to celebrate. The celebrations, however, were to be subdued. The Coalition did not want to be seen as gloating over its victory and hoped not to provoke members of the Alliance Party into violent or other provocative acts. One question that came up in relation to this was whether or not to raise the issue of election irregularities. There was strong evidence that the Alliance Party had tampered with, and in one case, switched ballot boxes. It was decided to let these and other such matters drop as a gesture of goodwill, in the hope of reducing the tension resulting from the Alliance Party's electoral defeat. Just how tense the situation had become was apparent when youths from homes of prominent Alliance Party members living near the Bavadras stoned the residence, and many Coalition members received telephone threats.

In his first address to the nation, Bavadra made a point of issuing a conciliatory statement concerning the Alliance Party and Mara in particular: 'We also acknowledge and greatly respect the contribution which Ratu Kamasese and the Alliance Party have made to the development of our nation. We look forward very much to their continuing contribution in the future and we sincerely hope that they will join and participate with us in the sacred task of nation-building and national development.'

After some delay, Mara acknowledged defeat and issued a statement expressing his disappointment and affirming his support of democracy. Behind a public face of acceptance, however, Mara clearly had not accepted defeat, a mood exemplified by his unwillingness to vacate the prime minister's official residence and to give up the prime minister's two Mercedes Benz cars. Bavadra did not press the matter, not wishing to contribute to the ill will that was evident. Mara and his family finally vacated the house with little grace and considerable pettiness. Mara's wife Adi Lala had plants in the garden torn out, and Mara sought sympathy by claiming to be having trouble finding a place to live. While still at the residence, Mara had called local Lauans and Tongans together to mourn the loss of their government.

Bavadra found it more difficult than he had anticipated to arrange a meeting with the governor general to form a new government. Initial telephone calls to Ratu Penaia Ganilau's secretary, the wife of Jim Ah Koy, met with excuses and delays. In particular, the Coalition was told that the governor general could not act until he had been 'officially informed' of the election results and that these had not been forthcoming. Upon being approached, the Registrar informed the Coalition that he was still awaiting some of the official results. The Coalition suspected at this point that the Alliance Party was stalling for time hoping for a repeat of 1977 whereby the National Federation Party and Fiji Labour Party members of the Coalition would be unable to reach an agreement over questions of leadership and the filling of cabinet posts. Protests by the Coalition finally resulted in the governor general agreeing to meet with Bavadra, by which time it was clear that he would have no trouble in forming a government.

The Alliance Party tried to bribe members of the Coalition to cross over. The Coalition leadership learned that at least one member had been approached, and it was suspected that a couple of others may have been approached as well. But nothing happened. The Alliance Party was having problems holding on to its own members, in large part because the collapse of the patronage system allowed the emergence of old grudges against Mara. Militoni Leweniqila and William Toganivalu, in particular, were seen as weak links who might defect if the opportunity arose. Beyond the parliamentary membership, it was clear that support for the Alliance Party was withering rapidly now that it no longer had control of state power and patronage. Mara was careful to distance himself from this dirty work. As in the past, this was to be left to his associates, in this instance Apisai Tora, Filipe Bole, and others.

A great deal has been made of Bavadra's selection of cabinet members. The previous Alliance Party cabinet had consisted of fourteen members: ten native Fijians, two Indo-Fijians, and two General Electors. As much as anything else, this raised serious doubts about the Alliance Party's claim of multiracialism. And after its defeat, one of the tactics employed by the Alliance Party to stir up communal support among native Fijians was to point to the overwhelming dominance of native Fijians in previous Mara cabinets. To avoid any chance of promoting internal rifts, it was agreed by the Coalition parliamentarians in advance that Bavadra's selection of his cabinet members would be accepted without question. As with most important matters, members of the party gave their advice, but the final decision was Bavadra's alone. In arriving at his decision, he made it clear that the party's championing of the principles of merit and multiracialism had figured prominently in his thoughts. The cabinet consisted of six native Fijians, six Indo-Fijians, and one General Elector.[13] The second week of May, Bavadra also named Ratu Filimone Ralogaivau to the newly created post of Minister of State for Fijian Affairs, thus giving native Fijians a majority. Nine of the cabinet members came from the Labour Party and five from the NFP.

While the cabinet meetings proved to be relatively open and democratic, in practice, four members were the most influential: Bavadra, Baba, Chaudhry, and Reddy. From this perspective, ethnic balance and Labour dominance was in evidence. Bavadra also had sought to ensure that native Fijians were given responsibility for those posts of most direct concern to the native Fijian community: responsibility for land, rural industries, and rural development. Placing Mahendra Chaudhry and Navin Maharaj in the key economic posts was a decision based on experience and a desire to assure the local and foreign business community of the soundness of the new government. Overall, compared with the previous Alliance cabinets, the Coalition cabinet was young (the average age was forty-five) and well educated. In addition to lawyers, businessmen, and civil servants, the cabinet included three academics (Satendra Nandan, Jo

Nacola, and Tupeni Baba) and two teachers (Krishna Datt and Joeli Kalou). What it was missing were chiefs and Lauans. The addition of Ralogaivau increased the native Fijian presence to a majority.

Nationalist Party leader Butadroka's response to the new cabinet, and to the Coalition victory, was ambivalent. In an interview, he expressed the view that he was satisfied that Bavadra had given native Fijians responsibility for those posts of most relevance to native Fijians, and he was certainly pleased to see Mara and some of the other chiefs out of the way. On the other hand, he was not happy to see so many Indo-Fijians in the cabinet. While he urged his followers to back the new government since it had won the election, he also saw its victory as demonstrating the need for constitutional reform.

The Alliance Party expressed no such ambivalence and immediately set about to launch a propaganda campaign aimed at picturing the cabinet as 'Indian-dominated.' In particular, it focused on Reddy's appointment as proof of what it had argued all along – that the Coalition was nothing but the Flower faction under another name. But it soon became evident that the Alliance Party had done more than simply launch a vocal campaign of criticism against the new regime.

On 19 April, a group of native Fijians led by Alliance Party stalwart Ratu Ovini Bokini, the Tui Tavua, erected a roadblock near Tavua and raised placards critical of the new government. Native Fijian villagers erected another blockade at Tunuk near Ba. Coalition members were suspicious of the involvement of Emperor Gold Mine manager Jeffrey Reid in the affair. Reid had been seen near the Tavua roadblock and had a close relationship with the Tui Tavua. The Coalition's suspicion was given some justification when some of its supporters in the Tavua area informed them of a meeting that took place at Reid's house the evening after release of the election results. The meeting involved a handful of prominent Alliance Party figures in the west such as the Tui Tavua and Apisai Tora. It was rumoured that at this meeting, plans had been made for a destabilization campaign against the Coalition government, with Reid providing the funds and Tora directing the campaign. If true, this news was extremely disturbing. But just as disturbing was the implication that Mara himself was involved because of his close relationship with the others at the meeting. Bavadra asked the police to investigate and informed the governor general of his concerns for security and public safety.

Opposition to the Coalition centred on a newly formed organization known as the Taukei Movement. The leadership of the movement was drawn largely from communal extremists associated with the Alliance Party. A couple of days after the roadblocks, Apisai Tora addressed a meeting of western chiefs convened by the Tui Vuda, a powerful Alliance Party supporter in the west, at Viseisei, near Lautoka. Tora and pro-Taukei chiefs turned the meeting into a Taukei rally, bringing with them hundreds of Taukei supporters. In his speech, Tora emphasized the need to maintain the paramountcy of native Fijian interests which he claimed were now being threatened: 'Today Jai Ram Reddy is the real Prime Minister and Bavadra his shield.' Referring to Bavadra as a 'prisoner' of a cabinet with an Indo-Fijian majority, Tora called for the cancellation of land leases for Indo-Fijians. He continued: 'Our independence is now shattered. Upon us is imposed a new colonialism, not from outside but from within our own country by those who arrived here with no rights and were given full rights by us, the *taukei*.'[14] When he had been with the NFP, Tora had used the term 'taukei' as he had sought to rally native Fijian support for the NFP. Now, it became the banner for the movement that he and others launched to destabilize the government, by stirring up communal fears and hatred.

The Taukei prepared a petition along the lines of Tora's speech asking the governor general to intervene to ensure the paramountcy of native Fijian interests. The petition stated that the new government had been elected by non-native Fijians and argued that the constitution should give priority to the protection of native Fijian rights and ensure that native Fijians would 'continue to control Government at all times.' It included 23,000 signatures and on 23 April, fourteen Alliance Party chiefs added their names. The plan was to present it to the governor general in Suva following a march through the city by Taukei supporters on the twenty-fourth.

The Taukei leaders said that they expected twenty thousand people to take part in the march.[15] The Taukei brought a large contingent of supporters from the west by bus. The government at this point became concerned about the Taukei's source of funds, which were rumoured to have come from a prominent expatriate. Tora sought to ensure that Mara was not too closely associated with the march, stating that he had told Mara that the march 'has nothing to do with you' and assuring the public that 'Ratu Sir Kamasese is not involved.'[16] The government allowed the march to proceed, and the turnout of an estimated five thousand, while large, was much smaller than the organizers had anticipated.

The Fijian Nationalists met in Suva on 24 April and condemned the roadblocks and other illegal acts by the Taukei, who they viewed simply as Mara's tool. They saw themselves as the true voice of

native Fijian communal chauvinism, and, viewed the Taukei Movement as yet another attempt by Mara and his cronies to manipulate
native Fijian sentiment towards their own ends. The Western United
Front issued a similar statement condemning the Taukei and
expressing concern about Mara's 'conspicuous silence' over the protests.

The Taukei did not receive the support from the governor general
that they had hoped for. He appealed to native Fijian commoners
and chiefs to uphold the law and to act in the interest of communal
harmony and said that he felt that no good could come from 'unlawful acts and actions that are designed to destabilise the Coalition
Government.'[17] To this was added a statement by Ratu George Cakobau which argued that inciting communal hatred would damage
Fiji's international reputation and that such actions and the calls to
change the constitution went against the principles of multiracialism, as well as native Fijian culture. He added his backing for the
governor general's call for the people of Fiji to respect the new government.

The Coalition government felt that the situation was under control. Later, on 24 April, Bavadra made a national broadcast over radio
in which he assured the nation that his government was in control:
'Let us not yield to the designs of a disgruntled few. Let us not
sacrifice the future of our beloved children to the greed of a small
minority.' He used the opportunity once again to review the Coalition government's policies on land and development, explaining
how they were framed to benefit all people.

In a public display of native Fijian support for the Coalition to
counter Taukei and Alliance propaganda, the Labour Party held a
large installation ceremony for Bavadra at the prime minister's official residence at Veiuto on Friday, 1 May. In addition to a large
contingent from the Suva and Rewa area, over two thousand native
Fijians came from the western and central divisions to attend the
ceremony. The people of the Vatububere mataqali performed the
naivakora ceremony from Western Viti Levu to install the new prime
minister, and almost the entire proceeding was held in the western
dialect of Fijian instead of Bauan. It was a dramatic event that served
for many as a symbol of a dramatic change in native Fijian politics.

That same day in the village of Kalokalevu, Butadroka and his
Nationalist Party supporters held their own ceremony (the quisi-ni-
loaloa) to celebrate the defeat of the Alliance Party. At the gathering,
Butadroka stated that he felt that the victory of the 'Indian-dominated' Coalition demonstrated the correctness of the Nationalist

claim that the constitution did not protect native Fijian rights and announced that his group was planning a demonstration.

Meanwhile, Mara was in Honolulu to attend his final meeting of the Pacific Islands Development Program at the East-West Center and to play golf with American officials, a trip that later prompted speculation about suspected American involvement in the coup. After resigning as head of the Pacific Islands Development Program, Mara returned to Fiji on 6 May.

Aware of Mara's special relationship with American officials and U.S. concern over the Coalition's foreign policy, the cabinet decided to mute its foreign policy initiatives by playing down its anti-nuclear and non-aligned stances. Plans were made to hold educational workshops for people in government and then around the nation on non-alignment and nuclear issues to create a greater awareness of these matters before pursuing them as matters of policy. These plans were seen as fitting in with the Coalition's desire to create a framework for greater popular participation in foreign policy decisionmaking and to make it more difficult for foreign powers or the Alliance Party to attack it on the basis of its foreign policy.

Shortly after assuming office, Bavadra had a tense meeting with American ambassador Edward Dillery in which he expressed his concern about U.S. AID official William Paupe, who had actively supported the Alliance Party during the campaign and who had since maintained close relations with Apisai Tora. Since the election, the government had received reports that Tora had received money from Paupe, and there was concern that this was being used to finance destabilization efforts. At the meeting, Dillery denied that Paupe was still funding Tora, but soon after leaving to return to the embassy he telephoned back, admitting that the relationship between Paupe and Tora had in fact continued after the election. The ambassador told Bavadra that he had asked Paupe to stop.

Less than two weeks after the election, on 30 April, American Ambassador to the United Nations, General Vernon Walters, arrived in Fiji for discussions which focused on whether the new government planned on banning visits by nuclear-armed and nuclear-powered ships. Since Walters was closely associated with other American destabilization efforts such as those in Brazil in the early 1960s, Chile in the early 1970s, and, more recently, in Nicaragua, his arrival made the government nervous and it sought to assure Walters that it represented no threat to American interests.[18] During lunch with foreign minister Krishna Datt on 1 May, Walters remarked jokingly that 'coups follow me around,' and he added, 'if a coup were to happen here that would be an accident. It would have nothing to do with me.' Despite these remarks, on balance, the Coalition government was optimistic that it had neutralized the American threat.

Shortly after ten o'clock at night on 2 May, while Mara was out of the country, molotov cocktails exploded in the law offices of Jai Ram Reddy in Lautoka. Alliance Senator Jona Qio, whose car had been seen near the incidents, was held for questioning and then released. The government ordered the police to investigate suspected links between the fire-bombings, the marches, the Taukei, and those who might be behind these activities. On Sunday, Police Commissioner P.U. Raman briefed Bavadra on what little progress the police had made in their investigations. Throughout the following week investigations continued amid rumours that the Coalition government was going to shake up the police to ensure a more responsive force.

Meanwhile, the Coalition announced reforms that would begin to build mass support, particularly among ordinary Fijians. On 5 May, following meetings with bus owners, Minister of Communications, Works and Transport Ahmed Bhamji declared that an agreement had been reached so that, starting 1 July, ex-servicemen, civil service pensioners, people on social welfare, and disabled persons would be able to travel free on buses between 9:00 A.M. and 3:00 P.M. The move was greeted very favourably by a number of groups, especially by spokesmen for former servicemen. A few days later, Minister for Health and Social Welfare Satendra Nandan announced the formation of three committees to study the provision of health care and to recommend improvements. In another popular initiative, Nandan eliminated basic fees for visits to hospitals and clinics which had made health care a burden for many poor Fijians. In both instances, the question asked by many was, why had these steps not been taken before? In response, members of the Alliance Party began spreading rumours, mainly in the eastern native Fijian villages, that the Coalition was receiving money from Libya to pay for these reforms.

On 5 May, the Alliance Party announced that it was going to challenge the legality of Bavadra's appointment of Jai Ram Reddy and Etuati Tavai to the Senate, claiming that the posts they had been appointed to fill (those of Ratu Napolioni Dawai and Balwant Singh Rakkha) were rightfully Opposition appointments. The challenge stood little chance of success but it did serve as an additional irritant, and it allowed the Alliance Party propaganda machine more ammunition out in the villages.

On 6 May, as behind the scenes preparations were going on for the opening of Parliament on Friday the eighth, those charged for erecting the roadblocks near Tavua on 19 April appeared in court in Tavua and Ba. The sixty-three who appeared in Tavua court, including the Tui Tavua, Ratu Ovini Bokini, were freed on bail of F$100 each and the case was adjourned until 13 May.

The Taukei sought a permit to hold a demonstration on Friday as Parliament opened. The government refused the permit and a meeting was held on Thursday at the Raiwai/Raiwaqa Community Centre, which had become something of a base of operations for the Taukei in Suva, to decide what to do. With Apisai Tora taking a leading role, the meeting was also attended by several Alliance Party parliamentarians, including Taniela Veitata, Apenisa Kurisaqila, Filipe Bole, and Viliame Gonelevu. A few busloads of Taukei supporters had been brought to Suva from the west to attend the meeting, and total attendance was in the neighbourhood of four to five hundred. In his address Tora said, 'I don't condone violence, but if it's God's will, we can't help it.' He and Veitata sought to brand the new government as 'belonging to the Indians.' Plans were announced for all sixteen native Fijian Alliance Party members of parliament to boycott the opening. Mara's lieutenants appeared to be turning up the pressure. A planned march by the Taukei in Labasa was called off, but a permit had been issued for one in Savusavu.

After only a few weeks of militant action, however, the Taukei Movement met with serious opposition from native Fijian leaders. Speaking on Radio Fiji, the president of the Methodist church, Josateki Koroi, issued a statement expressing concern about the racist tone of the Taukei marches and the involvement of Methodist ministers in the Taukei Movement. 'If by joining the movement,' he said, 'they are taking a stand of being anti-Indian or racist, and encourage violence, then they will have to answer to the church's conference.' To the surprise of many, on Thursday, upon his return from a brief trip to Australia, the important western chief and Alliance Party stalwart, the Tui Vuda, sought to distance himself from the Taukei Movement. He publicly withdrew his support for the movement and said that he was disturbed by the bombings. Asked about the 21 April meeting at Viseisei attended by a large number of Taukei supporters, he said that his intention was for it to have been a meeting solely of chiefs belonging to the Western Chiefs Association, but that Tora and others had brought their supporters with them and the numbers had grown to two thousand. The claim strained credibility, but it was an indication of changing political alignments, as one of the Alliance Party's primary agents in the west began to move to neutral ground.

Although Bavadra and other members of the Coalition government felt that the Taukei Movement was running out of steam, they
were still frustrated by delays in the police investigation into Taukei
activities, especially the Saturday night bombings, and they were
concerned about future Alliance Party 'tricks.' Alliance Party loyalists in the police force were not co-operating with the new government, and it was obvious that steps had to be taken to strengthen
the government's control over the police.

Bavadra was also engaged in discreet negotiations over the nomination of the Speaker of the House. He had approached Ratu William Toganivalu, who was considered one of the weak links in the
Alliance Party lineup. Bavadra was well aware that having a Speaker
from the Alliance Party posed some danger. But he felt that if someone could be convinced to break ranks with the Alliance Party, this
person would be sufficiently discredited by his Alliance colleagues
so as to be considered in the Coalition camp. William Toganivalu
said in confidence that he would accept the post, but in public he
refused to confirm or deny that he had even been approached. Telephone threats against those associated with the Coalition had
become commonplace and Toganivalu now began to receive them.
The Alliance Party placed considerable pressure on him in private,
using both threats and enticements of jobs with better benefits and
pay. At a parliamentary caucus meeting on Thursday, Mara and
others kept up the pressure. That evening he was harangued again
by Jim Ah Koy and Mosese Qionibaravi at the United Club, an
Alliance Party hangout. The pressure was sufficient for Toganivalu
to back down and the Alliance Party felt that it had outmanoeuvred
Bavadra.

The opening of Parliament on Friday did not go as well as anticipated for the Alliance Party. The day began well enough with a bomb
threat telephoned in just before 9:00 A.M., and government offices
had to be cleared and searched. Then came the opening of Parliament and the swearing-in ceremony. The call for a boycott was
heeded by all of the Alliance Party parliamentarians except Mara
(who, as usual, sought to portray himself as above such things), Jim
Ah Koy, Charles Walker, William Toganivalu, and Militoni Leweniqila. Those not in attendance did, however, let it be known that they
would attend on Monday to take the Oath of Allegiance. The native
Fijian boycotters held a brief meeting at the nearby offices of the
Fijian Affairs Board (still effectively an Alliance Party stronghold).
Then they moved to the Grand Pacific Hotel (owned by a Mara
associate) across the road from Parliament and attempted to put
together a group called the Fijian United Front. They claimed to be

trying to form a united front of all native Fijian parliamentarians, including those of the Coalition, and said that they had invited Bavadra himself to attend. The latter ploy accomplished little, and the Fijian United Front vanished as quickly as it had appeared.

So far things had gone as planned. The 'popular show of support' for the boycotters outside their offices, however, was a flop. Only about one hundred people turned up (the press reports greatly exaggerated the numbers), including a choir group from Rewa brought in to sing for the occasion and a large number of regular demonstrators from Taniela Veitata's dockworkers' union. If the Coalition needed confirmation that support for the opposition demonstrations was dwindling, this was it. Even worse was to come, when Alliance Party trouble-maker, Militoni Leweniqila, stood up to be sworn in as Speaker. Bavadra had pulled off a coup that left many in the Alliance Party stunned. Unknown to others in the Alliance camp, Bavadra, after being turned down by William Toganivalu late Thursday evening, had held discussions with a few others in the Coalition. He then had Etuati Tavai contact Leweniqila on his behalf and offer him the post. Leweniqila accepted, but the deal had been kept secret from others in the Alliance Party.

Mara was visibly shaken by Leweniqila's action and refused to shake his hand during the swearing-in ceremony. Jim Ah Koy also snubbed Leweniqila, but William Toganivalu and Charles Walker (who it was rumoured Mara had considered dumping before the election) came up to shake his hand. To some observers it looked as if Mara's Alliance Party stood to lose three of its members, rather than attracting a few cross-overs from the Coalition. After the event, the Alliance Party issued a statement that it had not been consulted by Leweniqila and that 'he has neither the support nor the confidence of the whole House.'[19] It also said that Leweniqila would be excluded from participation in Alliance Party affairs and that his membership in the party would be decided at a meeting of the Fijian Alliance. A Taukei meeting convened that afternoon criticized Leweniqila for abandoning his electorate and called for his expulsion from the Alliance Party.

The march in Savusavu led by a group of Cakaudrove chiefs also had a disappointing turnout. Only a couple of hundred people took part in the march, during which calls were made for a change in the constitution to guarantee native Fijian control of Parliament.

The Alliance Party tried to keep up the pressure over the weekend. On Saturday morning another fire was set, this time in Harish Sharma's law office in Nadi. In this instance, police had been asked by nearby residents to keep an eye on the office after suspicious people had been seen loitering nearby, but the police had failed to do so. Later in the day in Suva, Joveci Gavoka addressed a meeting of the Public Employees Union and demanded that the Coalition government take steps to improve the lot of blue-collar workers, again accusing the Labour Party of representing the interests of white-collar workers. It was apparent that the Alliance Party planned on using Gavoka, Veitata, and others among its trade unionists to harass the Coalition government on the labour front. Gavoka's own position was weakened a few days later when the Ministry of Industrial Relations and Employment recognized the recently formed Fiji Airport Workers Union, comprised of dissident airport workers in Gavoka's union. Without state support, it seemed that Gavoka's days as a unionist might be numbered.[20]

On Sunday the tenth, the Fiji Council of Churches held a special service for the dedication of members of Parliament in Suva. The service was attended by Bavadra, Governor General Ganilau, the chief justice, and most Coalition parliamentarians. For the Alliance Party, only Charles Walker and Narsi Raniga attended, while the other Alliance parliamentarians were notably absent. The service was addressed by the president of the Methodist church, Josateki Koroi, and Roman Catholic Archbishop Petero Mataca. The sermons stressed the need of the church to become involved in promoting the well-being of people and the archbishop noted that the church had an active role to play in the task of nation-building. The political message of the service was clear – the church hierarchy did not approve of the illegal attempts to destabilize the elected government.

On Monday, 11 May, the Alliance parliamentarians turned up to be sworn in and to listen to the governor general's address. In his address Ganilau said that the nation should be proud of the relatively smooth transition. He then reviewed the new government's policies, focusing on economic policies aimed at encouraging investment, increasing employment, and creating an atmosphere for more equitable economic growth. One section of the speech dealt with the Coalition's plans for the military. There was to be a review of the Royal Fiji Military Forces' 'role in the areas of defence, nation-building, internal security and international peace-keeping.' Two specific points made were that the government would continue Fiji's participation in Middle East peacekeeping and that 'in terms of nation-building, Government will expand the use of the RFMF in youth training.' These were all initiatives aimed at alleviating unease within the military. Foreign policy issues were played down, although the speech reaffirmed the Coalition's support for Kanak independence and its opposition to nuclear testing.[21]

The initial battle in Parliament over, another arena of conflict was shaping up over elections for membership on the Fijian Affairs Board. The native Fijian members of Parliament took part in the election: thirteen members of the Alliance Party and seven from the Coalition. Bavadra was chairman by virtue of his still holding responsiblity for the Fijian Affairs Ministry, but the Alliance Party used its numerical advantage to place eight of its members on the board.[22] Yet to come were two Council of Chiefs nominees. With such a commanding majority (ten to one) and given the individuals involved, it seemed likely that the Coalition would have a difficult time implementing any reforms falling within the jurisdiction of the ministry. Bavadra himself was optimistic that, with patience and by appealing to reason, reform still would be possible. Bavadra also moved towards creating a new portfolio for a minister of state for Fijian affairs, with Filimone Ralogaivau to be appointed to the post.

The same day, the government began to move against the conspirators. Apisai Tora was arrested at his house in Natalau and charged with sedition and inciting racial antagonisms, on the basis of his speech at Viseisei three weeks earlier. The charge of sedition carried a maximum penalty of a F$200 fine and two years in jail. After studying police files, the new acting director of public prosecutions, Mehboob Raza, had approved the arrest on Friday. Tora was released on F$400 bail pending his appearance in court on the twentieth to answer the two charges. The government was also now pushing for action against Emperor Gold Mine manager Jeffrey Reid. As soon as the compilation of evidence against him was complete within the week, the government planned to expel him from the country for violation of his work permit. In the meantime, Reid was seen around the government buildings, including the Ministry of Home Affairs offices, on a number of occasions. The Coalition was not overly worried, however, since it felt that the momentum was clearly on its side now, and that within a matter of days the destabilization conspiracy would be completely broken.

Also on Monday, police charged a senior clerk in Harish Sharma's law firm with carrying out the fire-bombing of the firm's office. Apparently, the bombing was tied to financial irregularities involving the clerk, and it was not a political act.

In Parliament on Wednesday, 13 May, opposition parliamentarian and Taukei activist Viliame Gonelevu accused the Coalition of seeking to destroy the chiefly system. Filimone Ralogaivau, the newly appointed minister of state for Fijian affairs responded:

> It is difficult to understand how a Government with only 28 members can be accused to do something which we have neither the desire nor the capacity to achieve ...
>
> There must be no feelings among the Fijians that they will be left out of development or isolated. The Government is concerned about all those who need special assistance – and there is no doubt that special assistance will be forthcoming to the Fijians.
>
> I plead trust and understanding. Let us break down the barrier that exists between us. Let us look on the Government as a Government for all and join hands with the Opposition on great issues which need a truly national perspective.
>
> I pledge myself today to protect the interests of the Fijians. I'm authorised to say that the Government will act with care and sensitivity on all matters relating to the Fijian administration and land.[23]

He then referred to the governor general's speech and his hope that it would help to dispel fear and uncertainty among native Fijians.

Away from Parliament an event took place that was later to play an important role as a justification for the coup. An Indo-Fijian bus driver was brutally murdered by a native Fijian at Bua Landing after an argument. The murderer was picked up by police a short time later, blood-stained, still holding the knife used in the murder, and with the cash box from the bus. It was simple robbery, albeit a brutal one, and such acts were not unknown in Fiji, which has one of the world's highest crime rates. However, an attempt would be made to use it as an example of communal tensions and to support contentions that widespread violence was likely if the Coalition remained in power.

In Tavua, meanwhile, the hearing into the April roadblocks was adjourned again until 3 July. The adjournment came about following an agreement to pursue 'traditional Fijian customs and traditions' to 'enable the defusing of the present situation in Tavua.' The hearing was also attended by Apisai Tora, Senator Inoke Tabua, and Dr. Sefania Tabua of the Taukei Movement. But the most important event of the day was the charging of Senator Jona Qio in Lautoka Magistrates Court on one count of arson and two counts of attempted arson. Ignoring prosecution arguments that Qio not be granted bail since there might be a recurrence of arson, the magistrate released him on F$10,000 bail bond, ordering him to surrender his passport and not to interfere with witnesses. Police also had learned that plans had been made to fire-bomb the law offices of Bavadra associate Tevita Fa located behind the government buildings in Suva on 16 May. It was hoped to catch the bombers in the act and then to be able to round up the remaining conspirators.

By 13 May the Coalition felt that the destabilization campaign had been crushed and it was time to turn to the business of government and reforms. Although the government recognised that reforms would not be easy, there was a feeling of optimism – and that the worst was over.

When the evidence is examined, it seems clear that the Alliance Party was behind much of the destabilization campaign. The most likely scenario is that Mara and his closest associates arranged for Alliance Party militants like Apisai Tora and Taniela Veitata to stir up communal antagonism to create a situation where the Coalition would no longer be able to govern. Coalition suspicions that funds for the campaign were coming from expatriate business interests and the United States are now probably impossible to prove. The military coup on 14 May stopped the investigation into Jeffrey Reid's involvement. Likewise, although proof had been obtained that u.s. AID director William Paupe continued to fund the Alliance Party after the election, the coup took place before it could be established how these funds were used or the extent to which Paupe was aware of Alliance Party backing of the destabilization campaign.

In addition to questions surrounding the conspiracy to orchestrate the destabilization campaign, there is the question of why it failed. One reason for the failure of the campaign is that the Coalition government did not panic and demonstrated considerable skill in outmanoeuvring those behind it. Beyond this is a more fundamental question as to why the appeals for communal solidarity failed to generate the level of support expected by the conspirators. The most important factor was the collapse of the Alliance Party's patronage system which meant that it no longer was in a position to give out favours. People who had benefitted under the old system had to ask themselves whether it was better to come out openly in opposition to the new government in the hopes that it would be overthrown or to wait and see whether it would remain in office, and if it did, try to gain favour with the new group in power.

At the outset, when the Coalition was new to office and it seemed possible that it might not be able to hold on to power, it was relatively easy for Tora and the others to gather crowds. But as time went on, and it looked as if the Coalition government was going to remain in office, fewer and fewer people were willing to openly defy the new government. Mara loyalists from his home islands of Lau still greeted the change of government with disbelief or anger, but by 13 May most people in Fiji were adjusting to life under a Coalition government with Mara and the Alliance Party in opposition. If the Coaltion was to be removed from power, other means would be necessary.

CHAPTER SEVEN

The May Coup

When Parliament met at 9:30 A.M. on Thursday, 14 May, Taniela Veitata, the newly elected Alliance Party M.P., stood up to speak. Veitata was a popular orator among conservative native Fijians, and he was well known for his racism and religiosity – having assumed the title of the 'Prophet' on occasion. He had been active in the movement to destabilize the Bavadra government and, along with members of the dockworkers' union of which he was general secretary, he played a prominent role in many of the disturbances of the previous weeks.

Veitata's speech was devoted to praising the past actions of former prime minister Ratu Mara, his predecessor Ratu Sir Lala Sukuna, and, more generally, the role that Fiji's eastern chiefly élite had played in nation-building. His speech had a strong Christian flavour. With respect to the history of chiefly rule, he noted that

> Christianity did not destroy the chiefly system, but found in it a ready-made plan whereby Christ's message of love could easily and effectively be filtered through to all the people. If that was so then naturally God must have had a hand to play in the formation of the chiefly system. And so, Saint Paul was right all the time when he said in his letter to the Romans, Chapter 13, that no authority existed without God's permission.
>
> Authority ... is really the right and the power to give orders which must be obeyed by the people ... The respect, honour and praise which our people had for their chiefs has been the base by which our chiefs were able to coerce their people into stricter discipline and unity.
>
> So, if Christianity did not destroy the chiefly system then obviously

it wanted the form of administration to persist and continue firmly in the course it was taking.[1]

Veitata went on to assert that 'our chiefs are really the guardians of peace in Fiji' and contrasted the peace of the chiefs with 'the political philosophy of Mao Tse Tung where he said that political power comes out of the barrel of a gun.' In this vein, he commented, 'In Fiji, there is no gun, but our chiefs are there.' Veitata also singled out Sakeasi Butadroka for criticism. Butadroka, a commoner and leader of the Fijian Nationalist Party, was a vocal critic of Mara and other eastern chiefs, and his party had played a role in the defeat of the Alliance Party in the election.

Among those in the audience were Lieutenant Colonel Sitiveni Rabuka, dressed in civilian clothes, and Mara's son, Finau Mara, who towards the end of the speech was to be observed suggesting to a couple of Fijian women about to enter the chamber that they remain outside. Shortly before ten o'clock, Veitata stopped his speech to ask the Speaker, 'How much more time do I have, Sir?' Receiving a nod to continue, he began shuffling through his papers and engaged in a brief exchange with Labour Party parliamentarians Joeli Kalou and Satendra Nandan.

Immediately after ten o'clock, a small group of soldiers, armed and wearing gas masks, entered the parliamentary chamber. The soldiers were later identified as a group that had received SAS training a couple of months earlier. They were led by Major Isireli Dugu, who made a loud noise and announced: 'Sit down everybody, sit down. This is a take-over. Ladies and gentlemen, this is a military take-over. We apologise for any inconvenience caused. You are requested to stay cool, stay down and listen to what we are going to tell you.'[2] The soldiers lined up behind the Coalition parliamentarians. Colonel Rabuka rose, moved towards where his uncle, Speaker of the House Militoni Leweniqila sat and faced Prime Minister Bavadra. After urging everyone to 'stay calm' he addressed the prime minister: 'Mr. Prime Minister, please lead your team down to the right.' When Bavadra refused, Colonel Rabuka repeated his command: 'Mr. Prime Minister, Sir, will you lead your team now.' The Prime Minister turned to the Speaker, who indicated that he should obey the command. Bavadra and the other Coalition parliamentarians rose and were led out with guns at their backs. Colonel Rabuka asked the Alliance parliamentarians to leave the chamber and retire to the Opposition offices.[3]

Speaking to an interviewer about the coup two weeks later, Timoci Bavadra commented: 'looking back now, it was like a dream, and nobody ever believed that it was actually happening, until Rabuka went up to the Speaker's chair and ordered us out.'[4] Another member of the Bavadra government said later that his initial reaction was that it was merely some kind of military game. It only took seconds, however, for all to realize that Rabuka and his cohorts were serious. The Speaker, rebel Alliance parliamentarian Militoni Leweniqila, who had himself served in the army, told Coalition members later that he had indicated that they obey the second command for fear that plans might have been made to shoot someone should a third order been necessary. One police officer in the chamber, who did move when the soldiers entered, was quickly covered.

The twenty-seven members of the Coalition government who had been in attendance (one was absent) were taken to two army trucks waiting outside. They were then driven to the army's Queen Elizabeth Barracks at Nabua, on the outskirts of Suva, where they were held, guarded under tight security. Troops also occupied the offices of the Posts and Telecommunications Department, halting communications for over four hours; and the Fiji Broadcasting Commission (FBC), which gave them control of Radio Fiji. They had, however, overlooked the private radio station, FM96. One of its reporters had been in the Parliamentary Press Gallery at the time of the coup and the station broadcast the news of what had happened within minutes of the event. It was not until 11 A.M. that Colonel Rabuka issued a statement in English over FBC's Radio Fiji. In his announcement, he stated that Parliament had been neutralized and the constitution suspended 'to prevent any further disturbances and bloodshed.'

There were indigenous Fijians in nearby government buildings – strong Alliance Party supporters – who greeted the news with joy: 'We are back in power!' In fact, some had begun to celebrate earlier in the day. Around 8 o'clock that morning, Lieutenant Colonel Edward Tuivanuavoa, a reservist out of active service for two years, had taken his uniform for dry-cleaning and requested that it be ready by noon. That afternoon, he was to appear in uniform at the Queen Elizabeth Barracks – the first of several reservists and civilians to don uniforms over the next few days and join forces with those in the army involved in the coup.[5] Alliance Party parliamentarians, for their part, began conferring excitedly with military personnel immediately after the coup, making plans for what to do next. Finau Mara, a government lawyer, led those seeking to prepare a legal basis for the change in government.

As news of the coup spread, people began to gather outside of the Parliament building. The emotions of those in the crowd were mixed, ranging from glee to fear and anger. For the majority, the reaction was one of stunned disbelief. Most were uncertain how to respond. Among those in the crowd who did react was longtime Mara foe, Fijian Nationalist Sakeasi Butadroka: 'Where is Kamasese Mara! Don't blame Bavadra, don't blame anybody. Blame Kamasese Mara, the bastard who sold Fiji. That's the fellow. Where is he? Where is he now? Where is Mara may I ask? The bloody Judas Escariot.'[6] Butadroka's remarks did not go unchallenged by supporters of the coup who were among those milling outside of Parliament – an assortment of young native Fijians mostly from Mara's home islands of Lau, or from the same area of the northern island of Vanua Levu as Colonel Rabuka (the Navatu-Natewa area, in particular).

Where was Mara? He was attending a meeting of the conservative Pacific Democratic Union at the Fijian Hotel near Sigatoka, on the other side of the island. Colonel Rabuka informed Mara of the coup over the telephone. Upon his return to Suva later in the afternoon, he came out in support of the interim government: 'I stand by my country and I stand by this [military] government.' His justification for doing so was that after devoting twenty years of his life 'to welding this country together with democratic government' he was 'not going to see it go down the drain.'[7]

Later in the afternoon, Kuini Bavadra, wife of the deposed prime minister, gave an interview, denying that she or her husband had had any idea that a coup was being planned. On first hearing the news at about half past ten that morning, she had not believed it: 'I thought it was a joke,' but then she recognized the man's voice 'and I knew that he was serious.' When asked of her reaction to the day's events, now knowing that her husband was alive, she stated: 'It's one of confusion, anger and total disillusionment with everything that's happened.' She had received a number of telephone calls from supporters of her husband's government and had urged them to remain calm. When questioned about how she thought most native Fijians felt about the coup, she responded that she believed that most of them would be confused: 'They don't know what's happening because this is totally new ... quite a number are confused and deeply disappointed about the turn of events.'[8]

The military issued repeated statements urging people to remain calm. But by midday, shops were starting to fill with people stocking up on food, and many were crowding the banks to withdraw money. Work throughout much of the city had come to a halt. There was talk of a general strike, but some of the most powerful trade union leaders were among those taken by the military in the morning, and many other labour leaders had gone into hiding. A small group talked quietly at the office of the Fiji Trades Union Congress, with no clear idea of what to do. Labour Party activists met around town to talk and share their sense of unease. Labour Party officials removed files from their office, but no other actions were taken.

After the coup, Leweniqila, who himself was later arrested by the army, telephoned Governor General Ganilau to inform him of what had happened. Thus, according to Leweniqila, when he called the governor general, Ganilau already knew and was still reeling from the shock of the take-over. After Parliament had been secured, Rabuka took Prime Minister Bavadra's car to the governor general's nearby residence. From others present, it would appear that the governor general expressed disbelief and then shock when he learned of the coup – unlike most Alliance parliamentarians who had shown little evidence of being surprised when the army walked into the parliamentary chambers.[9]

Upon entering the governor general's residence, Rabuka met one of his superior officers, Colonel Jim Sanday. Sanday was only to learn later that Rabuka had planned for him to be delayed at the governor general's residence until after the coup to keep him from interfering. Upon their meeting, Rabuka ordered Sanday to stay out of the way.[10] Sanday left after the meeting, staying with relatives that evening and then leaving town early the next morning. Rabuka informed the governor general, with whom he had a close personal relationship, of his plans to form an interim government. In suspending the constitution, Rabuka had terminated the post of governor general. Nevertheless, Rabuka assured Ganilau that he could remain at the residence and that Rabuka would appoint him president as soon as possible. The governor general did not agree to recognize the new regime or to the suspension of his office, nor did he offer any concrete support to Rabuka. His parting words to Rabuka were, 'Good luck. I hope you understand what you're doing.'

Rabuka summoned foreign diplomatic representatives to a meeting at 2:00 P.M. The governments of Australia and New Zealand had been quick to condemn the coup and directed their representatives not to attend. Prime Minister David Lange of New Zealand had called a meeting in Wellington of senior foreign affairs officials to discuss the coup at 11:00 A.M. A short time later, after talking to Lange over the telephone, Australian prime minister Bob Hawke met with Defense Minister Kim Beazley and acting foreign affairs minister Gareth Evans in Canberra. While ruling out unilateral military intervention, Lange issued a public statement deploring the coup, and left the door open for multilateral intervention. Hawke and his two ministers also debated intervention and, for the time being, ruled it out as well. Early in the afternoon, Hawke and Evans criticized Rabuka's actions in addresses to Parliament and called for a speedy return to parliamentary democracy in Fiji. Critical remarks were also forthcoming from opposition leader John Howard and other Australian politicians.

Elsewhere in the region, Papua New Guinea's foreign minister, Ted Diro, issued a statement directed mainly at Australia and New Zealand: 'The political developments in Fiji are a matter for the people of Fiji to resolve themselves' and 'I appeal to foreign powers to respect the sovereignty of Fiji.'[11] It should be noted that Diro was the former commander of the military in Papua New Guinea and he had led Papua New Guinean troops (with Australian backing) on their foray into Vanuatu in 1980 to assist the government of Walter Lini. A few months later, Diro was to admit to receiving funds from General Murdani of Indonesia to support his own political activities. Diro's statement was seized upon by Colonel Rabuka in his search for indications of overseas support and it was aired over Radio Fiji.

Other politicians in Papua New Guinea were more critical of the coup. Opposition leader and former prime minister, Michael Somare, expressed shock and disbelief. Deputy opposition leader John Momis stated: 'The Pacific has lost a shining example of democracy and a progressive government which was vigorously asserting the right of Pacific people to be free from interference by the nuclear powers. This is a victory for narrow racial prejudice and for those global powers who prefer to keep Pacific nations meek and quiet.'[12]

Responses from other countries in the region were slower in coming. While, generally, they too condemned the coup and called for a return to parliamentary democracy, their statements were more muted. In fact, the next day, Tonga, with its close ties to Fiji's eastern chiefly élite, sent a telegram supporting the colonel's actions. Elsewhere around the world, countries followed the line of Australia and New Zealand and deplored the military take-over.

The question of military intervention came up again that afternoon at a meeting between Prime Minister Hawke and the commander of the Fiji military, Brigadier General Ratu Epeli Nailatikau. Nailatikau was in Perth at the time of the coup, having gone there for the handing over of two patrol boats. Statements after the meeting, again, ruled out military intervention. Nailatikau condemned the coup, but stated that further comments would have to await his having discussions with people in Fiji. Meanwhile, the Australian government let it be known that two Australian naval vessels in Suva were not to become involved, except for providing communications.

Following the meeting with diplomatic representatives, where he had been flanked by Peter Stinson and Ahmed Ali, Rabuka met with local newspaper publishers and managers of radio stations and warned them to show caution in their reporting and to avoid 'sensationalism.' In the meantime, the FBC remained under military control, with Radio Fiji broadcasting only music, and news and bulletins approved by the military. Radio FM96 (which broadcast effectively only in the Suva area) and the two dailies, the *Fiji Times* and *Fiji Sun*, however, remained unoccupied by the military and under no formal censorship.

Rabuka's rationale for the coup and his plans for the future were spelled out to the press when he met them a little after 3:00 P.M.:

> Ladies and gentlemen, I believe that you are all now aware of the events of this morning. At ten o'clock this morning, members of the Royal Fiji Military Forces took over the government of Fiji. They have neutralised Parliament and by the same process have suspended the Constitution of Fiji ... Legal draftsmen are now in the process of putting together the draft interim constitution. You may ask whether the activities of this morning were absolutely necessary. In my position, as Chief of Operations in the Royal Military Forces, and after monitoring the events of the past few weeks and with the information about planned activities of certain groups in the community I believe it is in the national interest that I carry out the events of this morning – the takeover of the government ... Later today, I will be naming a Council of Ministers to run the government until the next elections. I reiterate that this is an interim measure to ensure the safety of the public and perhaps to effect some of the changes that I think are necessary to protect the interests of the communities in Fiji.[13]

In the question period that followed his statement, Rabuka made it clear that the changes he was concerned with had to do primarily with land issues and the chiefly system. He also announced the suspension of Brigadier General Nailatikau, Chief of Staff Jim Sanday, and the country's top three police officers. Rabuka assumed command of the military himself and placed Josefa Lewaicei, a relative from his home area, in command of the police.

Broadcasts over Radio Fiji in the Fijian language provided somewhat different reasons for the coup. As with Veitata's speech, broadcasts made frequent reference to God and the inspiration that He provided Rabuka in guiding him towards his decision to act. Rabuka claimed that he and his soldiers were the *liga-ni-wau* (club-men) for the paramount chiefs, and in his broadcast he addressed the paramount chiefs individually: the Vunivalu, Tui Cakau, Tui Nayau, Tui

Lau, and Roko Tui Dreketi. Rabuka also noted the threat of public disorder, and stressed the need to act to save Fiji from Libyan intervention. Before the coup, Alliance Party supporters had been spreading rumours in Fijian villages that Colonel Qaddafi and his fellow Libyans were helping to finance some of the Coalition government's reforms, such as the elimination of certain hospital fees and bus fares. Rabuka claimed to have documentary evidence of Libyan and Soviet involvement with the Fiji Labour Party. Such allegations might seem incredible, but the anti-Libyan hysteria, that was a regular feature in the region's media during the weeks and months prior to the coup, had paved the way for at least some Fijians to believe that Libya was helping to pay for Fijian pensioners to ride buses, and that even more sinister plans might be afoot.

Among the first public responses to the coup was a statement by the General Electors' Association (an arm of the Alliance Party) in support of the coup. A statement by the Fiji Council of Churches, however, was critical of those involved in the coup and called on the army 'to release the hostages and to surrender to the sovereign authority of the land.'

At the same time that Rabuka was meeting with the diplomatic corps, the chief justice, Timoci Tuivaga, visited the governor general to argue that the suspension of the constitution was 'illegal and invalid' and to urge Ganilau, as the Queen's representative, to take a stand against Rabuka. The result was that around 6:00 P.M. the governor general prepared a statement which the army sought to suppress. But a tape recording of the governor general reading his statement was smuggled out of his residence around 9:00 P.M. and taken to the Radio Fiji studio where soldiers sought to intercept it. The person carrying it escaped and went to the nearby offices of Radio FM96, which was able to broadcast the tape once, before it was seized by the military:

People of Fiji, I'm deeply disturbed by the events of this morning during the sitting of the national assembly.

The unlawful seizure of members of my government and some members of parliament has created an unprecedented situation which cannot be allowed to continue.

The executive power under the Constitution of Fiji is vested in Her Majesty the Queen which by law and convention I exercise on her behalf on the advice of the cabinet.

In the temporary absence of the Ministers of the Crown I have assumed that authority.

I have accordingly issued a proclamation that a state of emergency exists and I'm taking immediate steps to restore the lawful situation.

I wish to emphasise that the Constitution is the supreme law of Fiji and has not been over-ridden and that all public officers duly appointed as such remain in office.

As commander-in-chief in Fiji I now call upon all officers and men of the Royal Fiji Military Forces, the Royal Fiji Police and members of the Public Service to return to their lawful allegiance in accordance with the oath of office and their duty of obedience without delay.

For the sake of peace and the prosperity of our beloved country, I command the people of Fiji to respect and obey the Constitution.[14]

It was a command that went unheeded by those that mattered. The military continued to hold the Coalition parliamentarians at Queen Elizabeth Barracks, while Colonel Rabuka, Mara, and their associates went ahead with plans to form a Council of Ministers.

Negotiations went on much of the afternoon and evening over who was to be on the Council of Ministers, with the radio issuing periodic statements that the names of the ministers would be forthcoming soon. By the time the announcement was made, after midnight, most people had gone to sleep.[15] The names announced included a core group of Alliance Party parliamentarians and a few others associated with recent events. Rabuka named himself president and minister for home affairs. Mara became minister for foreign affairs. Among those closely involved in the destabilization efforts to appear on the list were Taniela Veitata and the Reverend Tomasi Raikivi (former secretary of the Fiji Council of Churches and, along with Rabuka, from the Navatu-Natewa area on Vanua Levu). Nine other native Fijians were named, all with Alliance Party backgrounds.[16] There were two Indo-Fijians (Ahmed Ali and Narsi Raniga) and one local European (Peter Stinson) who were also from the Alliance Party. Ali was given responsibility for information and broadcasting, and Stinson for finance. Attempts were made to recruit native Fijians who were not associated with the Alliance Party, such as Fijian Nationalist Party leader Sakeasi Butadroka, but these came to nothing. By and large, the new council looked very much like the old Alliance Party government.

Around 11:00 P.M. the Coalition parliamentarians were transferred from the barracks to the prime minister's official residence at Veiuto, where they were guarded by about thirty armed soldiers. Shortly after midnight, Timoci Bavadra was able to make a telephone call to the *Fiji Times*. He stated to the newspaper that he expected the situation to be resolved shortly and urged people to remain calm. He denied that his government had any intention of using the army against the people, noting that 'the Government's position has always been that the situation was fast returning to normal. And therefore, there was absolutely no reason for the action taken by Colonel Rabuka.'[17]

The military did not feel that it was necessary to impose a curfew that evening. The military left the international airport at Nadi open and allowed the two newspapers to go about preparing the morning editions unhindered. Colonel Rabuka, Mara and the others linked to the coup felt that the situation was under control and sought to promote a situation of normalcy. But there were few in Suva that night who saw the situation as anything approaching normal as the reality of what had happened and its implications for the future of Fiji began to sink in.

WHO WAS RESPONSIBLE?

After having described what happened on the day of the coup, what remains is the much more difficult task of discovering who was actually involved in the plot. Understanding any coup requires sorting out who was involved in its planning and implementation and the reasons for such actions. Determining the cast of characters and causes, however, is rarely easy, and debate and speculation can continue for years after the event. In fact, unravelling the events surrounding coups often takes on characteristics more commonly associated with detective novels than with history or political science. Unlike detective novels, however, the full story behind a coup may never be known.

Two things that most coups have in common are: (1) there is almost never a single cause, and (2) only rarely does the military act on its own without some foreign or civilian support. The causes of the first Fiji coup are indeed complex and controversial. In addition to the military, the potential cast of characters includes an array of local and expatriate civilians, but, in only a few instances, is there any conclusive evidence relating to their role in the coup. The possible participants include: (1) Rabuka and a small group of fellow officers, (2) Mara and his cohorts in the Alliance Party, (3) a group of corrupt businessmen with links to the Alliance Party, (4) private and perhaps not-so-private right-wing expatriates in Fiji around the time of the coup, and (5) officials associated with the U.S. government. Among the possible motivating factors are power, money, racism, cold war fanaticism, and traditional regional rivalries. Linking any of these parties, besides the military, to the coup also requires exploring the question of the extent to which the overall destabilization campaign in the weeks before the coup was tied to the coup itself, that is, was the coup part of the general destabilization plan devised by those with ties to the Alliance Party? Or was it a relatively independent event?

The official Mara/Rabuka version portrays Mara as an innocent who knew nothing;[18] the Taukei leaders acting independently to turn Fiji into a bloody racial battle ground because of their opposition to an Indian-dominated government; and Colonel Rabuka coming to the rescue in the name of God to preserve native Fijian rights, prevent bloodshed, and to rid the country of a socialist government that would turn Fiji into another Cuba. In this version, the United States does not appear at all as an actor.

At the other extreme is a conspiracy theory that views the coup as a CIA plot.[19] This theory highlights the strategic importance of Fiji to the United States and Mara's close relations with the U.S. government and American military personnel, in particular. Specifically, this thesis points to General Vernon Walters' visit to Suva prior to the coup, to Mara's trip to Honolulu shortly before the coup, and to the activities of the alleged CIA agent, William Paupe. Those adhering to this thesis raise questions concerning the claim that the American embassy, close to Parliament House, placed riot shutters over its windows fifteen minutes before the coup took place. This thesis also cites fragmentary incidents as evidence which include the following: (1) an American ship capable of carrying out an amphibious landing was stationed offshore at the time of the coup; (2) a number of American military planes landed in the country on the flimsiest of excuses shortly after the coup; and (3) a claim by one member of the Bavadra cabinet that the soldiers who seized Parliament were black U.S. Marines disguised as Fijian soldiers.

The Mara/Rabuka version seems incredible to anyone familiar with Fijian politics and seems a story dreamt up for a, hopefully, gullible public. As for the second version, it sounds like a tale told by someone who had seen a few too many James Bond movies. But sometimes events that are even stranger than fiction or the paranoia of conspiracy theorists do take place, and neither version should be dismissed out of hand.

There are also 'middle-ground' theses that focus on internal developments. One such thesis sees Mara and his business and chiefly cronies becoming increasingly desperate as their attempts at destabilization failed and support for the Taukei Movement evaporated. The conspirators then turned to the military, where they found a willing agent in Colonel Sitiveni Rabuka, to remove the Coalition government before the Alliance group was exposed for corruption and lost all chance of regaining power. Among other things, those adhering to this thesis point to 'the speed with which Colonel Rabuka was able to appoint a Council of Ministers – a Council of Ministers which read like an Alliance "who's who", including Ratu Mara' as an indication 'that the coup cabinet list had been prepared before the takeover.'[20] This version seems more plausible in light of the known facts and the nature of Fijian politics, but perhaps this ease of fit, if nothing else, should make one uncomfortable about accepting it as the true version too readily.

Mara himself is probably the best person to begin with. Was he the master-mind behind the coup? Was he a co-conspirator with the Americans? Was it simply a matter of his being aware of plans and giving his tacit approval? Or was he completely innocent? Firm proof of Mara's precise role in the coup is lacking and may never come to light. But there is considerable circumstantial evidence about his involvement.

That Mara should be suspected of being behind the coup is understandable. Mara had a long history of orchestrating events in such a way as to make himself appear to be a voice of moderation and the saviour of the nation. He often used racist extremists to stir things up, usually while he was conveniently absent from the country or at least a good distance away from the event itself, and then he would intervene to save the day. Mara's tactics had become some of the most clichéd aspects of Fijian politics. Many observers saw Mara's trip to Honolulu shortly before the coup, and then his presence at a conference on the other side of the island while the coup was in progress, as 'proof' of Mara's involvement. It is not proof of course, but the pattern is suspicious. Also, there is evidence that Rabuka informed Mara of developments in Suva 'around 9:00 A.M.,' or before the actual take-over.[21] Then there was his son Finau's involvement in the plot, demonstrated when he began work on a new constitution immediately after the seizure of power. Mara and his son were not always on the best of terms since Finau had a history of trouble with the police, and Mara had become an increasingly authoritarian father; but with a matter like this, it is doubtful that Finau would have acted without discussing the plan with his father.

Another event that is pointed to by those who believe in Mara's involvement is his meeting with Rabuka on the Sunday before the coup while playing golf at the Pacific Harbour resort. Rabuka and Mara have gone out of their way to try to convince a sceptical public that this was a chance encounter. Thus, E. Dean and S. Ritova in their book, *Rabuka: No Other Way*, make the assertion that the two men's paths crossed by accident while they were playing golf separately, and Mara invited Rabuka to join him for lunch with some Samoan guests.[22] The authors then write that as Rabuka sat down he remembered 'one rule very clearly: When Ratu Mara plays golf, he doesn't talk about anything else.' Having told us this, which is known by others from personal experience not to be true (Mara's golf games having assumed a central place in his political interactions, both nationally and internationally), the authors then discuss the lunch-time conversation: 'Local politics, naturally enough, were raised.' As to the specific content of this discussion, we are told:

> The Colonel was interested in Mara's opinion about the way things were heading and his views on the status of the 1970 Constitution. 'We were talking about politics, and I asked how can the Constitution be changed? He (Mara), said the Constitution could not now be changed. The only way to change it ... and to use his exact words ... is to throw it out and make a new one, and the likelihood of that is nil.' Rabuka thinks Mara was speaking lightly, more in jest than in seriousness, for the benefit of his guests. Equally, he feels that, when Mara's Samoan guests went away, they had the possibility of a coup in their minds. This would have been reinforced because Rabuka had deliberately sat on the floor next to Mara at lunch – but this was for reasons of Fijian protocol, the Colonel insists, and not collaboration.[23]

It is not surprising that the Samoan guests went away thinking that these two men might be referring to plans for a coup – so would anyone else who had been present. And to dismiss Mara's statement as a jest is more than a little hard to swallow and would have been very out of character for Mara. Similarly, the book's next assertion should not be taken too seriously:

> What impressed itself most on Rabuka about this chance meeting, and the luncheon conversation, was that Ratu Mara 'seemed resigned to being Opposition Leader. He told me that the people seemed to have accepted the change of Government, and we would all have to wait and see, and hope that they (the Coalition) could do a good job.'[24]

Mara had made such statements often enough for public consumption and may well have said such a thing in front of his Samoan guests, but it was quite clear at the time that Mara had far from accepted his status as leader of the opposition. One thing that the account in the book does do is reinforce the notion that Rabuka and Mara were on good terms, and in no way does it serve to convince one that the two men were not co-conspirators.

The golf course tale is followed in the book with a denial by Rabu-ka that Mara was in any way knowledgable of his plans to stage a coup, and that when he supposedly began planning the coup a few weeks before the Pacific Harbour encounter: 'I discussed my ability to execute a coup only with my father and my uncle.'[25] This claim of secrecy does not completely square with the facts. Rabuka was known by many in and around the military to have brought up the prospect of a coup, from time to time, over the course of a number of years. His interest in coups was no secret, certainly not to Mara. But interest in a coup and its actual implementation are very different matters. In this respect, some of those who believe that Mara was behind the coup assert that it is unlikely that Rabuka would have acted on his own without the blessing of those of high traditional authority. This has been countered by reference to Rabuka's inde-pendence of action after the coup. The two are not, however, neces-sarily linked, since it is clear that, in many ways, post-coup events took on a momentum of their own.

A short time after the coup, informants close to the military told some Labour Party supporters of Mara's involvement. Under the circumstances, further confirmation of the validity of these accounts was impossible. According to one account, Mara and a small group within the Alliance Party had approached a number of officers with close ties to the chiefly oligarchy about the possibility of staging a coup, if other measures to unseat the Coalition government failed. Not all of the officers approached were supportive of the idea. Infor-mants suggested that among those with reservations was the mil-itary's commander, Brigadier General Nailatikau, who therefore absented himself and went to Australia to avoid having to take a stand. In an interview after the coup, Sanday commented that he was surprised when Nailatikau told him he was going to Australia 'at a time when there were protests and demonstrations in the coun-try.'[26] Rabuka, with a known history of interest in coups, became the prime organizer of the possible coup, while other means of regaining power continued to be attempted by members of the Alliance Party. It should be remembered that, over the years during times of crisis, members of the Alliance Party government had discussed the use of military force, but that it had never proven necessary to resort to such measures. So why should they not consider a military option this time?

Wanting to take credit for the coup themselves, Taukei leaders some time after the events stated that the take-over was solely their idea – leaving Mara out altogether and making Rabuka their agent. In an interview with *Islands Business* a year after the coup, Taukei leader Inoke Kubuabola states that the idea of the coup was first hatched on 19 April, at a meeting between himself, Jone Veisama-sama, and Rabuka: 'we spent some time in prayer and options and we asked Rabuka to prepare his side of things, you know the military option ... We asked Rabuka to prepare that side and when the time, when we reach a stage when he must step in, he must be ready to step in.' Kubuabola claims to have been the Taukei Movement's 'direct link' with Rabuka, and indicates that military action was decided on only when it became apparent that neither Mara nor Ganilau were prepared to act against the Coalition. This decision, according to Kubuabola, was made on 11 May, after Mara's return from Hawaii. Another Taukei leader, Viliame Gonelevu, asked Mara at an Alliance Party board meeting if Ganilau had called him about a meeting with Bavadra. To this, Mara responded: 'He hasn't called me up and even if he called me up I would not go.' From that point, the Taukei conspirators felt committed to a coup. Kubuabola says that he went to see Rabuka and that they set 15 May as the date for the coup. They planned to use a roll-on roll-off ship at the wharf to transport the Coalition ministers to Makogai Island, where they were to be held. When the conspirators learned that Parliament would not sit on the fifteenth, they held a meeting at the office of the Bible Society of the South Pacific on the night of the thirteenth and decided to stage the coup on the following day.[27]

In part, at least, Kubuabola's story is probably true. It reflects how he and his fellow Taukei conspirators saw things, with, no doubt, additional elaborations over time after the success of the coup. But it is not necessarily the whole truth. While Rabuka's claims that a primary reason for his staging the coup was to prevent further civil disorder by the Taukei and that he, essentially, stumbled across their plans at a party at the house of Taukei leader Raikivi lack credibility, it is equally incredible to see Rabuka simply as a Taukei agent.[28] Nor does Kubuabola's account, even if true, rule out an ultimate Mara link. The possibility remains that at least some of the Taukei were in close contact with Mara and that the others, such as Kubuabola, were, in fact, Mara's unwitting tools. Thus, while Kubuabola's revelations one year after the coup fill in some of the gaps in the picture, much of it remains obscured, especially in regard to Mara's role in events.

Those who back the hypothesis of Mara's involvement also point to the question of Mara's fear of being exposed for corruption. As was noted in earlier chapters, as evidence of corruption in the Alliance Party government increased, a number of questions had been raised about Mara himself. How had he, on a prime minister's salary and the legitimate perks of a high chief, managed to amass a personal fortune estimated at between F$4 and F$6 million? How had he and his wife acquired so many business interests? And how had they come to own so much residential and agricultural property around the country? He was known to have received many favours from businessmen. His house at Lakeba had been built largely with funds provided by Mara's various friends in business. What had they received in return? There were also questions about his role in the development of the Fijian Hotel and Pacific Harbour Resort (in which Mara had been involved along with the well-known international arms merchant Adnan Khashoggi). What of Mara's involvement in the television deal with Kerry Packer? Or of the F$52,000 pay off from business interests in the garment industry at the time of the wages tribunal? What of his alleged involvement in the theft of artifacts from the Fiji Museum? Then there was Marella House and the Hurricane Relief Committee. The latter had been the subject of rumours concerning corruption since its inception. Most attention focused on the distribution of F$61 million in relief funds after two cyclones in January 1985. Mara chaired and chose the members of the committee, and reports of the proceedings of its meetings and the actions of individuals involved with the actual distribution of funds and goods seemed to lend substance to rumours of corruption.

The Coalition government had yet to lay charges against Mara, but investigations into irregularities were proceeding, and even if most of the allegations proved wrong and Mara was really unaware of and uninvolved in most of the corruption that had become rife in his government, it seems unlikely that Mara would have escaped completely unscathed. In fairness to Mara, the evidence of his involvement remains circumstantial. But it is circumstantial evidence that is too strong to dismiss lightly, and it certainly is at least as compelling as the denials.

Turning to Mara's associates in the Alliance Party, one can divide them into two interrelated groups. First, there are members of the chiefly oligarchy itself and individuals closely tied to it through kinship and a sense of loyalty (based, in part, on patronage). This would include important chiefs, such as Ratu Penaia Ganilau, and an assortment of individuals belonging to the Fijian Association, such as Jone Veisamasama, Taniela Veitata, and Filipe Bole. The second group is comprised of those whose allegiance to the oligarchy is perhaps 'less pure,' and includes such men as Peter Stinson, Jim Ah Koy, and Apisai Tora. There are three interrelated factors which motivated both groups of individuals to act to save the oligarchy's privileged position – power, spoils, and the fear of exposure for corruption – the same factors that may have motivated Mara.

The question of Ganilau's involvement has been the subject of considerable debate. His actions following the coup (discussed in the next chapter), in which he seemed disposed to support Rabuka, were seen by many as an indication of his prior knowledge, if not actual involvement. There is also a report that two Taukei leaders from Ganilau's home province of Cakaudrove, Kubuabola and Veisamasama, had shown him their plans to destabilize the Coalition government in April.[29] Countering this evidence was his apparent genuine surprise when informed that the coup had taken place, as indicated by Leweniqila's account of his conversation with Ganilau. The reticence on the part of some to link Ganilau to the coup was undoubtedly related to his holding the office of governor general and the extent to which this provided him with an aura of added respectability. Yet on closer inspection, Ganilau appears to be affected by many of the same pressures as Mara and others. In 1982 several individuals had raised questions about his use of funds for logging development.[30] A short time later, Ganilau, along with other prominent Alliance Party members, were the recipients of one of the lots in the controversial Muanikau land deal in Suva.[31]

Suspicion of Ganilau's involvement was also aroused by his close association with the army dating back to the 1940s. In particular, and more recently, there was the record of his support for Colonel Rabuka. He was known to have been fond of the colonel and to have avidly supported Rabuka's promotion through the ranks. The event that attracted most attention in this regard took place in 1985. Contravening orders, Rabuka had allowed a major under his command in the Sinai to return home for the funeral of his father. Brigadier General Nailatikau had sought to court-martial Rabuka, but Ganilau interceded and had the charges dropped. After the coup, Ganilau not only pardoned Rabuka for his 'insubordination' but went so far as to promote him to full colonel.

Some saw further evidence of Ganilau's involvement in the coup when two weeks before the coup steps were taken to make Ganilau the Tui Cakau, the Paramount Chief of the Tovata Confederacy. From the perspective of the 'tribal conspiracy' theory, which viewed the coup as directed by members of the Tovata Confederacy, the move to make Ganilau the Tui Cakau was seen as a pay-off for his acquiescence to the military takeover. The Tovata Confederacy included Cakaudrove, to which Rabuka owed allegiance, and also Lau.

The manner in which members of the Tovata Confederacy sought to make Ganilau the Tui Cakau raised a few eyebrows. Ganilau held the best claim to the Tui Cakau title on the death of the incumbent, Ratu Ratavo Lalabalavu, but the title was not his automatically. The offer of the title came during the ninety–day mourning period for Lalabalavu, and the offer was seen as a major breach of traditional protocol. Significantly, the initiative had come from Taukei leader Ratu Inoke Kubuabola.

Observers favouring the 'tribal conspiracy' theory noted that many of those involved in the coup and put in positions of power immediately after the coup were not only from Cakaudrove but, more specifically, many were from the Navatu-Natewa area of Vanua Levu. The Navatu-Natewa people are the traditional spear holders (*liga-ni-kau*) within Cakaudrove – a position that Rabuka made frequent reference to, during and after the coup. Thus, they were the 'hatchet men' for Ganilau and the other chiefs of Somosomo. In addition to Rabuka, others from Navatu-Natewa who were prominent in the events surrounding the coup were Rev. Tomasi Raikivi (Taukei leader and former secretary general of the Fiji Council of Churches), Jone Veisamasama (Alliance Party secretary general), Viliame Gonelevu (former vice-president of the Methodist church, Alliance Party M.P. for Cakaudrove, and related to Mara's wife), and Josefa Lewacei (a cousin of Rabuka's and police commissioner).

Again, Rabuka's own account denies that Ganilau knew anything about the plot. Rabuka presents his visit to the governor general after the take-over of Parliament as motivated by the need to gain his acquiescence and he reports that he had difficulty in convincing the governor general of the need for the coup: 'He was not convinced. I had, in fact, been counting on his support, but he made it clear that it should have been done some other way. Executing a coup was wrong in his book, and in the eyes of all democratic countries.'[32] What Rabuka reports the governor general as saying next, if true, is of more interest: 'Couldn't you have given them (the Coalition) time to carry out their policies? Perhaps they would have shown us in a few months' time that they were incapable of running the Government, anyway.'[33] The earlier destabilization campaign was based on the belief that with a little pressure, the Coalition government would collapse. It is quite likely that Ganilau continued to cling to this view (partly because he saw the Coalition as nothing more than another version of the National Federation Party), unaware of the extent to which the destabilization efforts had collapsed and that the Coalition had proven itself capable of resisting the destabilization campaign.

The conversation between Rabuka and the governor general took place after Lieutenant Col. Jim Sanday had left the governor general's residence and therefore lacks independent verification. If Rabuka's account is at least generally true, it indicates that rather than being an active participant in the coup and in earlier destabilization efforts, Ganilau may, indeed, simply have been a sympathetic bystander who hoped that less drastic measures would succeed in removing the Coalition from office. But enough questions remain to make it difficult to dismiss the prospect of Ganilau's complicity too easily.

What of the other Alliance Party parliamentarians like Apisai Tora and Peter Stinson? To understand why they and so many Alliance Party adherents were so anxious to see the Coalition government removed, one only has to remember that they had prospered as part of the extensive Alliance Party patronage network. A partial list of spoils linked to control of state power includes: Fiji Development Bank loans; government contracts; avoidance of close scrutiny by government agencies; Fijian Affairs Board patronage (jobs, scholarships, contracts, etc.); control of mataqali funds; preferential duties favouring crony businesses; various perks of office (housing, overseas travel, automobiles); deals with private firms in the form of payoffs and placement on boards; use of aid money for personal gain and patronage; and the list goes on. Such questionable practices reached far beyond Mara's cronies in office. For example, it soon became evident to the Coalition government that Alliance Party government patronage had helped to ensure the survival of many businesses owned by prominent members of the General Electors' Association through a seemingly endless stream of loan funds. Peter Stinson's financial troubles have already been alluded to, and he had become more dependent than ever on holding government office as could be seen from his driving around town in a small Japanese import after having to give up his ministerial Mercedes Benz. In fact, there was not a single minister in the Alliance government who had escaped the hint of scandal. But it is, perhaps, Apisai Tora who provided the most interesting case.

Tora had a long history of corruption dating back to his union days when he gained a reputation among fellow unionists for taking pay-offs. Apparently he had found his association with Jeffrey Reid to be a profitable one, as were the ones with his new-found friends from America, Valentine Suazo representing the Asian-American Free Labor Institute and local AID director William Paupe, both suspected of ties to American intelligence. Tora came to serve as an intermediary, disbursing aid funds to secure the allegiance of trade unionists and chiefs to the Alliance Party. Working with Suazo, he had sought to promote Alliance Party interests by dividing the trade union movement. Before and during the election campaign, he had used development funds from the United States and other sources to help secure the allegiance of important local chiefs for the Alliance Party. In one documented case in late 1984, Tora received a cheque for F$27,500 from Paupe to build a 'multicraft and training centre' in his home village of Natalau. In addition to the centre, it appears as if some of the money went towards construction of a new house for Tora himself.[34] It would be wrong to simply characterize Tora as an American agent, for he was far too independent for that, but he was a crucial element in the web of relationships that bound the Alliance Party's survival to perceived American strategic interests.

Tora and his wife had made it very clear after the election that they were extremely upset at the loss of their government house and his Mercedes Benz. That he became a ringleader of the destabilization campaign surprised nobody. During the days before the coup, he made remarks on numerous occasions, to the effect that the Coalition government's days were numbered, and he appeared less than disturbed by the legal net that seemed to be closing in on him. And, like many of the other Alliance Party parliamentarians, he took the military take-over in stride and seemed well prepared for the day's events. Maybe all of this was merely a matter of Tora's usual bluster, but circumstantial evidence would seem to indicate that there was a great deal more to it than a corrupt politician's bravado. Because of Tora's close relations with the Americans and his intimate involvement in the destabilization campaign (and perhaps the coup itself), questions are also raised about American participation in these events. We will return to the possibility of an American connection, shortly.

While discussing suspects from the Alliance Party, mention should also be made of Rabuka's uncle, Militoni Leweniqila. By his own admission, Rabuka had discussed the possible effects of a coup two weeks before the actual take-over. The discussion took place among relatives at Lewenqila's home in Suva: 'I told him if you are going to successfully execute a coup, you may have to take some lives ... I also told him that a coup will be economically disastrous for the country.'[35] Leweniqila's subsequent break with his Alliance Party colleagues would seem to indicate that by early May, at least, he did not expect a coup and supports his claim that, on the day of the coup: 'I had no idea what was in store.'[36] While he may not have been part of the conspiracy, however, he did not see fit to tell members of the Coalition government of the conversation with his nephew.

Next on the list of suspects is a small group of expatriate businessmen associated with Mara. Two of them stand out: Jeffrey Reid and Paul Freeman. Reid's relationship with Mara has already been discussed on several occasions. Having friends in government in the past had been important to his running of Emperor Gold Mine. Mara had helped him through labour troubles, and, at one point, the government had secured a F$2.5 million loan to Emperor Gold Mine. In addition, the government agency responsible had never looked too closely into problems associated with waste disposal at the mine. One allegation that particularly disturbed the Coalition government was that Reid was operating a gold-smuggling operation, using an extra labour shift and a front company in Hong Kong, and taking the gold out as tailings. Investigations into these charges had only just gotten under way when the coup took place. Reid's involvement in destabilization efforts and the growing likelihood of his being forced out of the country were probably responsible for indirect approaches made to the Bavadra government by others involved with the ownership of the mine who sought to distance themselves from Reid. Again, nothing has been proven to link Reid directly with the coup, but there is enough circumstantial evidence to justify suspicions.

The case of Paul Freeman is a little more bizarre. I first encountered Paul Freeman when he appeared as a guest lecturer before a class at the University of the South Pacific. During his lecture to a group of wide-eyed students, he described in detail, and with an ease that seemed astounding, his transfer pricing scams and use of bribery in the logging industry in the Solomon Islands. He also referred on several occasions to his friend Mara. He had run afoul of authorities in New Zealand, Vanuatu, and the Solomon Islands, but seemingly to little avail. It continued to be business as usual. Reporter Wendy Bacon has reviewed Freeman's controversial activities in New Zealand:

In 1975, Freeman, at the time a member of the National Party and a political lobbyist, was allegedly leaked a document by a friend in New Zealand's Security Intelligence Service, Rowan Jays. The document was a police record of an interview with Gerald O'Brien, M.P., that centred on long-range economic policy. *Truth* newspaper, also involved in the leak, called those discussions a 'socialist plot'.

Why Freeman was chosen to receive the document was never made clear. At the time, he told journalists he had CIA and SIS connections [a claim he later denied]. Whatever the reasons, the Labour Government reeled in the face of communist smears and allegations that it mishandled security matters.[37]

Freeman turned up in Fiji in 1977 and immediately established a close association with Mara. The two travelled together to China the following year. When William Paupe arrived in Suva in 1985, Freeman had found another friend to help advance his business interests – Paupe being a keen supporter of private-sector entrepreneurial initiatives. Meanwhile, Freeman found himself banned temporarily from Vanuatu and then the Solomon Islands.

It was Freeman's activities after the May coup and the activities of some of his associates that raised questions about whether he was involved in the coup. At the time of the coup, Freeman was managing director of the Fiji-based External Trade Organisation (ETO). Its chairman was Mara confidant John Falvey. Bacon comments on events relating to ETO the day before Fiji's second coup in September:

> That afternoon, Freeman, as managing director of ETO, had called a top level meeting. Present were none other than the second most senior officer in Fiji's Military Forces Colonel Pio Wong, a Fiji military intelligence officer Captain Samuela Matai, two retired officers from the United States military and Freeman himself. The two Americans were Richard Cyrus, just retired from the U.S. Navy special warfare team, the Seals, and Larrie McKenna, a retired airforce colonel.
>
> What exactly the five men discussed is not known, but the following day Freeman shut the office early and sent the staff home. Later, while a stunned Suva was still trying to come to grips with a second military coup, Freeman boasted that he had foreknowledge of military commander Colonel Sitiveni Rabuka's plans.
>
> Richard Cyrus, one of the Americans who attended the pre-coup meeting in the ETO offices, had flown in urgently from Hawaii. ETO project officer, David Watson, had been present two days earlier when Freeman had called Cyrus back from the U.S. Navy base at Pearl Harbor. Freeman, he remembers, was 'very, very upset and said that Dick had to be here for some very, very important meetings with the military ... he demanded that this man must get here and as soon as possible.[38]

During the period between the first and second coups Freeman had maintained a high profile close to the regime. In July, about two months after the May coup, Freeman travelled with Mara, Pio Wong, and four other military officers to several Asian countries, partly on a trade mission, but primarily to secure materials for the military. In fact, Freeman paid the expenses of those accompanying him and, during the trip, introduced them to a variety of contacts, including an arms merchant in Singapore. Back in Fiji, Freeman was often seen in the company of Pio Wong and other officers, mostly connected with intelligence. Bacon continues: 'ETO was fast turning from a commodities trading company into what Watson describes as a "front for clandestine activities." Watson's worry increased when he visited ETO and found Freeman and Cyrus discussing "the best form of surveillance aircraft and helicopters and areas for landing and training." '[39]

Despite convincing evidence, Rabuka denies that there was any link between Freeman and his regime. As Ritova and Dean write: 'Media claims about a connection between businessman Paul Freeman and the Army's Colonel Pio Wong are "wrong." Colonel Pio Wong had believed that Freeman was "a good talker," could help the Army in its post-coup role as a development agency. However, Rabuka says, Freeman did not become an officer in the Fiji Army, nor did he pay for a Fiji mission to Asia, led by Ratu Mara.'[40]

In this as in so many other instances, Rabuka's denial does not seem to square with the facts. For example, not only had Freeman told numerous individuals that he had been given a commission, but, in typical Freeman fashion, he had shown people, including former ETO project manager David Watson, his commission card signed by Rabuka. While it is obvious that Freeman was intimately involved with the military regime after the coup and that he probably knew of the second coup, there is, however, no specific evidence linking him with the first coup. The question that remains is whether he was involved, or whether he merely took advantage of the opportunity that it presented. It is also interesting to note that, despite claims by the United States that it had suspended all aid to Fiji after the coup, Paupe's office, in fact, continued to provide financing for Freeman's projects.

Richard Cyrus, a self-proclaimed 'extreme anti-communist,' turned up at the U.S. embassy a short time after the coup wearing his navy uniform. He was a lieutenant colonel in the U.S. Navy Special Warfare Force, otherwise known as the SEALS, and a veteran of the Vietnam War. When Coalition spokesman Richard Naidu asked Ambassador Dillery about Cyrus, he said that Cyrus was in Fiji on a private visit and 'the fact that he'd been in his naval uniform and appeared at the Embassy was a source of some embarrassment and concern to the Embassy because he was retired and it was against regulations for him to be in uniform.'[41] In fact, Cyrus was still in the military at the time and did not retire until September.

What of Freeman's other associate, Larry McKenna? McKenna is a retired colonel in the U.S. Air Force who owns a company called Pacific Gemini based in Newport, California. Late in 1986 his company bought the Kon Tiki Tourist Resort near Savusavu. While McKenna sought to present himself as a simple businessman with no formal links to Freeman, Freeman himself has a different version. As Wendy Bacon reports: 'Freeman insists on his links with McKenna. From a safe in the corner [of his office] he showed us a large file labeled "McKenna" who he descibed as a CIA operative.'[42] Mention should also be made of another Freeman associate, Bob McIntosh, who helped operate Freeman's timber operation in the Solomon Islands. McIntosh had been in the CIA for twenty years.[43]

Mention of Freeman's associates, Cyrus and McKenna, brings us to the next group under investigation: the assorted expatriate right-wing cold war warriors in Fiji in and around the time of the coup. Under the Alliance Party government their number had grown, many of them associated with religious bodies, with the U.S. Peace Corps, as well as various businesses. During its campaign, the Coalition had become aware that there were Peace Corps volunteers in some native Fijian villages actively supporting the Alliance Party's attempts to stir up communal tensions. Such activities did not end with the change in government. Shortly after the election, a native Fijian who worked with the Peace Corps was instrumental in the formation of the Fijian National League in Ra, purportedly to 'teach the Fijian language and culture.'[44]

More disturbing were the activities of a volunteer named Bill Derrenger. After Deputy Prime Minister Harish Sharma was released from captivity by the military, he went to rest at the Travellers Beach Resort Hotel. While there, he was shown a document by Derrenger, who said that he was working as an adviser to a native Fijian chief. Sharma recalled in a later interview: 'Well, I think he wanted to say that this was one of the ways in which the present crisis could be solved.'[45] The document was a plan to establish a republic without political parties that contained no provision to allow Indo-Fijians to vote. The same document later appeared as the Taukei proposal for a new constitution.

It is highly unlikely that people such as Derrenger had anything to do with the coup directly. The same cannot be said of another interesting character, Rod Kelly. Rod Kelly's name came to this author's attention in early 1986 as someone who was working closely with members of the Alliance Party. I was told that he was someone that people should be careful of, who was involved in some questionable activities. He was working through the Fiji Visitors Bureau (of 'Carroll report' fame). He also was known to have connections in France, and some felt that he he had something to do with Mara's increasingly close relations with the French.

When reporter Wendy Bacon visited Fiji in May 1986, she ran into Kelly at a resort outside of Suva: 'He told me he had lots of high level contacts and a silent number in Suva. He told me he was an Australian Trade Union Official, connected with the Australian Labor Party which he said hadn't decided yet whether it would support the new Fiji Labor Party. He told me the ALP [Australian Labor Party] was concerned about the large amount of foreign money which Dr. Bavadra had at his disposal – he suggested it came from the Soviet Union.'[46] Kelly's story was pure fabrication and he became very agitated when he learned later that Bacon was a reporter. A couple of days later, when I went to meet Wendy Bacon in the lobby of the Suva Travelodge, I witnessed Kelly threatening her if she reported the conversation that they had had at the resort.

Delving deeper, the Kelly story became even more interesting. There were rumours of Kelly's involvement with French intelligence and there were people who claimed to know Kelly under different names. Following up on the story back in Australia, Wendy Bacon discovered that Kelly had been actively involved in right-wing union activities in Melbourne and that he worked out of an office that housed an enigmatic organization called the Labour Association for Pacific Understanding.[47] Kelly also appeared to be associated with a right-wing Seychellian named Brian Hoffman, who worked as a mercenary in Southern Rhodesia and is reported to have advocated the overthrow of the leftist government in the Seychelles.

Late in 1986, as the election date was drawing near, Kelly moved into a house in Suva. Investigating Kelly's activities around the time of the coup, Wendy Bacon talked with witnesses in Suva 'who saw Fijian soldiers walking in and out of his home. They also recognised Bill Paupe. On the Sunday of the week leading up to the first coup, Kelly was at Pacific Harbour where Mara and Rabuka played golf. On Monday, Tuesday, and Wednesday, he left for appointments at 4 o'clock in the morning. The day after the coup, on the Friday, he suddenly packed everything up and disappeared.'[48] Coalition supporters were watching his house when he left: 'I heard of him leaving the country a day or two after the coup. In fact, a friend of mine followed him with all his equipment to the military camp.'[49] Once again, no firm proof of Kelly's involvement in the coup but enough information to raise questions nonetheless.

Possibly linked to the Kelly story is the fact that after he left Fiji, Taukei leader Ratu Meli Vesikula moved into the house that Kelly had occupied. Vesikula had returned to Fiji in 1984, after serving twenty-two years in the British army, along with his stepson who had just retired from British army intelligence. Both men had diffi-

culty in adjusting to civilian life in postcolonial Fiji and were particularly disturbed by what they perceived to be the breakdown of
native Fijian traditions and, especially, respect for the chiefs. They
were to emerge as key players in the destabilization efforts and in
political events after the coup. Although Kelly and Vesikula appear
to have been acquainted, the extent to which Kelly was involved in
Vesikula's political activities is still subject to debate.

The activities of Freeman, Kelly, and the others serves to highlight
the extent to which the nineteenth-century 'beachcomber tradition'
has been maintained by Mara and his fellow chiefs. During the early
years of European contact in the nineteenth century, individuals
such as Charles Savage were able to play an important role in
improving the political fortunes of chiefs in eastern Fiji. This was a
relatively common phenomenon in many parts of the non-Western
world at a time when access to Western military hardware and
know-how was still limited. But it was a phase that passed quickly
in most settings. The South Pacific remains one of the few corners of
the globe where a Western drifter can gain a position of influence
close to the centre of power. The reasons for this are to be found in
the small scale of the societies and their relative lack of sophistica-
tion. In the case of Mara, the maintenance of the beachcomber tradition is also tied to the nature of his personalistic rule; his love of
adulation, especially by foreigners, and his pattern of surrounding
himself with those whose loyalty, if not based upon kinship,
reflected dependency on royal favours.

The name that crops up repeatedly in connection with the individuals discussed above is William Paupe. My own interest in Paupe
began in relation to investigations into the activities of Valentine
Suazo, the representative for the Asian-American Free Labor Institute. I learned that the two men worked closely together, often in
conjunction with Apisai Tora. One usually reliable informant
employed by the Americans told me that Paupe was the CIA chief of
station. Such an assertion needed further proof, but it was enough
for me and others to pay more attention to his activities. Before and
after the coup, Paupe seemed to be supplying aid funds to help the
Alliance Party government maintain its patronage structure, and he
continued to be involved in local political affairs. After Paupe's
arrival in Fiji not only did the amount of American aid to Fiji
increase sharply but so did the AID office staff – reaching twenty-
four, which was more than worked in the embassy itself.

Who is William Paupe? U.S. officials claim that he is simply a man
who oversees the distribution of aid. New Zealand-based *Wellington
Confidential* reviews some of his suspected activities:

[Paupe was] reportedly involved in covert/special operations in South-east Asia in the Vietnam war years (when U.S. AID was a conduit for CIA programs such as "strategic hamletization" and the MSU training of S Vietnam police), Paupe was reportedly later involved in training Marcos palace guards together with British soldier of fortune Graeme Gibson, who is now a director of Tropic Images, a Sydney-registered possible CIA front company (U.S. AID money administered by Paupe supposedly ends up on island projects carried out by Tropic Images).[50]

In fact, Suazo and several other U.S. embassy staff shared a history of previous experience in the Philippines. Needless to say, Paupe described the allegation of his being a CIA agent as 'absurd' and claimed that he had never had any connection with the CIA in his thirty-two years of government service.[51]

During Mara's trip to Honolulu two weeks before the coup, he was accompanied by Paupe. It was reported that Mara and Paupe had visited CINCPAC headquarters in Honolulu on 29 April. CINCPAC sources responded with the claim that only Paupe had paid a visit. Then on 22 October, United States Information Service spokesman Michael Gould issued a statement claiming that Paupe had already left Honolulu on the twenty-ninth, while leaving the impression that Mara alone had visited CINCPAC. This was followed by a statement on 16 November by another American representative, William Lane, Jr., that 'neither Ratu Mara nor Mr. Paupe visited CINCPAC.'[52]

Paupe also seemed to take charge of Vernon Walters' visit to Suva and may have been responsible for the reported meeting between Walters and Rabuka. Paupe was to remain in Fiji until December 1987. When Ambassador Dillery left in July, Paupe was, in effect, the senior American representative. Some feel that Dillery's departure was related to the publicity surrounding Paupe's activities, which led to his being compared to Ollie North of 'Contragate' fame. The appearance of another Contragate star, Adnan Khashoggi, on the Fijian scene adds a nice touch to the comparison.

Paupe is not the only resident American official who received notice around the time of the coup. The other was the deputy chief of mission, Edrick Sherman, considered by many in Suva to have been a CIA agent. Sherman was reportedly seen with Rabuka on several occasions following the coup. The Bavadra government had also been disturbed by a report that four CIA agents had arrived in Nadi shortly before the first Taukei marches and fire-bombings. It was reported that they had gone to a building owned by Mara associate Motibhai Patel where discussions were held with Patel present. The Special Branch was asked to investigate. Reports after the coup indicated that at least three of the men had arrived in Nadi on 7 May, that two of them were identifed as being at Pacific Harbour on Sunday the tenth during the Mara-Rabuka golf game, and that one of them was in Parliament at the actual time of the coup.[53] Verification of these reports requires further investigation, which is highly unlikely at the present time, but it is easy to see why this, when combined with the activities of Paupe and others, led members of the overthrown Bavadra government to suspect u.s. involvement.

Another piece of evidence used by some who point to American involvement, has to do with Rabuka's charge that he had proof of Soviet and Libyan links with the Coalition government. One piece of the so-called proof was the by now thoroughly discredited 'Russian letter' from the 1982 election which resurfaced in Rabuka's hands. The assocation of this letter with Mara confidant John Falvey has been noted by some observers (see Chapter 3). Rabuka's wild claims about Libyan involvement were in keeping with a regional campaign that seemed to be under way at the time.

The press throughout the South Pacific was full of anti-Qaddafi stories. True, the Libyan presence had increased, but, in practical terms, it remained insignificant. And it was certainly hard to justify the kinds of stories that appeared in the media. Typical of the stories being printed were two articles which appeared on the front page of the *Sydney Morning Herald* on 27 April, beneath the headline 'World War in Pacific – Gaddafi.' One by Peter Fray reported on a conference in Tripoli and Qaddafi's plans 'to create a sphere of influence in the Pacific' and his support for 'violent revolutionary struggle in several Pacific islands, including Tonga, Vanuatu, New Caledonia, and Mindanao.' In the other article, Peter Hastings, while admitting that Libya's interests in the Pacific were a 'minor development,' nevertheless accused Qaddafi of seeking to 'destabilise the South Pacific in much the same way as Cuba saw Grenada as the weak link in the Caribbean.' The pro-Israeli Hawke government in Australia had been particularly susceptible to this propaganda.

The origins of this anti-Qaddafi media blitz were exposed in an article by Bob Woodward in the *Washington Post*, in which the contents of a memorandum from John Poindexter, the national security adviser under the Reagan administration, are revealed. The memorandum, dated 14 August 1986, proposed the launching of a major disinformation campaign against Libya.[54] During his trip through the South Pacific, Vernon Walters actively sought to promote anti-Libyan hysteria. This American link has led some Coalition supporters to view Rabuka's use of Libya as yet further evidence of CIA involvement in the coup, in that he had been supplied with false information either to help prompt him to act or at least to help justify his action. It is possible, however, to see Rabuka's claims simply as typical products of the Alliance Party propaganda mill.

Both Rabuka and the U.S. government have denied any CIA involvement in the coup. This is hardly surprising. Despite indications that the CIA may have been involved, there is still insufficient evidence to confirm any such involvement. What we have is a string of reports that indicate a high level of suspicious American activity in Fiji around the time of the coup, but the actual links that could connect Walters, Paupe, Rabuka, and Mara remain tenuous. That Walters and other right-wing Americans were concerned about developments in Fiji and about the overall geopolitical drift of the region is unquestionable, but this does not automatically translate into a plot to overthrow the newly elected Bavadra government. There is also the possibility that Paupe acted on his own or at least provided assistance and encouragement to his Fijian allies to destabilize and then overthrow the Bavadra government without the orders of his superiors, although this does not seem likely. Paupe's involvement in Alliance Party politics was evident, but it is necessary to be cautious before determining that a link existed between his distribution of funds and advice, and the coup. Certainly, it is unlikely that people such as Mara and Tora were willing simply to do the bidding of the Americans. Whether or not the coup plot itself originated with the Americans or with Mara and the Alliance Party or Rabuka, it is possible that the latter were given encouragement by Paupe or others associated with the Americans, and, at the very least, American government officials in Fiji before and after the coup do appear to have been inappropriately involved in Fiji's internal political affairs.

The scandal surrounding Oliver North and the so-called Contragate affair alerts us to the extent to which even privatized counter-revolutionary and destabilization efforts can ultimately be linked to American government intervention. This use of right-wing civilians leads us back to the intriguing question of the role played by Paul Freeman and the gang of anti-communist, right-wing fanatics at the External Trade Organisation, as well as the enigmatic Rod Kelly. Freeman and Kelly may well be con-men. The South Pacific abounds in them, and the Mara government seemed to attract them like flies. But this does not rule out the possibility of their involvement in the coup, at least at some level. The presence of Falvey as chairman of ETO on the one hand, and of the close relationship between Freeman and Paupe on the other hand, would seem to indicate some linkage between the Americans, ETO, and the Alliance Party. And Freeman's actions after the coup demonstrate that he had established close relations with the military regime. But, as noted above, this may well have been a matter of opportunism, and the actual link between the External Trade Organisation and the coup itself remains elusive.

At one level, actual proof of American, or even Mara's, complicity in the coup is not that important. Whether or not they were involved in its planning and implementation, they helped to contribute to the conditions that made it possible. Through specific actions, the Americans had contributed to the climate which made the coup possible: support for the patronage structure and the divide-and-rule tactics of the Alliance Party; the cynical use of anti-communist, anti-Libyan propaganda and disinformation; and assistance to a military force that was little more than a palace guard and that inevitably would become entangled in civilian political affairs.

As for Mara and his cronies, even in the unlikely event that they were not involved in plotting the military take-over, they were the ones primarily responsible for creating an atmosphere within which it could take place: indirectly, through a history of communal politics and promotion of anti-democratic sentiment; and, more directly, through their destabilization efforts aimed at the democratically-elected Bavadra government. This, of course, will not satisfy lovers of mystery and intrigue who must remain curious as to how the pieces in this extremely complex puzzle fit together. We have come a long way from simplistic notions of a valiant soldier acting on his own to save the dignity and rights of his race, but a good deal of sleuthing remains to be done before the mystery is solved.

Having noted the limitations in presenting an accurate picture of why and how the coup took place, this chapter will conclude with a probable scenario of the forces that may have precipitated the coup. The electoral defeat of the Alliance Party in early April created a crisis for various elements in Fiji: (1) Alliance politicians and cronies who would lose power; (2) the regional eastern chiefly élite who would lose power to the west; (3) the children of the old eastern chiefly élite who had anticipated inheriting the mantle of rule; (4) expatriate businessmen like Jeffrey Reid and Paul Freeman who had prospered under Alliance Party rule; and (5) the U.S. government which was concerned about the spread of anti-nuclear policies beyond New Zealand.

Attempts to destabilize the Coalition government got under way almost immediately after the election. All of the above-mentioned elements actively opposed the new government in one way or another, their efforts centring on the formation of the Taukei Movement. Ostensibly a spontaneous response to the victory of an Indian-dominated government with widespread popular backing among native Fijians, the Taukei Movement was, in fact, the creation of a few individuals backed by members of the oligarchy who sought to play upon the insecurities and communal sentiments of native Fijians. The public leadership of the Taukei was comprised of a mixture of communal extremists and a handful of other Alliance parliamentarians. Tora continued to receive American aid throughout this period and it seems likely that, at least at some level, the Americans were involved in promoting the destabilization of the Coalition government, although such involvement may have been fairly indirect.

Inititial attempts to destabilize the Coalition government included various ploys within Parliament and the mounting of demonstrations to stir up communal antagonism. As these efforts failed to shake the government or to generate the desired level of popular support, those who had lost power became increasingly desperate. This desperation led members of the Taukei to resort to violence in the form of fire-bombings of the offices of Coalition parliamentarians and supporters. At the same time, Colonel Rabuka began preparations for a possible military take-over, should the Taukei fail to dislodge the Coalition government. Following the election, there was widespread discussion among military officers about the possible desirability of staging a coup, but the origins of the actual plan to stage a coup remain controversial. Mara may have initiated the move – this would have been entirely in character – and, at the very least, it is difficult to believe that he was unaware that a coup was being planned. Involvement of the beachcombers and Americans is also unproven, although there is circumstantial evidence to suggest that men such as Freeman and Paupe might have participated in, or known, of the plans. Whoever was involved in planning the coup, its being carried out was the final escalation of a gradual process of destabilization that ultimately demonstrated the extent to which Fiji's oligarchy and its allies held democratic principles in disregard.

Following the coup, the oligarchy moved quickly to consolidate its power, but as events were to show, this was to prove more difficult than anticipated. The oligarchy found itself faced not only with widespread popular opposition and unexpected international condemnation, but elements in and around the oligarchy fell to fighting among themselves once Mara's supreme authority no longer was as firmly established, as it had been before the election.

CHAPTER EIGHT

Aftermath of the First Coup

Rabuka and the others involved in the coup had not anticipated any resistance once they had seized power. They expected the people of Fiji to remain passive in the face of military power and chiefly authority. It would be equally easy, so they believed, to install a new government composed of native Fijians from the Alliance Party with the backing of the military. After all, this was, in effect, the same crew that had run Fiji since independence – all that was missing was the pretense of democracy.

The plan was a simple one. First, the governor general swears in Colonel Rabuka's Council of Advisors. Next, over the weekend, a new draft constitution is prepared to add further legitimacy to the new regime. Then, the following week, the Great Council of Chiefs is convened to give the new government its blessing. The nation would thus be presented with a new government and political system that assured continued rule by the eastern chiefly establishment and that safeguarded the position of the business interests with whom the chiefs were associated.

The take-over of Parliament may have been carried out with a degree of military precision, but what happened in the aftermath was anything but precise. Before swearing in Rabuka's new council, Governor General Ganilau was advised that, legally, he could not swear in the council. Such independence on the part of the judiciary came as a surprise not only to those behind the coup, but also to many of its opponents who had grown cynical in a system where judges were often appointed on the basis of political patronage and a willingness to acquiesce to the demands of the oligarchy. What followed were several days during which it became almost impossible for local or foreign observers to figure out what the governor general was doing. His statements and actions frequently appeared contradictory and confused.

In the world beyond the governor general's residence, the situation also was becoming more difficult than had been anticipated by Rabuka and his military and Alliance Party cohorts. During the first day or two after the coup, the people did not know how to respond, but, gradually, resistance began to emerge as the shock wore off and was replaced with anger among Labour Party-NFP coalition supporters. Their resistance took the form of vigils outside the official prime minister's residence where members of the Bavadra government were being held, street marches, and distribution of pamphlets condemning the coup.

There were a few who desired to resist the military by force, but cooler heads prevailed. When a group of Indo-Fijian youths piled into a large truck 'to go run down soldiers,' their employer pleaded with them not to use violence and to channel their anguish into nonviolent forms of resistance. There was widespread fear that it would not take much to spark violent reprisals from the military. Most Fijians were all too aware that the smiling, friendly native Fijian was only part of the picture; there was another side of Fijian society where aggression was commonplace as was evident in the high incidence of violent crime and by acts of violence in the bars and on the rugby fields.

An additional problem for Rabuka was that the reasons given for staging the coup had not been widely believed. Few believed that the colonel's action had been motivated by the need to prevent bloodshed in the wake of escalating racial conflict, since it had been all too obvious in the days before the coup that support for the Taukei was dwindling and that, in fact, the new government had been able to contain the threats to stability. Rabuka's reference to the word of God and pernicious Libyan influence was given some credence in more isolated Fijian villages, but nowhere else. Most saw it simply as a power play by forces associated with the defeated Alliance government, and the onus for the violence was placed squarely on Rabuka.

In the face of such difficulties, the army launched a campaign to crush any signs of dissent. The regime began to harass and arrest those they identified as key figures in planning resistance. Assisted by supporters at the university and within the union movement, the regime compiled lists of those to be picked up, and the names were circulated among the police and army. The regime increased its control of the media and closed the nation's two daily newspapers. Rabuka's allies in the Taukei Movement, meanwhile, set about to provide substance to the myth of racial conflict by organizing attacks on Indo-Fijians. Taniela Veitata and his dockworkers provided the core of the organized violence. They were joined by gang members recruited from the public housing and squatter settlements in and around Suva. Gangs roamed the streets, broke into houses and entered Indo-Fijian squatter settlements where they terrorized the inhabitants and forced many to flee.

The Great Council of Chiefs met in Suva on 19 May to give its approval to the coup and to plans to establish a new racist regime. As mentioned previously, under the Mara government, the Great Council of Chiefs had assumed a role as the voice of the most conservative, and often most racist, elements in Fijian society. Members who were known to be opposed to the coup were excluded from the meeting (as, of course, were those members who had belonged to the Bavadra government), while many others remained silent in the face of the assertive posturing by the most extreme elements. Such extremists tended to be identified with the Taukei Movement, which had coalesced after the coup into a relatively organized political body representing diverse native Fijian communalist elements. The Taukei Movement remained largely under the control of Mara allies from the Alliance Party, but not completely.

After two days of meetings, the Council of Chiefs agreed to back an interim Council of Advisors under the nominal headship of the governor general, and this body was to govern until new elections could be held. This interim council was to replace Rabuka's Council of Ministers. When new elections would be held was not stated, but the intent was that they would not be held for some time and certainly not under existing rules. Fundamentally, this was a compromise between the moderate and more extreme elements within the native Fijian establishment and the intention was to legitimatize the original seizure of power from the Bavadra government.

In a move clearly intended to serve notice that no dissent was to be tolerated, as well as to highlight the need for the army to maintain order in the face of civil unrest, gangs of thugs organized by those supporting the coup attacked anti-coup demonstrators (and journalists) near the site where the Council of Chiefs was meeting on the twentieth. Over one hundred people were injured, and a number had to be hospitalized. Simultaneously, gangs that included members of Veitata's dockworkers launched attacks on Indo-Fijian stores and homes.

The army released the members of the Bavadra government on the nineteenth. Bavadra himself did not remain in Suva for long, preferring the relative safety of his home village of Viseisei in the west. It was in the west that the strongest signs of resistance to the military-backed regime began to emerge. There was even talk of secession or of setting up a 'government in exile' in the west.

Questions began to be raised as to whether the nation's thousands of cane farmers (most of whom were Indo-Fijians) would harvest their cane. Crushing had been scheduled to begin at the Labasa mill in the north on 19 May, but the date had to be deferred as a result of uncertainty over the supply of cane. There were also doubts about whether crushing would begin on schedule at the Lautoka and Penang (at Rakiraki) mills on the twenty-fifth, and at the Rarawai mill (at Ba) on 2 June. There were several acts of sabotage against cane fields. A fire on the night of 21 May, for example, destroyed cane on a farm on Vanua Levu belonging to Mara. Such moves threatened economic disaster for the country. Sugar exports the previous year had been worth over F$250 million, which accounted for 60 per cent of total export earnings and 15 per cent of GDP.

Many native Fijian villagers in the west indicated that they, too, were prepared to withdraw economic support from a regime that they viewed as having stolen the government from them. Ratu Osea Gavidi, leader of the Western United Front, told people in his area to stay in their villages and live at a subsistence level until the new regime collapsed. At a meeting in Viseisei on 23 May, a group of western Fijian chiefs passed resolutions opposing the military-backed regime and expressing their support for the Bavadra government.

There was opposition in the east as well. Sakeasi Butadroka, leader of the Fijian Nationalist Party, despite his reputation for anti-Indian sentiments, had been quick to condemn the coup (for which he blamed Mara). In interviews with foreign journalists shortly after the coup, he stated that he had been quite satisfied with the Coalition government's handling of native Fijian affairs and that he had turned down overtures to join the military-backed regime.

Indo-Fijian shopkeepers and businessmen began planning protest actions soon after the coup – many being upset not only by the coup's racial overtones, but also by its disastrous economic implications. Their actions involved shop closures, which began on a large scale on 18 May and continued intermittently thereafter. Significantly, among those involved were several individuals who had been prominent in the Indian Alliance (the Indo-Fijian wing of the Alliance Party).

The governor general's office named the nineteen members of the Council of Advisors on 22 May. With the governor general as its head, Rabuka was placed in charge of security and Mara, foreign affairs. The membership was heavily weighted in favour of the Alliance Party and prominent supporters of the Taukei Movement. A few more neutral members were included in an effort to make the new Council of Advisors at least look different from the previous Council of Ministers.[1]

Bavadra and deputy Coalition leader Harish Sharma were invited to participate as the only two representatives of the deposed government. The members of the Bavadra government met in the western town of Ba on the twenty-fourth and decided not to participate in the council, which was due to hold its first meeting in Suva the following day. The council soon lost another of its members when Daniel Mastapha resigned after attending the first meeting.

Colonel Rabuka had been pardoned by the governor general on 23 May for his exemplary behaviour after overthrowing the elected government and on the pretext of helping to restore normalcy. The governor general went even further on the twenty-nineth and promoted Rabuka to full colonel and commander of the military, effective from the date of the coup. Other officers who had taken part in the coup were promoted as well. From a regional perspective, the effect was to strengthen the position of officers from Cakaudrove at the expense of those from Lau and Tailevu.

Despite the presence of civilians on the governing council, Fiji was looking more and more like a military state. Troops were in evidence around the capital and at strategic points throughout the country, and in early June Rabuka announced plans to increase the strength of the army from four to eight battalions. Soon after the coup, the army began drafting civilian supporters, to lend the regime additional authority in the eyes of the people. These included individuals from important statutory bodies such as the Fiji Electricity Authority and Fiji Sugar Commission. Former Alliance Party parliamentarian Fred Caine was made a lieutenant and given responsibility for public relations. Finau Mara was made a captain and given the post of legal adviser to the army, while another native Fijian lawyer, Isikeli Mataitoga, was also made captain and given the position of legal adviser to the governor general. Alliance senator Jona Qio, who before the coup had been charged with involvement in acts of sabotage against Coalition ministers, was made a lieutenant.

Intimidation of anyone suspected of speaking or acting against the regime continued with short-term detentions becoming common. Soldiers became increasingly bold in threatening individuals and in searching for materials not to their liking. Soldiers went so far as to storm wedding ceremonies and ransack video rental shops.

Acts of violence (including an increasing number of rapes) by gangs of native Fijian youths became more widespread. On 1 June there were serious attacks by native Fijian youths against Indo-Fijians in Suva as well as on the northern islands of Vanua Levu (in Savusavu) and Taveuni.

Despite the growing military presence, extensive violence, and continued protests, the new regime attempted to present a picture, especially to the outside world, that the situation was returning to normal. One indication of this was that the newspapers were allowed to resume printing on the twenty-first, although the radio remained tightly controlled.

EXTERNAL RESPONSES

As noted in the last chapter, initial reactions to the coup by other governments had been fairly critical, but no firm proposals for action were immediately forthcoming. The United States, Britain, New Zealand, and Australia continued to make it clear that they recognized the Bavadra government as the only legitimate government of Fiji. India explored the possibility of joint Commonwealth action and asked Australia to consider imposing economic sanctions. While not prepared to impose trade sanctions, these countries did announce the suspension of development assistance to Fiji.

The rise to power of the Fiji Labour Party had been watched with considerable interest in Singapore and Malaysia, in large part, because of its policy of non-racialism. An editorial in the *Straits Times* was critical of the racial overtones of the Fiji coup, and on 25 May a Singapore government official was quoted in the press as saying the Fiji coup 'just goes to show how fragile democracy is in Third World countries, particularly those with multiracial populations.'[2] In Malaysia, while members of opposition parties were highly critical of the coup, the Mahathir government took a milder line and warned against outside interference in the internal affairs of Fiji.

The first responses of regional governments to the coup had been sympathetic to its racial aims, while generally not condoning the means of stopping what was seen as an 'Indian threat.' The king of Tonga had sent a telegram of support to Rabuka, but this had not been made public. The response of the other governments was much more muted. The first real test of how regional governments would respond to the coup came at the South Pacific Forum meeting held in Apia, Western Samoa, which began on 29 May. Prime Minister Bob Hawke of Australia discussed his position with respect to Fiji shortly before the Forum meeting: 'In this issue, as in all others in the region, we do not seek to interfere in the internal affairs of sovereign independent nations, but we assert that Australia has a real and legitimate interest in regional stability. And it is in that context that we will continue to press our view about the desirability of adherence to constitutional processes in Fiji ... Our obviously preferred position ... needless to say, is the reinstatement of the Bavadra Government, because we say that it is the only legitimate Government.' On the question of sanctions, he commented: 'In my thinking and in the discussions of the Cabinet, what has emerged is that we have decided to leave the question of sanctions, as it were, on the table. But I don't see, my colleagues in the Cabinet don't see, sanctions at this stage as an appropriate course of action.'[3]

Before the coup, Bavadra had intended to attend the Forum meeting since it was seen as an ideal means by which he could personally meet the region's heads of state and familiarize them with his government's positions. Bavadra recognized that most of the region's heads of government were sympathetic to Mara and he had hoped to put their minds at ease about any potentially destabilizing effect that the Coalition government might have on the region. The Coalition also felt that it was important to overcome the image that it had in the region as an 'Indian government.' Bavadra's lack of personal relationships with heads of other governments in the region and the view that the Coalition was dominated by Indo-Fijians were important factors in the lack of regional support for the overthrown government. Being unfamiliar with Bavadra and the new government it was all too easy for the regional governments to accept the racist rationales for the coup put forward by Rabuka, Mara, and others.

In an effort to help legitimate the new regime, Mara planned to attend the Forum meeting. When word reached Hawke that this was a possibility, he quickly made it known that he would not attend if the Fijian regime sent a representative. He then contacted the Western Samoan prime minister, who was hosting the meeting, to ask him to apply pressure on the regime not to attend. The New Zealand prime minister's position was similar. Such pressure resulted in the governor general announcing on 26 May that, because of the state of emergency in Fiji, it would not be possible for Fiji to send a delegation. At the same time, members of the Bavadra government announced that they would be sending three delegates to put their position to the Forum.

The way had now been cleared for Australia and New Zealand to attend the meeting. Questions remained, however, as to how to handle Fiji. Many states were anxious to avoid any formal discussion of Fiji, although a number were sympathetic to allowing unofficial discussions with representatives of the Bavadra government. Australia and New Zealand, for their part, were sensitive about not looking as if they were trying to bully the island states into taking a particular position; and the Melanesian states, in particular, had made it clear that they were completely opposed to any form of 'meddling' by Australia and New Zealand in Fijian affairs. The view of the Pacific island states was that the coup was an internal affair and that it was up to Fijians to settle the matter.

The representatives of the Bavadra government, Tupeni Baba and Krishna Datt, urged that a trade embargo be imposed, that the governments not recognize the regime, and that the Forum send a peacekeeping force to Fiji. On the question of non-recognition there was some support, but there was little sympathy for the imposition of trade sanctions or for sending a peacekeeping force. When Baba and Datt attempted to address the Forum delegates as they met in Samoa's Parliament House, they were forcefully ejected by police. They were able to talk to reporters and some delegates away from the meeting, but it was clear that the Coalition had little support among the Pacific islanders in attendance. One thing that was evident was that, for many of the delegates, racial considerations – and for the Polynesians, the maintenance of chiefly authority – overrode concern for the survival of democratic institutions. It was a fact that did not bode well for the future of such institutions elsewhere in the region.

The issue of democracy was of concern primarily to Australia and New Zealand. Over the weekend, talk at the Forum meeting did turn to Fiji. In fact, it became one of the main issues discussed. With Hawke leading the initiative and Lange supporting him, the Forum agreed to include a long reference to the coup in its final communiqué. The three Melanesian states expressed their concern about outside interference, but, in the end, were satisfied with the Hawke proposal. In general, the communiqué expressed concern and anguish at the overthrow of the elected government of Fiji. More specifically, in what was considered a diplomatic victory for Hawke, it was agreed to send a delegation to Fiji to discuss the coup on behalf of the Forum. The delegation was to be headed by Hawke, accompanied by the prime minister of the Solomon Islands and the head of the Forum secretariat. The delegation was only to be sent, however, if agreed to by Fiji's governor general.

The response of the governor general to the proposal was confusing, but it was sufficient for the Forum leaders to believe that it had his support. Plans were made to release the communiqué at 2:30 P.M. on Saturday. Just before the appointed time, however, word came from the governor general that it 'would not be practical' to send such a mission and he urged the Forum to stay away. Rumour of the governor general's turn-about had spread when Hawke called a press conference and failed to confirm whether he had any knowledge of the new development. Becoming angry with reporters, he did admit that he was 'not sure' of what the governor general had decided to do. Not too long afterwards, Hawke left Western Samoa – a full day earlier than scheduled. On his return to Australia, he sought to give the impression that there was still a chance of the Forum mission going ahead, but, in reality, it now appeared as if it would not. From the perspective of the governor general, Mara, and others associated with the regime, there had been little to gain by allowing the mission to go ahead since, by doing so, they ran the risk of providing yet another forum for their opponents to put forth their position which would further undermine the credibility of the reasoning behind the initial seizure of power.

It was left largely to overseas unions to take concrete steps against the military regime. At the request of the Fiji Trades Union Congress, unions in Australia and New Zealand placed cargo and passenger bans on ships and aircraft. The impact of such bans was considerable since these two countries provided Fiji with the bulk of its imported goods and with the majority of its tourists.[4] Whereas Australia and New Zealand provided Fiji with most of its imports of food, medical supplies, machinery, and petroleum products, Fiji exported small (but important to its economy) amounts of clothing, gold, timber, and agricultural products to these countries.

The bans immediately affected F$1.5 million worth of clothing due for export to Australia and several hundred thousand dollars worth of timber products on their way to New Zealand. A 9,000-ton cargo of wheat bound for Fiji was held up in Australia, and large shipments of onions and potatoes were threatened in New Zealand. The ban on timber exports came just as the F$50 million Drasa pine complex had opened, which employed around 400 people and was expected to generate tens of millions of dollars worth of exports within a couple of years. Fiji Forest Industries, the country's main exporter of timber products, reported that 85 per cent of its overseas orders were cancelled as the prospect of a shipping ban loomed. There were also several large hotel projects under way or under discussion that now seemed in question.

The suspension of development assistance was not without significance either. Australia and New Zealand announced that they were suspending aid to Fiji, which for 1987–88 was to have amounted to almost F$20 million. Even the United States suspended its aid program. At first the State Department had said that it was unclear whether American law, which required the suspension of aid to governments established by military coups, would apply in the case of Fiji. However, on 28 May, after the coup was endorsed by the Great Council of Chiefs, Rabuka was given a place in the governor general's interim government, and the Coalition rejected the notion of working with the new regime, the United States announced the suspension of remaining aid funds for 1987 and the blocking of 1988 funds. This included a F$1.3 million aid package and F$2.3 million worth of wheat shipments for 1987, and an aid program with a budget of over U.S.$6 million for 1988. The ban, however, did not include U.S.$2.2 million for the Peace Corps, which was allowed to continue operating in Fiji.[5] Japan and other aid donors were known to be considering what steps to take.

There was also the worry among some Fijians that international and regional bodies might move their offices out of Fiji, or at least direct more of their spending elsewhere. One regional body that was of particular concern was the University of the South Pacific, since it was known to be unpopular with leaders of the Taukei and the army, who viewed it as a breeding ground for radical ideas. Regional students began leaving soon after the coup until the vice-chancellor was finally forced to temporarily close the university. Several members of staff had been forced into hiding or had to leave the country. Not only was the military in evidence in and around the campus, but those sympathetic with the regime employed on the campus assumed the role of informers and actively intimidated other members of staff. Under the circumstances, there was the likelihood that the other countries in the region might decide to pull out of the university altogether.

Fiji's second most important industry, tourism, also was in serious trouble, as tourists cancelled reservations and airline flights declined. By early June, occupancy rates in Fiji's hotels had fallen to around 10 per cent, forcing management to begin laying off staff. Australia was Fiji's primary source of tourists, and union bans in Australia meant that Qantas would not carry tourists to Fiji. New Zealand was the second most important source of tourists and Air New Zealand stopped its flights to Fiji after an attempted hijacking on 19 May. The important American carrier, Continental, suspended its flights for at least a couple of months because of a drop in bookings. Other less significant international carriers (Canadian, JAL and Air Nauru) continued to fly to Fiji but were unable to pick up tourists bound for Fiji in Australia or New Zealand and their bookings sharply declined. The national airline, Air Pacific, was soon forced to reduce its international flights, and even internal carriers began to talk of reducing services.

The Coalition parliamentarians decided to travel overseas to lobby foreign governments and others directly for support. Bavadra himself left Fiji for Britain on 6 June. He stopped briefly in Melbourne, where senior government officials did not meet with him despite a request that they do so, and in Bombay, where he met with the Indian foreign minister, who expressed a willingness to help on behalf of the Indian government. Bavadra was unable to speak with the Queen, but talks were held with the Queen's secretary, William Heseltine, and with Commonwealth Secretary General Shridath Ramphal.

At the last minute, while in London, Bavadra decided to make a side trip to the United States to lobby for support in Washington. On the way back to Fiji, Bavadra had hoped to have an opportunity to talk with Prime Minister Hawke or Foreign Minister Hayden, but both men made themselves unavailable. Bavadra had also planned to visit Vanuatu for talks with Walter Lini. The Vanuatu visit was cancelled when a visit to New Zealand to talk with Prime Minister Lange was arranged by Bavadra supporters in New Zealand. Bavadra then returned to Fiji on 24 July.

The trip did not go particularly well. In Britain, the best that can be said is that Bavadra and those accompanying him were at least able to present their case directly to a few important individuals (although not the Queen), but little of anything concrete came out of these talks. The trip to the United States was handled very badly, but Bavadra was able to meet with a few sympathetic members of Congress who later supported passage of a motion condemning the coup.[6] The Hawke government had made it clear that it wanted to distance itself from Bavadra. In New Zealand, Prime Minister Lange modified his earlier strong support of the Bavadra government and urged Bavadra to take part in new elections proposed by the governor general. In retrospect, the time would have been better spent talking with Walter Lini and other Pacific island heads of government, none of whom Bavadra had met up to this point, but the Coalition had felt that the effort to lobby relevant Western powers had to be made.

More successful were bids to maintain union bans in Australia and New Zealand. Support was particularly strong from the New Zealand Federation of Labour and individual unions in Australia such as the Waterside Workers Federation. The importance of the bans can be measured by a statement from the governor general in early June threatening those lobbying for their retention, and by frequent critical reference to them in the press by others associated with the regime.

Propaganda efforts by the Fijian regime and pressure by business and political interests in Australia and New Zealand succeeded in having bans on shipments of essential foods and medical supplies lifted during the first week of June, but other bans remained in effect. The regime in Fiji responded to this by having union leaders close to it, such as Taniela Veitata, seek to have the executive of the Fiji Trades Union Congress vote for a lifting of the bans. A meeting of the executive of the Fiji Trades Union Congress was called for 6 June. The evening before, six members of the executive known to be hostile to the regime were picked up by the military, and Veitata arrived at the meeting the following morning accompanied by thugs from his union and observers from the military. Partly out of fear, many members of the executive did not attend. Despite such intimidation, the vote was a close one (a seventeen to seventeen tie, with the pro-regime president breaking the tie in favour of calling for a lifting of the bans). When the Australian Council of Trade Unions executive met in Melbourne on 12 June to discuss lifting the bans following the Fiji Trades Union Congress vote, only minor alterations were agreed to (specifically, a lifting of bans on Fijian timber exports to Australia), with most of the bans remaining in place.

Members of the regime felt that it was necessary to do something quickly about the drop in the number of tourists to avoid an economic catastrophe which would make the regime's hold on the country even more precarious. Lobbying by the regime resulted in overseas governments lifting travel warnings, but the number of flights was still reduced, and arriving planes remained virtually empty. In an effort to entice tourists from Australia during that country's vital school holiday in July, the regime launched 'Operation Bounceback' and announced that it would spend an additional F$500,000 on tourist promotion (above the F$1.5 million already budgeted in 1987 for the Fiji Visitors Bureau), and the national airline, Air Pacific, began to advertise bargain-level airfares. Two representatives of the regime travelled to Australia during the third week of June for talks with travel agents and others close to the tourist industry, while Bavadra supporters in Australia sought to counter these efforts by pointing to acts of violence (especially rapes and robberies) and other uncertainties facing would-be tourists.

By the end of the month, tourist arrivals remained low, with occupancy rates around 15 per cent, but travel writers and agents in Australia seemed to be responding favourably to the regime's initiative. As an added incentive, it was decided to fly a plane load of travel agents and writers to Fiji for free and, once there, to give them an all-expenses-paid look around the islands.

TOWARD A TAUKEI FIJI

Statements from extreme elements in the Great Council of Chiefs during its May meeting had supported the notion of a parliament with all representation in the hands of native Fijians or, at most, one that would give members of other ethnic groups a small token presence. After the meeting, discussion in this vein had continued throughout Fiji, with Taukei extremists led by Tomasi Raikivi, Taniela Veitata, and others, and egged on by Apisai Tora, seeking to gain support for their views. They frequently resorted to threats and intimidation, and stirred up racial antagonism in the process.

The governor general was presented with three proposals for constitutional changes on 9 June. The drafts represented the divergent views of those within the governing council as well as the Taukei Movement, the army, and the Great Council of Chiefs. All three favoured giving the majority of seats in the fifty-two-member House of Representatives to indigenous Fijians (the figure most commonly mentioned being 75 per cent or forty seats). Among the proposals was one to turn the Senate into a House of Chiefs with much greater powers than the present Senate.

Another issue concerned Fiji's relationship with the Queen. Loyalty to the Queen is very strong among native Fijians and much is made of the fact that she is the Queen of Fiji. Nevertheless, during the Great Council of Chiefs meeting, some members had expressed the view that Fiji should become a republic, if this was the only way to move ahead in forming a legitimate government that was completely in the hands of the chiefs. Mara and Ganilau had sought, at the time, to curtail support for such an idea, but it continued to be discussed as a firm possibility. In fact, the most extreme supporters of the Taukei Movement pushed the proposal vigorously, until, by the end of June, it seemed to have considerable support among the more conservative chiefs.

The governor general presented his own plan for Fiji's immediate political future on 11 June. His idea was to first appoint a Constitutional Review Committee and to then hold an uncontested election to restore parliamentary rule. According to the plan, the government elected under the scheme would then amend the constitution in accordance with the recommendations of the review committee. This done, Parliament would be dissolved and another election would be held under the new constitution.

The composition of the Constitutional Review Committee was spelled out on 23 June. It was to be comprised of sixteen members: four nominated by the governor general, four by the Great Council of Chiefs, four by Mara, and four by Bavadra. Thus, the Bavadra forces were to be given four seats, while those supporting the coup were likely to have twelve.

At the direction of the Great Council of Chiefs, discussions concerning constitutional changes shifted to the provincial level, where pro-coup forces sought to gain further support from the country's fourteen provincial councils (which represented rural-dwelling native Fijians). The Lau Provincial Council met in Suva on 17 June, with Mara scheduled to give an important address. Before the meeting, there was some debate regarding what Mara would say about the need to revise the 1970 constitution, of which he had been the principal architect. When he did speak, he stated clearly that changes were needed to enhance the power of native Fijians, but he warned that such acts alone would not improve the lot of the Fijian people and that economic success would depend on hard work. Those attending the meeting took the opportunity to present gifts to the army and to thank the soldiers for returning control of the government to them.

Taukei extremists were able to push their ideas through at a meeting of the Ba Provincial Council in the west, held the last week of June. A group of four Taukei, including Apisai Tora, had prepared a document in advance calling for constitutional reforms that would exclude non-native Fijians from Parliament. They also proposed turning Fiji into a republic. An attempt to present an alternative proposal by another member sympathetic to the Bavadra government was blocked, and the meeting was completely dominated by Tora and his associates.

The move to establish a republic in which non-native Fijians were virtually disenfranchised was often accompanied by statements to the effect that parliamentary democracy and related practices and institutions were foreign imports which had no place in the Fijian state that the Taukei extremists were seeking to establish. As one Taukei supporter, Finau Tabakaucoro (a prominent Alliance Party member and on the staff at the university), put it, 'democracy is a foreign flower.' A document prepared for the Council of Advisors by the Taukei during the latter half of June stated that democratic notions were 'contrary to the Fijian way of life where liberty exists only within one's own social rank and equality is strictly constrained by a fully developed social hierarchy.'[7] Such sentiments were not so much intended to assert native Fijian primacy over other ethnic groups as they were addressed to native Fijian commoners who had come to represent a growing threat to the eastern chiefs and their supporters.

RESISTANCE AND INTIMIDATION

While the Taukei were seeking to assert their control, the Bavadra government and its supporters took steps to counter them. Towards the end of May, Bavadra, through lawyer John Cameron (who was subsequently threatened with expulsion for his work on behalf of Bavadra), filed action in the Fiji Supreme Court challenging the dissolution of Parliament by the governor general and his declaration that the ministerial positions were vacant. It was a move to establish that Bavadra was still the legal prime minister.

On 4 June, five hundred western native Fijian supporters of Bavadra, led by Osea Gavidi and Etuati Tavai (a Labour Party senator), attempted to visit Ratu George Cakobau, the high chief (Vunivalu), at his home island of Bau, near Suva. Part of this group was turned back by David Toganivalu, who, backed by hundreds of his own supporters, told the westerners that the Vunivalu was too ill to see them. Members of the Vunivalu's family later denied that he was ill and stated that he had been awaiting the delegation. Other members of the delegation were stopped by the army, which, fearing any signs of solidarity among native Fijian opponents, had set up roadblocks in the area. The rumour was that the westerners were coming to Bau to ask Ratu George to head a government in opposition to the military-backed regime.

Resistance among Indo-Fijians was most apparent among cane farmers and cutters who continued to refuse to harvest sugar cane. The regime issued threats and even took steps to recruit native Fijian workers to harvest the cane by force, but the vast majority of growers and cutters remained adamant. Other, more violent, forms of resistance also began to emerge. On 11 June a group of eight men attempted to blow up a fuel line at Nadi International Airport with dynamite in the hope of sabotaging the regime's efforts to increase tourist arrivals.

Fiji Sugar Corporation management announced on 3 June that crushing would be postponed until 18 June. As a gesture of goodwill, it ruled out using the military to force harvesting. Talks between the Fiji Sugar Growers Association (representing cane farmers) and the Fiji Sugar Corporation began with the cane growers presenting a series of demands on what were referred to as 'nuts and bolts' issues. Before harvesting would commence the growers wanted military personnel removed from cane areas. They demanded that the balance still owed them from the 1986 harvest be paid and that they be paid on delivery for cane harvested in 1987. They also sought loans of F$14 million. The Fiji Sugar Corporation estimated that meeting grower demands would cost around F$70 million. It did not have the money and the growers, political considerations aside, saw no reason to harvest their cane with no guarantee of being paid for it. An impasse seemed to have been reached.

It soon became obvious that there would be insufficient cane to commence crushing on the eighteenth, and once again the start was postponed. Towards the end of June a few growers, mainly native Fijians (who accounted for only a small percentage of the crop), began to harvest their cane. Thus, by late June, only forty-seven out of 135 gangs on Vanua Levu had begun work – far too few to ensure an adequate supply of cane.

The Labasa and Penang mills began crushing on 25 June. At the Labasa mill (with a daily capacity of 2,200 to 2,600 tons) only about one-half of the 1,000 tons that had been delivered at the mill on the first day had been crushed before mechanical problems caused a shutdown. It was apparent that supplies would soon be depleted unless other growers were convinced to begin harvesting. The poor quality of much of the cane that had been delivered was also a matter of concern. Then, five hundred workers at the Penang mill threatened to walk out following an assault by army troops on one of the workers. And, on 29 June, hundreds of mill workers walked out at the Labasa mill in protest over harassment by the military which was occupying the complex. The management also reported problems arising from sabotage of machinery at the Labasa mill.

In the face of small and irregular supplies and worker discord, on 30 June the Fiji Sugar Corporation announced the discontinuation of crushing until the end of July. The 2,500 mill workers employed by the Fiji Sugar Corporation were stood down. A total of only 17,600 tons of cane had been crushed, producing 1,700 tons of sugar – enough for one month's local consumption. With the season growing late and the cane suffering the effects of a drought, worries increased as to whether Fiji would be able to export any sugar in 1987.

The regime enacted increasingly stringent emergency regulations as part of its effort to overcome opposition from sugar growers and merchants. The initial 'Emergency Regulations' issued by the governor general on 14 May included: the right to detain suspected persons, pending enquiries, for up to twenty-four hours; the right to exclude those suspected of, or likely to provoke, breaches of the peace from certain areas or to specifiy where they must reside; the right to control the entry and exit of persons from one area to another; and the right to detain and search persons on the basis of 'reasonable grounds' of suspicion. The regulations allowed authorities to ban or control meetings and to threaten or arrest those who criticized the regime.

On 12 June the regime issued additional 'Public Emergency Regulations,' which gave the regime the right to: direct the performance of employment in essential and necessary services, control sales of supplies, regulate transport priority, and 'get information from people.' In effect, authorities (which included a wide range of soldiers and police) were given the right to seize land, buildings, vehicles, and crops. Soldiers used the new regulations to allow them to requisition automobiles and they found various means of obtaining goods from stores with no intention of payment. To add a semblance of justification, the military publicized seizures of arms. Thus, on 25 June the army publicized the capture of a weapon and a small amount of ammunition from a farmer near Nausori and tried to link the incident with insurrectionary plans. They arrested a security officer, Rusiate Uluimoala, and accused him of conspiring to form the Kadavu Republican Army. Uluimoala later told journalists that he had been arrested after being asked by the soldiers if he were a Labour Party supporter.

Such measures were taken at a time when military harassment of civilians seemed to be increasing. Numerous incidents of armed soldiers threatening people were reported. There were raids on houses and offices, and assaults (one left a relative of Coalition parliamentarian Noor Dean in a coma). Soldiers' carelessness with their guns led one person from the tourist industry to express concern about the possible adverse affect that the sight of soldiers wandering the streets carrying guns by the trigger and taking wild shots might have on tourists. One incident that caused a diplomatic row took place on 2 June, when soldiers fired shots at the tires of a vehicle driven by diplomats from the British High Commission near the Suva wharf.

At the same time, gangs of native Fijian youths continued to cause problems in Suva and elsewhere. One incident on 1 July involved some fifty Fijian youths rampaging through an Indo-Fijian settlement in a village near Nausori. Reported rapes reached unprecedented levels – a fact strongly denied by the regime which played down such acts of lawlessness so as to not frighten tourists. Fear in the face of threats and acts of violence caused many parents to keep their children home from school. In late June it was estimated that nearly one-half of the nation's 160,000 school children were not in attendance.

There were also numerous acts of intimidation committed against journalists, trade unionists, academics, and members of the Bavadra government. A New Zealand journalist was arrested on 2 July after receiving a bullet and a warning note in an envelope. He was investigating financial dealings between close Mara associate Jim Ah Koy and Colonel Rabuka which involved a F$75,000 loan from the Bank of New Zealand to Rabuka to purchase a house from a company owned by Ah Koy. After trying to see Ah Koy at his home, the journalist was picked up and questioned for eight hours by police and soldiers (with civilian Taukei supporters present) and then told to leave the country. At one point he was accused of being an arms smuggler based on the evidence of the bullet that was found in his room.

On 25 June the military picked up a spokesman for Bavadra, Richard Naidu. The interrogators produced written summaries of telephone calls that he had held with Bavadra in London. Their admission of this particular instance of wire-tapping was advertised in the local press with the clear intention of intimidating others. On 1 July, three Labour parliamentarians (Tupeni Baba, Satendra Nandan, and Navin Maharaj) and about thirty others attending a prayer meeting in Suva were surrounded by soldiers, rounded up, and arrested. On the same day, thirty-one shopkeepers, who had refused to open their shops in protest against the regime, also were arrested in Suva.

Despite such intimidation, resistance continued. Cane growers and mill workers refused to co-operate and shopkeepers carried out periodic shutdowns. Labour Party and National Federation Party parliamentarians, both inside and outside Fiji spoke out in the face of arrests, abuse, and even death threats. More cane was destroyed by burning. Thus, nearly 4,000 tons of cane was destroyed in fields near Ba on 1 July, and about 800 tons of cane were burnt near Rakiraki on 5 July.

The Fiji Sugar Corporation radio station in Labasa (used for co-ordinating harvest activities) was burned on 2 July. There were also frequent bomb threats against Air Pacific flights. And, on 27 June, two former soldiers in the Fijian army announced in Christchurch, New Zealand that they were there to raise funds to buy weapons for an armed revolt against the regime. Two days later a letter threatening to carry out acts of sabotage was sent to media sources in Fiji from a group calling itself Fiji's Freedom Fighters.

Also important were remarks by the former commander of the military (and son of Ratu Edward Cakobau, former deputy prime minister and cousin of George Cakobau), Epeli Nailatikau, who had returned to Fiji from Australia on 29 May. He had been highly critical of the support given to the Taukei Movement by the Great Council of Chiefs and in a long newspaper interview discussed the need to 'cleanse' the army of those who had been involved in the coup. His presence in Suva, and the return of Colonel Jim Sanday from the countryside, raised speculation about a counter-coup.

The church was an additional factor to consider. Even before the coup, the church had been sharply divided and it remained so afterwards. Taniela Veitata, Colonel Rabuka, and others involved in the coup were lay preachers and sprinkled their political speeches with references to God and the Bible. The secretary of the Fiji Council of Churches, Tomasi Raikivi, had also been prominent in the Taukei Movement. But many within the church hierarchy were not pleased to see religion used to condone racism and violence. Raikivi had been forced to resign his position after leading anti-Indian demonstrations (he was subsequently given a post with the new regime as information adviser to the governor general).

The day of the coup, the president of the Methodist church, Josateki Koroi, and other church leaders had issued a statement condemning the coup and calling on the army to surrender. Prominent church leaders supported the efforts of the governor general to return the country to democracy. In its publication *Domodra*, the Methodist church urged reconciliation. In a letter to the *Fiji Sun* with the title 'Klaus Barbie & Fiji,' the Reverend Akuila Yabaki, communication secretary of the Methodist church, stated that 'racism is a heresy against God whether it is Nazi Germany, South Africa or Fiji' and commented that 'the link with recent events in Fiji is perhaps uncomfortably close' with those in Nazi Germany.[8]

ECONOMIC PROBLEMS

The union bans, the threat to the sugar crop, the diminishing number of 'coup-shy' tourists, and declining foreign reserves placed Fiji's economy in a precarious position. Foreign reserves had stood at F$160 million at the time of the coup. Two weeks later they were down to F$143 million, and at the end of the third week in June they had fallen to F$113 million. By the end of June, the economic situation had deteriorated to the point that the governor of the Reserve Bank decided to devalue the Fiji dollar by 17.75 per cent (the largest devaluation since independence). Steps were also taken to limit the flow of capital out of the country, especially by Indo-Fijian businessmen and migrants.

Employers in both the private and public sectors had laid off thousands of workers since the coup and reduced hours and wages for those still employed. The Fiji Electricity Authority, for example, reduced the hours for its 1,300 employees as electricity consumption dropped by 50 per cent (before the coup, hotels had accounted for 40 per cent of consumption). On 25 June, government departments were asked to find means to cut spending by 20 per cent. The next day, the Public Service Commission unveiled its 'Strategy for Economic Survival.' It included a proposal for a 25 per cent across-the-board pay cut starting 23 July, and a freeze on hiring and leave.

A meeting of the Joint Consultative Committee of the Tripartite Forum scheduled for 3 July to discuss the Public Service Commission plan had to be cancelled when the Fiji Public Service Association failed to attend. When a meeting was held on the seventh, the four public-sector unions expressed opposition to the proposal, but it was apparent that the regime would in all likelihood go ahead with the plan.

Lifting of union bans in Australia and New Zealand remained an important priority of the regime. The Australian school holidays were due to start shortly with Qantas staff still refusing to carry tourists to Fiji. The shipping bans meant that many goods were either held up at the wharf or were being air-freighted (especially needed machine parts) at considerable expense. The regime began to seek alternative sources of imports. Thus, negotiations were undertaken to purchase wheat from Europe and rice from Thailand – both items normally imported from Australia. In many instances, it was clear that goods acquired in this manner would be more costly than if they had been obtained from Australia or New Zealand, but Mara and Rabuka felt that it was important to diversify Fiji's sources of imports regardless of relative costs.

On 29 June, Australian airline unions agreed to lift bans on Qantas flying tourists to Fiji. But the Australian Council of Trade Unions executive decided at a meeting on 3 July to keep other bans in place. The feeling was that basic democratic and trade union rights in Fiji continued to be denied. The executive agreed to await the outcome of a meeting of the Fiji Trades Union Congress executive on 4 July before deciding what further steps to take. During this time, the Australian Council of Trade Unions and member unions were under considerable pressure from the Hawke government to lift the bans. The New Zealand unions maintained their bans, and six affiliates of the New Zealand Federation of Labour met in Wellington on 6 July to call on their executive to reaffirm its commitment to maintaining the bans.

The military seemed to have learned its lesson after the previous Fiji Trades Union Congress meeting and stayed out of the way at the meeting on the fourth. It left the task of getting a correct vote to pro-regime forces within the union movement itself, led by Taukei militant Taniela Veitata. With supporters from his dockworkers' union accompanying him, Veitata and three other unionists harassed the others present, issuing warnings should they not vote to lift the bans. This time Veitata and his allies won by a vote of twenty-seven to twenty-one, although, as noted by several observers, their support tended to come from smaller unions and from members of the Board of Management (of which there were only five voting members present) who did not represent any particular union. The Fiji Trades Union Congress meeting did not have its desired immediate effect of prompting an end to the bans. The Australian Council of Trade Unions and the New Zealand Federation of Labour postponed meeting on the issue and a proposed meeting on 9–10 July was cancelled (the Australian national election was due to be held on the eleventh). Meanwhile, a group of soldiers entered the Fiji Trades Union Congress offices on the ninth and arrested members of the executive who were holding a meeting, even though this group was known to be in support of lifting the bans. A few days later the governor general issued a statement regretting the incident, and Fiji Trades Union Congress president Jale Toki resumed calls to lift the bans.

The lifting of the Qantas ban and support from the Australian travel industry served to increase Australian tourist arrivals in Fiji. Both Air Pacific and Qantas reported higher levels of bookings by the middle of July, and industry representatives in Fiji reported that hotel occupancy rates were up to 25 per cent (40 per cent in the Coral Coast resort area). Despite such developments, there was an awareness that the recovery was only partial and that it remained very fragile. Furthermore, given the fact that flights and rooms were heavily discounted, and that the bulk of tourist dollars never come into the country or leak out (the so-called leakage rate being an estimated 75 per cent), the financial benefits to the country as a whole were likely limited.

Mara, never one to take criticism lightly, had been extremely upset by critical comments made about him for his support of the coup by Prime Minister Hawke and Prime Minister Lange shortly after the coup had taken place. He issued a warning on 21 June that Fiji might seek to redirect its trade away from Australia and New Zealand unless the two governments took steps to improve relations with the new regime. The negotiations with Thailand and European countries for food shipments served notice that this was a serious threat.

On 11 July the regime announced plans to use the National Marketing Authority as an agency for importing food, machinery, and medical supplies from other countries and raised the spectre of doubling duties on imports from Australia and New Zealand. Mara then set off on a trip to Japan and Southeast Asia to seek new trade ties. Mara was accompanied by New Zealand businessman Paul Freeman, as well as Colonel Pio Wong (who had been promoted after the coup) and five other army officers. Carrying letters of credit from local banks, they planned to visit Taiwan and South Korea for the purpose of negotiating the purchase of F$10 million worth of ammunition and uniforms for the expanded army. In addition, they were to explore the possibility of obtaining military assistance in the form of helicopters, armed personnel carriers, and other military equipment.

A RETURN TO NORMALCY

The Coalition parliamentarians held their first caucus since the coup on 28 June. The following day, Governor General Ganilau met with Bavadra in Lautoka. Ganilau was anxious to get Bavadra to support a call to end the cane harvest boycott and to convince him to take part in the Constitutional Review Committee, which was due to hold its first meeting on 6 July. Bavadra expressed his concern to Ganilau that the proposed structure of the review committee did not sufficiently safeguard the interests of non-native Fijians, and he also sought a reduced military presence around the country. The talks ended inconclusively. A follow-up meeting in Suva on 1 July also ended without agreement, with Bavadra expressing concern over the political imbalance of the review committee.

The Coalition now sought permission to hold a series of meetings to discuss the current situation. The authorities allowed only one hundred to attend a public meeting in Ra on 3 July. Those present passed resolutions in favour of retaining the present constitution and maintaining the harvest boycott. That evening, the Coalition parliamentary group met in Lautoka, and Bavadra made clear his intention to boycott the review committee meeting unless the terms of reference were changed.

A joint meeting of the Coalition's working committee and parliamentary board was held in Nadi on the fifth, with five hundred allowed to attend. Addressing the meeting, Labour Party senator Etuati Tavai and Ratu Mosese Tuisawau emphasized the extent of native Fijian support for the Coalition. Tuisawau warned that the

Taukei was trying to make Fiji a republic in order to eliminate the Privy Council from the Fijian judiciary and thus stop it from hearing the Bavadra case before it reached the Supreme Court. Those at the meeting passed resolutions similar to the ones at Ra.

Chaired by John Falvey, a longtime confidant of Mara and former attorney general, the Constitutional Review Committee held its first meeting, as scheduled, on the sixth, without the Coalition delegates in attendance. Jim Ah Koy's wife, Lavinia, was appointed secretary. She had served as secretary to the governor general previously, but at the time she and her husband were at the centre of a scandal involving the questionable transfer of F$200,000 out of the country a short time after the coup. The governor general sought to appease different interests and nominated one native Fijian (Isikeli Mataitoga), one Rotuman (Alfoa Varea), and two Indo-Fijians (Dr. Sahu Khan, a well-known constitutional lawyer, and Kantilal Parshotam).

There was no indication of any such sensitivity on the part of the Great Council of Chiefs or on the part of Mara. The Council of Chiefs' nominees represented conservative, pro-Taukei opinion: Jone Mataitoga, Adi Litia Cakobau, Aporosa Rakoto, and Rabuka. As for Mara, he nominated David Pickering (a General Elector and Alliance Party stalwart); Tomasi Vakatora (former Speaker of the House, known for his anti-Indian sentiments); and two Taukei activists: Filipe Bole (Mara's de facto representative in the Taukei) and Apisai Tora. The Indian Alliance was quick to express dismay at Mara's choices, being particularly upset by his failure to nominate a single Indo-Fijian. These nominees served to confirm the worst fears of the Coalition.

The governor general offered Bavadra revised terms of reference on 8 July. The initial terms of reference had read: 'To review the Constitution of Fiji with the view to proposing to the Governor-General amendments which will guarantee native Fijian political interests and in so doing bear in mind the best interests of other people in Fiji.'[9] As revised, it read: 'To review the Constitution of Fiji with the view to proposing to the Governor-General any amendments which will guarantee indigenous Fijian political interests with full regard to the interests of other people in Fiji.'[10] The sugar harvest boycott and overseas union bans clearly had served as a source of pressure to push the governor general to agree to the revision. An agreement was finally reached after a few more days of discussions. The review committee met on the fourteenth under the revised terms of reference, with four Coalition nominees in attendance. The meeting took place despite the fact that one of the nominees, Krishna Datt, had been picked up the day before and held overnight by the army, after having been intimidated by the army on several other occasions. Moreover, Coalition members privately expressed little optimism about the outcome of the review.

The Coalition decided that rather than Bavadra himself serving as a member of the committee, he would be replaced by another westerner, Mosese Tuisawau (with Etuati Tavai as an alternate). The other nominees were selected, in part, to provide an ethnic and regional balance. They included Joeli Kalou (a native Fijian from the east), Jai Ram Reddy (an Indo-Fijian lawyer from the west), and Krishna Datt (who was from the northern island of Vanua Levu). Since Kalou had not yet returned from a lobbying trip overseas, his place on the committee was taken by Tupeni Baba (who was from Vanua Levu).

The plan was for the review committee to hold hearings until 24 July and then to present its recommendations to the governor general on the thirty-first. A Council of National Reconciliation would then be convened. It would be chaired by the governor general and include all members of the former House of Representatives and Senate and the present Council of Advisors. It would serve as a constitutional conference to act upon the recommendations of the review committee and was to formulate means for a return to democracy. The Commonwealth Secretariat had agreed to provide the review committee with a constitutional expert.

Meanwhile, negotiations had resumed between the sugar growers and the Fiji Sugar Corporation. Progress with the talks between the governor general and Bavadra, as well as economic pressure on many growers, seemed to point to a settlement being at hand. Finally, both parties announced on 14 July that the ban was at an end.

The international union bans were lifted at a joint meeting between the executives of the Australian Council of Trade Unions and the New Zealand Federation of Labour in Wellington on 16 July, which was attended by James Raman from the Fiji Trades Union Congress. The unions decided, however, to send a fact-finding mission to Fiji within a few days to report on the situation and on trade union rights in particular.

Bavadra's case before the Supreme Court (which questioned the legality of the initial dissolution of Parliament) was due to be heard on 23 July. The week before, however, it was decided to postpone the case in order to give the two sides more time to prepare their cases.

While the constitutional negotiations were taking place, extremist Taukei were pressing ahead with their plans to declare Fiji a republic and to change the constitution in accordance with their objectives. Finau Mara was travelling around the country with a draft copy of a republican constitution, holding meetings to explain the document. Among the others involved in drafting plans for the Taukei were two university-based Fijians, Malaki Tewaki (associated with Mara and the Young Alliance) and Asasela Ravuvu, who helped to draw up the Taukei's submission to the Constitutional Review Committee which called for a republic headed by a president. An Upper House was to be drawn from the Great Council of Chiefs and a Lower House was to have sixty members, elected from twenty native Fijian provincial councils. Fijian was to become the national language and 'Taukei customary law' was to take precedence over English common law. Inspired by the Malaysian model, every commercial venture would be required to have at least 40 per cent native Fijian ownership, and no more native land would be released for use by non-indigenous people.

An inner circle of Taukei extremists (including Veitata and Tora) was holding daily meetings in the Ports Authority building to keep the pressure on. This group viewed Mara, and even Rabuka, as moderates and, under their influence, it was apparent that the governor general's standing among the Taukei and other conservative native Fijians was very weak. The Taukei had been able to gain the support of Fijian Nationalist Party leader Sakeasi Butadroka, who resumed his call for sending all Indo-Fijians to India and asking Britain to compensate them for the losses they would incur.

THE GREAT COUNCIL OF CHIEFS MEET AGAIN

The negotiations between the governor general and Bavadra, on the one hand, and the agitation of the Taukei, on the other hand, provided the background for the Great Council of Chiefs meeting on Monday, 20 July, in Suva. It was widely rumoured that the Taukei planned on asking the governor general to step down and then have the council declare Fiji a republic. There were also rumours that if they did not get their way, Rabuka would stage a 'second coup.' (Rabuka was already in the process of forming a new special force within the military to deal with internal security threats.) Taukei leaders Veitata and Tora addressed a meeting in Labasa during the weekend, where they stated that a republic was the only solution and hinted at violence should their aims be denied. The Taukei had requested permission to hold a mass rally in Suva for the opening of the Great Council of Chiefs meeting, but this was called off after talks with the military.

The council meeting was to be attended by around one hundred delegates representing the fourteen provincial councils and the provisional regime. Nine of the councils had passed resolutions calling for an immediate declaration of Fiji as a republic, while the other five had agreed to support a republic only if the governor general's initiative failed. All had come out in favour of a Parliament dominated by native Fijians, although there were different views as to whether, and the extent to which, non-native Fijians should be represented. One important difference between this meeting and the previous one was that, this time, those with views opposed to the regime were allowed to attend. Thus, Bavadra and other indigenous members of his government were invited to attend to express their views 'as Fijians.' The Coalition members decided to attend in an effort to put forward their case, even though Bavadra questioned the legitimacy of those involved to have called the meeting of the Great Council of Chiefs in the first place.

There was trouble even before the meeting began when early in the morning there was an explosion at the Nadi Travelodge, which broke windows and forced a number of tourists from their rooms. During the meeting, around one thousand Taukei supporters gathered in a nearby park. Later in the day, some four thousand Coalition supporters attended a meeting in Labasa and threatened again to halt the sugar harvest and call a general strike should the chiefs back the Taukei plans. Ratu Meli Vesikula spoke on behalf of the Taukei Movement at the first day of the meeting, urging the chiefs to revoke the 1874 Deed of Cession and declare Fiji a republic.

The second day of the meeting included submissions from Bavadra, the six other native Fijians in his government, and members of the Taukei Movement. Early in the morning Rabuka spoke, calling for the formation of a 'Christian democratic state' and retention of ties with the Queen, rather than a republic. He warned that he saw little chance of arriving at a compromise that was faithful to the original aims of his coup and threatened to resign from the Constitutional Review Committee. As the Coalition parliamentarians left the meeting they were threatened by Taukei supporters and Tupeni Baba was punched.

The Council of Chiefs' decision on Wednesday, the final day of the meeting, came as a surprise to many. The chiefs rejected, for the time being, the idea of declaring a republic, but reserved the right to do so in the future should the governor general's Constitutional Review Committee fail to come up with a satisfactory solution. Rabuka, having been unwilling to end Fiji's ties to the Queen, called the decision 'a consensus between the objectives of the Taukei Movement, the aim of my coup, and the wishes of the Great Council of Chiefs.'[11] The decision clearly was a defeat for the Taukei extremists, and moderate chiefs had forced them to agree to stop threatening violence should the council fail to move for a republic.

Specifically, the Council of Chiefs called for creation of a lower house with ten additional seats reserved for native Fijians: that is, thirty seats for native Fijians and twenty-two seats for Indo-Fijians. They would retain the present eight seats set aside for others, but change the composition to give one seat apiece to the ethnically distinct islands of Rotuma and Rabi (the existing structure only provided for Rotuman representation in the Senate). Most important, voting was to be strictly on a communal basis, with no national seats that allowed cross-ethnic voting. They also asked that senior positions in government such as prime minister and attorney general be reserved for native Fijians.

Mara was appointed to head a subcommittee that was to meet the following day and prepare the submission for the Constitutional Review Committee. The subcommittee proposed giving native Fijians thirty-two seats in a new Parliament. The additional ten seats were to be created by placing the ten chiefs in the Senate in the House. The proposal also supported having all voting on a communal basis. A group of Taukei went to the governor general to express their opposition to the Mara plan. They stated that they wanted a parliament that was 100 per cent native Fijian, but that they were prepared to accept 75 per cent of the seats. After this criticism from the Taukei, Mara threatened to resign. This was averted when a delegation from the Council of Chiefs went to Mara's home to ask foregiveness. This move by the chiefs did not stop the Taukei from continuing to attack the proposal since it did not guarantee native Fijian control of Parliament. Nor was the Coalition silent. At a rally at the village of Natokawawaqa on Saturday the twenty-fifth attended by around two thousand, Bavadra rejected the proposal for a fixed number of seats for chiefs and said also that he would not be part of any proposal that compromised the political rights of Indo-Fijians.

Mara left Fiji on Sunday for a two-week trade trip to avoid the potentially embarrassing meeting of the Great Council of Chiefs which was to be held on Monday to discuss his proposal. As Mara had feared, there was dissent, and it was not until Tuesday that an agreement was reached. The final proposal was for a single house of Parliament with seventy-one seats, forty-one of which were to be reserved for native Fijians, eight for General Electors, and twenty-two for Indo-Fijians. The native Fijian seats were to be allotted as follows: eight nominated by the Great Council of Chiefs, twenty-eight from the Provincial Councils, four by the prime minister, and one from Rotuma. Included among the eight General Electors was to be one seat for the Rabi islanders. The offices of governor general, prime minister, foreign affairs minister, finance minister, minister of home affairs, and minister of Fijian affairs were to be reserved for native Fijians as were 50 per cent of the posts in the public service. The speaker and deputy speaker of Parliament were to be appointed from outside of Parliament on the advice of the prime minister and leader of the opposition. If this demand was met, the Council agreed not to move to declare Fiji a republic.

The Taukei representatives stated that they accepted the proposal, and Rabuka said that the aims of his May coup would be achieved if it was accepted. A Coalition spokesman said that the Great Council of Chiefs had ignored the Coalition submission and succumbed to the demands of the Taukei. The proposal was now to be presented to the Constitutional Review Committee on Wednesday.

While the Council of Chiefs was debating proposed changes to the constitution, Rabuka delivered an address at Queen Elizabeth Barracks. He announced his intention to establish a cabinet-level body to monitor security intelligence as well as plans to increase the size of the army from 3,000 to 5,000 and boost the army's surveillance capabilities with helicopters. These steps were to be taken 'to maintain peace between the Fijian and Indian populations.' He went on to say: 'When people talk about normalcy, do they only mean getting back to a parliamentary democracy? I don't believe this is the case. We will need to maintain stability for the next 15 years. This is the time that it will take for all this to die down.' Rabuka was sounding more and more like every other military dictator. On Friday, 31 July, he was officially installed as commander of the army at a three-hour traditional ceremony before 1,500 invited guests. Rabuka commented: 'I am really here today as the representative of the great chiefs and the people of Fiji. I am doing this for you.'[12]

Following the meeting, Taukei criticism of Mara intensified, and for the first time Taukei extremists began to openly discuss a break with the Alliance Party. Former Suva mayor Joape Rokosoi (known primarily for his questionable business activities) addressed a Taukei rally on 8 August and accused some members of the former Mara government of 'secretly' collaborating with Indo-Fijians. He then said that the Taukei should disassociate itself from the Alliance Party and consider forming its own political party. He claimed that

Alliance Party moderates wished to retain the 1970 Constitution because they were afraid of losing what they now enjoyed. After the rally, six hundred Taukei supporters marched on the Indian High Commission to present a petition accusing the Indian government of assisting those opposed to the regime and asking it to stop doing so.

Many prominent native Fijian moderates had remained relatively silent since the May coup. But as the situation deteriorated and extremist elements appeared to be exerting more influence, they began to come together in an effort to present an alternative to the Taukei. Moderates from the Alliance Party joined forces with Coalition members and others opposed to the regime the final week of July to form the Back to Early May Movement. The movement sought to have the military return to the barracks and the dissolved Parliament recalled in order to form a government of national unity. Once this was done, it wanted there to be a referendum regarding proposed changes to the constitution and that there be a royal commission appointed to consider these changes.

A group of moderate native Fijians associated with the Alliance Party met with the governor general the first week of August to press for a government of national unity. Among those visiting the governor general were David Toganivalu (the recognized head of the moderate wing), William Toganivalu, Jone Madraiwiwi (who had been barred from the Council of Chiefs meeting), Mosese Qioniba-ravi (the second deputy prime minister in the Mara government), Epeli Kacimaiwi, Suliana Siwatibau, and Finau Tabakaucoro. Divisions were also noticeable within native Fijian villages between those supporting the Labour Party, moderates within the Alliance Party, and members of the Taukei Movement and Fijian Nationalists. Thus, on 14 August one youth was killed and fourteen had to be treated for injuries after a fight broke out among native Fijian villagers near Savusavu over political differences. Speaking to a Taukei rally on the same day, Jona Qio, the Alliance Party senator who had been indicted for his involvement in the fire-bombings before the coup, warned native Fijians not to be influenced by the Back to Early May Movement. He accused those in the movement of trying to divide the native Fijian people.

Such developments took place amidst continuing arrests, intimidation, and violence. Three members of an Australian film crew were arrested on 23 August while interviewing former attorney general Vijay Singh. But violence was no longer the exclusive domain of the Taukei. After the bomb in the Nadi Travelodge went off on 20 July, another bomb exploded in a Suva night-club on 22 July, and a third bomb went off in a rental car at Nadi airport on the twenty-fourth. In none of these bombings, however, were there injuries.

THE CONSTITUTIONAL REVIEW COMMITTEE

Representatives of the Coalition and the regime reached agreement on the membership of the Constitutional Review Committee the second week of July, and the committee met for the next five weeks to hear submissions and prepare its report to the governor general. Initially, the report was to have been submitted on 31 July, but the governor general agreed to extend the period into mid-August.

The Great Council of Chiefs presented its proposal to the committee on 29 July. Another, related, submission was that of the Fiji Muslim League, presented to the committee on 5 August. Its four-page submission expressed sympathy for moves to increase native Fijian representation in Parliament and supported the submission of the Great Council of Chiefs. It also asked for separate representation in Parliament for Muslims, specifying four seats. Arguing against retention of the 1970 constitution, the submission stated: 'Just as the 1970 constitution disinherited the Fijians ... so did it disinherit the Muslims.'[13] Two days later it became public that some officials of the Muslim League did not agree with the submission and, especially, its call for separate Muslim seats in Parliament. A handful of executive members, under the influence of Apisai Tora, had met and prepared the submission without consulting branch representatives or other members of the league.

To the surprise of almost no one, the fifty-six recommendations in the official report were, in effect, a replay of the Great Council of Chiefs submission for the creation of a seventy-one seat, unicameral Parliament, with voting on the basis of communal roles and with the highest offices reserved for native Fijians. The governor general was to be nominated by the Great Council of Chiefs for a term of five years. The new Parliament was called upon to pursue a policy of 'positive discrimination' in making laws aimed specifically at assisting native Fijians. The committee stated that it found little support for proposals to turn Fiji into a republic and urged that links with the Queen be retained.

The Coalition members of the committee had been under no illusion that they had much of a chance of swaying the other members, but felt that they could use the committee hearings as a forum to voice their opinions. Since most of the submissions had been ignored by those formulating the official report, the Coalition issued its own minority report.[14] The minority report recommended that the 1970 constitution 'be retained in its entirety' and characterized the recommendations in the 'majority' report as 'repugnant on the grounds that they will further segregate the various races.' The Coalition argued that the 1970 constitution provided adequate protection for native Fijian rights and noted that 'the majority of those who made submissions to the Constitutional Review Committee indicated that they were satisfied that these entrenched provisions [in the existing constitution] adequately protected Fijian, Rotuman and Banaban interests.' The Coalition criticized the recommendation to restrict native Fijian voting on a provincial basis on several grounds, including the fact that 'it would discriminate against urban Fijians who see their interests as inextricably related to opportunities and interests available in urban areas' and the likelihood that it would inhibit native Fijians from seeking educational and economic opportunities away from their traditional homes. This section of their report concluded by citing a well respected, educated native Fijian of the previous generation, Rusiate Nayacakalou:

'It seems to me that one of the greatest obstacles facing the Fijians today is the failure to recognise that there is a contradiction; they must now make the momentous choice between preserving and changing their way of life. The belief that they can do both simultaneously is a monstrous nonsense with which they have been saddled for so many years ... Further attempts to keep Fijian political development tied to the 'communal system' can seriously constrict the people for future political development.'[15]

The governor general responded after receiving the reports that he felt there was no general consensus in the country about the future of the constitution. Among the others to comment on the reports was Sakeasi Butadroka, who condemned both of them. He stated that unrest would continue until native Fijians were given two-thirds of the seats in Parliament.

THE ECONOMY

The serious economic impact of the first coup was still apparent in September. Savenaca Siwatibau, head of the Reserve Bank, reported in late September 'that the total of wages, salaries, profits of all businesses, income from rent and royalties will be some F$80m-F$100m lower this year than originally estimated.'[16] He also revealed that revenue receipts of the central government were estimated to be F$50 million short of budget predictions. Siwatibau's report led the government to announce in the third week of September that grants to statutory bodies would be reduced by 50 per cent. Emigrants had been taking out of the country around F$2.5 million a month since May (in contrast to F$1.8 million in April). And because of the drought, sugar growers had been able to plant only 2,500 hectares out of 13,400 hectares by the end of September, with the drought endangering what had already been planted.

Arson, a common form of political protest among western native Fijians, as well as fires resulting from the exceptionally dry weather were becoming another serious concern in Fiji's pine plantations. In a published statement in mid-November 1987, the management of the Fiji Pine Commission commented: 'The pine industry has taken 20 years to develop to a stage where it promises to make a major contribution to the national economy ... The pine fires have been so bad this year that the very existence of this new industry is under threat.'[17] Over a five-year period from 1982–86, there had been an average of seventy-nine fires a year, damaging an average of 575 hectares. In contrast, between January and early November 1987 there had been 445 fires, damaging 11,215 hectares of pine forest – 23.5 per cent of total pine forest area. It was estimated that arson was the cause of 53 per cent of the fires.

Nevertheless, there were signs of a gradual improvement in the economy. Cane crushing amounted to 1.3 million tons by late September (producing 173,000 tons of cane), and it was estimated that by the latter part of October, around two million tons of cane would be crushed, yielding over 250,000 tons of sugar. The first cruise ship since the coup had docked in Suva with 1,300 Australian and New Zealand tourists on 25 July. Visitor arrivals for the month of August numbered 20,762, representing a 37 per cent increase over July (although still down 21 per cent from the previous August), and a similar level was maintained for September. Australian tourists, responding to the low fares and discounted accommodation rates, accounted for around one-half of the arrivals (10,800 in August). Foreign reserves showed signs of stabilizing by late August. By the end of September foreign reserves amounted to U.S.$101.4 million, which was still U.S.$52.5 million lower than the figure a year earlier, but the trend now appeared to be upward. Siwatibau reported on 20 August that government bodies and statutory bodies were still operating within the budgets prescribed by Parliament.

Inflation continued to rise, reflecting the impact of the devaluation and of the drought, but the rate of increase was showing signs of easing, from 2 per cent in August to 1 per cent in September. Interest rates also appeared to be stabilizing, but remained relatively high.

Thus, according to the Reserve Bank of Fiji, average interest rates of the large deposits rose from 8 per cent in the June quarter to 20 per cent in the September quarter, and average lending rates of the banks rose to 14 per cent at end of September from 12 per cent at the end of the June quarter. Also, although the drastic firings of the months immediately after the coup were no longer so common, there was virtually no new hiring. For example, some 80 per cent of the staff in the tourist industry had been dismissed over a period of a couple of months after the May coup, and as of early September, despite improvements in tourist arrivals, very few had been reinstated.

Rabuka himself seemed unwilling to take steps to ease the economic situation. The army had grown to a strength of 7,100 by August (1,100 of these in the Middle East) and paying for these soldiers was producing a considerable strain on government finances. Responding to a request from the governor general, on 31 August Rabuka announced that he would reduce the force by 2,000. But he still had not followed through with his stated plan to reduce army wages.

A GOVERNMENT OF NATIONAL UNITY

The Back to Early May Movement presented a petition calling for a 'government of national unity' to the governor general on 13 August. It was signed by over one hundred thousand people, representing 35 per cent of the registered voters. Only about 10 per cent of the signatories were native Fijians, and, in an accompanying letter, the movement's leaders noted that 'our efforts to acquaint you with genuine public opinion was hampered greatly by people's fear of intimidation, particularly among indigenous Fijian people.' The letter also mentioned one known case where a soldier had destroyed two hundred petition forms containing two thousand signatures.

The parliamentary board of the Alliance Party met for the first time since the coup on 19–20 August to discuss proposed talks with the Coalition on national reconciliation. Mara supported moves towards a government of national unity and told the meeting that international recognition of the government was important to prevent the country from running into economic trouble. There were disagreements among those attending, especially between party moderates and the more extreme Taukei, and, at one point, Mara walked out of the meeting. After prolonged and often heated debate, those at the meeting agreed to support a proposal for a government of national unity and to hold talks with the Coalition on the issue, provided certain preconditions were met. The preconditions included a demand that Bavadra apologize for his 'insulting' remarks at the Great Council of Chiefs meeting in July and that he drop his Supreme Court case challenging the legality of the dissolution of Parliament after the May coup.

When these demands were made public the following day, Coalition spokesman Richard Naidu responded: 'Who is the Alliance Party to set preconditions on this meeting? That is not the way to go about the process of national reconciliation,' and Bavadra stated that he had nothing to apologize for.[18] Nevertheless, plans went ahead for talks between the Coalition and the regime.

In a radio broadcast on 31 August, the governor general stated that it was too early to say what constitutional changes might be necessary to attain consensus and national reconciliation, indicating his awareness of opposition from the Coalition and others to the review committee proposal. He also stated that his initial plan for an uncontested general election to pass constitutional changes that would ensure native Fijian control was now seen as only one possible option. Another option was the installation of a temporary caretaker government 'for the period in which arrangements for a permanent solution are being talked through and finalised.' A plan was to be decided on at the forthcoming meeting of the Council of National Reconciliation. The following day, the governor general addressed a gathering of about two hundred chiefs and urged them not to abuse their position and take rights away from people.

Talks began in Suva on Friday, 4 September among the governor general, Mara, and Bavadra, each heading a six-member delegation, to facilitate the proposed meeting of a Council of National Reconciliation. The night before, a fight erupted outside of Bavadra's Suva home between Coalition and Taukei supporters, and shots were fired in the direction of the house by soldiers. While the meeting was in progress, a group of Taukei, dressed as traditional warriors, prepared a *lovo* (earth oven) nearby, threatening to cook Coalition members and Supreme Court judges who were to hear Bavadra's case. Spotting Bavadra adviser Richard Naidu, about twenty of the Taukei chased him into the lobby of the Travelodge with spears and clubs and then assaulted him.

The behaviour of the Taukei led the Coalition to hold a public meeting on Saturday to discuss its response. That evening, Bavadra spoke with the governor general and informed him that the Coalition had decided to pull out of the talks unless their security could be guaranteed. On Monday, a letter from Bavadra outlining his reasons for withdrawing from the talks was delivered to the governor general. In the letter he stated: 'I am deeply concerned that extremist elements in our society can dig up government grounds, and light a fire, and threaten to kill people who take their grievances to a court of law, and threaten judges ... All this can happen without any intervention by the security forces.' The Coalition agreed on Thursday to resume talks the following day after the governor general guaranteed their safety.

In an effort to strengthen its position in native Fijian villages and to counter the activities of the Taukei, the Coalition launched Operation Sunrise calling for retention of the 1970 constitution, reinstatement of the Coalition government, and the return of Epeli Nailatikau as commander of the military. The plan was to hold meetings in native Fijian villages to explain the Coalition position and, especially, the extent to which the 1970 constitution guaranteed native Fijian rights. For the first time, the Coalition translated relevant sections of the Fiji constitution concerning native Fijian rights into Fijian – something that had not been done by the Alliance government (some argued on purpose to allow the government to play on peoples insecurities). Meetings were held in various parts of Viti Levu, despite intimidation and threats from the military and the Taukei. In addition, tape recordings were made of talks and passed among villagers.

The twenty-sixth meeting of Operation Sunrise was held on Thursday, 17 September in the village of Naboutini, Serua, about 80 kilometers from Suva. Bavadra addressed 150 native Fijians representing fifty western villages. In his address, he issued a warning that should the governor general not meet the demands of Operation Sunrise, many of his followers favoured forming a breakaway government in the west. The next day, the Coalition's parliamentary board met to decide whether to attend a meeting scheduled for the twenty-second with the governor general and Mara to discuss the government of national reconciliation.

Taukei efforts to maintain a sense of lawlessness and to undermine moves towards a restoration of civilian rule increased. Two militant splinter groups, calling themselves Black September and the Taukei Liberation Front, were formed, advocating the use of violence. They were said to be separate from the Taukei Movement, but most saw this merely as an attempt to create the image of the Taukei Movement as a more responsible body rather than as evidence of factional fighting. On 12 September, Taukei extremists burned six buildings in Suva. On the sixteenth, arsonists destroyed a medical laboratory belonging to Coalition supporter Dr. Karam Singh, and a group of Taukei supporters surrounded the house belonging to Richard Naidu's parents and smashed windows and set fires.

On the night of Thursday, the seventeenth, leading Taukei extremist Taniela Veitata arranged for a group of thugs to arrive in Suva from Lau. Under Veitata's direction (and apparently with the foreknowledge of the army), this group and local gangs went on a rampage of rioting, burning, and looting on Friday. One native Fijian was shot in the leg by soldiers, and twelve were injured. Thirteen were arrested. By evening, only soldiers remained on the streets in the city centre. On the same day, the army stepped up patrols in Labasa when the Taukei Liberation Front issued arson threats. The following week, many shops were closed for varying periods in Suva, Labasa, and Lautoka and threats of arson continued. The spate of incidents of arson had led Fiji's four insurance companies to announce on 24 September that they would no longer cover losses caused by arson or damage during riots.

On the evening of Monday 21 September, Taukei leaders and others extremists held a special meeting to discuss steps to be taken to put a stop to advances being made by moderate forces in the Alliance Party and the Coalition. The plans, as outlined in a secret letter written later that night by a senior army officer, and addressed to the Coalition, included the staging of an escape of prisoners from Naboro Prison, to be followed by raids and attacks on leading opponents of the regime.[19] The extremists called for destabilization efforts which would lead to another military coup should a caretaker government assume office, and further called for the declaration of Fiji as a republic with a Parliament in which all seats would be given to native Fijians. The letter also stated that members of the army were in league with those involved in recent acts of arson and looting and that Taukei Movement leaders, in turn, were working with leaders of youth gangs and ex-criminals. The letter pointed to Rabuka's personal involvement: 'On Sunday evening 7.30 pm 20.9.87 Rabuka went to the Central Police Station cell and had a private audience with five to eight members of those who were to appear in court on Monday morning 21.9.87 (arsonists). He took cigarettes and gave them. He had a secret discussion with them ... He ordered that the arsonists be released for a few hours that evening. He apparently entertained them and also briefed them.'

The meeting between Mara, Ganilau, and Bavadra began on Tuesday. The day before the meeting, on Monday, about two hundred native Fijians from the west and Ra arrived in Suva to serve as guards for the Coalition ministers. The army attempted to stop them. Those from Ra went around an army roadblock about 60 kilometers from Suva, swam across a river, and then walked until they were picked up by another vehicle closer to Suva. There was considerable tension in Suva, with soldiers erecting checkpoints in and around the city. The evening of the meeting prisoners set fires, and 114 of them escaped from Naboro prison outside of Suva. Fifty-two of them went to Lami and entered a liquor store where they remained until the next morning, holding cordial talks with soldiers and police. Wednesday morning they walked to Walu Bay where they were put on trucks and given placards by the army critical of Bavadra's Supreme Court case. Soldiers and police escorted them through town to Government House where they held a meeting with the governor general before he left for Pacific Harbour. After the meeting, the prisoners were returned to captivity, although the other escapees remained at large.

The military/Taukei plans to derail the Pacific Harbour talks did not work. On Wednesday, the Deuba Accord was announced. In order to reach the agreement, Bavadra had withdrawn his Supreme Court case which was due to be heard on 29 August. A twenty-member Council of State was to be formed the following week with the governor general as its head and portfolios to be divided between the two sides by the governor general after further talks with Mara and Bavadra. The role of the Council of State was to guide Fiji to a solution to its constitutional problems, to re-establish respect for law and order, and to take steps to put the economy back on a firm footing. While taking full account of the aspirations of native Fijians, the caretaker government was to provide a framework for 'a multi-racial society in which the rights and interests of all the communities are safeguarded.' Also, although 'due regard' was to be given to the recommendations of the recent Constitutional Review Committee, it was agreed that a new committee would be formed by the caretaker government to examine future constitutional needs. The new committee was to be comprised of three members from the Alliance Party and three from the Coalition, with 'an independent chairman from overseas.' The governor general was to make an address to the nation on Friday, calling on people to support the accord.

The Deuba Accord was a victory for the Coalition. Mara and other Alliance Party members had been forced to recognize the growing support for the Coalition among native Fijians and to respond to popular opposition to the military-backed regime. Mara himself had been placed in a difficult position. Had he failed to go along with the accord, he risked losing control of the Alliance Party to moderate forces associated with David Toganivalu and finding himself either off the political stage altogether or allied solely with the Taukei. The agreement meant that it was Rabuka and the Taukei exremists who were threatened with being marginalized.

The political turmoil that had rocked Fiji since the May coup seemed at last to be under control, and the Coalition and other forces of moderation appeared well on the way to containing those who had pursued violent and extreme measures to preserve the oligarchy. The strategy of the Coalition to rely on patience, argument, and moral integrity seemed vindicated. Yet could the clock be turned back to early May and a form of civilian rule that was not overly racist be reinstated? The forces of reaction, violence, and racism that had been unleashed five months earlier had been outmanoeuvred for the moment, but their advocates remained at large and were still a powerful force to be reckoned with.

CHAPTER NINE

The Second Coup and the Republic of Fiji

The optimism expressed by the Labour Party-NFP coalition and moderate forces within the Alliance Party over the Deuba Accord was understandable. It appeared as if Fiji, at last, might be on the road to a return to normalcy. Mara and his close supporters had been forced to break with Colonel Rabuka and the extremist faction of the Taukei. The Coalition recognized that Rabuka remained a dangerous force, but it was hoped that Mara would be able to exert control over him. As for the Taukei, the Coalition believed that without Mara or Rabuka to support them, they would quickly cease to be an important political force. Rabuka's response to the Deuba Accord was lukewarm:

> I am bound by the promises which I have made to the Fijian people at the time of the May 14 coup and, if at any stage I feel that the objectives of the coup – which was to safeguard the interests of the Fijian people by changing the Constitution to cater for them – are being compromised, I would withdraw my co-operation.
>
> I believe that this agreement that they have reached has some merits, but also some weaknesses. I am now looking at it with the hope that I can work out the next steps that I and my officers and men will have to take.[1]

The Taukei response was much more direct. Taukei spokesman Ratu Meli Vesikula referred to the agreement to divide the Council of State between the Alliance Party and Coalition as 'degrading and a sell-out.' He went on to say: 'If the right solution is to be accepted, then some force will have to be used, military or civilian. It's the way it's been done before. You can be assured we will be fighting it all the way. Before we get to the end of the road there will be bloodshed and some people will die.' Both the Taukei and the Fijian Nationalist Party called for an immediate declaration of a republic. Fijian Nationalist Party leader Sakeasi Butadroka called on Rabuka to declare himself president, with senior military officers serving as ministers.

By this time, the Taukei's hold on Rabuka was substantial, and both were angered at being left out of the accord. It appeared as if Mara had finally joined other Alliance Party moderates in deciding that it was time to put a stop to the havoc being wreaked by the forces that he had helped to unleash in May. This did not sit well with Rabuka's visions of himself as the saviour of the Fijian people, which the Taukei were trying hard to promote. Frustrated with negotiations going on among the civilian politicians and encouraged to act decisively by the Taukei, Rabuka had begun making contingency plans for a second coup in early September. After the first coup, he had declared that he had made a mistake holding it on Thursday and that if there was a next time it would be on a Friday.[2] On Friday, 25 September, at 4:00 P.M., Rabuka moved again, having decided to act before the caretaker government was in place.

Rabuka announced over Radio Fiji that he had assumed executive authority over the governor general. He promised swift implementation of the original aims of his first coup which were to guarantee native Fijian control of Parliament. The governor general had failed to do this he said, so he was 'taking immediate steps to bring about the desired constitutional changes in a manner which will bring about lasting peace and prosperity in our beloved country.'

Once again communications within Fiji and with the outside world were cut off. Soldiers entered the offices of FM96, the *Fiji Times*, and the *Fiji Sun* and ordered them closed. Entering the *Fiji Times* office, soldiers knocked telephones out of reporters hands and smashed them against the wall. The staff was told to leave the building and not allowed to take personal possessions. News editor Mark Garrett commented: 'The soldiers were very edgy, very jumpy. We got out.' Soldiers began rounding up foreign journalists and putting them in the Travelodge, where they were told to await possible detention. Radio Fiji continued to broadcast music and announcements from the army.

At the same time, a truck with about sixty soldiers arrived at the Bavadra's Suva home. Not finding Bavadra there, they ransacked the house and fired shots into the ceiling. Bavadra had left his home a short time before and was driving away from town towards the west when the coup occurred, and he was stopped and detained a short

time later. The governor general was placed under armed guard at
Government House. A total of about eighty-five persons were
known to have been arrested in Suva, Nadi, Lautoka, and elsewhere.
Among those detained were Bavadra and eight members of his government; Suva's Labour Party mayor Bob Kumar; trade unionists
James Raman, Micky Columbus, and Rakesh Maharaj; university
lecturer Claire Slatter; Justices Rooney and Govind; former police
commissioner Pramesh Raman; *Fiji Sun* editor Jim Carney and its
legal adviser Miles Johnson; *Islands Business* editor Robert Keith-
Reid; Radio FM96 manager William Parkinson; and Back to Early May
activists such as Kenneth Zinck. This time, there was no delay in
arrests, and the net was cast much wider to include as many potential trouble-makers as possible.

Rabuka announced an 8:00 P.M. to 5:00 A.M. curfew. All night-time
entertainment and Sunday sports were banned. Tourists were told
to obey the curfew and not to take photos of soldiers. Air traffic was
suspended. All Fijian nationals were banned from leaving the country. All territorial forces and reservists were told to report to the
barracks in the morning. Army patrols and roadblocks were stepped
up.

In Nadi, a group calling itself 'the murdering association' sent a
letter to the town clerk threatening to kill the people of the town
'like chickens.' Around the country, as word of the second coup
spread, Indo-Fijians prepared for the worst and many expressed fear
of a blood-bath – a 'night of the long knives.' Taukei leader Vesikula's
English-born wife told a reporter: 'We are very happy. There are
several celebrations going on. I hope things go quietly now.' And ten
chiefs who supported the Taukei movement sent Rabuka messages
of congratulations which were read over Radio Fiji.

Although effectively under house arrest, Ganilau maintained that
he was still the legal authority and refused to accept the second
coup. Moreover, it was obvious that many Fijian chiefs continued to
back the governor general. The former deputy prime minister in the
Mara government, David Toganivalu, strongly condemned the coup.
On Sunday, Rabuka and a group of senior military officers went to
Government House to meet with Ganilau, *tabua* (whale's tooth) in
hand, to apologize for 'slighting' their chief. It was an effort to avoid
a show-down with the governor general. Ganilau, however, refused
to co-operate.

Also on Sunday, the army picked up magistrate, John Small, who
was known to be opposed to the regime. The 'hit list,' which also
included the director of public prosecutions, John Raza, and five
other lawyers who were opposed to military rule, had been drawn

up by the military before the coup. Small was assaulted while under detention, an indication that things might be rougher this time around. Early Sunday morning, a bomb went off in a car near the university killing one and injuring two.

On Monday, the twenty-eighth, the chief justice and judges of the Supreme Court met with Colonel Rabuka and informed him that they would refuse to serve under a regime not recognized by the governor general and then threatened to resign. Rabuka also met with diplomats from eleven countries to inform them officially that he had suspended the constitution. The diplomats responded that they recognized only the governor general as the legitimate executive power in Fiji. Rabuka went to meet with the governor general once again later in the afternoon in a final effort to gain his approval before announcing his new interim government on Tuesday and to offer him the presidency of the new republic. Rabuka had already made it clear that he was prepared to dismiss Ganilau if it was necessary for 'legitimising my assumption of executive authority.' After the meeting, Rabuka reported that 'the Governor General did not accept' his offer to become president. Monday night, the army released twenty-two of those held in Suva, leaving another dozen still under detention.

Rabuka issued a statement at a press conference on Tuesday, the twenty-ninth, in which he announced that he had assumed full authority. He indicated that he would declare a republic shortly and offer the presidency to Mara. In addition to effectively dismissing the governor general, in the statement Rabuka also said that he would dismiss the country's senior judges and appoint new ones loyal to his regime. He also expressed concern about the effect of the coup on the economy, but felt that it would do no long-term harm. With him at the press conference were Lt. Col. Pio Wong representing the extremist pro-Taukei faction within the military and Rev. Tomasi Raikivi from the radical religious faction within the Taukei.

On the same day as the press conference, Rabuka visited Bau in an effort to gain the support of George Cakobau, the Vunivalu or high chief of Bau, who held considerable traditional authority and was known to harbour sympathies for Rabuka's opponents. Amidst reports of scattered violence around the country, including the fire-bombing of a house in Suva, the governor general refused to acknowledge the new regime and the judges reaffirmed their loyalty to him. Mara paid a visit to the governor general and placed his full support behind him. Ostensibly Mara was upset over Rabuka's presumption to mention the possibility of Mara becoming president without first talking to him about it, but behind this minor affront was a more serious issue concerning the extent to which Rabuka had acted independently of Mara in staging the coup. The second coup had brought into question the balance of power within, and even the very existence of the alliance between, the chiefly oligarchy and the military. Faced with the prospect of a new ruling alliance being formed among lesser chiefs, the military, and other conservative dissident groups of native Fijians, Ganilau and Mara closed ranks.

More detainees were released on Tuesday evening, on the condition that they stay away from the governor general. Among those released was journalist Robert Keith-Reid. In a meeting with Rabuka at the time of his release, Rabuka gave his reason for arresting the journalist: 'You were like the fellow with a lean, hungry look. I didn't like the look of you.'

By Wednesday morning, it appeared that Rabuka had decided to stop short of dismissing the governor general and thereby committing the supreme act of disloyalty to his paramount chief and setting himself and his supporters irrevocably against the chiefly oligarchy. Instead he decided on a less drastic course of action and set about to neutralize the governor general by isolating him physically and spreading disinformation. In the first of a string of lies to the press about the governor general, the regime issued a statement that Ganilau had not refused the offer of the presidency outright. Similarly, Rabuka claimed that George Cakobau, during his visit the day before, had offered his support. The truth was that the Vunivalu had expressed concern over the coup, but said that he could understand Rabuka's motives. Rabuka also met with Siddiq Koya, who, still anxious to regain political prominence, presented him with a compromise plan to change the constitution that would give native Fijians control. Radio FM96 was allowed to resume broadcasting, although it was to be censored, but it was announced that the newspapers would remain closed indefinitely. Bavadra's assistant, Richard Naidu, and university lecturer and anti-nuclear activist, Vijay Naidu, were picked up by the military and held in Suva (both were released on Friday after having been beaten while in custody).

Evidence of trouble within the army emerged midday on Wednesday when a brawl erupted in the officers' mess. It mainly involved supporters of the governor general and those backing the Taukei. Later in the day, Rabuka issued a statement that nothing had happened and that he was in firm control of the army. It was becoming clear that the position of the governor general was strengthening as army officers and a number of chiefs voiced their support for him. There was continued evidence of strong support for Bavadra from the west as well, and Rabuka's support among traditional leaders and some segments of the army was weak. The governor general met with Chief Justice Timoci Tuivaga for legal advice and was told that he remained the legal head of state and should stand firm.

Rabuka released Bavadra early in the afternoon (other Coalition parliamentarians were freed a short time later) and then held a series of meetings with Bavadra, Mara, and the governor general. As a result of these meetings, Rabuka delayed his plan to declare Fiji a republic. Speaking for the Coalition, Krishna Datt said: 'Today's discussions have opened the gap. We have to sit down and talk with Rabuka to get the man to see reason.' That evening, the governor general issued a statement that he had hopes of dialogue between the different parties and that a meeting among them was planned on Monday.

Rabuka's meeting with Bavadra, Mara, and Ganilau angered the extremist Taukei, who held a meeting with Rabuka on Thursday morning. Following the meeting, Rabuka abruptly renounced the peace talks. He issued Interim Military Government Decree No. 1 which abrogated the 1970 constitution and announced that he had resumed his plan to declare Fiji a republic and to proclaim a new constitution based on the Great Council of Chiefs July proposal. He said that he still planned to meet with the other political leaders on Monday, but only to ask them to agree with what he had done. He asserted that he had acted after receiving legal advice that a 'quick fix' to the constitution was not possible. In a radio broadcast, Rabuka warned that the Fijian economy would deteriorate further and urged people to become as self-sufficient as possible. He also expressed the hope that the governor general would accept the office of president. Vesikula commented that the Taukei were prepared to 'bundle up Western democracy and throw it out to sea in order to preserve Fijian values.' He went on to criticize Rabuka, the first time he had done so in public, as being naïve for thinking that a compromise could be reached with Mara and Bavadra.

Bavadra learned of Rabuka's action over the telephone while talking with reporters in the west at Viseisei. Visibly shaken, he responded: 'Well, he's made his decision. We'll just have to see it through. What else can be done? I feel terrible ... after having tried our best to come together to find a peaceful solution towards the restoration of democracy, this thing has come about.' That evening the chief justice stated that Rabuka's proclamation had no legal standing until the governor general was physically removed from office. More worrying for Rabuka was a message from the Queen accusing him of disloyalty which was broadcast once over the radio in the Fijian language before being suppressed by the military. The broadcast was to prove an important impetus to the growing support for the governor general among native Fijians.

The military released thirty more detainees in Nadi and Lautoka during the day. *Fiji Sun* manager Jim Carney, who had been released on Wednesday, was given twenty-four hours to leave the country. The newspaper's management decided to close the paper until further notice and paid off its eighty-nine employees.

In the face of strong opposition from prominent native Fijians who continued to rally behind Mara and Ganilau as representatives of the traditional oligarchy, Rabuka's coup seemed on the verge of falling part. His plan to sever links with the Crown, in particular, received considerable criticism from many high and lower chiefs. An indication of Rabuka's lack of support was the fact that he still had not been able to appoint a new Council of Ministers by Friday. Former National Federation Party leader Siddiq Koya, seeking a way to once again become a player in the nation's political events, visited Rabuka and sought to dissuade him from declaring a republic.

Rabuka faced problems from another quarter as well; the head of the Reserve Bank, Saveneca Siwatibau, warned him of grave economic consequences should the present situation be allowed to continue, and banks were closed amid rumours that large amounts of money were being shipped out of the country illegally. The first opposition pamphlet since the coup also made its appearance (based largely on news from Radio Australia). Perhaps the most telling evidence of Rabuka's isolation came when Bavadra and Mara conferred over the telephone to plan joint strategies to counter him. A short time later, the governor general convened a meeting of his own Council of Advisors at Government House to indicate that his was still the legitimate government.

Rabuka found himself besieged from all sides. If he had not issued the decree the day before, he risked losing control of the military to officers under him, who were hard-core Taukei supporters. The Taukei criticized Siddiq Koya and Jim Ah Koy, both supporters of the Rabuka regime, for trying to thwart plans to declare Fiji a republic. In an effort to regain their initiative, the Taukei announced plans to hold a rally in Suva on Saturday, 3 October. The rally was attended by only a small crowd of about five hundred. Without the oligarchy's financial and political backing, the Taukei found it hard to attract the much larger numbers of their April rallies. The group was addressed by Raikivi and Vesikula in a prayer-meeting fashion that indicated the close relationship between the extremist wing of the Taukei and fundamentalist Christianity. Raikivi spoke to an Australian reporter after the rally. Regarding the country's Indo-Fijian population, he commented:

> We are not praying to the same God. I don't call that a God. I am not concerned with what they are saying in their prayers. I'm only concerned with what I'm saying to my God. My God is the one and only ... To join us is inhuman. To be classed with an Indian is inhuman to my own race. I will never tolerate it. I live a Fijian, I'll die a Fijian. There is no limit to what must be done to ensure Fijian supremacy. The limit is when we succeed ... Beating up people in the street is not much ... you may call it violence, I don't see it that way. It is simply our way of getting what we want. If we can't get it legally then we will have to get it illegally.[3]

The hold that Christian fundamentalism had on the regime was evident the second Sunday after the second coup, when the regime sought to enforce a ban on picnics, swimming, and all travel except to attend church. The regime and its Taukei supporters, however, continued to be opposed by other Christians. In Suva's central Methodist church, four hundred people from all ethnic groups gathered to listen to prominent Back to Early May activist John Garrett (a lecturer in religious studies) in a demonstration of ethnic harmony.

On the other side of the island that Sunday, Bavadra drove a short distance away from Nadi for a secret meeting with the U.S. chargé d'affaires. Returning from the meeting around two o'clock in the afternoon, the car he was in was stopped by armed soldiers in civilian clothes. They were joined by a mini-bus full of soldiers in balaclavas who demanded that Bavadra go with them to the Nadi police station. As they drove under military escort, Bavadra and the others in the car decided to make a break and sped off. The soldiers gave chase until they neared Viseisei where the pursuers gave up. Bavadra then called the governor general and told him that he would not attend Monday's meeting unless it was moved to Lautoka. Rabuka himself was in Nadi at the time to attend a rugby match (Sunday sports had not yet been banned). That night a bomb exploded in a Nadi police station, injuring one person.

Beginning at 6:00 A.M., on 5 October, Radio Fiji broadcast a series of decrees for over an hour covering measures to establish a new military government. Initially this was seen as a major step towards consolidating the power of the new regime, but questions arose when, later, the text of the decrees was not made available, and they were not broadcast again.

On the same day, Bavadra, Mara, Ganilau, and Rabuka met in Lautoka in an effort to resolve the current crisis. The meeting was a clear indication of the weakness of Rabuka's hold on the country. Ganilau chaired the meeting, and Mara and Bavadra were accompanied by five members each from their respective parties. The meeting broke up forty minutes later. Rabuka offered to 'reinstate' the governor general and allow him to appoint an interim administration if Mara and Bavadra would agree in advance to certain constitutional changes: (1) there was to be a unicameral parliament with sixty-seven seats, thirty-six of which were to be reserved for native Fijians; (2) native Fijians were to be guaranteed the offices of prime minister, foreign affairs and home affairs; (3) the governor general was to be appointed on recommendation of the Great Council of Chiefs and not the prime minister; (4) elections were to be held on the basis of a communal roll; (5) there was to be a mandatory review of the constitution every ten years; and (6) there was to be a 'Christianity clause' banning sports and commercial trading on Sunday.

Mara and Ganilau, representing the chiefly oligarchy, agreed to the demands, but Bavadra refused. Bavadra initially was prepared to at least consider accepting the demands for the sake of national reconciliation and in an effort to keep the negotiations going, but changed his mind after further discussion with his colleagues and rejected them outright. Speaking after the meeting, Bavadra said, 'I am shocked and saddened by the Alliance Party's acceptance of terms that strike at the very democratic process and at the multiracial basis of our country.'

An hour after the meeting had broken up, Rabuka returned for private talks with Ganilau that lasted for another hour. The two came to a compromise allowing the governor general to act 'in his own deliberate judgement.' Ganilau was now seen to have two options: he could resign and clear the way for a republic or he could ask the Queen to accept changes to the constitution approved by him. That night, the governor general contacted the Queen and asked her to consider a constitution with sweeping changes that entrenched native Fijian paramountcy at the expense of the Indo-Fijian population. Commenting on the governor general's initiative to approach the Queen, an editorial in *The Australian* commented: 'He apparently wishes her to establish a procedure for legitimising coups d'etat in those countries of which she is monarch, to seek no advice from Dr. Bavadra and the other ministers who have been unconstitutionally removed from office, and to endorse the violent repudiation of the Constitution that provides her legal authority as Queen of Fiji.'[4]

Australia's response to the second coup was much more muted. Those in Foreign Affairs congratulated themselves on this as a sign of Australia's ability to handle the situation much more maturely than had been the case with the first coup. Although a week before the coup, staff from the Australian and New Zealand high commissions had heard Rabuka say that he was not happy with the Deuba Accord and that he 'might have to have another coup,' this had not been taken seriously in Canberra. Australian officials in Foreign Affairs had first learned of the coup through the press, but once it was known, a meeting of top government officials was quickly convened. Australia's minister for foreign affairs, Bill Hayden, sent a message to Rabuka on his arrival back in Australia on Monday informing him that Australia continued to recognize the governor general's authority. The Australian Council of Trade Unions imposed maritime bans on Fiji once again, but airline unions decided to hold off on a decision concerning bans on flights. Naval ships were put on alert in case there was a need to evacuate the nearly five thousand Australian tourists who had been lured to Fiji by the cheap fares, and Australians were warned to defer unnecessary travel to Fiji.

New Zealand sent an unarmed ship towards Fiji in case it was necessary to evacuate its one thousand or so citizens from the country. British foreign secretary Geoffrey Howe warned that Fiji would be expelled from the Commonwealth and that Britain would withdraw aid to the country if Rabuka went ahead with his plans to make Fiji a republic. Both government and opposition parliamentarians in Papua New Guinea called on other nations not to intervene in Fiji's internal affairs. No countries, however, were immediately willing to recognize the new regime.

THE REPUBLIC OF FIJI

At midnight on Monday, 5 October, Rabuka made a broadcast confirming that Fiji was a republic. After his meeting with the governor general in the afternoon, he had come under pressure from the Taukei and its supporters in the army. The seven points outlined in his announcement made no specific mention of the governor general. No details were given of the new constitution other than that it would be founded on the teachings of Jesus Christ. Ganilau and Bavadra were already asleep by the time the broadcast was made. As it went to air, troops stepped up their presence around key points, especially Government House.

Wednesday morning, Ganilau issued a statement proclaiming that he was still the head of government. Rabuka responded by saying that there was no going back on his midnight proclamation. At a press conference, Rabuka said: 'You may all be aware that the citizens of Fiji have reverence for the Queen and the institutions that represent her. However, because of the difficulties faced in finding a solution to the present crisis, we have taken the only feasible way out.' Rabuka held another meeting with the governor general, but there was no resolution of the impasse between the two men.

This time, Rabuka named a Council of Ministers. He named himself head of state, as well as minister of home affairs and head of the public service. There were twenty other cabinet ministers.[5] The majority on the cabinet were identifiable as Taukei, but matters were far from this simple since the Taukei Movement itself was divided between Christian extremists who tended to side with the National-ists and those who had sympathies for, if they were not outright supporters, of Mara.

In effect, the cabinet was divided into three factions – those with loyalty primarily to Rabuka, the Taukei extremists and Nationalists, and the Mara faction – with the Mara faction being by far the largest, having at least ten members. Initially, the cabinet demonstrated a degree of unity, but it was not long before major divisions appeared. The Rabuka group was relatively neutral, sitting between the other two factions, whose differences became more pronounced as the Taukei extremists within the cabinet aligned themselves with the anti-Mara Nationalists, and the others (such as Apisai Tora and Filipe Bole) came out more clearly in support of Mara and the oli-garchy. Nationalist leader Sakeasi Butadroka had been given the important Ministry of Lands and Mineral Resources, and he found ready support from Taukei extremist ministers such as Raikivi and Vesikula.

The cabinet also contained one former member of the Coalition, Ratu Filimone Ralogaivau. Ralogaivau, from Bua, had been the suc-cessful Coalition candidate for the Vanua Levu North and West Fijian national seat and had been made minister of state for Fijian affairs by Bavadra. Since the first coup, he had been put under considerable pressure by Mara and Taukei supporters to break with the Coalition, and his defection, while not completely unexpected by the Labour Party, nevertheless was seen by them as a blow.

Rabuka also announced that he would be naming a new judiciary and that there was to be a 15.25 per cent devaluatation. In an attack on Fiji's unions, Rabuka said that he planned a 'thorough rethinking and reformation ... of the basic motivations and rationale for the existence of trade unions.' He referred to the Singapore model of trade unions and said that unions could continue to operate provided that they did not cause disruption.

The Coalition parliamentarians refused to recognize the declaration of a republic, reaffirmed their support for the governor general and the judiciary, and threatened, once again, to have the Western Division secede. In private discussions, secession was seen as a last resort, and it was understood that establishing a separate government would require assurances of recognition from overseas powers. Mahendra Chaudhry criticized Rabuka's statements concerning trade unions.

Irene Narayan, who Rabuka had named as minister for Indian affairs, told reporters that she had not been consulted in advance about taking a post on the council and that she had not made up her mind about serving. This proved not to be the case, and her denial seemed to be more of a face-saving device in an attempt to retain some credibility while she was trying to work a personal deal with Rabuka.

Thursday morning, troops moved in and closed the offices of the Fiji Trades Union Congress and Fiji Public Service Association. It was announced that the offices would be closed for seven days. Chaudhry went into hiding to avoid being detained again. With the blessing of both Ganilau and Rabuka, Mara left for London, stopping on the way in Melbourne to talk with Prime Minister Hawke (who, it will be recalled, had refused to speak with Bavadra under similar circumstances after the first coup). In hope of holding talks with the Queen before she left for the Commonweath Heads of Government Meeting in Vancouver, Mara was trying to find a way to retain Commonwealth membership and Fiji's links with the Crown. The Queen, however, made it clear that she would not see Mara personally and, like Bavadra, he would have to speak to her secretary, William Heseltine.

The Council of Ministers was installed on Friday, 9 October, with Irene Narayan declining to attend. Before the ceremony, Rabuka warned the ministers (several of whom had criminal records) that he expected them to behave properly. They were to receive a reduced salary of F$10,000, but would be provided a free car and housing. Rabuka also mentioned that elections would be held in one year. The promise of elections was seen by many as an attempt to win much desired international support rather than a firm pledge to restore parliamentary democracy.

On the twelfth, in a broadcast over the BBC (and reported over Radio FM96), the governor general claimed that he still held legitimate executive power, but also said that he felt that the only way to maintain stability was to change the constitution. He claimed that the changes would not disenfranchise the Indo-Fijian population: 'They have rights. We want them to remain, to carry on their businesses.' His statement caused dismay among those opposed to the regime, but delighted its supporters. The next day he prepared to leave Suva for his home village on Taveuni to ponder what to do next – whether to step down or whether to accept the presidency. Indications were that he had already decided to resign. His wife, a trained nurse, was rumoured to be looking for work. Later, Mara, in his interview with Australian journalist Stuart Inder, said that Ganilau had told him over the telephone in London that he thought that he should resign because he had become 'an embarrassment to the Queen.' Mara's response to Ganilau was that he should hold on for a few more days, at least until the Vancouver meeting was over so that 'they would have no excuse to cut the link with the Commonwealth.'[6]

After a meeting with the minister for justice, the chief justice and seven Supreme Court judges ended their stand against the regime on Wednesday and announced that they would resign. Most other members of the judiciary also had declined to work for the regime. The following day, on the fifteenth, after the minister for justice visited the chief justice at his home in an unsuccessful attempt to try to convince him to reconsider working for the regime, the chief justice and others were told to quit their offices and chambers by Monday.

Ignoring Mara's advice, the governor general announced his resignation on Friday, the sixteenth. In a message to the Queen, he stated: 'Owing to the uncertainty of the political and constitutional situation in Fiji I have now made up my mind to request Your Majesty to relieve me of my appointment as Governor-General with immediate effect. This I do with the utmost regret, but my endeavours to preserve constitutional government in Fiji have proved in vain, and I can see no alternative way forward.'[7] The Queen responded: 'The Queen accepts that it must be for the people of Fiji to decide their own future and prays that peace may obtain among the people of all races in that country.'[8]

In a radio broadcast, Rabuka thanked Ganilau for 'graciously relinquishing his post.' Early that evening a bomb exploded outside the Morris Hedstrom store in central Suva, causing no casualities. Mara returned from London on Saturday, and Ganilau returned to

Suva from Taveuni the same night. The way now seemed clear for Rabuka and the Taukei to consolidate their hold on the Republic of Fiji.

Questions remained about the political futures of Mara and Ganilau. Mara had considerable support in the cabinet, but Rabuka held ultimate power, making it impossible, at this point, for Mara to translate his cabinet backing into concrete power over decisionmaking. He was extremely angry with Rabuka for the officer's disloyalty but was not in a strong enough position to openly challenge Rabuka. As for Rabuka, as indicated by the cabinet he chose, he was aware of the extent to which he needed the backing of Mara and his supporters to form a stable government. Ganilau was in a tricky position in that, while his personal inclinations might have been simply to go along with Rabuka, his position as governor general made this extremely difficult. All three men desired to make a deal, but they needed to do so without appearing to lose face.

The impasse seemed broken when Mara and Ganilau issued statements apparently aimed at making peace with Rabuka, on 19 October. Ganilau said that he would consider the presidency if it was under an acceptable constitution, although he also stated that he felt such a constitution should be put to a referendum. Mara commented to the press that the Taukei members of the government should be given time to prove themselves.

Rabuka's other concern was the creation of at least a façade of Indo-Fijian support. This proved extremely difficult, and it was obvious that it would be impossible to secure any significant backing within the Indo-Fijian community. The best that he could do was to put forward two individuals who were already seen as traitors by most Indo-Fijians. Irene Narayan finally was sworn in, and she was joined by Ahmed Ali, who became minister without portfolio. The regime tried portraying this as a breakthrough in gaining support within the Indo-Fijian community, but given the two individuals involved, few saw it quite in this light.

THE COMMONWEALTH HEADS OF GOVERNMENT MEETING

The Commonwealth Heads of Government Meeting (CHOGM) scheduled to be held in Vancouver in mid-October became an important forum for testing international support for the Rabuka regime. The primary issue at stake at the meeting was Fiji's continued membership in the Commonwealth (which was made up of forty-nine independent states formerly under British rule).

In late July, the Canadian government, as host of the meeting, sounded out a number of other Commonwealth members concerning whether Fiji's governor general should be invited to attend the meeting. Australia announced that it would not oppose inviting the governor general since it recognized his authority. The opinion was shared widely enough that it was expected that Ganilau would be invited. The move did not go unchallenged, however, and it was likely that his presence in Vancouver would lead to controversy. Commonwealth Secretary General Shridath Ramphal, in a move clearly seen as an attempt by him to avoid controversy at the meeting, stated in an address while on a visit to Australia on 29 August that he did not expect the governor general to attend nor did he anticipate that Fiji would be an issue at the meeting since it was essentially an internal matter.

In the end, the governor general was not invited to attend the meeting, but efforts to keep Fiji from being discussed failed. Mara's dash to London in an attempt to convince the Queen to go along with his and Ganilau's plan for consitutional reform failed in its primary aim. Moreover, his trip did succeed in helping to ensure that the Fiji question figured in media coverage surrounding the CHOGM meeting which the Queen was on her way to attend. By the time of the Commonwealth meeting, a range of positions regarding recognition of the regime had emerged. On the one hand, there were those adopting a relatively hard-line approach. India was the strongest advocate of this and, in public and private, had maintained strong support for the Bavadra government. The Indian government announced on 10 October that it would be suspending trade with Fiji. A more moderate stance was pushed by the Thatcher government in Britain, with Prime Minister Thatcher voicing her sympathy for the Fiji regime.

The CHOGM meeting was to begin in Vancouver on Tuesday, 13 October. Before the meeting began, the heads of government of the South Pacific islands decided to hold talks on the Fiji issue, with Papua New Guinea prime minister Wingti urging that Fiji be left alone to sort out its internal problems. Something of a furor was created on Monday, when Australian prime minister Hawke, upon his arrival in Vancouver after a stopover in the United States to meet Secretary of State George Shultz, told the press that there was 'an indication' that the Queen would be making a statement concerning Fiji within a few days. He said further that the statement was likely to entail the severing of links between Fiji and the Crown and the Commonwealth on the grounds that Colonel Rabuka's actions had implied that Fiji had cut its links with the Queen. However, the Queen's press secretary and senior officials of the Commonwealth

Secretariat denied knowledge of any impending statement. That evening, Black African members of the Commonwealth called for Fiji's expulsion from the Commonwealth, while Britain's Margaret Thatcher refused to commit herself to support any course of action.

On Tuesday, Wingti said that although he would not mind if a statement was issued at the meeting deploring the military take-over in Fiji, he doubted that any stronger steps would be taken and indicated that his government might recognize the military regime: 'Whichever authority is in charge in Fiji, we have to recognise and deal with. We cannot change events in Fiji.' In a meeting with the Queen, Prime Minister Hawke urged her to clarify the matter of Fiji before the meeting adjourned for a retreat. This was seen as putting pressure on the Queen to act. Hawke was supported by New Zealand prime minister Lange, who expressed impatience with the meeting for not deciding on how to handle Fiji. Thatcher, however, expressed opposition to pressing the Queen to act and called for 'tolerance,' stating that 'it is wrong to abandon countries in their moment of greatest need.' The Queen herself, in her first statement on Fiji since the second coup, described the situation as 'very sad.' Her secretary, William Heseltine, undertook to send a message to the governor general stating that it would be appreciated if he could clarify his position within twenty-four hours.

During the first full working day of the meeting on Wednesday, Hawke sought to placate the Pacific island leaders by strongly condemning the French in New Caledonia. He then seemed to be backing down on Fiji when, on Thursday, Hawke joined with Wingti in calling for recognition of the military regime in Fiji ('no one now questions de facto recognition – that the Rabuka regime is the authority in Fiji'). But those seeking to avoid a strong statement on Fiji or even its expulsion came up against strong lobbying in support of the Bavadra government by several leaders – Rajiv Gandhi, in particular. As a compromise, Hawke had proposed that Fiji suffer a 'period of exile' from the Commonwealth, after which it could be considered for re-admission. That evening, the governor general's position was clarified when he phoned Heseltine and submitted his resignation. Hawke called a press conference and claimed that events had vindicated his position. The following morning the texts of the Queen's and governor general's statements were released.

The Bavadra government had sent a small delegation to Vancouver, which included its minister for education, Tupeni Baba. It had no official standing, but was able to conduct some lobbying. It sought to link Fiji's situation with that of South Africa, an issue which also figured prominently at the meeting, arguing that the

Rabuka/Mara regime was seeking to create a political structure in Fiji that was based on race and that this structure was in many ways similar to the one found in South Africa.

The Commonwealth leaders now left for their retreat at Lake Okanagan, where they were to settle how to handle the thorny issues of South African sanctions and Fiji. The retreat saw further evidence of the strained relations between Hawke and Thatcher as Thatcher continued to lobby for keeping Fiji in the Commonwealth, supported by Papua New Guinea's Wingti. Hawke, however, succeeded in having the leaders endorse his plan under which Fiji would be expelled from the Commonwealth for up to two years, after which time it could re-apply for admission. Since any member state could veto an application for membership, the hard-line states such as India, after considerable lobbying by Hawke, agreed to the compromise. In part, to placate the Pacific island members, the meeting did not issue a strong condemnation of the military coups and instead noted that it viewed the developments 'with sadness' and offered the 'good offices' of the Commonwealth in trying to solve Fiji's problems. Margaret Thatcher commended the decision to avoid 'hasty action,' but Rajiv Gandhi warned that 'Fiji cannot be a member if there are any racial overtones to their government or in their constitution'.

Commenting on the CHOGM decision, the Fijian regime's foreign minister, Filipe Bole, stated that the government was in no hurry to re-apply for membership and sought to give the impression that the regime was not overly disturbed by the development. In private, it was clear that members of the regime were extremely upset since this served to erode its legitimacy even further in the eyes of the people of Fiji, who continued to hold the Crown in high regard and to associate it closely with the legitimacy of the chiefs.

CONSOLIDATION OF THE REGIME

A handful of decrees were quietly issued on 9 October outlining the basic policies of the regime. They included a name change for the regime from the 'Interim Military Government' to the 'Military Government.' The decrees were not announced in public, however, until 23 October. Even then, there was no mention of them over Radio Fiji nor did the Ministry of Information release a statement.

Two of the decrees were of particular importance. Decree No. 10, the 'Fiji Public Service Commission and Public Service (Amendment) Decree 1987,' proclaimed that at least one-half of the positions actually held at all levels of the public service would be reserved for native Fijians and Rotumans; that all public officers were to be denied existing rights of appeal on such matters as transfer, promotion, and discrimination; and that the Public Service Commission was to be given the right to dismiss any civil servant when deemed in the public interest. It also reduced the compulsory retirement age from sixty to fifty-five years and made it an offence for public officers to leave Fiji without the consent of the Public Service Commission. One of the immediate consequences of this decree was that many senior civil servants, who were not native Fijians, were told to resign from their posts or face dismissal. Others were transferred to a newly created Department of Indian Affairs.

Decree No. 12, the 'Fundamental Freedoms Decree 1987,' was devoted largely to the denial of various freedoms. After affirming the various rights usually found in democratic countries, the decree then overrode them 'in the interests of the security of the Republic of Fiji ... or public order or morality.' The decree absolved the regime of any responsibility for persons killed 'for the purpose of suppressing a riot, insurrection or mutiny'; upheld freedom of expression and then suspended it in cases of 'political activity by whatever party, group or affiliation in the interests of public order and public safety'; suspended freedom of assembly and association, singling out any actions by unions and protest marches and demonstrations; stated that anyone detained by the military would be provided with written grounds for their detention within seven days and that such notice was to be reviewed by a tribunal after one month, and, subsequently, at no more than six monthly intervals (but then stated that the authorities were not required to act in accordance with any of the recommendations of the tribunal); granted the government broad powers to 'acquire or use' property; disallowed the use of public funds for legal aid to detainees appearing before a tribunal; and established preferences for customary native Fijian traditional law over other law.

The provisions in these decrees were not entirely new. They were built upon the legal system devised under the British, and strengthened by the Alliance Party, to deny individual freedoms and allow the government to control or coerce people. Reform of such laws had been a priority of the Coalition government. The military regime now sought to strengthen existing contraints on personal freedoms and move Fiji closer to becoming a totalitarian state.

The regime also sought to consolidate its position by stepping up intimidation of the civilian population. The use of harassment, intimidation, and detention without trial became widespread. While some of the acts were arbitrarily aimed at the population at large, many focused on Coalition supporters, unionists, and other anti-regime activists. While falling short of the brutality exhibited by military regimes elsewhere in the world, these acts represented a significant escalation of human rights violations in Fiji which had many worried that even worse might be in store.

Trade unionists Joeli Kalou (Coalition minister for labour and industrial relations) and Shiva Shankaran (industrial relations officer of the Air Pacific Employees' Association) were arrested in October, despite the agreement between Fiji Trades Union Congress secretary James Raman and the regime's minister of employment and industrial relations, Taniela Veitata, to end union harassment in an effort to appease Australian and New Zealand unions. Shankaran was interrogated and beaten by a squad of five police officers led by the deputy commissioner of police, Qalo Bulatiko, who had gained a reputation as the most brutal, senior-ranking pro-Taukei policeman. Questions were asked concerning union activities and details of the Coalition's Operation Sunrise. After suffering a broken nose, black eyes, and bruises to the liver and kidney region, Shankaran was instructed on his release not to engage in further union activities.

As the 'brain drain' continued, the regime also took steps to stop professionals with needed skills from leaving the country. In mid-October a medical doctor was pulled off an international flight and forced to return to work. However, such acts of coercion combined with restraints on taking funds out of the country, did not prove very effective, and skilled personnel continued to leave Fiji.

The military regime named new magistrates and judges on 27 October. Included were two European, three Indo-Fijian, and two native Fijian judges, and seven Indo-Fijian and three native Fijian magistrates. Rabuka encountered trouble, however, in finding a chief justice. A retired British judge, Justice Williams, was invited, but negotiations proved too difficult when he responded that he wished to appoint his own bench and to retain the Privy Council as Fiji's final court of appeal. Consideration was then given to Sailosi Kepa, a Lauan closely related to Mara through marriage.

The economic consequences of the coups and the limitations of Taukei (Pacific Way) economics – which emphasized a return to precolonial subsistence activities and a turning away from modern forms of production and exchange – began to dawn on Rabuka by early November, as it came time to think of drawing up a national budget for the following year. In a frank and rather grim appraisal of Fiji's immediate economic future, the head of the Reserve Bank, Savenaca Siwatibau, warned the regime of impending economic disaster if corrective steps were not taken quickly. The government was largely reliant on revenues from taxes and duties, and neither of these had been forthcoming in large quantities since the first coup. Rumours spread that the regime had printed an additional F$33 million to cover its liquidity crisis. The original 1987 military budget of F$10.5 million was easily more than double that amount. Overall, the budget deficit, which had been F$23 million in 1986, was at risk of exceeding that amount by two to three times by the end of 1987. Sugar payments had helped to stabilize the loss of foreign exchange for a while, but the situation was once again deteriorating rapidly, and prospects for a further devaluation of the currency were high.

As a means of allowing the army to help pay its own way, in addition to being part of his plan to win the hearts and minds of the Fijian people, Rabuka authorized the army to begin commercial ventures in construction, fishing, agriculture and similar fields, especially in more isolated parts of the country. There was little likelihood, however, that these enterprises would prove commercially viable and it was even less likely that they would make the army more self-reliant to any significant degree.

Sugar payments towards the end of 1987 were based on the previous year's production and this ensured that a significant amount of money would be coming into the economy for a brief period. Also, gold production and tuna exports were holding up. Overall, however, the economic picture was far from bright. Sugar output for 1987 looked like it would be around 350,000 tons. This amount was around 100,000 tons below the year's initial target, indicating a drop in sugar earnings of at least 30 per cent. Moreover, while British prime minister Margaret Thatcher's support for the military regime seemed to assure that the lucrative European Economic Community contract (that allowed Fiji to sell 175,000 tons of sugar at two to three times world market prices) would not be lost, the picture elsewhere was not so rosy. The last week in October, the New Zealand cabinet voted to impose economic sanctions which included scrapping a trade accord giving preferential prices for about one-half of the 60,000 tons of sugar that New Zealand bought each year from Fiji.

Other industries also were suffering. Fiji's copra industry was in crisis as production continued to fall off sharply. The tourist industry also remained a disaster. Investments in tourist resorts, amounting to hundreds of millions of dollars, had been lost or were held in abeyance. Japan Airlines, Continental, and Air New Zealand had suspended service as bookings dropped, and wholesalers had begun cancelling tours. By mid-October, hotel occupancy rates were around 20 per cent.

Despite the Taukei's constant invocation of the Christian divine, God did not seem to be entirely on Rabuka's side either. The drought that had begun earlier in the year continued throughout October and early November. In early November, the Fiji Meteorological Service reported that the current rainfall deficiency was 'the worst for at least the last 100 years' and that the wet season might not start at all. The dry weather that had helped raise the sugar content of the cane harvested earlier in the year, was now threatening to destroy the prospects for next year's crop being planted at all. Moreover, concern was being expressed for the prospects of local food crops in general. And still ahead was the cyclone season which meant that when rain did come, it might not be in a very welcome form.

There was also the question of just how much further the people of Fiji could be pushed. Taukei militant, Tomasi Raikivi, spoke of the economic hardships being endured by the people of Fiji as being 'to witness their faith,' but few on the receiving end saw the situation in such spiritual terms. The number of people out of work was growing, and wages continued to be cut. Poorer people living in Suva were finding it increasingly difficult to make ends meet. A survey conducted by members of the Catholic church in Raiwaqa parish in late October found that, although most homes had at least one income-earner, many workers were suffering from reduced paid working hours and pay cuts or were in danger of losing their jobs. Many families were having to borrow to meet their weekly expenses, whereas others were only just able to get by. Interestingly, when questioned about the Australian Council of Trade Unions bans, the survey found that, despite the realization that the bans might affect people living in the area, a number of respondents said that they supported the bans because of their concern over the deterioration of workers' rights: 'Without fair and adequate representation for workers there is a danger of increasing exploitation.' In the countryside, people were suffering from depressed market conditions in the towns and from the effects of the drought.

But appeals to economic rationality carried little weight with those members of the regime committed to the Taukei ideology of Christian fundamentalism and the idealization of village life. Individual cabinet ministers were keen to implement their own pet policies in areas over which they now had power. The pro-Taukei elements in the cabinet, in particular, were anxious to get on with the business of creating the 'New Fiji' of their dreams. Others simply had old grudges to settle.

Ratu Filimone Ralogaivau, minister for education, allowed Ahmed Ali (who had served for a period as education minister in the former Alliance Party government and was known for his extreme views) to control educational policies and draft releases. One institution singled out for attack was the University of the South Pacific, which Ali especially disliked. He made it clear that not only would the Fiji government not increase university funding (Fiji contributed about 70 per cent of the university's budget) to compensate for its economic decline since the first coup, but that funding would probably be reduced. To continued losses of expatriate staff, a situation that worried many regional members of the university who were concerned about deteriorating academic standards, Ali's response was that dissidents could be replaced by native Fijians. Warnings were also given to stop moves to remove Taukei ideologue Asesela Ravuvu as head of the Institute of Pacific Studies. The situation sent university Vice-Chancellor Geoffrey Caston scurrying to Australia to plead for further assistance, especially in the form of aid-funded staff to replace those leaving, and also led the Solomon Islands, Western Samoa, and Tonga to threaten to pull out of the university and send their students elsewhere.

Arguments within the cabinet became quite heated when Minister for Lands Sakeasi Butadroka unveiled plans for radical changes in land policies without first discussing them with his fellow cabinet ministers. The first issue of the *Fiji Times*, since it resumed publication after the second coup on 5 November, contained an announcement by Butadroka suspending all transactions involving Crown land (about 9 per cent of total national land) and indicating that, in the future, all transactions would require his approval. He justified this step by arguing that his intent was to curb speculation.

Then, on 17 November, Butadroka declared that all Crown land would have the same status as Native land. Land councils were to be established in each province to facilitate the take-over by delineating boundaries and establishing traditional ownership rights. The Native Land Trust Board would then assume administrative responsibility. Butadroka also announced that future sales of freehold land (the remaining 8 per cent of national land not already identified as native-owned) would require his personal approval and that the first option of sale should go to the original native Fijian owners. He said that the military government would set up a fund to assist native Fijians in the purchase of land that had been alienated from them. The stage was set for the removal of Indo-Fijian tenants and landowners throughout the country, and the regime committed itself to a lands policy that promised to drain it of its already diminished financial resourses.

Butadroka's plans did not go unchallenged within the regime. On 5 November the pro-Mara minister for economic planning, trade and industry, Isimeli Bose, stated that there had been 'no change in the status of freehold land' and that no plans were being made to change the status of freehold property.[9] On 16 November the regime instructed Radio Fiji not to broadcast a report on Butadroka's new land policies. Three days later, Rabuka himself stated in public that Butadroka's policies were 'inconsistent with the land policies of the interim government' and were merely the personal views of Butadroka.[10] Following Rabuka's statement, Attorney General Kelemedi Bulewa, a Taukei supporter who had been responsible for drafting the new land legislation, handed in his resignation (which Rabuka declined to accept). Bose and others from the Mara and Rabuka camps apparently had been concerned that Butadroka's plans would undermine attempts to attract new overseas investment and, in particular, jeopardize plans to establish a 'free trade zone' being promoted by business interests close to Mara. This was the first defeat within the regime for the extremists and seemed to indicate that Mara loyalists were getting the upper hand largely on the basis of economic arguments.

The regime's efforts to purge Indo-Fijians from the upper reaches of the civil service also were slowing down. Members of the regime who were not Taukei extremists were concerned over the impact that such moves were having on the running of the government. By late November, faced with some six hundred vacant posts in the public service, the government quietly began to ask some of those who had been purged to return.

Despite evidence of political disarray within the cabinet, the regime continued efforts to consolidate its position. Even though the number of arrests and incidents of harassment by the military had died down, most restrictions remained in force. Some opponents of the regime were denied permission to travel overseas, and others were forced to agree that they would make no public statements while abroad before being given permission to travel. During the final week of November, it was announced that there would be no further town council elections and that administrative officers would now be appointed. There was also talk of appointing trade union officials. The Taukei's prayers also seemed to have been answered when the drought broke briefly in the middle of

November – with floods that resulted in one death. Sugar planting, however, remained in doubt.

FOREIGN RELATIONS

The new regime's foreign policy essentially sought to pursue and consolidate trends already under way before the second coup. The assumption was that the traditional close ties with Australia, New Zealand, Britain, and the United States had been strained by the second military take-over and that relations with the these countries were likely to remain limited for the foreseeable future. The Indian government was seen as hostile. The new regime sought to strengthen ties with sympathetic Asian countries, including Malaysia, Indonesia, Singapore, South Korea, and China, and with France, Israel, and South Africa. In concrete terms, it was hoped that these new allies would be able to provide military assistance as well as non-military trade to lessen Fiji's reliance on its traditional partners and to help it escape from its current economic problems. Foreign Minister Filipe Bole announced plans to establish trade missions in Indonesia, China, and Malaysia.

Immediately after the coup, the Australian government had refused to recognize the new regime, but had stopped short of taking any further economic or political actions. The left wing of the Australian Labor Party continued to push for the Hawke government to take a stronger stand, but Hawke and Foreign Affairs Minister Hayden chose to pursue a more moderate course, and at the CHOGM meeting, Hawke had indicated that he was prepared to recognize the Rabuka regime, although he did not do so at the time. After the governor general's resignation, the Hawke government recalled the Australian high commissioner in Fiji 'for consultations' and issued a statement that Australia 'naturally wishes to maintain its friendly links with the people of Fiji' but that the nature of relations with the new regime 'remained under consideration.'

New Zealand's prime minister Lange had declared on 7 October that his government did not recognize the legality of Rabuka's new regime, and, on 22 October, New Zealand announced that it was imposing limited economic sanctions and recalling some of its diplomats and most of its aid workers from Fiji as part of a policy of maintaining 'more distant and cooler relations' with the Rabuka regime. This was despite lobbying efforts on behalf of the Rabuka regime by Maori militants.

Having initially raised the prospect of economic sanctions against the new Rabuka regime, the Thatcher government quickly reversed itself and, by the CHOGM meeting, had emerged almost as a champion of the regime. Towards the end of October, the British high commissioner in Suva was advised by his government to begin routine contacts with ministers of the military regime. When told of this decision, the regime's foreign affairs minister, Filipe Bole, informed the press that he was 'greatly encouraged' by the decision and termed it a 'realistic understanding of the situation in Fiji.'

On 6 August, Republican congressman Robert Dornan, at the behest of Coalition supporters in California, had introduced a resolution expressing support for efforts 'to forge a political compromise in Fiji which preserves its traditions of parliamentary constitutional democracy and guarantees the rights of its citizens.' The bill was passed on to the Subcommittee on Asia and Pacific Affairs, where it languished until October. Spurred by the second coup, the bill was finally introduced by the subcommittee's chairman, Democrat Stephen Solarz, on 27 October. As passed, it was a gentle slap on the wrist that committed the United States to no precise action.

The United States also announced in October that it 'had not engaged in official contacts with the military Government or taken other actions that would imply recognition of the interim Government' but that 'for the time being, our embassy has maintained informal contacts with the de facto authorities in Fiji to ensure that U.S. citizens and interests are protected, to express our concerns over human rights abuses and to express the need for a return to democratic processes.' The communique also stated that the newly appointed U.S. ambassador to Fiji would remain in Washington for the time being. In the meantime, the effective head of the United States mission in Suva was William Paupe. Although most American aid to Fiji had stopped, Paupe continued to distrubute small amounts from funds under his personal direction, and the Peace Corps remained active.

Among the Pacific island nations, sentiments regarding the new regime were mixed, but there was a general sense of sympathy. What emerged clearly was that few Pacific islanders had any idea of what was actually going on in Fiji and most perceived the coup in limited racial terms as an assertion of indigenous rights. Thus, one member of Parliament in Papua New Guinea, Jim Yer Wim, stated that 'the coup in Fiji must be a signal to expatriates and naturalised citizens who think that they can ride rough-shod over ethnic Papua Guineans.' The government of Tonga had been very supportive of the Mara/Rabuka regimes, recognizing its close affinity to the segment of Fijian society involved, and the crown prince of Tonga paid a visit to Suva in early October. On 11 October, the military regime announced that the crown prince had delivered Rabuka a message indicating support and recognition of the new regime. Tonga later equivocated on the question of recognition, but the initial message was an accurate expression of the sentiment of the Kingdom of Tonga and it served to bolster support for Rabuka among Fijians of Tongan ancestry.

Indonesia was emerging as a particularly important new ally. Under the previous civilian governments, relations between Fiji and Indonesia had been minimal, reflecting, in part, the Melanesian nations' disapproval of Indonesia's treatment of the Melanesian people in Irian Jaya. Relations between Indonesia and Pacific island nations had been improving, however, especially relations with Papua New Guinea. Rabuka and other officers allied with him were open in expressing their admiration for the 'Indonesian model,' which allowed the military to play a central role in political and economic affairs. They also expressed interest in using the Indonesian constitution as an inspiration for the Republic of Fiji's new constitution.

As a follow-up to two earlier visits by representatives of the Rabuka regime, an unofficial eight-member Indonesian trade mission arrived in Fiji for talks with Filipe Bole on 3 November – the first such foreign delegation since the second coup. The mission announced that President Suharto had offered Fiji up to 25,000 tons of rice on credit and special financing facilities, as a goodwill gesture. Means of boosting Fiji-Indonesia trade were discussed, as were plans for joint operations between Air Pacific and Garuda to serve Japan, Papua New Guinea, and Indonesia. The mission led to the approval of trade deals by which Indonesian rice, petroleum products, and other commodities were to be exchanged for Fijian sugar.

General Benny Murdani, commander of Indonesia's armed forces, also took an interest in the Rabuka regime. On 13 November, following close on the heels of the trade mission, it was announced in Jakarta that plans approved by General Murdani were at an advanced stage to send a high-level military delegation to Fiji with the aim of establishing a security alliance between the two countries. This was part of what was emerging as a comprehensive plan to enhance Indonesian influence in the South Pacific. It reflected a view by Murdani that the United States and Australia were proving 'incompetent' in maintaining security in the Asia-Pacific region. The extent of Indonesia's growing involvement in the region was amplified when it was revealed that Murdani had provided the former commander of the Papua New Guinea military with nearly A$200,000 for his campaign in the 1987 national election. In the debate that followed this revelation, on 17 November , Bernard Nara-kobi, of the opposition Melanesian Alliance, claimed that the money was part of a larger Indonesian plan to 'dominate the entire Pacific region.'[11]

Indonesian foreign minister Mochtar Kusumaatmadja called for closer ties with Fiji, but stopped short of supporting recognition of the regime and was more cautious in his approach than Murdani. He felt that closer ties should be fostered in part to minimize the effects of superpower rivalry in the South Pacific. He noted, however, that Indonesian relations with the Rabuka regime 'must be such that it does not give the impression Indonesia tolerates unconstitutional actions and sides with a certain ethnic group' in Fiji. While hoping that military co-operation would be possible in the future, he stated that 'Indonesia should give its immediate response to Fiji's request for help, initially through the private business sector.' Thus, while wishing to take advantage of a situation that promised to provide Indonesia with a greater role in the South Pacific, Mochtar did not wish to be seen as supporting positions or actions that were politically sensitive for Indonesia itself.

Malaysia was also assuming an increasingly important role in the regime's foreign relations. Prime Minister Mahathir saw that by supporting the Rabuka regime he could further legitimate his own increasingly authoritarian communal policies. Malaysian foreign minister Abu Hassan arrived in Fiji on 30 November, leading the first official delegation by a foreign government to visit Fiji since the second coup. The foreign minister said that Malaysia would do all in its power to help the Rabuka regime and urged other countries to understand and not impede the regime's 'efforts at consolidation.' He said that Malaysia understood the regime's desire to entrench the political domination of native Fijians. Trade was emphasized, with Malaysian exports of cooked oil, textiles, and rubber products being cited, and recognition of the Rabuka regime was not mentioned. Ten officers were sent to Malaysia for training in business to strengthen the army's auxiliary unit and to help ensure it a continued role in Fijian society.

France, too, sought to strengthen ties with the military regime. The French saw this as an opportunity to drive a wedge among Pacific island nations by stepping in to fill the void created by Australia and New Zealand's refusal to recognize the military regime and by their suspension of aid to Fiji. It was a move that alarmed the Australians considerably. Although the amount involved was not made public, it became widely known that the French were providing the Rabuka regime with substantial amounts of money in assistance during the latter half of the year (rumoured to be in excess of F$10 million). Without such support, it is clear that the economic picture for the regime would have been much worse than it was and that the military would have had a much harder time holding on to power. It is also worth noting that France was the only nation among Fiji's new-found friends that was in a position to provide substantial amounts of assistance to replace what had been lost since the coup.

After the 1982 election, relations between Israel and the Mara government had begun to increase slowly. Israel seemed to view Fiji as a potentially useful ally in the international arena, and Mara was sympathetic to the conservative Israeli government. Israeli advisers worked in the country in a variety of capacities and, with the help of the Asian-American Free Labor Institute, the Israeli trade union body Histadrut had begun to promote training activities for Fijian unionists. Israeli president Chaim Herzog had visited Fiji in November 1986. He had received a warm welcome from the Fiji government ('as the Prime Minister of the country where Jesus was born'), but his request to upgrade existing ties so as to allow for a resident diplomat was turned down. The denial was motivated, in part, by internal political considerations since the Alliance government did not want to do anything that might threaten its support among Fiji's Muslims. (It is interesting to note that Fijian troops in the Middle East referred to the Arabs as 'Indians.') After the May coup, relations between Israel and the new regime became increasingly cordial. One week before the September coup, the deputy director of the Israeli Foreign Ministry, Avraham Tamir, visited Fiji and agreed to open an embassy to facilitate economic and other forms of assistance. Following the September coup, observers became aware of the presence of Israeli army officers in Fiji helping the military with surveillance and intelligence work.

China, which had growing political and economic ties with Fiji before the coups, had failed to recognize the new regimes. Foreign Minister Filipe Bole visited China between 3–8 December in an effort to 'drum up' financial and diplomatic support for the military regime. The visit was not reported in the Chinese media and diplomatic support was not forthcoming, but promises of continued economic activities were made by Chinese authorities who were not anxious to risk losing this foothold in the South Pacific.

The viability of some of the regime's foreign policy initiatives was questionable. Under the Mara government, it had become increasingly difficult to finance the operation of Fiji's overseas missions, leading the Bavadra government to formulate plans to scale them back considerably. The plans of the Rabuka regime to open new trade missions seemed to have little chance of getting off the ground under current economic circumstances. Similarly, an earlier attempt by Air Pacific to fly between Fiji and Papua New Guinea had been abandoned after only a few months. Moreover, the regime still had not been recognized by any of Fiji's major traditional allies.

The reasons behind Rabuka's seizure of power in September are clear enough – Mara had planned to dump him. But in staging the coup, Rabuka had pitted himself against the oligarchy in whose name he had staged the first coup. His hold on power remained precarious, even after he was able to form a cabinet and declare Fiji a republic. His allies among the Taukei and Nationalists lacked not only the numerical support, but their leaders in cabinet proved themselves incapable of governing. Rabuka found himself caught between them and Mara's supporters, on whom he became increasingly dependent to keep the government functioning. Once again the real world of twentieth-century Fiji seemed to be confounding the plans of the military strategist.

CHAPTER TEN

Mara's Return

Ratu Sir Kamasese Mara once again became prime minister in late 1987. He assumed the post with the backing of Rabuka, and it looked as if the chiefly oligarchy had regained its control of the country. As events were to show, however, Mara's rule was to be an uneasy one. He remained heavily dependent on the military to remain in power in the face of popular opposition not only from Labour Party and National Federation Party supporters but also from extremists associated with the Nationalists and the Taukei.

The Mara faction within the Rabuka regime's cabinet had begun to get the upper hand during the month of November. Four factors played into Mara's hands: the continuing economic decline, difficulties in gaining international recognition, factional squabbling within the cabinet, and the obvious incompetence of some of the ministers. Rabuka found himself caught in the middle of the fight between the most extreme Taukei and the Mara loyalists. The Taukei continued to claim that they were not worried about the impending economic ruin of the country, arguing that it was the price to pay for racial supremacy and a return to tradition. But many others who supported the basic aims of the two coups, including Rabuka himself, were worried about the economic viability of the existing government.

While two draft constitutions were being prepared for the consideration of the Great Council of Chiefs in December and while the Taukei lobbied to enhance their power and have one of their supporters named as president, Rabuka held discussions with Ganilau and Mara about the possibility of handing power over to them in an effort to extricate Fiji from the current mess. The two chiefs set conditions for their acceptance of the offices of president and prime minister, respectively. Ganilau stated that he would agree only if there was to be a constitution that was acceptable to all Fijians and that was also more democratic than the one proposed by the Taukei extremists. The two men also wanted the judiciary returned to its earlier state with the Rabuka appointees being dismissed. Finally, Mara insisted on his right to select the cabinet so that he could eliminate those individuals, such as Sakeasi Butadroka, who were openly hostile to him, along with others (that is, non-Mara Taukei) who were no longer needed.

In mid-November, Mara complained of a slight heart problem and used this ailment as an excuse to leave Fiji for treatment in Sydney while awaiting resolution of the negotiations. It was a typical Mara manoeuvre. While in Sydney 'recuperating,' Mara held an interview with the well-known apologist for the eastern chiefly establishment, Australian journalist Stuart Inder. Previously, Mara had found Inder a willing vehicle through which he could deny his involvement in the first coup in May. Inder's article presented Mara as a man 'who has spent that last six months working to prevent his country from being destroyed' and who was 'disappointed and frustrated' by recent developments.[1] Mara emphasized once again that he had known nothing in advance of either coup, and Inder reported that 'he had been kept at a distance by members of the ultra-nationalist Taukei Movement because they considered him too moderate, too accommodating to the Indians during his leadership.' Mara lay part of the blame for the second coup on Ganilau: 'By dragging his heels [after the Deuba Accord] Ratu Ganilau allowed the destructive forces to mobilise.' Ganilau was thus portrayed as a weakling in a clear effort to ensure that Mara would be seen as the dominant force in the government that was soon to be formed. The interview was reprinted in the recently reopened *Fiji Times*, and it helped to set the stage for Mara's return to power.

Shortly after Mara's return from Sydney, Rabuka, Mara, and Ganilau met on 30 November and 4 December to discuss handing over the government. In typical Mara fashion, his supporters arranged for delegations to visit Mara 'urging him to resume the mantle of leadership.' Mara and Rabuka reached an agreement on Saturday, 5 December, and, that evening, in a ten-minute radio broadcast, Rabuka announced that the government would be turned over to Mara and Ganilau, with Mara assuming the prime ministership. In his broadcast, Rabuka commented that he hoped that Ganilau would lead Fiji 'to a point where the historic link with the Crown would be re-established.' Rabuka ordered the troops back to their barracks and presented Ganilau with a tabua as a token of appreciation.

In an article appearing in the *Sydney Morning Herald* the following month, Rabuka, seeking to explain his deal with Mara, criticized Sakeasi Butadroka and several other ministers for using their positions 'to achieve their own ends.' Pointedly, he commented: 'They were becoming more of an embarrassment than anything else.'[2]

Several Taukei leaders were quick to criticize Rabuka's deal. After a meeting of the Taukei and Fijian Nationalist Party on Sunday evening, 6 December, Taukei extremist Meli Vesikula accused Rabuka of giving in to pressure from 'political and military tyrants' and criticized him for not waiting to refer matters to the Council of Chiefs. 'It's another coup,' he said, and 'there is no guarantee that the Constitution will be changed to meet the aspirations of the Taukei Movement and the Fijian people generally.' He said that the Taukei were shocked: 'We are faced with a crazy situation and have become the laughing stock of the whole world.' As for Mara's new regime, Vesikula commented that 'Mara's not interested in us, he will only have cronies.' The executive members of the Taukei Movement individually swore that none of them would accept positions in Mara's cabinet.

On Monday, 7 December, Rabuka issued a warning to the Taukei that they should not resort to violent acts against the new regime and that they must accept his decision in order to help revive the economy and speed international recognition. After Mara and Rabuka met to discuss the composition of the new cabinet, Mara presented Ganilau with a tabua to thank him for helping in the change of government. The following day, Mara held a similar ceremony for Rabuka to help reassert his influence over the military. In a radio broadcast on Tuesday night, Mara asserted that he was not an 'opportunist' and that his acceptance of the prime ministership had been done solely in the national interest. He also stated once again that he had not been involved in either of the coups: 'My hands are clean.'

The oligarchy appeared to be back in the saddle. Despite public shows of unity, however, relations between the two men apparently remained tense. Circumstances had forced Rabuka to deal with Mara; he had not done so voluntarily. Moreover, Rabuka retained considerable power and clearly did not view himself as being relegated to the role of a mere follower of Mara.

On Tuesday, 8 December, one of the initial agents in the destabilization campaign, Jona Qio, died in an automobile accident in western Fiji. Initially, the incident did not draw much attention, but later, when others in and around the regime and in the Alliance camp died as well, people recalled the death of Qio and began to wonder if it was an accident.

A significant split emerged in the Taukei between those willing to go along with Mara (many of them had been Mara loyalists all along such as Filipe Bole and Taniela Veitata) and those unwilling to compromise. The pro-Mara faction presented a letter to Ganilau on Tuesday pledging their support for the new regime. The letter contained one thousand signatures (not all of them necessarily coming from actual Taukei). The extremist faction, known as the 'angry faction,' which included Ratu Inoke Kubuabola and Vesikula, pledged to continue its struggle. Later, the two factions assumed separate identities with Veitata leading the pro-Mara faction under the name of the *Domo ni Taukei* and Vesikula leading the anti-Mara faction which retained the name of the Taukei Movement.

Mara named his cabinet on Wednesday, 9 December. There had been some speculation that he might seek to enact some of the conditions of the Deuba Accord and thereby to provide the Coalition with a place in the new cabinet, but most realized that this was unlikely since Mara was now in a position to assume power without having to share it with members of the government he had seen overthrown. The main problem from Mara's perspective was ensuring that those who opposed him among the Taukei were kept under control once they were removed from office. For this he needed the support of his allies within the Taukei Movement and the military. His cabinet was a mixture of Mara loyalists and useful political allies.

Mara named twenty-one ministers, keeping the foreign affairs and the Public Service Commission portfolios for himself.[3] Thirteen of the ministers had been Alliance Party members of Parliament in the pre-coup government, with the other posts being divided among the military and a handful of Alliance Party/Mara loyalists. Rabuka was made minister of home affairs. Significantly, three Mara allies within the Taukei Movement were also named as cabinet members (Filipe Bole, Apisai Tora, and Taniela Veitata). Missing were all of the anti-Mara Taukei and Fijian Nationalist Party leader Sakeasi Butadroka. Also missing was the leader of the moderate faction within the Alliance Party, David Toganivalu. Mara had selected mostly native Fijians within the Alliance Party who were from Lau, several of whom were related to him. Those who were not from Lau (such as William Toganivalu and Apisai Tora) were chosen to provide some regional balance, but they did little to alter the overall picture. It was, as Taukei Movement leader Vesikula had predicted, a cabinet of Mara cronies.

The 'angry faction' of the Taukei had sought unsuccessfully to convince Veitata not to join the Mara cabinet shortly before the swearing-in ceremony. Both Tora and Bole had made it clear that their loyalties lay with Mara. That the militant Taukei's influence was on the wane was made abundantly clear when they were denied a police permit to hold a joint meeting with the Fijian Nationalists to form a new political group. Unexpectedly, after the first coup, this band of extremists had been able to assert more power than Mara and others around him would have predicted. It had taken time for Mara and his supporters to manoeuvre the militant Taukei to a position where they were no longer needed or were no longer in a position to influence Rabuka. But, they had finally accomplished this, and now it was time to push the Taukei out of the way and get on with ruling the country in the interests of the oligarchy.

Mara was given some encouragement by Prime Minister Hawke of Australia, who stated that Mara's return to power was 'a step in the right direction.' While saying little about the illegitimacy of the new Mara government and less about the fate of the Bavadra government, he chose to focus on economic and geopolitical questions. He stated that he had been concerned that under the Rabuka regime there had been a 'tendency to divert away from Australia, for instance, some of its sourcing of imports and, if you like, some of its strategic associations.' But now Hawke hoped for a 'reversal of those tendencies.'

On Friday, 11 December, Timoci Bavadra issued a statement which characterized the Mara regime as a military government in a 'civilian cloak.' Members of the Labour-NFP coalition were not overly upset with the composition of the new cabinet. They had not wanted or expected to be part of the new government. Moreover, since it was clear from the composition of the cabinet that the new government was little more than a Lauan regime with military backing, the Labour Party anticipated that this regional bias would strengthen its own hand among non-Lauan native Fijians. In addition, as one Coalition member noted, 'At least we can talk with a few of these people.' The Labour-NFP coalition would continue to expand its influence among native Fijians in the countryside through Operation Sunrise, by which it sought to demonstrate to native Fijians the extent to which the 1970 constitution safeguarded their interests, and it was hoped that some of the worst vestiges of repression and harassment under the Rabuka regime would disappear.

Fears of a continued military presence in the government proved well founded. In addition to the four officers given cabinet posts, other military personnel appeared in key government positions. The army chief of staff, Lt. Col. Isikia Savua, was quoted in the *Sydney Morning Herald* as saying that this move 'was consistent with the military's initiative to move more strongly into the Government.'[4]

These appointments reflected the balance of power within the regime and the extent to which Mara and Rabuka were dependent on one another in an uneasy coalition.

Amid rumours that Mara was going to appoint him high commissioner to Britain as a reward for staying out of the way, Brigadier General Epeli Nailatikau paid a visit to Rabuka on 11 December at army headquarters. The visit was to congratulate Rabuka for surrendering the government to Mara and to present a public face of goodwill between the two men. Rabuka told those present that there never had been any ill feelings between the two and that if 'there ever were any, it's all over.'

One of the first problems to confront the new Mara regime was a secessionist movement on the island of Rotuma. Secessionist sentiment on Rotuma, which had been annexed by Britain in 1881 and joined administratively with Fiji, had been growing under the Alliance government during the 1980s. Placating the Rotumans had become an issue in the 1987 national election and in subsequent discussions of constitutional reform. Led by self-proclaimed king, Gagaj Sau Lagfatmaro, the Mulmahau clan on Rotuma declared that the island had cut its ties with Fiji after the country had declared itself a republic. The secessionists informed Rabuka of their action by letter during the first week of December. The islanders were divided on the issue, and tensions on Rotuma were running high. The chairman of the Rotuman council, Victor Rigamoto, informed Rabuka that the council still considered Rotuma a part of Fiji, and he felt that Rotumans living elsewhere in Fiji supported the republic. Police and troops in Suva were put on alert the second week of December, awaiting possible deployment to Rotuma, but were not sent until 1 February 'to restore order.' In April, however, the Mulmahau clan suspended seven chiefs who had agreed to Fiji becoming a republic without first consulting the clan and replaced them with individuals who favoured secession, an event that prompted the regime to send another contingent of police to Rotuma, the first week of May.

The Fiji Trades Union Congress, for its part, was quick to voice its opposition to some of the plans of the new Mara regime. In particular, it was critical of the proposed 'tax-free zones' promoted by some of Mara's business associates. Significantly, Fiji Public Service Association general secretary Mahendra Chaudhry announced that his union was contemplating a strike at Nadi airport after the government issued termination notices to Civil Air Authority employees who had been suspended after the first coup for being 'security risks.' A number of people also expressed concern over plans announced by the Mara regime in mid-January to license news media, noting that the licenses could be revoked at any time for 'irresponsible reporting.'

And the 'angry faction' of the Taukei continued to fulminate against the new regime: 'Already, in only a week,' complained one faction member, 'we have seen that conditions set by the army on the basis that power would be handed back to Ratu Sir Penaia have been withdrawn. Why must everybody suffer? Must we have three or four coups before our objectives are achieved?' Another faction spokesman complained that the agreement to transfer power had ignored the Great Council of Chiefs. But this time, few seemed to be listening.

About thirty members of what had come to be referred to as the Taukei Movement/Fijian Nationalist Party Front (the so-called 'angry faction') sought to hold a demonstration in central Suva on 18 December, but they were dispersed by police and soldiers before Nationalist leader Sakeasi Butadroka arrived to address the group, and two were held for questioning. Not wishing to take any chances, many shops in downtown Suva remained closed for the day. Later, Butadroka warned: 'We are planning more serious things for the future.' In a move aimed at further reducing the influence of Taukei extremists, a group of pro-Mara Taukei led by Inoke Tabua (a long-time Mara ally) again pledged their support to the new regime. Tabua criticized members of the 'angry faction,' stating that 'they have no support' and promising that pro-Mara Taukei were willing to turn out in large numbers in support of the regime.

In a rather bizarre incident, a few days later on 22 January, three members of the 'angry faction' broke into the Fiji Museum, stole a war club and sword that had belonged to Ratu Sukuna, and tried to capture Radio Fiji. They demanded to be allowed to broadcast plans to take over the government, but police were called and over-powered the men before the broadcast could be made.

Moderate forces within the Alliance Party had lost one of their members earlier when Mosese Qionibaravi died in hospital. They were now to be dealt a much more serious blow when David Togani-valu (fifty-four years old), leader of the moderate faction within the Alliance Party and Mara's primary rival for party leadership, died on 18 December. The official version was that he was killed when his car went off the road north of Suva shortly after he had left a social function. But rumours linking his death to political rivalry spread quickly, some saying that his neck had been broken in 'traditional

Fijian fashion.' Whatever the true story, his death left Mara firmly in control of the Alliance Party and in a position to pick his own successor.

ECONOMIC CONDITIONS

The Mara regime's budget for 1988 – its first concrete statement about its plans for the country's economic future – was announced on 17 December by Finance Minister Josefata Kamikamica. The F$421 million budget aimed to cut government expenditure by 30 per cent. It contained few new sources of income and, in a bow to the business community, reduced duties on a wide range of items needed for manufacturing and agriculture. The regime planned to meet some of the projected F$119 million deficit through overseas borrowing. In March, the Hong Kong and Shanghai Bank offered to lend the regime U.S.$20 million. The regime also was helped by increased receipt of foreign aid, which rose to an official F$14 million from F$2 million the year before (this not counting unreported sums received from France, Israel, and other sources).

The most important economic initiative involved the regime's decision to develop export-processing zones. In conjunction with this were widespread moves to grant tax-free status to local businesses owned by Mara cronies and to continue advocacy of wage restraint. Fiji's growing garment export industry had been singled out for promotion by the regime, exemplifying its commitment to the development of Fiji as a low-wage exporting nation. In 1987, garment exports had totalled F$8.8 million, and it was hoped that this total would reach F$12 million in 1988. Government planners spoke of the industry eventually employing 25,000 workers with exports worth F$300 million, but few took these statements seriously.

By early March 1988, twenty companies had applied for tax-free status. This included ten existing local companies and ten foreign-local joint ventures. Among these was Forest Products (Fiji) Limited; a New Zealand-Hong Kong joint venture that intended to purchase wood from Tropik Woods in Lautoka to produce prefabricated houses; a Fiji-Pakistani joint venture to export towels to Australia, New Zealand, and North America; and several existing garment industries. On 22 March, the government-owned tuna cannery, PAFCO, was also given tax-free status. Since average wages in New Zealand were NZ$7 per hour compared to F$0.45 per hour for Fiji's 6,000 garment workers, clothing workers in New Zealand were becoming alarmed over the prospect of the loss of jobs. In early May, two Irish experts on tax-free zones, who were sponsored by UNIDO, arrived to help the regime with its plans. By the end of May, the government had awarded fourteen companies tax-free status, and had another twenty-four under consideration.

The regime also stated that it wished to promote privatization. In accordance with this policy, in the first week of March, it was announced that telecommunications would be privatized by 1989 and that negotiations were in progress with the World Bank for funds to help establish the new company. The intent here was clearly to use development funds to set up a private company in the hands of Mara or his associates. Indeed, Government economic policies were often enacted primarily to assist Mara's business associates. For the population at large, Mara offered up speeches on the need for hard work, efficiency, and ending corruption. These themes dated back to his early days in the colonial administration and they were greeted with considerable cynicism since his previous government had been tainted with corruption and inefficiency. While employees at the public service continued working at the reduced salaries imposed the year before, Mara's cabinet ministers voted themselves wage increases of over 21 per cent. The Fiji Public Service Association responded by demanding the restoration of full salaries for all public servants and a comparable wage increase. At the same time that the regime reduced revenue by eliminating business taxes for Mara's cronies, it increased its revenue from those not so fortunate.

One issue that had cane farmers particularly upset was the revision of valuations for cane land sharply upward – a move that led to protests by farmers in Ba and elsewhere and led to even greater dissatisfaction with the way that Siddiq Koya and his associates were running the Sugar Cane Growers Council. The Rabuka regime had gazetted the new rates on 29 September and they remained in force under the Mara regime. The increase was substantial for better-off farmers who saw the rates for 'first class land' go from a maximum of F$2,225 per hectare to F$4,500 per hectare. But it was the poorer farmers who were hit the worst, as rates for 'third class land' went from a maximum of F$495 per hectare to F$1,650 per hectare. In addition, there were price increases of about F$3 per bag for fertilizer and a price rise from F$27 to F$56 a gallon for herbicides.

On 22 March Finance Minister Kamikamica announced that the regime had decided to impose a wage freeze until June. He noted that the freeze was to apply to wages only and not to prices, service charges, or rents. Fiji Trades Union Congress president Jale Toki, usually silent on controversial issues, condemned the freeze as 'Draconian, unfair, unjust.' Mahendra Chaudhry, who had replaced

James Raman as the general secretary of the congress, called the freeze 'morally indefensible and a form of corruption' and asked 'does this mean that the government ministers would refund their increases or that they would go back to the $10,000 per year salaries?'[5] The response of many in the business community was lukewarm. The Fiji Employers' Consulative Association did not issue an immediate statement, but many individual businessmen were critical of the move: 'Government is killing trade and making it harder to attract skilled staff' commented one businessman. The regime's reaction was to backdate the freeze to 1 January. A short time later the Fiji Employers' Consultative Association issued a statement stating that the freeze was an impediment to encouraging investment and, like the Fiji Trades Union Congress, wrote to the regime opposing the freeze. Opposition to the freeze, primarily from the employers' association, led the government to modify the freeze before signing it into law on 14 April. The regime agreed that price controls would remain in effect on items already under control and that some wage increases would be permitted (for example, to retain scarce skills or, in some cases, where increases had not been paid for the previous year). As if the new wage freeze was not enough, on 15 April, the minister for housing and urban development, Tomasi Vakatora, threatened tenants in arrears with evictions. Out of 15,000 borrowers, 7,000 were in arrears, and tenants in 1,500 out of 2,300 rental flats were behind in their payments.

Evidence of the improved economic situation was provided by the country's foreign reserves, which reached F$223 million on 2 March (a record high in Fiji dollar terms), largely as a result of year-end sugar payments. Total sugar production had exceeded 440,000 tons, producing earnings of F$215 million. The Fiji Sugar Corporation stated that it hoped production would reach 500,000 tons in 1988. The annual rate of inflation by January 1988 was down to 6.2 per cent, but in February it had begun to rise again, and by April it had reached 8.7 per cent. To this could be added the industrial production index figures for the first quarter of 1988, released in late May, which were down by 6.2 per cent from 1987 overall, with the unadjusted figure (basically not including sugar) down by 50.7 per cent.

Perhaps the most worrying sign for Fiji's economic future was a lack of faith by members of the business community. Mara tried to paint a glowing picture of the economy, pointing to the effects of the devaluation and new tax incentives such as thirteen-year tax holidays for foreign investors. While some, especially those close to Mara who saw new chances for plunder, shared such a positive view, many in the business community thought only of getting out with as much money as possible. One aspect of this was the growing black-market money trade which amounted to as much as A$10 million a month, a considerable amount in such a small economy. With the official rate for the Australian dollar being F$0.97, the black-market rate was between F$1.05 and F$1.18. Added to this was a brisk market in passports.

Fiji's high level of foreign reserves was seen by some as an indication of economic stagnation rather than as a sign of economic recovery. Customs receipts for imports in January were down by 30 per cent compared to the previous January. If translated in constant dollars, the figure was even more alarming. In addition, the country's banks were finding themselves faced with a money glut rather than a shortage, as had been the case earlier. Borrowing was at its lowest level since independence, and the private banks had F$30 million sitting in the Reserve Bank earning no interest. Interest rates had dropped, but this had done little to stimulate demand.

The most important problem undermining prospects for eventual economic recovery was the continued loss of trained personnel. Medical facilities were in a poor state. At least one-half of the country's doctors and other medical professionals had left since the first coup, and there were serious shortages of supplies. Thus, in mid-December, the Lautoka Hospital, the primary hospital in western Fiji, announced that it would only perform emergency operations because of 'cost-cutting measures.' The Ministry of Health reported in mid-March that there was a shortage of ninety-seven doctors (before the coup there had been a total of 450 doctors and medical assistants in Fiji). In February, the Ministry of Education reported that it had been able to fill only 374 vacant teaching positions, 209 of them by reappointing teachers who had retired or resigned, and that 167 posts remained unfilled. The same month, Posts and Telecommunications reported that it had lost seventy employees in 1987, mostly in technical areas. Emigration figures for the month of January totalled 689: 571 Indo-Fijians, 50 native Fijians, and 68 'Others,' including 87 professionals (70 Indo-Fijians, 7 native Fijians, 5 Chinese, and 2 Europeans), and 73 categorized as clerical/supervisory.

Among those leaving Fiji was Savenaca Siwatibau, the head of the Reserve Bank who almost single-handedly had sought to save the national economy from the ravages of the Rabuka/Mara regimes. He had taken leave to accept a visiting position at the Australian National University in February 1988, and then in April announced that he was resigning to take up a post with the U.N. Economic and Social Commission for Asia and the Pacific (ESCAP) in Vanuatu; thus, one of the few remaining obstacles in the way of Mara and his cronies for assuming complete control of the country's finances was removed.

Tourism had recovered slightly. In February 1988, cruise ships resumed visits to Suva, and, by April, hotel occupancy rates were reported to be up to 35–45 per cent (compared to precoup levels of 75–85 per cent). Overall, however, arrivals remained low. Arrivals for the month of January were down 36 per cent from the year before, and for the six-month period to January there was a decline of 39 per cent from the same period in 1986. Continued adverse publicity was blamed, in particular, for the continued lack of tourists from Australia and New Zealand. In late February, the regime reached an agreement with Seaboard Airlines to begin charter flights from the United States in mid-June. It was claimed that this would generate 50,000 new arrivals a year, but the projection appeared to most observers to be highly optimistic. Cheap package tours from Australia (A$599 for airfare and seven nights accommodation), like the year before, had lured a number of tourists from Australia during the first few months of the year, but, once again those who came tended to be small spenders. Moreover, the number of tourists arriving from other countries continued to be off sharply (especially from the United States).

The economic crisis also had an important effect on crime. Figures released in late March for the months of January and February indicated a sharp increase in the crime rate nationwide over the comparable period in 1987. The figures for violent crime were ninety-two reported incidents versus thirty-five for the year before. For other robbery-related crimes (stealing, housebreaking, burglary, and break-in), the figure rose from 443 to 672.

Superficially, it appeared as if Fiji's economy was improving since the return of Mara, but signs of an ominous future abounded. Perhaps the most troubling aspects were the extent to which the nation's economic infrastructure had been undermined with the loss of so many people in business and the professions and by the lack of constraints on Mara's cronies to stop them from looting the country and driving wages down even further. The boosterism and 'cooked' figures that were becoming increasingly common in the media and government pronouncements fooled few who were knowledgeable about the actual state of the economy.

FOREIGN RELATIONS

Mara was trying once again to play the role of international statesman that he loved so much; sending a letter, for example, congratulating Reagan and Gorbachev on the signing of the intermediate-range nuclear forces treaty (and making sure that this was publicized in the local media). Mara also resumed his round of social events to ensure that his photo was constantly in the press. He continued to promote relations with his new allies. France had been presented with a request for development and military assistance in December, and, in mid-January, France announced that it would be providing Fiji with U.S.$12.72 million in development aid in the form of grants and bank credit guarantees. A decision had not yet been reached on whether to provide Fiji with military assistance as well, although, during the week, a French warship paid a five-day 'courtesy call.'

There were strong indications of Fiji's growing ties with another ally when, the following week, the regime announced that it would be sending more military officers for training in Malaysia. Prime Minister Mahathir saw parallels between his own country and Mara's Fiji, and to show his support for the Mara regime, sugar imports from Fiji were increased by 30,000 tons in April. In late February, Mara left for South Korea, stopping briefly in Japan to discuss aid matters. Mara's talks in South Korea focused on bilateral aid and joint business ventures. After his return to Fiji, the regime announced that South Korea was considering soft loans to construct new bridges at Ba and Sigatoka.

Relations having cooled slightly while Rabuka was in power, China responded to the Mara regime by increasing its aid to Fiji, and ten doctors were sent to help overcome the shortage in medical personnel (a further thirty-six doctors were to be provided under a UN Development Program scheme). In February, the Chinese proposed to spend U.S.$100,000 to set up two television stations (to replace the Australian Publishing and Broadcasting project that had been withdrawn earlier) and agreed to fund a four-year F$4 million rural electrification project to include hydroelectric facilities in Ba and on Vanua Levu. Apisai Tora was quick to use the latter for propaganda purposes in an effort to undermine support for the Labour Party in western Viti Levu.

In mid-April, Mara made a visit to Taiwan to strengthen relations and gain additional financial support. The immediate result of the trip was a U.S.$2 million loan on favourable terms for development projects. In early May, Taiwan upgraded its representation in Fiji to the status of a trade mission. It was a move that upset the Chinese representatives, but they took no concrete steps to indicate their displeasure. Meanwhile, Singapore's new ambassador, Joseph Conceicao, stated in mid-March that he hoped for increased co-operation and closer political and economic ties between Singapore and the Mara regime.

On 26 March, Mara left to visit Britain and France. Prime Minister Margaret Thatcher had proven a strong ally, and Mara hoped to gain further economic benefits from both nations. When Mara met with Thatcher on the twenty-ninth, she expressed her desire to see Fiji reinstated in the Commonwealth, offered assistance in drafting Fiji's new constitution, and reaffirmed her government's commitment to continued technical assistance and support for military training programs. In France, Mara praised the role of the French in the Pacific and referred to France as 'an important Pacific country' – an incredible statement, even for Mara, given the situation in New Caledonia at the time. He also signed an economic co-operation agreement under which the French would provide his regime with a F$8.5 million development grant and a F$7.5 million low-interest development loan. While in Paris, Mara also arranged additional aid from the European Economic Community.

Mara's relations with his Pacific island neighbours remained relatively strong. In the case of the Polynesian states, this was to be expected, but the warm reception that he received from the Melanesian states was surprising. Before 1987, Mara had sided with his Polynesian allies on regional issues and had expressed little sympathy for causes of concern to the Melanesian states. However, the Melanesian governments had responded favourably to the racist stance of the Rabuka regime, and this support continued when Mara assumed the prime ministership. In mid-March, Papua New Guinea's foreign minister, Akoki Doi, visited Fiji to see if Mara was interested in joining the Melanesian Bloc formalized in Port Vila, Vanuatu, on 14 March. After meeting Mara and Rabuka, Doi expressed confidence in the regime: 'We were the first country to recognise Fiji's new government and our position is that we will not isolate our brother in the Pacific.'[6] Such warm words did not convince Mara to join the Melanesian Bloc, however, and he remained aligned with his Polynesian kin.

Despite Mara's close ties with France, even the Kanak independence front, the FLNKS, in New Caledonia was sympathetic to the Mara regime. During a visit in early May, Yann Celene Uregei of the FLNKS met with Rabuka and played down the importance of French assistance to the regime. Mara rewarded Uregei for his support by issuing a mild rebuke to the French for shelling a Kanak village, but, for the most part, he continued to support the French position on New Caledonia.

Australia's decision on 19 January 1988 to change the basis for recognizing foreign nations as states rather than looking at new governments on a case-by-case basis was seen as opening the way for the Hawke government's recognition of the Mara regime. Lobbying in favour of restoring ties with Fiji had increased in response to news of France's new aid package which many feared would squeeze Australia out in Fiji. The move was quickly criticized by opponents of the regime in Australia, and Bavadra issued a statement, which was published in Australia, urging the Hawke government not to recognize the Mara regime.[7] But on the twentieth, the acting Australian high commissioner in Suva met with Ganilau, and, on the twenty-second, Prime Minister Hawke confirmed that Australia would recognize 'the state of Fiji' and raised the possibility of a meeting with Mara the following week when both men would be in Sydney to attend a cricket match.

Australia resumed aid to Fiji on 1 March. This included funds for five projects amounting to F$2.25 million, including almost F$1 million for staffing assistance to help overcome personnel shortages. The aid money was an important help to the Mara regime, especially in its efforts to improve its image in rural areas through the use of patronage; but, on a more basic level, it also enabled the regime to carry out many functions that had been impaired through widespread resignations. Additional Australian aid was used by the regime to expand Fiji Forest Industries and to pay off its debts to native landowners on Vanua Levu, thereby hopefully defusing a situation that had become a political problem for the regime.

Indicative of Australia's propensity to ignore the repressive and racist nature of the regime, the new Australian ambassador to Fiji, Robert Cott, stated on 1 April that 'there have been clear signals that the government intends to assure economic stability and progress for the country. It has set guidelines for a return to constitutional rule. It is engaged in the processes of consultation which would lead to elections in the next two years.'

The ambassador's statement came only a little over a week after Bavadra had flown to Australia to attend a conference of progressive parties in the South Pacific which was sponsored by the Australian Labor Party. After Bavadra became president of the newly formed South Pacific Progressive Parties Association, Hawke and Hayden were keen to have their photos taken with him and to be seen holding talks with him (one hour in Canberra). It was a far cry from earlier days when both men had sought to avoid contact for fear of offending the Mara/Rabuka regimes. The move undoubtedly had something to do with Hawke's desire to placate the left of his own party around the time of the disastrous New South Wales state election. But, as indicated by the new ambassador's statement, it did not indicate a substantive change in the government's policy of tacit support for Mara.

After his return to Fiji, Bavadra responded to the Australian ambassador by calling on Australia to cut aid to the Mara regime and on the regime itself to set a timetable for the restoration of democracy. His call was ignored. On 26 May, Minister of Finance Kamikamica led a delegation to Australia to discuss an additional aid package of F$12 million. The Australian government agreed to this in late August as part of a 'coup rehabilitation' package.

Relations between New Zealand and the Mara regime were slower to warm, but gradually they too improved. After a visit to Fiji, the New Zealand minister for Pacific island affairs announced that discussions with the Mara regime had 'progressed towards a point where New Zealand could restore full links' and aid was partially restored with payment of u.s.$340,000 to assist Fiji's pine industry. Prime Minister Lange, however, told the press that New Zealand would wait until the format of the new constitution was known before making its decision about full restoration of ties. A short time later, New Zealand took steps to restore the balance of its aid that had been suspended over the past twelve months, amounting to a further F$1.8 million. Bavadra left for a visit to New Zealand on 7 April in an effort to lobby for continued support. Meetings were held with Prime Minister Lange and Minister of Foreign Affairs Russell Marshall and some assurances were given, but it was obvious that New Zealand was moving towards full restoration of relations with Fiji as well.

During the third week of January. a representative of the u.s. government announced in Singapore that the United States wanted to move as quickly as possible to normalize relations with the Mara regime and, in particular, to resume aid. Then, on 26 February, the u.s. government informed the press that its ambassador designate, Leonard Rochwarger (another political appointee from upstate New York), was to arrive in Fiji on 10 March. Before setting out for Fiji, Rochwarger praised Fiji as 'a beautiful country with a long tradition of constitutional democratic rule and ethnic cooperation' and stated that he was encouraged by the military's return to the barracks. A few days later he was sworn in as the new ambassador by Ganilau, who, at the same time, also swore in the new Israeli ambassador.

Thus, while Fiji's traditional Western allies continued to express disapproval of the regime, gradually they were coming to learn to live with it. Perhaps the most important motivating factor was geopolitical, that is, whether they liked the government in power or not, these countries did not feel that they could afford to ignore the state of Fiji. The Australians, in particular, did not like the regime's growing ties with France. Beyond this was the general fear that had also made the Western powers wary of the foreign policy objectives of the Fiji Labour Party, that is, the fear of a Fiji that was too independent. The desire of the Western allies, with the possible exception of France, was to keep Fiji firmly within its traditional geopolitical position. From the perspective of the Mara regime, however, improved relations with these countries did not imply that it should turn away from those who had supported it initially. For the regime, it was not an 'either/or' situation but rather one of expanding the range of potential aid donors to make the regime's survival more likely.

Mara's only remaining immediate trouble spot overseas was with the international union bodies. A nine-member union delegation from the International Confederation of Free Trade Unions (ICFTU), including Simon Crean from Australia and Ken Douglas from New Zealand, arrived in Suva on 14 January for a three-day visit to report on the state of union rights in Fiji. As expected, the mission recommended that trade bans not be reimposed, but that the situation continue to be monitored. At the World ICFTU Congress in Melbourne in the middle of March, a threat was issued to renew union bans unless the Mara regime improved conditions for Fijian unions. The regime's minister for employment and industrial relations, Taniela Veitata, called the ICFTU statement 'a declaration of war.'

POLITICAL CONSOLIDATION AND OPPOSITION

On 14 January Mara let it be known that there would be no elections before 1989 at the earliest. Meanwhile, there remained the matter of creating a new constitution. Mara announced his cabinet committee to prepare a new draft constitution on 23 February. Significantly, the committee was to base its proposal on the recommendations presented by the Great Council of Chiefs, Constitutional Review Committee, and Fiji Military Forces. Comprised of staunch Mara loyalists, the twelve-member committee was headed by William Toganivalu, the minister for lands and mineral resources, who was Mara's 'man in Tailevu,' responsible for overcoming opposition in that province.

The committee held its first meeting on 2 March. The majority of committee members favoured a single-chamber parliament of sixty-six or seventy members (this including four non-voting appointees of the prime minister), all elected on a communal basis: 36 Fijian, 22

Indian, and 8 General Elector, with 28 of the Fijian seats being drawn from the Provincial Councils, and 4 of the Indian seats reserved for Muslims. This proposal was opposed by the 'angry faction' of the Taukei since it did not include clauses increasing native Fijian representation so as to guarantee that any future government would have a native Fijian majority.

After the first coup, Mara had been extremely upset when he lost control of the Great Council of Chiefs. Extremists within the Taukei Movement had subsequently sought to bolster the power of the Great Council of Chiefs to enhance their own position and, in part, keep Mara from regaining power. Mara now realized that it was essential for him to ensure his complete dominance over the Great Council of Chiefs in order to consolidate his power.

In early February, Mara's minister for Fijian affairs, Colonel Vatiliai Navunisaravai, announced plans to revamp the Great Council of Chiefs. He argued that since the 1970 constitution had been abrogated, the present Great Council of Chiefs had no legal standing. Mara planned on using this situation as an opportunity to reduce the number of members of the council from its present 154 to fifty-one and to concentrate power in the hands of the high chiefs, while reducing the influence of lesser chiefs. Navunisaravai argued that in growing from its original forty members at the time of independence, the council had become unwieldy and that commoners had assumed too prominent a role. 'While we appreciate the contributions made by commoners to the Great Council of Chiefs,' Col. Navunisaravai stated, 'it is becoming increasingly obvious that the chiefs can be outnumbered. What we want is for the commoners to act as advisers while the decision-making is left entirely to the chiefs.' What was not mentioned, of course, was that it had grown in size through Mara's own patronage.

Grasping its implications, the extremists within the Taukei Movement were quick to denounce the proposal. Taukei Movement leader Kubuabola told the press that 'the Alliance government is trying to play around with the composition of the Great Council of Chiefs so that it becomes easier for them to promulgate their constitution.' He noted that at no point since the April 1987 election had the Alliance Party been given a mandate to run the country. Rather, he argued, the Great Council of Chiefs had been given the mandate. The Taukei Movement contended that the existing Great Council of Chiefs was legal and that no changes should be made to its composition until a new constitution was in place. Wary of Mara's initiative, a Taukei spokesman stated: 'We see ourselves as the only meaningful opposition to government at the moment safeguarding Fijian interests.'

In an effort to present itself as a respectable opposition, the Taukei later issued a fifteen-point policy declaration, claiming that its two main aims were constitutional reform and support for the regime's plans to stabilize the economy. But there were lingering questions about the movement's sincerity, especially since, only days before, its members had been blamed for placing a bomb under the house of Lt. Col. Ratu Tomasi Korovakaturaga – Ganilau's son, commander of the Northern Division, and manager of the Labasa sugar mill. There were also rumours that Taukei extremists were seeking to secure arms. Such opposition reflected a growing sense of disillusion among Taukei and Nationalist followers who felt that Rabuka had sold out to the chiefly oligarchy and who were also angered to see Mara and his cronies reestablishing themselves in power.

While attending a party hosted by conservative American multimillionaire Malcolm Forbes on his island of Laucala on 13 March, Mara made a speech that delighted cynics. Praising Forbes for his support of the regime, Mara assured those gathered on the island 'that the stability of Fiji is assured' and that 'there will not be a third coup' before handing over the government in two years' time.[8] Speaking on behalf of the Taukei Movement, Kubuabola commented: 'Reading between the lines of his statement, one cannot help but see the subtle insinuation that he seems to know when coups are likely to take place.'[9] The following week the Taukei Movement issued a statement calling on the Mara regime to step down and hand over the government to the Great Council of Chiefs: 'As far as we are concerned, Ratu Mara, along with those he could work with, have had 20 years to deliver their promises, but they have failed miserably.'

The regime announced creation of a National Flag and Anthem Committee on 7 March to come up with a new flag and anthem for the republic. As was now common, the committee's membership was made up entirely of Alliance Party supporters. To the dismay of many, its secretary was to be Eliki Bomani, who earlier had been at the centre of a scandal involving compensation payments by the Alliance Party government.

Bavadra's response to Mara's talk of no more coups came in a statement in which he noted that political stability could only be achieved with the participation of the Labour-NFP coalition. Drawing attention to the extent to which the military was 'entrenching itself in the political and civilian life of the nation,' Bavadra stated that the people will only believe that there will be no more coups when steps are taken to reduce the size of the military.

There was ample evidence to support Bavadra's claim of growing military involvement in civilian life. And the size of the army itself remained at close to eight thousand, with new recruits continuing to be inducted. The army was engaged in numerous development projects around the country. Thus, in Labasa, in an effort to improve the regime's image in the Indo-Fijian community, troops were being used to build the Bulileka Sanatan Dharam Primary School. The army had become particularly active in the eastern outer islands. In February, for example, soldiers were sent to the island of Totoya, in the Lau Group, at the request of islanders, to hunt wild cattle and pigs. Ex-soldiers had long played an important role in Fiji's business community. This was even more evident now. In mid-February the Carpenters Group announced that former chief of operations, Lt. Col. Edward Tuivanuqvou, was to become a division manager. Other former military officers were also much in evidence. Colonel Paul Manueli, an Alliance Party stalwart, was appointed chairman of the National Bank of Fiji on 22 March.

The military also continued with its Operation Yavoto, which was ostensibly aimed at rooting out corruption. By and large this meant 'investigating' perceived enemies of the regime, but the investigators also found themselves confronted with the problem of the Hurricane Relief Committee and its close association with Mara and other members of his regime. Thus, they uncovered one instance in the Navosa district where 440 of 660 houses, supposedly supplied as part of a relief program, had never materialized. The Taukei Movement urged the army to continue with its investigations of corruption, pointing to the collapse of the Native Land Development Corporation in particular. As with the Hurricane Relief Committee, however, the situation in the Native Land Development Corporation once again implicated those associated with Mara, and Taukei concern over corruption highlighted the extent to which extremist members of the Taukei Movement saw Mara, as much as the Coalition, as 'the enemy.' Such sentiments were shared by some army officers as well. In fact, on 31 March, a couple of officers presented a paper to other high-ranking officers in the army which recommended that Mara and Ganilau be removed. Although a majority of officers did not support the proposal, it served to point to the continuing tension between Mara and the military.

Both Mara and Rabuka were concerned with opposition to the regime within the army, and a number of soldiers were posted in the Ministry of Foreign Affairs in order to neutralize possible sources of friction in the military. The best example of this practice was the appointment of the former commander of the military, Brig. Gen. Epeli Nailatikau, as ambassador to the United Kingdom, in February. At around the same time, the regime had Col. Pio Wong, who was seen as an extremist, posted to the ministry's Suva office. It was also decided to post Lt. Col. Isikia Savua, who was chief-of-staff of the army, to the United Nations and to replace him with Lt. Col. George Konrote (Wong was later posted back to the army).

Although the most active opposition to Mara came from the Coalition and Taukei extremists, Mara's uneasy alliance with the Vunivalu, Ratu George Cakobau, and other chiefs of Tailevu Province simmered in the background, and disagreements surfaced again in April. On 19 April, Ratu George's son, Ratu Epenisa Cakobau, expressed concern that Mara had gone to London to discuss restoring links with the Crown without discussing the matter with Ratu George. He was disturbed, moreover, by Mara's suggestion of using the title Tui Viti for the Queen, a title which Epenisa said belonged to his father. A couple of days later, Epenisa Cakobau was suspended without pay from his post as assistant Roko Tui Tailevu (assistant to the chief provincial officer). The Ministry of Fijian Affairs accused Epenisa of 'questioning the ability of the Prime Minister and President to lead the country.' Epenisa responded by asking the ministry to withdraw the charges and stated that his suspension was a breach of the standing orders of the ministry.

When the Tailevu Council met on the twenty-eighth, there was heated debate over the suspension of Epenisa Cakobau. Pro-Mara forces only managed to keep things under control because the council meeting was chaired by Mara ally, William Toganivalu.[10] Epenisa Cakobau then took the Fijian Affairs Board to court (represented by Vijaya Parmanandan), and on 27 May the High Court ruled that the board had no power to suspend him.

Meanwhile, the chiefs of Lau, Macuata, Bua, and Cakaudrove gathered at Somosomo in early April in a show of solidarity to install Ganilau as the Tui Cakau (the paramount chief of the Tovata Confederacy to which they belonged). This move had been initiated shortly before the May coup and subsequently had served to fuel suspicion of Ganilau's involvement in the coup. In an interesting development shortly before the installation, members of the chiefly mataqali of Cakaudrove (the Valelevu mataqali) requested that Ganilau resign as president after his installation and come home to his lineage. Ganilau turned down the request, but many were curious as to what had prompted it. Over one thousand people gathered at Somosomo for the ceremony which was intended to unify the eastern chiefs behind the regime, and most of those attending were transported at government expense. The chiefs of Lau were led by Finau Mara, whose father continued in his efforts to bolster support for his son.

The Tailevu Provincial Council meeting had taken place shortly before the *Bose ni turaga* (chiefs) were to meet in Tailevu Province to rubber-stamp Mara's proposed changes in the constitution and Council of Chiefs. Upset in general by his treatment by Mara and specifically by the way the regime had treated his son, on 30 April, George Cakobau sent a letter to Ganilau stating that he did not approve of the Bose ni turaga meeting being held in Tailevu. The letter was ignored and the meeting went ahead as scheduled.

As the chiefs arrived at Lodoni on 2 May, troops patrolled the area in case pro-Cakobau forces attempted to block the roads or cause some other form of disturbance. George Cakobau did not attend the meeting because of 'the grave discourtesy and disrespect' shown to him and his son. Epenisa Cakobau claimed that the chief leading the Tailevu delegation, Ratu Tu'uakitau Cokanauto, had no right to do so since this was the prerogative of the Vunivalu.

Ganilau opened the meeting and praised the chiefs for supporting him in 'leading the country back to normalcy.' One of the more interesting developments was a proposal by a group of western chiefs to establish a fourth confederacy in the west, as the existing Burebasaga, Kubuna, and Tovata confederacies represented eastern chiefly interests. The previous week, at a meeting of the Ba Provincial Council, there had been a proposal to create such a confederacy – to be known as Yasayasa Vakara – by having the western region break away from the Kubuna and Burebasaga confederacies. The initiative was not a new one, having first been proposed by Ratu Napolioni Dawai in 1968 (when it was voted down), and this time it was motivated by the desire of some of the western chiefs to improve their position in negotiations with the regime. The pro-Mara forces in the west led by the Tui Vuda, Ratu Josaia Tavaigia, however, were able to block the proposal from coming up for discussion at the Lodoni meeting.

His henchmen having cleared the way, Mara addressed the meeting on the fourth. He gave his, by now, standard reasons for changing the 1970 constitution and mentioned the need to rejoin the Commonwealth before links with the Crown could be reestablished. As expected, the chiefs pledged their support for the regime. In addition, the Tailevu delegation deplored the actions of Epenisa Cakobau and others, who they accused of 'misleading' George Cakobau.

The chiefs approved the plan for a two-tiered Great Council of Chiefs with power concentrated in the hands of the oligarchy. Next, the chiefs endorsed the July 1987 Great Council of Chiefs proposal for a seventy-one-member, single-chamber parliament which effec-

tively disenfranchised both Indo-Fijians and native Fijian commoners. The stage now appeared to be set to impose a form of centralized chiefly rule over Fiji. Columnist Mosese Velia, himself a native
Fijian, wrote of these developments: 'Now with the chiefs committed to having a constitution rigidly racial in complexion, with Fijians
holding power out of proportion to their numbers in the population,
it seems we are locked into a confrontation situation, where the
immigrant Indians, now the majority group, cannot help but
bemoan the injustice of it.'[11]

Bavadra criticized Mara's speech as 'rife with contradictions' and
pointed to its 'multiracial rhetoric' which belied the fact that he was
pushing for complete control by native Fijian chiefs. He also felt that
Mara had little chance of restoring links with the Commonwealth
and the Queen under the proposed constitution. In a demonstration
of the rather twisted logic that was predominant in the regime, the
minister of information, Josefata Kamikamica, responded on Mara's
behalf, stating that 'Dr. Bavadra is living in the past and not facing
the realities of the present.' 'As a Fijian,' he continued, 'Dr. Bavadra
should respect the decisions on the new constitution rendered by
the Great Council of Chiefs.'

Problems on Rotuma also continued to plague the regime. Secessionist leader Gagaj Sau Lagfatmaro (otherwise known as Henry
Gibson) had been unsuccessfully seeking overseas support in New
Zealand and Tonga, accompanied by lawyer Tevita Fa. Among the
initiatives was a proposal that Rotuma become a protectorate of
New Zealand. This, however, was rejected by Prime Minister Lange.
Using the constitutions of Niue and the Cook Islands for models, Fa
had drafted a constitution for an independent Rotuma. Speaking
from Tonga, on 8 May he announced that Rotuma was to secede on
Friday the fourteenth. On the tenth, thirty soldiers were dispatched
to Rotuma, and seven Rotuman chiefs were arrested and charged
with sedition.

The Sunday bans remained a thorny issue and they were opposed
by many. In mid-March, the Fiji Council of Churches called on the
regime to revoke the bans: 'Worship cannot be enforced by threat of
punishment and force of arms.' In March, the army set up roadblocks around Suva to stop people from breaching the Sunday Ordinance Decree. Nevertheless, under growing pressure, Rabuka
hinted in late April that the Sunday bans might be relaxed, and on 11
May the regime altered the ordinance to allow rice and cane transport, family picnics, pharmacies to remain open, and the holding of
funerals. For the militants, many of whom were fundamentalist
Christians, the Sunday bans had assumed considerable symbolic

significance in their pursuit of a Taukei Fiji. For them, even a partial lifting of the bans was too much, and, in protest, three thousand Methodist fundamentalists staged a march in Suva. Rabuka stood by Mara on the lifting of the bans, in a show of solidarity with the oligarchy, while the remaining Taukei split once again. To the surprise of many, one of the original ringleaders at the time of the May coup, Vesikula, held discussions with Bavadra and indicated that he had been wrong to have sided with Mara. The remaining militants were led by the Reverend Manasa Lasaro, who was joined by Butadroka. The Lasaro-Butadroka group now formed the militant vanguard, and the Methodist church became their primary battleground.

Harassment of Labour Party and National Federation Party supporters by the military and police was widespread. The regime had allowed Bavadra, his wife, and a few of his colleagues to travel overseas and to return to Fiji, but the freedom to travel had not been restored, and it remained necessary to ask for permission. Labour-NFP coalition member Navin Patel was prevented from leaving the country in mid-April since his name was on the 'blacklist,' although he was later allowed to board a plane. In April, the NFP branch in Ba was denied permission to hold a meeting. On 9 May, former Bavadra adviser Richard Naidu was barred from returning to Fiji.

Mara had allowed Fiji's unions to continue to function, largely to avoid further censure from overseas unions and to assist in restoring relations with Australia and New Zealand. But harassment of Fiji's trade unions and trade unionists had not ended. As was noted above, the regime had sought to divide the Fiji Public Service Association along ethnic lines. The Viti Civil Servants Association was recognized by the Public Service Commission on 24 March (having been registered in October 1987). It was to cater to native Fijian, Rotuman, and Banaban public servants. Its president, Dr. Filimone Wainiqolo, argued that 'The FPSA [Fiji Public Service Association] is too closely affiliated with the FTUC [Fiji Trades Union Congress] and FLP [Fiji Labour Party].'[12] Similarly, supporters of the regime formed the Fiji Sugar Association in late March and sought to recruit native Fijian and General Elector workers in the industry.

Unions were also suffering from loss of membership due to an employment situation in which many members had lost their jobs and in which the newly created jobs in the garment and other industries were not unionized. At the annual general meeting of the National Union of Factory Workers in April, union general secretary James Raman noted that since the first coup the union's membership had dropped from about five thousand to around three thousand.

On the positive side, meetings began in April between the Central Planning Office, the Fiji Employers' Consultative Association, and the Fiji Trades Union Congress to 'map out a working relationship.' And on 24 May the regime backed down on the freeze and announced that it would be replaced with wage guidelines in June.

At its annual general meeting on 8 April, Fiji Public Service Association members voted to give the executive a strike mandate over the pay freeze and the 15 per cent pay cut. As in other recent meetings, Mara sought to run candidates against union general secretary Mahendra Chaudhry (who had also replaced Raman as general secretary of the Fiji Trades Union Congress) and his allies in an effort to split the union along ethnic lines. A short time before, the regime had recognized the Viti Civil Servants Association which provided native Fijians with an alternative to the Fiji Public Service Association. The leader of the regime's union sought to run against Chaudhry, but his candidacy was declared invalid. The Mara faction, however, was able to run a candidate against Fiji Public Service Association president Dhriendra Singh. Singh won by a vote of 1,965 to 772 – a safe margin, but the lowest margin of victory yet recorded, indicating the extent to which Mara had succeeded in splitting the union.

Moves were afoot by Mara and his supporters to entrench ethnic distinctions even further within the government. In mid-April, David Pickering, the minister for tourism, civil aviation and energy, directed statutory bodies in his ministry to ensure that native Fijians and Rotumans constituted 50 per cent of their staff. This was in accordance with the regime's Decree No. 7 and was made easier in the wake of mass resignations since the first coup, although it did mean waiving concern for qualifications. The desire to help Mara's cronies, while further entrenching the communal nature of Fijian society, was also evident in moves to promote native Fijian participation in business by establishing guidelines for native Fijian involvement. On 20 April, the Ministry of Trade and Commerce announced that the national rice import quota would be reserved for companies with at least 50 per cent native Fijian ownership.

Attempts by the regime to present a multiracial image met with little success, and Mara found it difficult to attract Indo-Fijian supporters beyond the handful of opportunists who had been with him from the start. Irene Narayan remained the most prominent of these. Thus, in one speech in early March she had referred to Rabuka as 'a sensible, kind-hearted and honest man.' When she was invited to address the Sanatan Dharam convention, which was an important Hindu organization, on 2 April, many of its members announced that they would boycott the meeting, and Narayan sought to save face by cancelling at the last minute because of 'ill health.'

There were worrisome signs in the way the judicial system was being reorganized. The regime announced plans to abolish the supreme court and increase the jurisdiction of local magistrates, thereby putting judicial matters more firmly in the hands of those who were most likely to be biased towards the regime. Among the other initiatives of the regime was a move to license the nation's media, with the warning that the licenses would be revoked for 'irresponsible reporting.' Mara also gave the minister for housing and urban development the power to appoint new city and town councillors. The minister justified the suspension of council elections by citing the need for 'by-passing the political confrontation anticipated with such elections at this stage of Fiji's recovery.' The regime also announced on 10 March that it was amending the Sugar Industry Act to delay the election of new officers in the Sugar Cane Growers Council for one year – in effect, to allow Siddiq Koya and his associates to stay in power. Taking advantage of the regime's support, the Sugar Cane Growers Council passed a record F$614,530 budget in late August, most of which was to go for salaries and members' expenses.

The University of the South Pacific continued to be a target of the regime, which viewed the university as a centre of Labour Party support. In mid-February, one expatriate lecturer who had been critical of the regime, Robbie Robertson, was ordered to leave the country. The propaganda film about Rabuka, *Operation Surprise*, produced by right-wing interests in Australia, was premiered in Suva on 20 April, following the release of the associated book about his exploits, *Rabuka: No Other Way*.[13] Both, essentially, were part of the attempt to build a Rabuka cult not unlike that built around Sukuna. At the film's première, seven protesters were carted off by police. On 21 April, a university student was detained and questioned for three hours for taking notes at a screening of *Operation Surprise* and told not to use the material for making statements against the regime. While the Rabuka book was being heavily promoted, publication of a slender volume by a handful of Labour Party supporters at the university, entitled *Coup and Crisis: Fiji a Year Later*, resulted in the university coming under pressure from the regime to stop its instructors from engaging in such activities.[14]

The regime prepared for the first anniversary of the 14 May coup with a military buildup. All territorials were called up on the twelfth. Meanwhile, on the thirteenth, Mara celebrated his sixty-eighth birthday – and, clearly, he had a great deal to celebrate that year –

and Rabuka opened a new military wing of the Tamavua Hospital. On the day of the anniversary, Rabuka held a military parade at Queen Elizabeth Barracks where he handed out service medals. In his address at the parade, Rabuka said once again that the coup had been the will of God and that its aim had been the protection of native Fijian interests.

Bavadra marked the occasion with a prayer meeting led by Rev. Paula Niukula, former president of the Methodist church, in his village of Viseisei. He also published an 'Address to the Nation' on the state of Fiji one year after his government had been overthrown (see Appendix B). There was no declaration of secession in Rotuma, as had been planned, since many of the leaders were under arrest and security forces remained on the island. There were, however, other quiet protest demonstrations held around the country to mark the anniversay. In the morning, a group of protesters began to gather at Sukuna Park in Suva. Police immediately arrested eighteen of them, including individuals from the university, the anti-nuclear movement, the church, and legal profession, and some teachers. Some of the protesters had a history of political activism but there were also several ordinary citizens with no prior involvement in political activities. Others involved in the protest were arrested later in the day.

On 16 May, the Fiji Law Society represented those charged. Speaking on behalf of the Law Society, John Falvey referred to the police actions as a 'mindless exercise of authority.'[15] The eighteen protesters were released without bail 'on condition that they did not take part in any protest meetings against the government or any political meetings until the case had been heard.' The presence of Falvey at the hearing, Mara's close confidant for decades, served to highlight the isolation of the regime.

MARA'S TRIUMPH?

After his initial successes, by mid-1988, things seemed to have stalled for Mara. True, the economy continued to recover, mainly as a result of sugar export earnings, and many of Mara's cronies began to reap the profits brought about by Mara's return, but, politically, he and his allies seemed unable to consolidate their position. Not only did the Coalition-based opposition remain, but tribal rifts and communal militants continued to plague the regime, and Rabuka proved adept at expanding and consolidating his own position.

Rather than assuming a secondary position under Mara, Rabuka continued to wield considerable power. Since the May 1987 coup, the army had grown in size from around 2,500 to some 8,000, until it was larger than the civilian public service. Moreover, while Mara's position stagnated, the military expanded its presence within Fijian society. Pursuing what was sometimes referred to as an 'Indonesian model,' the army engaged in anti-corruption drives, a host of civic activities in native Fijian villages, and promoted notions of the civic role of the military.

The regime's struggle with its opponents took an important turn the first week of June 1988 when Australian authorities in Sydney announced that they had discovered a large shipment of arms bound for Fiji.[16] It was immediately assumed that the arms were intended for opponents of the Mara-Rabuka regime. Three Fijian nationals were held and a search was launched for two others, including an arms merchant by the name of Mohammed Kahan. In Fiji, the authorities claimed that the arms found in Sydney were linked to an earlier shipment of twelve tons of Czechoslovakian-made armaments that had been shipped into Fiji via Lautoka in April. One crate was recovered but two others were supposedly missing.

On the night of Sunday, 5 June, the police and army launched a series of raids in western Viti Levu. They claimed to have discovered fourteen machine-guns and ninety-seven AK-47 rifles on six properties. On Monday, the search turned to Suva, where twenty-eight people were taken in for questioning, including one Labour Party and one NFP parliamentarian. Then on Tuesday, twenty-one individuals were charged in connection with arms smuggling and held without bail. Among those arrested was Labour Party activist and longtime Mara foe, Ratu Mosese Tuisawau. During the following week, more than one hundred people were taken in for questioning, including Mahendra Chaudhry who was held for twenty-nine hours, and dozens of homes were raided (and, in several cases, looted). The arms search then moved to Labasa, where more Labour Party and NFP supporters were harassed.

The hysteria drummed up by the regime over the arms culminated in promulgation of an Internal Security Decree on 16 June. The decree was modelled on Singapore's Internal Security Decree and provided for life imprisonment for anyone found to be in possession of illegal arms, ammunition, and explosives. A week later, ten people were arrested under the new decree. These included Labour Party lawyer Tevita Fa, the secretary of the Fiji Law Society, and university lecturer Som Prakash, who recently had published a critical review of Dean and Ritova's book, *Rabuka: No Other Way*. Rather than being individuals seriously suspected of arms smuggling, these were simply prominent opponents of the regime.

On 23 June, the regime announced a one-month amnesty for anyone turning in illegal arms – a deadline that was later extended until 5 September. Only small quantities of weapons and bullets not associated with the arms shipment were reported to have been turned in until, on 12 July, the army announced that it had received nineteen assault rifles and a few boxes of grenades which, it claimed, were part of an arms shipment. The weapons were presented but further details were sketchy. In the meantime, the regime arrested six nationals and a West German tourist on the suspicion that they were paid mercenaries, while finally releasing Tuisawau and Prakash.

After the initial announcement that arms had been smuggled into Fiji, Bavadra issued a statement denying that the Labour Party had anything to do with it. In fact, there was widespread speculation within Fiji that the whole episode had been cooked up by the regime to legitimate a crackdown on Labour-NFP supporters. The pattern of arrests added to this suspicion as did the continued 'failure' of the regime to find the missing arms. It was apparent that the mercenary scare had no basis in fact, and the small arms cache 'discovered' on 12 July appeared to have been planted by individuals associated with the regime.

Speculation was rampant as to who was involved in the scheme. Among those suspected were the Israelis (who were assisting the regime), various members of the Taukei Movement, and Rabuka himself. But there was no firm evidence one way or another. Subsequently, Mohammed Kahan claimed that the arms had been purchased with the assistance of Adnan Khashoggi, with whom Mara had prior dealings, on behalf of Mara loyalists in their struggle against Rabuka. In the meantime, the regime extended the amnesty, stepped up raids on people's houses, and left the Internal Security Decree in place – adding yet another piece to the structure of authoritarian rule.

In the midst of the crackdown, leaders of the two Taukei factions met in an effort to reunite the movement. Taukei Movement leader Vesikula visited military officers in early June to discuss unification. A meeting of the factions on 18 June, however, ended in a deadlock, and plans for a Taukei march in Suva the following week were dropped as relations between Taukei extremists and the regime remained strained.

Unease among backers of the regime spread when prominent Alliance Party and Taukei member Jone Veisamasama was found dead on 22 July. The police reported that he had 'accidently shot himself' but word from the coroner's office was that he had been shot in the back. Members of Apisai Tora's family were seen racing away from their home near Nadi not too long after the murder, apparently fearful that Tora too might be the target of an assassin. A little later, police picked up coup 'groupies' Fred Caine and Tony Stephens, who they suspected of involvement in the murder. Caine was beaten during the course of interrogation, but neither man was charged in connection with Veisamasama's death. On 1 September the two men were sentenced to fifteen months in jail for possession of illegal arms and ammunition – far less than the maximum penalty of life imprisonment – and Caine, smiling as he left the courtroom, had his sentence suspended. Amidst recollections of the deaths of Jona Qio and David Toganivalu, there was once again widespread speculation about power struggles among those associated with the regime, but few facts.

A row erupted in mid-August when the *Fiji Times* ran an interview with Rabuka which it had received over the wire from New Zealand. In the article, Rabuka was quoted as saying about Mara that 'the Prime Minister is not calling the shots.'[17] The newspaper's editor, Vijendra Kumar, was awakened at 2:30 A.M. and taken in for questioning by the military. Rabuka denied that he had made the statement and apologized to the cabinet, and later it appeared as if there had been an error and that 'not' should have read 'now.' Whether true or false, the statement attributed to Rabuka further added to speculation in Fiji that Mara's power was once again on the wane and that the military was reasserting control of the government behind a civilian mask.

The 'conspirators' charged in the Lautoka gun-smuggling case were eventually released, and the scheme seemed to have done little to dampen opposition. The Internal Security Decree was lifted on 17 November, amidst rumours of a third coup arising out of military 'exercises' around Suva. Such rumours had become commonplace, as the military sought to flex its muscle periodically in a seeming effort to remind everyone, including members of the oligarchy, that it was still a force with which to be reckoned. The point was brought home in December when Rabuka, speaking at a village meeting, warned that the army would resume control unless satisfactory progress was made in implementing the proposed constitution, a constitution which many considered racist.

In fact, the regime was having unexpected difficulty with its new constitution. Mara had named a fourteen-member committee on 15 September to tour the country to promote the new constitution. But after only a few meetings, it was obvious that there was considerable disagreement. Among native Fijian commoners, many cared little for the prospect of their own disenfranchisement, while others felt that the draft still did not go far enough in disenfranchising Indo-Fijians.

The regime decided to ease the Sunday bans further on 18 December to allow cane milling, general farming activities, and the operation of public transportation. Led by Lasaro and Butadroka, militant Methodists set up roadblocks around Suva in protest. They even held up Mara's wife, Adi Lala, on her way to visit Mara, who had been hospitalized with a heart complaint. This time Rabuka's response was different. Rabuka met with Lasaro the following day and told those present that he was in accord with Lasaro's views. After a cabinet meeting, Rabuka's support for Lasaro was denied, and a potential rift between Rabuka and Mara was once again patched over. When the militants organized further roadblocks on 25 December, 150 were arrested, including Lasaro.

The situation did not remain quiet for long and on 3 February 1989, Lasaro and his followers staged a coup of their own seizing the Methodist headquarters in Suva and declaring church president Josateki Koroi deposed. Koroi and many church leaders had been critical of the May coup and subsequent acts by the regime; from a pillar of support for the oligarchy, the church hierarchy had become a moderate but vocal critic. But the oligarchy had been loath to take on the church leadership openly: a task it left for the lower ranks of fundamentalist preachers aligned with the Taukei. As it broke with the Taukei, however, the oligarchy placed itelf in a very weak position in its relations with the church and created an opportunity for the militants to assert their position. Given the overwhelming importance of the Christian churches in the native Fijian community, this posed a serious problem for the oligarchy.

In April, faced with so many political difficulties, Mara fell back on another of his standard ploys. On 12 April he announced that he might step down by the end of the year, setting the stage for his loyal followers to plead with him to stay on as leader, to stay on 'for the good of the nation.'[18] Mara's announcement occurred at a time when criticism of the proposed constitution had become increasingly widespread, with even the army saying it had some reservations. After mid-April, the most vocal and publicized criticism came from several provincial councils and the Soqosoqo Vakamarama. They argued for a delay of three more years before implementing the changes, while the regime, under Mara's leadership, prepared the nation for a smooth transition. Bavadra claimed that this was part of an orchestrated campaign by Mara forces for Mara to stay on.

Weight was added to Bavadra's allegation when, as calls for delay became more persistent, Mara announced that he was taking a one-month holiday in August.

Mara's 'threat' to resign served to strengthen his position, but it did not put an end to his problems with Lasaro and Rabuka. Turning to Lasaro first, Methodist president Koroi took the matter of the headship of the church to court, and the court ruled in his favour against Lasaro. Lasaro ignored the court decision, moving the Methodists ever closer to a split. By now it seemed obvious to the oligarchy that Lasaro had emerged as an important political figure and one with whom Rabuka had sympathies. In an effort to defuse the situation, Ganilau and Mara agreed to accompany Rabuka to visit Lasaro to receive a petition from him. But Lasaro and his followers continued to press for control of the church. There were further roadblocks in July, and Lasaro was given a six-month jail sentence. Rabuka visited Lasaro in jail on 10 August, and two days later, without discussing the matter with cabinet, Rabuka ordered Lasaro and fifty-six of his followers released, giving as his reason a desire to avoid escalation of tensions.

But the newly freed Lasaro was in no mood to try to resolve his differences with Koroi and other church leaders, nor with the oligarchy. The annual conference of the Methodist church was due to be held later in August, and Lasaro threatened to hold a separate conference. With Mara expressing exasperation and Ganilau urging reconciliation, Koroi and his followers sought to hold a series of meetings with the Lasaro forces. Finally, the two groups did come together at a single conference, but the outcome proved a disaster for the moderates. Koroi escaped a vote of no confidence, but Lasaro emerged from the conference with his supporters in a dominant position and himself in full control of the key office of general secretary.[19]

Rabuka's freeing of Lasaro in early August was only one of a series of independent acts on his part that placed further strain on his alliance with Mara. Rabuka met with Mara and Ganilau in June 1989 and presented them with a program drawn up by senior military officers that reiterated an earlier notion of his for the military to run the state for the next ten to fifteen years.[20] During this period of rule, the military would oversee the implementation of 'a program of Fijian Democratic Socialism' that would consolidate chiefly and military power. The report represented the most extreme proposal put forward by Rabuka to date. It called for executing opponents of the regime, abolishing the trade union movement, eliminating opposition within the church and judiciary, and taking other measures to strengthen the position of the military and the Great Council of Chiefs. His plan was to place the proposal before the Great Council of Chiefs for implementation in December 1989.

Rabuka's plan may well have represented nothing more than a bargaining chip for the military, for past experience had demonstrated the problems he faced when acting unilaterally. It is important to recognize the continued insecurity of both Mara and Rabuka in the face of their repeated failure to gain a secure hold over state power. Both men had been trying to achieve such security for almost two years and it had proven elusive. Rabuka's plan was also of some potential use to Mara, in that it allowed him to resort to another of his longstanding ploys – 'let me have my way or look at what you will get.'

In September, pro-Mara forces stepped up their campaign for Mara to stay on beyond 5 December. On 28 September, Mara announced that he would indeed stay on beyond December, until new elections were held. But he would only do so if Rabuka would agree to one of three options: (1) resign from the cabinet to serve only as commander of the military, (2) retain his military command and agree to restrict his cabinet portfolio solely to military affairs, or (3) resign his military commission and accept a position as one of two deputy prime ministers. Apparently, Rabuka at first sought to hold on to his military command and to be given the deputy prime ministership, but this was unacceptable to Mara. Rabuka held a series of meetings with senior military officers and then met with Ganilau before announcing on 3 October that he would leave the cabinet in December and return to the barracks.[21]

The day after Rabuka's announcement, Ganilau delivered a radio address making it official that Mara would remain in office after December. The Constitutional Inquiry and Advisory Commission had presented its report to Ganilau on 30 August. A final proposal was now to be prepared for presentation to the Great Council of Chiefs, which was to meet in December to discuss the constitution and give its blessing to Mara's new cabinet. This, so Mara and his allies no doubt hoped, would mark the final step to achieving secure control of the state as any election under the proposed constitution provided no opportunity for the population at large to take power away from them again.

A few weeks later, Mara's political fortunes seemed to have been given a further boost when Timoci Bavadra died on 3 November, after a prolonged period of illness. It was a tremendous blow to the opposition, which the regime now hoped would factionalize and lose some of its international support. But the Coalition responded to the challenge with determination and the leadership was passed smoothly on to Timoci Bavadra's wife, Adi Kuini Viukaba Bavadra.[22] The continued extent of support for the Coalition was to be seen when a crowd estimated at between twenty thousand to fifty thousand attended Bavadra's funeral a short time later, and Adi Kuini made it clear very quickly that she was a force to be reckoned with in her own right.

WHAT DOES THE FUTURE HOLD?

In early 1990, the political situation in Fiji seems closer to resolution, even if it is a resolution that might not seem desirable to many. But the oligarchy is unlikely to achieve total hegemony or to enjoy the stablility of rule that it so desires for a number of reasons. First, there is the matter of the constitution. Reform of the constitution has been of primary importance to the military and the oligarchy because of the promise that it holds for achieving the security they desire; after all, the 1970 constitution did allow Mara to hold on to the state for seventeen years, with some difficulty, but with far greater ease than at present. But a constitution is only useful if enough people accept its legitimacy or at least are willing to go along with the rules of the game it lays down. At present, there does not seem to be such support for the draft constitution, and its structure is so unfair to the majority of Fijians that it is unlikely ever to enjoy the degree of support that existed (and still exists) for the 1970 constitution. The new proposed constitution, in fact, will probably only serve to create even greater political pressures for change, given the extent to which it runs counter to the interests of so many segments of the population.

Second, there is the continuing problem of the communal and religious zealots which the oligarchy's desire for power helped to create in the first place. These zealots have created an instability in national politics that has proven to be extremely difficult to bring under control and which shows little indication of coming to an end. After all, the broader social and economic conditions of rapid change that led to the rise of many of the communal tensions and to the support for Christian fundamentalism – conditions beyond the cynical manipulation of Mara and his cohorts who served to exacerbate the situation – still exist and are likely to worsen.

Third, there is the military. Rabuka's return to the barracks in December does not signify that the army is to resume its pre-coup role as loyal servant of the oligarchy. Rabuka and his fellow soldiers will continue to exert considerable influence over the population, and as the memory of the post-September 1987 mess fades, they will perhaps be more willing to engage in acts of adventurism. The Mara regime is also faced with the common problem of having to satisfy the military's ever growing financial demands, which by doing so, strengthens the military and makes it easier for the military to intervene.

Closely associated with the problem posed by the military is another potential difficulty facing the oligarchy. The regime remains populated by numerous corrupt and incompetent individuals. Moreover, there is every indication that the new generation of chiefs is even more corrupt and even less competent than the present generation. One only has to compare Kamasese Mara with his son Finau to recognize that something has been lost between the generations. This would indicate a continued reliance by the chiefs on talented commoners: a pattern going back over generations and one that helped give rise to the Fiji Labour Party in the first place. Among the commoners on whom the oligarchy has depended are those in the military and, as we have seen, this group of commoners has shown itself to be relatively assertive since May 1987.

And these are not the only political problems still confronting the Mara regime. The problem of western Fiji, as seen in the initiative for the fourth confederacy, remains a potent one. One also needs to remember that a large percentage of the population supports the Coalition. Kuini Bavadra herself is from the eastern chiefly class and moves easily in chiefly circles. While her style might prove to be more conciliatory than that of her husband's, there is no doubt that she will remain an energetic opponent of many of the regime's policies.

There is one other problem that bears mention: the economy. Increased sugar revenue, a resumption of aid, and improved tourist arrivals have helped to buoy the economy at present, but the improbability of arriving at an adequate solution to the land problem, the continuing drain of talent,[23] the sheer greed of those in and around the regime, and the growing financial demands of the military do not augur well for the country's economic future. And future economic troubles will only contribute further to the country's political instability, which seems all too likely to continue.

Finally, what about the future of democracy in Fiji? Obviously, in the short run, any meaningful form of democracy in Fiji is unlikely. A new Parliament building is due to open near Mara's and Rabuka's official residences, and Fiji may well have a constitution and even an election one of these days; but the election certainly will not be democratic, nor the Parliament representative of the vast majority of

Fijian people. Yet, the democratic principles espoused by so many Fijians have not disappeared from the political horizon. Democratic opposition to the regime persists and has proven to be resilient. Before April 1987, it seemed impossible that a non-racial, democratic socialist party could assume state power in Fiji. Yet this is precisely what did happen, if only for one month. It would therefore seem presumptive to deny the future prospects for democratic forces to regain state power on a more lasting basis – just not any time soon.

Appendixes

A: Candidates and Voting by Seat
for the 1987 Election

North Eastern. **Ishwari Bajpai (Alliance Party)**: a Tavuan shopkeeper who initially built his business on the basis of its close proximity to the Vatukoula gold-mine; with the help of Alliance Party patronage, he was later able to expand his operations to Suva and elsewhere. **Ahmed Bhamji (Coalition)**: mayor of Ba; age 37 (youngest mayor in the country); holder of a B.A. in economics; had worked for Coopers Lybrand and then for his family's business. Bhamji's popularity and energy were thought to make him a strong candidate for this seat, regarded as the west's most marginal seat. The seat was narrowly won in 1982 by Iqbal Khan of the NFP. **Voters registered:** 14,706 Indian, 11,225 Fijian, 285 General Elector, Total 26,216. **Results**: 12,786 **Coalition**, 9,946 Alliance Party.

East Central. **K.R.Latchan (Alliance Party)**: the sitting member. **Madho Prasad (Coalition)**. This was considered a relatively safe Alliance Party seat. **Voters registered:** 7,995 Indian, 18,714 Fijian, 421 General Elector, Total 27,130. **Results**: 15,939 **Alliance Party**, 6,397 Coalition.

South Central. **Narsi Raniga (Alliance Party)**: age 44; born in Ba; received a B.A. from the University of Queensland in 1964; taught for a number of years and then went to the University of Auckland and Cambridge University for postgraduate courses; on his return, was made a district officer; has held numerous government posts since then (including several overseas in the diplomatic corps); held posts as permanent secretary of commerce and industry, of economic planning and development, foreign affairs and civil aviation, of education, and of the Public Service Commission; with twenty-two years experience, the most senior civil servant standing in the election; had to resign his position to run for election and by so doing gave up benefits that would have accrued to him if he had waited to retire at the minimum age of forty-five. The seat was held for the Alliance Party by Ramanlal Kapadia. Kapadia applied to stand for the seat again, as did former Suva mayor Maan Singh, Senator Raojibhai Patel, and Raniga. It was considered a relatively safe Alliance Party seat. **Dr. Som Prakash (Coalition)**: age 43; from Ba; B.A. and M.A. from Auckland University; a lecturer in education at the University of the South Pacific, with no previous political experience. The initial Coalition choice had been a 28-year-old teacher, Praveen Kumar Sarup, who was replaced when Prakash agreed to stand. **Voters registered**: 4,763 Indian, 17,614 Fijian, 1,040 General Elector, Total 23,417. **Results**: 12,796 **Alliance Party**, 4,592 Coalition.

Lau / Cakaudrove / Rotuma. **Dr. Ahmed Ali (Alliance Party)**: the sitting member. **Aindra Deo Sharndil (Coalition)**. A safe Alliance seat usually reserved for an Indo-Fijian closely associated with Mara. **Voters registered**: 1,504 Indian, 19,889 Fijian, 724 General Elector, Total 22,117. **Results**: 17,698 **Alliance Party**, 1,247 Coalition.

Vanua Levu North and West. **Joseph Kanahilal Maharaj (Alliance Party)**: a Suva lawyer originally from Macuata, he moved to Labasa to open a law office after receiving the Alliance Party nomination. **Govind Swamy (Coalition)**: age 38; born in Labasa; worked as an industrial arts teacher for eighteen years, but resigned to stand as the Coalition candidate. The seat had been held by Dr. Santa Singh, who was dropped by the Coaliton, but remained a Coalition supporter. Neither candidate had any prior political experience. Veteran NFP politician Subramani Basawaiya of the NFP splinter group also contested the seat. Despite Basawaiya, it was considered a safe Coalition seat. **Voters registered**: 22,526 Indian, 12,256 Fijian, 585 General Elector, Total 35,367. **Results**: 17,196 **Coalition**, 12,938 Alliance Party, 702 NFP splinter group.

Suva. **Irene Jai Narayan (Alliance Party)**: age 54; born in Lucknow, India; her husband is principal of Indian College in Suva; winner of the Suva Indian communal seat for the NFP in 1966 and has held the seat since then. The Suva national seat had been held by Minister for Employment and Industrial Relations Mohammed Ramzan. It had been clear before nominations that Ramzan was unlikely to stand for the seat again. It was considered a difficult seat for the Alliance Party to hold on to. Irene Narayan had been popular in Suva, having held a Suva seat for years, but many felt that she had lost much of her credibility by going over to the Alliance Party, after having been an outspoken critic of the party. Maan Singh, Suva branch president of the Indian Alliance, threatened to run against her as an independent Alliance candidate after he and others complained that the Indian Alliance had been ignored in her selection. **Navin Maharaj (Coalition)**: age 48; born in Nadi (his father had been one of the first three Indian members elected to the Legislative Council); worked for Reddy Fletcher Construction Company for sixteen years starting in 1957, and then formed his own construction company; served two terms as mayor of Suva, first with the Alliance Party and then with the NFP; led the campaign for Jai Ram Reddy against Siddiq Koya as NFP party leader; became a member of the Suva City Council as an independent; resigned from the council to run against Narayan; has strong ties with the local Indo-Fijian community and was considered by the Coalition to be a strong candidate with a good chance of defeating Narayan. **Voters registered:** 16,257 Indian, 12,969 Fijian, 2,823 General Elector, Total 32,049. **Results:** 12,431 **Coalition**, 11,772 Alliance Party.

North Central. **Uday Singh (Alliance Party)**: the sitting member; defeated Mahendra Chaudhry of the Labour Party in the 1985 by-election; owns a large amount of freehold land near Ba, with numerous Indo-Fijian tenant cane farmers; is the brother of Coalition candidate James Shankar Singh. **Navin Patel (Coalition)**: had held the Ba Indian communal seat. The North Central seat had been held by Siddiq Koya and its fate was considered to depend in part on whether or not Koya decided to stand as an independent. It was thought that a split brought on by Koya running would give the Alliance Party a chance. **Voters registered**: 20,795 Indian, 8,245 Fijian, 291 General Elector, Total 29,331. **Results:** 15,369 **Coalition**, 11,142 Alliance Party.

North Western. **Kumar Sivam (Alliance Party)**: owner of a real estate firm. **Davendra Singh (Coalition)**: age 37, sitting member for the Lautoka Indian communal seat; former youth president of the NFP Lautoka branch; successful candidate of the Youth Wing of the NFP against the Koya-backed candidate in the 1986 Lautoka Indian communal by-election.The North Western seat was won in 1982 by Jai

Raj Singh of the NFP by a landslide of 4,000 votes. **Voters registered:** 19,965 Indian, 9,590 Fijian, 914 General Elector, Total 30,469. **Results:** 15,596 **Coalition**, 10,183 Alliance Party.

South Eastern. **Major Veer Vijay Singh (Alliance Party):** age 47; born in Tamavua; served in various administrative posts in the government, including assistant clerk in Parliament; joined the army and rose to the rank of major; served as a company commander in Sinai and Lebanon and as an operations officer in Sinai; after having to leave the army, established a real estate consulting firm in Suva. Singh was chosen by the Alliance Party over a local businessman, Ben Rambisheswar, the sitting member, and it soon became apparent that this was not a popular move among Indo-Fijians in the area. Singh was also a relative unknown among local native Fijians. Former Alliance Party senator Kaur Battan Singh had sought the seat until advised not to contest it by Mara. The nomination then seemed to be between Rambisheswar and Young Alliance president Nirmal Singh. In the end, neither was given the nod. Singh's nomination angered the Young Alliance president, who felt that a number of Young Alliance candidates had been overlooked. **Fida Hussein (Coalition):** age 40; born in Rewa; became a member of the police force in 1964; resigned in 1981 to become a sales representative for the *Fiji Times* and later became a sales consultant for a publishing firm; had long been active in Muslim organizations, but had no previous political experience; had been one of the few Muslims to come out actively in support of the Labour Party when it was founded and had campaigned for Labour candidates among Muslims during the Suva City Council election. The seat was regarded as an Alliance stronghold. **Voters registered:** 15,220 Indian, 18,786 Fijian, 647 General Elector, Total 34,653. **Results:** 14,138 **Coalition**, 13,341 Alliance Party.

South Western. **Narayan Reddy (Alliance Party):** aged 60; former secondary school principal in Labasa. **Nitya Nand Reddy (Coalition):** age 37; B.A. (Economics) from the University of the South Pacific; had been an accountant for the Fiji Sugar Corporation since 1973 and served as president of the Sugar Milling Staff Officers Association for four terms; was a founding vice-president of the Labour Party and ran as the Labour Party's candidate in the 1986 Lautoka City Council election in 1986; in an apparent case of victimization, was dismissed by the Fiji Sugar Corporation in mid-1986. This was considered a safe NFP seat. **Voters registered:** 18,798 Indian, 12,558

Fijian, 236 General Elector, Total 31,592. **Results**: 15,589 **Coalition**, 8,462 Alliance Party.

INDIAN COMMUNAL SEATS

Suva Rural. **Mohammed Afzal Khan (Alliance Party)**: age 32; law degree from New Zealand; works as a lawyer in Suva; comes from a family of strong Alliance Party supporters. **Dr. Satendra Nandan (Coalition)**: age 47; born in Nadi; holds a B.A. and B.ED. from Delhi University, an M.A. from Leeds University, and a PH.D. from Australian National University; worked as a journalist and teacher and then joined the staff of the University of the South Pacific in 1969, where he was employed in the School of Education. Nandan was elected on the NFP ticket for the Nasinu-Vunidawa Indian communal seat in 1982, following the death of the respected incumbent. He broke with the NFP, along with Irene Narayan and other independents, and then became the first former NFP parliamentarian to join the Labour Party. **Results**: 7,453 **Coalition**, 1,081 Alliance Party.

Suva City. **Vinod Singh (Alliance Party)**: age 39; worked for the Suva City Council; in the early 1970s went to work at Pacific Harbour resort, where he is the director; served as secretary to the NFP Flower faction in 1977 and secretary to the reunited NFP in 1981; held a Suva City Council seat for the NFP; switched to the Alliance Party in 1986. **Harilal Manilal Patel (Coalition)**: age 46; received a law degree from the University of Auckland in 1968; joined the law firm of prominent NFP member K.C. Ramrakha upon his return to Suva; formed his own firm in 1977 when Ramrakha emigrated to Australia; served as an NFP member of the Suva City Council, had been president of the Suva branch of the NFP, and was a founding member of the NFP Youth Movement; stood for the seat as an NFP Flower faction candidate in 1977 and lost; withdrew from political activities after the two factions reunited; decided to return to politics after the formation of the Coalition. Suva mayor Bob Kumar of the Labour Party had expressed interest in running for the seat; when he was passed over he threatened to stand as an independent, but nothing came of the threat. This was regarded as a safe seat for the Coalition. **Results**: 8,247 **Coalition**, 1,068 Alliance Party.

Nasinu/Vunidawa. **Mahendra Sukhdeo (Alliance Party)**: age 46; born in Nadi; received a B.ED. and M.A. in politics from Bombay University; worked as a lecturer at the University of the South Pacific for two years; worked for the Suva City Council; became general secretary of the National Union of Municipal Workers; had been a Labour Party vice-president and secretary of its Nasinu/Vunidawa branch and was elected as a Labour Party candidate to the Suva City Council in 1985. He had not been popular with some prominent members of the Labour Party and his defection was not greeted with surprise or concern. The Alliance Party had offered him a prominent post should he win and assured him of its support after the election even should he loose. Gaining his support was part of a larger Alliance Party push to divide white-collar and blue-collar workers. **James Shankar Singh (Coalition)**: age 62; born in Ba; founding member of the Alliance Party; served as president of the Indian Alliance for several years. As an Alliance Party member of Parliament he held several cabinet portfolios. He had a falling out with Mara in 1982 and did not seek re-election. He later joined the NFP and was its candidate for the 1985 North Central Indian national seat by-election, running against his brother Uday Singh (Alliance) and Labour candidate Mahendra Chaudhry. This was considered a safe seat for the Coalition. **Results**: 8,535 **Coalition**, 679 Alliance Party.

Nausori/Levuka. **Brij Bhan Singh (Alliance Party)**: age 41; born at Raralevu; worked for Desai Bookshops, becoming a branch manager; later became a taxi proprietor and grocery and liquor shop owner; member of the Nausori Advisory Council since 1971 and chairman of the council since 1974; also president of the Rewa Taxi Association. **Mahendra Chand Vinod (Coalition)**: age 65; born in Nacokaika, Naitasiri; holds a B.S. from the University of Hawaii and a journalism diploma from New Delhi; worked in the public service for forty years, retiring in 1979; became editor of the Hindi language newspaper *Shanti Dutt* in 1981; resigned his editorship to stand as the Coalition candidate. The sitting member is Koya loyalist Shardha Nand, who decided to stand as a member of the NFP splinter group. Some members of the Coalition disagreed with the nomination of Vinod, and another Coalition member, Ram Yadav, also sought the nomination. Despite the divisions, this was a relatively safe seat for the Coalition. **Results**: 6,222 **Coalition**, 879 Alliance Party, 751 NFP-splinter group.

Ba/Lautoka Rural. **Surya Deep Singh (Alliance Party)**. **Mahendra Chaudhry (Coalition)**. Early in December, Jai Ram Reddy had been suggested as a candidate for this seat, but he decided not to stand. This was a safe Coalition seat. **Results**: 8,858 **Coalition**, 2,894 Alliance Party.

Tavua / Vaileka. **Gopalan Nair (Alliance Party)**: age 60; born in Samabula; a retired school teacher; had served on the executive of the Fiji Teachers Union for several years. **Samresan Pillay (Coalition)**: age 46; born in Penang, Ra; received a diploma in education from the University of the South Pacific; son of former NFP President Ram Sami Gounder; after working for the Department of Agriculture, joined the British army in 1961; left the army in 1969 to work as a co-operatives officer and then teacher; worked as a warden at the University of the South Pacific between 1981 and 1983 and then resumed teaching in Ra. This was considered a safe Coalition seat. **Results**: 7,314 **Coalition**, 1,462 Alliance Party.

Ba. **Velaydan Nair (Alliance Party)**: age 59; born in Ba; began teaching in 1947; received some tertiary education and later became a head teacher, then education officer; became a senior education officer in 1977. **Dr. Balwant Singh Rakkha (Coalition)**: age 46; born in Tavua; had gone to India to study medicine and remained in India for fourteen years, where he was influenced by the political ideas of Nehru and Gandhi; established a practice in Ba; joined the NFP in 1975, serving as Ba branch president since 1977. This was his second election, having failed to win a seat previously. The seat had been held by Navin Patel of the NFP, who was moved to the North Central Indian national seat. There had been some sentiment to give the seat to Ba mayor Ahmed Bhamji, but it was decided to give Bhamji the more difficult North Eastern Indian national seat. There had also been some thought of having Bhupendra Patel stand. The NFP splinter group ran candidate Ram Sundar as a candidate, but he was seen to have little support. This was considered a safe seat for the Coalition. **Results**: 8,226 **Coalition**, 1,961 Alliance Party, 610 NFP-splinter group.

Lautoka. **Deo Lingham Reddy (Alliance Party)**: age 45; worked in auto sales; active in the Indian Alliance, served as a councillor and deputy mayor of Lautoka between 1981 and 1983; ran against Nitya Reddy in the 1986 Lautoka City Council election. **Vinubhai Patel (Coalition)**. The seat had been held by Davendra Singh, who was shifted to the North Western Indian communal seat. The seat was considered an NFP stronghold and thus a likely win for the Coalition. The Alliance Party had become optimistic about the seat in December when there was indication that a number of prominent NFP figures were joining the Alliance Party. However, the Lautoka Indian Alliance was not pleased with the choice of Reddy as a candidate. It wanted to run Dr. Arumugam Pillai, a former mayor of Lautoka, who it was felt had a better chance of winning. This was another example of the Indian Alliance being upset with the decision of the Alliance Party selection committee. **Results**: 8,875 **Coalition**, 1,493 Alliance Party.

Nadi. **Himmat Raniga (Alliance Party)**: age 52; born in Ba; worked for the Health Department from 1953 to 1961; worked for Qantas until 1981, by which time he had become property manager; began a land development business the following year and is involved in the development of residential and industrial land as well as growing cane. **Rishi Shankar (Coalition)**: age 53; born at Vitogo Lautoka; worked as a policeman between 1953 and 1965; then attended Victoria University, Wellington, where he received a law degree; upon his return, went back to the police force and in 1974 joined the Office of the Director of Public Prosecutions; left the government in 1976 to join a law firm based in Ba and later formed his own firm; served as a Nadi Town Councillor between 1982 and 1985. This was considered a safe Coalition seat. **Results**: 10,090 **Coalition**, 2,026 Alliance Party.

Sigatoka. **Mohammed Azam Khalil (Alliance Party)**: age 36; born in Maro, Nadroga, where he lives and works as a cane farmer and businessman. **Harish Sharma (Coalition)**: age 54; born Nausori; worked for the government and then a private insurance company; attended the University of Tasmania in 1960, where he received an LL.B. in 1964; first worked for the Koya law firm and then joined the law firm of NFP founder A.D. Patel; formed a new law firm upon Patel's death in 1969 which he continues to run; was nominated to the Senate by Koya after independence; was elected to Parliament in 1972 and is the sitting member for the seat; replaced Koya as opposition leader in 1986.This was a safe Coalition seat. **Results**: 8,929 **Coalition**, 2,023 Alliance Party.

Labasa / Bua. **Shiromaniam Madhavan (Alliance Party)**: age 43; born in Labasa; his father, James Madhavan (now deceased), was a founder of the NFP and a long-serving member of Parliament; was a founder of the Air Pacific Employees' Association in the 1960s (served as secretary and president); active in NFP politics since 1963; elected to Labasa Town Council in 1973, nominated to the Senate in 1974; elected mayor of Labasa in 1978; elected to Labasa Town Council as an independent in 1982. His decision to stand for the Alliance Party caused a division within his family, which supports the Coalition. The seat had been held by Labasa lawyer Mohammed Sadiq, who was dropped by the Coalition in favour of former Suva mayor Noor

Dean. **Noor Dean (Coalition)**: born in Suva; worked as a school teacher and then became a lawyer; served as an NFP Suva City Councillor and in 1982 was elected lord mayor; his law firm has an office in Labasa; is the organizing secretary of the NFP. There was some dissent, and a breakaway group threatened to field a rival candidate, but nothing came of this. **Results**: 8,754 **Coalition**, 1,840 Alliance Party.

Savusavu / Macuata East. **Ram Deo (Alliance Party)**: age 44; born in Labasa; worked as a farm adviser for the Fiji Sugar Corporation; continued to farm after retirement and went into business as owner of Sita Ram Bargain Centre. **Krishna Datt (Coalition)**: age 42; general secretary of the Fiji Teachers Union; former high school principal in Suva; general secretary of the Labour Party; considered a 'home town' candidate on Vanua Levu. Labasa town councillor Dewan Shankar of the Labour Party had applied for the seat. He expressed considerable anger after not being chosen, accusing them of being 'a pack of liars.' Mainly to try to give Datt trouble, the NFP splinter group ran Raman Singh, but he was not viewed as a very strong candidate. The seat was considered an easy win for Datt. **Results**: 8,640 **Coalition**, 1,392 Alliance Party, 447 NFP-splinter group.

FIJIAN NATIONAL SEATS

Vanua Levu North and West. **Emosi Vuakatagane (Alliance Party)**: from Macuata. **Ratu Filimone Ralogaivau (Coalition)**: age 48; the Tui Solevu (the largest district in Bua) and nephew of the Tui Bua; employed as a labour officer in the Ministry of Employment and Industrial Relations; chairman of the Bua Provincial Council from 1974 to 1980 and its nominee to the Great Council of Chiefs. After noting the neglect of Bua since independence despite election promises, he commented: 'In the past no Bua man has ever been chosen to fight this seat and the Bua Provincial Council is fed up.' He was also forced to resign from his job to stand for the seat. The sitting member is Ratu Soso Katonivere of the NFP (from Macuata). He chose to run for the NFP splinter group. With a strong candidate, it was considered one the Coalition should be able to win. **Voters registered**: 12,256 Fijian, 22,526 Indian, 585 General Elector, Total 35,367. **Results**: 17,265 **Coalition**, 12,712 Alliance Party, 538 NFP-splinter group.

Lau / Cakaudrove / Rotuma. **Ratu Sir Kamasese Mara (Alliance Party)**: nomination opposed; one of the safest Alliance seats in the country. **Sivinia Vakarewa (Coalition)**: age 42; a Savusavu farmer and national secretary of the 1,000-member Cocoa Growers' and Producers' Association. Vakarewa had been a vocal critic of the government's treatment of native Fijian cocoa farmers since 1980, and increasingly of government corruption. The Coalition realized that it had little chance of winning but felt it important to make a showing, in part, to divert the prime minister's attention away from other areas. Vakarewa stated that he was running to prove a point that not all native Fijians in the eastern islands thought that the Alliance Party was doing a good job. Initially, Dr. Tupeni Baba was suggested as a possible candidate, but it was eventually decided that he should run against David Toganivalu in Suva, a seat whose outcome would play a crucial role in deciding who won the election. **Voters registered:** 19,889 Fijian, 1,504 Indian, 724 General Elector, Total 22,117. **Results:** 17,814 **Alliance Party**, 1,160 Coalition.

South Central. **Sakiasi Waqanivavalagi (Alliance Party):** age 55; employed as assistant secretary to the Fiji Stevedoring Union from 1961 to 1972 and then served as general secretary of the Fiji Mine Workers Union; elected to the Legislative Council in 1966 and remained in Parliament from 1970 until he lost his seat in 1982; appointed minister for commerce, industry and co-operatives in 1973, and in 1981 became minister for lands. Josua Cavalevu (former permanent secretary for Fijian affairs and ambassador to the EEC) had also expressed interest in this seat. **Solomone Momoivalu (Coalition):** age 59; from Kadavu; served in various administrative positions during colonial rule and fought in the Malayan campaign from 1951 to 1955; joined the Alliance Party in 1966; was passed over for this seat in 1972, but decided to run against the official candidate and lost; elected to Parliament for the Lomaviti/Maunikau seat in 1977 as the Alliance Party candidate and for the South Central seat in 1982; served as minister of state for information and as minister for home affairs between 1977 and 1982: re-elected in 1982, but not given a ministerial portfolio (serving as government whip instead); did not reapply to stand and expressed a desire to quit politics while at the same time holding private discussions with Bavadra about the possibility of his standing for a seat for the Coalition; was considered an important addition to the Labour Party. Atunaisa Lacabuka contested the seat for the Western United Front and Isireli Vuibau for the Nationalists. It was considered a safe seat for the Alliance Party. **Voters registered:** 17,614 Fijian, 4,763 Indian, 1,040 General Elector, Total 23,417. **Results:** 11,718 **Alliance Party**, 3,795 Coalition, 2,593 Fijian Nationalist Party, 243 Western United Front.

East Central. **Ratu Timoci Vesikula (Alliance Party)**: current holder of the seat and minister of state for rural development. **Josua Waqawai (Coalition)**: age 31; from northern Tailevu; had been a teacher and then went to study law at Otago University in New Zealand; took leave from his studies to fight the election for the Labour Party. This was a safe Alliance Party seat. **Voters registered:** 18,714 Fijian, 7,995 Indian, 421 General Elector, Total 27,130. **Results:** 15,868 **Alliance Party**, 6,454 Coalition.

North Eastern. **Meli Waqa (Alliance Party)**: formerly employed by the University of the South Pacific; currently involved in various business activities in Suva. **Joe Nacola (Coalition)**: a lecturer in education at the University of the South Pacific with a strong following in the Ra area. The Coalition was considered to have a good chance of winning. **Voters registered:** 11,225 Fijian, 14,706 Indian, 285 General Elector, Total 26,216. **Results:** 13,230 **Coalition**, 9,491 Alliance Party.

Suva. **Ratu David Toganivalu (Alliance Party)**: nomination unopposed; age 53; holder of the seat; from the chiefly Massau mataqali of Bau; entered parliament in 1966; served as parliamentary secretary for Fijian affairs, 1966–68; a member of cabinet from 1973, holding portfolios in Commerce and Industry and Information; became the country's first deputy prime minister in 1984 as well as minister for Fijian affairs. He had been seen by many for some time as a possible replacement for Mara as party leader and was considered to be more moderate than Mara and more genuinely committed to multiracialism. Toganivalu had strong support among both native Fijians and the local Indo-Fijian business community. Nevertheless, the seat was considered to be a difficult one this time because of the urban support of the Labour Party and there had been some speculation that Toganivalu would be given a safer seat. This was countered by the need to have a strong candidate to ensure that the Alliance Party retained control of the seat. **Dr. Tupeni Baba (Coalition)**: age 43; received an M.A. in education from the University of Sydney and a PH.D. from Macquarie University; became a lecturer at the University of the South Pacific and then registrar from 1981 to 1984, after which he became Reader in Education. Baba had been minimally involved in the Alliance Party in the past. He was viewed by many as a spokesman for younger, educated native Fijians. From Vanua Levu, he was related through marriage to the governor general. He had become increasingly active in the Labour Party during the latter part of 1986 and had put a great deal of effort into helping Labour during the Suva City Council election. The Alliance Party arranged for former Labour member Iliesa Duvuloco to run as an independent in the hope of taking votes away from Baba and also as part of its general push to split union votes. It was considered one of the most important seats in the election. **Voters registered:** 12,969 Fijian, 16,257 Indian, 2,823 General Elector, Total 32,049. **Results:** 12,452 **Coalition**, 11,902 Alliance Party.

North Central. **Aporosa Rakoto (Alliance Party)**: former Fiji Sugar Corporation field officer; a graduate of the University of the South Pacific; a member of the Senate, the Ba Provincial Council, and the Great Council of Chiefs. **Temo Sukanaivalu (Coalition)**. This was considered a safe Coalition seat. **Voters registered:** 8,245 Fijian, 20,795 Indian, 291 General Elector, Total 29,331. **Results:** 15,737 **Coalition**, 10,786 Alliance Party.

North Western. **Dr. Sefanaia Tabua (Alliance Party)**: private doctor in Lautoka. **Dr. Timoci Bavadra (Coalition)**. The seat was held by Koresi Matatolu for the NFP who agreed to shift to the Bua/Macuata Fijian communal seat. This was considered a relatively safe seat for the Coalition. **Voters registered:** 9,590 Fijian, 19,965 Indian, 914 General Elector, Total 30,469. **Results:** 15,990 **Coalition**, 9,882 Alliance Party.

South Eastern. **Ratu George Tu'uakitau Cokanauto (Alliance Party)**: age 40; director of the Centre for Applied Technology and Development (funded by the West German Hans Siedel Foundation), which was active in promoting training programs for young members of the Alliance Party; resident of the constituency (living in Caubati), but considered to be an outsider. As was noted in one Alliance Party report: 'People of Rewa regard Ratu Cokanauto as an outsider and have interpreted his selection as an attempt by Kabuna to dominate Rewa. This is an extension of the age old rivalry between the Kubuna and Burebasaga confederacies in the 25-year Bau-Rewa war. Rewans have usually occupied the seat.' Mara's wife is from Rewa and there was some hope that she would be able to sway voters, but she herself appeared to be losing popularity in the delta. The present sitting member is Semesa Sikivou, the minister for foreign affairs, who decided to quit politics. **Joeli Kalou (Coalition)**: age 47; from a village on Ovalau; received a B.A. from Massey University and served as a teacher for the next twenty-two years; decided to give up teaching in 1984 and devote himself full-time to trade union activities as general secretary of the Fijian Teachers Association; was a vice-president of the Labour Party and also a member of the Great Council of Chiefs; a controversial trade unionist known for his radicalism with a strong following in the Suva area and on his home island. The Fijian Nationalist candidate, Emoni Rakadrudru, a commercial farmer, stood unsuccessfully for the seat in 1982 and ran again in 1987. This was thought to be a crucial seat in the election. **Voters registered:** 18,786 Fijian, 15,220 Indian, 647 General Elector, Total 34,653. **Results:** 13,445 **Coalition**, 12,506 Alliance Party, 2,474 Fijian Nationalist Party.

South Western. **Isikeli Bakewa (Alliance Party):** a prominent official in the Fijian Association. It was initially hoped that Dr. Mesake Biumaiwai, the permanent secretary for health, would stand for the seat for the Coalition, but, in the end, the choice was Mosese Volavola. **Mosese Volavola (Coalition):** age 39; holds diplomas from the Netherlands and New Zealand in surveying and has worked as a public servant for twelve years; is assistant director of Lands and Surveys, a post he had to resign to run for office. Sitting member Isikeli Nadolo of the Western United Front decided to contest the seat on the Western United Front ticket. The Coalition was thought likely to win the seat. **Voters registered:** 12,558 Fijian, 18,798 Indian, 236 General Elector, Total 31,592. **Results:** 15,127 **Coalition**, 8,308 Alliance Party, 3,612 Western United Front.

FIJIAN COMMUNAL SEATS

Naitasiri. **Livai Nasilivata (Alliance Party):** age 60; from Naikurukuru, Naitasiri; taught for six years and then enlisted in the army in 1951; served in Malaya between 1951 and 1956, and was commissioned as a second lieutenant; remained in the army until 1960 and then worked as a fire officer at Nadi airport; was a Great Council of Chiefs nominee to the Senate in 1970; was elected to Parliament for the Naitasiri seat in 1972 and has held it ever since; was appointed minister for works and communications in 1979 and then in 1982 became minister for co-operatives, from which he resigned in 1985; has served as chairman of the Naitasiri Provincial Council since 1967 and is also a prominent lay preacher in the Methodist church. **Kavekini Navuso (Coalition):** age 45; holds a B.A. from University of Hawaii; worked as a teacher and co-operative manager until joining the Bureau of Statistics; resigned from his post to contest the election even though it was considered a relatively safe Alliance seat. The Fijian Nationalists also fielded a candidate for this seat, Suva businessman Viliame Savu. It was regarded as an easy Alliance win.

Results: 7,379 **Alliance Party**, 1,445 Coalition, 1,673 Fijian Nationalist Party.

Tailevu. **Ratu William Toganivalu (Alliance Party)**: the sitting member and formerly minister for home affairs (with a questionable financial reputation). It was known that Mara would have liked to have replaced him, but the Toganivalu's political power in Tailevu precluded this. **Sailasa Verebasaga (Coalition)**: a retired Nadi Airport fire officer who had been active in the FPSA. There were several contenders for the Coalition slot. Among the others was Alisi Dobui, a senior nursing services official in the ministry of health. This was a safe Alliance seat. **Results**: 8,813 **Alliance Party**, 974 Coalition.

Rewa / Serua / Namosi. **Tomasi Vakatora (Alliance Party)**: age 52; from Navilaca, Rewa; worked as a civil servant and was secretary for labour when he retired in 1974; elected to Parliament in 1977 and has held several ministerial portfolios; is the sitting member for the seat; elected Speaker of the House in 1982, where he quickly gained a reputation for a lack of impartiality; known for his anti-Indian views; his actions as Speaker led Jai Ram Reddy to leave parliament and eventually step down as NFP leader. **Apenisa Seduadua (Coalition)**: age 44; from Vutia, Rewa (a member of an important chiefly clan); received a diploma in English from the University of the South Pacific; worked for the Fiji Electricity Authority as an accounts officer; became general secretary of the Fiji Electricity Authority Staff Association in 1982; served as a member of the Rewa Provincial Council since 1984. The seat was held by Sakeasi Butadroka until 1977, when he lost it to Vakatora. Butadroka lost the seat to Vakatora again in the 1982 election. Butadroka decided to try again in 1987 on the Nationalist ticket. A report prepared for the Alliance Party in late January indicated that Butadroka was making a strong showing and that the Alliance Party was in danger of losing the seat to the Nationalists. The seat was also contested by Vitati Babaseru for the Western United Front and Epeli Kacimaiwai as an independent. Bavadra had sought unsuccessfully to convince Kacimaiwai to run on behalf of the Coalition. **Results**: 6,002 **Alliance Party**, 4,102 Fijian Nationalist Party, 351 Coalition, 84 Western United Front.

Lomaviti / Muanikau. **Mosese Qionibaravi (Alliance Party)**: age 56; from Nasau, Koro; holds an M.A. in economics from New Zealand; first elected to parliament in 1972; became Speaker of the House in 1977; appointed minister for foreign affairs and tourism in 1982; became minister of finance in 1983 after Charles Walker resigned from the post; appointed the second deputy prime minister by Mara in 1984. **Ratu Isimeli Cokasiga (Coalition)**: age 43; a mataqali head from the chiefly village on the island of Nairai in the Lomaviti Group (the mataqali has connections with Bau); began as a teacher in 1962; received a B.ED. from the University of the South Pacific and then resigned as a teacher in 1980 to study at the University of London, where he received a M.A. in comparative education in 1982; is assistant registrar at the University of the South Pacific. He is an opponent of mixing the chiefly system with politics, which he says corrupts the chiefly system. One of his reasons for running is concern over lack of development in the Lomaviti Group under the Alliance Party government: 'I have a lot of respect for Mosese as a politician, but where Lomaviti is concerned he has failed.' This was considered a safe Alliance seat. **Results**: 8,307 **Alliance Party**, 763 Coalition.

Kadavu / Tamavua / Suva Suburban. **Taniela Veitata (Alliance Party)**: age 48; born in Somosomo, Taviuni, but with ties to Naceva, Kadavu; went to work on the Suva waterfront after leaving school; elected assistant secretary of the newly formed Dockworkers' and Seamen's Union and then in 1969 became the union's general secretary; stood for Parliament unsuccessfully in 1972 under the banner of his own Liberal Party; an unsuccessful candidate again in 1977, this time running for the NFP. He was known as a militant trade unionist in the 1970s, but after his union came under severe pressure from the government he became an ardent supporter of Mara, for which he and his union were rewarded. As general secretary of the Fiji Port Workers' Union and a well-known lay preacher (who at times referred to himself as 'the Prophet' and claimed to hear the voice of God), he was considered a strong candidate. On receiving word of his selection, Veitata told reporters: 'I'm a trade unionist, prophet and now politician.' Through Alliance Party patronage he had been made a board member of the Ports Authority, as had other prominent Alliance Party supporters, and a director of the cargo ship *Tui Cakau*. His dockworkers form an important part of the backbone of the Fijian Association. The seat had been held by Minister for Home Affairs Akariva Nabati who was passed over this time, partly because of several scandals linked to financial irregularities (most recently the so-called 'Tony Stephens case'). The permanent secretary of primary industries, Josua Cavalevu, had also applied to the Alliance Party to stand for the seat. Cavalevu was known to have had discussions with the Labour Party and his loyalty was thus suspect. **Ema Druavesi (Coalition)**: age 40; born in Suva; graduated from Fiji Institute of Technology; worked as a chemistry laboratory assistant at the University of the South Pacific; a firm Alliance Party supporter until 1982, and in that year she became president of the University of the South Pacific Staff Union. As she became increasingly involved in trade union affairs, she became radicalized in her politics and moved away from the Alliance Party and was especially critical of its record on women's rights. The Nationalists ran Ratu Tevita Nasodrodro for the seat. It was considered a fairly safe seat for the Alliance Party given the respective strengths of the two candidates. **Results**: 9,727 **Alliance Party**, 1,020 Coalition, 100 Fijian National Party.

Ra / Samabula / Suva. **Isikeli Kasami (Alliance Party)**: age 35; from Ra; received a diploma in development studies from the University of the South Pacific; worked in various capacities for the government; currently a youth worker, president of the Ra Youth Council, and an advisor to the Ra Provincial Council. The sitting member for the Alliance Party since 1982, Ra businessman and cane farmer, Kolinio Qiqiwaqa, announced that he would stand as an independent for this seat after he was passed over by the Alliance Party. In Parliament, he had been a critic of the administration of the Native Lands Trust Board and called for more native Fijian land to be put into production, but his criticisms had been muted by a sense of loyalty to the Alliance Party. After meetings with Bavadra, he was expected to be named as the Coalition candidate for the seat since the person expected to be named by the Coalition, community worker Jo Banuve, was unable to stand. This did not happen, however, and, in the end, Qiqiwaqa stood as an independent. **Isikeli Naitura (Coalition)**: age 47; from Rakiraki; joined the civil service in 1961 and retired as an agricultural officer in 1986. This was a relatively safe Alliance Party seat. **Results**: 6,333 **Alliance Party**, 1,137 Coalition.

Lau / Rotuma. **Filipe Bole (Alliance Party)**: nomination unopposed; age 50; from Mualevu, Vanuabalavu; holds teaching degrees from Auckland University; was appointed education officer (secondary) in 1968 and rose to permanent secretary for education in 1974; was appointed Fiji's representative the U.N. and the United States in 1980; returned to Fiji to serve as permanent secretary for foreign affairs and then became director of the Pacific Islands Deveopment Program in Honolulu. All of the later posts were Mara appointments and his relationship with Mara was a close one. He came back to Fiji in 1985 to stand for the Lau/Rotuma by-election and was seen as an important Mara political protégé. He replaced Ahmed Ali as minister for education in 1986. **Jioji Areki (Coalition)**: age 46; born in Vatukoula, but considered from Lakeba; joined the British army, which he left in 1980 to return to Fiji and work as an engineer. This was a very safe seat for the Alliance Party. **Results**: 6,620 **Alliance Party**, 122 Coalition.

Nadroga / Navosa. **Dr. Apenisa Kurisaqila (Alliance Party)**: nomination unopposed; age 55; from Voua, Nadroga; the sitting member and minister for health; studied medicine at the Fiji School of Medicine and worked as a government doctor for twenty years; retired in 1979 and set up a private practice in Nadi. The seat was won by Ratu Osea Gavidi for the Western United Front in both 1977 elections, but he lost the seat to Dr. Kurisaqila in 1982. **Rev. Mosese Naisoroi (Coalition)**: age 46; from Raiwaqa, Ruwailevu, Nadroga; became a policeman in 1961 and then resigned in 1978 to go overseas for studies; received a diploma in theology in New Zealand and set up a religious counselling office in Suva on his return and worked as a lay preacher. The Coalition initially planned on giving this seat to Gavidi, but when negotiations with him to join the Coalition failed, the seat was given to Naisoroi and Gavidi stood for the seat under the Western United Front banner. A toss-up between the Alliance Party and the Western United Front with the Alliance having a slight edge. **Results**: 4,829 **Alliance Party**, 3,791 Western United Front, 406 Coalition.

Ba / Nadi. **Apisai Tora (Alliance Party)**: the sitting member and minister for communications and works, with a long history as a trade unionist and political figure in Fiji (formerly with the NFP). Senator Aporosa Rakoto had also expressed interest in the seat, but there was little chance of it not being given to Tora. **Simione Durutalo (Coalition)**: a member of the sociology department at the University of the South Pacific, on leave on a PH.D. scholarship in the United States; was active in the founding the the Labour Party; considered one of the Coalition's top potential native Fijian candidates, strongly identified with western Fijian interests. After the announcement of his candidacy, there remained some doubt as to whether he would return from the United States to stand. It was finally announced that he would stand, but he did not physically arrive in Fiji until mid-March, having taken leave from his studies to contest the election. He was not considered to have a good chance of winning the seat, but was expected to make a strong showing and to help swing votes to other Coalition candidates (such as Labour Party leader Bavadra). **Results**: 7,868 **Alliance Party**, 2,597 Coalition.

Vuda / Yasawa. **Ratu Sir Josaia Tavaiqia (Alliance Party)**: age 56; born at Viseisei, Vuda; worked as a customs officer and then as a hotel manager from 1958 to 1972; was installed as the Tui Vuda in 1972; nominated to the Senate by the Great Council of Chiefs; won election to the House of Representatives in 1977 and 1982 for the Vuda/Yasawa seat and has served as minister of state for forests (a position created to try to placate western landowners as a result of disputes in the pine industry). The title of Tui Vuda provides him with strong traditional support in the area and he is seen as a key figure in maintaining Alliance Party power in the west. He is also chairman of the Ba Provincial Council and serves on a number of government bodies (such as the Native Land Trust Board and Native Land Development Corporation). Interest in the seat was also expressed by Young Alliance member and present senator Jona Qio, but there was little chance of the seat not being given to Tavaiqia. **Etuate Tavai (Coalition)**: age 52; also from the village of Viseisei; worked for the Agriculture Department, in the hotel industry, and then for the Polynesian Cultural Center in Hawaii; went to work for the Native Land Trust Board in 1971; resigned from the NLTB when he was not awarded study leave to attend university; received a B.A. degree from the University of the South Pacific in 1976 and then returned to work for the NLTB; resigned from the NLTB again in 1982 and returned to Viseisei to work as a cane farmer; served as president of the Lautoka Rugby Union and as a representative on the Sugar Cane Growers Council; has been an Alliance Party member of the Lautoka City Council; accused the Alliance Party of not serving the interests of poor cane farmers. The Western United Front put forward Semisi Nadriubalavu as a candidate. This was a safe seat for the Alliance Party, but the Coalition was hoping for a good showing. **Results**: 8,569 **Alliance Party**, 1,221 Coalition, 609 Western United Front.

Bua / Macuata. **Militoni Leweniqila (Alliance Party)**: age 50; from Udu Point, Macuata, Vanua Levu; the sitting member; worked for the NLTB and then entered Parliament in 1972; held a number of ministerial positions until the end of 1985, first as assistant minister for Fijian affairs and rural development in 1977 and then he was promoted to full cabinet rank in 1979 as minister of state for lands and mineral resources and then minister for housing and urban development; became minister for home affairs in 1985. His relations with Mara were strained, especially after he had been removed from his ministership, and it was thought that he would not be renominated for the seat. After being made to step down as minister of home affairs (under a cloud of allegations of corruption), Leweniqila had been appointed to a high salaried post as managing director of the Macuata Development Corporation, a move that stirred considerable controversy. (The corporation secured a F$500,000 loan from the Fiji Development Bank and questions quickly arose over use of the funds. The corporation was forced to close down in April 1988 for failure to repay the loan.) Paula Sotutu had resigned as head of the Pacific liaison unit of ESCAP (a post he had held for six years) and returned to Fiji to stand for the seat. In the end, Mara decided to stay with Leweniqila, who was known to have a strong base among the constituents, and Sotutu decided to stand as an independent. **Koresi Matatolu (Coalition)**: age 48; born in Suva (but with kinship ties in Bua); graduated from Marist Brother's High School; trade unionist and cane farmer; first became a member of Parliament in 1978 in a by-election on the Flower ticket for the North West Fijian national seat (which he won again in 1982); associated with Jai Ram Reddy. Deputy Opposition Leader Matatolu agreed to give up his North Western Fijian national seat to Bavadra and move to Bua-Macuata, which is his home area (and the home area of Bavadra's first wife), and he served as chairman of the Bua Provincial Council. Matatolu had been approached by the Alliance Party to run as an independent against Bavadra, but he had refused. Although it was considered a safe Alliance seat, Sotutu's candidacy and Matatolu's base of support raised the possibility of a tough campaign. **Results**: 7,634 **Alliance Party**, 662 Coalition.

Cakaudrove. **Viliame Gonelevu (Alliance Party)**: age 46; from Vanuavou, Cakaudrove; received a Bachelor of Engineering degree from the University of New South Wales (is the only qualified hydro engineer in Fiji); worked for the Fiji Electricity Authority until he resigned following a union-related dispute; worked as a teacher and then as educational secretary for the Methodist church; made chairman of the Fiji Electricity Authority and the Civil Aviation Authority of Fiji by Mara and placed on the board of the Fiji Broadcasting Commission; adviser to the Cakaudrove Provincial Council, serving on its business committee. Gonelevu was given the ticket instead of the Alliance incumbent, Jone Naisara (minister for energy), in a nod to local sentiment (the move was endorsed at a meeting of the Cakaudrove Provincial Council and known to be backed by Ganilau). Naisara, a long-serving member of Parliament, was faced with growing opposition in the province due to what was perceived as his relative inactivity. **Tevita Daugunu (Coalition)**: age 52; born of a chiefly Cakaudrove family; is popularly known around the province as 'the Headmaster'; educated at the University of the South Pacific;

served as head teacher at Vanuavou primary school for the past fifteen years; active in rugby union; a member and founder of two musical groups; a lay Methodist preacher; resigned from his post to run for office, being highly critical of the lack of development in Cakaudrove after seventeen years of Alliance Party rule. This was a safe Alliance Party seat. **Results**: 9,994 **Alliance Party**, 519 Coalition.

GENERAL NATIONAL SEATS

Southern. **Peter Stinson (Alliance Party)**: age 41; born in Suva; attended Auckland University, joined the family business, Stinson Limited, in 1966; in 1967 became managing director of the Stinson Pearce Group; left Fiji for a period to work in Hong Kong for Jardine Matheson; returned to Fiji in 1981 and went back to the Stinson Pearce Group as chief executive and then as chairman; his business affairs were intertwined with Mara and others in the Alliance Party; elected to Parliament in 1982; served as minister for energy and mineral resources until mid-1983, when he resigned from the cabinet to enable him to devote more time to the failing family business; rejoined the cabinet in early 1985 as minister for economic planning and development, planning and tourism. Stinson was a target for allegations of corruption in the Alliance government, especially with respect to his alleged association with known criminal figures and individuals with gambling interests from Australia and to question-able real estate deals in Fiji. **Andrew Miller (Coalition)**: age 49; born at Vatukoula; worked for an insurance company for a few years and then established his own business in Suva. The Fijian Nationalists also fielded a candidate for this seat, sixty-year-old retired mechanical engineer Fred Elbourne. The Alliance Party was considered likely to win, but a Coalition victory could not be counted out because of the Fijian Nationalist Party vote. **Voters registered:** 3,863 General Elector, 30,583 Fijian, 21,020 Indian, Total 55,466. **Results**: 23,610 **Alliance Party**, 16,138 Coalition, 3,075 Fijian Nationalist Party.

Eastern. **Jim Ah Koy (Alliance Party)**: age 51; worked for Burns Philp and then Armstrong and Springhill; established his own business, Office Equipment Limited, in 1967, which later bought out Armstrong and Springhill; sold Office Equipment Limited to Burns Philp in 1976; in 1971, had set up another company, Kelton Investments, and later Kelton Marketing; is chairman and managing director of a number of companies owned by the Kelton Group; is a close Mara associate (Mara's personal financial adviser); first entered Parliament in 1982, winning the Suva and Central communal seat. The Eastern seat had been held by Charles Walker, who took over the Vanua Levu seat for the 1987 election. **David Eyre (Coalition)**: age 36; born in Suva; employed by Air Pacific as an aircraft maintenance engineer since 1969; became president of the Air Pacific Employees' Association in 1984 and later a vice-president of the Labour Party; had initially been picked for the Western communal seat. This was thought to be a safe Alliance Party seat, but there was some concern on the part of the Alliance Party. **Voters registered:** 1,068 General Elector, 37,500 Fijian, 23,215 Indian, Total 61,783. **Results:** 29,608 **Alliance Party**, 20,502 Coalition.

Northern. **Vincent Lobendahn (Alliance Party)**: former secretary of the Fiji Nurses Association who had sought unsuccessfully to counter growing Labour Party influence in the association. **Edmund March (Coalition)**. This was considered a safe Coalition seat. **Voters registered:** 576 General Elector, 19,470 Fijian, 35,501 Indian, Total 55,547. **Results:** 28,742 **Coalition**, 20,503 Alliance Party.

Western. **Tony Wilkinson (Alliance Party)**. **Chris Work (Coalition)**: age 47; an engineer and Fiji Electricity Authority supervisor at Sigatoka. This was a safe Coalition seat. **Voters registered:** 1,150 General Elector, 22,148 Fijian, 38,763 Indian, Total 62,061. **Results:** 34,077 **Coalition**, 18,905 Alliance Party.

Vanua Levu/Lau/Rotuma. **Charles Walker (Alliance Party)**: age 58; finance minister, 1979–83; minister for primary industries in the latest Mara government. The seat had been held by Minister for Housing and Urban Affairs Edward Beddoes. Beddoes had lost popularity and the party decided that he had become a liability. Walker had held the Eastern General national seat. **William Heritage (Coalition)**. This was considered the safest General national seat for the Alliance Party. **Voters registered:** 1,309 General Elector, 32,145 Fijian, 24,030 Indian, Total 57,484. **Results:** 30,814 **Alliance Party**, 19,120 Coalition.

GENERAL COMMUNAL SEATS

Northern and Eastern. **Leo Smith (Alliance Party)**: age 47; born in Savusavu; studied accountancy at Victoria University, Wellington; returned to Fiji in 1973 and went into business as a customs and shipping agent; became national secretary of the General Electors' Association in 1975; member of Alliance Party management board; prime minister's nominee to Senate in 1986; has interests in the copra industry and Mara appointed him to several boards in the coconut industry. **Stanley Simpson (Coalition)**: age 34; attended the University of the South Pacific for one year and then worked for the Fiji Sugar Corporation as a field officer for nine years and an estate manager for the NLTB for four years. The Coalition originally had named Labasa town councillor Charles Johnson as its candidate. It was considered a safe Alliance Party seat in the past, but there was dissatisfaction with the choice of Smith as a candidate. Hugh Thaggard had been the sitting member (he had run unopposed in 1977 and had received 1,138 out of 1,523 votes against two other candidates in 1982), and there were those who wanted him to run again. Thaggard decided to run as an independent. One worry for the Alliance Party was that Thaggard's relatives outnumbered Smith's relatives, and a three-way split was seen as endangering the Alliance Party hold on the seat. **Results**: 896 **Alliance Party**, 123 Coalition.

Western. **David Pickering (Alliance Party)**: age 50; born in Lautoka; worked for the Public Works Department for twenty-six years; became deputy permanent secretary for works and then joined the Fiji Electricity Authority, serving as general manager for the past eight years; active in the Alliance Party and in supporting Alliance Party policies for many years. **Daniel Johns (Coalition)**: age 50; born in Lautoka; studied for the priesthood in New Zealand and spent twelve years in the Catholic ministry in Fiji; left the priesthood in 1975 to work as a sales manager for Hooker (Fiji) limited; went to work for W.A. Flick and Company in 1976; set up his own pest control business in 1980; well-known in sports circles, having served as an officer for several sporting associations, managed the Fiji contingent to the 1983 South Pacific Games, and worked as a part-time sports announcer over Radio Fiji. This was a fairly safe seat for the Alliance Party if it was able to maintain its traditional General Elector loyalty. **Results**: 1,323 **Alliance Party**, 197 Coalition.

Suva/Central. **Archie Seeto (Alliance Party)**: age 53; a part-European/part-Chinese, born in Kadavu, raised in Suva, and educated in both Fiji and China; worked in the family business on his return from China in the late 1940s; became the town council clerk in Suva in the early 1950s and remained with the council for twenty-three years; resigned to take up a post as secretary and general manager of Naviti Investments and in 1978 joined the New Zealand firm, Bowring, Burgess, Marsh and McLennan; then spent three years in New Zealand on a familiarization program; was convinced to resign from the company to run for office in the 1987 election. **Quake Raddock (Coalition)**: age 33; born in Suva, from a prominent Alliance Party family; worked as a clerk for Coopers & Lybrand between 1973 and 1982, and then Colonial Mutual Life; resigned to take up sports training and became a champion weightlifter (he was the Fiji National Power Lifting champion); founded the Workout Inn in 1984. Timoci Bavadra became a regular at the gym and was seen as Raddock's political mentor. he was thought to be the Coalition's best chance to pick up a General communal seat. **Results:** 2,887 **Alliance Party,** 711 Coalition.

Appendixes

B: An Address to the Nation
Dr. T.U. Bavadra

A year ago, the Government that you elected, based on a democratic, mutually accepted Constitution, was ousted through the force of arms. Following that unprecedented event in this country, Fiji has faced a very difficult time.

It has gone through five successive governments and faced a tattered economy, a massive devaluation, a reduction of salaries, a rise in the level of unemployment, a deterioration in medical and other government services, a devastating loss of many professional and technical people, and a deteriorating law and order situation – not to mention a virtual collapse of our sense of self-respect and national pride.

All these events have brought untold suffering on our people; it has sharpened the divisions in our country in racial, religious and regional terms. It is sad indeed to think that all these difficulties need not have arisen.

Hardly two years ago, our country was described 'as a symbol of hope' in the world. Most of us believed this despite the fact that we had differing opinions on the way our beloved country was actually being run.

I need not remind you of the hopes we had as a newly elected government to address many of the problems that had previously been undetected or ignored: problems of the ordinary people; of the young people as well as the old, problems of the sick, the poor and the unemployed. You know how we were deeply concerned about the way our women were being treated as second and third class citizens. We had hoped to address the problems of our Fijian brothers and sisters, particularly those problems relating to land, culture, education, and their economic advancement. We were also aware of the fears and aspirations of our Indian brothers and sisters and their special contribution and needs. In fact we were fully awake to the needs and aspirations of all the people of this bountiful, beautiful, multiracial nation of ours. We are also aware of the fact that we were scarcely given the chance to fully put our policies into practice. I hardly have to remind you of that. But despite the setbacks of the last 12 months we are as determined as ever to reestablish a firmer basis for a free, democratic and peaceful society; one that would help rebuild the confidence of our people in our country; in themselves, in one another – irrespective of race, religion or creed.

I extend to all our citizens in these most difficult times my sincere sympathy. I particularly remember those who have lost jobs; those who have been harassed for no fault of their own; those whose properties have been damaged or devalued; those who have lost friends and loved ones; those who experience a sense of gloom, uncertainty and insecurity; those who have almost lost their faith in humanity.

At the same time I must congratulate those of you who have stood firm in upholding the traditional values of compassion, love and respect for one another as equals – because you have courageously resisted the communal pressures that have fanned hatred, violence and racism. I need not remind you that it is through these positive values of love, compassion and understanding that we have the basis for a secure, enduring and peaceful society.

From time to time we are told not to look back to the past. People who make this special pleading do so out of political convenience or a guilty conscience. And yet it is the same people who want to take us back to the past by proposing to introduce regressive Constitutional changes that will promote communalism rather than multi-racialism. I am afraid such proposals will do the greatest harm to those who are being denied the positive benefits of a modern society. Sadly, those who do not understand the past are in danger of repeating the mistakes of the past. I need not remind you that the present is intricately tied up with the past, and that we cannot understand the present or the future, without understanding our past. Let there be no doubt that the present crisis the people of Fiji are undergoing is the direct result of the drastic events of a year ago.

We have had a proud past and I believe that we need to project into the future some of the enduring values we have developed and which made our country once an envy of many. Let us not too easily give up what is sound, fair and just. Let us not too easily be misled by the rhetoric of expediency. We must hold firmly on to the tested values embedded in our religions, and in our common heritage.

Our future will depend on how we now approach some of the tasks that are before us. I, for one, do not accept that there are good enough reasons to reject totally our 17-year-old Constitution. To reject the 1970 Constitution substantially is to deny the wisdom derived from our experience. Unless we have a fair and just Constitution, our chances of acceptance into the Commonwealth will be fraught with difficulties. Our standing in the eyes of the international community will largely be determined by the quality of the Constitution we have. We must therefore continue to push for nothing short of equality of all our people irrespective of race. This does not mean that we do not recognise the special needs of our ethnic Fijians or the weaker members of our society. Whilst these special needs have to be addressed, we must make sure that it does not erode the concept of equality, justice and fairness, the cornerstone of any responsible Constitution.

We must also ensure that the Judiciary is independent and free from interference, which will ensure that we attract high quality judges from here and abroad. At this time in our history, we must make sure that justice is not only done but also it is seen to be done.

We cannot be isolated anymore. We need the support and friendship of the Commonwealth, both in terms of our trade and economic relations, but more so because we believe equally in the Commonwealth Principles of equality, democracy and our common opposition to any form of racism. Our longstanding relationship with the Commonwealth therefore needs to be reestablished as soon as practicable. We are all sadly aware of how the recent events have led the government to the severance of our ties with our beloved Queen. The Crown and the Commonwealth are inseparable. Personally speaking, not once in the last year have I, even for a moment, given up the idea of regarding the Queen as the Queen of Fiji. The abrogation of the Constitution and the severing of our connection with the Crown and the Commonwealth is, I am sure, deeply regretted by the vast majority of our people who would regard this insult not in keeping with our time-honoured tradition.

I, therefore, believe that we must work to re-establish that cherished connection, a wish in keeping with the wisdom of our chiefs and with wishes of the overwhelming majority of our people.

We have a lot of work ahead of us but I know that all of us, and certainly those who work with me, are ready and willing to begin the task of reconstruction. Let us therefore rededicate ourselves to restoring the hopes and visions of our people. Let us help restore our people's confidence in themselves, in one another and in their nation. Let us once again show the world that even in the depths of despair and uncertainty, we have the strength and the will to make our country once more a symbol of hope in a real way.

Let us pray for Fiji at 10 o'clock on May 14 and ask God to forgive us our trespasses and to give us the courage to face the challenges ahead of us and to grant us the wisdom to recognise the dignity and worth of every human being.

God bless Fiji
God bless the Queen

[Saturday, 14 May 1988]
[Printed in the *Fiji Times*]

Notes

1 Most of these dialects are mutually intelligible, and the majority of native Fijians are fluent in the Bauan dialect as well as their own dialect.

2 Examples of works that view Fiji from a plural society perspective are: E.K. Fisk, *The Political Economy of Independent Fiji* (Canberra: Australian National University Press 1970); and R.S. Milne, *Politics in Ethnically Bipolar States* (Vancouver: University of British Columbia Press 1981).

3 Discussions of the various theoretical perspectives in Pacific islands scholarship are provided in the essays included in a special issue of the *Journal of Pacific Studies* 9 (1983), entitled 'Social Science in the South Pacific.' Among the works that approach the study of Fiji from a class perspective are: 'Atu Bain, 'Vatukoula Rock of Gold: Labour in the Gold Mining Industry of Fiji, 1930–1970' (PH.D. thesis, Australian National University 1985); Simione Durutalo, 'Internal Colonialism and Unequal Development: The Case of Western Viti Levu' (MA thesis, University of the South Pacific 1985); S. Durutalo, *The Paramountcy of Fijian Interest and the Politicization of Ethnicity*, South Pacific Forum Working Paper No. 6 (Suva: USP Sociological Society 1986); William Sutherland, 'The State and Capitalist Development in Fiji' (PH.D. diss., University of Canterbury, New Zealand 1984); and Michael C. Howard and Simione Durutalo, *The Political Economy of the South Pacific to 1945*, Centre for Southeast Asian Studies, Monograph No. 26 (Townsville: James Cook University 1987). A number of these works fit within the framework of labour history which has gained greater attention in the South Pacific over the past few years, and this has allowed a more thorough understanding of the class nature of Pacific island societies and politics. Of relevance in this regard is, Michael C. Howard and Linda Searcy Howard, *Industrial Relations in the*

South Pacific: A Preliminary Bibliography, South Pacific Forum Working Paper No. 4 (Suva: USP Sociological Society 1985).

4 For a critical review of the concept of the 'Pacific Way' and its political implications, see Michael C. Howard, 'Vanuatu: The Myth of Melanesian Socialism,' *Labour, Capital and Society* 16:2 (1983), 176–203.

5 Attention to resistance to colonial and chiefly rule is featured in the studies cited in note 2. Two other works that deal with resistance from a different theoretical perspective are: Alex Mamak and Ahmed Ali, eds., *Race, Class and Rebellion in the South Pacific* (Sydney: George Allen & Unwin 1979); and Peter Hempenstall and Noel Rutherford, *Protest and Dissent in the Colonial Pacific*, Institute of Pacific Studies (Suva: University of the South Pacific 1984).

6 Until the coup in Fiji, Papua New Guinea's military had been almost the sole subject of scholarly attention: see Peta Colebach, 'To Find a Path: The Army in Papua New Guinea' (PH.D. thesis, University of Sussex 1974); P. Mench, *The Papua New Guinea Military* (Canberra: Australian National University Press 1978); Ralph Premdas, 'Keeping the Military Out of Papua New Guinea's Politics,' *New Guinea Quarterly* 8:2 (1974); and U. Sundhaussen, 'The Army: A Political Role?' *New Guinea Quarterly* 8:2 (1974). In addition to Fiji, Vanuatu and Tonga are the other countries in the region where the possibility of military intervention in politics has been the subject of informal discussions.

CHAPTER TWO: COLONIAL AND PRECOLONIAL FIJI

1 See entries in the Bibliography on Roth and Scarr.

2 W.R. Geddes, 'Fijian Social Structure in a Period of Transition,' in *Anthropology in the South Seas*, ed. J.D. Freeman and W.R. Geddes (New Plymouth, New Zealand: Avery 1959), 210.

3 G.K. Roth, *Fijian Way of Life* (Melbourne: Oxford University Press 1953), 1.

4 Ibid., 4.

5 Peter France, *The Charter of the Land: Custom and Colonization in Fiji* (Melbourne: Oxford University Press 1969), xiv. The chief in question was Ratu Bonaveidogo of Macuata, giving evidence on the position of the Tui Macuata in 1958.

6 John Clammer, 'Colonialism and the Perception of Tradition in Fiji,' in *Anthropology and the Colonial Encounter*, ed. T. Asad (London: Ithaca Press 1973), 213.

7 See entries in the Bibliography for Lal and Durutalo. Also see Simione Durutalo, 'The Liberation of the Pacific Island Intellectual,' *Review* (University of the South Pacific) 4:10 (1983), 6–18; and 'Buccaneers and Chiefly Historians (D. Routledge, Matanitu: The Struggle for Power in Early Fiji),' *Journal of Pacific Studies* 11 (1985), 117–56.

8 John Gibbons and F. Clunie, 'Sea Level Changes and Pacific Prehistory: New Insights into Early Human Settlement of Oceania,' *Journal of Pacific History* 21:2 (1986), 58–82. Portions of this chapter have been taken in revised form from Michael C. Howard and Simione Durutalo, *The Political Economy of the South Pacific to 1945*, Centre for Southeast Asian Studies, Monograph No. 26 (Townsville: James Cook University 1987).

9 R.A.Derrick, *A History of Fiji* (Suva: Government Press 1950), 9.

10 Ibid., 204.

11 Ibid., 201.

12 France, *The Charter of the Land*, 109.

13 Solomon Islands labourers remained in Fiji after the recruitment of indentured labourers from the Solomon Islands ended in 1911, working primarily on copra plantations in the northern portion of the colony. Some also drifted into Suva where they took up odd jobs, especially around the wharf. They were forced to move from Suva in 1940 and scattered to several nearby settlements. Today, the largest settlement of Solomon Islanders in Fiji is at Wailoku, a 285-acre site on the outskirts of Suva which is leased from native Fijian landowners and administered by the Anglican church. There are six villages at the Wailoku site, occupied by approximately 1,200 Solomon Islanders. There is another settlement of Solomon Islanders at Wainiloku near Levuka, and others are to be found living near Labasa, Savusavu, Vatukoula, and Navua, as well as on the islands of Taveuni and Kadavu. They are easily the poorest ethnic community in the country, suffer from an insecurity based on their lack of land rights, and are almost completely lacking in political power or influence.

14 K. Buckley and K. Klugman, *The History of Burns Philp* (Sydney: Burns Philp 1981), 76.

15 See Timothy J. Macnaught, *The Fijian Colonial Experience: A Study of the Neotraditional Order Under British Colonial Rule Prior to World War II*, Pacific Research Monograph No. 7 (Canberra: Australian National University 1982).

16 Ibid.

17 Peter Worsley, *The Trumpet Shall Sound* (London: MacGibbon & Kee 1957), 29.

18 *The Cyclopedia of Fiji* (Sydney: The Cyclopedia Company of Fiji 1907), 214.

19 Macnaught, *The Fijian Colonial Experience*, 75, 79.

20 William Sutherland, 'The State and Capitalist Development in Fiji' (PH.D. diss., University of Canterbury, Christchurch 1984), 231.

21 Cited in Macnaught, *The Fijian Colonial Experience*, 90.

22 See Kevin Hince, 'The Earliest Origins and Suppression of Trade Unionism in the Fiji Islands,' *New Zealand Journal of Industrial Relations* 10 (1985), 93–101.

23 'Atu Bain, 'Labour Protest and Control in the Goldmining Industry of Fiji, 1930–1970,' *South Pacific Forum* 3:1 (1986), 39.

24 Cited in K.L. Gillion, *The Fiji Indians* (Canberra: Australian National University Press 1977), 11.

25 A.J. Chapelle, 'The Fijian Voice in Fiji's Colonial History,' *Journal of Pacific Studies* 1 (1975), 57.

26 Sukuna advised the colonial government on the selection of commoners for tertiary education and government positions. In 1945, reacting to the growing number of commoners seeking higher education, 'Sukuna warned the Council of Chiefs that education would increasingly vie with rank in the recruitment of the administrative and political elite' (from Legislative Council Paper 10 (1945), cited in Robert Norton, *Race and Politics in Fiji* (St. Lucia: University of Queensland Press 1977), 187.

27 Cited in Deryck Scarr, *Fiji: A Short History* (Sydney: Allen & Unwin 1984), 139.

28 Ibid.

29 Bain, 'Labour Protest and Control in the Goldmining Industry,' pg. 39.

30 Michael Moynagh, *Brown or White?: A History of the Fiji Sugar Industry, 1873-1973*, Pacific Research Monograph No. 5 (Canberra: Australian National University 1981), 170.

31 Bain, 'Labour Protest and Control in the Goldmining Industry,' 44–5.

32 Moynagh, *Brown or White?* 164.

33 An establishment view of the workings of Fijian Administration is provided by G.K. Roth in his *Fijian Way of Life* (Melbourne: Oxford University Press 1953), Ch. 4. Other views are provided by Cyril Belshaw, *Underneath the Ivi Tree* (Berkeley: University of California Press 1964), Ch. 18; and R.R. Nayacakalou, *Leadership in Fiji* (Melbourne: Oxford University Press 1975).

34 Cited in Ahmed Ali, *Plantation to Politics: Studies on Fiji Indians* (Suva: Institute of Pacific Studies and Fiji Times Herald 1980), 147.

35 John Wesley Coulter, *The Drama of Fiji: A Contemporary History* (Rutland, VT: Charles E. Tuttle 1967), 126.

CHAPTER THREE: ALLIANCE PARTY RULE

1 Simione Durutalo, *The Paramountcy of Fijian Interests and the Politicization of Ethnicity*, South Pacific Forum Working Paper No. 6 (Suva: USP Sociological Society 1986), 1.

2 Ibid.

3 Michael C. Howard, 'Vanuatu: The Myth of Melanesian Socialism,' *Labour, Capital and Society* 16:2 (1983), 180–1.

4 Ibid., 181.

5 *Fiji Times*, 29 August 1977.

6 For an interesting discussion of 'Russophobia' in the South Pacific with particular reference to the Soviet-Kiribati fishing agreement, see Uentabo F. Neemia, 'Russophobia and Self-determination in Kiribati,' *South Pacific Forum* 3:2 (1986), 136–49.

7 The discussion of labour relations is taken from Michael C. Howard, 'The Evolution of Industrial Relations in Fiji and the Reaction of Public Employees' Unions to the Current Economic Crisis,' *South Pacific Forum* 2:2 (1985), 115–16.

8 For a more detailed discussion of the 1959 strike, see Peter Hempenstall and Noel Rutherford, *Protest and Dissent in the Colonial Pacific*, Institute of Pacific Studies (Suva: University of the South Pacific 1984), 73–86.

9 For more details concerning the 1960 strike and founding of the Federation of Cane Growers, see Michael Moynagh, *Brown or White? A History of the Fiji Sugar Industry, 1873-1973*, Pacific Research Monograph No. 5 (Canberra: Australian National University 1981).

10 Oskar Spate, *The Fijian People: Economic Problems and Prospects*, Council Paper No. 13 (Suva: Legislative Council of Fiji 1959), 77.

11 Ibid., 93.

12 Ibid., 98.

13 Ibid., 97.

14 Alan Burns, *Report of the Commission of Enquiry into the Resources and Population Trends of the Colony of Fiji*, Council Paper No. 1 (Suva: Legislative Council of Fiji 1960).

15 Ibid., 29.

16 *Fiji Legislative Council Debates*, 1960, 634; cited in Ahmed Ali, 'Fiji: Political Change, 1874–1960,' in *Politics in Fiji*, ed. Brij Lal (Sydney: Allen & Unwin 1986), 39.

17 Norman Meller and James Anthony, *Fiji Goes to the Polls: The Crucial Legislative Council Elections of 1963* (Honolulu: University Press of Hawaii 1968), 3–4.

18 Robert Norton, *Race and Politics in Fiji* (St. Lucia: University of Queensland Press 1977), 35.

19 Roderic Alley, 'The Emergence of Party Politics,' in *Politics in Fiji*, ed. Brij Lal (Sydney: Allen & Unwin 1986), 31.

20 See Jacqueline Leckie, 'The Functioning of Civil Service Unions During the Colonial Era in Fiji,' *South Pacific Forum* 3:1 (1986), 11–36.

21 Simione Durutalo, 'Internal Colonialism and Unequal Regional Development: The Case of Western Viti Levu, Fiji' (MA thesis, University of the South Pacific 1985), 407. Also see R.R. Nayacakalou, *Leadership in Fiji* (Melbourne: Oxford University Press 1975), 95–6.

22 *Fiji Times*, 26 August 1961.

23 *Fiji Times*, 15 August 1961; cited in Durutalo, 'Internal Colonialism and Unequal Regional Development,' 409.

24 Broadcast over Radio Fiji and reproduced in the *Fiji Times* cited in Durutalo, 'Internal Colonialism and Unequal Regional Development,' 405.

25 Meller and Anthony, *Fiji Goes to the Polls*, 28.

26 Alley, 'The Emergence of Party Politics,' 32–3.

27 Ibid., 32.

28 Ibid., 33. Nayacakalou was a commoner who had received a PH.D. in anthropology in London under the supervision Raymond Firth and then taught at the University of Sydney. At the urging of Sukuna, he had returned to Fiji to work with the Fijian Administration. Although, in some ways, he was clearly a part of the native Fijian establishment, after his return to Fiji, his voice was one of moderation.

29 Ibid., 35.

30 Deryck Scarr, *Fiji: A Short History* (Sydney: Allen & Unwin 1984), 170.

31 Norton, *Race and Politics in Fiji*, 205.

32 Ibid.

33 Scarr, *Fiji: A Short History*, 35.

34 Cited in Norton, *Race and Politics in Fiji*, 124.

35 The Alliance Party won all of the thirteen seats in Ba, defeating NFP candidates in eight seats (including Tora). The Alliance Party and independents polled 4,795 votes to 768 for the NFP. The Alliance Party and independents won seven of the nine seats in Nadroga-Navosa, with the NFP winning two. The voting total was 3,931 to 678. The NFP had managed to win 17 per cent of the votes.

36 Trevor Gould, *Report by Sir Trevor Gould, Kt., LL.M., on the Trade Dispute between the Airport, Hotel and Catering Workers' Union and Qantas Empire Airways Ltd.*, Council Paper No. 34 (Suva: Legislative Council of Fiji 1967).

37 A.T. Denning, *The Award of the Rt. Hon. Lord Denning in the Fiji Sugar Cane Contract Dispute 1969*, Supplement to the Royal Gazette (Suva: Government Printer 1970); see also Michael Moynagh, *Brown or White? A History of the Fiji Sugar Industry, 1873-1973*, 235–6.

38 On the constitutional talks, see R.K. Vasil, 'Communalism and Constitution-making in Fiji,' *Pacific Affairs* 45:1 (1972).

39 Ahmed Ali, *Plantation to Politics: Studies on Fiji Indians* (Suva: Institute of Pacific Studies and The Fiji Times Herald 1980), 164.

40 *Fiji Times*, 26 November 1971, cited in Durutalo, 'Internal Colonialism and Unequal Regional Development,' 413.

41 Ibid., 413–14.

42 Alexander Mamak, *Colour, Culture and Conflict: A Study of Pluralism in Fiji* (Sydney: Pergamon Press 1978), 150.

43 Ibid., 153.

44 Ibid.,155.

45 Robert Norton, *Race and Politics in Fiji*, 136.

46 Ibid., 136.

47 Ibid., 140.

48 Ibid.

49 Mamak, *Colour, Culture and Conflict*, 171.

50 The discussion concerning industrial relations is taken from Howard, 'The Evolution of Industrial Relations in Fiji and the Reaction of Public Employees' Unions to the Current Economic Crisis,' 120-3.

51 Cited in C.H.Brown, 'Ethnic Politics in Fiji: Fijian-Indian Relations,' *Journal of Ethnic Studies* 5:4 (1978), 1; see also R.K. Vasil, *Politics in Bi-racial Societies* (Delhi: Vikas 1984), 137.

52 Durutalo, 'Internal Colonialism and Unequal Regional Development,' 34.

53 Ibid.

54 Discussion of the pine controversy is drawn from Durutalo, 'Internal Colonialism,' 421-37.

55 Ibid., 428.

56 Ibid., 433.

57 Ibid.

58 Ibid., 434.

59 *Report of the Royal Commission Appointed for the Purpose of Considering and Making Recommendations as to the most Appropriate Method of Electing Members to, and Representing the People of Fiji in, the House of Representatives*, Parliamentary Paper No. 24 (Suva: Parliament of Fiji 1975).

60 Ibid., 3.

61 Ibid.

62 Evidence from the two parties is summarized on pages four and five of the report.

63 Among those preparing this submission were Amelia Rokotuivuna, Joan Yee, Venessa Griffen, Claire Slatter, and Waden Narsey. Several of these people were responsible for publication of an early critical look at the political economy of Fiji, entitled *Fiji: A Developing Australian Colony* (Melbourne: International Development Action 1973), and some of them were to later become involved with the Fiji Labour Party around the time of the 1987 election.

64 *Report of the Royal Commission* (1975), 6.

65 Ibid., 19-20.

66 Ali, *Plantation to Politics*, 209.

67 *Fiji Times*, 7 April 1977 ('Election Special') and 9 April 1977; see also D. Murray, 'The Governor General's Constitutional Crisis,' *Politics* 13:2 (1978), 230-8.

68 For a more detailed discussion of the second 1977 election see Ralph R. Premdas, 'Elections in Fiji: Restoration of the Balance in September 1977,' *Journal of Pacific History* 14:3/4 (1979), 194-207.

69 Ibid., 197.

70 'Reddy Sets New Leadership Style,' *Fiji Times*, 14 August 1981.

71 The four proposals are discussed at length in Durutalo, 'Internal Colonialism and Unequal Regional Development,' 314-38.

72 The Phoenix Foundation is a right-wing American organization linked to backing the separatist movement on Santo in Vanuatu in 1980 and involved in seeking to set up a separate state on Minerva Reef, between Fiji and Tonga.

73 Durutalo, 'Internal Colonialism and Unequal Regional Development,' 438-9.

74 The founding of the Western United Front is discussed in Durutalo, 'Internal Colonialism,' 458-68.

75 *Report: FTUC/ILO National Seminar of Rural Workers Organisation: Nadi (Fiji)*, 13-17 August 1979 (Suva: FTUC/ILO 1979), 7.

76 Brij Lal, 'The Fiji General Election in 1982: The Tidal Wave that Never Came,' *Journal of Pacific History* 18:2 (1983), 134.

77 *Fiji Times*, 11 January 1982.

78 *Report of the Financial Review Committee*, Parliamentary Paper No. 17 (Suva: Parliament of Fiji 1979).

79 The text of the report was published in, *Report of the Royal Commission of Inquiry into the 1982 Fiji General Elections, the Hon. Sir John White, M.B.E., November 1983*, Appendix X, Parliamentary Paper No. 74 (Suva: Parliament of Fiji 1983).

80 Ibid.

81 *Fiji Sun* and *Fiji Times*, 4 July 1982.

82 *Fiji Times*, 18 July 1982.

83 *Fiji Times*, 10 August 1982. Previously Mara had accused the Indian high commissioner, Soonu Kochar, and her husband of being Soviet agents and of meddling in Fijian politics. These allegations led to a deterioration of relations between the two countries.

84 Robert Keith-Reid, 'Cold War in the House,' *Islands Business*, September 1982, 18.

85 Robert Keith-Reid, 'Queen of the Islands,' *Islands Business*, November 1982, 20.

86 Robert Keith-Reid, 'Could Unity Rule Work?' *Islands Business*, January 1988, 30-2.

87 *Report of the Royal Commission of Inquiry into the 1982 Fiji General Elections, the Hon. Sir John White, M.B.E., November 1983*, Parliamentary Paper No. 74 (Suva: Parliament of Fiji 1983). See also, Robert Keith-Reid, 'Poll Probe Marathon,' *Islands Business*, May 1983, 22-3.

88 See 'The $1 million Question,' *Islands Business*, June, 1983, 25.

89 Ibid.

90 Robert Keith-Reid, 'Fiji's Inquiry Collapse,' *Islands Business*, September 1983, 26.

91 *Fiji Sun*, 24 April 1986. Mara was among the witnesses summoned in

connection with the case.

92 *Fiji Times*, 13 June 1986.

CHAPTER FOUR: FIJI AND THE WORLD

1 See Michael C. Howard, 'Myth of the Soviet Menace in the South Pacific,' *Economic and Political Weekly* 21:7 (15 February 1986), 308–15.

2 Ibid., 311; see also John C. Dorrance, 'Coping with the Soviet Pacific Threat,' *Pacific Defence Reporter*, July 1983; and Richard Herr, 'Preventing a South Pacific Cuba,' *New Zealand International Review*, March/April 1982.

3 Howard, Myth of the Soviet Menace,' 311; see also 'Interview: Reagan's Pacific Isles Policies,' *Pacific Magazine*, May/June 1984, 64–5.

4 See Robert Keith-Reid, 'War on Tuna Pirates,' *Islands Business*, August 1984; and Graham S. Sem, 'Cooperation Management of Fisheries and Regionalism,' *South Pacific Forum* 3:2 (1986), 113–35.

5 See Uentabo F. Neemia, 'Russophobia and Self-determination in Kiribati,' *South Pacific Forum* 3:2 (1986), 136–49.

6 Suliana Siwatibau and B. David Williams, *A Call to a New Exodus: An Antinuclear Primer for Pacific People* (Suva: Lotu Pasifika Productions 1982); and James E. Winkler, *Losing Control ... Towards an Understanding of Transnational Corporations in the Pacific Islands Context* (Suva: Lotu Pasifika Productions 1982).

7 Senate Standing Committee on Foreign Affairs and Defence, *Australia's Defence Co-operation with Its Neighbours in the Asian-Pacific Region* (Canberra: Australian Government Publishing Service 1984), 27.

8 'How to Stop Hi-jacking,' *Pacific Islands Monthly*, March 1984.

9 Mara selected Mosese Qionibaravi to replace him as minister for foreign affairs. Qionibaravi later was replaced by Semesa Sikivou. Saunders was replaced as permanent secretary by Jone Kotobalavu, who was subsequently replaced by James Maraj. Maraj had come to Fiji from Trinidad as vice-chancellor of the University of the South Pacific. Securing Mara's favour, he left the university to assume the government post, and later there was speculation about his running for office for the Alliance Party.

10 Upon independence Semesa Sikivou was named permanent representative to the United Nations; R. Nair, high commissioner to Australia; and Josua Rabukawaqa, high commissioner to the United Kingdom. Upon expiration of these terms in 1976, Sikivou and Nair retired from the Public Service, and Rabukawaqa became Fiji's first representative and high commissioner to the Forum Island Countries as well as undersecretary of foreign affairs and chief of protocol (he retired in 1979). Sikivou was replaced by Berenado Vunibobo, Nair by Epeli Kacimaiwai, and Rabukawaqa by Joseph D. Gibson.

11 S.N. Nandan was the first ambassador to the EEC. He was succeeded in

1981 by Josua Cavalevu, who was followed in turn by Poseci Bune.

12 Relations between the Pinochet regime in Chile and Fiji grew partly as a result of ties between prominent Alliance Party chief David Toganivalu and members of the Pinochet regime in Chile. Diplomatic relations were established with Chile in 1973, and President Pinochet was invited to pay a visit to Fiji. Upon his arrival, Pinochet was greeted by a large number of protesters who were organized by unionists and church leaders. With the promise of further trouble, the remainder of the visit was cancelled and Pinochet left. The event proved an embarrassment for both the Mara government and for Pinochet, and relations between the two countries were dormant until after 1982 when a Chilean consul was appointed and Chilean diplomats again visited Fiji.

13 'Statement by the Chairman of the Fiji Delegation, the Right Honourable Ratu Sir K.K.T. Mara, K.B.E., Prime Minister of Fiji; Twenty-fifth Regular Session of the U.N. General Assembly, New York - 1970,' *Report on Foreign Affairs*, Parliamentary Paper No. 19 (Suva: Parliament of Fiji 1974), 22.

14 Ibid., 23.

15 Ibid.,1.

16 Ibid., 7.

17 Ibid., 10.

18 Ibid., 3.

19 See Sem, 'Cooperation Management of Fisheries and Regionalism'; G. Kent, *The Politics of Pacific Island Fisheries*, (Boulder, CO: Westview Press 1980); P.J. Ridings, *Resources Use Arrangements in Southwest Pacific Fisheries*, Pacific Islands Development Program (Honolulu: East-West Center 1982); and J. Van Dyke and S. Heftel, *Tuna Management in the Pacific* (Honolulu: East-West Environment and Policy Institute 1981).

20 See Michael C. Howard, 'Vanuatu: The Myth of Melanesian Socialism,' *Labour, Capital and Society* 16:2 (1983), 176-203.

21 Ralph Premdas and Michael C. Howard, 'Vanuatu's Foreign Policy: Contradictions and Constraints,' *Australian Outlook* 39:3 (1985), 183.

22 Palau, the Federated States of Micronesia, the Marshall Islands, Papua New Guinea, the Solomon Islands, Nauru, and Kiribati.

23 Howard, 'Vanuatu: The Myth of Melanesian Socialism,' 184-5.

24 Foreign borrowing amounted to F$5.1 million and foreign grants, F$2.0 million.

25 Government expenditure in 1983 was F$341.7 million. Government revenue that year was F$291.2 million (including F$9.1 million in foreign grants), with a deficit of F$50.5 million.

26 The UNDP and UNFPA provided F$1.4 million in assistance in 1983.

27 Richard Herr, 'Strategy and Security: The Choices are Few,' in *Foreign Forces in Pacific Politics*, ed. R. Crocombe and A. Ali, Institute of Pacific Studies (Suva: University of the South Pacific 1983), 298.

28 *Fiji Sun*, 14 April 1984 (this statement was made around the time of Eckert's departure). Eckert maintained ties with Mara after returning to the United States in 1984 and was to try to assist Mara after the 1987 coup by raising funds in the United States to help the financially strapped Rabuka regime.

29 *Fiji Focus*, 10 September 1982, 8–9. *Fiji Focus* began publication after the 1982 election and served primarily as a means of publicizing the activities of Alliance Party members of government.

30 *Fiji Times*, 16 May 1984.

31 See Robert Keith-Reid, 'Calling on Washington,' *Islands Business*, January 1985, 27.

32 Suazo had run into political trouble in India and was eventually expelled by the Indian government. The AAFLI had established a centre in Ahmedabad, Gujarat, which was used for promoting antagonisms among workers. Following publication of articles in the Indian press pointing to AAFLI's activities and linking the organization and Suazo to the CIA, the AAFLI was forced to leave India in early 1984.

33 'Ratu Sir Penaia Tells of Army Values,' *Sunday Sun* (supplement, 'The Royal Fiji Military Forces: 1873-1984'), 16 September 1984, 23.

34 Information based on a conversation between Ron Crocombe and Ganilau in 1972.

35 *Fiji: Eighth Development Plan 1981-1985: Volume 1* (Suva: Central Planning Office 1980), 274.

36 Ibid.

37 Eddie Dean and Stan Ritova, *Rabuka: No Other Way, His Own Story of the Fiji Coup* (Sydney: Doubleday 1988), 28.

CHAPTER FIVE: THE FIJI LABOUR PARTY

1 On the origins of the Fiji Labour Party also see Michael C. Howard, 'The Evolution of Industrial Relations in Fiji and the Reaction of Public Employees' Unions to the Current Economic Crisis,' *South Pacific Forum* 2:2 (1985), 106-63; and Michael C. Howard, 'The Trade Union Movement in Fiji,' in *Fiji: Future Imperfect?* ed. Michael Taylor (Sydney: Allen & Unwin 1987), 108-21.

2 A.F. Hurst and H.W. Nicol, *Report of the Public Service Review Team: 1981–82* (Suva: Government Printer 1984).

3 *Fiji Times*, 13 September 1983.

4 *Fiji Sun*, 29 September 1983.

5 *Fiji Times*, 23 March 1984.

6 *Fiji Times*, 23 July 1984.

7 *Fiji Times*, 10 November 1984, and 15 November 1984.

8 Bob Kumar was replaced as president of FANG in 1985 by University of

the South Pacific sociologist Vijay Naidu.

9 Statements by Chaudhry and Raman cited in Michael C. Howard, 'The Evolution of Industrial Relations in Fiji and the Reaction of Public Employess' Unions to the Current Economic Crisis,' 144.

10 *Fiji Sun*, 22 December 1984.

11 Michael C. Howard, 'The Evolution of Industrial Relations in Fiji and the Reaction of Public Employees' Unions to the Current Economic Crisis,' 146.

12 Ibid., 148.

13 See Michael C. Howard, 'Vanuatu: The Myth of Melanesian Socialism', *Labour, Capital and Society* 16:2 (1983), 176-203.

14 See Vijay Naidu, *The Fiji Labour Party and the By-elections of December 1985: A Report*, School of Social and Economic Development, Working Paper No. 2 (Suva: University of the South Pacific 1986).

15 Position statements by the parties on the national name issue appeared in the *Fiji Sun,* 18 February 1986, 3.

16 *Fiji Sun*, 8 April 1986.

17 *Fiji Sun*, 26 March 1986.

18 *Fiji Times*, 25 March 1986.

19 *Fiji Times*, 19 February 1986.

20 Ibid.

21 *Fiji Sun*, 21 February 1986.

22 *Fiji Sun*, 23 March 1986.

23 *Fiji Sun*, 24 March 1986.

24 *Fiji Times*, 14 March 1986.

25 *Fiji Sun*, 15 March 1986.

26 *Fiji Sun*, 25 May 1986.

27 Ibid.

28 *Fiji Sun*, 11 June 1986.

29 *Fiji Sun*, 16 June 1986.

30 Ibid.

31 *Fiji Sun*, 17 June 1986.

32 *Fiji Times*, 23 June 1986.

33 *Fiji Times*, 28 June 1986.

34 *Fiji Times*, 29 June 1986.

35 Conference Papers, Fiji Labour Party: First National Convention (19 July 1986).

36 Ibid.

37 *Fiji Times*, 17 August 1986.

38 Ibid.

39 Plan for Establishing a Landowners' Council and a National Lands and Resources Commission, Fiji Labour Party (no date).

40 Ibid.

41 'The Workers' Challenge,' *Pacific Islands Monthly*, November 1986, 22.

CHAPTER SIX:
THE 1987 ELECTION AND THE COALITION GOVERNMENT

1 Among the former Koya supporters who decided to remain with the Coalition were Noor Dean, Dr. Balwant Singh Rakkha and Senator Harnam Singh Golian. The main individuals forming the anti-Coalition group were longtime Koya stalwarts Vijaya Parmanandan, Subramani Basawaiya, and Shardha Nand.

2 *Fiji Sun* and *Fiji Times*, 28 January 1987.

3 *Sunday Sun*, 2 February 1987, 1.

4 *Fiji Times*, 14 March 1987.

5 *Fiji Sun*, 18 November 1986.

6 The advertisements were found in both the *Fiji Times* and the *Fiji Sun*.

7 "Trying Time for New Government," *Pacific Islands Monthly*, June 1987, 19.

8 *Fiji Sun*, 8 March 1987.

9 *Fiji Times*, 8 February 1987.

10 *Fiji Times*, 22 March 1987.

11 *Fiji Times*, 19 March 1987.

12 'Fiji Elections: Mara Government Defeated,' *Pacific Islands Monthly*, May 1987, 10.

13 The ministers in the Coalition government were as follows: **Timoci Bavadra**: prime minister/Public Service/Fijian Affairs/Home Affairs (Labour); native Fijian, trade unionist, medical doctor. **Jo Nacola**: Agriculture, Fisheries and Forestry (Labour); native Fijian, academic. **Tupeni Baba**: Education, Youth and Sports (Labour); native Fijian academic. **Joeli Kalou**: Labour and Immigration (Labour); native Fijian, trade unionist, teacher. **Mosese Volavola**: Lands, Energy and Mineral Resources (Labour); native Fijian, civil servant. **Temo Sukanaivalu**: Rural Development, Rehabilitation and Relief (NFP); native Fijian. **Satendra Nandan**: Health and Social Welfare (Labour/NFP); Indo-Fijian, academic. **Krishna Datt**: Foreign Affairs and Civil Aviation (Labour); Indo-Fijian, trade unionist, teacher. **Ahmed Bhamji**: Communications, Transport and Works (NFP); Indo-Fijian, businessman. **Mahendra Chaudhry**: Finance and Economic Planning (FLP); Indo-Fijian, trade unionist. **Harish Sharma**: deputy prime minister/Housing and Urban Affairs/Information (NFP); Indo-Fijian, lawyer. **Navin Maharaj**: Trade, Industry and Tourism (NFP); Indo-Fijian, businessman. **Jai Ram Reddy**: attorney general/Justice (NFP); Indo-Fijian, lawyer. **Chris Work**: Co-operatives and Consumer Affairs (Labour); Gen. Elector, engineer.

14 *Fiji Times*, 22 April 1987.

15 The leadership of the Taukei at this time included Inoke Kubuabola, Jone

Veisamasama, Apisai Tora, Jona Qio, Inoke Tabua, Viliame Gonelevu, and
Rev. Tomasi Raikivi. The first meeting of those who were to form the
Taukei Movement apparently took place in Suva on 15 April (*Islands
Business*, May 1988, 15). Subsequent meetings of Taukei leaders tended to
be held at the offices of either the Ports Authority or the Bible Society of
the South Pacific.

16 *Fiji Times*, 25 April 1987.

17 Ibid.

18 See Jeff Stein, 'Mystery Man of American Diplomacy,' *Boston Globe Maga-
zine*, 29 August 1982, 12; Michael Massing, 'America's Top Messenger
Boy,' *New Republic*, 16 September 1985, 22; and Ellen Ray and William
Schaap, 'The Modern Mithridates: Vernon Walters, Crypto-diplomat and
Terrorist,' *Covert Action Information Bulletin*, No. 26 (Summer 1986), 3–8.

19 *Fiji Times*, 9 April 1987.

20 The May coup gave Gavoka's union leadership a new lease, but he was
forced to step down as head of the Public Employees Union in the middle of 1988 because of ill health and he died a short time later.

21 The governor general's address was reported in both the *Fiji Times* and
Fiji Sun, 12 May 1987.

22 The Alliance members of the board included William Toganivalu, Timoci
Vesikula, Filipe Bole, Viliame Gonelevu, Mosese Qionibaravi, Apisai Tora,
and Taniela Veitata.

23 *Daily Hansard*, 13 May 1987.

CHAPTER SEVEN: THE MAY COUP

1 'Resumption of Debate on His Excellency's Address,' *Daily Hansard*, Parliament of Fiji, 14 May 1987, 139.

2 Ibid., 142. Captain Dugu's second in command in the take-over was Captain Savenaca Draunidalo, the former husband of Kuini Bavadra.

3 The account of events in the parliamentary chamber comes from interviews with several parliamentarians and others who were present at the
time of the coup, as well as published accounts in the *Fiji Times*, *Fiji Sun*,
Sydney Morning Herald, and *Islands Business* (June 1987 issue).

4 'Dr. Timoci Bavadra Interview,' *Four Corners* program (ABC), reporter
Greg Wilesmith, 25 May 1987.

5 David Robie, 'Evidence of Tribal Conspiracy in Fiji Coup,' *Dominion Sunday Times* (New Zealand), 21 June 1987, 6.

6 Transcript, *Four Corners* program (ABC), reporter Marian Wilkinson, 18
May 1987.

7 Ibid.; see also 'The Agony of 6 Days in Captivity at Veiuto,' *Fiji Times*, 21
May 1987, 8.

8 Transcript, *Four Corners*, 18 May 1987.

9 *Islands Business*, May 1988, 16.

10 Ibid.; see also Jim Sanday, 'The Coups of 1987: A Personal Analysis,' *Pacific Viewpoint* 30: 2 (1989), 116–31.

11 'Aust, NZ, "Disturbed" by Army Takeover,' *Fiji Times*, 15 May 1987, 2.

12 Ibid.

13 Press Release by Fiji Ministry of Information; see also *Four Corners* program, 18 May 1987; and 'Leader Justifies Military Coup,' *Fiji Times*, 15 May 1987, 3.

14 'G-G Talks to Nation,' *Fiji Times*, 15 May 1987, 3.

15 'Suva Showdown: Hope Rises for an End to Fiji's Crisis, as G-G Steps In,' *Time*, 25 May 1987, 16.

16 The others on the Council of Ministers included: William Toganivalu (Fijian Affairs), Apenisa Kurisaqila (Health), Litia Cakobau (Women and Culture), Filipe Bole (Education), Kelemedi Bulewa (Justice), Jone Veisamasama (Housing and Urban Affairs), Timoci Vesikula (Rural Development), Viliame Gonelevu (Telecommunications and Civil Aviation), and Josaia Tavaiqia (Forestry). Among those missing were Charles Walker, Mosese Qionibaravi (who was in hospital), David Toganivalu (who had lost his seat in the election and was seen as a rival to Mara for leadership of the Alliance Party), and Apisai Tora (a leading activist in the destabilization efforts and, at the time, charged with sedition in connection with his activities).

17 'Bavadra Speaks,' *Fiji Times*, 15 May 1987, 1.

18 The best example of someone promoting the 'Mara the Innocent' perspective is longtime Mara apologist Stuart Inder; see his 'Exlusive: Ratu Mara Puts His Case,' *The Bulletin*, 26 May 1987, 21.

19 Examples of writings that adhered closest to the CIA conspiracy thesis are: Max Watts and Mark James, 'The U.S. in Fiji: A Coup in Question,' *Covert Action*, No. 29 (Fall 1987), 7–10; Mark Lillyman and Max Watts, 'Strangers in Paradise,' *Playboy* (Australia), October 1987, 38, 40, 112–3; and Joann Wypijewski, 'The Fiji Coup: Was the U.S. Behind It?' *The Nation*, 15/20 August 1987, 117–20. A more balanced assessment from this perspective is found in: 'US Involvement in the Fiji Coup,' *Wellington Confidential*, No. 36 (June 1987).

20 An example of the middle-ground approach that focuses on internal politics, while not completely dismissing the possibility of U.S. involvement, is David Robie, 'Why the Fijian Plot Theory is Gaining Ground,' *Times on Sunday*, 12 July 1987, 12.

21 See Brij Lal, *Power and Prejudice: The Making of the Fiji Crisis* (Wellington: New Zealand Institute of International Affairs 1988).

22 Eddie Dean and Stan Ritova, *Rabuka: No Other Way, His Own Story of the Fiji Coup* (Sydney: Doubleday 1988), 80.

23 Ibid.

24 Ibid., 80–1.

25 Ibid., 81.

26 *Islands Business*, May 1988, 16.

27 Ibid., 18.

28 The party at Raikivi's is discussed in Dean and Ritova, *Rabuka: No Other Way*, 49–50.

29 K. Mingnall, *Sunday Star* 15 May 1988. Inoke Kubuabola gives some credence to this idea in his revelations (*Islands Business*, May 1988, 18) when he says that the Taukei approached Ganilau on 24 April asking him to intervene so that a coup would not be necessary.

30 This was related to formation of a F$1.8 million joint venture between Fiji Forest Industries and Kubuna Holdings (with which the governor general was associated) underwritten by Australian aid during the latter part of 1982. Rumours circulated that the deal was a political pay-off arranged between Mara and Ganilau and, moreover, that Ganilau himself had profited from the deal. See Michael C. Howard, 'Transnational Corporations: The Influence of the Capitalist World Economy,' in *Foreign Forces in Pacific Politics*, ed. Ahmed Ali and Ron Crocombe, Institute of Pacific Studies (Suva: University of the South Pacific 1983), 271–2.

31 The Muanikau land deal was a scandal involving the 'sale' of government lands in the central residential area of the Domain and Muanikau to Alliance Party cronies at a fraction of their value. Ganilau obtained a choice lot on Ratu Sukuna Road on which he built a large house (questions were raised about the source of funding for this as well) which was subsequently rented to the local European Economic Community representative. This and the Kubuna Holdings deal were among the earliest post-1982 election scandals involving the Mara government.

32 Dean and Ritova, *Rabuka: No Other Way*, 75.

33 Ibid.

34 David McKnight, 'U.S. Aid Funds Used to Grease Political Palms in Fiji,' *Sydney Morning Herald*, 26 March 1988, 1, 18.

35 *Islands Business*, May 1988, 16.

36 Ibid.

37 Wendy Bacon, 'Somebody's Man in Fiji,' *NZ Listener*, 26 December 1987, 20; see also Wendy Bacon, 'Paul Freeman: Fijian Army Officer with Friends in CIA,' *Times on Sunday*, 24 January 1988, 25; 'Who is Paul Freeman?' *Fiji Sun*, 9 July 1987, 1–2.

38 Bacon, 'Somebody's Man in Fiji,' 18.

39 Ibid., 20.

40 Dean and Ritova, *Rabuka: No Other Way*, 81–2.

41 'Fiji,' *Four Corners* program (ABC), reporter Wendy Bacon, 16 October 1987.

42 Ibid.

43 'McIntosh is listed in the 1983 Membership directory of the Association of former Intelligence Officers, and J. Mader's Who's Who in the CIA, and in Microassociates database is shown as having been stationed in Germany 1960–61, Japan 1967–8' (*Wellington Pacific Report*, No. 7 [January 1988], 3).

44 'Learn More About Fijian and Culture,' *Fiji Times*, 13 May, 1987, 10.

45 Bacon, *Four Corners.*

46 Ibid.

47 Wendy Bacon, 'The Company They Keep,' *The Eye*, March 1988, 18.

48 Bacon, *Four Corners.*

49 Ibid.

50 'US Involvement in the Fiji Coup,' *Wellington Confidential*, No. 36 (June 1987), 2.

51 'U.S. Coup Involvement Denied,' *Christchurch Press*, 18 June 1987.

52 See 'Fiji: Did Ratu Mara and/or William Paupe visit CINCPAC?' *Wellington Pacific Report*, No. 6 (December 1987), 2; see also 'Fiji Coups – The Mythology of U.S. Involvement' (Sydney: Consulate General of the United States of America [9 November 1987], 2).

53 *Sydney Morning Herald*, 18 May 1987; and *Dominion*, 26 May 1987.

54 *Washington Post*, 2 October 1986; see also Bill Schaap, 'The Endless Campaign: Disinforming the World on Libya,' *Covert Action*, No. 30 (Summer 1988), 76, 69–74.

CHAPTER EIGHT: AFTERMATH OF THE FIRST COUP

1 The relatively neutral members of the new council included Savenaca Siwatibau (from the same area in Cakaudrove as Rabuka and the governor of the Reserve Bank, whose presence was seen as important to minimize the economic damage done by the coup), Mumtatz Ali (a Muslim and one of the very few Indo-Fijians willing to be identified in public with the regime), and Rev. Daniel Mastapha (the highly respected former president of the Methodist church of Fiji and, at the time, its acting president).

2 *Straits Times*, 22 May and 26 May 1987.

3 *The Australian*, 30–31 May 1987, 19.

4 Trade between Fiji and Australia amounting to some F$250 million a year.

5 Other non-official aid bodies such as the Asia Foundation, which were closely associated with the American government, also continued to operate in Fiji.

6 The bill was House Resolution 248, introduced by Robert K. Dornan (Rep. of California) in August and finally agreed to by a voice vote of the House in late September 1987. The resolution expressed concern over developments in Fiji without committing the United States to any partic-

ular course of action.

7 The principal author of the report was Asesela Ravuvu, director of the Institute of Pacific Studies at the University of the South Pacific. Privately, Ravuvu had been an important supporter of the Fijian Nationalists for many years and now had become active with the Taukei. Academically, he had been a protégé of the former director of the institute, Professor Ronald Crocombe.

8 *Fiji Sun*, 9 July 1987.

9 *Report of the Constitutional Review Committee July/August 1987*, Parliamentary Paper No. 21 (Suva: Parliament of Fiji 1987).

10 Ibid.

11 *Fiji Times*, 23 July 1987.

12 *Fiji Times*, 1 August 1987.

13 *Report of the Constitutional Review Committee July/August 1987*, 22-4.

14 Ibid., 62-82.

15 Ibid., 81.

16 *Fiji Times*, 25 September 1987.

17 *Fiji Times*, 11 November 1987.

18 *Fiji Times*, 22 August 1987.

19 The Coalition did not publicize the letter immediately, as they were suspicious of its reliability and purpose. Once they felt that it was genuine, they decided to show it to the governor general. The letter was sent to the Fiji Independent News Service in Sydney for distribution to the Australian media, late on the afternoon of 24 September.

CHAPTER NINE:
THE SECOND COUP AND THE REPUBLIC OF FIJI

1 *Fiji Times*, 25 September 1987.

2 See Jale Moala, 'Regional Support,' *Islands Business*, September 1987, 7-8.

3 *Sydney Morning Herald*, 5 October 1987, 7.

4 *The Australian*, 7 October 1987, 10.

5 The members of the Republic of Fiji's first cabinet were as follows: **Col. Sitiveni Rabuka**: head of state/Home Affairs/head of Public Service; Filipe Bole: Foreign Affairs and Civil Aviation; Alliance M.P. and Mara's right-hand man in the Taukei. **Isimeli Bose**: Economic Development, Planning, Trade and Industry; Alliance Party campaign manager in 1982 and 1987 elections, political appointment by Mara to head Ports Authority (where offices used for Taukei meetings). **Kelemedi Bulewa**: attorney general/Justice; Taukei, lawyer with little previous experience. **Sakeasi Butadroka**: Lands and Mineral Resources; leader of Fijian Nationalist Party and strongly anti-Mara. **Litia Cakobau**: Women and Culture; former air-hostess, daughter of Ratu George Cakobau, very close to Rabu-

ka. **Josua Cavalevu**: Finance; Alliance Party, former ambassador, Methodist lay preacher and born-again Christian from Cakaudrove, landlord with financial problems. **Viliame Gonelevu**: Primary Industries; Alliance Party M.P. for Cakaudrove communal seat, related to Mara's wife through marriage, Methodist lay preacher. **Lt. Col. Ilaisa Kacisolomone**: Youth and Sports; army chief of staff, cricketer, loyal to Rabuka. **Inoke Kubuabola**: State and Information; Taukei, born-again Christian, secretary of the Fiji Bible Society. **Dr. Apenisa Kurisaqila**: Health; long-serving Alliance Party M.P., Mara devotee on the verge of bankruptcy. **Irene Jai Narayan**: Indian Affairs; defected from NFP to Alliance Party in 1987 election, now a Mara supporter. **Livai Nasilivata**: Housing and Urban Affairs; former Alliance Party minister in Mara camp. **David Pickering**: Tourism and Energy; Alliance Party M.P., strong Mara supporter, related to Mara's wife. **Rev. Tomasi Raikivi**: Social Welfare; leader among Taukei extremists. **Filimone Ralogaivau**: Education; Labour Party defector from Bua. **Josaia Tavaiqia**: Forests; Alliance Party M.P., important Mara stalwart in the west. **Apisai Tora**: Communication, Works and Transport; Alliance Party M.P., Taukei leader, willing to support whichever side likely to help him most. **Jone Veisamasama**: Rural Development; Taukei, former Alliance Party secretary, part of Mara faction but not an ardent loyalist. **Taniela Veitata**: Employment and Industrial Relations; Alliance Party M.P., Taukei leader and gang organizer, another important pro-Mara figure in the Taukei. **Meli Vesikula**: Fijian Affairs; Taukei extremist leader.

6 *Times on Sunday*, 29 November 1987.

7 Robert Keith-Reid, 'Fiji Under Colonel Rabuka,' *Islands Business*, November 1987, 7.

8 Ibid.

9 *Fiji Times*, 6 November 1987.

10 *Fiji Times*, 20 November 1987.

11 See 'Trouble in the Trees,' *Islands Business*, December 1987, 6–8; and Frank Serge, 'Diro Scandal Escalates,' *Pacific Islands Monthly*, December 1987, 14–5.

CHAPTER TEN: MARA'S RETURN

1 *Times on Sunday*, 29 November 1987.

2 *Sydney Morning Herald*, 13 January 1988.

3 Members of Mara's December 1987 cabinet were as follows: **Mara**: prime minister/Foreign Affairs; **Brig. Gen. Rabuka**: Home Affairs (military); **Col. Ilaisa Kacisolomone**: Youth and Sport (military); **Col. Apolosi Biuvakaloloma**: Rural Development and Rural Housing (military); **Col. Vatiliai Navunisaravai**: Fijian Affairs (military); **Apisai Tora**: Communications, Works and Transport (Mara-Taukei/Alliance M.P.); **Taniela Veitata**:

Employment and Industrial Relations (Mara-Taukei/Alliance M.P.); **Filipe Bole**: Education (Mara-Taukei/Alliance M.P.); **Josefata Kamikamica**: Finance and Economic Planning (Mara), General Manager of the Native Land Trust Board; **Charles Walker**: Information (Mara/Alliance M.P.); **Berenado Vunibobo**: Trade and Commerce (Mara), Fiji's U.N. ambassador (1975–80), recent high commissioner in London; **Sailosi Kepa**: attorney general/Justice (Mara), diplomat under Alliance Party government and lawyer, from Lau; **Irene Narayan**: Indian Affairs (Mara/Alliance M.P.); **Ishwari Bajpai**: Co-operatives and National Marketing Authority (Mara), President of the Indian Alliance; **Viliame Gonelevu**: Primary Industry (Mara/Alliance M.P.); **Apenisa Kurisaqila**: Health (Mara/Alliance M.P.); **David Pickering**: Tourism, Civil Aviation and Energy (Mara); **Josaia Tavaiqia**: Forests (Mara/Alliance M.P.); **Finau Tabakaucoro**: Women's Affairs and Social Welfare (Mara-Taukei); **Tomasi Vakatora**: Housing and Urban Development (Mara/Alliance M.P.); **William Toganivalu**: Lands and Mineral Resources (Mara/Alliance M.P.).

4 *Sydney Morning Herald*, 22 January 1988.

5 *Fiji Times*, 23 March 1988.

6 See 'Why We're Uniting: The Melanesian Bloc View,' *Islands Business*, April 1988, 26, 29.

7 *Weekend Australian*, 16–17 January 1988.

8 *Fiji Times*, 14 March 1988.

9 *Fiji Times*, 15 March 1988.

10 With respect to the status of Ratu George Cakobau, on 11 May, a high-ranking army officer from Tailevu made the point that last year's Great Council of Chiefs meeting had been illegitimate since it had not been convened by the Vunivalu.

11 *Fiji Times*, 9 May 1988.

12 *Fiji Times*, 25 March 1988.

13 Eddie Dean and Stan Ritova, *Rabuka: No Other Way, His Own Story of the Fiji Coup* (Sydney: Doubleday 1988).

14 Satendra Prasad, ed., *Coup and Crisis: Fiji – A Year Later* (Suva: no publisher, 1988).

15 *Fiji Times*, 17 May 1988.

16 See C. Harder, *The Guns of Lautoka: The Defence of Kahan* (Auckland: Sunshine Press 1988).

17 *Fiji Times*, 16 August 1988.

18 Mara's announcement fueled speculation about a possible successor – the most common name to crop up being Deputy Prime Minister and Finance Minister Josefata Kamikamica, a commoner who possesses a reputation as an honest technocrat as well as a loyal servant of the oligarchy.

19 It was disclosed the last day of the Methodist Conference that Lasaro

had negotiated an agreement with the conservative West German Konrad Adenauer Foundation to provide F$1.2 million over a three-year period, starting in 1988, to support rural projects by the church's Youth Fellowship Taskforce. Lasaro had bypassed normal channels within the church in acquiring and then using the funds (F$718,000 having been spent by the time of the conference). It was apparent that these funds had been used to support Lasaro's activities, at least to some extent, and Koroi, and those associated with him, accused the Konrad Adenauer Foundation of providing money to destabilize the church.

20 Rowan Callick, 'Fijian Army at the Ready to Assume Control,' *Australian Financial Review*, 25 September 1989, 1, 10.

21 Chris Sherwell, 'Rabuka to Leave Cabinet Job,' *Financial Times* (London), 4 October 1989, 4.

22 See Davendra Sharma, 'Adi Kuini Takes up the Fight,' *Islands Business*, December 1989, 14–21.

23 From the time of the May 1987 coup until early 1990, the population of Fiji declined by some 23,000 people, with primarily non-native Fijians (including a large number of professionals) leaving Fiji. In an effort to overcome personnel shortages, the regime has recruited doctors from Thailand and China; engineers, magistrates, and accountants from Sri Lanka; and senior staff for the Fiji Sugar Corporation from Britain and the Philippines.

Bibliography

Academic writing on Fiji has been dominated by the disciplines of anthropology, history, and geography and, more generally, by conservative theoretical perspectives. Only in recent years has the scope of Fijian scholarship broadened to provide readers with a more comprehensive picture of Fiji, past and present, from differing points of view.

The more traditional writings have been sympathetic to the eastern chiefly establishment and have portrayed Fiji as a plural society in which native Fijians and Indo-Fijians have little in common. Thus, much of the historical writing has presented Fiji from the view of the colonial authorities or eastern chiefs. Indo-Fijians have been treated mainly in separate historical studies, and in more general works they have been seen largely through the eyes of the eastern chiefs. Over the past few years, historians have begun to shift their perspective away from formal, establishment historiography to social history that pays more attention to the underdogs – workers, native Fijian commoners, peasant farmers, and the like.

Anthropological writings have been dominated by British social anthropology and its regional variants with the functionalism of Raymond Firth providing the most important theoretical influence. American anthropology of the Boasian and later ecological perspectives has been represented by a few writers. Most ethnographic research has taken place in eastern Fiji among native Fijians so that the anthropological view of Fiji has a decided bias in favour of the eastern chiefs. Relatively little ethnographic research has been conducted among Indo-Fijians or, more generally, among those living away from the smaller, more isolated villages. Most geographical writings during the postwar years also have taken a plural society perspective, but several recent works have adopted a political economy point of view and have sought to place ethnic relations within this broader context.

The list of works included in this bibliography is not complete. I have

sought to include what I consider the most important works on Fiji as well
as some of those items that have received sufficient attention to warrant
comment.

Ali, Ahmed. *Plantation to Politics: Studies on Fiji Indians*. Suva: Institute of
    Pacific Studies and Fiji Times Herald 1980. A collection of seven essays of
    varying quality on Indo-Fijian politics from the 1870s to the mid-1970s.
    Among the more important are those on the 1920 and 1921 strikes, the
    March-April 1977 election, and the origins of Muslim separatism.
    Although some of the work has been superceded by subsequent research
    and writing, it remains a useful volume. It is also of interest because of the
    political role of the author in Fijian politics and represents his early
    attempt to gain recognition as a radical and a scholar, which by the 1982
    election, any hint had vanished.
Bain, Kenneth. *Treason at 10: Fiji at the Cross Roads*. London: Hodder &
    Stoughton 1989. A personal account of events in Fiji during 1987 written
    for a general audience.
Bayliss-Smith, T., R. Bedford, H. Brookfield and M. Latham. *Islands, Islanders
    and the World: The Colonial and Post-colonial Experience of Eastern Fiji*. Cam-
    bridge: Cambridge University Press 1988. A useful collection of essays on
    the smaller islands of eastern Fiji by four geographers. Good discussion of
    environmental factors and the vulnerability of small peripheral societies.
    Includes several village case studies.
Belshaw, Cyril S. *Underneath the Ivi Tree: Social and Economic Growth in Rural
    Fiji*. Berkeley: University of California Press 1964. A detailed ethnographic
    study of native Fijian life in the Sigatoka valley region as it was in the late
    1950s, with an emphasis on questions relating to economic development
    with respect to the administration and organization of native Fijian
    society. The work has achieved the status of a classic of its genre and
    provides a good picture of rural life during the 'transition to indepen-
    dence' period.
Bienefeld, Manfred. *Work and Income for the People of Fiji: A Strategy for More
    Than Just Survival: The Final Report of the Fiji Employment and Development
    Mission*. Parliamentary Paper No. 66. Suva: Parliament of Fiji 1984.
    Although the recommendations of the report concerning steps to over-
    come Fiji's severe economic problems were quickly overtaken by political
    developments surrounding the rise of the Fiji Labour Party, the report
    remains a valuable source of economic and social data.
Brewster, A.B. *The Hill Tribes of Fiji*. London: Seeley, Service 1922. One of the
    few studies of western native Fijians by a colonial administrator with
    considerable experience in Fiji. It is an important alternative to other early
    works that view Fiji exclusively from the perspective of the eastern chiefly
    regions. The work contains useful descriptions of the Tuka and other cults

in western Viti Levu. While important, the book is far from being an unbiased, scholarly account. The author views Fiji from the perspective of a paternalistic colonial administrator who is not above promoting his own self-importance and employing sweeping generalizations about 'the natives' (e.g., 'Fijians jump to conclusions quickly').

Britton, Stephen G. *Tourism and Underdevelopment in Fiji*. Development Studies Centre. Monograph No. 31. Canberra: Australian National University 1983. An excellent study of the development of the tourist industry in Fiji, from a critical perspective. In addition to its thorough analysis of the tourist industry in Fiji as of the late 1970s, it also provides a very good history of the industry.

Brookfield, Harold, Frank Ellis, and R.G. Ward. *Land, Cane and Coconuts: Papers on the Rural Economy of Fiji*. Research School of Pacific Studies. Department of Human Geography Pub. No. 17. Canberra: Australian National University 1985. Three essays by scholars associated with the Fiji Employment and Development Mission (the mission report itself was published by the Fiji government in 1984). The papers focus on questions relating to land use, copra production, and the sugar industry. The book augments the coverage of these topics found in the Michael Taylor volume listed below.

Burns, Alan. *Report of the Commission of Enquiry into the Resources and Population Trends of the Colony of Fiji*. Council Paper No.1. Suva: Legislative Council of Fiji 1960. The report argues for the restructuring of the Fijian Administration so as to put an end to paternalism and the stifling of individual freedom. The new structure favoured in the report would allow greater personal autonomy and initiative as a means of promoting economic development and greater freedom for native Fijian commoners.

–. *Fiji*. London: Her Majesty's Stationery Office 1963. Provides a history and overview of Fiji from the perspective of an important colonial administrator during the postwar period. His brief discussion of Fiji's problems mirrors the perspective of the Burns Commission report.

Chandra, S. *Agricultural Development in Fiji*. Canberra: Australian Universities International Development Programme 1983. A useful overview of agricultural development in Fiji as it was perceived in the early 1980s. The book, however, suffers from several problems. Thus, the author argues that agriculture in Fiji has been the 'poor relation' of tourism and industry and that returns in agriculture have been lower than in these other two sectors. Empirical work by others, in fact, has not borne this out and instead have shown, for example, that income levels in agriculture compare favourably with unskilled labour in urban areas. More generally, a major fault of the book is its failure to place Fiji's agricultural sector within its political context.

Chapple, W.A. *Fiji: Its Problems and Resources*. Auckland: Whitcombe and

Tombs 1921. Not strong on insights, but the volume is useful as a source of basic information on Fijian society and the Fijian economy during the early part of the twentieth century.

Clammer, John. *Literacy and Social Change: A Case Study of Fiji*. Leiden: E.J. Brill 1976. An interesting study of the impact of literacy on native Fijian society based largely on published and other written sources. The chapters include discussions of the early introduction of literacy and education by Christian missionaries, religious cults, and the attitudes of the chiefly élite to education.

Cole, Rodney, and Helen Hughes. *The Fiji Economy May 1987: Problems and Prospects*. National Centre for Development Studies. Pacific Policy Paper No. 4. Canberra: Australian National University 1988. Rodney Cole served in Fiji under the Alliance government as secretary of finance. Economist Helen Hughes attracted attention in Fiji in late February 1987 when she changed the prepared text of a paper she was to give at a national meeting of accountants held in the midst of the 1987 election campaign. She dropped portions of the paper critical of Alliance Party government economic policies to avoid having her statements 'misused' by the Labour-NFP coalition. The Cole and Hughes paper begins with a background section in which it describes the sluggish Fijian economy from the mid-1970s to early 1987, viewing poor economic performance as contributing to the May coup. The remainder of the paper examines the economic effects of the May coup and speculates about the long-term economic prospects of the country.

Coulter, John Wesley. *Fiji: Little India of the Pacific*. Chicago: University of Chicago Press 1942. A rather simplistic overview of Fijian society that adds little to our knowledge beyond the occasional passage that is of interest primarily to the specialist.

– *The Drama of Fiji: A Contemporary History*. Rutland, Vermont: Charles E. Tuttle 1967. An uninspiring history, weak on insights, and not overly useful. Possibly the worst history of Fiji published.

Dean, Eddie and Stan Ritova. *Rabuka: No Other Way, His Own Story of the Fijian Coup*. Sydney: Doubleday 1988. If it were not for the serious nature of the subject matter, this book would best be viewed with a sense of humour. It is a self-serving piece of propaganda containing much that is of dubious validity. Nevertheless, taking its numerous shortcomings into account, the book does provide insights into the often confused mind of Rabuka himself, and serves to highlight the extent to which he has sought to invoke Christianity in support of his actions. Perhaps the work should be seen as lineal descendant of Scarr's biography of Sukuna – an attempt to create a new cult.

Derrick, R.A. *A History of Fiji: Volume One*. Suva: Government Press 1950. An important work that surveys the period of early European contact through the signing of the Deed of Cession. It suffers from a Eurocentric bias (for example, the role that Derrick assigns to the early beach-combers), but, nevertheless, is essential reading for anyone interested in this important period in Fiji's history.

Durutalo, Simione. *The Paramountcy of Fijian Interest and the Politicization of Ethnicity.* South Pacific Forum Working Paper No. 6. Suva: University of the South Pacific Sociological Society 1985. A critical examination of the chiefly oligarchy and its use of ethnicity to maintain itself in power. Contains a critique of the 'three-Fiji's' thesis espoused by Fisk (see below) and other pluralists by which the three major ethnic communities in Fiji (native Fijian, European, and Indo-Fijian) are divided according to economic function and political affiliation. Durutalo seeks to replace this with an analysis of the forces that have created, maintained, and manipulated ethnicity in terms of class and colonial-neocolonial rule by a national oligarchy.

'Internal Colonialism and Unequal Development.' M.A. thesis, University of the South Pacific, Suva 1985. Written by a politically prominent native Fijian from western Viti Levu, the thesis was greeted with considerable interest in Fiji when it appeared. It is a sociological and historical work that views Fiji from the perspective of western rather than eastern Fiji, as usually has been the case. The thesis contains important material on the development of the pine industry in western Fiji and the political responses in the west to the Alliance government's handling of the pine industry leading to the formation of the Western United Front.

Fisk, E.K. *The Political Economy of Independent Fiji.* Canberra: Australian National University Press 1970. A pluralist analysis of Fijian society that articulated what became known as the 'three Fiji's' perspective, dividing Fijian society into three relatively distinct groups: Europeans, Indo-Fijians, and native Fijians. With little attempt at explanation, the work suffers from many of the shortcomings of pluralist analyses, but, nevertheless, it remains an important study.

France, Peter. *The Charter of the Land: Custom and Colonization in Fiji.* Melbourne: Oxford University Press 1969. A very important work on the foundation of the chiefly establishment under colonial rule, and a book that caused considerable controversy in Fiji when it first appeared. Its coverage overlaps with that of Derrick and Legge and is in many ways more perceptive than either of these works in its treatment of the rationale behind the structure of indirect rule and the manner in which it was put in place.

Geddes, William R. *Deuba: A Study of a Fijian Village.* Polynesian Society Monograph. Wellington: Polynesian Society 1945. A standard ethnographic study of a native Fijian village on the coast, a short distance from Suva. Not an overly important work, but it does provide information on native Fijian society in an area that has been largely ignored by anthropologists.

Gillion, K.L. *Fiji's Indian Migrants: A History to the End of Indenture in 1920*. Melbourne: Oxford University Press 1962. The most important history of Indian migrants to Fiji during the indenture period. This, and its sequel, provide essential reading on the background of Indo-Fijian society.

–. *The Fiji Indians: Challenge to European Dominance, 1920-1946*. Canberra: Australian National University Press 1977. A sequel to the earlier volume, covering the period from the end of indenture through the Second World War. Includes chapters on the 1920 strike and subsequent efforts to organize Indo-Fijians along economic and political lines.

Harder, Christopher. *The Guns of Lautoka: The Defence of Kahan*. Auckland: Sunshine Press,1988. A personal account of events surrounding the 1988 Lautoka arms-smuggling case by the lawyer defending Mohammed Kahan. Includes a discussion of the attempted secession of Rotuma.

Hocart, Arthur M. *The Lau Islands of Fiji*. Bishop Museum Bulletin No. 62. Honolulu: The Bishop Museum 1929. The classic ethnographic account of native Fijian society in the Lau Group based on four years residence in Fiji and written under the influence of the diffusionist tradition within anthropology. It was published around the same time as Hocart's first major theoretical work, *Kingship*, in 1929. Concerned with the diffusion of culture, Hocart argued that the initial occupants of eastern and central Fiji had been overwhelmed by 'barbarians' from the west and were either driven out or absorbed by these invaders. Perhaps the most important legacy of the monograph is its establishment of Lau as the lens through which native Fijian society came to be viewed by future scholars.

–. *Northern States of Fiji*. Occasional Publication. London: Royal Anthropological Institute 1952. A survey that is essentially volume two of the 1929 work and written along the same diffusionist lines. To the central question of the extent to which Lau is Polynesian, Hocart argues that 'Lau is fundamentally Fijian' in contrast to Taveuni or Cakaudrove which are much more Tongan in character. While the extent of Polynesian influence on native Fijian society continues to interest scholars, other questions pursued in the volume are of little concern today, even though they elicited heated debate in the early part of this century. Thus, Hocart seeks to use his Fijian material to answer whether primitive peoples are subject to 'decadence' just as are 'civilized' peoples. He answers this in the affirmative: 'We can recognize faded gentility, demoralization and decay ...'

Howlett, R.A. *The History of the Fiji Military Forces, 1939–1945*. London: Crown Agents 1948. The book is of interest mainly because it is one of the few published sources of information on the history of the Fijian military. It covers Fijian involvement in the Second World War.

Knapman, Bruce. *Fiji's Economic History, 1874–1939: Studies of Capitalist Colo-*

nial Development. National Centre for Development Studies. Pacific Research Monograph No. 15. Canberra: Australian National University 1987. Essentially a study of the enclave economy of colonial Fiji prior to the Second World War. Knapman argues that, despite the shortcomings of the form of economic development pursued, there was no real alternative, and that, rather than undermining the country's long-term developmental prospects, the colonial economy increased the absolute level of incomes in Fiji and provided a foundation for later economic expansion.

Knapman, Claudia. *White Women in Fiji: 1835–1930, The Ruin of Empire?* Sydney: Allen & Unwin 1986. The book seeks to counter the view that European women played a negative role in race relations in colonial Fiji. The work looks carefully at the lives of European women in colonial Fiji, focusing attention on those factors relating to European women's relationships with members of other ethnic communities. It is an important addition to our understanding of colonial society in Fiji which, to too large an extent, remains recorded only in broad impersonal terms.

Lal, Brij V. *Girmityas: The Origins of Fiji Indians*. Canberra: Journal of Pacific History 1983. A brief study of the backgrounds of the people recruited from India to work in the cane fields of Fiji. It provides a useful supplement to Gillion's work.

–, ed. *Politics in Fiji*. Sydney: Allen & Unwin 1986. The papers contained in the book are uneven in quality. Some of the chapters are very disappointing and add little to the existing literature. Easily the best chapters are those by Alley, on the emergence of party politics in Fiji, and Lal, a survey of Fijian politics from 1970 to 1982. The book also reprints Timoci Bavadra's speech at the inauguration of the Fiji Labour Party.

–. *Power and Prejudice: The Making of the Fiji Crisis*. Wellington: New Zealand Institute of International Affairs 1988. Provides a good summary of political developments leading up to the May coup and of subsequent events during the remainder of 1987. Includes a reprint of the governor general's 11 May 1987 speech outlining Coalition policies.

Lasaqa, Isireli. *The Fijian People: Before and After Independence, 1959–1977*. Canberra: Australian National University Press 1984. Not so much a scholarly work as an ideological statement by an ardent defender of chiefly privilege in Fiji and a loyal Mara follower.

Legge, J.D. *Britain in Fiji, 1858–1880*. London: Macmillan 1958. A history of the transition to colonial rule and the early Gordon administration that essentially takes up where Derrick leaves off. Legge saw his book as rectifying the African bias in studies of native administration and notes how Gordon's administrative structure was a forerunner of Lugard's indirect rule in Nigeria. In relation to Fiji, specifically, Legge seeks to answer two questions. First, in light of the fact that Gordon's views were decidedly unusual for the time, how did his contemporaries view Britain's role

in Fiji? Second, he seeks to establish the reasons for Britain finally deciding to establish colonial rule in Fiji. Arguing against the view of some
scholars that it was simply an outcome of the imperialist Disraeli's
assumption of the prime ministership in England, Legge considers that
the decision did not represent a significant change in British policy, but
rather that it was merely the next step in a consistent policy of gradual
colonial expansion in the southwest Pacific.

Lloyd, D.T. *Land Policy in Fiji*. Department of Land Economy. Occasional
Paper No. 14. Cambridge: Cambridge University 1982. A useful survey of
land policy in colonial Fiji with a brief chapter on the early postcolonial
period. The book is of value primarily to someone desiring more information on Fiji's complicated structure of land use. What is missing from the
analysis, however, is adequate attention to the political dimension of land
policy.

Macnaught, Timothy J. *The Fijian Colonial Experience: A Study of the Neotraditional Order Under British Colonial Rule Prior to World War II*. Pacific
Research Monograph No. 7. Canberra: Australian National University
1982. Focusing on the period from 1900 to the onset of the Second World
War, the work is of particular interest as one of the few attempts to
examine the activities of Apolosi Nawai, the populist native Fijian who
challenged the rule of the chiefly oligarchy in the early part of the twen-
tiethth century.

Mamak, Alexander. *Colour, Culture and Conflict: A Study in Pluralism in Fiji*.
Sydney: Pergamon Press 1978. An anthropological study of Fiji as a plural
society in the period just after independence. It is an uneven work that
reads like an unedited PH.D. thesis, but its shortcomings are compensated
for by useful discussions of trade unions, the 1972 national election, and
other aspects of urban Fijian society around the time of independence.

Mayer, A.C. *Peasants in the Pacific*. London: Routledge & Kegan Paul 1961
(2nd ed. Berkeley: University of California Press 1973). Along with the
work of Chandra Jayawardena, Mayer's writings comprise the most
important ethnographic accounts of Indo-Fijian society. The first edition
was based on field-work conducted in 1951 in three villages, two on Viti
Levu and one on Vanua Levu. The second edition includes a new chapter
reporting on a brief restudy of two of the villages in 1971.

Meller, Norman and James Anthony. *Fiji Goes to the Polls: The Crucial Legislative
Council Election of 1963*. Honolulu: East-West Center 1968. A detailed study
of the important 1963 Legislative Council election.

Mishra, Vijay, ed. *Rama's Banishment: A Centenary Tribute to the Fiji Indians,
1879–1979*. Auckland: Heinemann Educational Books 1979. The work contains seven brief essays on Indo-Fijian society, history, and politics. The
essays are of very uneven quality. Perhaps the two most interesting ones

are those by Chandra Jayawardena on Indo-Fijian society during the indenture period and Jim Wilson on Indo-Fijian Hinduism.

Moynagh, Michael. *Brown or White?: A History of the Fiji Sugar Industry, 1873-1973*. Pacific Research Monograph No. 5. Canberra: Australian National University 1981. An important study of Fiji's major industry from its early years in the 1870s until the large Australian sugar company which dominated the industry, csr, was replaced by the state-owned Fiji Sugar Corporation in 1973.

Narayan, Jay. *The Political Economy of Fiji*. Suva: South Pacific Review Press 1984. A partially successful attempt to employ a dependency perspective for an understanding of the political economy of colonial Fiji. The work is of interest mainly because it represents an early effort to break with the pluralist tradition.

Nation, John. *Customs of Respect: The Traditional Basis of Fijian Communal Politics*. Development Studies Centre. Monograph No. 14. Canberra: Australian National University 1978. An establishment historical work on chiefly rule and communalism. The book does contain some useful descriptive material.

Nayacakalou, Rusiate R. *Leadership in Fiji*. Melbourne: Oxford University Press 1975. A study of native Fijian chieftanship and its role in colonial Fiji by one of the more thoughtful members of the native Fijian leadership. Most of the work was completed in 1964 and it contains a long discussion of native Fijian chieftanship during the postwar period. The book includes a foreword by Mara.and a brief epilogue by J.N. Kamikamica.

Nayacakalou, Rusiate R. *Tradition and Change in the Fijian Village*. Institute of Pacific Studies. Suva: University of the South Pacific 1978. Published version of the author's M.A. thesis based on research conducted in 1954. The study was of three native Fijian villages, one near Sigatoka, and two others along the Rewa and Wainmala rivers near Suva. The book includes a short foreword by Ron Crocombe and Asesela Ravuvu (who comes from one of the villages studied). The perspective in both of Nayacakalou's works is influenced by the functionalism of Raymond Firth.

Norton, Robert. *Race and Politics in Fiji*. St. Lucia: University of Queensland Press 1977. The book is poorly organized, but, nevertheless, is a major contribution to scholarship on Fiji that seeks to provide a balance to the prevailing eastern chiefly orthodoxy. It contains numerous gems of information on Fijian politics in the 1970s and is highly recommended.

Overton, John, ed. 'Fiji Since the Coups.' Special issue of *Pacific Viewpoint* 30: 2 (1989). A mixed batch of eight articles focusing, largely, on various aspects of the economic impacts of the coups. Includes a personal analysis by Jim Sanday, who was a senior officer in the Fijian military, and an essay by Richard Bedford on migration.

Pollard, Caryl J. 'Domestic Service in Suva, Fiji: Socio-economic Factors Affecting Change.' PH.D. thesis, University of the South Pacific, Suva 1987. A thorough study of domestic service in Suva based on over 350 interviews of female domestic servants, hotel housemaids, employers, and heads-of-household. It carefully documents the reasons females become domestic servants and their lives as maids and housegirls. The survey pays special attention to ethnicity and related economic and cultural factors.

Prasad, Satendra, ed. *Coup and Crisis: Fiji – A Year Later*. Suva: no publisher, 1988. A collection of brief critical essays, mostly by academics at the University of the South Pacific, assessing the situation one year after the first coup. Printed in a limited edition with no information as to the publisher for fear of reprisals by the regime, the work evoked an angry response from the Mara regime even though the essays were relatively mild in their criticisms. The book has since been reprinted in Australia.

Qalo, Ropate R. *Divided We Stand?: Local Government in Fiji*. Institute of Pacific Studies. Suva: University of the South Pacific 1984. A brief overview of municipal councils, the Fijian Administration, and rural advisory councils. The work is of interest primarily to those desiring a better undertanding of the workings of local government bodies in Fiji, although it is weak on analysis of the political dimension of such bodies.

Quain, Buell. *Fijian Village*. Chicago: University of Chicago Press 1948. A very good ethnography based on field-work in the village of Nakaroka in Bua Province, Vanua Levu, conducted in 1935-36. It is the only detailed ethnography of native Fijian society in this area of strong Tongan influence. The book includes a final chapter, compiled by Ruth Benedict after Quain's death, which discusses the 'dissonance between theoretical hierarchy and the random and confused determinants of status.'; It is thus very useful for an understanding of contemporary political issues.

Ravuvu, Asesela. *The Fijian Way of Life*. Institute of Pacific Studies Suva: University of the South Pacific 1983. A highly idealized version of traditional native Fijian culture by an important supporter of the Fijian Nationalists and later the Taukei Movement. From a scholarly perspective the book is terrible, but it is worth reading to get a sense of how conservative and populist native Fijian politicians have sought to portray their society.

Robertson, Robert, and A. Tamanisau. *Fiji: Shattered Coups*. Sydney: Pluto Press 1988. Robertson was a lecturer in the Department of History and Politics at the University of the South Pacific in Suva at the time of the May coup and subsequently was expelled from Fiji by Rabuka. This book describes events surrounding the May and September coups.

Rokotuivuna, Amelia, et al. *Fiji: A Developing Australian Colony*. Melbourne: International Development Action 1973. A pioneering work offering a critical analysis of the political economy of Fiji. Among those involved in its writing were several individuals who later became involved in progressive politics in Fiji The work focuses on Australian foreign investment in Fiji and contains several useful summaries of the activities of the leading foreign companies in the country in the early 1970s.

Roth, G.K. *Fijian Way of Life*. Melbourne: Oxford University Press 1953 (2nd ed. 1973). The colonial establishment's view of native Fijian society. The book contains chapters on village life, land customs and the structure of native Fijian society, the major ceremonies, and the Fijian Administration. It includes a preface by the governor of Fiji at the time, Ronald Garvey, and the second edition also has a brief preface by G.B. Milner. The native Fijian administration is also discussed in an earlier publication, *Native Administration During the Past 75 Years*. (Occasional Paper No. 10. London: Royal Anthropological Institute 1951).

Routledge, David. *Matanitu: The Struggle for Power in Early Fiji*. Institute of Pacific Studies. Suva: University of the South Pacific 1985. A history of chiefly conflict in precolonial Fiji. The book is a slightly revised version of the author's 1965 PH.D. thesis. Although somewhat dated, the work does contain empirical information that fills in a few gaps, as well as some interesting photos. The author's claim that the book 'leans towards the tenets of what is sometimes called social history,' is not borne out by what is fairly standard traditional Pacific historiography along the lines of that written by Scarr and Macnaught.

Sahlins, Marshall D. *Moala: Culture and Nature on a Fijian Island*. Ann Arbor: University of Michigan Press 1962. An ethnographic account of native Fijian society on the eastern island of Moala. The monograph is of interest largely because of its author, who subsequently became a leading advocate of what is commonly referred to as symbolic anthropology. His work in recent years has taken on a very conservative orientation, and in Fiji he has come to be viewed by many local scholars as an apologist for the chiefly oligarchy.

Scarr, Deryck. *Ratu Sukuna: Soldier, Statesman, Man of Two Worlds*. London: Macmillan 1980. An uncritical biography of Sukuna that is probably best read for its usefulness as propaganda for the chiefly oligarchy. Under Mara's government, which sought to promote what amounted to a 'Sukuna cult' as a pillar of chiefly rule, Scarr came to be treated as the de facto official historian of the chiefly oligarchy.

–, ed *The Three Legged Stool: Collected Writings of Ratu Sir Lala Sukuna*. London: Macmillan 1983. Produced as a further contribution to the 'Sukuna cult,' the work contains a few gems in some of the letters, especially among those demonstrating the close relationship between Sukuna and the European colonial establishment.

–. *Fiji: A Short History*. Sydney: Allen & Unwin 1984. This book should have

been the culmination of Scarr's years of writing as the leading establishment historian of Fiji and defender of its chiefly oligarchy. The author's
ideological bias aside, it is a very disappointing book. Scarr is at his best in
his coverage of the the colonial period, whereas his section on postcolonial Fiji is very superficial. Even the writing on the colonial era, however, is
spotty – at times exasperatingly so.
The Politics of Illusion: the Military Coups in Fiji. Sydney: University of New
South Wales Press 1988. A rather bizarre little book. Essentially a personal
apologia for the actions of the chiefs and the army in 1987.

Spate, Oskar. *The Fijian People: Economic Problems and Prospects*. Council Paper
No. 13. Suva: Legislative Council of Fiji 1959. This important report provides a summary of the social and economic problems facing native Fijians under the paternalistic system of administration during a period of
rapid change and recommends major reforms to promote the rights of
individual native Fijians.

Spencer, Dorothy. *Disease, Religion and Society in the Fiji Islands*. American
Ethnological Society Monograph No. 2. New York: J.J.Augustin 1941.
Based on a year's research in 1935–36 in the village of Nasaucoko in Colo
West, it is a useful account of western native Fijian society, drawing
attention to the fact that, at the time, chiefly titles implied relatively little
authority. Most of the work focuses on medical concerns. There is a short
chapter on religious beliefs and, unfortunately, an equally brief discussion
of social organization.

Taylor, Michael, ed. *Fiji: Future Imperfect?* Sydney: Allen & Unwin 1987. An
important work on the political economy of Fiji. The eight essays in the
volume focus on the mid-1980s and raise significant questions about Fiji's
future with policies under the, then, Alliance Party government. There are
two excellent chapters by Michael Taylor, one an overview of development issues and the other an analysis of business organizations. The other
chapters are also generally of high quality: John Connell on population
issues, R.G. Ward on the future of native Fijian villages, Harold Brookfield
on commerical agriculture, Steve Britton on tourism, Christopher Kissling
on transportation, and Michael Howard on the trade union movement.

Thomas, Nicholas. *Planets Around the Sun: Contradictions and Dynamics of the
Fijian Matanitu*. Oceania Monograph 31. Sydney: University of Sydney
1988. Another study of precolonial chiefs in eastern Fiji. Focusing on élite
marriage alliances and factional conflict, Thomas presents a study of
chiefly rule during the early contact period with the intent of improving
our theoretical understanding of social stratification in the Pacific. Overlaps to some extent with Routledge's work.

Thompson, Laura. *Fijian Frontier*. San Francisco: American Council, Institute
of Pacific Relations 1940. A good ethnographic description of native

Fijian society on the island of Kabara in the southern Lau Group, with an introduction by Bronislaw Malinowski.

Thomson, B. *The Fijians: A Study of the Decay of Custom*. London: Heinemann 1908. A somewhat personal account of native Fijian society in the late nineteenth century by an important colonial administrator. Thomson was a member of a commission in 1893 which investigated the marked population decline among native Fijians, and this provides the basis of this book. He saw the work as concerned primarily with the transition from 'customary law' to 'modern competition,' associating the former with stagnation and the latter with modernization, on the part of 'a race that is peculiarly tenacious of its institutions.' Paying no attention to the extent to which the colonial administration, of which he was a part, contributed to this 'racial proclivity,' the work nevertheless does contain a wealth of empirical data.

Tinker, Hugh, et al. *Fiji*. Report No. 75. London: The Minority Rights Group 1987. A very disappointing report, hastily prepared after the first coup, which contains a number of factual errors and questionable interpretations of events. Its select bibliography contains only seven entries, and one has to wonder what criteria was used to include the likes of Lasaqa's book but not the edited volume on Fijian politics by Lal.

Utrecht, Ernst, ed. *Fiji: Client State of Australasia?* Transnational Corporations Research Project. Sydney: University of Sydney 1984. The work contains eight essays on the political economy of Fiji. The four essays by Utrecht are survey chapters that contain a good deal of useful economic data. The other chapters are by Randy Thaman on food dependency, Simione Durutalo on the forest industry, Michael Howard and Anand Chand on Australian companies in Fiji, and Neil Karunaratne on economic policy. Some of the chapters tend to ramble at points, but, overall, it is a good contribution to the literature.

Varley, R.M. *Tourism in Fiji: Some Economic and Social Problems*. Cardiff: University of Wales Press 1978. Another study of tourism in Fiji that includes information that augments what is available in Britton's study.

Ward, M. *The Role of Investment in the Development of Fiji*. Cambridge: Cambridge University Press 1971. This book is most useful as a source of statistical material on Fiji around the time of independence. It treats Fiji as a plural society of distinct ethnic communities and views the problems facing the new government accordingly, in terms of creating a nation out of a multi-ethnic population.

Ward, R.G. *Land Use and Population in Fiji: A Geographical Study*. London: Her Majesty's Stationery Office 1965. A useful overview of land tenure and agriculture in Fiji during the latter part of the colonial period (including a regional appraisal of agriculture). Among its findings is that it is 'impossible for the rural areas of Fiji to support more than a small proportion of the expected increase in the workforce,' and it is argued 'that a much greater proportion of the Colony's development capital and economic planning should be devoted to promoting industry.' As might be expected from this analysis, the following decade witnessed a pronounced movement of people to urban areas. Unfortunately, government policy and academic studies continued to focus on rural areas and problems, largely ignoring urban Fiji, which today represents well over one-third of the population (with another large proportion of the population living in close proximity to urban areas).

Watters, R.F. *Koro: Economic Development and Social Change in Fiji*. Oxford: Clarendon Press 1969. A good study of four villages (two in western Viti Levu, one in eastern Viti Levu, and the fourth on the island of Koro) focusing on the relationship between native Fijian 'traditionalism' and problems of economic development. This work, like the one by Belshaw, fits within the overall perspective of the Spate and Burns reports.

Whitehead, C. *Education in Fiji: Policy, Problems and Progress in Primary and Secondary Education, 1939–1973*. Pacific Research Monographs No. 6. Canberra: Australian National University 1981. One of the few published studies on education in Fiji, the work focuses on the 'transition to independence' period.

Williams, Thomas, and James Calvert. *Fiji and the Fijians*. 2 vols. Suva: Fiji Museum 1982 (originally published in 1858). The most important of the early missionary works on Fiji. The first volume is an account of native Fijian society, and the second volume a history of the early activities of Christian missionaries.

Young, John. *Adventurous Spirits: Australian Migrant Society in Pre-Cession Fiji*. St.Lucia: University of Queensland Press 1984. An interesting study of settler society in Fiji from 1804 to 1873, with a concluding chapter on 'the politics of culture contact.' Provides useful supplementary material to earlier historical works.

Young, John A. *The Lovoni Land-purchase Project: A Case Study in Native Fijian Agricultural Development*. South Pacific Forum Working Paper No. 2. Suva: University of the South Pacific Sociological Society 1984. A study of an important 'showcase' development project on the island of Ovalau. The project later became a major disaster and embarassment for the Alliance government.

Index